# Leveraging Drupal®

# Leveraging Drupal®

# Leveraging Drupal®

## Getting Your Site Done Right

Victor Kane

WILEY

Wiley Publishing, Inc.

# Leveraging Drupal®: Getting Your Site Done Right

Published by
**Wiley Publishing, Inc.**
10475 Crosspoint Boulevard
Indianapolis, IN 46256
www.wiley.com



Published simultaneously in Canada

ISBN: 978-0-470-41087-5

10 9 8 7 6 5 4 3 2 1

Library of Congress Cataloging-in-Publication Data

Kane, Victor, 1946-
Leveraging Drupal : getting your site done right / Victor Kane.
p. cm.
Includes index.
ISBN 978-0-470-41087-5 (paper/website)
1. Drupal (Computer file) 2. Web sites — Design — Computer programs. 3. Web site development. I. Title.
TK5105.8885.D78K36 2009
006.7'6 — dc22

2008049818

*To my parents, John and Helena Kane, who made huge sacrifices in order to guarantee their children's educations. To my son, Guillermo, who has taught me so many things. To my loving life partner, Elena, who shares with me life, love, and struggle, and who has taught me the meaning of determination; and to all our sisters and brothers.*

# About the Author

**Victor Kane** is a process engineer and system architect who focuses on mentoring services and Agile approaches to web application development. For the past several years, Victor has been building website applications and helping others to do so using the Drupal CMS Framework, with an emphasis on building a cookbook of proven recipes capable of meeting modern requirements, based on best practices and a test-driven approach to application construction.

Victor has been an active participant in the Drupal community, with its forums, locally based Drupal groups, and Drupal camps and conferences, and is a proud "graduate" of the Drupal Dojo knowledge sharing group originally founded by Josh Koenig on `http://groups.drupal.org`. Since then he has frequently shared his experience and insights on his personal blog, `http://awebfactory.com.ar`.

# Credits

**Executive Editor**
Carol Long

**Development Editor**
Maureen Spears

**Technical Editor**
Joel Farris
Dan Hakimzadah
Benjamin Melancon

**Production Editor**
Rebecca Coleman

**Copy Editor**
Cate Caffrey

**Editorial Manager**
Mary Beth Wakefield

**Production Manager**
Tim Tate

**Vice President and Executive Group Publisher**
Richard Swadley

**Vice President and Executive Publisher**
Barry Pruett

**Associate Publisher**
Jim Minatel

**Project Coordinator, Cover**
Lynsey Stanford

**Proofreader**
Andrew Phillips, Windhaven Press

**Indexer**
Jack Lewis

# Acknowledgments

The Drupal Community at http://drupal.org, who have managed to bring together a hugely talented and motivated network of talent, and who owe their success to their ability to begin to transcend national boundaries, must be acknowledged in first place.

In second place, the unknown and unwitting poster to the forums and handbooks of drupal.org, having provided the answers in the nick of time on countless occasions.

I must acknowledge also the Drupal Dojo group (http://groups.drupal.org/drupal-dojo), an incredibly selfless ''share the knowledge'' self-teaching group that started operations in January 2007 and is now getting ready to launch Drupal Dojo 2.0.

Also, I thank the kind people at Wiley Publishing including Carol Long, who helped me make this book a reality, and Maureen Spears, who was my lifeline. In addition, I'd like to convey a word of thanks to the technical editors — Joel Farris, Dan Hakimzadah, and Benjamin Melancon as well as Robert Douglass of Acquia — who all were instrumental in shaping the code and text; as well as Miguel Martinez, of Buenos Aires, who took my photograph for the cover.

All who post. All who test. All who post issues in the Bazaar.

# Contents

# Introduction

Drupal is an Open Source, community-based Content Management System (CMS) and Website Application Development Framework that allows individuals, organizations, businesses, government agencies, and social classes to create interactive, media-based database-driven websites where they can carry out a significant portion of their activities.

What does this mean for you?

- **Open Source** — Not only is Drupal a software product readily available free of charge, but it is also licensed under the GPL license. This means, among other things, that its source code is completely open and readily accessible to all. It also means that all upgrades are available free of charge.

  *For more on the GPL license, see* `www.gnu.org/licenses/gpl-faq.html#WhatDoesGPLStandFor`. *For an interesting discussion of how business can make use of GPL-licensed software without having to publish the way they actually put Drupal to use, see* `http://jeff.viapositiva.net/archives/2006/02/drupal_and_the_gpl_as_i_understa.html`.

- **Community-Based** — Not all Open Source software is community-based. Some large corporations release a portion of their code under a GPL license, but the user community cannot participate in the production of the code. It is important to understand that because Drupal is actually produced by a huge developer base, with a publicly accessible and tremendously active issue queue, Drupal enjoys a considerable gain in the quality of its software.
- **Content Management System (CMS)** — Once installed and configured, Drupal allows an authenticated user granted the appropriate permissions to create, edit, manage, and publish content without any more specialized knowledge than being able to use a modern word processor. And it allows graphic web designers and stylists to alter the look and feel of that content.
- **Website Application Development Framework** — Drupal goes way beyond being *only* a CMS: Off the shelf, it allows for the publishing of dynamic content capable of changing and adapting to different contexts, conditions, or kinds of users. It allows developers to implement web applications based on business objects and listings generated by flexible, real-time queries generated on the fly. And it allows developers to integrate the system with countless external web applications and Web Services in a thoroughly modular fashion.
- **Individuals, Organizations, Businesses, Government Agencies, and Social Classes** — In a word, you. You can use Drupal to create a modern, interactive website that can become part and parcel of your day-to-day activities and communications.

But this book is not just about Drupal. It is about *leveraging* Drupal. It explains the best possible set of approaches toward making Drupal work for you to get your site done right and, as such, views Drupal, together with a series of additional methods and best practices, as a way of getting things done.

By working with this book, you will gain insight into how to work with any of the most recent Drupal releases, and you will learn how to set up shop, how to approach your project using an Agile and test-driven approach to software development, how to plan for deployment, and how to avoid pitfalls along the way.

## Whom This Book Is For

This is a book you have to read. This is a book you have to work through, because it is so closely pegged to actually working with Drupal that an all-inclusive index would be longer than the book itself.

It is my earnest hope that the contents of this book may be shared with many kinds of Drupal users. But it must be said that this is neither a book on Drupal programming dedicated only to highly trained technical staff, on the one hand, nor is it a book designed to walk the casual Drupal end-user through its many features — although it might benefit both.

However, the problem this book attempts to solve — and in this sense, it is perhaps unique — is the sad but true fact that the development of any website today involves the ability to master, with at least a practical level of solvency, a huge number of disciplines. You need to be, in a certain sense, the Renaissance kind of person capable of either dealing with or (and this is extremely important) delegating, when you cannot, an extremely wide range of skills. This means that you are very often in the position of needing to get up to speed on a wide variety of issues. This book attempts to bring them into a single, convenient space.

In short, this is a book designed for people who, given a set of website requirements and a community of users who need to use that website, have to learn how to fashion Drupal to their needs, how to domesticate Drupal — in short, how to get it done.

And how to get it done *right*: This book is designed for those who are convinced that in order to successfully achieve a nontrivial purpose, it is necessary to stand on the shoulders of giants and adopt an industry's set of best practices in order to avoid a host of common pitfalls that can cost a great deal of time and money, and even cause your project to fail entirely.

So, taking into account that the book is directed at an extremely wide range of skill sets, you definitely form part of the audience of this book if you are:

- ❑ A website developer interested in looking over the shoulder of experienced Drupal developers and learning all the steps and how-tos of all the processes that they need to master in order to efficiently harness Drupal
- ❑ A website developer interested in learning how to set up a professional Drupal shop, including practical examples of best practices in business modeling and requirements capturing, iterative and incremental development, testing and deployment, and maintenance in regard to the Drupal website development life cycle

- Anyone interested in finding out the shortest path between what his or her clients need, on the one hand, and how Drupal can be used to get there
- An IT professional with experience in developing website applications using other frameworks and technologies, who is now interested in either using Drupal for a specific project, or in evaluating it
- A web designer who is interested in finding out how to convert XHTML/CSS designs into working Drupal sites
- A project manager who needs to understand the dimensioning of what is entailed in various kinds of website development using Drupal
- Untrained end-users who are having a Drupal-based site delivered to them and need to school themselves realistically in terms of what it means to own and house-train a modern website
- Anyone curious about how anything Drupal actually gets done

# What This Book Covers

This book attempts to be Drupal release-agnostic, and a large part of what is covered is applicable to website development with Drupal whether you are using Drupal 5.x, 6.x, or even 7.x and later.

And most importantly, it also focuses on a wide range of disciplines, tools, and best practices you need in order to optimize the way you approach development projects built on this CMS and framework.

# How This Book Is Structured

The book is structured around a real-world example of a website application based on Drupal, the On-Line Literary Workshop. As such, its organization mirrors the development life cycle as a whole, with the exception of Chapter 10, which covers the development of an entire real-world application from start to finish.

- **Part I: Launching Your Website as a Software Project**
  - **Chapter 1** — The first chapter takes you from the business vision and scoping of the project to the laying out of an Agile approach tailored to Drupal website application development based on an iterative and incremental approach with frequent builds and prototyping, oriented toward a maximum of client participation.
  - **Chapters 2 and 3** — The second and third chapters deal with gradually setting up a complete, no-nonsense development environment — including development, test, and production sites — using version control and issue-tracking tools. As you work through these chapters, you analyze, design, and implement your first cut of business objects while working with Drupal itself to get an initial prototype up and running.
  - **Chapter 4** — The fourth chapter is a fully fledged planning sprint, starting with the refinement of the project user stories, their final assignment to phases and iterations, and the test-driven implementation of the first batch. The architectural baseline, concerned

with mapping Drupal modules and architecture to the design and implementation of the project's functionality, is completed.

- **Part II: Getting Your 5.x Site Up-To-Date**
  - **Chapters 5 and 6** — The fifth and sixth chapters cover various implementation sprints. You use development documentation and project tracking to extend a project within the project and find it a home as part of the website itself, which becomes self-documenting.
  - **Chapter 7** — The seventh chapter covers more user story implementation, but also concentrates on explaining how the Drupal theming system works and how it cleanly separates content from presentation and styling. A great deal of hands-on practice is included, as well as a concrete recommendation and demonstration for using the Zen theme as a systematic starting point for all your Drupal theming.
- **Part III: Upgrading Your Drupal Site**
  - **Chapter 8** — The eighth chapter is an aside on upgrading from Drupal 5.x to 6.x, taking my blog, `http://awebfactory.com.ar`, as a real-world example.
  - **Chapter 9** — The ninth chapter is a hands-on, step-by-step approach to upgrading the On-Line Literary Workshop to Drupal 6.x, including the upgrading of all content and modules, including CCK, Views, Organic Groups, Pathauto, Private Messaging, and more.
- **Part IV: Getting the Most out of Drupal 6.x**
  - **Chapter 10** — This chapter covers the development of an entire real-world application from start to finish.
  - **Chapter 11** — Chapter 11 takes the development of the On-Line Literary Workshop a great leap forward with the implementation of another round of user stories and also includes a section on how to turn a standard XHTML/CSS template into a Drupal theme for use with your project.
  - **Chapter 12** — This is the jQuery chapter. Enough said.
- **Part V: Drupal 7 and the Road Ahead**
  - **Chapter 13** — This chapter deals with the Drupal 7 release, its roadmap and the philosophy behind it, and its feature list and architectural style; it also covers its installation and use.
  - **Chapter 14** — This chapter completes the On-Line Literary Workshop deployment, explaining how to use the Advanced Help module to provide customized context-sensitive help and how to turn your whole project into a reusable installation profile anyone in the community can download and use.
  - **Chapter 15** — Looking ahead, and with the objective of exploring as many alternatives as possible as a basis for serious Drupal development and use, Acquia Drupal is explained and explored in Chapter 15 as an Enterprise-ready commercial services-based distribution of Drupal. This chapter brings you the possibility of starting out with enhanced off-the-shelf functionality, monitoring, and support.

# What You Need to Use This Book

At a minimum, you should have access to at least one working Drupal website that you have installed yourself, or else have had installed, with all administration permissions granted. That pretty well defines the hardware and throughput characteristics also.

In order to do serious development, a workable setup would include the following:

- A development server (this could very well be a laptop) capable of running Drupal, on any modern operating system. Your favorite version control system (CVS, SVN, Git, etc.) client should be installed also.
- A development environment (may be the same laptop or computer acting as your development server), including at least a file manager and a simple text editor (or maybe an IDE development environment) in order to edit PHP, CSS, and other kinds of text files; a client for whatever version control system you are using (CVS, SVN, Git, etc.); and a dependable and decently fast Internet connection that will allow you to connect with your test and production sites and your version control system. Ideally, you should have an ssh client (putty in Windows, ssh in Linux or OS X), along with at least some form of graphic editing application (such as Gimp or Adobe Photoshop or Fireworks).
- A test site running Drupal to which you ideally have both FTP or SFTP as well as command line access via ssh. It should be capable of running a version control client.
- A production site, of course, if this is a real-world project, with at least similar characteristics to the test site.
- A version control repository either installed on one of your own hosting servers, or else a specialized version control repository account.

# Conventions

To help you get the most from the text and keep track of what's happening, we've used a number of conventions throughout the book.

> **Boxes like this one hold important, not-to-be forgotten information that is directly relevant to the surrounding text.**

*Notes, tips, hints, tricks, and asides to the current discussion are offset and placed in italics like this.*

As for styles in the text:

- We *highlight* new terms and important words when we introduce them.
- We show keyboard strokes like this: *Ctrl+A*.
- We show filenames, URLs, and code within the text like so: `persistence.properties`.

- We present code in two different ways:

```
We use a monofont type with no highlighting for most code examples.
```

```
We use gray highlighting to emphasize code that's particularly important in the
present context.
```

# Source Code

As you work through the examples in this book, you may choose either to type in all the code manually or to use the source code files that accompany the book. All of the source code used in this book is available for download at `www.wrox.com`. Once at the site, simply locate the book's title (either by using the Search box or by using one of the title lists) and click the Download Code link on the book's detail page to obtain all the source code for the book.

*Because many books have similar titles, you may find it easiest to search by ISBN; this book's ISBN is 978-0-470-41087-5.*

Once you download the code, just decompress it with your favorite compression tool. Alternately, you can go to the main Wrox code download page at `www.wrox.com/dynamic/books/download.aspx` to see the code available for this book and all other Wrox books.

# Errata

We make every effort to ensure that there are no errors in the text or in the code. However, no one is perfect, and mistakes do occur. If you find an error in one of our books, like a spelling mistake or faulty piece of code, we would be very grateful for your feedback. By sending in errata you may save another reader hours of frustration and at the same time you will be helping us provide even higher quality information.

To find the errata page for this book, go to `www.wrox.com` and locate the title using the Search box or one of the title lists. Then, on the book details page, click the Book Errata link. On this page you can view all errata that have been submitted for this book and posted by Wrox editors. A complete book list including links to each book's errata is also available at `www.wrox.com/misc-pages/booklist.shtml`.

If you don't spot "your" error on the Book Errata page, go to `www.wrox.com/contact/techsupport.shtml` and complete the form there to send us the error you have found. We'll check the information and, if appropriate, post a message to the book's errata page and fix the problem in subsequent editions of the book.

# p2p.wrox.com

For author and peer discussion, join the P2P forums at `p2p.wrox.com`. The forums are a Web-based system for you to post messages relating to Wrox books and related technologies and interact with other readers and technology users. The forums offer a subscription feature to e-mail you topics of interest of your choosing when new posts are made to the forums. Wrox authors, editors, other industry experts, and your fellow readers are present on these forums.

At `http://p2p.wrox.com` you will find a number of different forums that will help you not only as you read this book, but also as you develop your own applications. To join the forums, just follow these steps:

1. Go to `p2p.wrox.com` and click the Register link.
2. Read the terms of use and click Agree.
3. Complete the required information to join as well as any optional information you wish to provide and click Submit.
4. You will receive an e-mail with information describing how to verify your account and complete the joining process.

*You can read messages in the forums without joining P2P but in order to post your own messages, you must join.*

Once you join, you can post new messages and respond to messages other users post. You can read messages at any time on the Web. If you would like to have new messages from a particular forum e-mailed to you, click the Subscribe to this Forum icon by the forum name in the forum listing.

For more information about how to use the Wrox P2P, be sure to read the P2P FAQs for answers to questions about how the forum software works as well as many common questions specific to P2P and Wrox books. To read the FAQs, click the FAQ link on any P2P page.

# Part I

# Launching Your Website as a Software Project

**Chapter 1:** Keeping It Simple

**Chapter 2:** Taking Baby Steps

**Chapter 3:** Getting Organized

**Chapter 4:** Getting Up to Speed

# 1

# Keeping It Simple

"Keep It Simple" is really a synonym for "Get a Grip."

If you are reading this book, you probably have some degree of responsibility in getting a website application up and running. If you are reading this chapter and you are searching for a series of steps you can actually assimilate and follow toward fulfilling that goal, then you are in the right place.

First of all, in a software project (and because of its complexity, that is what a website application is), you are either controlled by circumstances or you succeed — but only if you can maintain your grip on things. That's only if, after receiving all the advice, you are able to fashion your own means of zooming into detail, return to the overview, keep it going, and know at all times where your bookmarks are . . .and if you can pilot the process of each layer making up the project, on every front: the purpose, the design, the usability, the navigation, the function, the data, the push and pull and flow of actions and results, the emission and reception of messages, the completion of tasks, the updating, the classification, and relation of content.

Which is to say, if you keep it simple and keep it all in view, or at least know where to look for it, then you can marshal your own approach to truly leveraging a powerful, open-ranging, and dynamically productive framework such as Drupal, the "Community Plumbing" Content Management System framework middleware powerhouse, featuring:

- Significant off-the-shelf functionality
- Tremendous extensibility through nearly 3,500 contributed modules
- Based on one of the most active Open Source communities in existence

Drupal is all of these things.

Add to the mix that Drupal itself is evolving at a fairly brisk pace, as you'll see in later chapters, and you definitely need to come to Drupal with your own approach.

Because you are using Drupal for world domination (a favorite geek metaphor among Drupaleros), then you had better have a program. And you had better make sure that everyone involved gets on that program and stays there.

# Getting with the "Program"

The "program" means that you must start out with a clear idea of how your client defends her interests with the website application in the works. In the program, keeping it simple does not mean splitting it apart and losing the richness of vision, nor does it mean oversimplifying.

This chapter lays out a method that you follow throughout the rest of the book. Then, you can either adopt it lock-stock-and-barrel or roll your own. But we definitely recommend following some kind of Agile approach and have developed a lean, mean methodology checklist. We find that this means, at a bare minimum, maintaining a policy for:

- ❑ **Vision and Scope** — The business vision and scope
- ❑ **Visitors and Users** — Who's going to use the website?
- ❑ **User Stories** — Narratives telling us what the users are going to use the website for
- ❑ **Analysis and Design** — What needs to be done so they can do that?
- ❑ **Planning and Risk Management** — When should you do that?
- ❑ **Design and Usability** — What should it look like?
- ❑ **Tracking and Testing** — Making sure you're getting what you really want
- ❑ **Technology Transfer and Deployment** — Turning over the helm to those who will be managing the website application each and every day

Figure 1-1 shows a basic main process workflow for this book's example project. The workflow is strongly influenced by Mike Cohn's book *User Stories Applied* (`http://amazon.com/User-Stories-Applied-Development-Addison-Wesley/dp/0321205685`).

The Perl programming language, in common with Drupal, has been one of the major Open Source success stories of all time, answering a burning need in an intelligent and synthetic way, backed by an extremely active community led by very smart people. And, like Drupal, given a problem, it provides an enormous number of alternatives offering themselves as solutions. "There's more than one way to do it" has always been their slogan, and the same holds true with Drupal: there is always more than one way to do it. So, of course, you can substitute your own process workflow and find your own solutions along the way. The important thing is to recognize that the development of a website application is a complex process. To get it done right and to leverage a powerful, dynamic, and productivity-enhancing framework like Drupal, you need to develop your own independent approach and method as you gain experience yourself. The method you'll use throughout this book is a "starter set" you will adapt and tailor to your own needs, as you develop the Literary Workshop community website.

In a nutshell, the main process workflow makes the first task the identification of the customer and, by extension, the business vision and scope of the project as well as the complete list of stakeholders involved. Then comes the identification of the roles — the different kinds of users who will use the site. For each role, you write a series of user stories, identifying all the possible interactions the role will have with the website application. Doing it this way (asking who will use the site, and, for each of the roles, what they are going to do when they interact with it) guarantees that you can cover all the functionality required and come up with a complete list of user stories.

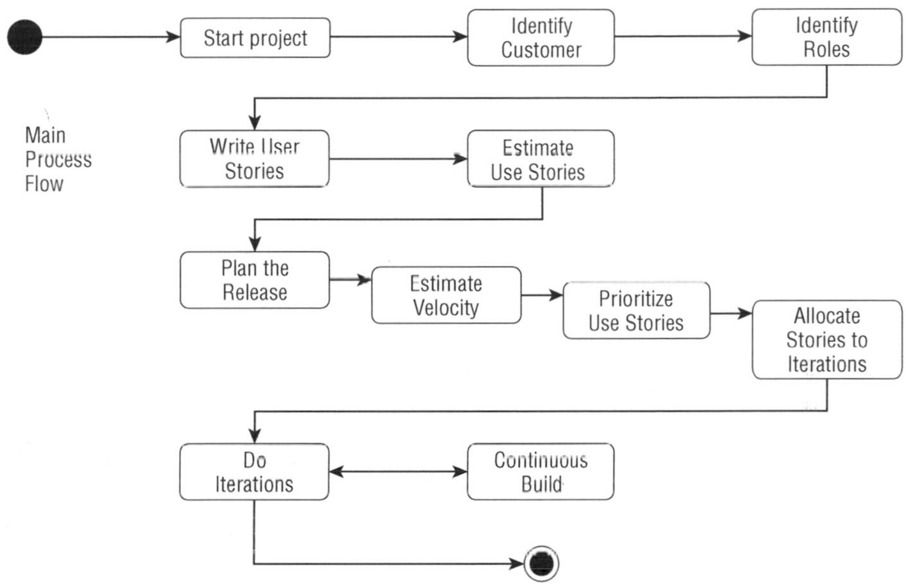


**Figure 1-1**

At this point, you have all your user stories, perhaps written on 3×5 cards and spread out on a table in front of you, or on a magnetic board, or taped up to the wall, or whatever. So you can do the planning. This involves making an initial estimate for each user story, taking advantage of the fact that each user story is a semi-autonomous chunk of functionality that can be dealt with independently. Then, you create a way of putting the estimates in context on the basis of the velocity of the team. (Is this our first time? Any extra-special technical areas of difficulty, like dealing with a text messaging gateway, or with specialized web services?)

Next, you are ready to prioritize the user stories. If they are indeed 3×5 cards, this means unshuffling the deck and putting them in order. The two most significant criteria for this should be: which ones does the client think are the most essential, and which ones need to be tackled first because they involve some kind of risk that needs to be mitigated at as early a stage as possible.

This process dovetails into the next important planning task, which is allocating the stories to iterations. You want to have several iterations, at least four to six for a medium site, even more for a large site, following the Agile principle of "frequent releases." One reason for this is so that the client, who should be considered part of the development team, can give really effective feedback in time for the architecture of the site not to be adversely affected by any "surprises" that may crop up: If implementation is straying far from the client expectations of what the website is supposed to actually do, you want to find out about that sooner rather than later. Another is so that work can be expressed as much as possible using the semantics of the solution domain, rather than the problem domain — which means that people can think much more clearly when something concrete is up and running, rather than being forced to work in the abstract.

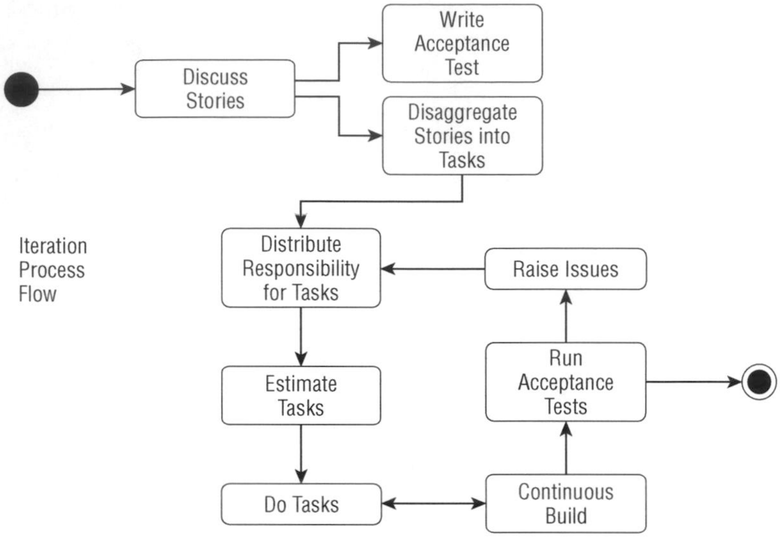


**Figure 1-2**

So now, you have planned your iterations, and you have on the table (and hopefully on the wall), or else entered into your favorite issue tracking system, essentially four to six piles of no more than five user stories (more iterations and more user stories per iteration if it is a bigger website, also depending on estimated team velocity).

Basically, you want to grab the first pile (the first iteration) and implement it. Now, for each planned iteration, or phase (sometimes people group iterations in phases), you use the workflow shown in Figure 1-2.

To do this, you take each story and discuss it, the client takes a major responsibility for writing the acceptance test for it, and you list all the tasks that need to be carried out in order to actually implement the functionality involved in the user story. The acceptance test is basically a semi-formal to formal statement of precise criteria according to which the work has actually been done right.

According to the Extreme Programming website (`http://extremeprogramming.org` — a great starting point to finding out more about a lot of the methodology we are talking about and using in this book, as is Kent Beck's ground-breaking work on the subject, *Extreme Programming Explained: Embrace Change*; `http://amazon.com/Extreme-Programming-Explained-Embrace-Change/dp/0201616416`):

> Acceptance tests are black box system tests. Each acceptance test represents some expected result from the system. Customers are responsible for verifying the correctness of the acceptance tests and reviewing test scores to decide which failed tests are of highest priority. Acceptance tests are also used as regression tests prior to a production release.

Essentially "getting your site done right" means that all the acceptance tests pass for all user stories. You'll be learning about acceptance tests and other forms of testing, like unit testing, below in the book.

In any case, it should be clear that the acceptance tests must be written before any work is actually done. Once written, and all the tasks necessary to implement a given user story are listed, each task can be taken up by a pair (hopefully) of developers. (It's much more productive for two people to work together on a task, but we won't get involved in any religious wars here; also, you might be working by yourself, so just be prepared to put on a lot of hats!) The developers will take the task, make an estimate, carry it out, and immediately integrate their work into the development test site. Later, the client will run the acceptance tests for the user story, and if they pass, the work just got done! Otherwise, an issue is raised in whatever issue tracking system you are using (more on this later), and the work is recycled, until the acceptance tests all pass.

Let's get our lean-and-mean methodology checklist straight now, starting with the task of mapping the business vision and scope.

## Starting with a Map for Business Vision and Scope

Experience at succeeding has shown that to achieve the benefits of the "KISS" approach, you actually have to dig down deep to the roots of what is an organic, dynamic process. It is not a question of over-simplification for the sake of simplification.

To succeed, you need to stand "commonsense" on its pointy head, at least for a while, and acquire a deep vision: It is not only that those who lack a business plan will not enjoy financial success. While true, what you are concerned with here is that without first identifying the business plan, there is no way you can build a website application that meets your clients' needs and fits right into their regular activity. Real needs cannot be translated into an analysis and design, analysis and design into implementation, implementation into a working model for testing, a working tested model into a deployed website application — the website application the client needs will never be born.

In traditional Information Technology terms, this is called a *Business Model* (see Wikipedia). The importance of business rules is present in the context of Agile Modeling, as well. Business Modeling is a difficult subject to master in its own right, but thankfully, you can cut to the chase here, and draw yourselves a Web 2.0 picture of the relationship between the business rules, the feature list, and the offerings of a website application: a meme map.

*For more on Business Models, see Wikipedia at* `http://en.wikipedia.org/wiki/Business_model`. *For more on Agile Modeling, see* `http://agilemodeling.com/artifacts/businessRule.htm`. *For more on meme maps, see "Remaking the Peer-to-Peer Meme," by Tom O'Reilly,* `http://oreillynet.com/pub/a/495`.

A meme map shows the deep relationship between the internal activities of a business or organization, their strategic positioning, on the one hand, and that business' outward, public face, on the other, including the website applications and their functionality, which is what it is you actually have to develop. Everything is clear at a glance. This is just what you need to get started. Look at Figure 1-3 (which shows a meme map for a Drupal-based Literary Workshop website application) and the comments following it.

- At the top, there are three bubbles containing the main public functionality of the website application.
- In the middle, the core is shown as a rectangle housing the positioning strategy and guiding principles (which may well differ with someone attempting a similar kind of site, but which will have a big impact on what you will be doing anyway).

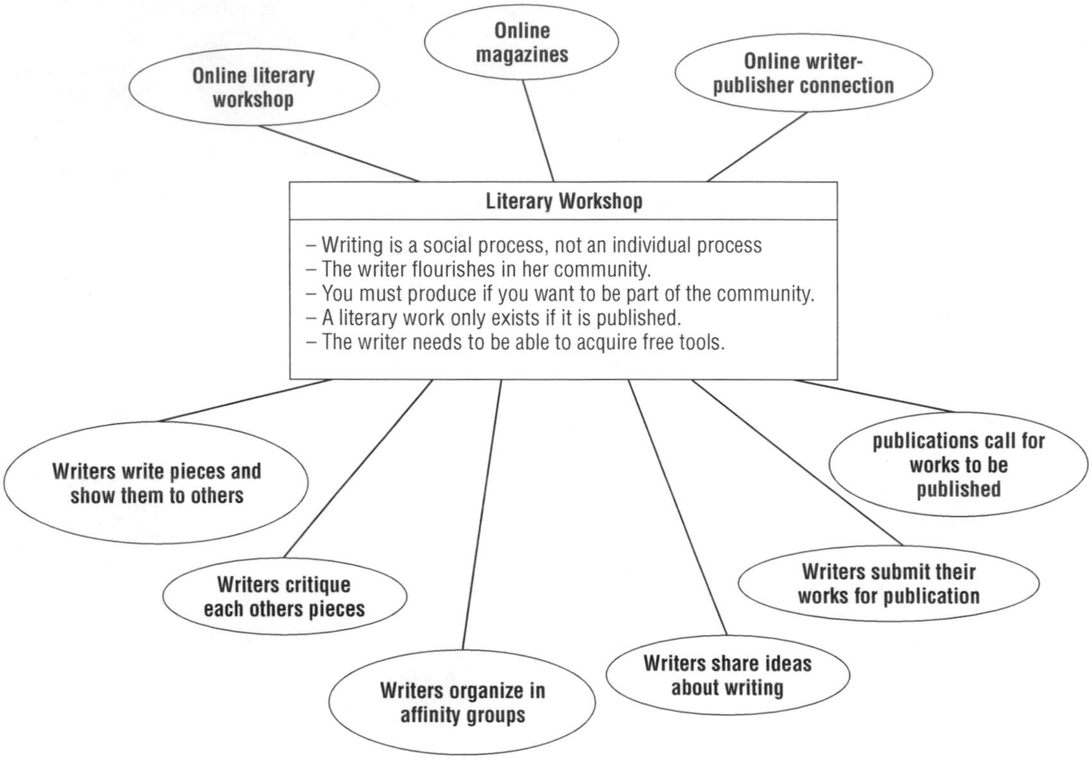


Figure 1-3

- ❑ Below are the regular business activities housing and forming the material basis and personal interactions supporting the rest.

From this point on, "Keeping It Simple" is going to mean banishing anything that isn't directly connected to your business vision, automatically and constantly getting rid of the fluff.

Going to the heart of the matter, and keeping that present, will enable you to get a grip right from the start.

There is a website where you can make your own meme maps (Do It Yourself Meme Map Generator, `http://web.forret.com/tools/mememap.asp`), so you can try it out yourself. Or you can use any diagram drawing tool. Or use pencil and paper (that will work!). In any case, I strongly recommend that you follow along in this book by actually developing your website application as I develop mine. Practice makes perfect.

## Who's Going to Use the Site?

This question really goes to the identification of the actual users of the website itself, and also the users of the website in a business sense.

Perhaps a sector of the back office, for example, will never actually use the site as such, but will be interested in receiving periodic statistics, say, as a weekly email. They must be included, of course, in the list of roles. Here's a list of roles for the Literary Workshop website application:

| Role | Description |
|---|---|
| Workshop Leader | The person who actually runs the workshop, decides who to accept, monitors whether members are complying with requirements, and also participates along with the other members |
| Workshop Member | Someone who has joined the workshop and actively participates in it |
| Publisher | Someone publishing a magazine, on and off the site |
| Webmaster | Technical administrator of the website |

The main thing is that every possible user of your website application needs to be taken into consideration in order to truly capture the complete set of requirements that need to be met in the implementation of the project. At the same time, a complete list of all interactions with the site (their user stories) for each of these users completes the picture.

## What Are They Going to Use It For?

Let's make a list of user stories, then, for each of the Roles we have previously identified.

| Role | User Story |
|---|---|
| Workshop Leader | Can approve applications to join the workshop (from members and magazine and book publishers) |
| | Can suspend members and publishers |
| | Can manage affinity groups |
| | Can broadcast messages to members |
| | Can do everything workshop members and publishers can do |
| Workshop Member | Can post literary pieces |
| | Can make any post public, private, or visible to an affinity group |
| | Can critique public posts |
| | Can browse public pieces and critiques |
| | Can send and receive messages to and from all members, publishers, and the workshop leader |
| | Can start an affinity group with its own forums |
| | Can post to forums |
| | Can maintain their own literary blogs |

| Role | User Story |
|---|---|
| Publishers | Can browse public content |
| | Can broadcast a call for pieces to be submitted for a publication |
| | Can select content for inclusion in a publication |
| | Can manage an on-line publication |
| | Can manage an on-line blog |
| Webmaster | Can administer the website configuration |
| | Can install new updates and functionality |

## What Needs to Be Done So They Can Do That?

You will be taking each user story and doing some analysis and design aimed at discerning what can be reused from the giant Drupal storehouse of core and contributed functionality, and what needs to be added on — perhaps contributing back to the community in the process (you'll learn why this is a great idea later on in the book).

But that isn't enough. The answer to this question is actually to be found during the course of the iteration planning workflow as well as in the user story implementation workflow. During the planning stage, when we are prioritizing user stories and assigning them to iterations, we would do well to bear in mind the organization of iterations established by both the Rational Unified Process (see `www-306.ibm.com/software/awdtools/rup` as well as `http://ibm.com/developerworks/rational/library/content/03July/1000/1251/1251_bestpractices_TP026B.pdf`) and the Open Unified Process (see `http://epf.eclipse.org/wikis/openup/index.htm`) into four phases, or groups of iterations:

| Phase | Iterations | Description |
|---|---|---|
| Inception | Usually a single iteration, with a resulting prototype | Vision, scope, and feasibility study enables the initiation of the project based on cost and schedule estimates. Initial requirements, risks, and mitigation strategies are identified, and a technical approach is agreed on. |
| Elaboration | Usually two iterations, prototype confirming architectural decisions | During the elaboration phase, the requirements baseline and the architectural baseline are set. Iterations are planned. Planning, costs, and schedule are agreed on. A lot of work gets done, and the test site is up and running with successive development releases. |
| Construction | Enough iterations to get the job done | Change management is in force from the onset of this phase. Alpha and Beta release will be completed, and all Alpha testing completed by phase end. |

| Phase | Iterations | Description |
|---|---|---|
| Transition | Usually a single iteration | Release 1.0 of the website application has been deployed on the live site and accepted by the client and is in production. All documentation and training have been completed, and an initial maintenance period has elapsed. |

Well, here we are getting to some pretty rigorous language. But, these phases actually occur in any project, and it is best to be conscious of the whole process, so as to manage it instead of being managed.

The main thing to understand here is that as the basic workflow is followed, two baselines emerge, relatively early in the project — a requirements baseline (the sum of all user stories) and an architectural baseline. Now, the decision to use Drupal in the first place settles a slew of architectural decisions. But you need to decide exactly how required functionality will be supported. Here are a few examples:

- Which modules will support the use of images? Will images be Drupal *nodes* in their own right, or fields in a node?
- What editing facilities will different kinds of users have at their disposal? Will a wiki-style markup approach be chosen, or will a rich text editor be necessary? Which one? And once it is chosen, how will it be configured?
- Will part of the site's content find its origin in external sources? Will those sources be news feeds? Will specialized multimedia modules be necessary? Will that content simply be listed, or will it be incorporated into the database also?
- To what extent will the website need to scale?
- In terms of support for foreign languages, will there be a need for localization (the process of adapting the user interface, including menus, currency and date formats, to a particular locale, or language, locality, and their customs, commonly abbreviated as l10n)? Will there be a need to make the content of the site multilingual through the use of internationalization modules (the process of making one or more translations into various different languages available for each content item, commonly abbreviated as i18n)?
- What is the basic content model? What classes of content and what content types need to exist, and what is the relationship between them?

And then there is also a whole other area of things that need to be attended to that are ongoing throughout the project, namely, setting up development, testing, and production sites; setting up a build and deployment procedure, including a version control system; and setting up an environment for everyone working on the project, with all the necessary (compatible) tools and workstations. You guessed it — this will be dealt with in detail in upcoming chapters.

*To delve even further into the whole question of software development process engineering (really getting it done right!), check out the CMMI website (''What Is CMMI?'' at* `http://sei.cmu.edu/cmmi/general`*). There are also books on the subject, specifically* CMMI Guidelines for Process Integration and Product Improvement, *by Mary Beth Chrissis, Mike Konrad, and Sandy Scrum* (`http://amazon.com/CMMI-Guidelines-Integration-Improvement-Engineering/dp/0321154967`)*, as well as* CMMI Distilled (`http://amazon.com/CMMI-Distilled-Introduction-Improvement-Engineering/dp/0321461088`)*. These sources give* *a good overview and grounding for this model. This model has been proven totally compatible with Agile approaches (*`www.agilecmmi.com/` *is just one example), and while it may definitely be overkill for most readers of this book, it may make all the difference in the world for some.*

## When Should You Do That?

The answer to this question is: during the whole project! There will be constant imbalance and balance struck again between two apparent opposites: the need to decide what to do and then do it, on the one hand, and the need for change, on the other. So this calls for an incremental and iterative approach, providing frequent opportunity for client feedback and for taking stock, and providing entry points for change and its impact to be repeatedly evaluated.

The mistake has been made time and time again, of using the so-called *waterfall model* approach to website development as a way of keeping things simple. "We will decide exactly what we want to do, and then we will do it." Experience has shown that this is a recipe for disaster and must be replaced with an incremental and iterative approach.

*For more information on the Standard Waterfall Model for Systems Development, see* `http://web.archive.org/web/20050310133243` *and* `http://asd-www.larc.nasa.gov/barkstrom/public/The_Standard_Waterfall_Model_For_Systems_Development.htm`.

Now, keeping it simple is actually the opposite of banishing change. Change is actually the mechanism by means of which clients understand what they really want and make sure the final product embodies their needs. That is why there need to be frequent iterations.

So, progress in the project means that various models are actually being built at the same time. The architectural big picture emerges and takes shape on a par with the requirements baseline, sometime in the third or fourth iteration, which is to say, together with actual deliveries of prototypes. By that time, all the user stories are written, estimated, and prioritized, and the iterations to implement them are planned.

But as the team starts plucking the next user story off the wall and starts seeing how to implement it, and as the client begins to see his or her dream more and more in the flesh, subtle and not so subtle changes will occur. If the planning has been good, then the user stories with the biggest likelihood of affecting the architecture will be among the first to be tackled. Then their impact will be positive and will help to shape the architectural baseline.

The catastrophe scenario to be avoided (and it is not always so easy to avoid) is a user story that gets implemented very late in the game and turns out to have a huge impact on architecture. You find out, for some reason, that the editing user interface simply has to be done in Flash, so we need to solve the problem of how to integrate Adobe's Remoting protocol with Drupal via, say, the Drupal Services module. Well, it's all good, but you really need to know about things that have that kind of impact earlier on.

The more the work is planned around iterations that are constructed in terms of a basic architectural vision and constantly checked by all concerned, the less likelihood there is of that kind of high-cost impact catastrophe occurring.

## What Should It Look Like?

Isn't it nice that this is just one more little section of this chapter? Too often a project is reduced to its bells and whistles (see the next section, "Making Sure You're Getting What You Really Want").

Well, because having a "Web 2.0 design" really is a concern of many clients, a good way of understanding what that means and what elements go together to constitute it, is the article "Current Web Design" (`http://webdesignfromscratch.com/current-style.cfm`).

But, most of all, you should be concerned about usability. You should concern yourself about form following content and being dictated by content. The best way to do that is to get the functionality of the site going first, and then and only then imposing the graphic design. That is the method you will be using in this book.

> *The obligatory read here is Steve Krug's book,* Don't Make Me Think *(*`http://sensible.com`*). However, I have recently seen this book cited in the Drupal forums as a reason why people in general, including developers, shouldn't have to think. No, for the end-user of a website not to have to think (that is what it's about), a lot of thinking has to go on: Drupaleros have to do a lot of thinking to get their websites done right.*

The main lessons are:

- The importance of usability testing
- The need to start out with a clear home page instead of ending up with a home page that is out of control
- The importance of usability testing
- The need to base your site navigation and design on how people really use the Internet
- The importance of usability testing

Drupal is great for this kind of approach — first, because, as you shall see, it is its own greatest prototyper, and second, because of its great theming system. With Drupal, the functionality is really skinnable, on a high level of detail and in a very flexible manner. But, of course, you have to know what you are doing. However, once you learn the secrets, you can leverage an extremely powerful theming system that has also proven itself to be very SEO friendly.

## Making Sure You're Getting What You Really Want

You should be concerned about testing, with the discipline of avoiding being driven by the bells and whistles instead of by what you really need. You should also be concerned about "Feature Creep," with quality control, and with building, which is understood as the integration of dependable blocks and units.

There are two basic principles involved here, and getting what you really want depends on both of them being observed:

- Unit testing forms an important part of the responsibility of implementing a piece of functionality. Unit tests must be written in such a way that they cover the maximum possible number of key functional points in the code.

- The whole process of development should be test-driven, by which we mean acceptance test-driven. Acceptance tests are black box tests; they test how the website application should behave. In website applications, usability testing forms an important part of acceptance testing.

While there are other forms of testing that should be included, such as stress and load testing, these two — unit tests and acceptance tests — are two you absolutely cannot do without. Indeed, the PHP SimpleTest framework is becoming part of Drupal. The module page can be found at `http://drupal.org/project/simpletest`, while great documentation is centralized at `http://drupal.org/simpletest`.

We have already defined acceptance tests, and here simply need to stress that they should be written and executed by the client, even though he or she will need to count on your assistance throughout the project in order to do so.

## Turning Over the Helm

At some point, the artist must be dragged kicking and screaming from her masterpiece and told: "It's done. It's not yours any longer; it belongs to the final user." This, too, must be planned for and implemented throughout the project. Its easy accomplishment is another beneficial result from getting the client involved, early and actively, in the project. Seeing the client as someone to keep at a distance like a bull in a china store will result in a difficult delivery of the website to those who will be using it thereafter.

Again, an iterative approach will help, and is actually indispensable, in order to avoid the all-too-often witnessed scenario of finishing a site and having no one to deliver it to, or else, delivery constituting itself as an almost insurmountable obstacle.

From the start, the responsibilities must be clear. One example scheme could be the following:

- Client is responsible for testing and acceptance.
- Client is responsible for administering website users and setting their permissions.
- Developer is responsible for updating Drupal core and modules.
- Client is responsible for contracting hosting.
- Developer is responsible for initial installation on production site.

This is why the phase is called *Transition* in the Unified Process approach. The website application itself must be deployed after all testing is completed. A maintenance plan must be in place. But there must also be documentation (manuals and/or on-line Help) and training in order to empower the client and the final users to actually use what they have acquired, for them to really take ownership.

In the case of website applications, the tight schedules they usually have and the fact that the resources actually required are generally overwhelming compared to what the client may actually have been thinking at the outset, so the more gradually this is all done, the better.

In this book, therefore, there will be a fictionalized client who will also be very much present throughout the project and who will actually motorize everything.

# Information Architecture and an Agile Approach for the Rest of Us

Best practices fans and refugees will discern throughout this chapter a dependency — a "standing on the shoulders of giants" — in relation both to the Agile approach to software development and to the discipline of information architecture (see `http://webmonkey.com/tutorial/Information_Architecture_Tutorial`; see also a more advanced article: `http://articles.techrepublic.com.com/5100-22_11-5074224.html`). Here I am drawing from a huge body of materials, and given the practical character of this book, I run the risk of treating these subjects superficially.

I hope that in the course of working through this book, it will be clear that I am not "name-dropping" buzzwords, but, rather, extracting from vast areas of expertise just what you need, and no more, in order to succeed at a task that is sold to you as simple and straightforward and that is simple and straightforward compared to doing everything from scratch, but that is neither simple nor straightforward.

So everything mentioned in this chapter will be used thoroughly, and you will gain a practical familiarity with all these tools.

So whether you are a project manager with specialized departments working under you, or someone who practically has to do the whole project alone, your responsibility in getting this site done right will very much make you a Renaissance person. You will learn much more about CSS and tools like Firebug than you may care to, more about navigation and menu systems than you may care to, even more about "templates" and PHP than you may care to. Indeed, in using Drupal, you may learn much more about "Views," "content types," "Taxonomy," and "clean URLs" than you ever dreamed of. You may find yourself checking out from CVS and SVN repositories and apt-get installing whole operating systems, or organizing and/or supervising others who do that as part of their everyday work.

You will find yourself involved in sending in "patches" to module maintainers. You may even be involved in theme or module development. You will find yourself concerned about unit test "coverage" and usability tests.

It is hoped that you will end up with a site done right together with a stack of passed acceptance tests that truly document the system requirements.

# The Example Used throughout This Book

As mentioned, you will be developing the Literary Workshop website application as an example project to illustrate the material presented in this book. Using a version control system and a standardized deployment procedure, you will be able to move forwards and backwards in time to all stages of development as part of your practical exploration.

As well, in the course of working your way through this book, you'll discover a whole series of what are termed reusable "Website Developer Patterns." These are collectible challenges, solutions, and secrets that crop up time and time again and need to be dealt with in project after project, and a systematic approach must be found for them in order to get your site done right.

So, let's get to it.

## Summary

In this chapter, you have been introduced to the methodology to be followed in this book in order to get the most out of the Drupal CMS framework, and to the nontrivial example you will be working with throughout. The methodology is based on an Agile approach to any kind of software development, and has been tailored to the development cycle required to develop a Drupal website application. In the next chapter, you will take your first practical steps and get the functional prototype up and running.

# 2

# Taking Baby Steps

This book is all about keeping it simple, but to be useful for those wishing to leverage Drupal, the experience of working through this book must be based on a reasonably complex real-world example. So, before diving right in, perhaps a recap is necessary.

In Chapter 1, the following questions were asked and answered in the context of using an Agile approach in the development of the example site worked on throughout this book, the *On-Line Literary Workshop*:

| Question | Answer |
|---|---|
| What's the website for? | A business model was created using a meme map. |
| Who's going to use the site? | It was emphasized that all user roles must be discovered in order to be able to capture all of the requirements. Four roles were discovered for the On-Line Literary Workshop: Workshop Leader, Workshop Member, Publisher, and Webmaster |
| What are they going to use it for? | Several user stories were identified for each user role. |
| What needs to be done so that they can do that? | An incremental and iterative method was adopted for planning of the development to be undertaken, dividing the work into four major phases (Inception, Elaboration, Construction, and Transition to Deployment) by assigning the user stories to them, ordered by the client's priorities and the development need to mitigate risk through the early tackling of tasks having a heavy architectural impact. |

During the initial, Inception, phase, Chapter 1 explains that a Vision is developed, outlining the scope and feasibility of the project based on cost and schedule estimates; initial requirements, risks, and mitigation strategies are identified, and a technical approach is agreed on, including a working prototype.

So now you are coming out of the Inception Phase of the project, the Literary Workshop website application. We have a Vision and scope and identification of the customer based on the meme map and the identification of user roles and user stories. Also, if we did the job right, we at least have a text file somewhere outlining a list of risks: In this case — "We're using several technologies we're not familiar with." "Shared hosting is becoming downright impossible to use for any serious undertakings." "A friend told me Drupal is very database-intensive." "Our client lives in Alaska, and there will be no face-to-face meetings." "The client's best friend is doing the graphic design, and who knows when that will be ready?" — And finally, we have settled upon a technical approach: We are definitely going to use a LAMP stack CMS framework deployed upon VPS hosting, with Drupal as our first choice.

The big job ahead of us now, as outlined in Chapter 1, is to embark on the Elaboration Phase in order to set the Requirements and Architectural baselines, and elaborate the planning.

For the Requirements baseline, you need to get the client to write the user stories you have outlined. But you want her to see and experiment with a running prototype before she does that, so you all know what you are talking about. This prototype will also allow you to experiment with different modules and theme approaches in Drupal so that you can move toward the fixing of the Architectural baseline, and — hopefully — make a dent in the risk list also.

In this chapter, you will work on the first two of the following list of tasks, wrapping up all of them by the end of Chapter 5. So you certainly have your work cut out for you:

- Creating an initial environment
- Whipping up our initial prototype
- Getting initial feedback from the client
- Finishing the user stories with the client
- Planning the project
- Working on the architectural baseline
- Getting the team organized and with the program

# Creating an Initial Environment

Figure 2-1 shows your initial working environment.

I can hear lots of you saying, "Hey, wait a minute, this isn't NASA, we're not sending a man to the moon." Well, you may not believe it, but you will be an expert in stuff like this, and you will get used to it in no time. And you will be very happy you did. And don't worry — you can simplify things in lots of ways. Referring to Figure 2-1:

- The Developer Workstation can be your own Mac or Ubuntu notebook.
- The Test Site can be practically any Drupal-friendly shared hosting.
- The Resource Repository can be automatically set up for you very cheaply using a paid service (such as — no endorsement intended — `unfuddle.com`, `cvsdude.com`, or `svnrepository.com`).
- The Client Workstation is simply the computer the client uses to view the website.

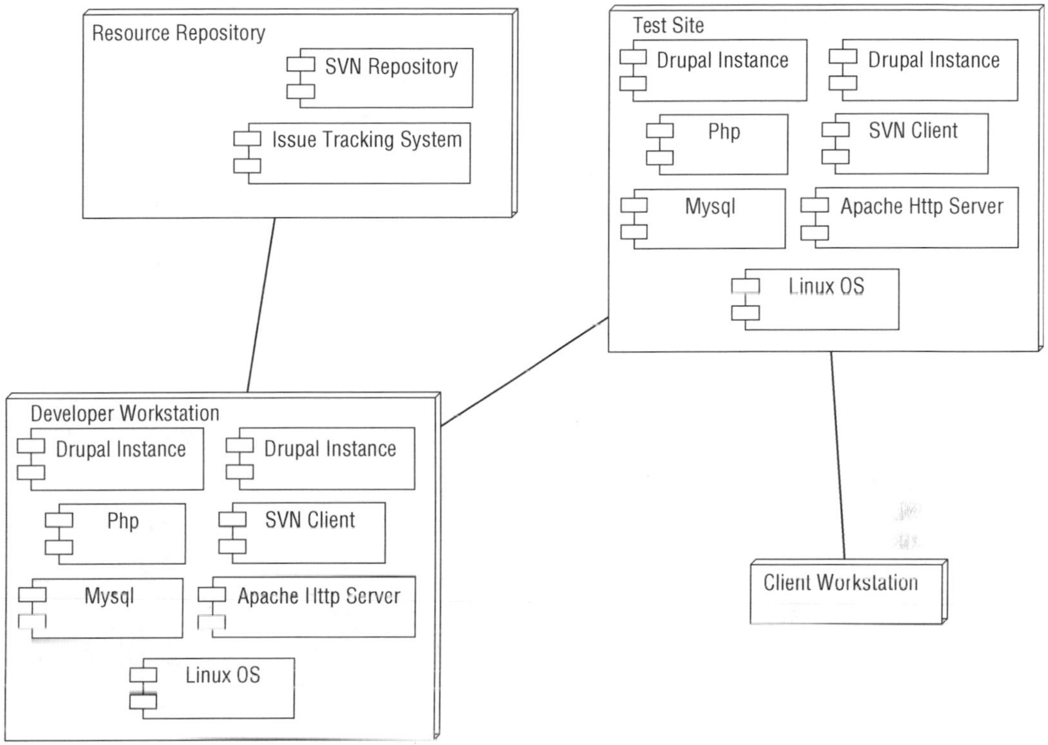


Figure 2-1

In Chapter 3, you will concentrate on the niceties and details of setting all of this up. In this chapter, you concentrate on getting Drupal installed in a typical shared hosting environment as a test site. And while not recommended, it is even possible to finish the remainder of the chapter with just that running (although if you don't have an issue-tracking system, you will have to put documentation somewhere handy for both you and your client: these days, something like shared Google docs can be more than enough).

By the way, before you go any further, the Drupal Documentation Handbooks (`http://drupal.org/handbook`) are required reading for this book. They are getting better and better all the time, thanks to a dedicated team of volunteer contributors. Please see the overview at `http://drupal.org/node/23743`, where you can find out how to contribute yourself!

As mentioned on that page, the Drupal Dojo project (`http://groups.drupal.org/drupal-dojo`) is also a great place to find a mutual help society as you climb the Drupal learning curve. That's where I got my start!

## Installing Drupal as a "One-Click" Pre-Installed Script

So there's more than one way to do it. Speaking of which, in order to install Drupal on a typical shared hosting site, many people simply use the "single-click," "pre-installed script" Fantastico approach, even though this is a frowned-on practice in the Drupal community.

Of course, simply for prototyping, it's no biggie. But you'll only have to uninstall later, simply because experience has shown that when a security update comes out, Fantastico may not offer that for you right away, and even if they do, your hosting provider may take even more time to update. So for production purposes and any serious use, even as a personal blog, it is out of the question. If you want to go directly to learning how to install Drupal right, skip to the next section.

However, in case you want to do this because just for prototyping you feel it may be best for the time being (we don't favor getting involved in religious wars here), follow these steps:

1. Log into your shared hosting control panel, and look for the Fantastico icon. Figure 2-2 shows it in a typical shared hosting control panel.

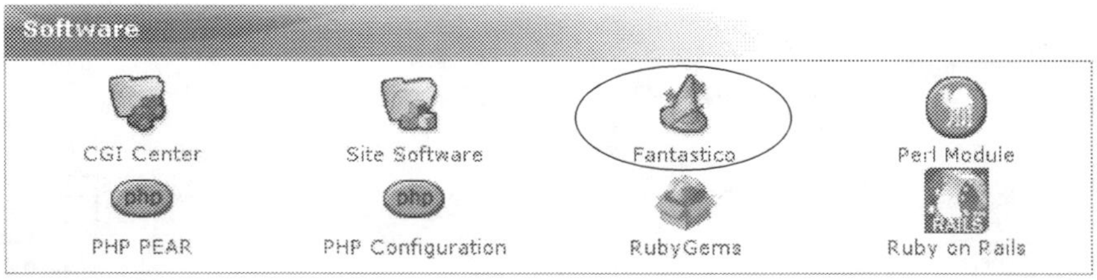


Figure 2-2

2. Click the Fantastico icon. Then, click Drupal, to be found in the list under the Content Management section (see Figure 2-3).

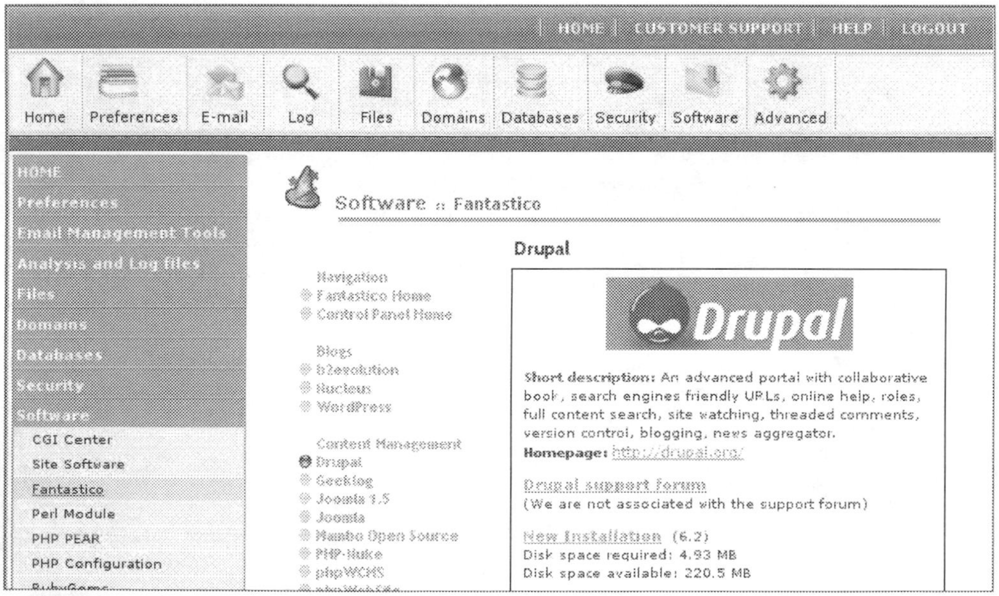


Figure 2-3

3. Click New Installation, and fill in the required details in the Fantastico installation form (see Figure 2-4). The domain in which the Drupal instance should be installed will be chosen for you by Cpanel. If you want, you can leave the "Install in directory" field blank

to install in the root document directory of your website, or else, you can type **workshop** to install into `http://example.com/workshop`. (Throughout this book, the mythical "`http://example.com`" URL will be used whenever a canonical URL is indicated.) To finish up, you need to specify an administrator username and a password, plus an administrator e-mail. And you're done.

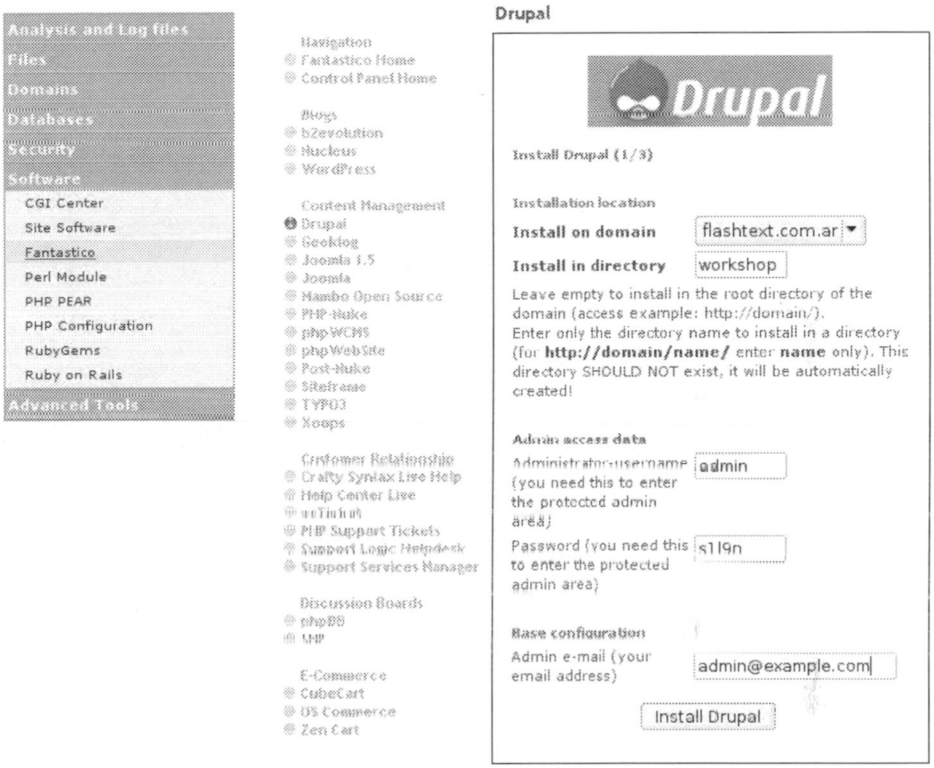


**Figure 2-4**

4. Click on the Install Drupal button. You are then given some summary info as shown in Figure 2-5.

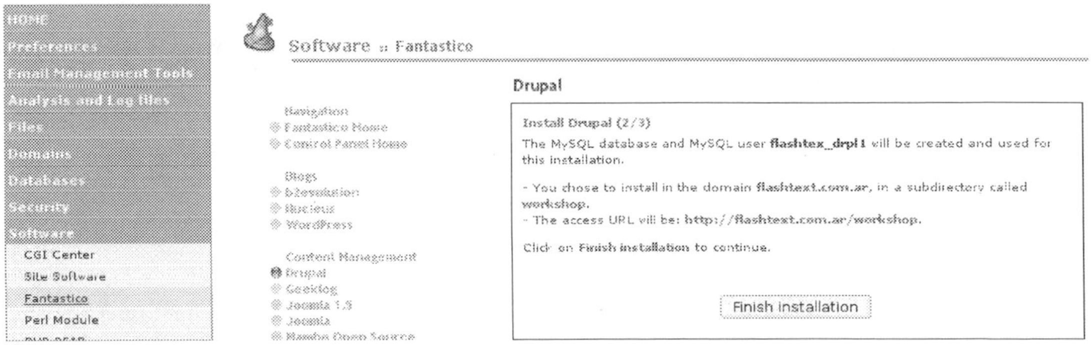


**Figure 2-5**

5. Click on the "Finish installation" button so that the installation can actually proceed. After a relatively short while, you should be rewarded by a final summary page (see Figure 2-6).

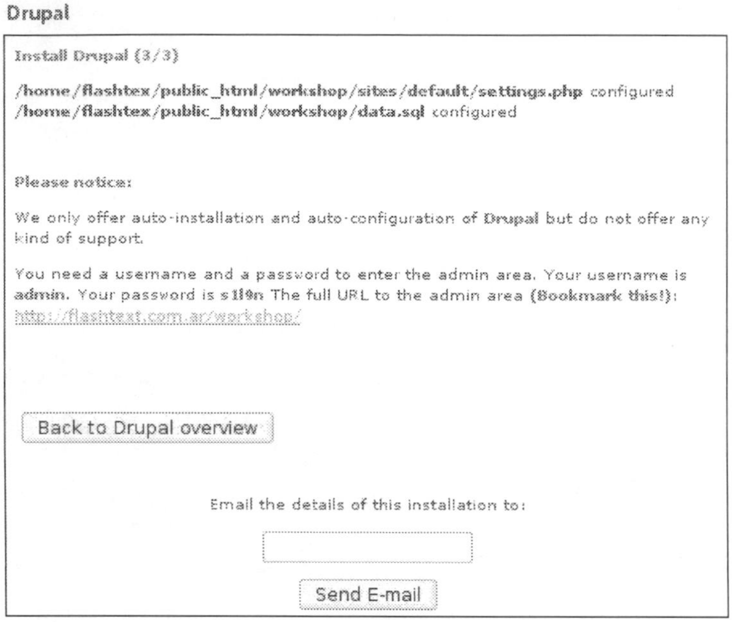

Drupal
Install Drupal (3/3)
/home/flashtex/public_html/workshop/sites/default/settings.php configured
/home/flashtex/public_html/workshop/data.sql configured
Please notice:
We only offer auto-installation and auto-configuration of Drupal but do not offer any kind of support.
You need a username and a password to enter the admin area. Your username is admin. Your password is s1l9n The full URL to the admin area (Bookmark this!):
http://flashtext.com.ar/workshop/
Back to Drupal overview
Email the details of this installation to:
Send E-mail


Figure 2-6

6. Jot down the admin username and password, e-mail the details of the installation to some lucky person, and/or bookmark and go directly to the URL of your new Drupal installation. (Figure 2-7 shows the freshly installed Drupal.)

## Installing Drupal Right

You can use the Fantastico installed Drupal for the prototyping you need to do now, but eventually you'll need to do a manual installation of Drupal, which is actually pretty straightforward. Because you definitely need to learn how to do this, the best thing is to learn that now.

There are many resources on installing Drupal at `http://drupal.org`, plus several video resources around the Internet (e.g., see the two videos published by Addison Berry on the Lullabot site in the References section at the end of this chapter).

What is involved in installing Drupal, exactly?

In Drupal 5.x, you just need to take these few steps and you're done. The steps are as follows and are detailed in the following sections:

1. Create a MySQL database and a user with full privileges to only that database. You can do this in one of three ways — using a control panel provided by your hosting company (such as CPanel or Plesk), using phpMyAdmin (recommended), or using the command line.

2. Download Drupal, and unpack the tarball. Again, you have several options for making this happen. You can use FTP, download it via the command line, or use CVS. Of these, I consider using CVS the best way of all!
3. Make sure the settings file is filesystem-writable.
4. Point your browser at the Drupal installation.
5. Create your first users.

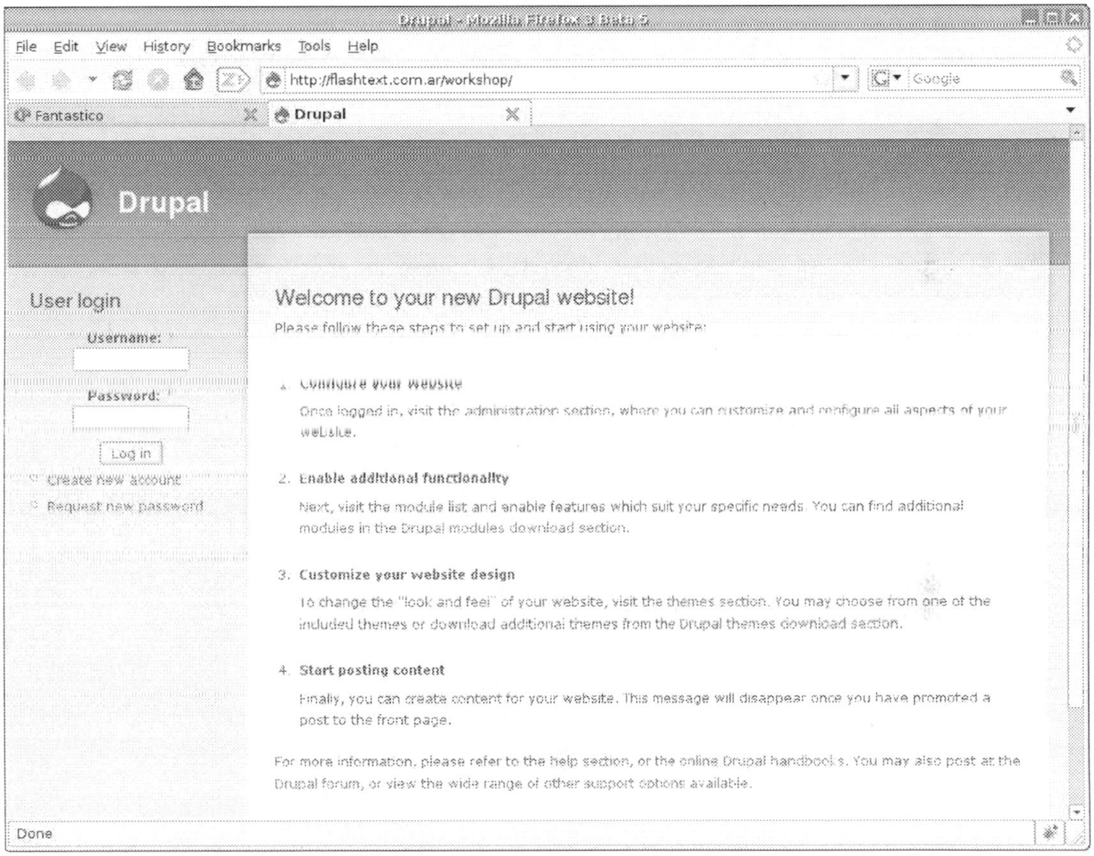


Figure 2-7

## Creating a MySQL Database

As stated before, the first step in installing Drupal right is by creating a MySQL database and then creating a user with full privileges to only that database. You have three ways to do this:

- **Using CPanel** (or other control panel) — These days, CPanel offers a MySQL Database Wizard. Basically, you are going to provide a name for the database (**workshop**), then on the next page, a username (seven characters maximum: **wrkshop**) and password (**workshop99**, which we are told is of 50% strength, so try to do better; in any event, you type that in twice). On the next page, the username and password are displayed (write it down), and you click on "All

Privileges" to indicate that this new user has all privileges to this, and only this, database (which is what you want). Then you click Next again, and you are informed that your work is done: "User xxxx_wrkshop was added to the database xxxx_workshop." Here "*xxxx*" refers to your CPanel username, which is automatically prepended. So the upshot is that you have three items of info, which is all you need for the Drupal installation Wizard:

- MySql username
- MySql user password
- MySql database name to which the user has all privileges

- **Using phpMyAdmin** — If you are using CPanel, the odds are that you will have to follow the above procedure to create a database for your Drupal installation, but if your hosting provider tells you that you can use phpMyAdmin to create the database, or you have your own setup with phpMyAdmin installed, here's the quickest and easiest way to do it (this is the recommended method for creating a database for Drupal in this book):

1. Go to myPhpAdmin, and click the Privileges link shown in Figure 2-8. If it isn't there, use the previous method directly from CPanel.

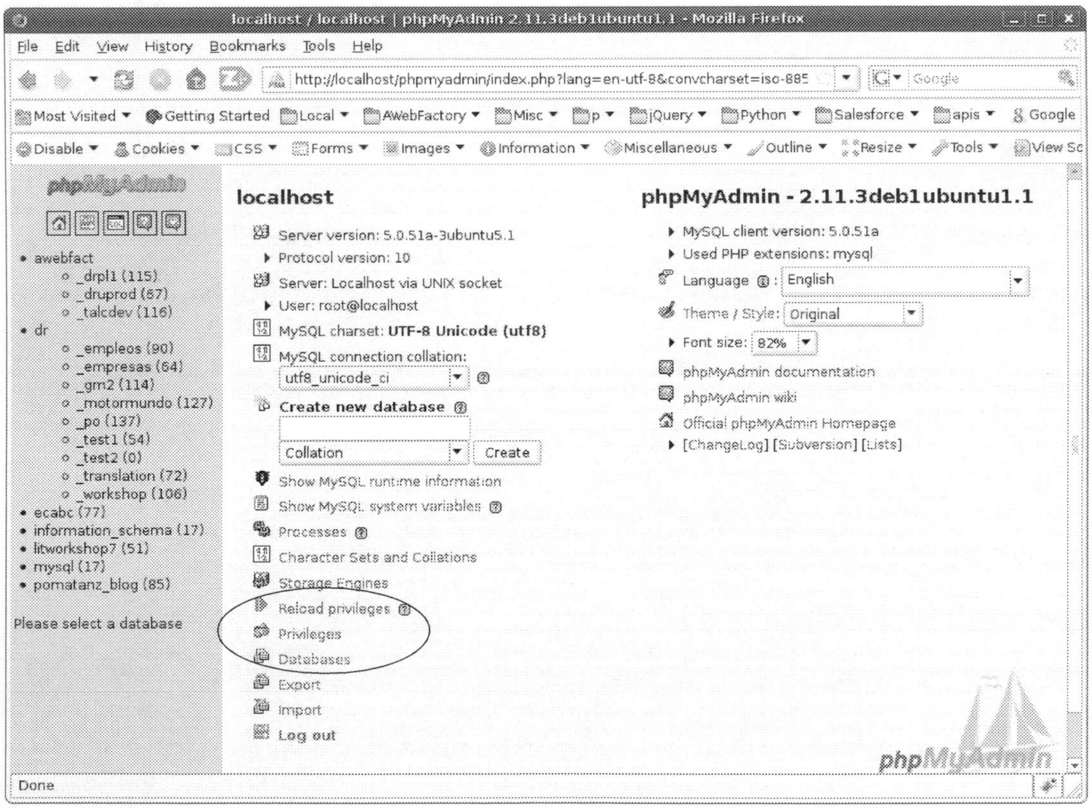

Figure 2-8

2. Click on "Add a new User," as shown in Figure 2-9.

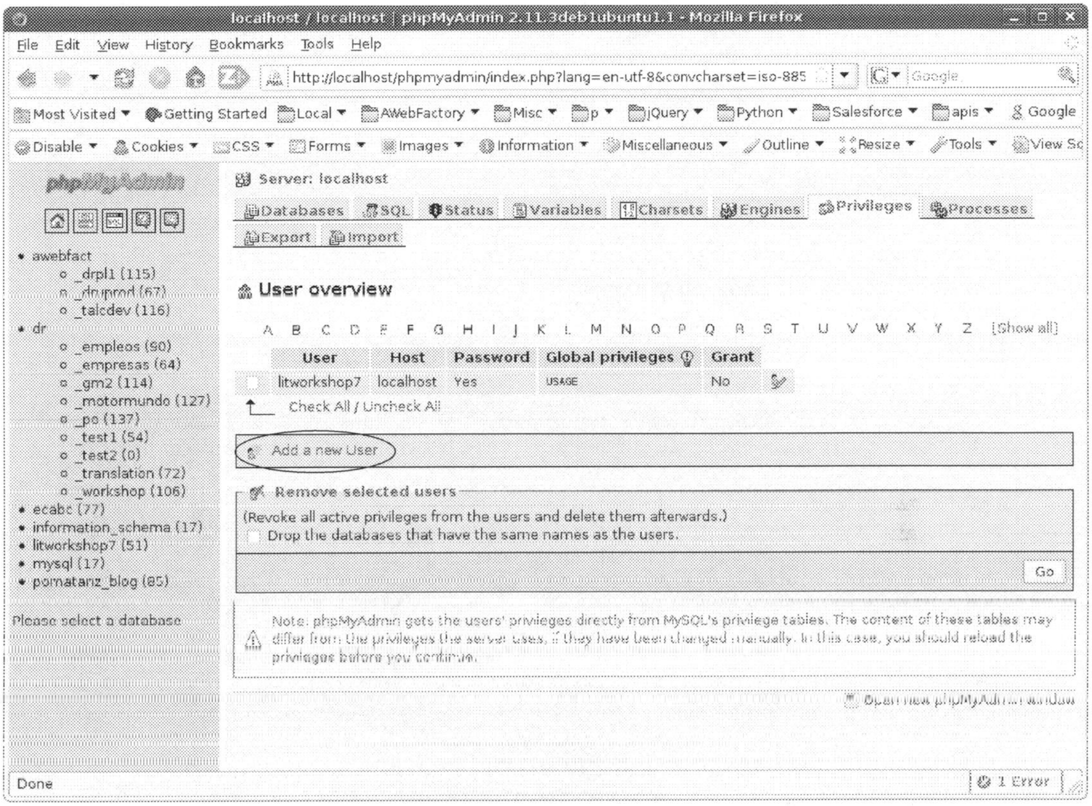


Figure 2-9

3. On the following page (Figure 2-10), fill in a username, make sure to indicate "Local" for host (**localhost** will automatically be filled in to the right), and provide a password. Be sure to select the checkbox labeled "Create database with same name and grant all privileges."

4. Click on the Go button on the bottom of the page. On the following page, you're informed that the new user has been added, and in the SQL query shown, which is the one phpMyAdmin used to create the database, you can see that the database has been created and that the user has full privileges on that database.

- **Using the Command Line** — Some of us would just as soon install on the command line. Nowadays, this assumes that you have access to ssh (Secure Shell) on your hosting server. If you don't have that, ask your hosting provider to grant you that access, and often they will. They may ask you for a reason, and you can simply say, "I want to download and install Drupal from the command line."

### About the Command Line

The command line is definitely making a comeback. Undoubtedly, GUI (graphical user interfaces) have been fundamental and essential for the generalized adoption of the personal computer. But sometimes it's just plain easier and more straightforward to punch out a few commands at the prompt in a terminal window than going through a complex series of mouse strokes and drags, especially with tasks that are repeated often.

This is recognized by the recent introduction of the amazing Ubiquity extension for the Firefox plug-in, which allows you to do quick calculations and even searches and translations from a command line that pops up with a shortcut key.

So for many of the tasks you need to do throughout this book, a command-line version is almost always included, and sometimes it's the most direct and even the only way to accomplish some tasks.

A clear example of this is downloading a module to your server. The easiest way is to right-click on the download link on `http://drupal.org` and copy the link URL. Then, log in via a terminal window (gnome-terminal in Ubuntu, putty in Windows, iTerm, etc.) to your website server, change directories to a convenient modules repository, and perform the following command:

```
$ wget {module-download-URL}
```

That's it! Otherwise, you have to download it to your local laptop or workstation and then upload it via FTP or SFTP.

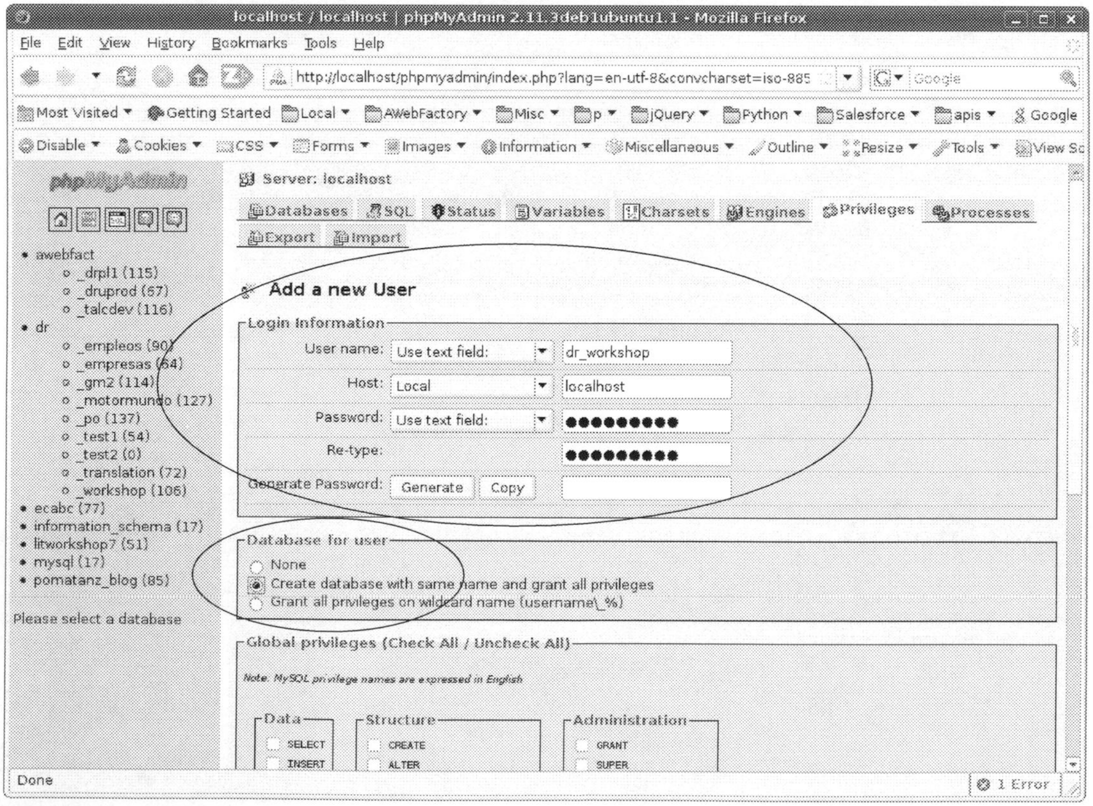


Figure 2-10

**A word to the wise: if you have just installed MySQL yourself, or you are in a brand-new VPS or dedicated server installation, make sure that the root user has a password. If you are not sure, do the following:**

```
# mysql -u root
ERROR 1045 (28000): Access denied for user 'root'@'localhost'
(using password: NO)
```

**If you do not see this error, but instead are given the mysql prompt, then no password has been set. Set it as follows:**

```
mysql> USE mysql;
mysql> UPDATE user SET Password=PASSWORD('new-password')↵
WHERE user='root';
mysql> FLUSH PRIVILEGES;
mysql> quit
Bye
```

**Now go back into MySQL as root, this time invoking use of the password, and create the Drupal user and database as follows (putting in a secure password where it says *password*, of course):**

```
mysql> CREATE DATABASE dr_workshop;
mysql> GRANT ALL ON dr_workshop.* TO dr_workshop@localhost
IDENTIFIED BY↵
 'password';
mysql> quit
```

Again, you have the Drupal database and user, together with the password. Now to download Drupal, unpack it, point your browser at it, fill in the database info, and we are done!

## Downloading Drupal

Next, you want to download Drupal and unpack the tarball into the appropriate directory. Naturally, there are many, many ways to do this. This section outlines four in the sections that follow.

### Using FTP

You could download the Drupal installation tarball onto your workstation, unpack it using your favorite file manager, and then upload all the files to the appropriate directory on your hosting server using FTP. To download Drupal 5.x in the first place, point your browser at `http://drupal.org`, and in the top-right-hand corner, click the release you are interested in downloading. In this case at this point, it is Drupal 5.x., so click the latest 5.x release, which at the time of this writing was Drupal 5.7 but could well be Drupal 5.11 or later for you. Download the file, which will be named something like `http://ftp.drupal.org/files/projects/drupal-5.7.tar.gz` (with the *.7* changing with the point release version, e.g., to *.11*). Then you can unpack it and upload it to your server using your favorite FTP client.

**A word to the wise: Make sure you upload the .htaccess file in the Drupal root directory. You may have to configure your FTP client to not hide files starting with a dot. Failure to upload this file will cause you all kinds of problems.**

### Doing It on the Command Line

If you want to place your Drupal installation into a subdirectory of the document root of your hosting server (maybe you redirected a subdomain to point there), this is pretty straightforward. From the Drupal Download page, instead of clicking the Drupal release download link, right-click on it and choose Copy Link Location. Then from your document root, type **wget** on the command line, leave a space, and paste in the download URL for the Drupal tarball. After pressing Enter, you should see something like this:

```
# wget  http://ftp.drupal.org/files/projects/drupal-5.7.tar.gz
--18:28:36--  http://ftp.drupal.org/files/projects/drupal-5.7.tar.gz
          => 'drupal-5.7.tar.gz'
Resolving ftp.drupal.org... 140.211.166.134
Connecting to ftp.drupal.org|140.211.166.134|:80... connected.
HTTP request sent, awaiting response... 200 OK
Length: 754,688 (737K) [application/x-gzip]

100%[=======================================>] 754,688      249.00K/s

18:28:40 (248.33 KB/s) - 'drupal-5.7.tar.gz' saved [754688/754688]
```

Then, simply untar in the following manner (notice typical output):

```
# tar xvzf drupal-5.7.tar.gz
drupal-5.7/
drupal-5.7/includes/
drupal-5.7/includes/bootstrap.inc
drupal-5.7/includes/cache.inc
... (all the subdirectories and files)
drupal-5.7/themes/pushbutton/tabs-option-hover.png
drupal-5.7/themes/pushbutton/tabs-option-off.png
drupal-5.7/themes/pushbutton/tabs-option-on.png
```

You will now have a subdirectory named something like *drupal-5.7*. Simply rename it as follows, and you are done:

```
# mv drupal-5.7 workshop
```

### Installing Drupal into the Root Directory

As an example, this is if it is the main application running on your site. This method is just a tad trickier. For this, you simply make use of the tmp directory or any other handy location. Assuming that your server document root is at /home/myaccount/public_html, do the following:

```
# cd /tmp
# wget http://ftp.drupal.org/files/projects/drupal-5.7.tar.gz
# tar xvzf drupal-5.7.tar.gz
# cd drupal-5.7
# cp -r * /path/to/public_html
# cp .htaccess /path/to/public_html
```

### Doing It with CVS

This is the best way of all! Concurrent Versions System CVS (`www.nongnu.org/cvs/`) is a version control system built atop historic *nix tools, on which Drupal bases its releases. This may or may not look very intimidating to you at first, but actually what it does when you issue the appropriate command is grab a whole complete file-tree from the Drupal repository and stick it just where you want it on your server.

And that's not all: as you'll see in the next chapter, with the issue of a very simple command, you can carry out updates of various kinds, on Drupal itself as well as on functional add-on components.

As explained in the Drupal Documentation Handbooks (`http://drupal.org/node/320`), after navigating to the directory where you keep all your sites (on a typical shared hosting, that might be *public_html*; on your own development box, that might be */var/www*), you can check out a fresh copy of Drupal to a subdirectory called *drupal*, which can then be renamed to whatever you wish by issuing the following command:

```
# cvs -z6 -d:pserver:anonymous:anonymous@cvs.drupal.org:/cvs/drupal co -r ↵
DRUPAL-5-7 drupal
```

So this will check out Drupal 5.7 into the subdirectory drupal. For other release core branch names, see `http://drupal.org/node/93997`. You can even find instructions on this same Drupal handbook page on how to create an "alias" in your bash shell so that you can just type out a simple command for this, such as **checkout5-7** or **checkout6** or **checkouthead** (to check out the development branch in order to experiment for non-production sites).

Because of the way Drupal is packaged in the CVS repository, if you need to install Drupal into the web root directly, you need to do the same as above, and then copy to the web root. Don't forget the .htaccess file! Supposing you have unpacked Drupal 5.7 into the /tmp/drupal-5.7 directory, navigate to the web root directory and do something like the following:

```
$ cp -R /tmp/drupal-5.7/* .
$ cp /tmp/drupal-5.7/.htaccess .
```

## Making Sure the Settings File Is Writeable

Now you are almost ready to point your browser to where you have unpacked Drupal, provide the database information, and get started. But because the automatic install Wizard will be writing your database settings to a settings file (appropriately enough: ./sites/default/settings.php), you need to make that filesystem writeable. While this can certainly be done using your FTP client, supposing you were doing this on the command line, you would simply do the following, directly from the document root:

```
# chmod 666 sites/default/settings.php
```

and then once you finish running the browser-based Drupal installation Wizard, you re-protect the file with the following command:

```
# chmod 644 sites/default/settings.php
```

*See more about filesystem permissions at* `http://drupal.org/server-permissions`.

## Pointing Your Browser at the Drupal Installation

Supposing you were installing Drupal on your personal development workstation or laptop, you would point your browser at `http://localhost/workshop` and fill in the information (if you are running PHP5, which you actually most certainly should be, use the "mysqli" option — see Figure 2-11 — Drupal 6 does this for you):

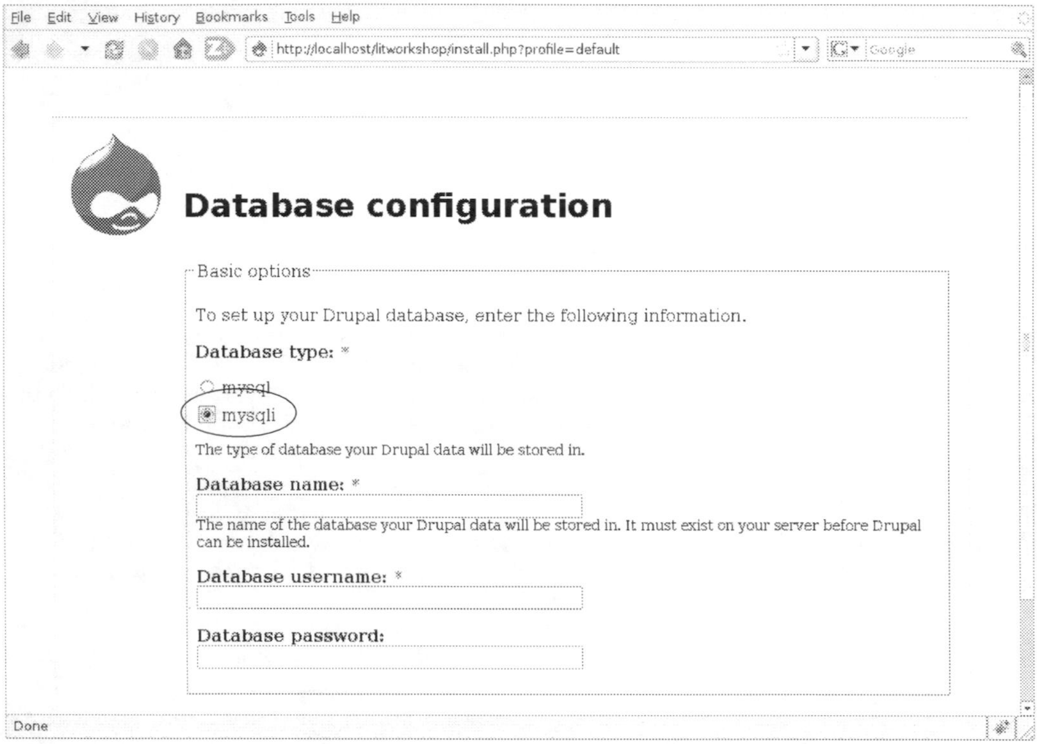


Figure 2-11

After hitting the Save configuration button, you can see that you are done (see Figure 2-12):

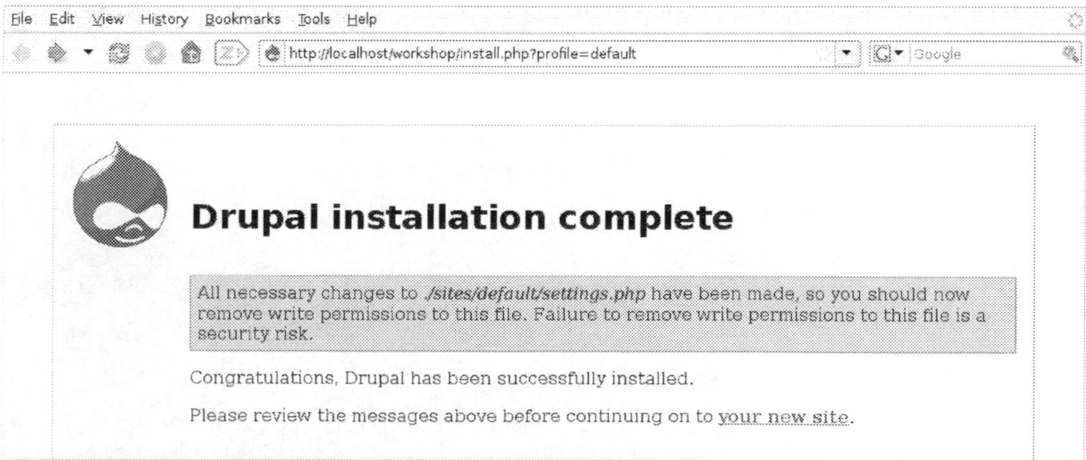


Figure 2-12

You are warned about removing Write permissions from ./sites/default/settings.php, as described above, and after taking care of that, you can click the link taking you to your new site.

### Creating Your First Users

Click on the "Create the first account" link, which now appears on the Welcome to Drupal page (included until the first content is created), and follow the instructions, naming this user **admin**. As the instructions say, "This account will have full administration rights and will allow you to configure your website." For this reason, most experienced Drupal users only use this user on rare occasions, for upgrading and other superuser actions, to protect the session from ever being hijacked.

So after creating your *superuser* admin, you're told the automatically created password, which you should change at this very screen: Fill in the new password in the Password and Confirm password fields, and hit the Submit button at the bottom of the page.

At this point, consult the "Configure Your Website" section of the Drupal Documentation Handbooks (found for Drupal 5 at `http://drupal.org/getting-started/5/install/configure`), and follow the instructions there for configuring your site and creating a special administration role and everyday administrator user.

## Whipping up the Initial Prototype

At this point, you should be interested in getting the initial prototype going in order to get feedback from the client on whether or not all the roles have been created and the list of user stories is complete. Then the user stories can be written.

At DrupalCon Barcelona 2007, I gave a presentation called "Using Drupal Itself to Prototype Your Drupal-Based Web Application" (see `http://barcelona2007.drupalcon.org/node/512`). There I quoted Dries as having recommended the article "Death to Visio Site Maps! How Clear Ink Uses Drupal for Information Architecture, Prototyping, and Project Management" (see `http://clearnightsky.com/node/318`). There, one method of prototyping is outlined, and we certainly share the sentiment that Drupal is its own best prototyper.

In the next sections, you are going to create the necessary roles, create some users, and get some basic functionality going according to our list of user stories.

### Implementing Roles

For each role, you are going to . . .create a role! Log in to your Drupal site with your everyday admin user ID (let's call that *dev*).

Dev, by the way, is an important user, fulfilling an important role. To create it, follow these steps:

1. First create the role by going to Administer ➤ User management ➤ Roles and simply adding the *admin* role. Then you assign it all permissions without exception either by clicking "Edit Permissions" or else by proceeding to Administer ➤ User management ➤ Access control (where you can see the permissions granted to all roles simultaneously) and doing the same. Figure 2-13 shows the screen for setting permissions.

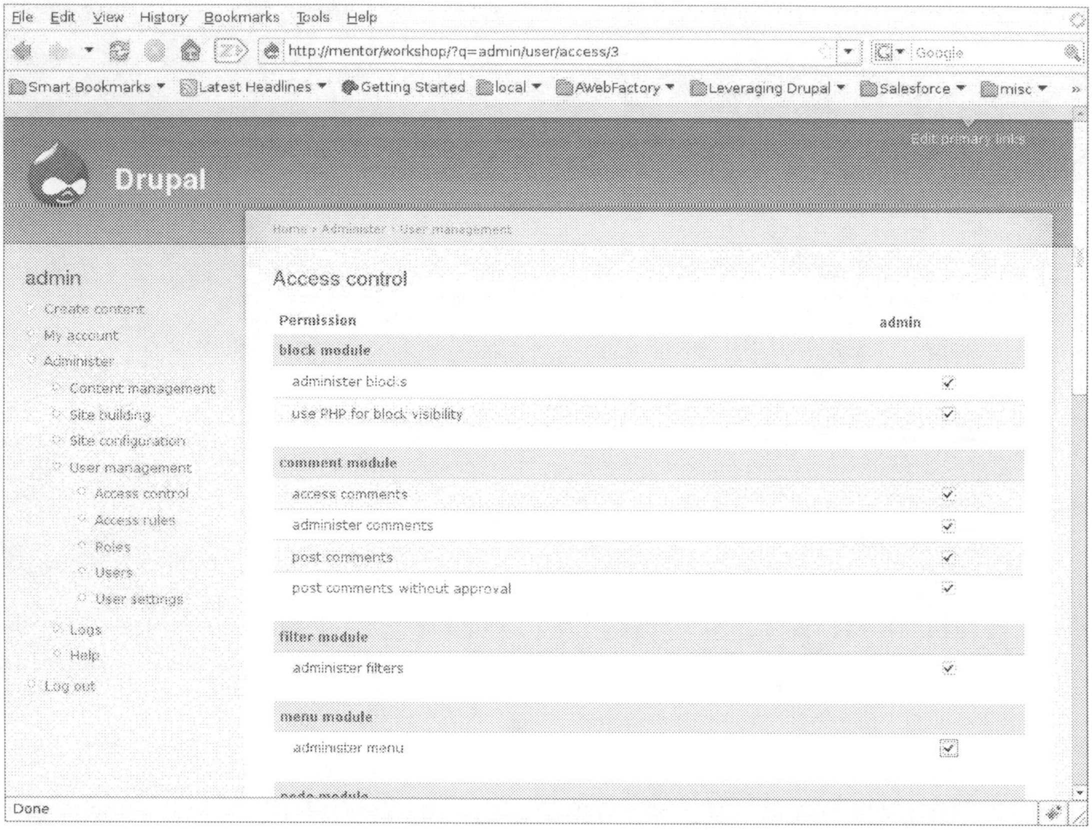


Figure 2-13

2. Now go to Administer ➤ User management ➤ Users and create the dev user, as shown in Figure 2-14.

3. Log out as admin, and log back in as user dev on an everyday basis for the duration of the project (except for superuser tasks such as core and module updates). User dev should have full Administer privileges; if that is not the case, log back in as admin and make sure that all permissions have been granted to the admin role.

4. As dev, go to Administer ➤ User management ➤ Roles, and create the following roles, on the basis of our requirements captured so far (see Chapter 1):

    - Workshop Leader
    - Workshop Member
    - Publisher
    - Webmaster

5. Assign the permissions to the various roles, and create example users in a bit, after creating your business objects. For now, you should have what you see in Figure 2-15, which shows the roles for the Literary Workshop website application.

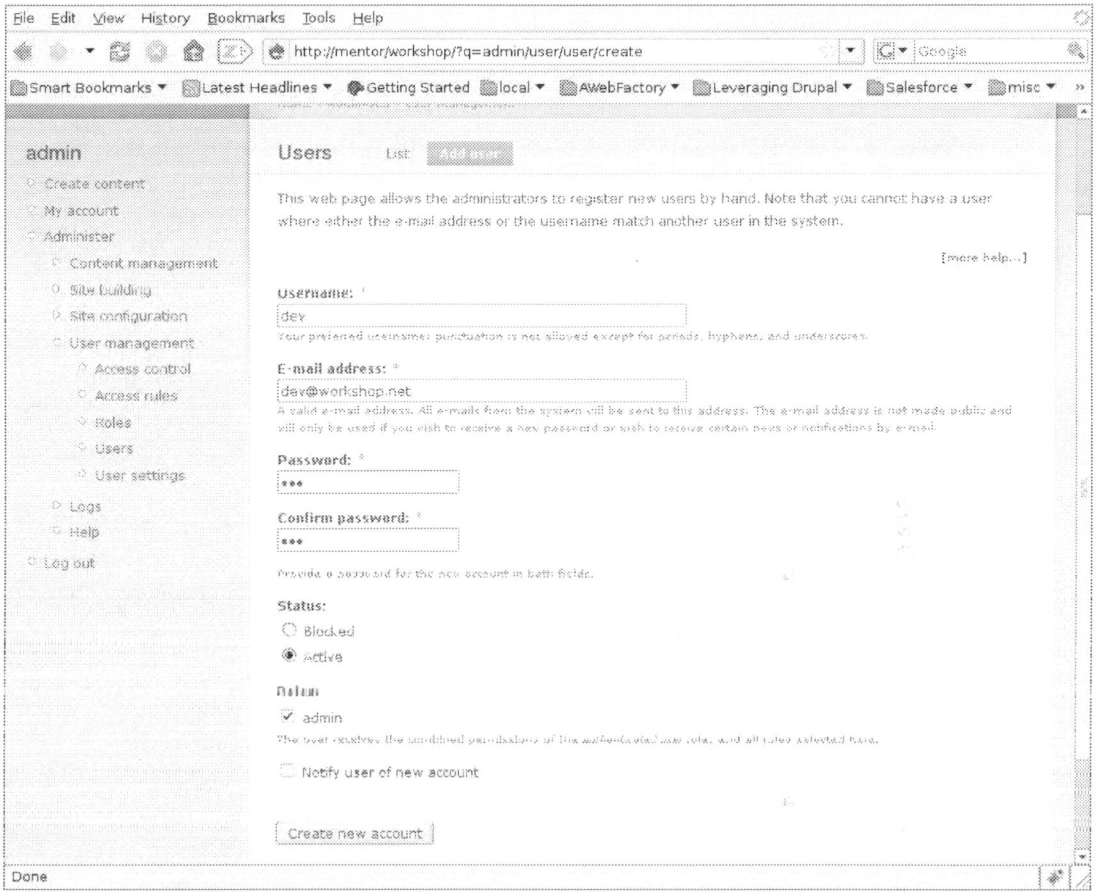


Figure 2-14

## Implementing the Business Objects

In Chapter 1, a first-cut list of user stories was identified (see the table in the section "What Are They Going to Use It For?" in Chapter 1). The basic objective in creating the initial prototype is to implement the user stories corresponding to each role on a very simple level. This involves a workflow by means of which users of each role can act on a series of business objects: They should be able to create, list, select, modify, and/or delete them.

With the stock, default Drupal you have installed right now, you can create stories (for simple articles) and pages (for static content such as an About page). If you enable the core modules packaged with Drupal — blog, forum, and book — you can create these additional forms of content. On the navigation menu (headed *dev* when you are logged in as user dev, and *navigation* for unregistered users), on the left-hand side of the screen is the option Create Content. Clicking that link brings up a list of content types currently supported by the system. But apart from this basic Content Management functionality that comes with Drupal out-of-the-box, you need to have a way to define content types (business objects) capable of being handled separately, and capable of supporting specialized data attributes, or fields.

You need a "posted work" with a word count field, for example, and an "application for membership" content type as well.

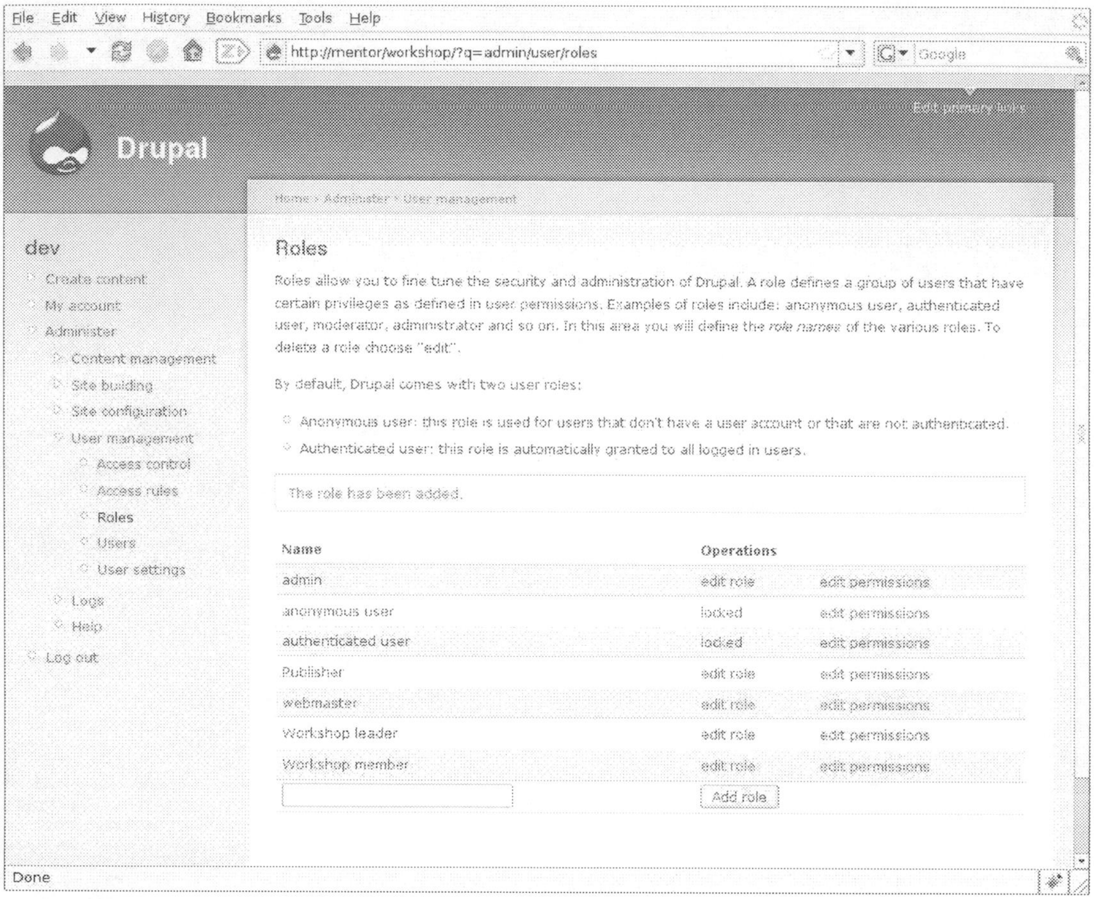
File Edit View History Bookmarks Tools Help
http://mentor/workshop/?q=admin/user/roles
Google
Drupal
Home › Administer › User management
dev
Create content
My account
Administer
Content management
Site building
Site configuration
User management
Access control
Access rules
Roles
Users
User settings
Logs
Help
Log out
Roles
Roles allow you to fine tune the security and administration of Drupal. A role defines a group of users that have certain privileges as defined in user permissions. Examples of roles include: anonymous user, authenticated user, moderator, administrator and so on. In this area you will define the role names of the various roles. To delete a role choose "edit".
By default, Drupal comes with two user roles:
Anonymous user: this role is used for users that don't have a user account or that are not authenticated.
Authenticated user: this role is automatically granted to all logged in users.
The role has been added.
Name
Operations
admin
edit role
edit permissions
anonymous user
locked
edit permissions
authenticated user
locked
edit permissions
Publisher
edit role
edit permissions
webmaster
edit role
edit permissions
Workshop leader
edit role
edit permissions
Workshop member
edit role
edit permissions
Add role
Done
**Figure 2-15**

Historically, in order to create a custom content type with additional fields of various kinds, you had to write a node module in PHP. But starting with Drupal 4.7, the Content Construction Kit (CCK) module (`http://drupal.org/project/cck`), like the (now essentially deprecated) flexinode module before it, enabled non-programmers to create additional content types from the administration panel, without programming, and also allowed for additional fields to be specified for the new content types.

In Drupal 5.x, the functionality for actually creating the content type was included in Drupal core, with the functionality for creating additional fields left in the contributed module, which means that to add fields, it is necessary to download and install the module.

So that is what you're going to do right now. At this point, of course, you should read the instructions "Installing Contributed Modules" in the Drupal handbook (`http://drupal.org/node/70151`), and then consult the README.txt file that comes with the module itself. But I would like to show you the steps I happened to follow now, and also take the opportunity to underline one important consideration:

> **Word to the wise: Do not install contributed modules in the modules directory where core modules are placed.**
>
> **When you download a fresh Drupal installation, there are two subdirectories, Modules and Themes, where core elements are placed. The reason you never want to store your own or downloaded modules and themes there is that when it comes time to update your Drupal core, it is going to be a very painstaking process to have to pick and choose what directories and files need to be overwritten and which should not be. You need to be able to confidently unpack a new Drupal release right on top of the current one, run the update script, and be on your way. So you must store anything that is not core and comes pre-packaged with a fresh Drupal installation in its own place.**

That place for most people using Drupal, for a single Drupal site installation, is usually ./sites/all/modules and ./sites/all/themes (see ./sites/all/README.txt). That way, you have your sites subdirectory full of site-specific stuff, and all the rest of the installation is pure off-the-shelf freshly downloaded Drupal. The only exception here is the files directory (images, videos, etc.), which can either reside below ./sites also, or else on the top level.

So to install CCK you need to download it, unpack it, and stick it under ./sites/all/modules. Here are the basic steps:

1. Here is the original directory structure for sites:

```
sites
|-- all
|   '-- README.txt
'-- default
    '-- settings.php
```

2. Modify it as follows by creating Modules and Themes directories under sites/all:

```
victorkane@mentor:/var/www/workshop$ cd sites/all
victorkane@mentor:/var/www/workshop/sites/all$ mkdir modules themes
```

You can see your new directory structure by stepping back and looking at the sites directory tree:

```
victorkane@mentor:/var/www/workshop/sites/all$ cd ../..
victorkane@mentor:/var/www/workshop$ tree sites
sites
|-- all
|   |-- README.txt
|   |-- modules
|   '-- themes
'-- default
    '-- settings.php

4 directories, 2 files
victorkane@mentor:/var/www/workshop$
```

3. From the command line, change the directory to ./sites/all/modules, grab the CCK module using `wget` (go to the CCK module page, right-click on the download link, and select Copy link location or similar, then paste it as an argument to `wget`) and then unpack it under ./sites/all/modules. Step by step:

```
victorkane@mentor:/var/www/workshop$ cd sites/all/modules
victorkane@mentor:/var/www/workshop/sites/all/modules$ wget ↵
http://ftp.drupal.org/ ↵
files/projects/cck-5.x-1.7.tar.gz
--15:26:45--  http://ftp.drupal.org/files/projects/cck-5.x-1.7.tar.gz
           => 'cck-5.x-1.7.tar.gz'
Resolving ftp.drupal.org... 140.211.166.134
Connecting to ftp.drupal.org|140.211.166.134|:80... connected.
HTTP request sent, awaiting response... 200 OK
Length: 130,633 (128K) [application/x-gzip]

100%[===================================>] 130,633        95.71K/s

15:26:47 (95.54 KB/s) - 'cck-5.x-1.7.tar.gz' saved [130633/130633]
victorkane@mentor:/var/www/workshop/sites/modules$ tar xvzf
cck-5.x-1.7.tar.gz
cck/
cck/po/
cck/po/cck.pot
cck/po/da.po
...
cck/theme/field.tpl.php
cck/theme/node-content_example.tpl.php
cck/theme/template.php
cck/LICENSE.txt
```

4. Now, you can either copy the module tarball to a storage space of your own or (as shown below) delete it directly:

```
victorkane@mentor:/var/www/workshop/sites/all/modules$ ls
cck  cck-5.x-1.7.tar.gz
victorkane@mentor:/var/www/workshop/sites/all/modules$ rm
cck-5.x-1.7.tar.gz
```

That's it. In Drupal itself, go to Administer ➢ Site building ➢ Modules, and enable the CCK module.

Quick admin aside: But wait, what's that red warning when you visit the main Administer page? The following table shows initial site-housekeeping tasks:

| Problem | Solution |
|---|---|
| Administration page warnings | Click the status report link (shown in Figure 2-16) to see what needs to be done. |
| Configuration file not protected | Remove Write permissions on ./sites/default/settings.php:<br>`# cd sites/default/`<br>`# ls -l`<br>`total 8` |

| **Problem** | **Solution** |
|---|---|
| | `-rw-rw-rw- 1 victorkane victorkane 5983 2008-05-31 19:21`<br>`settings.php`<br>`# chmod 644 settings.php`<br>`# ls -l`<br>`total 8`<br>`-rw-r--r-- 1 victorkane victorkane 5983 2008-05-31 19:21`<br>`settings.php`<br>`#`<br>`The warning will no longer be present. (Note: this task can also be accomplished by using your favorite FTP client.)` |
| `cron` maintenance tasks | Run `cron` manually (if search is enabled, search indexing will progress).<br>Or, set up `cron` tasks on the system. This can be done directly through the CPanel in shared hosting, or else via the command:<br>`# crontab -e`<br>This allows you to edit the `cron` tasks in your system.<br>Afterward, it should be possible to visualize the `cron` tasks with the following command:<br>`# crontab -l`<br>`# m h dom mon dow command`<br>`0 3 * * * wget 0 q`<br>`http://example.com/cron.php`<br>`#`<br>If you visit Administer ➢ Log ➢ Recent log entries, you will eventually see the message "Cron run completed." See Drupal Documentation Handbook, "Configuring cron Jobs," at `http://drupal.org/cron`. |
| Filesystem not writeable | Using either your favorite FTP client or else the command line, create a file directory in the main Drupal root directory, and make sure the HTTP server has write permissions to it. Try to do this without giving out full permissions indiscriminately.<br>For example, on an any Linux system (where www-data is the HTTP server user and group), you can do the following (where `/var/www/workshop` is the web root):<br>`# cd /var/www/workshop`<br>`# mkdir files`<br>`# chown www-data:www-data files` |

To enable the CCK module, visit Administer ➢ Site building ➢ Modules, where you'll now see the Content and associated modules listed. You need to enable all of them and hit the "Save configuration" button at the bottom of the page, to receive the following confirmation:

- ❑ The content fields table *content_type_page* has been created.
- ❑ The content fields table *content_type_story* has been created.
- ❑ The configuration options have been saved.

Now, the dev user already has "Administer content types" permission, so you don't need to set any additional permissions for the content types. You can move directly to implementing the business objects you require.

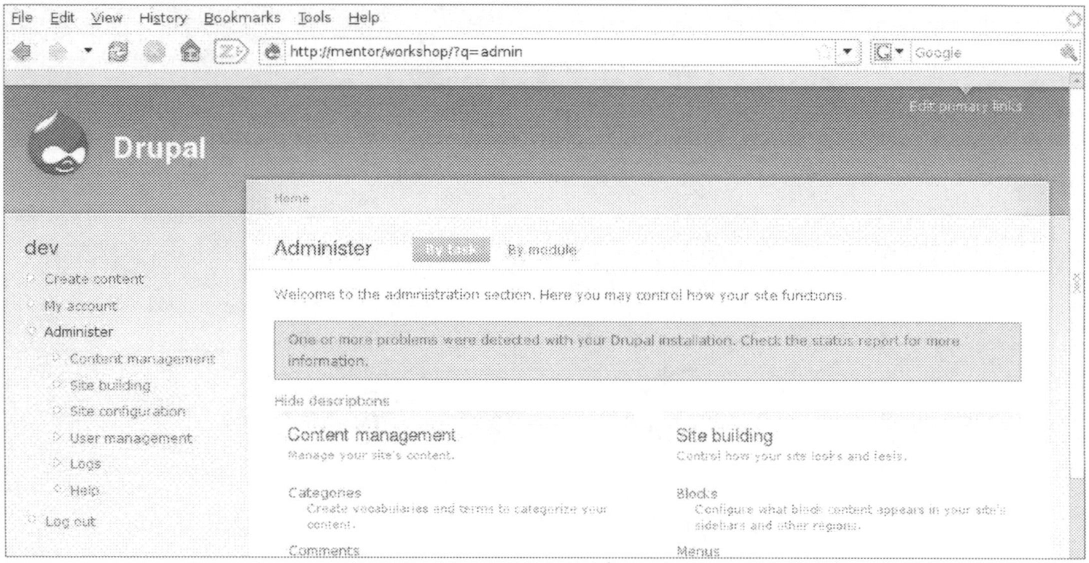


Figure 2-16

Now, which business objects do you require? You make a stab at answering that question by making a lexical semantic analysis (see Figure 2-17). You do this by circling significant nouns.

| Role | User Story |
|---|---|
| Workshop Leader | can approve applications to join the workshop (from members and magazine and book publishers).<br>can suspend members and publishers.<br>can manage affinity groups<br>can broadcast messages to members.<br>can do everything workshop members and publishers can do. |
| Workshop member | can post literary pieces<br>can make any post public, private or visible to an affinity group.<br>can critique public posts.<br>can browse public pieces and critiques<br>can send and receive messages to and from all members, publishers and the workshop leader.<br>can start an affinity group with its own forums<br>can post to forums.<br>can maintain their own literary blog. |
| Publishers | can browse public content<br>can broadcast a call for pieces to be submitted for a publication<br>can select content for inclusion in a publication.<br>can manage an on-line publication.<br>can manage an on-line blog. |
| Webmaster | can administer the website configuration.<br>can install new updates and functionality. |

Figure 2-17

This gives us the chance to do two things: to identify all the business objects, and, where there are ambiguous synonyms, to unify and tighten up our lexicon, yielding the following domain model. Figure 2-18 shows the initial domain model for the Literary Workshop website application, based on the nouns circled in the user story text.

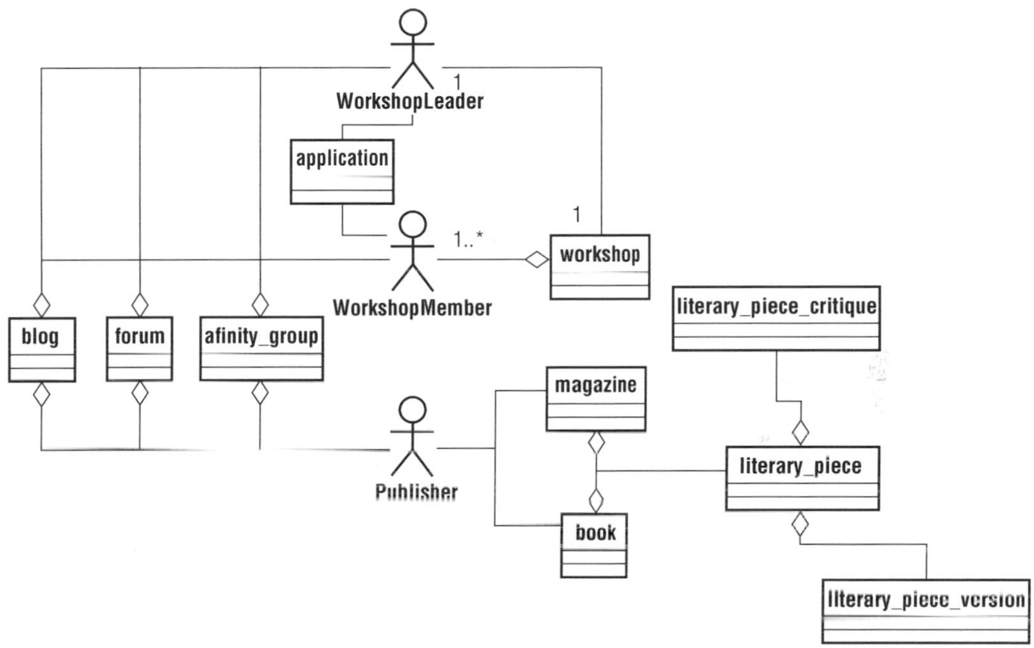


Figure 2-18

Some of the content types are built right into Drupal and implemented in the core (such as blog, forum, book). And others are available as well-respected and high-quality contributed modules (affinity_group and workshop, to be implemented with the Organic Groups module). The business objects shaping up as being application specific are:

- literary-piece
- (possibly) literary_piece_critique (unless these are simply core comments)
- magazine
- application

Let's create the application for membership first. You could simply use the core supported contact form, but you might need extra handling and historical persistence, so this fills the bill for requiring a custom content type.

To create it, follow these steps:

1. Go to Administer ➤ Content management ➤ Add content type.
2. Fill in **Application** in the Name field, then the machine-readable name of the application, together with a brief Description: **The Application is filled out by those applying for membership in the Literary Workshop**.

3. Because this is an application form, "Title" in the Title field label isn't very meaningful. You actually need to have a composite title created according to what is typed into other fields you'll be creating, such as first and last name, or an e-mail. Because this functionality is not available in a fresh Drupal installation, simply type **E-mail**, although in a later chapter, you'll learn how to achieve automatically created and hidden titles with the excellent Automatic Nodetitles module (`http://drupal.org/project/auto_nodetitle`), which will be forming part of your "must have" repertoire of contributed modules.
4. Erase the word *Body* from the "Body field label."

> **Word to the wise: You practically never want to use the deprecated content type field *Body* when you're creating a custom content type. If you want a textarea, you should add it yourself so that it gets treated the same as all your other fields.**

5. In the Workflow section, de-select the "Promoted to front page" checkbox, and select the "Create new revision" checkbox to leverage the fantastic, built-in Drupal version control system. Click on the "Save content" button to create the content type. This takes you to Administer ➤ Content management ➤ Content types, where you see your newly created content type listed together with its description, along with the built-in Page and Story, along with an info box telling you:

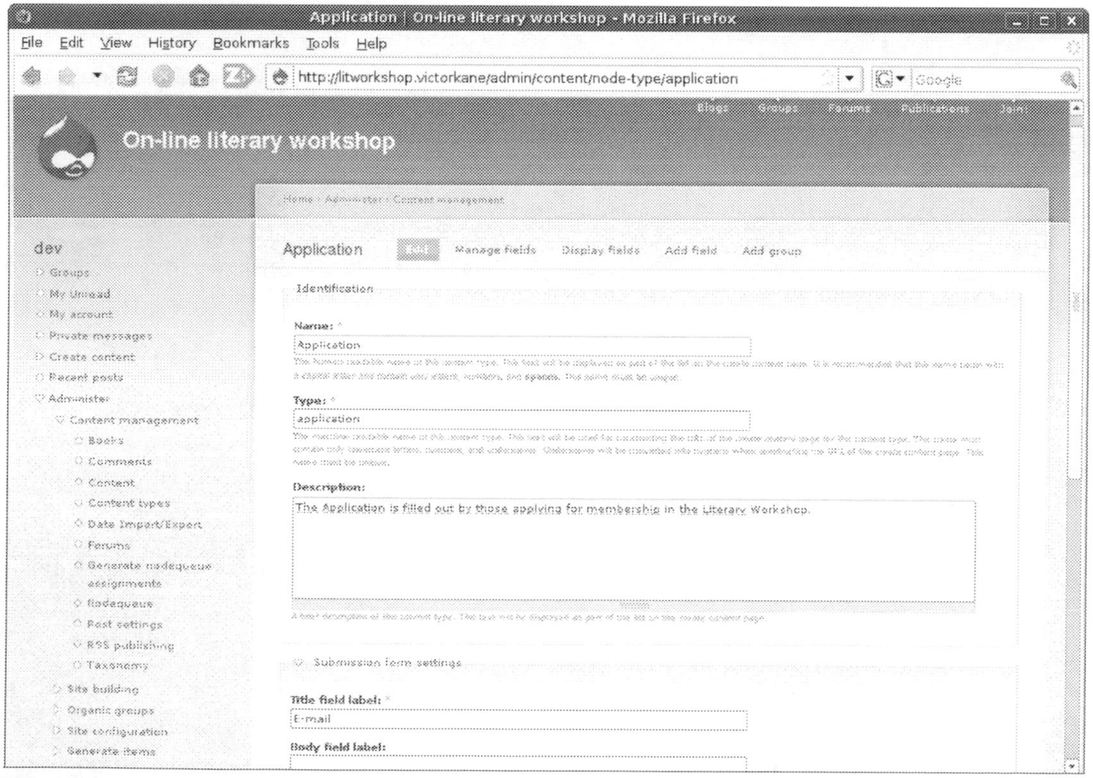


Figure 2-19

- The content fields table *content_type_application* has been created.
- The content type *Application* has been added.

This kind of content type creation is supported in every fresh Drupal installation.

6. You're now going to add some additional custom fields, thanks to the fact that you've installed the CCK module, starting with a textarea enabling those applying to say what their reasons are. To do so, click on the Edit link associated with the Application content type, and then click on the "Add field" tab (see Figure 2-19).
7. In the Name field, type in a machine readable name: **application_motives**.

> **Word to the wise: Always use a prefix with all machine-readable field names, so that they may be easily identified in long selection lists while creating views, and so on. The prefix should identify the content type at a glance.**

8. Because the data you want to hold is text, select "Text Field" under Text. Then click on the "Create field" button (see Figure 2-20). This takes you to the second page of the Wizard, where you are informed that the field *application_motives* has been created.

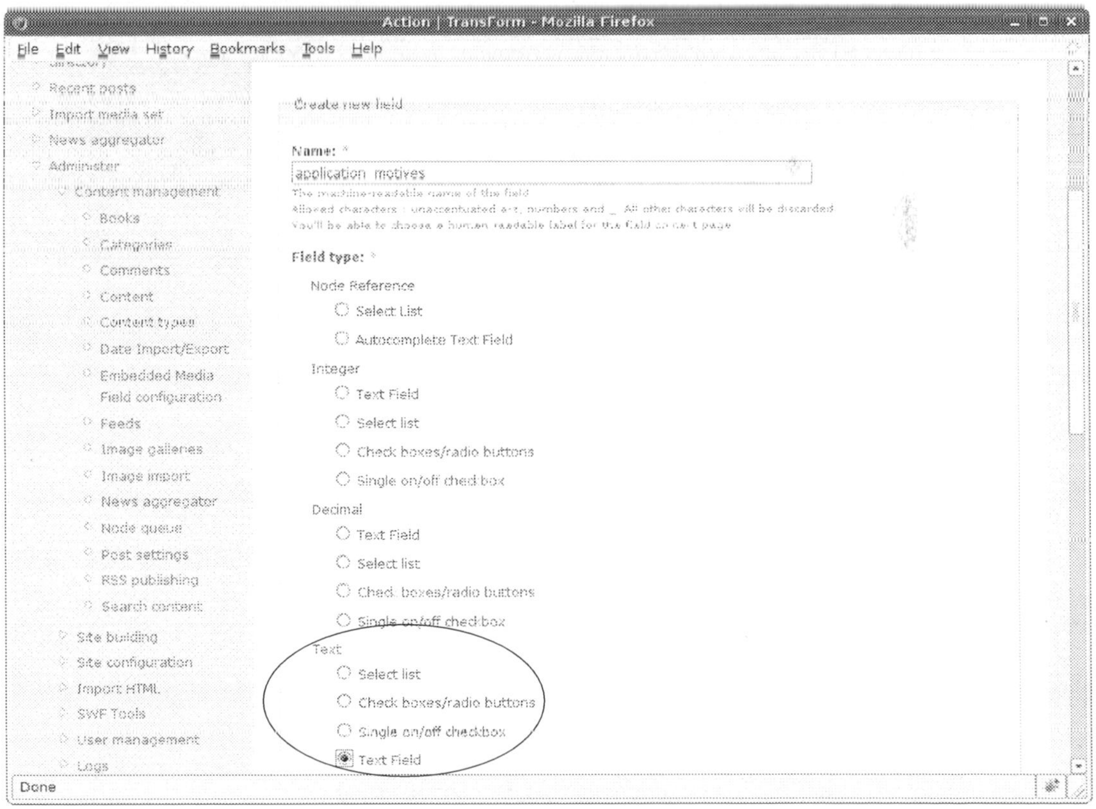


Figure 2-20

9. CCK lets you share field types across content types, so the second page of configuration has Widget settings, which affect the presentation of the field on the current content type and Data settings, thus affecting the field on any content type where it is used. In the Label field, replace the machine-readable name *application_motives* with *Reasons for wanting to join the workshop*. Because you want a textarea and not a single line, specify **7** as the number of rows. Fill in something suitable as Help text, and click on the "Save field settings" button at the bottom of the page. You're taken to the "Manage fields" tab as shown in Figure 2-21.

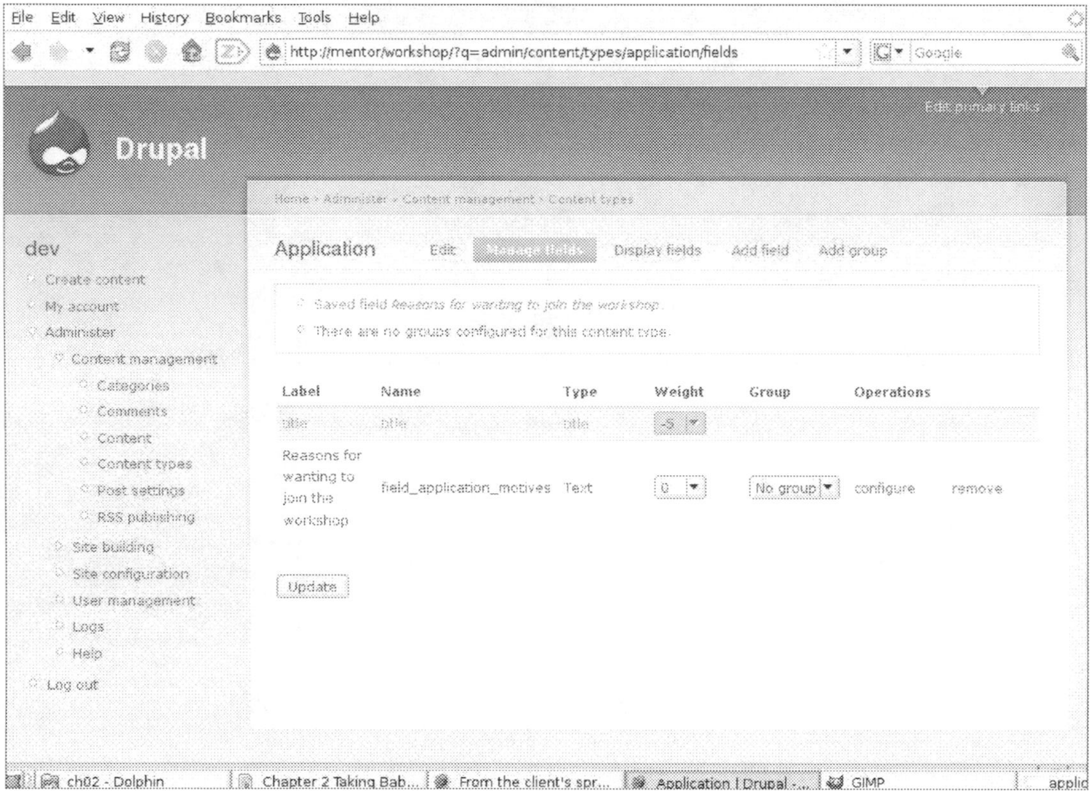


Figure 2-21

10. Now click on the "Add Field" tab again to create the following fields:

| Label | Machine-Readable Name | Field Type Category | Field Type | Number of Lines |
|---|---|---|---|---|
| First name | application_first_name | Text | Text Field | 1 |
| Last name | application_last_name | Text | Text Field | 1 |
| Published | application_published | Text | Checkboxes/radio buttonsYes/no | |

The Published field is a different type from the previous example and is covered below.

**11.** For the Published field, on the second page of the Wizard, under "Data settings" in the "Allowed values list," place **Yes** and **No** on consecutive lines, and then click on the "Save field settings" button (Figure 2-22).

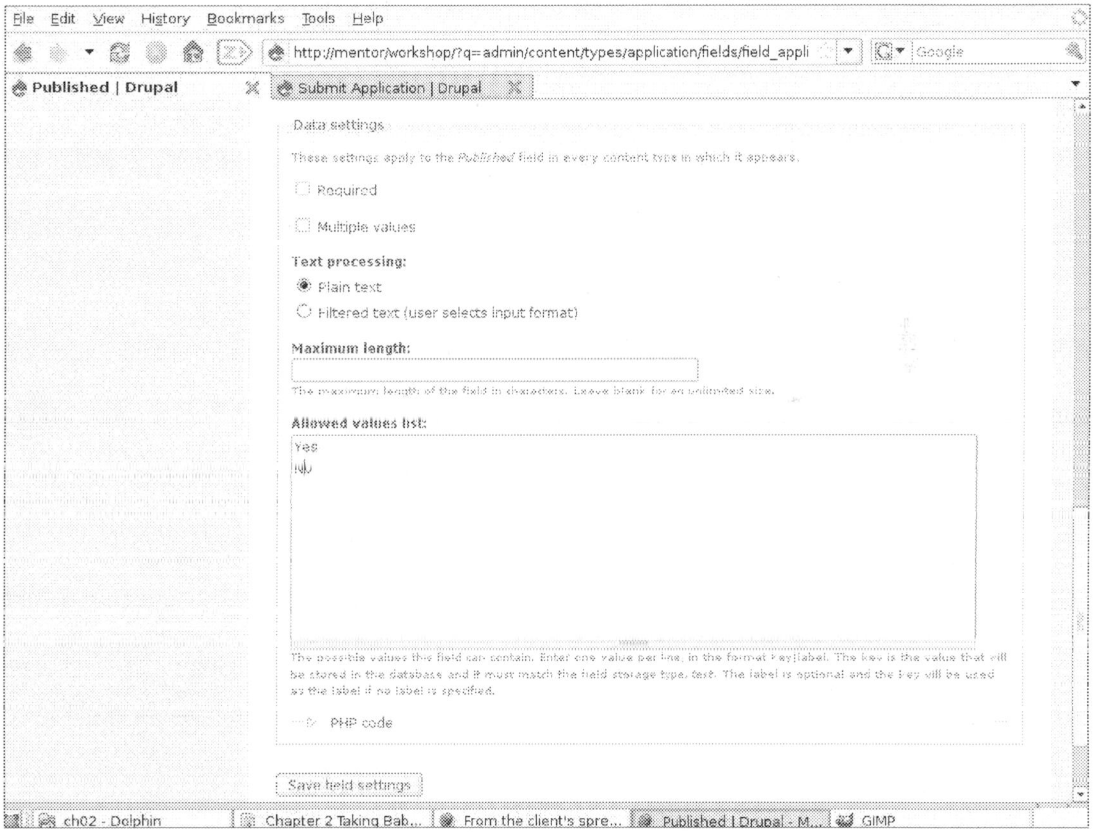


Figure 2-22

You're taken back to the "Manage fields" tab, and at this point should have something like what you see in Figure 2-23.

**12.** You just need to do one more thing: explicitly specify the order in which fields should appear in the form. Do this by selecting the Weight for each field and then clicking on the Update button, giving us something like Figure 2-24.

**13.** Moving right along in this initial prototyping, you're going to put this application form on the Primary menu and test how it works for first-time visitors to the site. Go to Administer ➢ Site building ➢ Menus, and under the Primary links menu, click on the "Add item" link. Type **Join!** in the Title field, **Join the literary workshop** in the Description field, and **node/add/application** in the Path field, as shown in Figure 2-25.

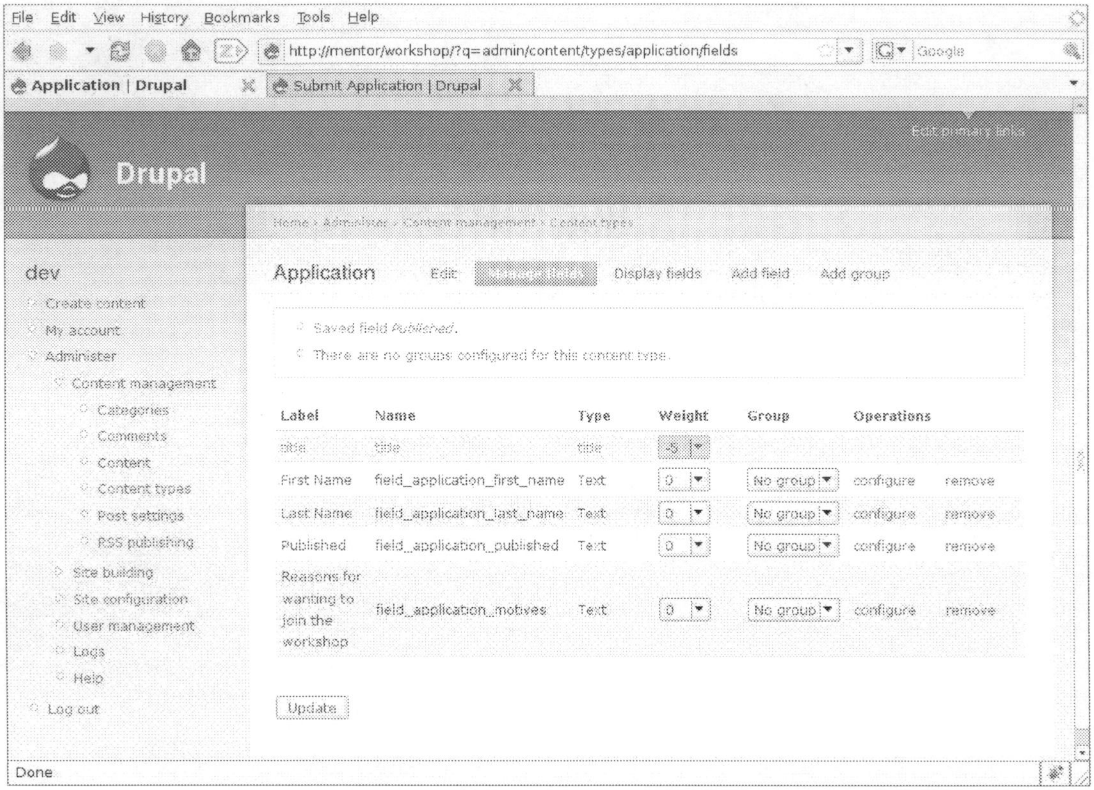

Figure 2-23

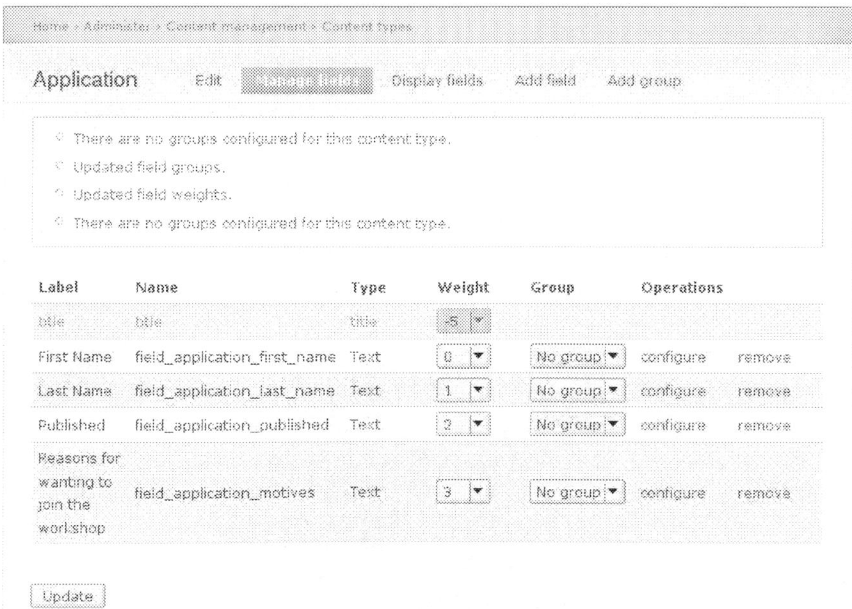

Figure 2-24

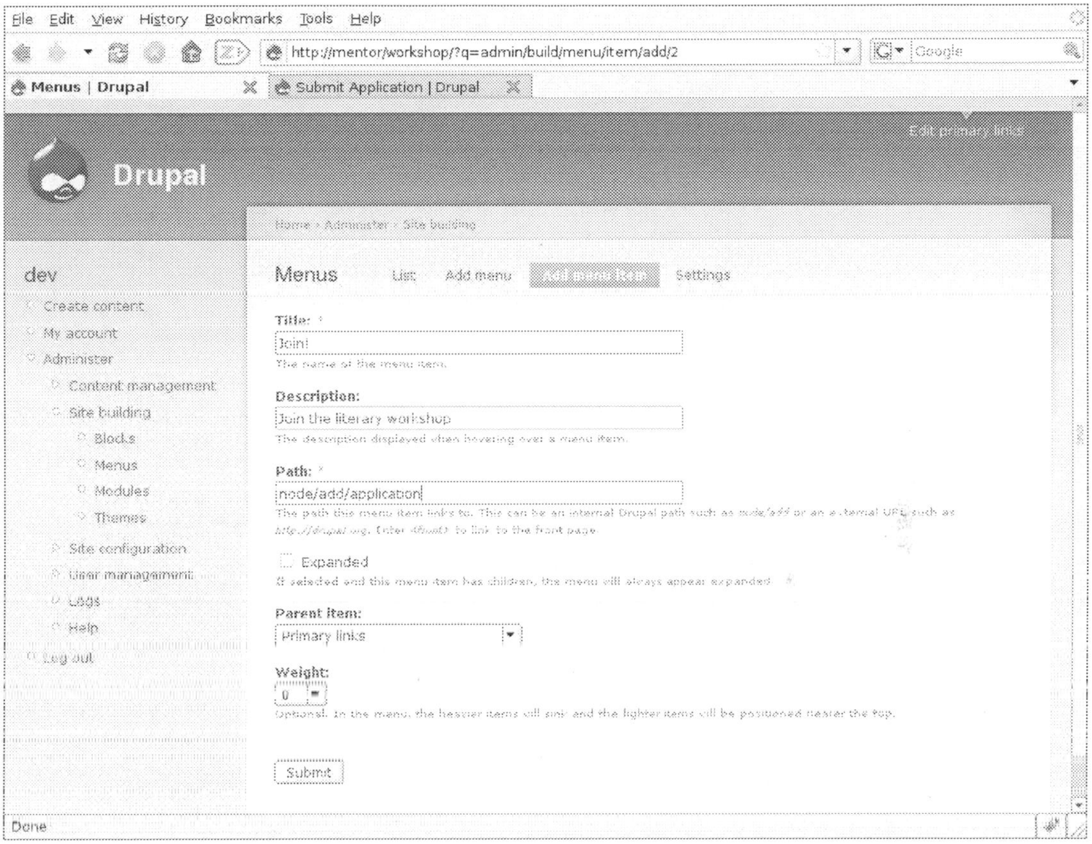


Figure 2-25

**14.** Click on the Submit button at the bottom of the form. From now on, in the upper-right-hand corner of the screen, you'll see the *Join!* Menu item. A mouse-over reveals what you typed in the Description field, and clicking on the mouse-over brings up your newly created Application form. Go ahead and do so, just to see what the form looks like, without actually submitting it for now (see Figure 2-26).

**15.** Hmm. The Published field isn't clear at all. Try adding a Help text. In this case, you're going to add **If you like, tell us if you have ever published your work before**. The automatically created N/A option plays nicely here. Go to Administer ➢ Content management ➢ Content types, and click Edit for the Application content type. Click on the ''Manage fields'' tab, and then click to configure the application_published field. Fill in the Help text field, typing **If you like, tell us if you have ever published your work before**, and click on ''Save field settings.''

To quickly go over our mini-workflow here: A visitor will come to the site, click on the Join! link, and fill out an application form (see Figure 2-25). This will be added to the database as an ''application'' instance. Then the Workshop Leader will come along, list all the application forms, and act on them, accepting them or not into the workshop, and will then mark the application as having been dealt with.

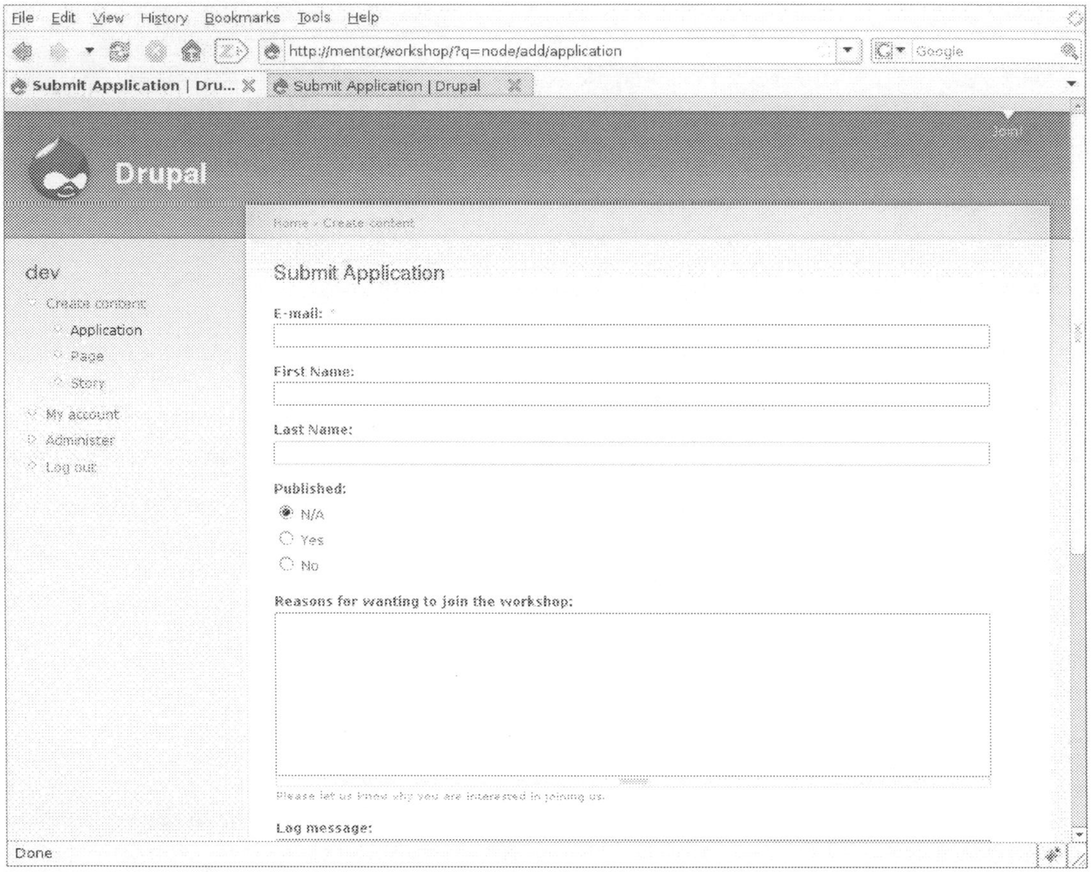


**Figure 2-26**

When we say "Drupal rocks" and is its own best prototyping tool, it is because we can actually do that right now without any coding at all!

So you need to do the following:

- ❑ Give admin role users all permissions to the new content type you have created.
- ❑ Give anonymous users the right to create an application content type (i.e., fill out an application form).
- ❑ Give users of the Workshop Leader role the right to edit application forms.
- ❑ Create a Workshop Leader user.
- ❑ Test.

To do this, go to Administer ➢ User management ➢ Access control. Give anonymous users permission to create application content so that when they enter the site, the Join! menu item will be visible to them. Give the Workshop Leader permission to create and to edit application content. And make sure that the admin role has all permissions. Figure 2-27 shows the screen where you click checkboxes to activate permissions. Please note that because you have to scroll to see the screen, the screen had to be broken into two different screenshots.

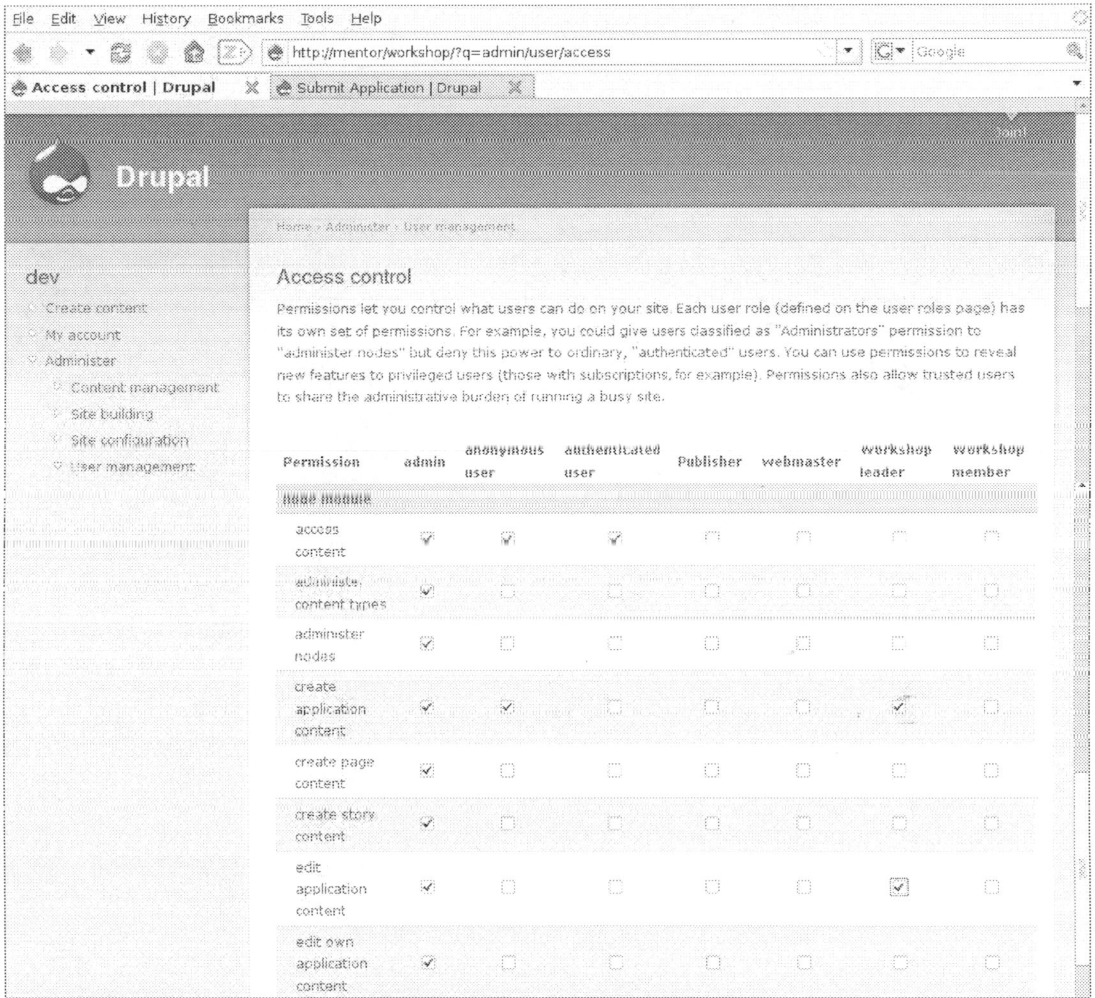


Figure 2-27

Now, test your workflow, by following these steps:

1. In another browser, without logging on as the dev user, enter the site.
2. Hmm. You can do better than "Welcome to your new Drupal website" even if this is a whipped-up prototype. In the browser where you are logged in as dev, click "Create content" and then click "Story." Type in **Literary Workshop** as the Title and **Welcome to our on-line literary workshop** as the Body. Under publishing options, you will see that "Promoted to the front page" is selected by default. That will do fine for now. Click Submit.

3. While you're at it, just give the site a name. Go to Administer ➢ Site configuration ➢ Site information, and enter a site name to replace *Drupal*, together with an e-mail address and a slogan and/or mission, if you like. Then click on the "Save configuration" button at the bottom of the page.

4. Now refresh the browser being used by the anonymous user. It should look something like Figure 2-28.

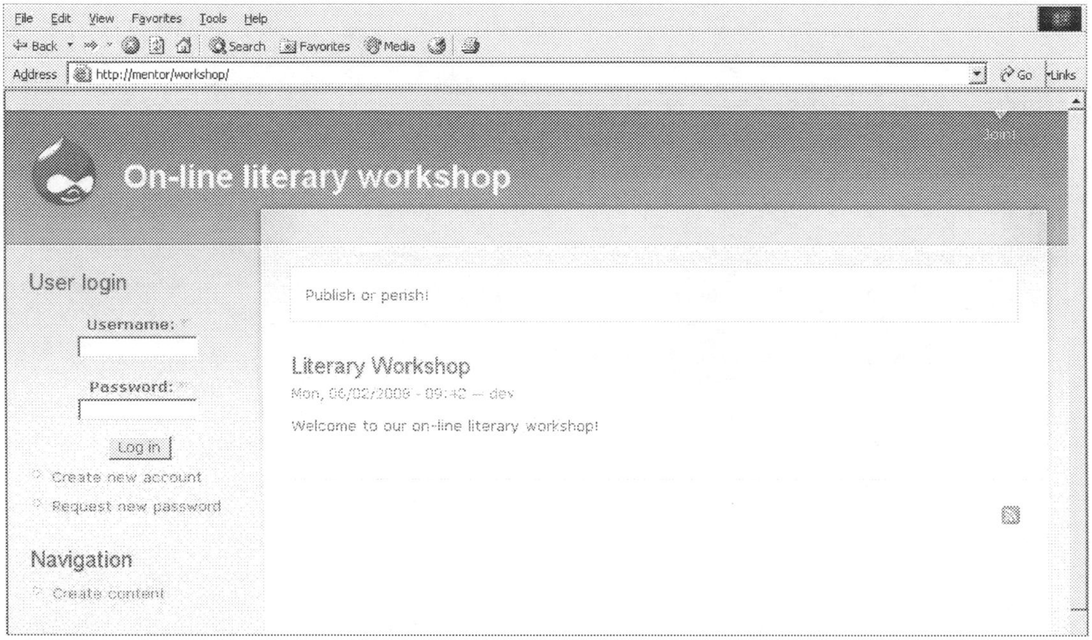


**Figure 2-28**

Now the site visitor can click Join! and click Submit to enter his or her application to join the workshop, as shown in Figure 2-29.

This has been a long haul. If you sense you're rounding off your first cut of tasks, and that you have something to show for your work, you're probably right. If you can just get the initial workflow going for the Workshop Leader, you can postpone the rest of the tasks to the second iteration in the next chapter and go for a walk or game for a couple of hours.

## *Putting the First Role to Work (Initial Basic CMS Workflow. . .)*

You still need to create a Workshop Leader user and test the workflow. To do so, follow these steps:

1. Go to Administer ➢ User management ➢ Users, and click on the "Add user" tab. Fill in **pam** for the Username, provide an e-mail and a password, and check the Workshop Leader role.

If applicable, check the "Notify user of new account" box. Click "Create new account." The new user pam is listed as active and of the Workshop Leader role.

2. Reviewing the workflow you want to implement, you may have realized that pam will list all application forms and then act on them. That is, she will need to have permissions to create new users. So re-visit Administer ➤ User management ➤ Access control, and grant the following permissions to the Workshop Leader role:

   a. In the Node Module section, permissions to access content, administer nodes, create application content, and edit application content

   b. In the User Module section, permissions to access user profiles, administer access control, administer users, and change own username. (You trust her a lot — after all, she is the Workshop Leader!)

3. Now log out, and log in as pam, as shown in Figure 2-30.

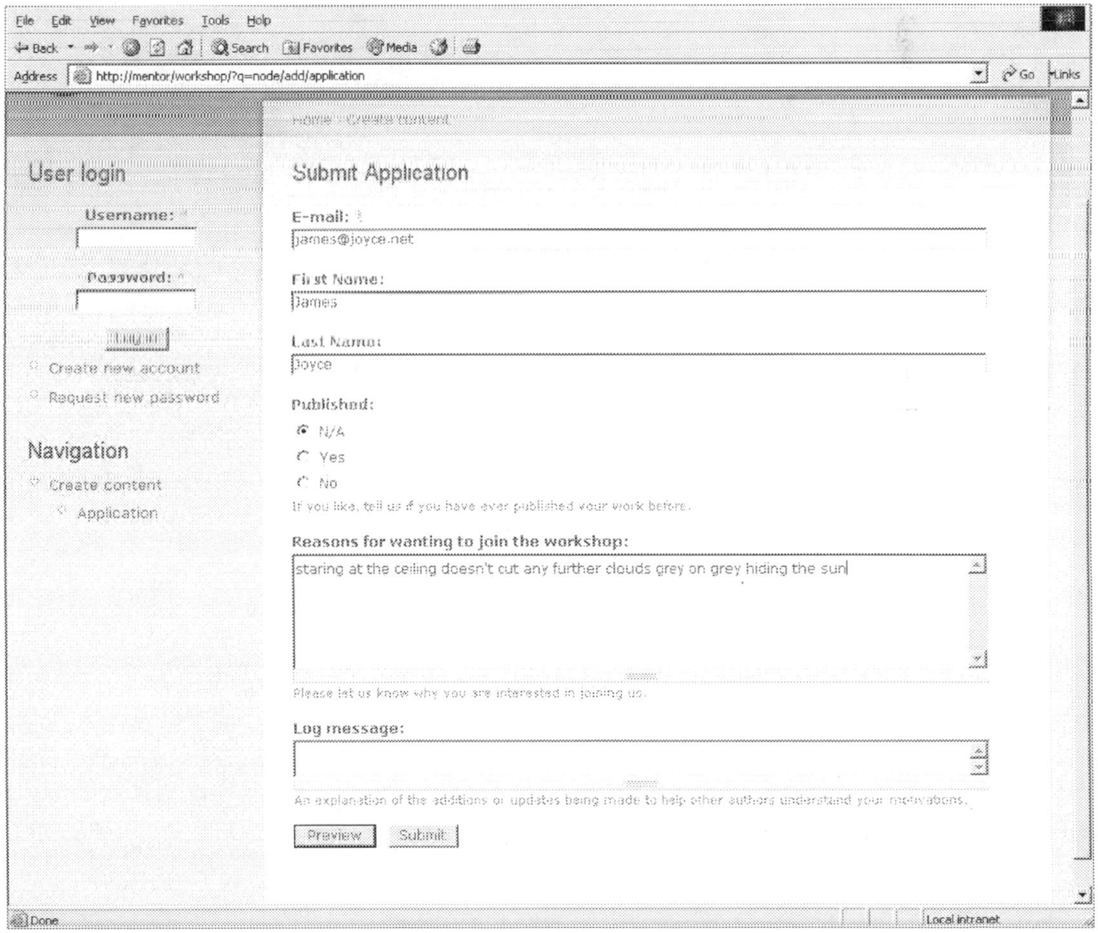


Figure 2-29

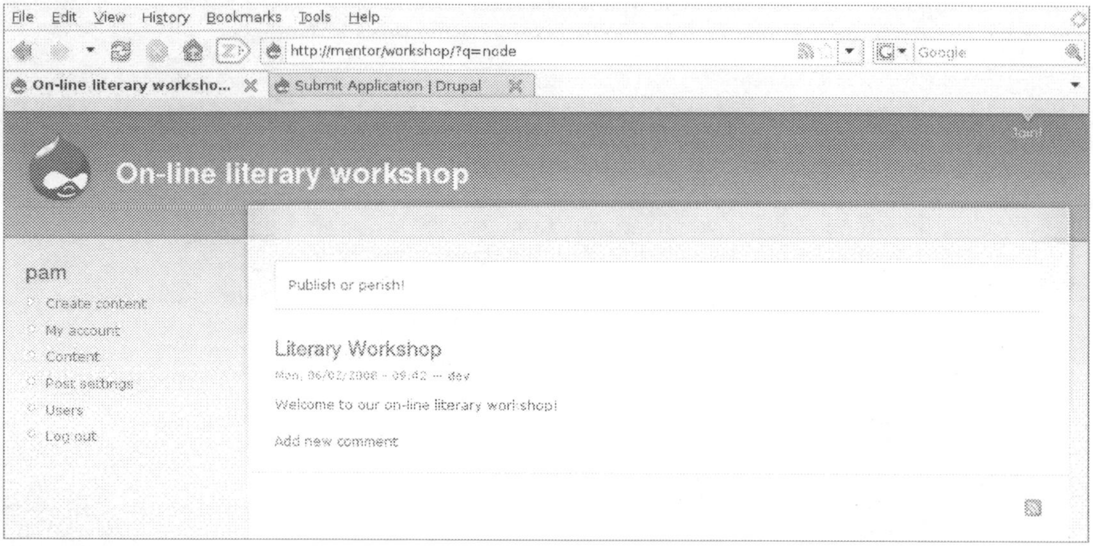


Figure 2-30

The Workshop Leader user pam can now hit Content in order to list application forms. Right now, there are only two items of content in the system, the application form submitted by you from another browser posing as a site visitor, and the Story promoted to the front page.

pam clicks on the application content and reads it and decides what to do. In this case, she feels that the applicant is worthy, so she right-clicks Users from her menu and opens up Administer ➤ User management ➤ Users in another window or tab while still being able to visualize the application form she is reviewing. She clicks on the ''Add user'' tab and creates the user with Name *buddingauthor* and the corresponding e-mail and password. She leaves Status as Active, selects the role of Workshop Member, and selects the ''Notify user of new account'' so that they will receive an e-mail telling them that they can now log into the system as a Workshop Member.

To complete the workflow, one method pam has of indicating that she is done working with that particular application form is to label it as *unpublished*. A little study of how the filters work on this page will show how it is possible to filter the content in the database to only those of type ''application'' and of status ''published.'' Very powerful stock content management tools! Drupal rocks!

# Summary

OK, you have certainly accomplished a lot for a day's work. You have seen several detailed descriptions of all the steps required to install Drupal, including recommendations for best practices. And you have gotten to work on the initial working prototype of the On-Line Literary Workshop, implementing roles and user permissions, business objects as Drupal content types. Finally, a primitive CMS workflow is established allowing the Workshop Leader to manage applications for membership.

In the next chapter, we will work to flesh out these tasks.

# References

1. Berry, Addison, Installing Drupal 6, www.lullabot.com/videocasts/installing-drupal-6
2. Berry, Addison, Install a Local Web Server on Ubuntu, www.lullabot.com/videocast/install-local-web-server-ubuntu
3. "Death to Visio Site Maps! How Clear Ink Uses Drupal for Information Architecture, Prototyping, and Project Management," http://clearnightsky.com/node/318
4. Concurrent Versions System, http://en.wikipedia.org/wiki/Concurrent_Versions_System
5. Drupal Documentation Handbooks, http://drupal.org/handbooks
6. Drupal Dojo Project, http://groups.drupal.org/drupal-dojo

# 3

# Getting Organized

So you've started the project and identified your customer and her objectives, and identified the roles: the distinct kinds of users who will be interacting with the website application. You've installed Drupal and begun getting your prototype on the road by creating your first cut of business objects based on a lexical analysis of the user story titles. You are almost at the point where you can ask the client for feedback to make sure the roles and list of user stories look complete, and to write the user stories. Coherency will be enhanced by her using the semantics offered by the list of business objects and the limited functionality you have started to put together based on input received so far.

Figure 3-1 shows the elaboration iteration as it looks now.

It doesn't look like it, but you have actually done quite a lot of work already. Still, there's plenty left to do. Let's see how much we get done in this sprint, starting with the third task: get initial feedback from the client Pam (who actually does live in Alaska!) on Skype, and show her the website deployed to the test site (see Chapter 2).

Before that, though, let's just review how the first task, creating an initial environment, is implemented and how you can synch up your development box and your test site on a daily basis so that the client can always check out the latest relatively stable version on the test site.

## Reviewing the Initial Environment

To build upon a solid foundation, it is necessary to deal with the whole question of version control, the source code and assets repository, and issue tracking, and get that started right now. You are going to be doing all your work on your development box in whatever cubicle world you inhabit. When you get everything to a particular point (as, e.g., at the end of the last chapter), you are going to be committing what you have to a Subversion repository and then updating the test site from that same repository.

- ✓ Create an initial environment
- ✓ Whip up the initial prototype
- Get initial feedback from the client
- Finish the user stories with the client
- Plan the project
- Work on the architectural baseline
- Get the team organized and with the program

**Figure 3-1**

*Subversion* (`http://subversion.tigris.org`), *or SVN as it is referred to, is an Open Source version control system. For some background on version control systems in general, see* `http://en.wikipedia.org/wiki/Revision_control`.

I use a Trac instance to visually review my repository and the commits, and to document the project Milestone planning and tracking. To do this, I contract a Subversion + Trac hosting service. You can choose your own (either free or commercial) from the list on the Trac wiki (`http://trac.edgewall.org/wiki/CommercialServices`), or set up your own if you feel so inclined on your own server (hosting companies like Dreamhost and Site5 allow this even on shared hosting).

*Trac, another Open Source project, is "an enhanced wiki and issue tracking system for software development projects" (see* `http://trac.edgewall.org`*). Bugzilla is another excellent alternative, among many, but Trac's "minimalistic" approach is very attractive. For background on issue tracking systems, see* `http://en.wikipedia.org/wiki/Issue_tracking_system`.

The basic features to look for, apart from price and reliability (which you will find out about only through experience), are:

- Separate repositories and Trac instances for each project
- Enough user accounts to make the setup usable for your team, together with the capability to give users (and hopefully user groups) access to different projects and Trac instances
- Capability of importing existing SVN repositories
- The capability to download a dump of the repository and Trac instance to keep as a safe backup, or to reuse with another service

There are many reasons why Subversion + Trac makes a good lightweight alternative for version control and issue tracking. At the very least, Trac allows you to:

- Easily browse your *changesets* (all the files added, modified, or deleted in a single, atomic commit).
- Compare various versions of any individual file.
- Create milestones and actually plan your project, and reference concrete commits and files.

- ❑ Actually manage your issue queue, again, in direct reference to changesets and individual files.

*Check out David Murphy's* Managing Software Development with Trac and Subversion *(2007, Packt Publishing). For more background on Subversion itself, and good usage and best-practices details, see the SVN homepage at* `http://subversion.tigris.org` *and the on-line documentation "Version Control with Subversion"* (`http://svnbook.red-bean.com/`)*, as well as books like* Practical Subversion *by Daniel Berlin and Garrett Rooney (2006, Apress).*

So as a practical example, here's what you do:

1. Create an SVN repository and a Trac instance using the tools provided by the service you have chosen.
2. Decide on the main directory structure for Drupal and for the repository.
3. Import what you have so far as your initial commit to the repository.
4. Install a fresh copy of Drupal on your test site.
5. Get your test site working as a mirror of the latest stable version of your development site by checking out the initial revision from the repository.

Let's take a more detailed look at these tasks.

## Housekeeping the SVN Repository and Trac Instance

If you happen to choose `svnrepository.com` as your repository provider, you simply log into your control panel, fill in a name for the repository (no spaces), and click on the "Create New Repository" button (see Figure 3-2).

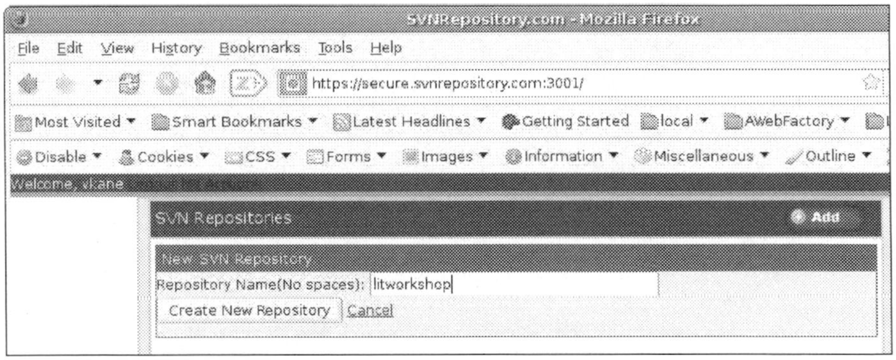


**Figure 3-2**

Figure 3-3 shows how you are then greeted with confirmation and access info for the newly created SVN repository.

With the control panel, you make any necessary user accounts and grant access to your new repository, which is now listed as in Figure 3-4.

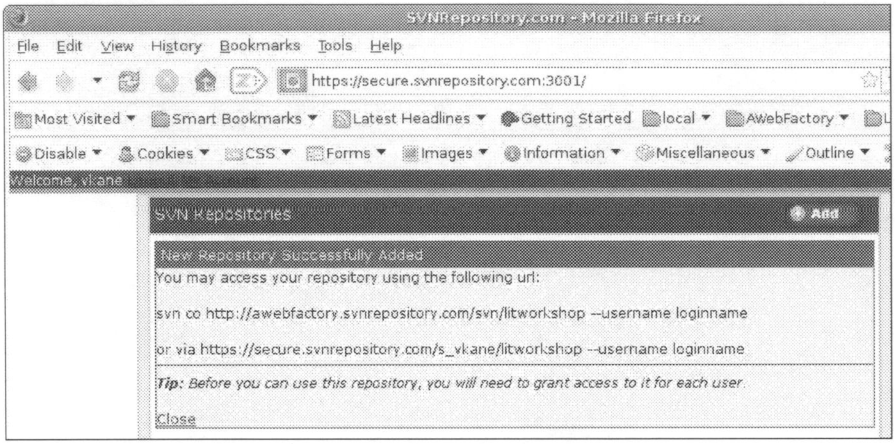


Figure 3-3

Figure 3-4

When you click on the Setup Trac link, you are told that Trac was successfully set up and are given information about how to restrict admin access to the newly created Trac instance should you wish to do so. You now want to make sure you have jotted down somewhere handy the access path to check out a working copy from the SVN repository together with the access path to the Trac instance.

*I always place an admin directory for each project on my development machine containing such things as usernames and passwords, URLs, and other contact information. You don't want to waste an hour looking through old e-mails when your client requests access to the repository, or if you need to go back to an old project.*

In this example, the links are always available on the control panel where your repository is listed, together with other handy features, like a Commit Notification Email List. The full Subversion + Trac instance entry in your control panel, once it is set up, is shown in Figure 3-5.

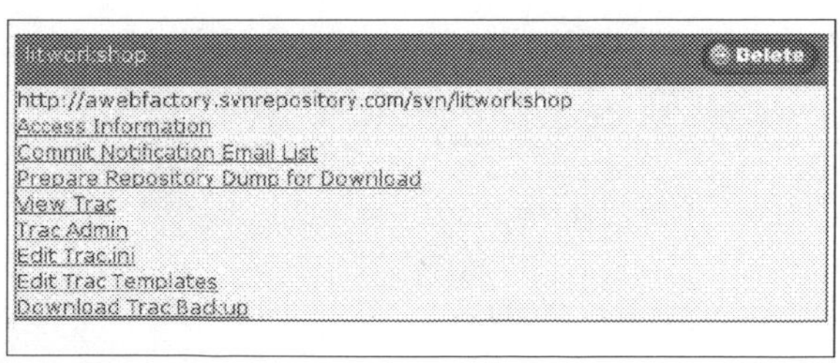


Figure 3-5

## Main Directory Structure for Drupal

As will be repeated many times throughout this book, "There's more than one way to do it," or *Tim Toady* for short (see `http://en.wikipedia.org/wiki/There_is_more_than_one_way_to_do_it`). So you may choose to do things differently from this example. Here I use CVS to manage Drupal core release installation and updating, and SVN for versioning the actual development project itself. Now, although it is absolutely necessary to version the development on the website (this is actually everything below the sites directory), it makes no sense whatsoever to version Drupal itself. That would be redundancy supreme, because best practices really dictate never to change, or *hack*, the Drupal core. Furthermore, you had better make sure that you can easily do things like unpack a new Drupal security release (say, Drupal 5.9) over your Drupal 5.8 site, for example, without having to worry about any overwriting of files. That is, you should always be able to cleanly upgrade Drupal releases without affecting your own versioned project.

**On *Hacking* the Drupal Core**

Drupal prides itself on being a clean and solid piece of software engineering, and it is. It is thoroughly extensible on all fronts (modules, themes, etc.), and there is no reason, unless you have some dire "exception that confirms the rule," to "hack the core," as you are forced to do with some other frameworks to achieve the functionality or look-and-feel you need. See "Do Not Modify Core Drupal" (`http://drupal.org/node/144376`). For a humorous, although somewhat advanced and very accurate, description of "Top 10 Ways a Developer Can Send a Drupal Project to Hell," see "The Road to Drupal Hell," by Nick Lewis (`http://drupal.org/node/77487`). This is a piece you should come back to after reading this book.

So, your Drupal installation looks as follows (this is the "Drupal document root directory"):

```
victorkane@mentor:/var/www/workshop$ tree -L 1
.
|-- CHANGELOG.txt
|-- INSTALL.mysql.txt
|-- INSTALL.pgsql.txt
|-- INSTALL.txt
|-- LICENSE.txt
|-- MAINTAINERS.txt
|-- UPGRADE.txt
|-- cron.php
|-- files
|-- includes
|-- index.php
|-- install.php
|-- misc
|-- modules
|-- profiles
|-- robots.txt
|-- scripts
```

```
|-- sites
|-- themes
|-- update.php
'-- xmlrpc.php
```

**So it is the sites directory, and that directory only, which you need to version, because all the rest comes straight out of a fresh Drupal release tarball.**

Under the sites directory, at this point, if you have been following the Literary Workshop development project, you have something like the following:

```
victorkane@mentor:/var/www/workshop$ tree sites
sites
|-- all
|   |-- README.txt
|   |-- modules
|   |   '-- cck
|   |       |-- CHANGELOG.txt
|   |       |-- LICENSE.txt
|   |       |-- README.txt
|   |       |-- UPGRADE.txt
|   |       |-- content.css
|   |       |-- content.info
|   |       |-- content.install
|   |       |-- content.module
...
|   |       |-- po
|   |       |   |-- cck.pot
|   |       |   |-- da.po
|   |       |   |-- de.po
|   |       |   |-- es.po
...
|   |       |-- userreference.install
|   |       '-- userreference.module
|   '-- themes
'-- default
    '-- settings.php
```

Here, you will be placing all of your installed contributed and custom modules (some people put contributed modules in a contrib folder and custom modules in a custom folder) and themes.

That leaves a couple of thorny questions: When you make a commit, how do you version the state of the Drupal database? Second of all, are you going to version your content assets (images, audio files, downloadable documents)? Let's deal with the database in a moment. As far as your image and document assets are concerned, when you upload an image or text document as an attachment to a page, it will be placed in the files directory (part of basic Drupal configuration), the only one with Write privileges for the HTTP server user and group (www-data on a Ubuntu server, e.g.). For this project, let's opt for not versioning these binary assets with the SVN repository, because you should be mostly concerned with development (coding and theming) rather than with content per se.

## Using Version Control

Moving the files directory under the sites directory is an efficient way to easily place image and document file assets under version control if desired.

Note that the files directory must be writeable by the HTTP server. You can create the directory and set its permissions by using an FTP client if you do not have access to a secure shell. The following table shows some common problems and solutions using version control:

| Problem | Solution |
|---|---|
| The files directory has already been created in the Drupal document root. | Delete it (which leads to next problem):<br>`# rmdir files` |
| Files directory is non-existent. | Create it. Change to the Drupal document root directory. Then:<br>`# mkdir sites/all/files`<br>`# chown -R www-data:www-data sites/all/files` |
| Drupal doesn't have the faintest idea where the files directory is. | Logged in as admin (dev in the workshop website), go to Administer ➢ Site configuration ➢ File system, specify the "File system path" (no leading slash), then press the "Save configuration" button (see Figure 3-6). |

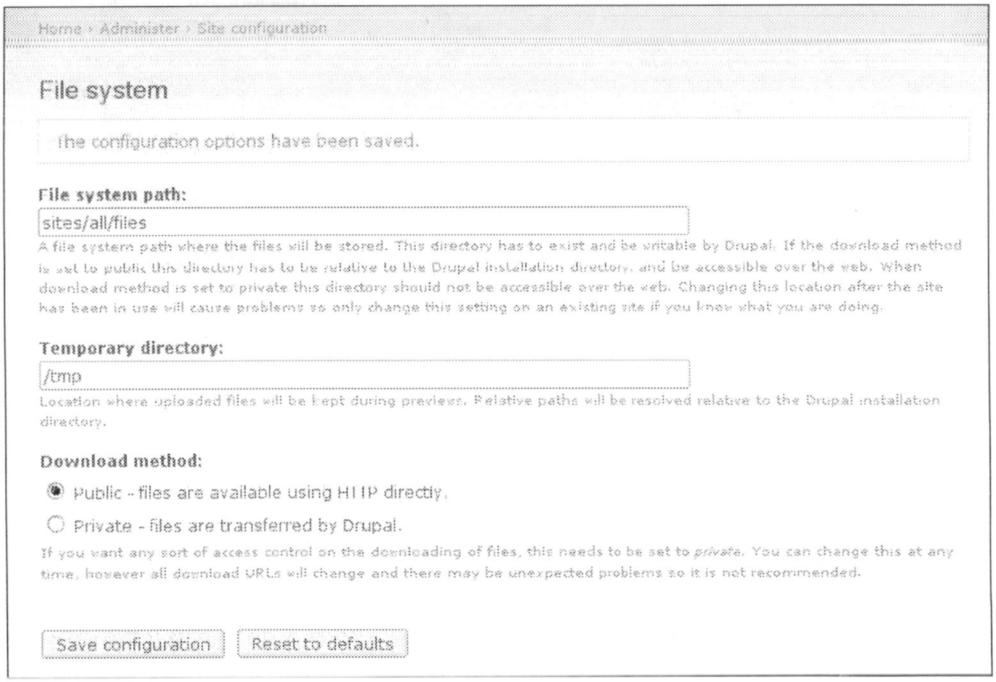


Figure 3-6

So it is settled: you will place ./sites and all its subdirectories under version control.

## What to Do about the Database

It must be admitted that Drupal has one serious area of difficulty, which will always crop up from time to time: the database contains content, but it also contains configuration (and darn important configuration too, as we saw when we configured our business objects with cck) and even (although we try to keep it down to a dull roar) code snippets, in blocks and panels, as you shall see.

> **That means that to commit a true snapshot of the project at a given point in time, you must include the database.**

Under development, at least, the database will probably not be too large. Fortunately, the command `mysqladmin` allows you to dump it to a text file (of SQL commands) so that it can be placed under version control relatively efficiently. But you need to find a home for the dumped SQL file somewhere in the directory tree. Again, there is more than one way to do it, but let's adopt the convention of placing the dump at ./sites/all/backup/db/litworkshop.sql. To do so, use the following commands:

```
# mkdir sites/all/backup
# mkdir sites/all/backup/db
# cd sites/all/backup/db
# mysqldump -u dr_workshop -p dr_workshop > litworkshop.sql
Enter password:
#
```

It's just that last command you will be needing on an everyday development basis, so be sure to write it down in a handy place, along with the password (should you forget, the info is in ./sites/default/settings).

Now you have:

```
#ls -l
total 128
-rw-r--r-- 1 victorkane victorkane 126735 2008-06-10 18:02 litworkshop.sql
#
```

## Using phpMyAdmin

A lot of on-line tutorials tell you how to create a MySQL dump of your database in SQL format, which can be used later to restore or deploy, but they often omit a very important detail: the inclusion of `DROP TABLE` statements so that the file can overwrite existing tables and can be easily imported without having to empty the database first by hand. First of all, bring up your Drupal database in phpMyAdmin, then click on the Export tab. Next select the "Add DROP TABLE/DROP VIEW" checkbox. As shown in Figure 3-7, press the Go button, and save the file to ./sites/all/backup/db in the Drupal filesystem tree.

Later on, when you are checking out the sites file tree from the repository to make a working copy on your test site, you insert the SQL file back into the database, either with the phpMyAdmin import facility, or else on the command line, as follows:

```
# ls -l
total 128
-rw-r--r-- 1 victorkane victorkane 126735 2008-06-10 18:02 litworkshop.sql
```

```
# mysql -u dr_workshop -p dr_workshop < litworkshop.sql
Enter password:
victorkane@mentor:/var/www/workshop/sites/all/backup/db$
```

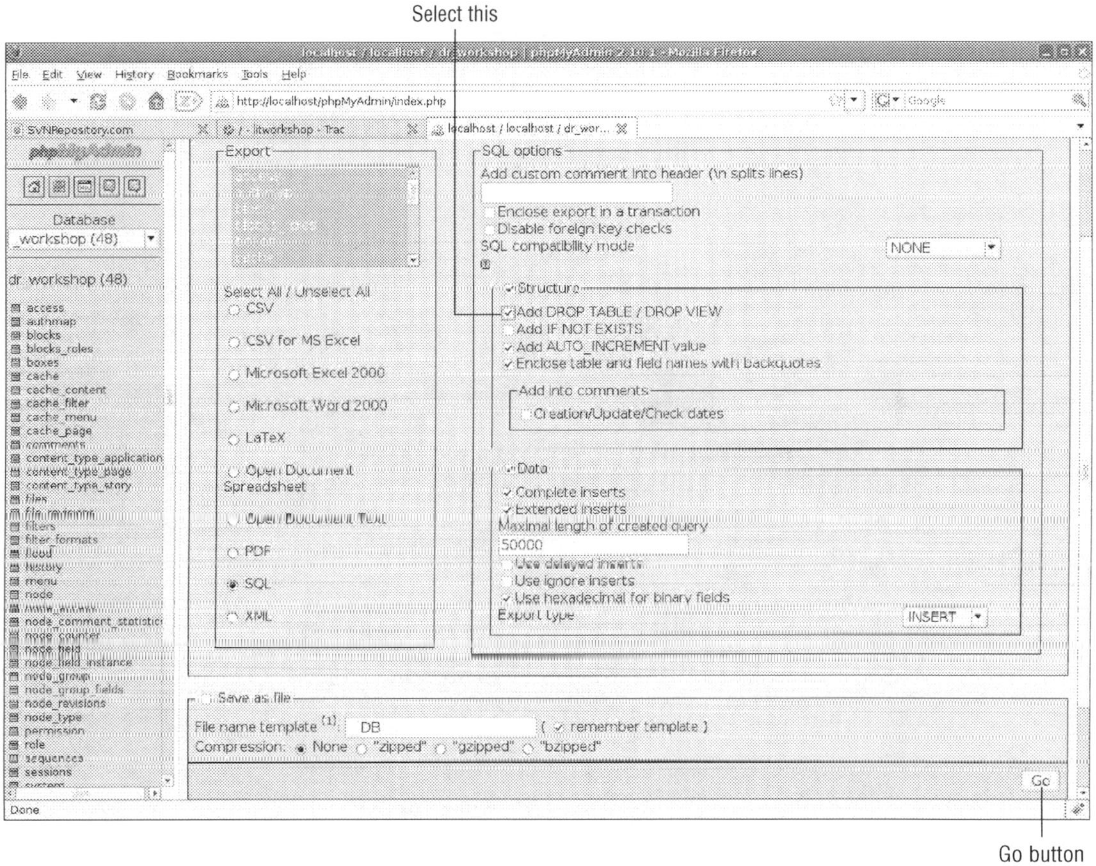


Figure 3-7

Notice the use of the `mysql` command to insert the SQL file into the database, as opposed to the `mysqldump` command we used to dump the database to the SQL text file.

## Main Directory Structure for the Repository

Now that you have created your repository and have your Drupal instance all set up to import into the repository for the first time, it's time to set up the main directory structure for branches and tags within the repository itself using the command line. Of course, you can achieve the same results with any of several GUI clients, available for all Operating System platforms.

> *See "Subversion UI Shootout," by Jeremy Jones, at* www.onlamp.com/pub/a/onlamp/2005/03/10/svn_uis.html RapidSVN. *For Linux, see* http://rapidsvn.tigris.org/, *and for Mac, see "Syncro Subversion Client" at* www.syncrosvnclient.com/.

The repository directory tree structure can then be verified by using the Trac instance you set up earlier. Follow the classic setup (see the Reference section for Subversion books and manuals) by executing the following (all one line; provide password where prompted; the `-m` switch allows you to include a log message directly):

```
# svn mkdir http://awebfactory.svnrepository.com/svn/litworkshop/trunk ↵
http://awebfactory.svnrepository.com/svn/litworkshop/branches ↵
http://awebfactory.svnrepository.com/svn/litworkshop/tags --username ↵
username -m "initial repo infrastructure"

Committed revision 1.
```

Let's just list the repository to make sure we got what we wanted:

```
# svn list http://awebfactory.svnrepository.com/svn/litworkshop
branches/
tags/
trunk/
```

As mentioned, you can also check out your "repo" with Trac. Point your browser at the link you saved earlier (or return to the control panel, and click "View Trac for the litworkshop repo," or follow the instructions given by your repository hosting provider), then click on the Browse Source menu item. You should see something similar to Figure 3-8, showing your initial repository structure.

Figure 3-8

## Initial Import of the Codebase into the Repository

On your development box filesystem, navigate to the Drupal document root. Your target "sites" directory is visible as a subdirectory, or "folder," if we are using a GUI file browsing tool.

> **Before you do the actual importing, however, temporarily remove ./sites/default/settings.php just this one time because it is not convenient to place this site-specific file under version control.**

*Continued*

```
# mv sites/default/settings.php /tmp
```

**Be sure to put it back later; otherwise, your site will be broken! Do:**

```
# mv tmp/settings.php sites/default
```

**If you are using the command line, then you simply have to do this one time. SVN will not commit unversioned files to the repository. However, some IDEs may do so, so you might want to consider using the SVN `propset ignore` command (a command to set properties on folders and files) in this case. Do:**

```
# cd sites default
# svn propset svn:ignore settings.php .
```

**Don't forget the trailing dot — it refers to the directory where the property is to be set. And you're all set; from then on, SVN will ignore that file.**

Now import the sites subdirectory into an appropriate place in the repository as follows:

```
# svn import sites http://awebfactory.svnrepository.com/svn/litworkshop/
trunk/sites ↵
-m "import roles and initial cut of basic functionality"
```

This will take a little while, depending on your connection speed. You will see:

```
Adding          sites/default
Adding          sites/all
...
Adding          sites/all/modules/cck/README.txt
Adding          sites/all/modules/cck/number.module
Adding          sites/all/README.txt
```

**Move your settings file back in, and you are done:**

```
# mv /tmp/settings.php sites/default
# ls sites/default/
settings.php
```

**When checking out or updating later on, it will not be overwritten because it is not under version control.**

Phew! Now you are going to get the test site working and create a virtual server setup on your development box to match, so your super website factory is almost set up.

## Getting the Test Site Up and Running

Some of this stuff may seem like a bit much, but from my own experience, I really wish someone had spelled it out from the beginning when I got started, because you are going to be saving bellyache upon bellyache by doing it right. (I will spare you the ugly details, but gone is the ugly prospect of having gotten things just right, and then accidentally ruining everything by installing a new module the next day: you just use the versioning system to revert back to life as it was yesterday.)

And again, I am presenting one way of doing it right. Two ways, actually — What you have to do in a nutshell, and then a more detailed approach suitable for those of you using a VPS (see `http://en.wikipedia.org/wiki/Virtual_private_server`) or a dedicated server (see `http://en.wikipedia.org/wiki/Dedicated_hosting_service`) you are managing yourself, as recommended in this book.

## In a Nutshell

If you have shared hosting or some kind of managed hosting, first of all, simply set up a subdomain `http://litworkshop.example.com`, associated with (redirected to) a subdirectory off your document path. You should be able to do this relatively easily with the CPanel or other site-management panel provided by your hosting provider. Then, create a database for the website, unpack the Drupal tarball into that subdirectory, and from its document root do a checkout of the SVN repository, as shown below, into the sites directory. Then edit the settings.php with your site-specific settings. Once you have placed the versioned database snapshot ./sites/all/backup/db/litworkshop.sql into the database, either from the command line or else by using phpMyAdmin, you are done. Your client and your staff can access via a separate ftp account to the subdomain directory, and will not have to have access to your whole site. All of this can be set up via CPanel; simply follow your hosting provider's instructions.

But because shared hosting tends to be oversold and suffer from sudden drops in performance making things difficult even for development and testing purposes, a lot of folks are turning to a more stable and dependable VPS or even dedicated server, now that the prices of these services are dropping to quite competitive levels.

## Using a Dedicated Server or VPS

If you have a dedicated server or a VPS you are managing yourself (that is really recommended in this book, and since you are going to get a lot of help on this throughout, your best bet is to do so), you get to create a system user with the same name as the application, so your client and staff can have secure shell and sftp access to the application, also without having to have root access to your server. Again, all of this may look pretty advanced, but the more at home you get with stuff like this, the more you can leverage Drupal, and you will have a smoother ride and fewer headaches in the long run. If you can wade on through it, you will find it extremely useful on this and many projects to come.

So, to do this, you want to create a database for the website, just as you did when you created the initial environment in Chapter 2. Then (assuming a LAMP–Linux, Apache, MySQL, PHP–server setup):

1. Logged into your server as root, create a system user and set of user directories to match:

```
root@example.com:~ # adduser litworkshop
Adding user 'litworkshop' ...
Adding new group 'litworkshop' (1006) ...
Adding new user 'litworkshop' (1006) with group 'litworkshop' ...
Creating home directory '/home/litworkshop' ...
```

```
Copying files from '/etc/skel' ...
Enter new UNIX password:
Retype new UNIX password:
passwd: password updated successfully
Changing the user information for litworkshop
Enter the new value, or press ENTER for the default
   Full Name []:
   Room Number []:
   Work Phone []:
   Home Phone []:
   Other []:
Is the information correct? [y/N] y
root@example.com:~ #
```

2. We still need root permissions for just a little more configuration, and then afterwards the user `litworkshop` can take it from there. Logged in as root, navigate to the newly created user's directory, and unpack a fresh Drupal tarball there. You should see something like the following:

```
root@example.com:/home/litworkshop # ls -l
total 4
drwxr-xr-x 9 1080 1080 4096 2008-01-28 19:10 drupal-5.7
root@example.com:/home/litworkshop #
```

3. Then do this:

```
root@example.com:/home/litworkshop # mv drupal-5.7/ public_html
root@example.com:/home/litworkshop # chown -R litworkshop:litworkshop
 public_html/
root@example.com:/home/litworkshop # ls -l
total 4
drwxr-xr-x 9 litworkshop litworkshop 4096 2008-01-28 19:10 public_html
root@example.com:/home/litworkshop # mkdir public_html/files
root@example.com:/home/litworkshop # chown www-data:www-data
public_html/files/
```

4. That's it. Now log in as the new user. Or, directly from your root session:

```
root@example.com:/home/litworkshop # su - litworkshop
```

5. Move the existing plain Drupal sites subdirectory out of there and check out your application from the repository:

```
litworkshop@example.com:~$ cd public_html/
litworkshop@example.com:~/public_html$ svn co ↵
http://awebfactory.svnrepository.com/svn/litworkshop/trunk/sites sites ↵
 --username loginname
Authentication realm: <http://awebfactory.svnrepository.com:80> ↵
awebfactory.svnrepository.com
Password for 'loginname':
A    sites/default
A    sites/all
```

```
...
A    sites/all/modules/cck/README.txt
A    sites/all/modules/cck/number.module
A    sites/all/README.txt
Checked out revision 2.
```

That's it.

## settings.php File

Now deal with the site-specific settings.php file.

```
litworkshop@example.com:~/public_html$ cp sites.old/default/settings.php sites/↵
default/
```

The last command installs a fresh settings.php, which you should then edit (important!) with your site-specific info. Line 93 or so of sites/default/settings.php should look something like this:

```
...
 * Database URL format:
 *   $db_url = 'mysql://username:password@localhost/databasename';
 *   $db_url = 'mysqli://username:password@localhost/databasename';
 *   $db_url = 'pgsql://username:password@localhost/databasename';
 */
#$db_url = 'mysql://username:password@localhost/databasename';
$db_url = 'mysqli://dr_workshop:big_secret@localhost/dr_workshop';
$db_prefix = '';
```

1. Remove the useless sites.old subdir, and shove the SQL file into the database:

```
litworkshop@example.com:~$ cd public_html/
litworkshop@example.com:~/public_html$ ls
CHANGELOG.txt  INSTALL.mysql.txt  MAINTAINERS.txt  scripts
UPGRADE.txt
cron.php       INSTALL.pgsql.txt  misc             sites
xmlrpc.php
files          install.php        modules          sites.old
includes       INSTALL.txt        profiles         themes
index.php      LICENSE.txt        robots.txt       update.php
litworkshop@example.com:~/public_html$ rm -rf sites.old
litworkshop@example.com:~/public_html$ cd sites/all/backup/db/
litworkshop@example.com:~/public_html/sites/all/backup/db$ ls -l
total 128
-rw-r--r-- 1 litworkshop litworkshop 126735 2008-06-10 18:51
litworkshop.sql
litworkshop@example.com:~/public_html/sites/all/backup/db$ grep mysql ↵
../../../default/settings.php
 *   $db_url = 'mysql://username:password@localhost/databasename';
 *   $db_url = 'mysqli://username:password@localhost/databasename';
#$db_url = 'mysql://username:password@localhost/databasename';
```

```
$db_url = 'mysqli://dr_workshop:workshoppw22@localhost/dr_workshop';
litworkshop@example.com:~/public_html/sites/all/backup/db$ mysql-u
dr_workshop -p ↵
dr_workshop < litworkshop.sql
Enter password:
litworkshop@example.com:~/public_html/sites/all/backup/db$
```

2. On a dedicated server or VPS you are managing yourself, someone has to tell the Apache HTTP server where the litworkshop website application is! This is a job for root, of course, because you need to deal with system configuration. But it's quite painless. Log in as root, and add the following snippet to your Apache configuration file. On an Ubuntu server, we edit `/etc/apache2/sites-enabled/000-default` and tack on the following to the end of the file:

```
<VirtualHost *>
  ServerName litworkshop.textworks.com.ar
  DocumentRoot /home/litworkshop/public_html
  <Directory "/home/litworkshop/public_html">
    Options Indexes FollowSymLinks MultiViews
    AllowOverride All
  </Directory>
</VirtualHost>
```

3. Restart the Apache server for the configuration to take effect:

```
root@example.com:~ # /etc/init.d/apache2 force-reload
 * Reloading web server config apache2                    ↵
                         2904
                                                     ↵
                [ OK ]root@example.com:~ #
```

Of course, this command will vary according to your server OS. Even on Ubuntu, you could have restarted Apache with:

```
root@example.com:~ # apache2ctl restart
```

On a Centos system, on the other hand, the command might be:

```
# /etc/init.d/httpd restart
```

Hey, am I done yet? Just about! You just need to ensure now that the whole world knows that the subdomain `http://litworkshop.example.com` points to the same IP as the server itself by editing your DNS server settings (which will vary according to how your VPS or dedicated server or shared hosting is set up; see Chapter 4 for instructions on that).

You can now be rewarded by pointing your browser at `http://litworkshop.example.com` and see that you have successfully installed your test server.

Awesome. Now, do something gratifying for a while, because then you must come back and repeat the exact same process on your local development box, ending up with a fresh Drupal installation with its sites directory checked out as a working copy of your repository, and implemented as a virtual host also.

> **You want to make sure that all of your sites are "Document Root" sites (domain or subdomain URLs). In this way, whether the domain is `example.com` or `litworkshop.example.com`, within a content item you can consistently link to the files directory where all your images and other assets are stored using /files/images/pic1.jpg, for example. So you never want to be fooling around with Drupal installations that are subdirectories, or you can wind up with inconsistencies in the linking of assets.**

At this point, the filesystem on our development box contains the first historical version of your work. This is what you imported into your repository. But it is not a working copy of the repository, and on your development box you need to be working with a checked-out working copy of the repository, so that when you make changes, you commit them to the repository and then update test and production sites accordingly. So to finish up, you need to create your local working copy, and then you can simply delete the original files. That may seem like a wicked and heartless thing to do (and even frightening, so you can save a tar or zip of that if you prefer), but get used to it: It's a repository-centric world!

In my case, I made a brand-new home for my local working copy in a www folder under my home user directory (i.e. /home/dev) and did the following:

```
dev@laptop:~/www$ tar xvzf
/media/store/downloads/Drupal/release/drupal-5.7.tar.gz
dev@laptop:~/www/litworkshop$ mv drupal-5.7/
litworkshopdev@laptop:~/www$ ↵
cd litworkshop
dev@laptop:~/www/litworkshop$ mkdir files
dev@laptop:~/www/litworkshop$ sudo chown www-data:www-data files
[sudo] password for victorkane:
dev@laptop:~/www/litworkshop$
dev@laptop:~/www/litworkshop$ ls
CHANGELOG.txt   index.php         INSTALL.txt      modules     themes
cron.php        INSTALL.mysql.txt LICENSE.txt      profiles
update.php
files           INSTALL.pgsql.txt MAINTAINERS.txt  robots.txt
UPGRADE.txt
includes        install.php       misc             scripts
xmlrpc.php
dev@laptop:~/www/litworkshop$ rm -rf sites
dev@laptop:~/www/litworkshop$ svn co ↵
http://awebfactory.svnrepository.com/svn/litworkshop/trunk/sites ↵
sites  --username username
```

Then, because you already have the database set up from your original work before you imported everything into the repository, you can simply copy ./default/settings.php over to this working copy:

```
dev@laptop:~/www/litworkshop$ cp /var/www/workshop/sites/default/settings.php ↩
sites/default/
```

All that is left is to create a virtual host pointing to the working copy and then use your /etc/hosts file to fool your browser into thinking that `http://litworkshop.mydomain` is a subdomain.

You add a similar Virtual Host snippet to /etc/apache2/sites-enabled/000-default, just as you did on the test site server, taking into account the location of your local working copy and the name of your development box (`mentor`, in my case):

```
<VirtualHost *>
  ServerName litworkshop.mentor
  DocumentRoot /home//dev/www/litworkshop
  <Directory "/home/dev/www/litworkshop">
    Options Indexes MultiViews FollowSymLinks
    AllowOverride All
    Order deny,allow
    Deny from all
    allow from all
  </Directory>
</VirtualHost>
```

then restart the Apache HTTP server in the same way.

All that remains is to make that phony subdomain on your development box by editing your /etc/hosts file in the following way:

```
192.168.1.7 laptop laptop.mydomain.com litworkshop.laptop
```

Now you can point your browser at `http://litworkshop.laptop`, and see the rewards of your labor. You can work, happy and care-free, on your development box, commit your work, and update your working copy on the test site in order to painlessly deploy your work where Pam can see it. Awesome again! Finally.

# Building on Your Initial Prototype

Getting back to doing some socially useful work (actually building the site for the client), the main purpose at this point is to build a minimum amount of functionality so that your initial prototype will do more good than harm to the client as a semantic springboard for her writing the user stories. If Pam has seen a literary piece and a literary piece critique in the flesh, even in primitive form, then at least you and she and the rest of the staff on both sides (not to mention the coders and themers and graphic design people) will be using consistent language to identify content types in the very language of the user stories. "Finding a common language" is a key part of the process in software development of any kind. So everyone will be getting off to a good start.

**While we are on the subject of semantics, let's bear in mind that the Drupal community uses the term *content types* to signify business objects. That's because it doesn't know if it's a web application framework or a content management system, so it's both. Not to worry.**

### On Finding a Common Language

There is, of course, a wealth of literature and resources on this and related software engineering topics. On the need for finding a common language, check out Doug Rosenberg and Matt Stephens, "Robustness Analysis," in *Use Case Driven Object Modeling with UML*, Chapter 5 (2007, Apress) and the "finding a common language" topic as it is dealt with in the Open Unified Process ("Unified Process," `http://en.wikipedia.org/wiki/Unified_Process`) and the IBM Rational Unified Process ("Rational Unified Process," `http://en.wikipedia.org/wiki/Rational_Unified_Process`), as well as in Scott Ambler's "Agile Unified Process" and the Agile Modeling site (see both "Scott Ambler's Unified Process," `http://en.wikipedia.org/wiki/Agile_Unified_Process` and the Agile Modeling home page, `www.agilemodeling.com/`).

So, using the same process in the litworkshop Drupal site as you did in Chapter 2, and working on your local development box, you're going to:

1. Create the literary_piece content type.
2. Enable comments for this content type, and show them as being literary piece critiques for now.
3. Use Drupal's built-in outlining to create some magazines and books.
4. Set up some forums so that Pam can say which forum structure and which forum topics she wants.
5. Set up blogs.
6. Put forums, blogs, books and magazines, and a global literary workshop on the primary menu along with the Join menu item.
7. Prepare for commit (including database dump) and commit to repository, then tag as initial prototype so if things go badly tomorrow you can go back and bravely set out once again.
8. Deploy to the test site.

Then, talk to Pam!

## Creating the literary_piece Content Type

You create the literary piece content type in exactly the same way as you created the application content type in Chapter 2. You go to Administer ➤ Content management ➤ Content types, and then click on "Add content type." Here is a table to serve as a reference in creating just a first cut of this content type (remember to leave the body field blank so as not to use this deprecated field, not to promote to front page, and to select "Publish" and "Create new revision" in the Workflow/Default options section; additionally, make sure that Comments are enabled for this content type and set to Read/Write):

| Field Label | Machine-Readable Name | Field Type | Widget | Configuration | Required Field | Required Modules |
|---|---|---|---|---|---|---|
| Title | title (default) | | | | Yes | cck |
| Text | literary_piece_text | Text | Text Field | 10 rows | Yes | cck |

Since Pam does not want people overly explaining the texts they submit for critiques, it is entirely possible that we will not be needing any additional fields.

### Importing and Exporting Content Types

Content types implement business objects and allow you to enter records with a custom-designed form with as many different fields as you like. While this is very powerful, once I design a content type on one system to hold my data, if I want to use the same content type on another system, do I have to go through the whole content type creation process again?

This is not necessary. Did you know you can export and import content types to and from text files?

To do so, make sure that the `Content Copy` module (already present as part of the CCK package) is enabled (Administer ➤ Site Building ➤ Modules — CCK section) and that your admin user dev has the necessary permissions (Administer ➤ User management ➤ Access control — Node module — Administer content types).

Then, for example, in order to import the Chapter 3 version of the file literary_piece.txt from the Leveraging Drupal website to avoid having to create this content type manually, you would go to Administer ➤ Content management ➤ Content types, and click on the Import tab. Leaving the Content type dropdown list on <Create>, paste the contents of the text file into Import data, as shown in the figure below, and click on the Submit button.

*Continued*

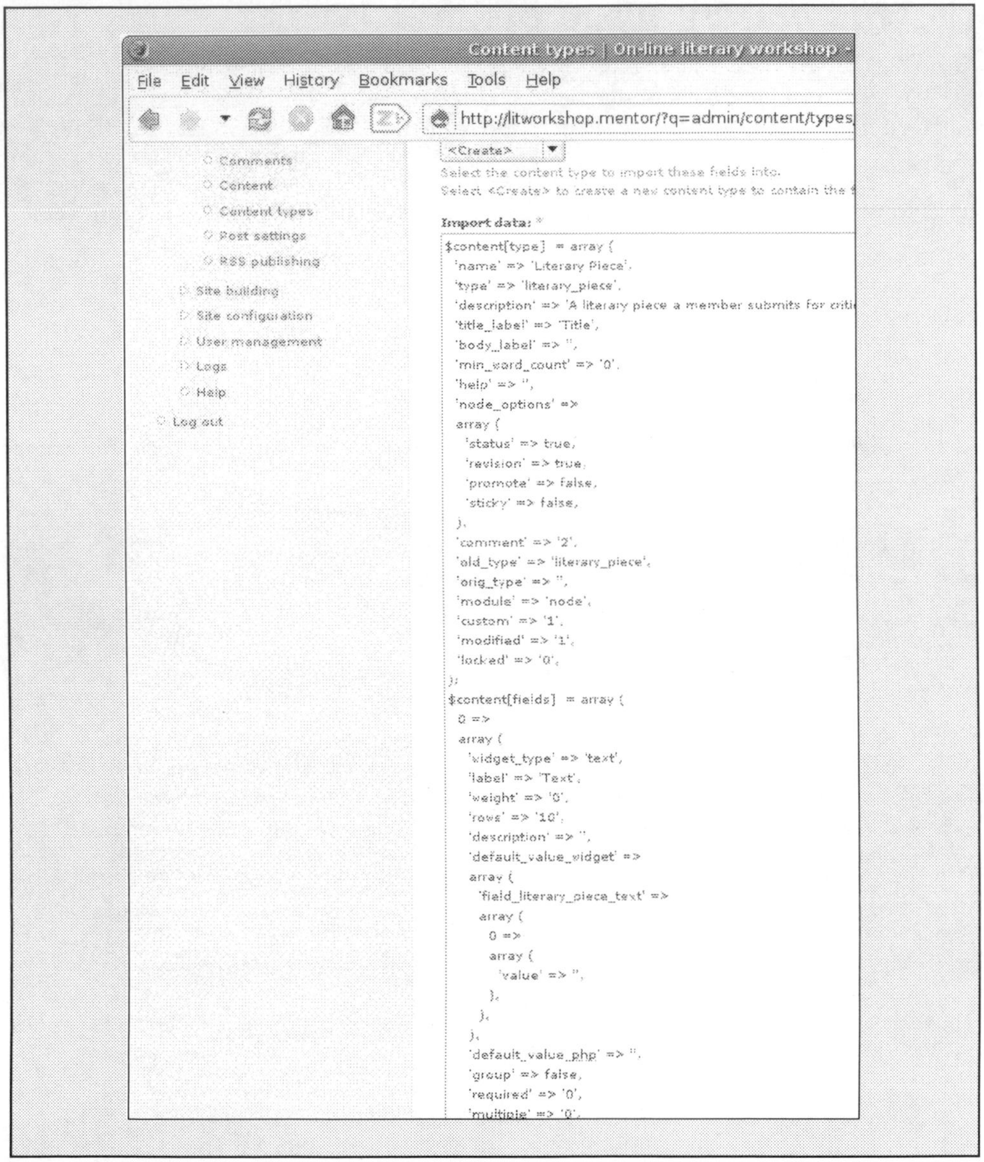


## *Enabling Comments for the literary_piece Content Type*

Next, you want to submit a couple of literary pieces and enter a few critiques of other pieces. Still logged in as user dev, do the following:

1. Create a couple of test member users, named, aptly enough, *James* and *Joyce*.
2. Set permissions for the Workshop Member role.
3. Log in as *James* and create two pieces.
4. Log in as *Joyce* and create two pieces.

To do this, you want to follow these steps:

1. Go to Administer ➢ User management ➢ Users, and click on the "Add user" tab.
2. Fill in the Username field with **james**, and provide a valid e-mail address and a suitable password. Select the role "Workshop Member" and "Create new account." Repeat the process for **joyce**.
3. To set permissions for the Workshop Member role, go to Administer ➢ User management ➢ Access control, and select the following permissions:

| Module | Permissions |
|---|---|
| Comment module | Access comments |
| | Post comments without approval |
| Node module | Access content |
| | Create literary_piece content |
| | Edit own literary_piece content |
| | View revisions |

4. Click on "Save permissions."
5. Now on the Navigation menu (titled *dev* since you are logged in as dev), click on the "Log out" link. Then log in as user james, and click on "Create Content." Now, user james has the option to create Applications (as do even unauthenticated users) and Literary Pieces.
6. Click on the Literary Piece link. In order to fill in the title and the Text body, you're going to avail yourself of the marvelous Lorum Ipsum site, which provides Latin dummy text. (See `www.lipsum.com/`. This site explains the history of Lorem Ipsum apart from limitless Latin dummy text creation!) Quickly hit Submit, and then create another. Log out and create two literary pieces logged in as user joyce.
7. Log in as pam to survey your current status. Click the Content option from the left-side navigation menu. Pam can survey the content items created so far, what types they are, on what dates they were created, and who created them, as shown in Figure 3-9.

So far so good. Let's move on.

## Creating Some Magazines and Books

Let's get the Publisher role into the act. Before you do this, you need to make sure the book module is enabled, because this allows for the creation of ad hoc hierarchical "publications" consisting of book pages. Follow these steps:

1. Log in as dev, and go to Administer ➢ Site building ➢ Modules. You can see that Drupal ships with quite a lot of core modules, which can be optionally enabled as per requirements. In the Core–Optional section, select Book, and then click on the "Save configuration" button.
2. Still logged in as dev, go to Administer ➢ User management ➢ Users, and click on "Add user." Create a Publisher called **alfred**, remembering to assign him the role of Publisher.

3. To set permissions for the Publisher role, go to Administer ➢ User management ➢ Access control, and select the following permissions for both the Workshop Leader and Publisher roles:

   - ❑ Book module (check all permissions for role admin as usual)
   - ❑ Create book pages.
   - ❑ Create new books.
   - ❑ Edit book pages (Workshop Leader only).
   - ❑ Edit own book pages.
   - ❑ Outline posts in books (Workshop Leader only).
   - ❑ See printer-friendly version (all roles, for now).

4. Click on the "Save permissions" button.

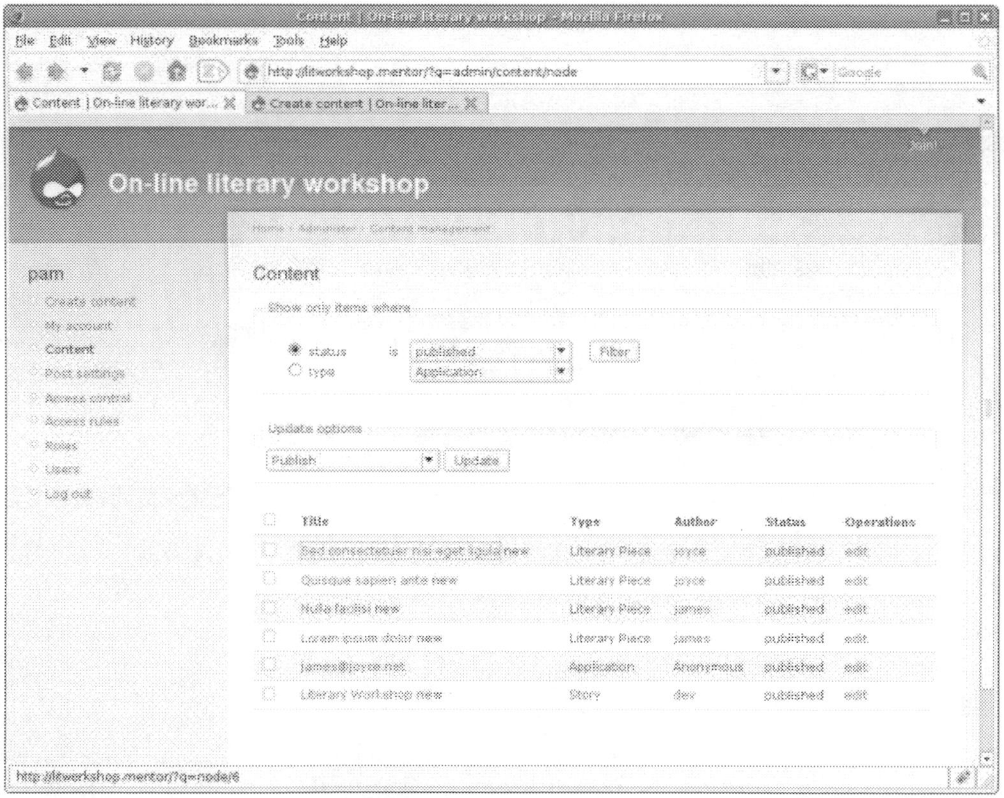


Figure 3-9

> **A Word on Core Modules**
>
> Core modules are modules shipped with Drupal. (See `http://drupal.org/node/937#module` for a precise definition of this independently packaged add-on element of software code that extends Drupal's functionality.) They are separated

into two groups, those that must be enabled in order for Drupal to work at all (Core–Required), and those that may be optionally enabled (Core–Optional), like Book, Forum, and Blog. Additionally, there are third-party modules, also called *contributed modules*, like the CCK module you have already added on to litwork-shop, which you can download from the Drupal site, install, and also enable (see `http://drupal.org/project/Modules`).

If you now log in as alfred, you can create a magazine called *Magazine*. Hit "Create content," click on the Book page link, enter **Magazine** as the title, and then fill in some Latin for the body and click on the Submit button. On the bottom of the page, click on the "Add child page" link. Fill in **Article one** as the title (notice that Magazine is automatically selected as the hierarchical *Parent*), and then some more Latin as the body. After clicking on the Submit button, click on the Up link, and again click on the "Add child page" link to create an *Article two* and then an *Article three* book page. After clicking on the Up link again, you should have something like Figure 3-10 — a magazine containing articles! Great for the prototype anyway.

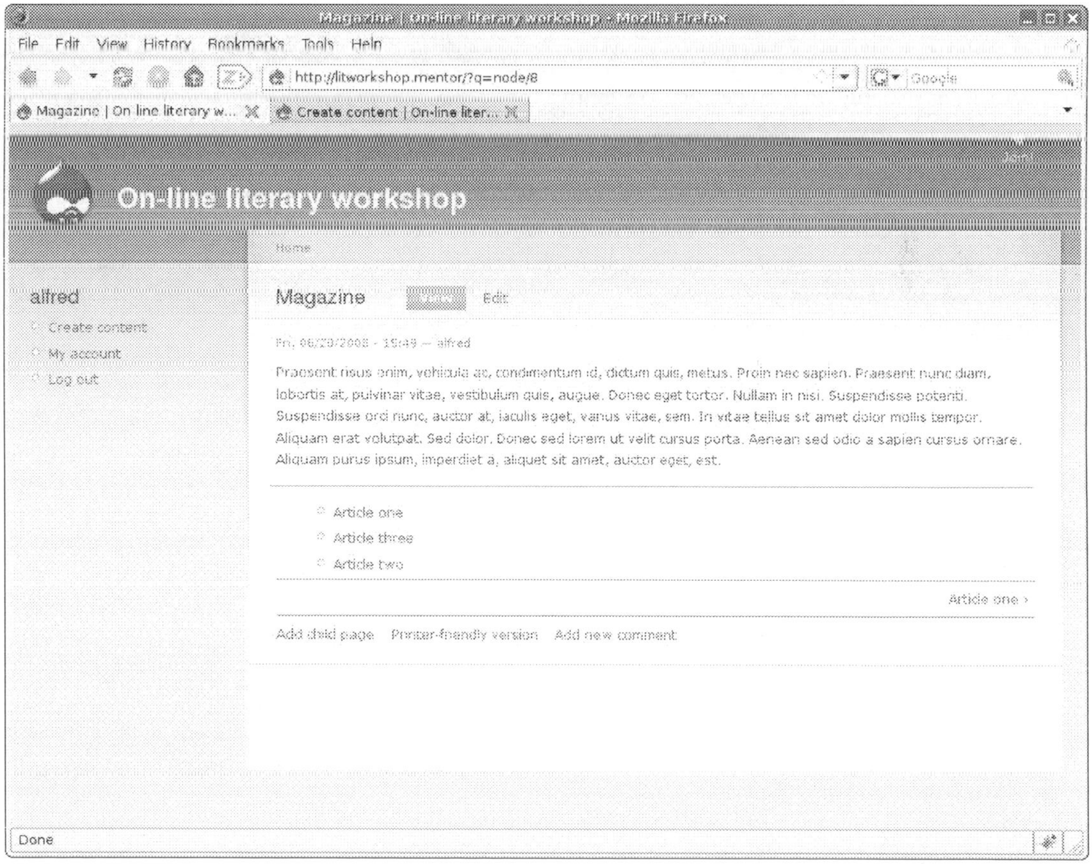


Figure 3-10

Drupal even has built-in content outlining capabilities off-the-shelf. First of all, when you view any content type, you can also add it to any existing book by clicking on the Outline tab. Let's suppose that Pam has made a book called *Literary Workshop Hall of Fame*. And she likes a certain literary piece so much that she wants to include it in her book. She can.

Suppose Pam logs in and goes to Administer ➢ Content Management ➢ Content. She filters the content listed there in order to list only the most recent literary pieces (select the radio button type, choose "Literary Piece" from the dropdown list, and click on the Filter button). She can view any literary piece in another window (or tab if she is using a recent browser) while maintaining this view, as seen in Figure 3-11. Notice how the filter is now set to Literary Piece (it is persistent during the sessions, so it stays that way until Pam hits the Undo button). So Pam can check out all the new pieces to see if the latest crop has any hidden gems.

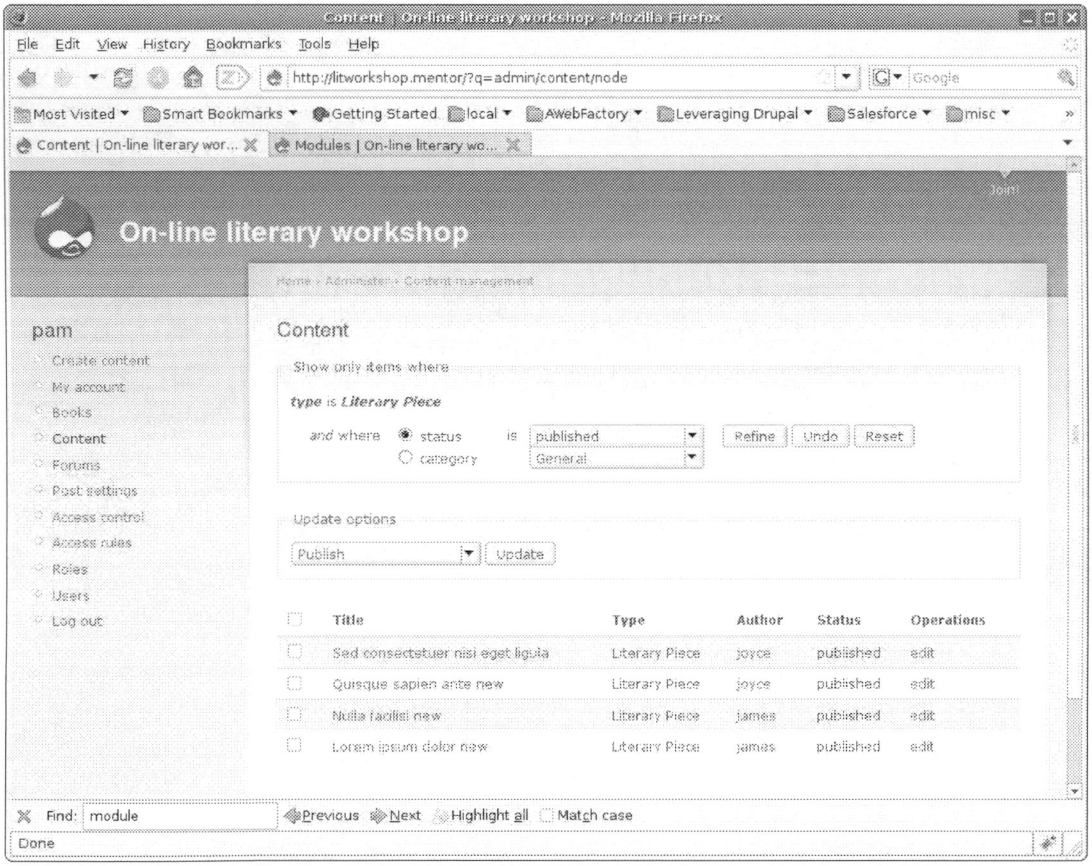


**Figure 3-11**

And she finds one. james's *Nulla facilisi* shows real promise and deserves to be inducted into the *Hall of Fame* Magazine. You already know how to create books: you simply create a book page from the "Create content" link, and then start adding child pages to it. Go ahead and just create the top-level parent page for the new magazine, then view the *Nulla facilisi* Literary Piece. Just to the right of the View and Edit tabs, there is an Outline tab (if there isn't, Pam doesn't have the right permissions as described earlier). See Figure 3-12. Pam clicks "Outline," selects *Hall of Fame* Magazine from the Parent dropdown list, then clicks on the "Add to book" outline button. She then clicks on the Up link to see the new magazine with its initial article.

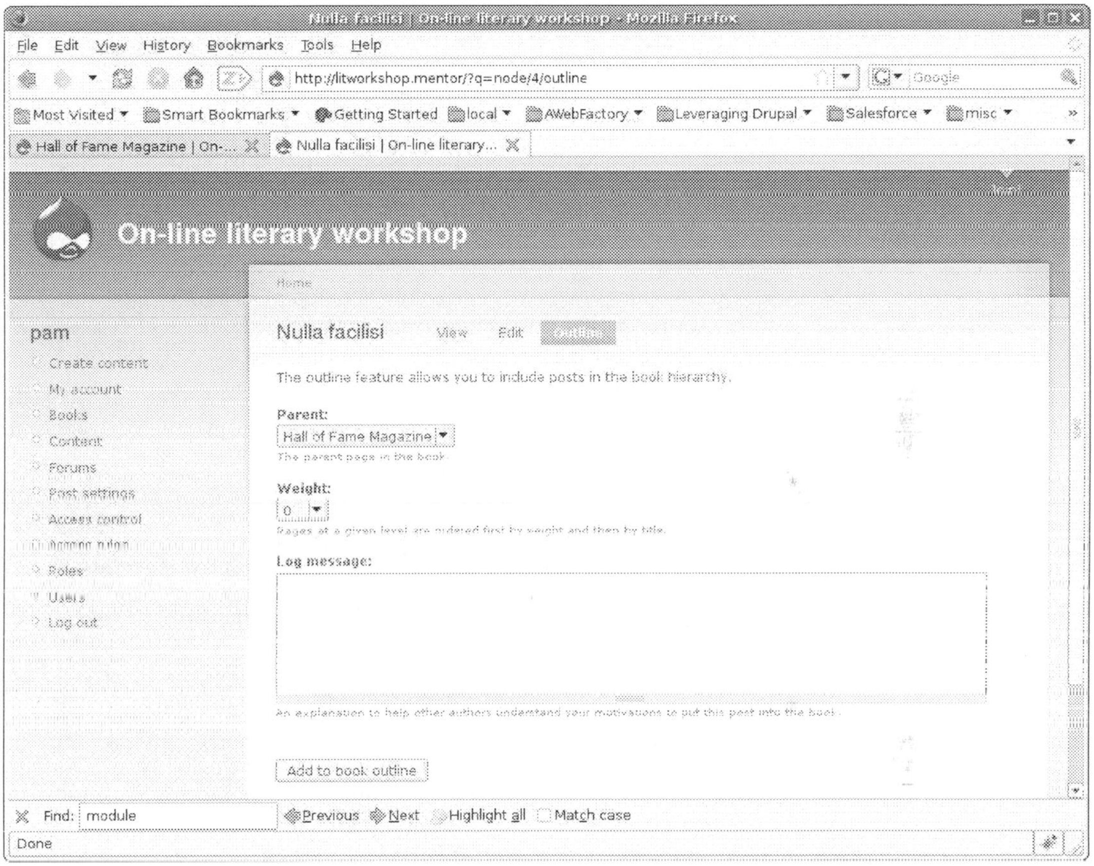

Figure 3-12

It's that easy to create a magazine in Drupal. We'll come back to this in a little bit. But first, you have a bigger problem to solve. Clicking on the "On-Line Literary Workshop" link at the top of the page, or else on the Home link in the breadcrumb, takes us to the Home page. There you have a bit of a shock.

The front page is filled up with all kinds of content, as if it were a blog. This is because Drupal by default sends, or *promotes*, certain kinds of content to the front page. This is great for some applications, like a blog, but doesn't jive with our understanding, even at this early stage, of Pam's requirements. Fortunately, Drupal allows you to configure this behavior for each content type:

1. Log in as dev, go to Administer ➢ Content management ➢ Content types, and click on the Edit link corresponding to the Book page content type.
2. Near the bottom of the page, in the Workflow section, de-select the "Promoted to the front page" option, and while you're at it, select "Create new revision" to allow you to take advantage of Drupal's built-in content version control system.

3. Click on the "Save content type" button. This should look familiar because it is what you did for both Application and Literary Piece content types.

4. While you're here, make sure that these settings apply to all content types, including blogs, and leave the story content type alone as one whose content will automatically be promoted to the front page, in case you need a quick edit at some point along these lines.

5. Returning to the front page, the first impression is that you haven't solved the problem at all. That is because changing the configuration of a content type will affect nodes created from that point on, but is not retroactive to nodes created before then. Those still reflect the configuration in effect at the time of their creation (they are clones of the configuration at that point of time).

*A* node *is an independent piece of content based on any content type (page, story, blog entry, etc.) entered by a user and stored in the database. It can be considered the basic atom of content in Drupal.*

So do you have to go in and de-select the front page promotion option from each one individually? That would be a lot of work, and error-prone too. Fortunately, Drupal allows you to deal with this problem:

1. Simply go to Administer ➢ Content management ➢ Content, and set a filter for book pages (as you did before for Literary Pieces).

2. Just below the "Show only items where" filter section, you can see the "Update options" section. Choose "Demote from front page" from the dropdown list, and select the check-all checkbox on the left-hand side in the content listing table header (see Figure 3-13). Then you simply click on the Update button.

3. Go back to the front page to test whether the problem is solved. There you should just see the Welcome page, as before. To test that your new configuration settings are correct, go ahead and log in as pam again, hit the books link from the navigation menu, click "*Hall of Fame* Magazine," and then click on the "Add child page" link. Type in **Second piece** for the title and some Latin filler for the body, and then click on the Submit button. Now go to the front page just to be sure your new configuration for book pages is in effect and only the Welcome page is seen there. Awesome.

## *Setting up Some Forums*

As an exercise, go ahead and follow the Drupal handbook instructions ("Forum: create threaded discussions": `http://drupal.org/handbook/modules/forum`) for setting up a forum for magazine publishers (you will need to enable the optional core module just as you did for the book), and then for flash fiction, Haibun, and Sonnet aficionados.

> **Make use of forum containers when planning your forum structure. For example, in this context, you might want a General and a Literary Forms forum container, and then specific forums within each of those.**

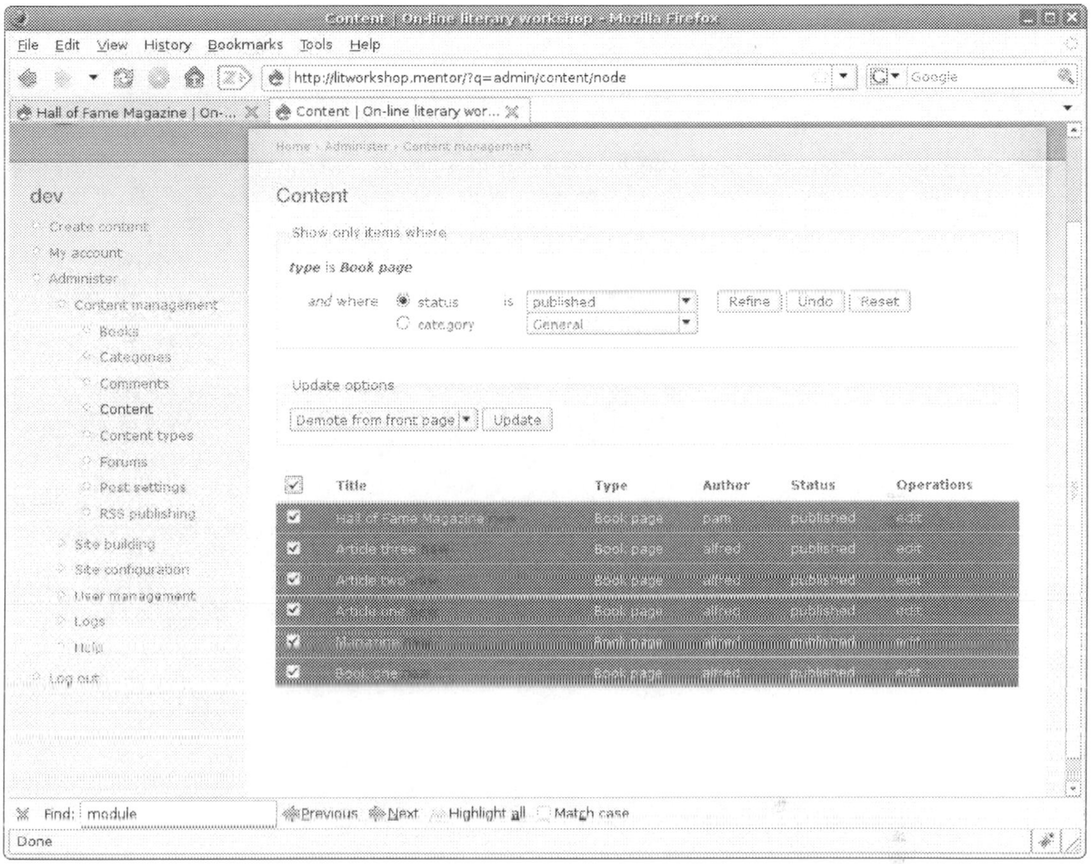

Figure 3-13

Later Pam will be able to go to Administer ➢ Administer ➢ Content Management ➢ Forums and carry it on after the first meeting.

If you followed the instructions, you should see something like Figure 3-14. Notice the use of Containers and Forums.

## Setting up Blogs

Blogs are also enabled by activating an optional core module. For prototyping purposes, enable blogs for all authenticated roles, with comments enabled also:

1. You enable the Blog module from Administer ➢ Site building ➢ Modules as usual, and then set permissions as before at Administer ➢ User management ➢ Access control.
2. Set "edit own blog" permissions and "access comments," "post comments," and "post comments without approval" for all authenticated roles.

3. Just one more little thing: go to Administer ➢ Content management ➢ Content types, edit the Blog entry content type, and de-select the "promoted to front page" option.
4. Log in as alfred the Publisher, and write a couple of entries; log in as pam, and write a couple of entries.
5. Click on the "My blog" link on the Navigation menu, and then on "Post new blog entry."

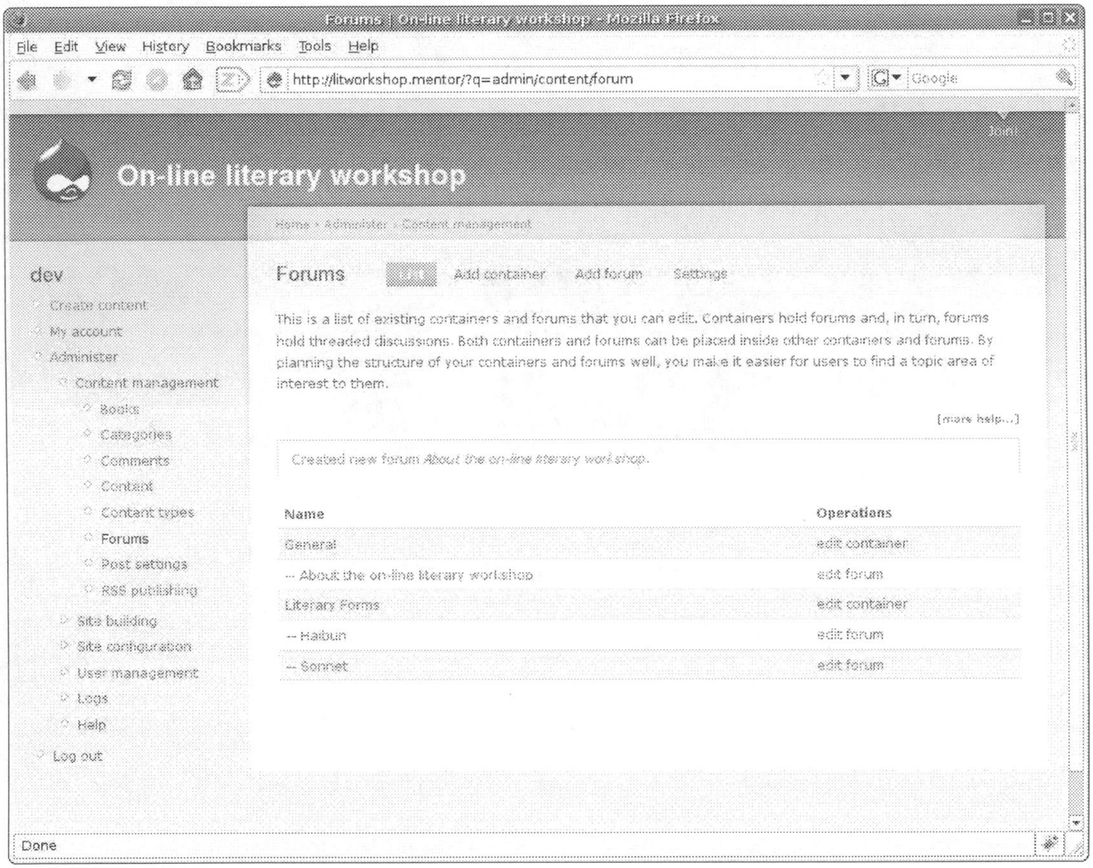


**Figure 3-14**

By now you should be starting to feel more at home around Drupal.

## Completing the Primary Menu

You've really got the initial prototype coming together! Now, one of the great things about Drupal is how it separates functionality from presentation, and within that, esthetics from navigation. In fact, there is a whole completely configurable and extremely power Navigation menu system built right into Drupal, and you're going to leverage that now to tie your package up, all ready to show to Pam!

Let's set up something like this:

Main Menu
- Blogs
- Forums
- Books and Magazines
- Join

Log in as dev, and go to Administer ➤ Site building ➤ Menus. The first menu listed on the page is called *Primary links*, and it is the menu including the menu item Join! you have already placed there. Just above the table listing Join!, click "Add item." Fill in the data for Blogs, as per the following table, and then insert the other items in the same way.

| Title | Description | Path (No Leading/Character) | Parent Item (Automatically Selected) | Weight |
|---|---|---|---|---|
| Blogs | On-Line Literary Workshop Blog Central! | Blog | Primary links | 0 |
| Forums | Discussion forums | Forum | Primary links | 2 |
| Publications | On-line books and magazines | Book | Primary links | 4 |
| Join! | Join our literary workshop | Node/add/application | Primary links | 6 |

Test out your new Navigation menu. It should look something like Figure 3-15, which is viewing Blog Central.

## Committing to the Repository and Tagging the Initial Prototype

Well, you have certainly done a good bit of work. Enough already. You are definitely at a point where you would want to commit your work to the repository and call it a day. You will be doing this a lot, every time you finish an atomic piece of work in the future (roughly corresponding to each section or subsection in this chapter). So let's just review these three quick easy steps:

1. Dump the database: You can do this via phpMyAdmin if the database isn't too big (and it won't be for quite a while, certainly during development), or else from the command line (which is actually the easiest way and is recommended in this book). In case you need a refresher, refer to the section "Main Directory Structure for the Repository" above. The main thing is to wind up with litworkshop.sql in ./sites/all/backup/db.

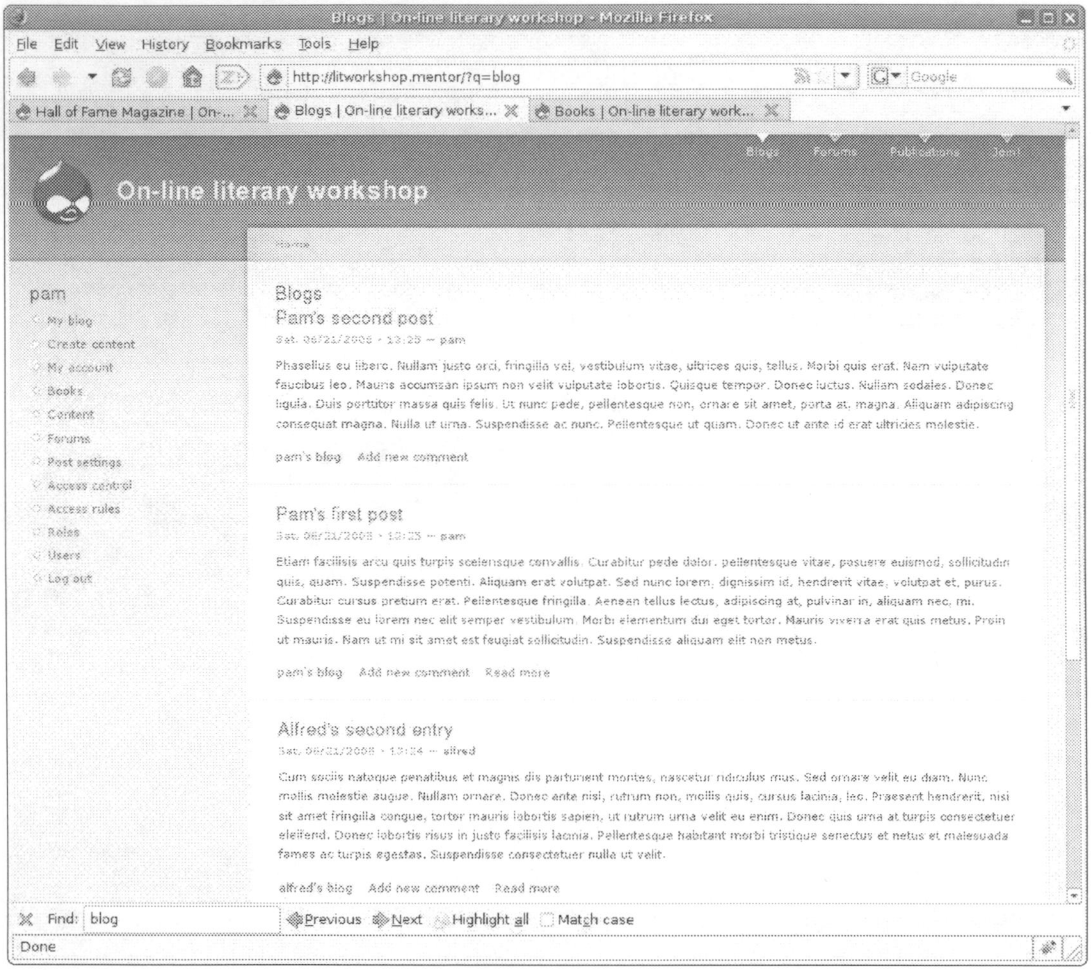


Figure 3-15

> **Clear the cache before dumping the database in order to commit a working copy snapshot to the repository.**

2. Navigate to the ./sites directory: # cd /path-to-working-copy/sites.
3. Commit to the repository. It's been a while, so let's see the status of the working copy as compared to the repository:

```
$ svn status
?      default/settings.php
M      all/backup/db/litworkshop.sql
$
```

Yes, all your work, in terms of both content and configuration, has been persisted in the database itself. Commit:

```
$ svn commit -m "prototype to show Pam for initial feedback and↵
 requirements capture"
Sending        all/backup/db/litworkshop.sql
Transmitting file data .
Committed revision 4.
$
```

> **One way to do this quickly right now is to log in as dev, go to Administer ➤ Site Building ➤ Modules, and hit the Submit button as if you were enabling a module. Later, you will see other alternatives.**

## Deploying to the Test Site

By this time your hosting provider, whoever it is, has had ample time to enable your secure shell. So you have just four steps to deploy this version to the test site so Pam can see it:

> ssh *is an abbreviation, and also the command for, a secure shell. On Linux, you've already got that. On Windows, use putty, an excellent Open Source solution. (For putty, see* `www.chiark.greenend.org.uk/~sgtatham/putty/`. *For background on ssh, see* `http://en.wikipedia.org/wiki/Secure_Shell`.*)*

1. **Log into the Test Site** — On Ubuntu, or any other Linux distribution, or on a Mac OS terminal, just do:

   ```
   $ ssh litworkshop@example.com.com.ar
   Password:
   Linux   textworks.com.ar   2.6.23.17-linode43   #1   Wed   Mar   5   13:57:22
   EST 2008 i686

   litworkshop@example.com:~$
   ```

   > *If this is your first time connecting to that host, you will be asked to confirm saving the remote site information in the local database. Just say Yes.*

   If for some reason you are on a Microsoft Windows system and trying to do this, just use putty (see above note). Just download it (e.g., to C:\Program Files\putty\putty.exe) and double-click on it. Fill in the hostname where your test site is located. Click on the SSH radio button, and the Port filed will automatically change to **22**. Use this unless you know otherwise. If you want to save this session info for the future, fill in a Saved Sessions name, and click on the Save button. Then click on the Open button.

   > *If this is your first time connecting to that host, you will be greeted with a scary warning window entitled, "PuTTY Security Alert," saying "WARNING — POTENTIAL SECURITY BREACH!" which gives a pretty darned good explanation of the fact that PuTTY has no idea if you are connected to the server you want to be connected with or to some other server just pretending to be that server. Since we expect this to happen the first time, again, we just say Yes.*

The terminal window appears and prompts for the username with "Log in as: "." Fill in **lit-workshop** if you have followed the instructions earlier in the chapter, or else whatever is the appropriate user. You are then prompted for the Password, and then you are in and should have a terminal window looking something like Figure 3-16 (which also shows the whole sequence necessary for deployment to the test site).

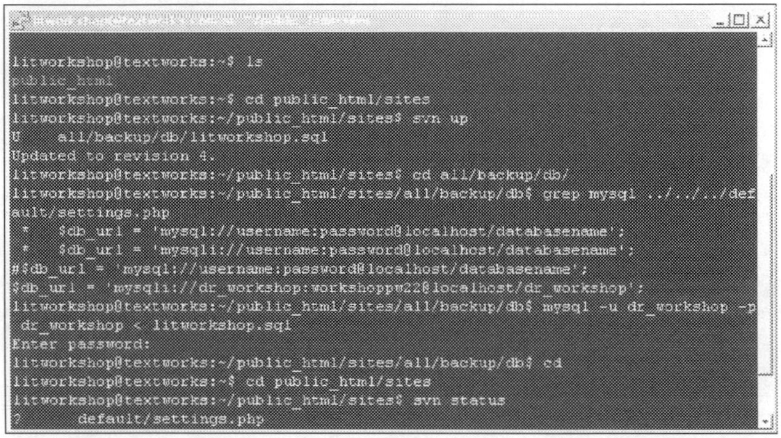


**Figure 3-16**

2. **Navigate to /path-to-working-copy/sites** — litworkshop@example.com:~$ cd public_html/sites.

3. **Update to Latest Version from the SVN Repository**

```
litworkshop@example.com:~/public_html/sites$ svn up
U    all/backup/db/litworkshop.sql
Updated to revision 4.
litworkshop@example.com:~/public_html/sites$
```

4. **Load the Database with the Current Database State** — Grab the details of the mysql database you are using, or else locate that info right in the ./sites/default/settings.php file. (That's why you set its permissions so it cannot be seen by anyone except the logged-in user.)

```
litworkshop@example.com:~/public_html/sites/all/backup/db$ grep mysql ↩
../../../default/settings.php
 *   $db_url = 'mysql://username:password@localhost/databasename';
 *   $db_url = 'mysqli://username:password@localhost/databasename';
#$db_url = 'mysql://username:password@localhost/databasename';
$db_url = 'mysqli://dr_workshop:workshoppw22@localhost/dr_workshop';
```

Load the database with the database state.

```
litworkshop@example.com:~/public_html/sites/all/backup/db$ mysql -u dr_workshop -p ↩
dr_workshop < litworkshop.sql
```

```
Enter password:
litworkshop@example.com:~/public_html/sites/all/backup/db$
```

Now point your browser at your test site and enjoy the fact that you have deployed your current state-of-the-art quickly and accurately!

# Getting Initial Feedback from the Client

Because the bottleneck now is getting the client to confirm the Roles and to start writing some short, pithy user stories, contact your client on Skype and look over the site together. The discussion at this point is basically an interview, wherein you first show the list of users and their roles and ask if any important role is missing. Then you confirm the first cut list of user stories. You struggle against "user story explosion," making sure to keep to the main ones only. Then you confirm the domain model. Then you compare that to the content types that have actually been created in accordance with the domain model. Pam finds out how to create content types here using the basic navigation interface (Drupal menu: Create content, Content). And you finish up the meeting by discussing the next step to be taken, namely, that of writing up all the user stories!

Pam enjoyed the fact that there was something up and running so quickly. She logged in, checked out the site, and then clicked Roles, which we have discussed. She agreed that the list was indeed exhaustive for the initial website launch, so we were all set to go on that score.

We then checked over the user stories (I had published the first cut list in a blog on the site itself) and got right down to work. In a few days, we had the whole set written and ready to finish off together as a collaborative effort between developer team and client.

# Summary

You did some real trapeze work in this chapter. First, you imported a snapshot of your existing Drupal website prototype into a spanking new SVN version control repository, after straightening out your directory structure for both the filesystem and repository. Then you checked out the initial snapshot of your work directly to the test website, where you created a user and a filesystem home for the website and configured everything, including the MySql database and the Apache HTTP server so that your checked-out working copy was actually up and running as a mirror of what you had done on your test box.

Then you got so confident about what you were doing that you up and erased the original work on your development box and checked out a more permanent working copy as home for your development efforts, and got that working too.

You then turned your attention to the job at hand and really leveraged off-the-shelf Drupal and set up a more-than-adequate working model to serve as a springboard to requirements captured from your client as both of you navigated a fully functional prototype while carrying out that interview. The model went a long way toward laying the basis for a common language to be used by all those working on site development, and you were able to sign off on the list of Roles and User Stories. After that, Pam was able to finish writing the first draft of all the remaining user stories in just a few days.

# 4

# Getting up to Speed

At this point, the Elaboration phase is looking like Figure 4-1:

Pam, the client, and Victor, the developer, have been applying an agile approach to the development of the On-line Literary Workshop website application in the last few chapters. Agile development demands the highest possible level of client participation in the development process itself, so Pam has had the task of writing the User Stories, which describe the functionality which needs to be implemented. Once the User Stories have been completed, perhaps with some help from the developer, the process can move forward and a fully functional prototype can be set up. So let's get right down to it.

## Finishing the User Stories with the Client

User Story 4-1 (which follows) is the first user story Pam wrote and revised after we went over the list (the complete set is included in the downloadable chapter resources ZIP file). We struggled to keep the user stories as short as possible, noting that it is better to have more stories than any longish stories. And we agreed that at the same time we should try to avoid "user story explosion," only adding more if they are absolutely necessary.

### More Information on the First User Story

For general background on the first user story, see `http://en.wikipedia.org/wiki/User_story` and the references listed there, particularly `www.extremeprogramming.org/rules/userstories.html`. In this book, I am using the general approach found in the book *User Stories Applied* by Mike Cohn (2004, Addison Wesley Professional), with the concise "Card," "Conversation," and "Confirmation" sections in Chapter 1 of that book that are attributed to Ron Jeffries, "Essential XP: Card, Conversation, and Confirmation," *XP Magazine* (August 30, 2001).

## User Story 4-1: Workshop Leader Can Approve Applications to Join the Workshop

### *Card*

The Workshop Leader can list all the outstanding membership applications and approve, reject, or postpone action on them.

### *Conversation*

Victor notes that the application corresponds to the Application content type and that it might be an application for membership as Publisher or Workshop Member.

Pam explains that membership applications may be new, approved, rejected, or postponed.

Pam says it would be nice if applications could be approved, rejected, or postponed with a single click and without leaving the Membership Application Administration page.

Victor says this should be a subordinate user story and that it should be postponed to a later rather than earlier iteration.

Pam agrees that, for the first iteration, this user story should be included, even if it takes extra clicks at first.

### *Confirmation*

**Test 1** — When the Application content type is created, a Drupal user must be automatically created at the same time.

**Test 2** — When the Application is set to Approved, the Drupal user must be automatically activated, and an e-mail must be sent notifying the new user and giving her access and login links.

**Test 3** — Workshop Members and Publishers can be approved in just a couple of clicks.

- ✓ Create an initial environment
- ✓ Whip up the initial prototype
- ✓ Get initial feedback from the client
- Finish the user stories with the client
- Plan the project
- Work on the architectural baseline
- Get the team organized and with the program

Figure 4-1

# Planning the Project

Now all the functional requirements are in, divided into a sequence of user stories. These actually become the raw material for the planning process:

1. Estimate each user story in terms of how many good days each one requires for implementation.
2. Estimate the team velocity (how many user stories can be implemented in a 2-week iteration, or sprint) of the development team and the client. This calculation will take into account whether or not they have worked together previously, how much confidence and trust exist among them, and so on.
3. Conclude how many iterations you need to get the project done.
4. Assign each user story to an iteration, based mainly on the client's desires, but also on the need to mitigate risk by assigning "risky" user stories (those that have a high impact on architecture, because choices will be made during the course of their implementation that might affect how a large part of the rest of the project gets done: these have to be dealt with as early as possible, in one of the early iterations).

## Doing It on the Dining Room Table

What you really have to play with is a deck of cards.

Think of every user story as a proverbial 3 × 5-inch card. In fact, they *should* be (or some printed-out variation). Do the following:

1. Shuffle the cards, and spread them out on the table.
2. Order the cards in terms of which ones Pam wants implemented first. Now divide the cards into five to six groups, in order. You have your first cut of iteration planning.
3. Review all the cards, starting from the last group, and check and see if there aren't some user stories that have been placed in a relatively late iteration (group of user story cards) that really need to be dealt with sooner rather than later.

These are the items that may not be "hot" but are high in risk and architectural impact. The whole idea of implementing the user stories in iterations is basically to show Pam frequent releases so that feedback and test results can show you where you are really standing, and also to be able to have early implementation act as prototyping aimed at confirming the architecture upon which you are basing the project.

Let's take Pam's need for single-click approval/rejection of membership applications. What is the architectural basis for this going to be?

*You guessed it: While you are planning the project you are also working on the architectural baseline in parallel. It is impossible to really separate one activity from the other.*

In other words, does any existing Drupal functionality support this? If not, is there any existing Drupal functionality that could support it if it were tweaked in some way? Just how much tweaking might be necessary? Are there contributed Drupal modules that could support what you are trying to do? What do you know about the reputation of these modules, in terms of doing the job well, in terms of resources needed, in terms of impact on other modules we might be using?

These questions need to be answered sooner rather than later.

## Doing It with Trac

So you have your clumps of user stories on the dining room table. To move on, bring in your laptop, and document this in a usable fashion. If you decide to use Trac (part of the SVN repository hosting you began to use in Chapter 3) to do this, you will get a few nice surprises: Trac will enable you to actually do the planning also.

Figure 3-7 showed your source code tree, accessed by clicking on the Browse Source menu item. Log into your Trac instance now, if you have one, or just watch and learn — it will be useful anyway:

1. Click on the Roadmap menu item. You'll see a listing of four Milestones (see Figure 4-2).

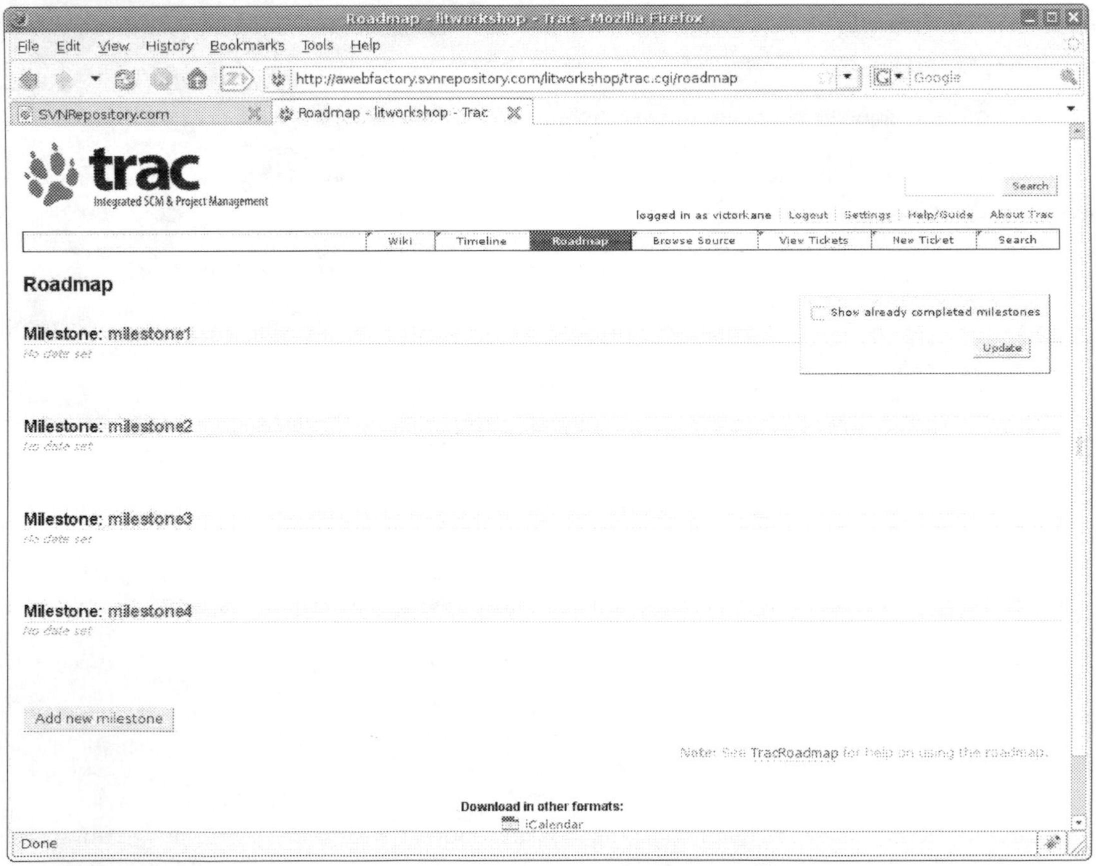


Figure 4-2

2. Click on the milestone1 link. You should see something like Figure 4-3. Click on the "Edit milestone info" button shown there.

3. For now, just change *milestone1* to **Prototype**, fill in a due date approximately 15 days away, and then click on "Submit changes." Then click on the Roadmap again, and edit the remaining three milestones, labeling them **Beta**, **Final release**, and **Launch**, due within 30, 45, and 60 days, respectively. Trac will order your milestones by due date, and your roadmap should now look like Figure 4-4.

4. Now, going to the main menu bar once again, click "New Ticket." In the "Short summary" field, enter **Workshop Leader can approve applications to join the workshop**, choose "task" from the Type dropdown list. In the "Full description" text area, enter the **Card**, **Conversation**, and **Confirmation** sections, and in the "Ticket Properties" section, choose Prototype. The result will look like Figure 4-5.

5. Click on the "Submit ticket" button. The task appears rendered on a yellow background and can be edited further down the page. Files can be attached, changes can be added, and ticket properties can also be altered. The interesting thing is that the ticket can be linked to any existing milestone. So at this point the plan is to add the remaining 19 user stories, dividing them up among the various milestones. The Prototype milestone will contain the first five user stories, the Beta Milestone the next five, and so on. After adding the 20 user stories as tasks allocated over the four Milestones, your Roadmap should look something like Figure 4-6.

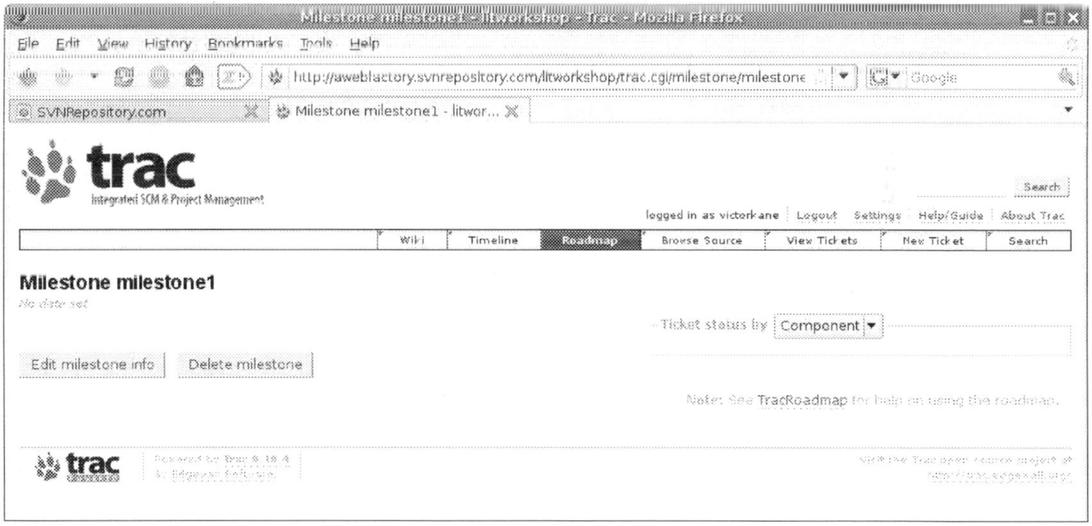


Figure 4-3

All that's left now is to see if any of the user story implementation tasks scheduled for one of the later iteration milestones should be brought forward to an earlier one. Click on the "View Tickets" menu item, and then click on the "Active Tickets" link (*Report {1}*). This list of all active tickets can be sorted by any of the headings. Click on the "Ticket heading" link to get a clean listing ordered by ticket number. Let's study the plan as it appears in Figure 4-7.

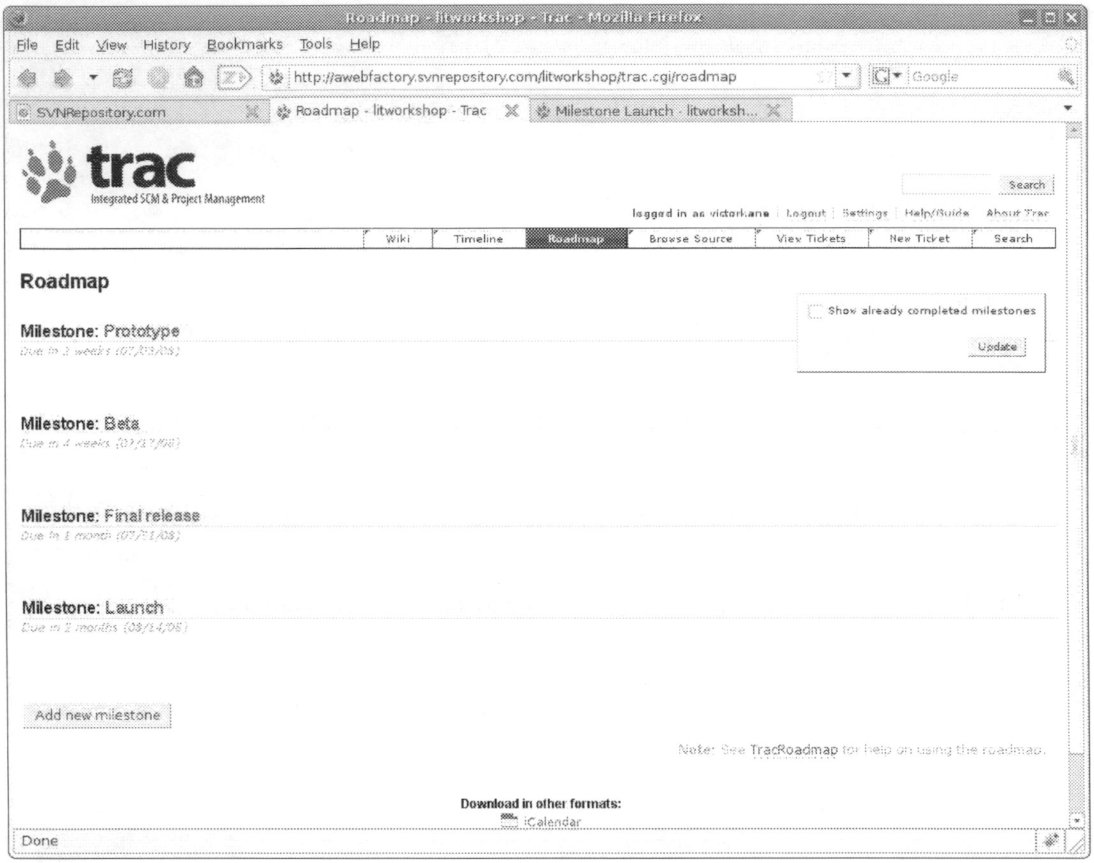


Figure 4-4

The last two tasks are:

- "A Webmaster can administer the website configuration."
- "A Webmaster can install new updates and functionality."

Actually, these tasks have more to do with training than implementation, since Drupal supports that functionality off-the-shelf, but the site needs to be handed over to the new webmaster, and experienced website developers know that that is work too! Of course, some additional Launch Milestone tasks need to be added in, having to do with deployment, so you should add those in immediately.

In terms of the rest of the planning, the question you have to ask yourself now is, "Are there any tasks allocated to the later iterations that represent leaving too much risk of architectural impact in the implementation of unknowns until it might be too late to handle adequately, for example, going with a mitigation plan B?"

Looking over the list, one might get the impression that there is some "easy stuff" earlier on, and "harder stuff" to be implemented later on, and that things perhaps should be the other way around. However, you do want to get started with all of the architectural, navigation, and usability components from the ground up. As you see in the next section, which deals with the architectural baseline that should be set as early as possible in the project after trying out different candidate alternatives, the architectural components are made up of Drupal modules in Drupal core and those contributed by third parties, as well as custom-coded modules you may have to write yourself.

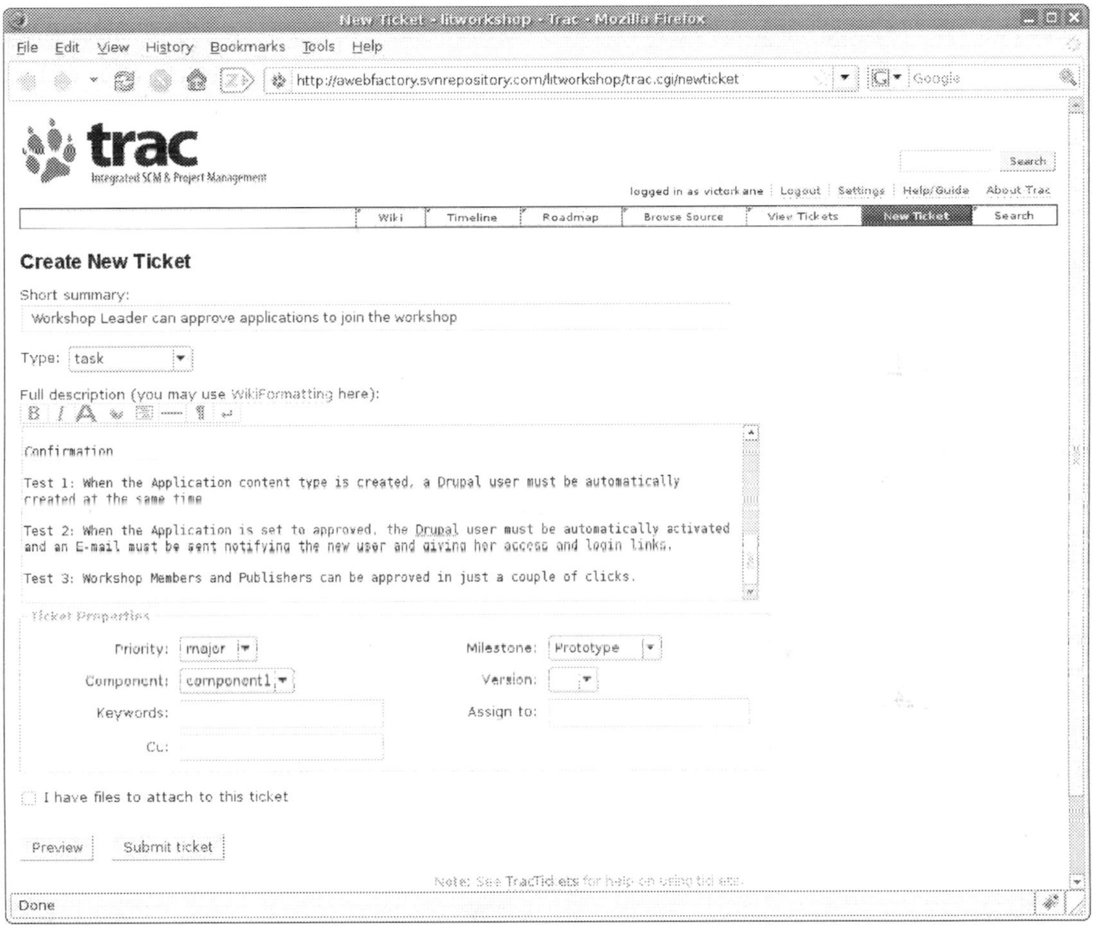


**Figure 4-5**

You will also be adding bugs (issues) and enhancements as tickets. (Trac will allow you to create your own issue categories.) Anyone (staff or client) can add bugs when an acceptance test fails. And anyone can add enhancements (that's usually going to be the client) as change requests for additional functionality not originally provided for in the agreed-upon 20 user story requirements baseline.

For example, Pam had seen some strange URLs being used in the prototype being developed in Drupal, like "?q=blog/2", and is concerned about whether she will be stuck with URLs like that; she says that in WordPress, the URL is created right from the title, and there are no weird characters in it either. So you need to add in enhancement-type issues for "clean URLs" and automatic SEO (Search Engine Optimization)-friendly paths. And you might as well add those to the first iteration, because clean URLs are handled right off-the-shelf (although they might require some tinkering with the Apache HTTP server configuration), and SEO-friendly paths can be generated automatically by the pathauto module.

### Organizing Groups of Iterations into Phases

If the complexity of the project so warrants, in order to better orient your development process, you could divide the iterations into groups, corresponding to the Inception, Elaboration, Construction, and Transition phases outlined in Chapter 1. For example, you could have the first Milestone correspond to the Inception phase; the second and third to the Elaboration phase; the third, fourth, and fifth to the Construction phase; and the last to the Transition phase.

Figure 4-8 shows the current state of affairs for each of the Milestones. You have your work cut out for you.

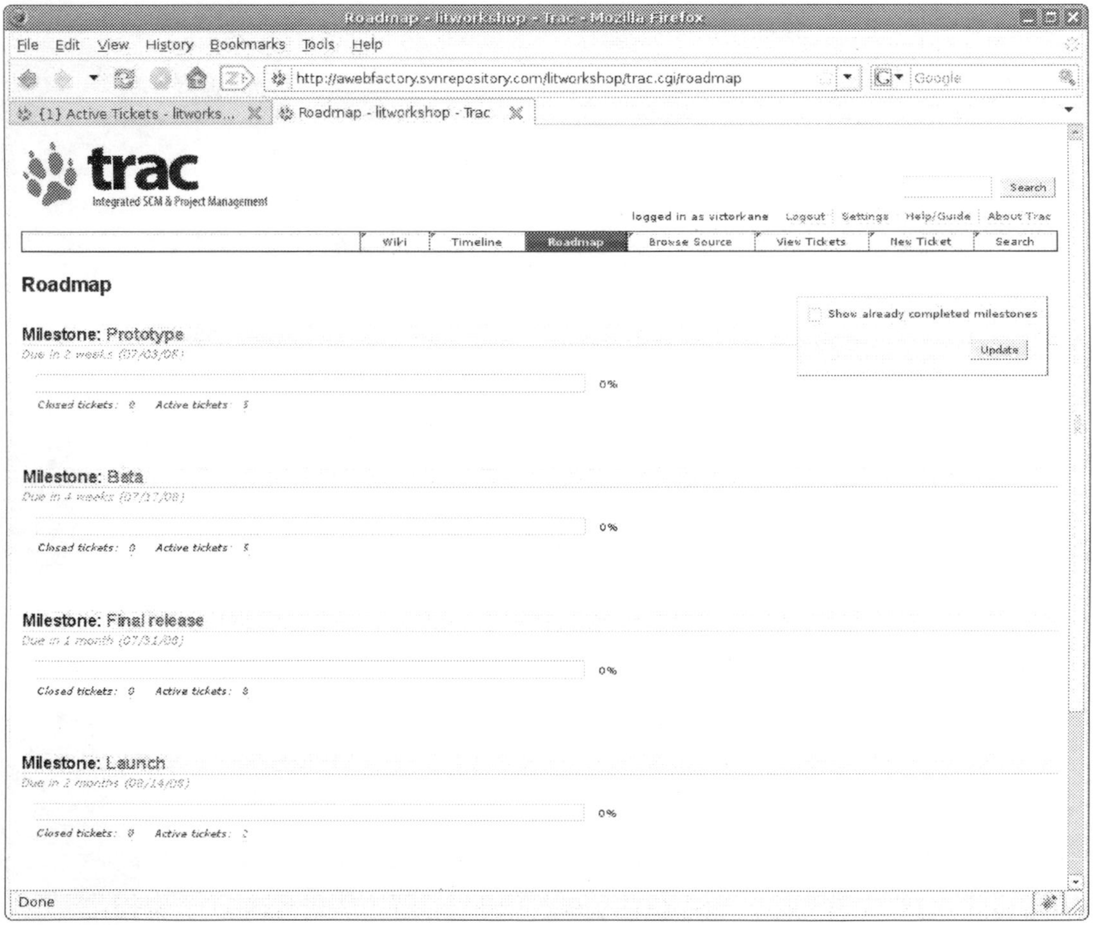


Figure 4-6

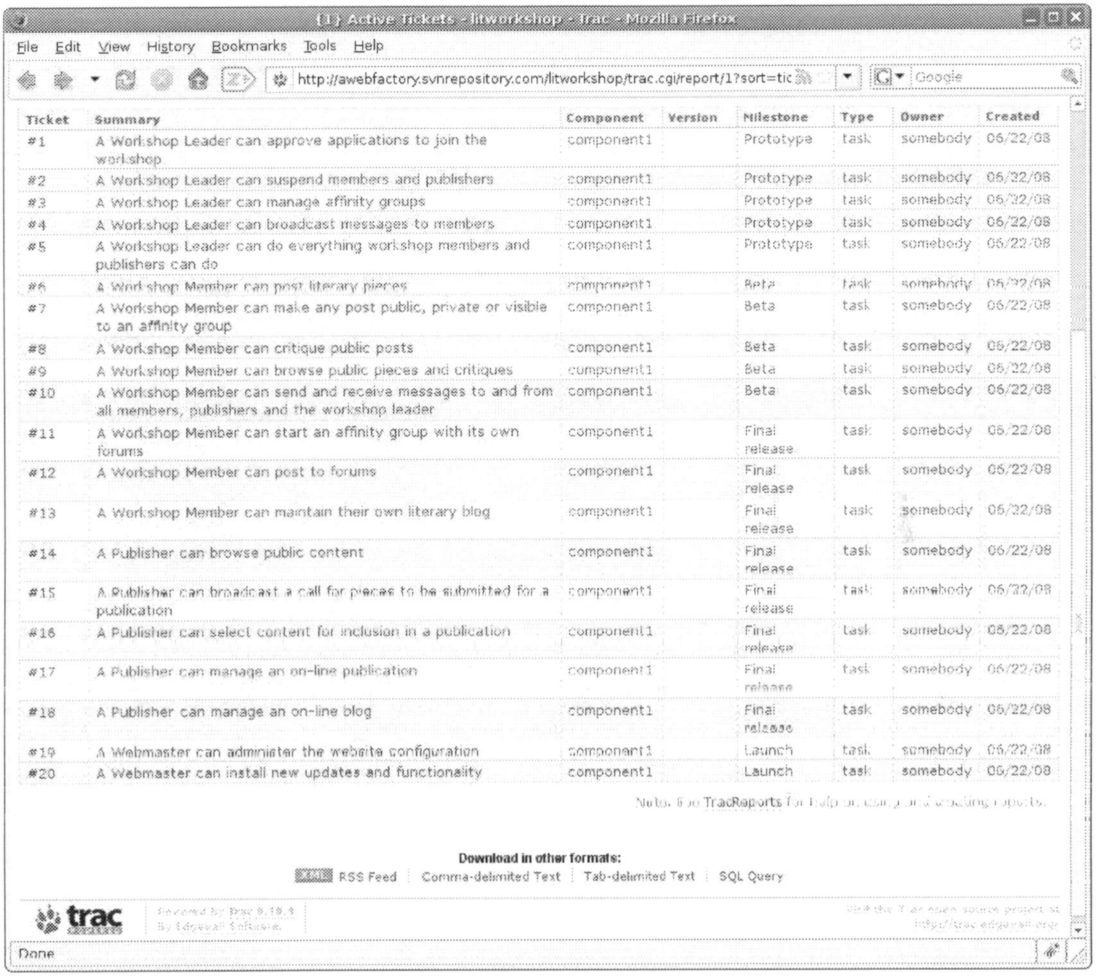

| Ticket | Summary | Component | Version | Milestone | Type | Owner | Created |
|---|---|---|---|---|---|---|---|
| #1 | A Workshop Leader can approve applications to join the workshop | component1 | | Prototype | task | somebody | 06/22/08 |
| #2 | A Workshop Leader can suspend members and publishers | component1 | | Prototype | task | somebody | 06/22/08 |
| #3 | A Workshop Leader can manage affinity groups | component1 | | Prototype | task | somebody | 06/22/08 |
| #4 | A Workshop Leader can broadcast messages to members | component1 | | Prototype | task | somebody | 06/22/08 |
| #5 | A Workshop Leader can do everything workshop members and publishers can do | component1 | | Prototype | task | somebody | 06/22/08 |
| #6 | A Workshop Member can post literary pieces | component1 | | Beta | task | somebody | 06/22/08 |
| #7 | A Workshop Member can make any post public, private or visible to an affinity group | component1 | | Beta | task | somebody | 06/22/08 |
| #8 | A Workshop Member can critique public posts | component1 | | Beta | task | somebody | 06/22/08 |
| #9 | A Workshop Member can browse public pieces and critiques | component1 | | Beta | task | somebody | 06/22/08 |
| #10 | A Workshop Member can send and receive messages to and from all members, publishers and the workshop leader | component1 | | Beta | task | somebody | 06/22/08 |
| #11 | A Workshop Member can start an affinity group with its own forums | component1 | | Final release | task | somebody | 06/22/08 |
| #12 | A Workshop Member can post to forums | component1 | | Final release | task | somebody | 06/22/08 |
| #13 | A Workshop Member can maintain their own literary blog | component1 | | Final release | task | somebody | 06/22/08 |
| #14 | A Publisher can browse public content | component1 | | Final release | task | somebody | 06/22/08 |
| #15 | A Publisher can broadcast a call for pieces to be submitted for a publication | component1 | | Final release | task | somebody | 06/22/08 |
| #16 | A Publisher can select content for inclusion in a publication | component1 | | Final release | task | somebody | 06/22/08 |
| #17 | A Publisher can manage an on-line publication | component1 | | Final release | task | somebody | 06/22/08 |
| #18 | A Publisher can manage an on-line blog | component1 | | Final release | task | somebody | 06/22/08 |
| #19 | A Webmaster can administer the website configuration | component1 | | Launch | task | somebody | 06/22/08 |
| #20 | A Webmaster can install new updates and functionality | component1 | | Launch | task | somebody | 06/22/08 |



Figure 4-7

# Doing It

One of the beautiful things of using an issue-tracking system is that what you have effectively done is split a complex problem — namely, that of developing and launching a website application — into bite-sized chunks that can be done at any point. This is actually the beauty of the Agile approach to software development itself. A member of the development team can just pluck a user story card from the (virtual or real) wall and get it done at any time, and a fixed percentage of the whole task gets accomplished.

Figure 4-8 shows your amended Prototype iteration user story implementation and associated tasks. Let's grab one and do it right now. Take: #21 — "Clean URLs and automatic generation of SEO friendly paths." These two tasks are, of course, interrelated, so they have been placed on the same "ticket."

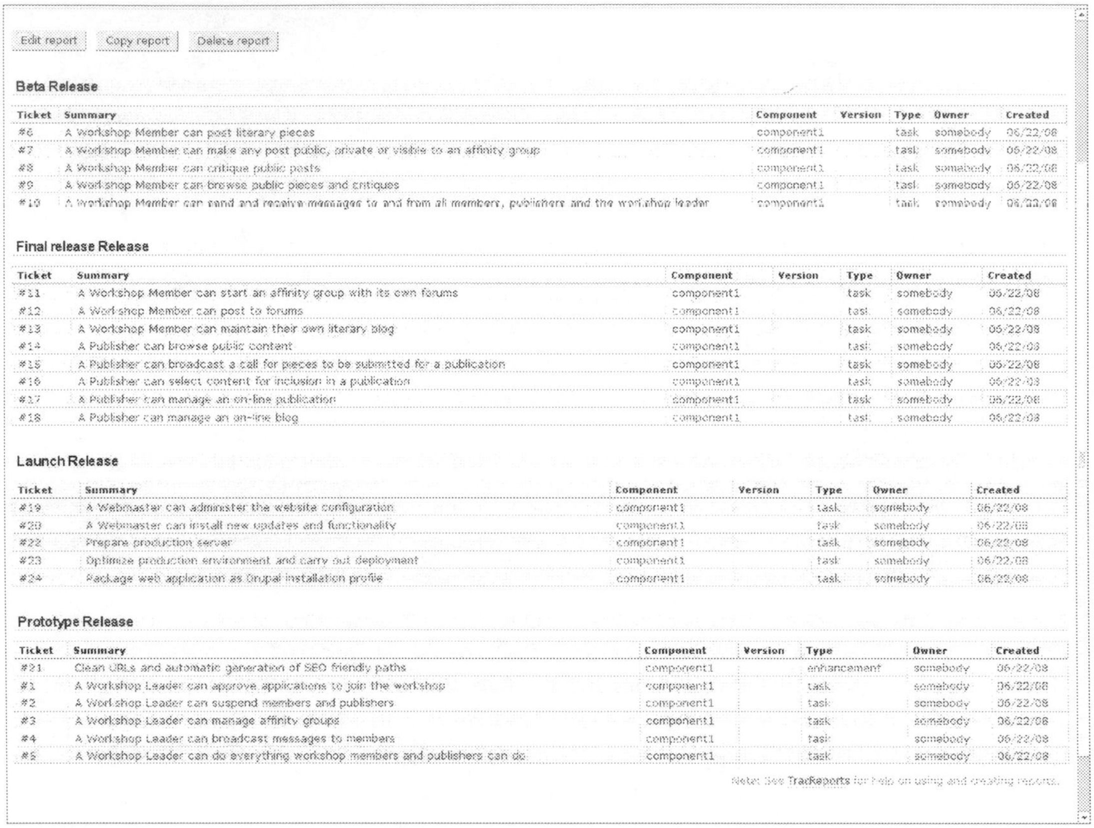

Edit report | Copy report | Delete report

**Beta Release**

| Ticket | Summary | Component | Version | Type | Owner | Created |
|---|---|---|---|---|---|---|
| #6 | A Workshop Member can post literary pieces | component1 | | task | somebody | 06/22/08 |
| #7 | A Workshop Member can make any post public, private or visible to an affinity group | component1 | | task | somebody | 06/22/08 |
| #8 | A Workshop Member can critique public posts | component1 | | task | somebody | 06/22/08 |
| #9 | A Workshop Member can browse public pieces and critiques | component1 | | task | somebody | 06/22/08 |
| #10 | A Workshop Member can send and receive messages to and from all members, publishers and the workshop leader | component1 | | task | somebody | 06/22/08 |

**Final release Release**

| Ticket | Summary | Component | Version | Type | Owner | Created |
|---|---|---|---|---|---|---|
| #11 | A Workshop Member can start an affinity group with its own forums | component1 | | task | somebody | 06/22/08 |
| #12 | A Workshop Member can post to forums | component1 | | task | somebody | 06/22/08 |
| #13 | A Workshop Member can maintain their own literary blog | component1 | | task | somebody | 06/22/08 |
| #14 | A Publisher can browse public content | component1 | | task | somebody | 06/22/08 |
| #15 | A Publisher can broadcast a call for pieces to be submitted for a publication | component1 | | task | somebody | 06/22/08 |
| #16 | A Publisher can select content for inclusion in a publication | component1 | | task | somebody | 06/22/08 |
| #17 | A Publisher can manage an on-line publication | component1 | | task | somebody | 06/22/08 |
| #18 | A Publisher can manage an on-line blog | component1 | | task | somebody | 06/22/08 |

**Launch Release**

| Ticket | Summary | Component | Version | Type | Owner | Created |
|---|---|---|---|---|---|---|
| #19 | A Webmaster can administer the website configuration | component1 | | task | somebody | 06/22/08 |
| #20 | A Webmaster can install new updates and functionality | component1 | | task | somebody | 06/22/08 |
| #22 | Prepare production server | component1 | | task | somebody | 06/22/08 |
| #23 | Optimize production environment and carry out deployment | component1 | | task | somebody | 06/22/08 |
| #24 | Package web application as Drupal installation profile | component1 | | task | somebody | 06/22/08 |

**Prototype Release**

| Ticket | Summary | Component | Version | Type | Owner | Created |
|---|---|---|---|---|---|---|
| #21 | Clean URLs and automatic generation of SEO friendly paths | component1 | | enhancement | somebody | 06/22/08 |
| #1 | A Workshop Leader can approve applications to join the workshop | component1 | | task | somebody | 06/22/08 |
| #2 | A Workshop Leader can suspend members and publishers | component1 | | task | somebody | 06/22/08 |
| #3 | A Workshop Leader can manage affinity groups | component1 | | task | somebody | 06/22/08 |
| #4 | A Workshop Leader can broadcast messages to members | component1 | | task | somebody | 06/22/08 |
| #5 | A Workshop Leader can do everything workshop members and publishers can do | component1 | | task | somebody | 06/22/08 |

Note: See TracReports for help on using and creating reports.

Figure 4-8

1. Go to Administer ➤ Site configuration ➤ Clean URLs, logged in as user `dev`. But wait, when you go to Administer (`http://litworkshop.example.com/?q=admin`), you may see an Administration warning message:

```
One or more problems were detected with your Drupal installation.
 Check the status report for more information.
```

Administration warning signs may pop up from time to time, which is why you have to be nimble in Drupal and learn how to mentally stack two or three tasks you might be doing all at the same time.

2. Click on the Status Report link to see what's going on. Warnings may appear for one or several reasons. A common issue can come from file permissions. On your local development box, when you created the working copy, perhaps you never attended to the operating system permissions regarding the files directory. This problem can carry over if you decided to place it under version control, in which case you will see the "File system–Not writable" warning in red:

```
File system     Not writable
The directory sites/all/files is not writable. You may need to set the
correct
```

```
Directory  at the file system settings page or change the current
directory's
permissions so that
it is writable.
```

See http://drupal.org/server-permissions for more information.

3. Click the File System Settings page link, and make sure that the directory ./sites/all/files is writeable for the Apache HTTP server.

   This is a Drupal moment: "Where was I?" Get used to it: you must learn to multi-task if you are going to leverage the power of Drupal and be a Renaissance woman or man into the bargain.

   You were about to implement #21 — "Clean URLs and automatic generation of SEO friendly paths."

4. So, right, go to Administer ➢ Site configuration ➢ Clean URLs. You'll immediately notice that the radio buttons Disabled/Enabled are grayed out. It turns out that you have to perform a test first. So click on the "Run the clean URL test" link. The odds are that you will pass, which will simply result in the radio buttons being freed up, so select "Enabled," and click on the "Save configuration" button. Where before you had:

```
http://litworkshop.example.com/?q=admin/settings/clean-urls
```

   you now have

```
http://litworkshop.example.com/admin/settings/clean urls
```

O Brave New SEO friendly World!

But wait, you're not done yet.

5. Go to Administer ➢ Content management ➢ Content, and mouse over the Content items. All of them have paths ending in */node/5* or */node/10*. Issue #21 says to implement SEO-friendly paths.

Fortunately, there is a contributed Drupal module of excellent quality and reputation, wonderfully maintained, called *pathauto*. Its home page is http://drupal.org/project/pathauto. Download the most recent, stable version for the Drupal release you are working with, and unpack it into the {path to Drupal root}/sites/all/modules directory, just as you did for the cck module in an earlier chapter.

This time, let's start a new habit of always reading the README.txt file that accompanies well-maintained contributed modules. One of the things it explains, apart from how to configure this very flexible and powerful module, is that it depends on the core module "path" also being enabled, and it also requires the Token module and recommends a couple of others. This is getting complicated very quickly. Another Drupal moment. Not to worry. Let's just do this:

1. Download and unpack two more modules: the Token module (because pathauto requires it; located at http://drupal.org/project/token) and the Global Redirect module (absolutely necessary to guarantee that you keep your path aliases' housekeeping in-line with what search engines expect; located at http://drupal.org/project/globalredirect).

2. Once these two modules are downloaded and unpacked under the ./sites/all/modules directory, go to Administer ➢ Site building ➢ Modules, select the Path module in the Core — Optional section, and click on the "Save configuration" button.

3. Then, in the Other section, the Global Redirect, the Pathauto, and the Token modules, click "Save configuration."

4. Now go to Administer ➢ User management ➢ Access control, and enable the following permissions:

| Module | Permissions | Roles |
|---|---|---|
| Path module | Administer URL aliases<br>Create URL aliases | Admin, Webmaster<br>Admin, Publisher, Webmaster, Workshop Leader, Workshop Member |
| Pathauto module | Admin pathauto<br>Notify of path changes | Admin, Webmaster<br>Admin, Webmaster |

There is no configuration necessary for the Global Redirect and Token modules. Let's finish up by quickly creating an initial configuration for Pathauto and making that configuration retroactive to existing content.

5. Go to Administer ➢ Site configuration ➢ Pathauto (`http://litworkshop.example.com/admin/settings/pathauto` in our spanking new clean URL system).

   Instead of getting dizzy for the moment with all the options, bells, and whistles you can fine-tune later (especially after Pam gets a chance to see what's going on with this), let's just do this:

6. Open the Blog Path Settings section, select "Bulk generate aliases for blogs that are not aliased," and click "Save configuration" at the bottom of the page.

   You should see something like this at the top of the page:

   > The configuration options have been saved.
   >
   > Bulk generation of user blogs completed, 6 aliases generated.

7. Now, hit the Blogs menu item you configured earlier, which takes you to `http://litworkshop.example.com/blog`, and hit the link to Pam's blog. You will find that takes you to `http://litworkshop.mentor/blogs/pam`. Awesome. Now, hit one of the posts: `http://litworkshop.mentor/node/17`. Not awesome.

8. Back at Administer ➢ Site configuration ➢ Pathauto, open up the "Node Path Settings" section. Leave the default path pattern as is for the time being. In the "Pattern for all Blog entry paths" field, enter:

```
blog/[author-name-raw]/[title-raw]
```

9. In the "Pattern for all Literary Piece paths" field, enter:

```
texts/[author-name-raw]/[title-raw]
```

10. You can open up the Replacement patterns section to see all the options available (courtesy of the Token module). Now, select the "Bulk generate aliases for nodes that are not aliased" checkbox, and click "Save configuration."

Awesome, yes! Checkout Administer ➢ Site building ➢ URL aliases to survey the results of your pain and labor: what was *node/15* is now *blog/alfred/alfreds-second-entry*; what was *node/6* is now *texts/joyce/sed-consectetuer-nisi-eget-ligula*. Awesome again. Now you need Pam's feedback in the form of an acceptance test, so you can truly complete the task.

## Committing, Deploying to Test, Testing, Tracking

Go ahead and commit your work to the SVN repository, so that all your work can then be deployed to the test site, where it can be tested by developers and clients alike, and then tracked (e.g., bugs or change requests can be raised as tickets in Trac).

1. Click on the "Save configuration" button in Administer ➢ Site building ➢ Modules to clear the cache, and then dump the database to ./sites/all/backup/litworkshop.sql

2. Change the directory to ./sites, and check the svn status:

```
$ cd sites
$ svn status
?       default/settings.php
M       all/backup/db/litworkshop.sql
?       all/modules/token
?       all/modules/globalredirect
?       all/modules/pathauto
victorkane@mentor:~/work/AWebFactory/Wiley/litworkshop/sites$
```

3. You don't want the settings file under version control, but you should add the contributed modules. Even though they are versioned with CVS in the Drupal repository, a true snapshot of what you have must contain the contributed modules you actually have installed, with their current version, and so on. So you add those to the repository and commit:

```
$    svn    add    all/modules/token/    all/modules/globalredirect/
all/modules/pathauto/
A         all/modules/token
A         all/modules/token/po
...
A         all/modules/pathauto/pathauto_user.inc
A         all/modules/pathauto/INSTALL.txt
A         all/modules/pathauto/pathauto_taxonomy.inc
```

```
$
$ svn commit -m "Initial implementation #21 Clean URLs and automatic \
generation of SEO friendly paths"
Sending        all/backup/db/litworkshop.sql
Adding         all/modules/globalredirect
...
Adding         all/modules/token/token_taxonomy.inc
Adding         all/modules/token/token_user.inc
Transmitting file data ........................................
Committed revision 6.
```

Notice that "#21" is included in the commit message for revision 6. This will allow you to navigate directly from the log message to the issue documentation and constitutes a truly minimalistic yet thorough implementation of what CMMI calls bidirectional traceability of requirements.

4. Click "Browse Source in Trac" and then on the Revision Log link just under the menu bar on the right-hand side. You can see the expression *#21* as a link in the revision 6 entry. Click on it, and you are taken directly to Ticket #21! In the Add/Change #21 text area, type in **Initial implementation r6**, and near the bottom of the page in the Action section, select "Resolve as worksforme" (Pam can reopen it with the Acceptance Test later on). Click "Submit changes."

5. Now, "r6" is also a link. Click on it, and you are taken to the changeset (all the files affected) for revision 6. And you can see a link back to the issue ticket *#21*, crossed out since it is labeled "resolved." Now click "Roadmap," and you can see, as in Figure 4-9, that you have actually done some real work!

6. Now you deploy to test by logging into your test site operating system and updating the project from the repository:

```
litworkshop@textworks:~$ cd public_html/sites
litworkshop@textworks:~/public_html/sites$ svn up
U    all/backup/db/litworkshop.sql
A    all/modules/token
A    all/modules/token/LICENSE.txt
A    all/modules/token/token.module
...
A    all/modules/pathauto/po
A    all/modules/pathauto/po/da.po
A    all/modules/pathauto/po/ru.po
A    all/modules/pathauto/po/es.po
A    all/modules/pathauto/po/de.po
A    all/modules/pathauto/po/pathauto.pot
Updated to revision 6.
litworkshop@textworks:~/public_html/sites$ cd all/backup/db/
litworkshop@textworks:~/public_html/sites/all/backup/db$ mysql \
-u dr_workshop -p dr_workshop < litworkshop.sql
Enter password:
litworkshop@textworks:~/public_html/sites/all/backup/db$
```

7. Point your browser at your test site, and test the new functionality added by Ticket #21. For now, this is informal, but in the future, you will see how to run through a test suite, with different kinds of tests designed both to test what's new as well as to make sure the new functionality hasn't broken anything we have already tested (regression tests).

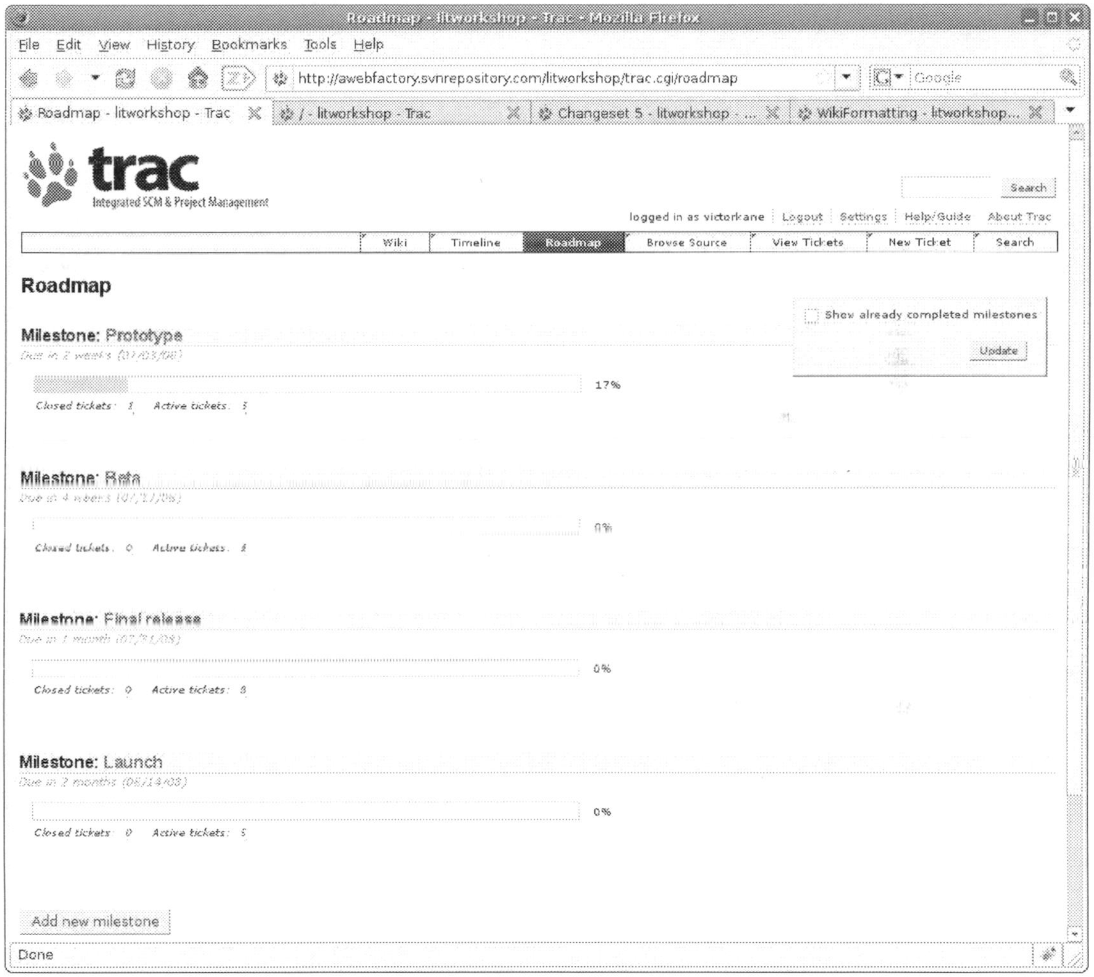


Figure 4-9

# Working on the Architectural Baseline

Up till now you have seen the high-level domain model sketched out in chapter 2. You need to verify and extend it and put together a minimalistic document set to prepare the way for the completion of all major decisions as to the architecture of your website application.

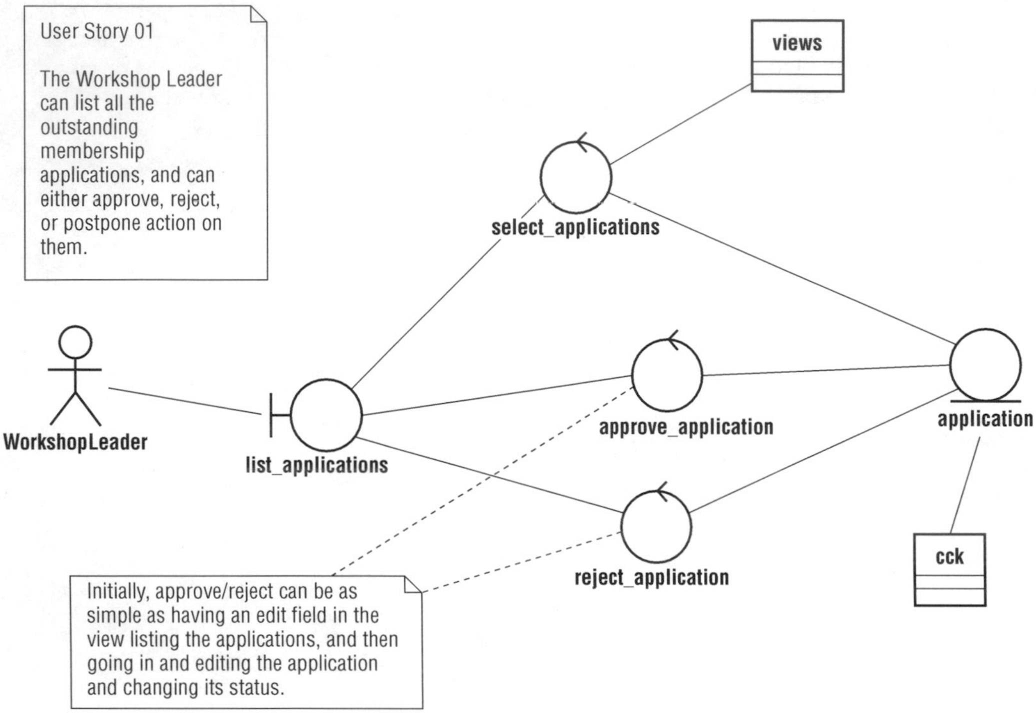
User Story 01
The Workshop Leader can list all the outstanding membership applications, and can either approve, reject, or postpone action on them.
views
select_applications
WorkshopLeader
list_applications
approve_application
application
reject_application
cck
Initially, approve/reject can be as simple as having an edit field in the view listing the applications, and then going in and editing the application and changing its status.

Figure 4-10

I recommend using a robustness diagram (see the "On Finding a Common Language" sidebar in Chapter 1, and Figure 4-10) in order to test the consistency of the user stories taken as a whole, and to create your first detailed bridge between *what* functionality you want and *how* exactly you are going to implement it. Robustness diagrams can replace the need for a formal site map or detailed storyboard or anything like that, at least until the work matures somewhat, especially taking into account the fact that your Drupal prototype is its own storyboard and navigational model. Robustness diagrams also aid in the consolidation of the building of a common language, which was mentioned in the last chapter.

A robustness diagram is actually needed for each user story. In order to normalize the common language of the project, you should be working on the domain model, the user story texts, and the robustness diagrams at the same time.

First of all, see `www.agilemodeling.com/artifacts/robustnessDiagram.htm` for an example from Scott Ambler's site. You've got your site visitor who interacts with a *boundary* (interface), and any action invokes a *controller* (functioning code — Drupal) on the server side, which performs actions and sorts out what data needs to be persisted (stored) as an *entity*.

**Scott Ambler uses a more formalized and objectivized artifact, called a *use case*, rather than "user stories." In our present context, the more classic user story (which is not at all the same thing as a use case) is much more a propos, so we are going with that.**

Therefore, let's take User Story 4-1. Figure 4-10 shows one possible Robustness Diagram for this user story, which not only serves as a partial site map, but also provides us with a vision of the necessary architecture as well. We are guided in the creation of the diagram by asking ourselves the question, "Which boundaries, controllers, and entities do we need to implement the user story?" And, of course, "Which Drupal modules can be associated with identifiable functionality?"

We'll take this up again in the next chapter.

# Getting the Team Organized and with the Program

As head cook and bottle washer, or pointy-headed project manager (someone has to do it), you need a team. On some very small projects, a team could mean taking a break (or not) and simply wearing a different hat. But for any nontrivial project, the complexity of even a simple website application demands top-notch skill sets in some specialized areas.

## *Whom Do You Need?*

Here are the minimum skill sets you need to marshal to get the job done on a nontrivial (more than five to seven user stories) website application:

- A project manager
- Someone completely at home with graphic design applications such as The Gimp, Adobe Photoshop, and Fireworks
- A Drupal themer
- An experienced Drupal module mashup integrator
- A Drupal module developer, should it be necessary to develop a module
- A Webmaster who can administer the target hosting operating system environment and Drupal installations, preferably of the "train the trainer" variety, since it will be very important to prepare the client (in terms of personnel and infrastructure) to administer the website application after launching

Look again at `http://drupal.org`. On the title bar, it still says "Community plumbing." The end-users of the Drupal CMS Framework tend to be website developers and not individuals, organizations and companies who need a website, and the website reflects this technically oriented atmosphere. But those individuals, organizations and companies need orientation and guidance in terms of their own concrete use of the CMS framework.

A common mistake is to confuse a website developer with someone who will administer the site and maintain it during its initial live launch and ongoing production. The developers need someone to whom they can deliver the end result, otherwise disaster will strike. If the developers have no one to relate to on a technical level, the deployment tasks will be compromised. So either make sure that there is someone in your organization able and willing to take on this role, or hire someone who can. The only exception may be if the developer is willing to take on that role, although be aware that there will normally be a separate charge for this service.

Additionally the above list will need to be beefed up if scaling and high-traffic sites are involved.

## *"Who You Gonna Call?"*

This depends entirely on your own objectives. You may want to learn how to do some or all of the tasks yourself, but almost certainly not all of them — which means that you should begin to gather around yourself a trustworthy group of professionals or make sure that resources are properly earmarked in your company.

You can advertise on the Drupal Paid Services forum at `http://drupal.org/paid-services`. Be sure to read "Hiring a Drupal Site Developer" (`http://drupal.org/node/51169`) first, along with several excellent comments present on that page.

Another place to advertise is at `http://groups.drupal.org`.

Although by no means do any guarantees exist, you are probably very much better off hiring someone involved in the Drupal Community with a profile showing membership for a year or so and the contribution of documentation, translations, themes, patches, or modules.

# Elaboration Phase Cleanup

The Elaboration phase will be completed once the tasks allocated to the Prototype Release Iteration Milestone are completed, and both the requirements and architectural baselines are set. That will most probably happen during the next chapter, but by this time, you have certainly built up a good head of steam.

You probably want to take advantage of Trac's wiki functionality to add a few additional project management artifacts, which cannot be easily reduced or included in user stories or acceptance tests. These are included in the following table:

| Name | Description |
|---|---|
| Risk list | A list of risks associated with the project. They are generally sorted so that the most important items are at the top. Each risk should include a short statement describing mitigation and/or contingency actions ("Plan B"). |
| Creative brief | This is a document that should be made available to the graphic design and theming people, which addresses a host of factors such as the business model and objectives, example designs, color schemes, imagery, and typography, as well as usability goals and the kind of atmosphere that should be achieved. |
| Styles and Standards Document | Apart from graphic and presentation styles, this document should set the norm for naming and coding standards in the project, which in the case of a Drupal project should follow the Drupal coding standards. (See `http://drupal.org/coding-standards`. As explained here, these are based on the PEAR coding standards; see also `http://pear.php.net/manual/en/standards.php`.) |

# Summary

You followed up on your first functional prototype-based meeting with Pam, your client, and she has written all the user stories, which include relevant dialog with you, together with testing suggestions. You have then made use of recommended on-line resources in order to plan the iterations of the project and have exercised the develop-commit-deploy-test-track cycle on an initial task.

You then used robustness diagrams in order to advance in the setting of the architectural baseline for the project, with a glimpse at which contributed Drupal modules will actually answer the question of how to implement the user stories. And you have given thought to what human resources will be necessary to get the litworkshop website application successfully launched.

# Part II

# Getting Your 5.x Site Up-To-Date

# 5

# Finishing up the Elaboration Phase

As the Milestone checklist shows (see Figure 5-1), you are almost done with the Elaboration phase. However, some additional work needs to be done on the first one, "Create an initial environment," and there is a little unfinished business regarding the second, "Whip up the initial prototype." Finally, there is one major milestone, "Work on the architectural baseline," where there is still a lot to be done.

## Creating an Initial Environment

You've already gotten your hands dirty when you worked on your development box, then saved everything to the repository and deployed to the test site via that repository. Now you just need to get a more focused view of how you are going to tool yourself up on this project, with some development modules to make your life a little easier, and a clearer, more polished idea of the process work flow. Luckily, there are a few modules that came to the fore during the tail end of the Drupal 5 life cycle that are really going to make your life easier, plus one old favorite that's been around, fortunately, for a long while — Devel:

- Update status module: `http://drupal.org/project/update_status`
- Drupal shell module: `http://drupal.org/project/drush`
- Devel module: `http://drupal.org/project/devel`. Even for Drupal 5.x, this module "for Drupal developers and inquisitive admins" is a real lifesaver, as a perusal of its features will show. Later on in this book, you will find out about the fabulous support for real-time theming debugging contributed by this module.

And you want the answer to two questions you may have been asking yourself:

- How am I going to update the Drupal release easily?

| | |
|---|---|
| ✓ | Create an initial environment |
| ✓ | Whip up the initial prototype |
| ✓ | Get initial feedback from the client |
| ✓ | Finish the user stories with the client |
| ✓ | Plan the project |
| | Work on the architectural baseline |
| ✓ | Get the team organized and with the program |

Figure 5-1

- ❑ How am I supposed to update modules easily and cleanly and reflect all that in the version control repository without painstakingly adding, removing, and committing individual files?

You'll see how this pans out as you do stuff throughout this chapter and the rest of the book, but your basic workflow is going to be:

1. Provision, develop, and test on the development box.
2. Deploy to testing (and eventually production) from the repository.

So your environment is all set.

## How Can I Easily Update the Drupal Release?

This first question is answered in a word: CVS.

If you used CVS to check out your virginal copy of the current Drupal 5.x release, you did so with the command:

```
$ cvs -z6 -d:pserver:anonymous:anonymous@cvs.drupal.org:/cvs/drupal co
-r DRUPAL-5-12↵
drupal
```

This checks out the project *drupal* to a subdirectory. The *-z6* switch says to use gzip compression during the checkout (co) process, and the *-d* switch sets the repository path, with the *-r* switch specifying the revision to check out.

Now, of course, you have replaced the sites subdirectory with your own themes and modules, and your own default settings file. Before you update to, say, Drupal 5.8, there is just one thing you need to do: Tell CVS to ignore the sites subdirectory and especially the default settings file. To do this, create a file in the main Drupal directory, which tells CVS to do this: .cvsignore, so that when you update to the next Drupal release, your settings file will be left undisturbed.

Study the following example to see how to do this:

```
$ cvs -z6 -d:pserver:anonymous:anonymous@cvs.drupal.org:/cvs/drupal co \
-r DRUPAL-5-6 drupal
$ cd drupal
```

Now create a file called *.cvsignore* to protect settings:

```
$ cat sites/default/settings.php > .cvsignore
```

Edit the settings file so that the mysql URL string reflects your database settings. Mine has:

```
$db_url = 'mysql://thisproject:mysecret@localhost/thisproject';
```

Now update from Drupal 5.6 to Drupal 5.7:

```
$ cvs update -dPr DRUPAL-5-7
```

View your mysql URL string, to confirm that it was left undisturbed.

The actual update command says to create any directories that are in the repository but not in the sandbox (-d), to not include empty directories (-P), and to update the working copy to revision DRUPAL-5-7. This is the command that works best for *automagically* updating Drupal core to a new release on a filesystem originally checked out with CVS:

```
$ cd {Drupal document root}
$ cvs update -dPr DRUPAL-5-8
```

**Question: Why CVS?**

Answer: Because Drupal is still using it `http://drupal.org/node/289117`.

**Question: Am I Done?**

Answer: Remember to always run update.php as admin after updating the Drupal core or any module, so that any necessary database modification scripts can be run. So, no, not quite.

## *How Can I Update Modules Easily and Cleanly?*

. . . and reflect all that in the version control repository without painstakingly adding, removing, and committing individual files?

Here's the thing: you want to be able to deploy a unique snapshot of your project at any time from the repository, which will be as easy as plunking down a SVN checkout or update on top of a fresh Drupal release install. You saw in the previous chapters how this involves including in this project a state snapshot including all the modules (third-party ones you have installed, together with any you might develop yourself) together with the database dump. Now, modules get updated, either because new features are developed, bugs are fixed, or a new security fix might be released.

To update the code in the module directory, if you weren't using version control, you would simply delete all the files in the module directory and then copy in the new, probably by *untarring* (unpacking) the files. Suppose one file was removed entirely and another new one was added, say, a translation. When you go to commit the directory to the SVN repository, subversion will protest because it can't find a file previously under version control. And even worse, the new file will be ignored altogether.

So, you download the module tarball, open it up and review the list of files, copy the files into the module's directory, and then do an `svn add` for all the new files, and an `svn rm` for all the files no longer part of the module's code. And, finally, you need to do an `svn commit`.

What if there were a Drupal module that does all of that for you? W00t! There is! Enter the fabulous Drush module, which works in tandem with the update status module to become, almost, an "apt-get" system for Drupal, or at least a running start in that direction.

> *apt-get is part of apt, the Advanced Packaging Tool, "a user interface that works with core libraries to handle the sometimes difficult process of installing software on Linux." See* `http://en.wikipedia.org/wiki/Advanced_Packaging_Tool`.

Download the latest version of Update Status (this will be the second-to-the-last time you have to do that!). In itself, it is a boon, telling us exactly what you have installed, and what you need to update. Install it by following the instructions in the accompanying README.txt file, and go to Administer ➢ Logs ➢ Available updates. Figure 5-2 shows where you are with litworkshop.

Right, so Global Redirect and Pathauto (another pair of modules that work in tandem, as explained in Chapter 4) have come out with a new version. You can read the Release notes right from the admin page, and there is a download link too.

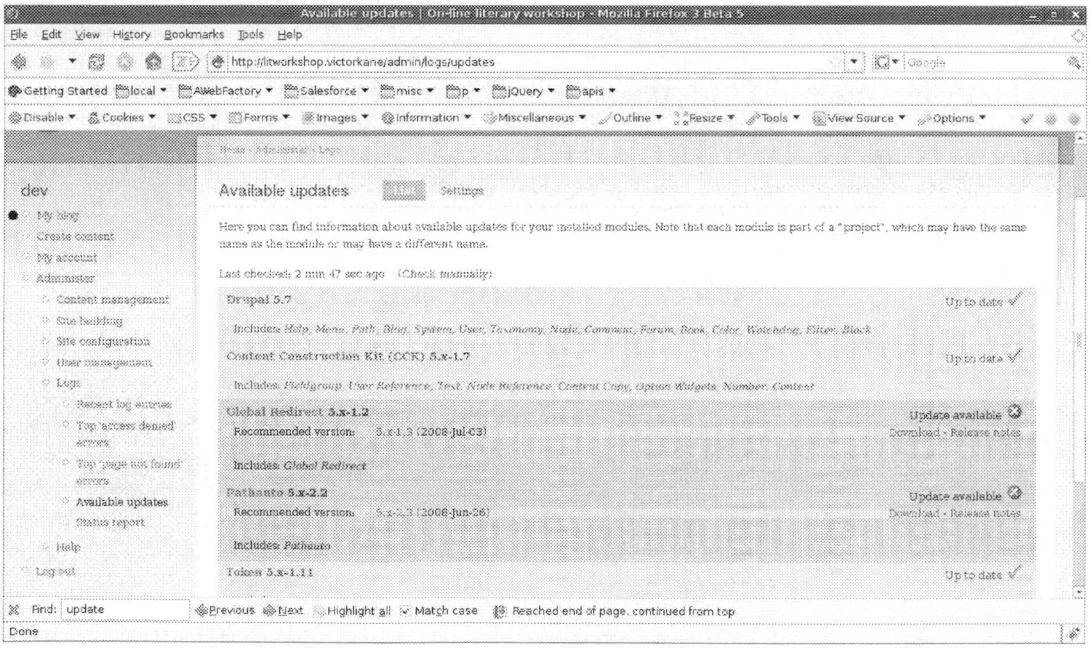


Figure 5-2

But you are going to outdo yourself now, and install the Drush module, and let the CPU do the walking.

Download the latest version of Drush (this will be the last time you have to do that!), and install it by following the instructions in the accompanying README.txt file (any decent contributed module worth its salt has an accompanying README.txt file that tells you how to install it and get it going, sometimes with the aid of an INSTALL.txt file). What you should do is enable the Drush module and the following submodules:

- ❑ Drush Package Manager
- ❑ Drush Package Manager SVN Support
- ❑ Drush Package Manager wget Support
- ❑ Drush SQL commands
- ❑ Drush Toolbox

Then, from the command line in the Drupal root directory, you can run the following and read the results:

```
$ php sites/all/modules/drush/drush.php help
```

If your screen looks something like Figure 5-3, you have successfully installed both modules.

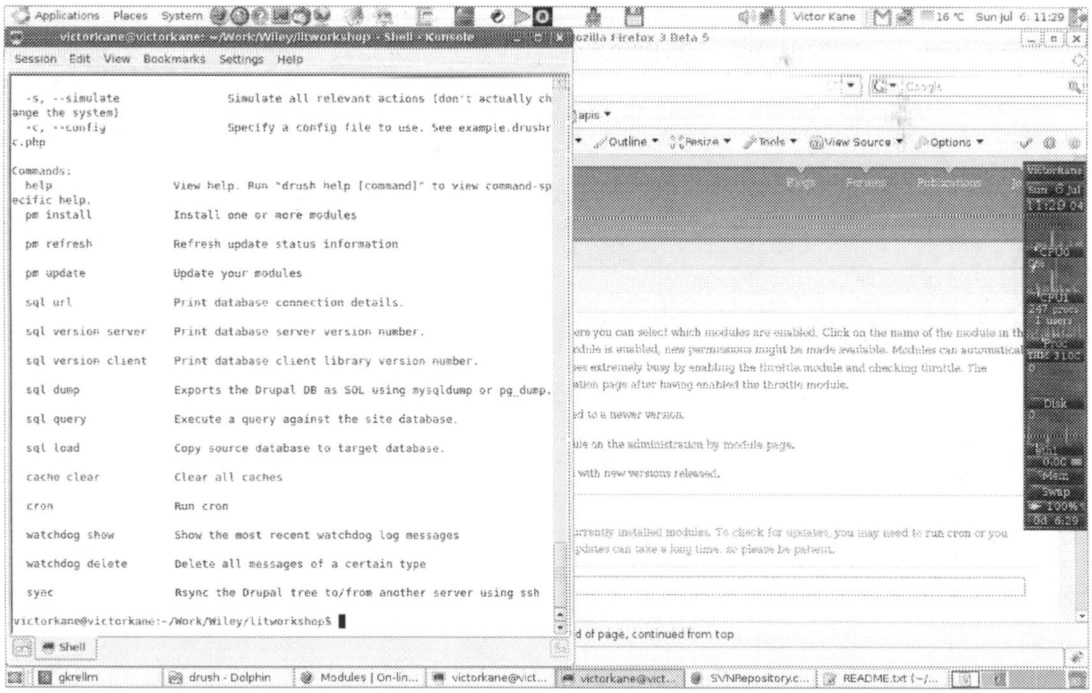


Figure 5-3

**Question: What Now?**

Answer: Place the two module directories under version control and commit to the repository. By the way, don't forget to dump the database state first into sites/all/backup/db/litworkshop.sql. You can do that with the `drush sql dump` command (see below on how to create a Drush alias):

```
$ drush sql dump > sites/all/backup/db/litworkshop.sql
```

then:

```
$ cd sites
$ svn add all/modules/drush
$ svn add all/modules/update_status/
$ svn commit -m "finally got smart and installed update-status\
and drush modules"
```

### More about Aliasing

Assuming that you are using the bash shell as your terminal, or another shell that supports command-line aliasing, you can populate your ~/.bash_aliases file with something like the following:

```
alias drush='php sites/all/modules/drush/drush.php'
alias checkouthead='cvs -z6
-d:pserver:anonymous:anonymous@cvs. drupal.org:/cvs/drupal \
checkout drupal'
alias checkout6='cvs -z6
-d:pserver:anonymous:anonymous@cvs. drupal.org:/cvs/drupal \
co -r DRUPAL-6-6 drupal'
alias checkout5-11='cvs -z6
-d:pserver:anonymous:anonymous@cvs. drupal.org:/cvs/drupal \
co -r DRUPAL-5-11 drupal'
alias checkout5-12='cvs -z6
-d:pserver:anonymous:anonymous@cvs. drupal.org:/cvs/drupal \
co -r DRUPAL-5-12 drupal'
```

In Ubuntu at least, the .bash_aliases file is read by the ~/.bashrc file; you may have to make sure the following three lines are uncommented/present:

```
if [ -f ~/.bash_aliases ]; then
    . ~/.bash_aliases
fi
```

With the appropriate `alias` installed in your bash shell environment, updating the Pathauto and Global Redirect modules becomes as easy as carrying out these steps:

1. Update Pathauto and Global Redirect in the filesystem and repository.

```
$ drush pm refresh
$ drush pm update --svnsync
```

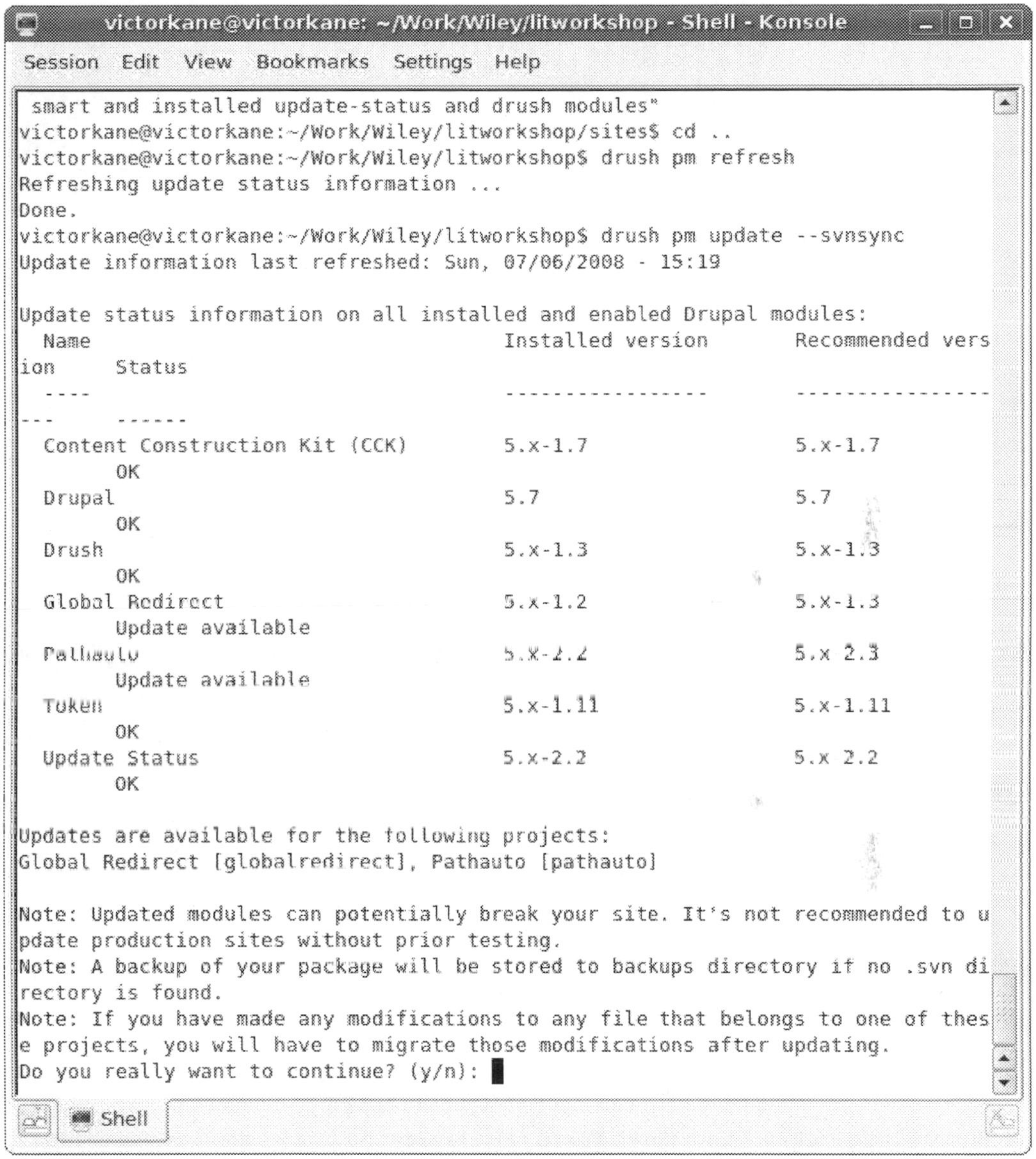

victorkane@victorkane: ~/Work/Wiley/litworkshop - Shell - Konsole
Session Edit View Bookmarks Settings Help
smart and installed update-status and drush modules"
victorkane@victorkane:~/Work/Wiley/litworkshop/sites$ cd ..
victorkane@victorkane:~/Work/Wiley/litworkshop$ drush pm refresh
Refreshing update status information ...
Done.
victorkane@victorkane:~/Work/Wiley/litworkshop$ drush pm update --svnsync
Update information last refreshed: Sun, 07/06/2008 - 15:19
Update status information on all installed and enabled Drupal modules:
Name Installed version Recommended version Status
Content Construction Kit (CCK) 5.x-1.7 5.x-1.7 OK
Drupal 5.7 5.7 OK
Drush 5.x-1.3 5.x-1.3 OK
Global Redirect 5.x-1.2 5.x-1.3 Update available
Pathauto 5.x-2.2 5.x-2.3 Update available
Token 5.x-1.11 5.x-1.11 OK
Update Status 5.x-2.2 5.x-2.2 OK
Updates are available for the following projects:
Global Redirect [globalredirect], Pathauto [pathauto]
Note: Updated modules can potentially break your site. It's not recommended to update production sites without prior testing.
Note: A backup of your package will be stored to backups directory if no .svn directory is found.
Note: If you have made any modifications to any file that belongs to one of these projects, you will have to migrate those modifications after updating.
Do you really want to continue? (y/n):
Shell


Figure 5-4

(By default, Drush will show you what it intends to update and solicits confirmation — see Figure 5-4.) Upon answering Yes, Drush completes the job and tells you how to finish up:

```
Do you really want to continue? (y/n): y
Project globalredirect was updated successfully. Installed version is
now 5.x-1.3.
```

```
You should consider committing the new code to your Subversion repository.
If this version becomes undesirable, use Subversion to roll back.
Project pathauto was updated successfully. Installed version is now 5.x-2.3.
You should consider committing the new code to your Subversion repository.
If this version becomes undesirable, use Subversion to roll back.
You should now run update.php through your browser.
victorkane@victorkane:~/Work/Wiley/litworkshop$
```

2. Run update.php as usual when updating Drupal core or modules.
3. Complete the snapshot with the database state.
4. Test.
5. Commit (this can be done with the `drush -svncommit` switch, but it is better to test first).

I ran update.php (I set the variable `$access_check` in the update.php file to `False` because I wasn't logged in as user number 1, then changed it back to `True` afterward) and created a blog entry, and the module changes were looking good. So I committed and then checked how the repository looked in Trac. See Figures 5-5 (Revision Log) and 5-6 (Changeset).

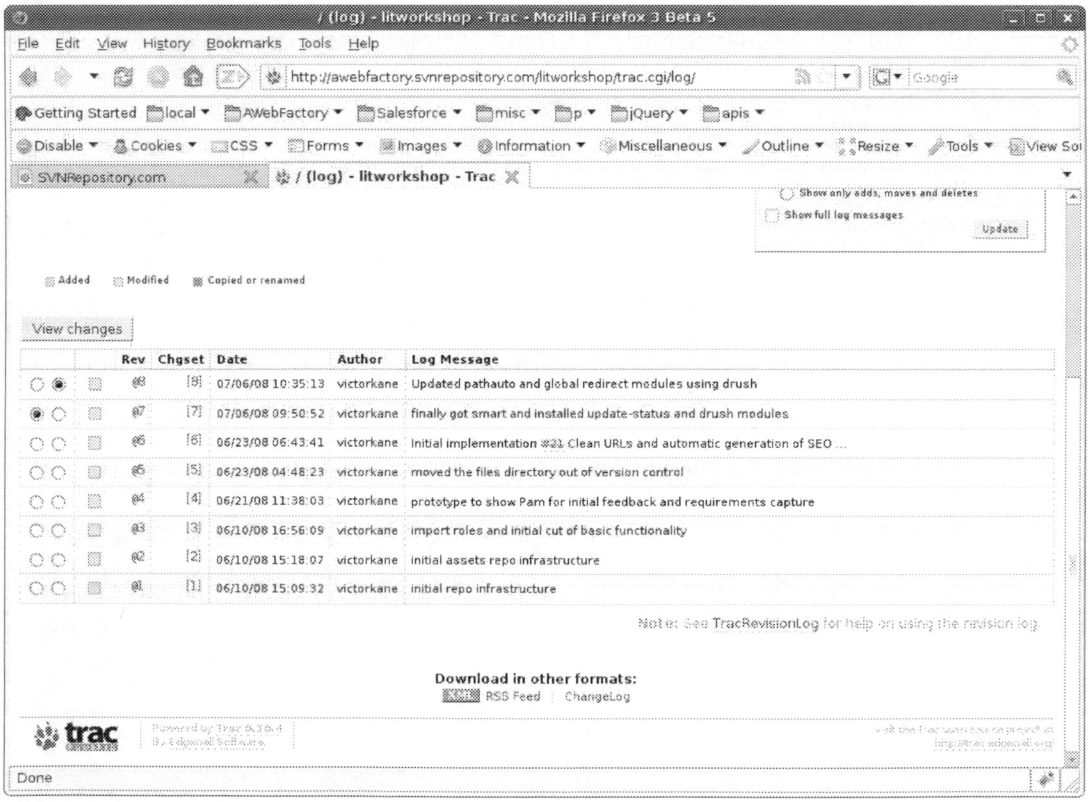

Figure 5-5

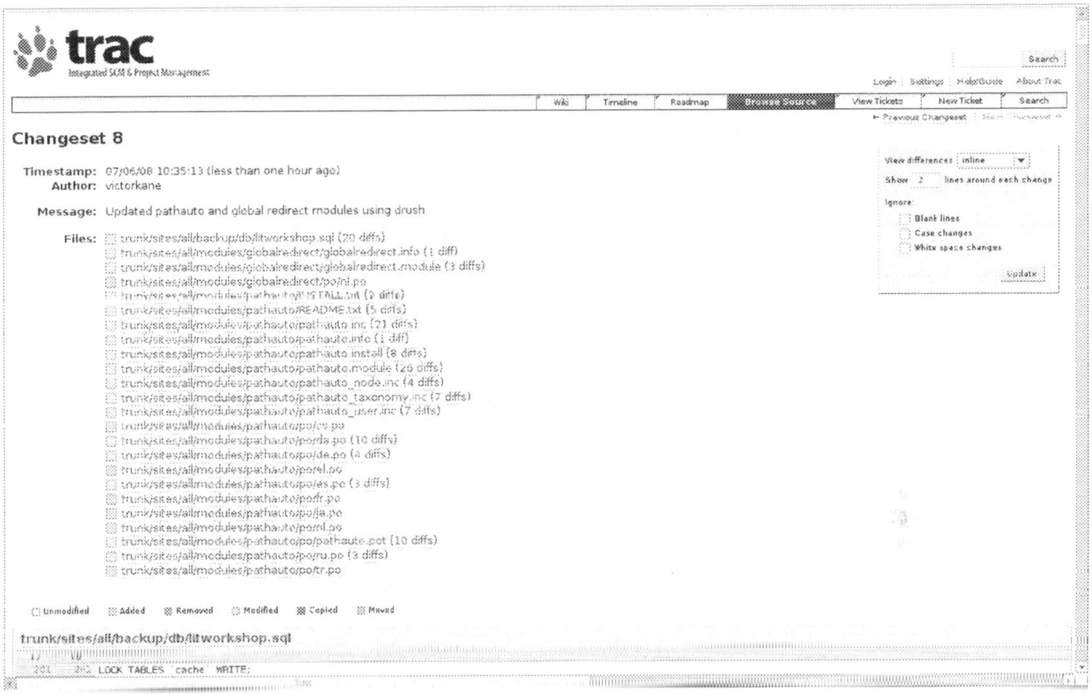

Figure 5-6

# Whipping up the Initial Prototype

At one of our first meetings with Pam, I explained about acceptance tests. So Pam wrote one for the ticket "Clean URLs and automatic generation of SEO friendly paths," and for the other user stories slated to be implemented during the initial Prototype Milestone. Acceptance Test 5-1 illustrates this and shows how every Acceptance Test (which strives to search for bugs and is not satisfied simply by code coverage) consists of a series of scenarios or concrete uses of the features being tested.

**Demystifying Testing**

Testing is a broad subject. But you won't get any nontrivial site done without dealing with testing. Code coverage (see `http://en.wikipedia.org/wiki/Code_coverage`) strives to make sure that every line of code and every function and every conditional statement and every entry/exit point and every parameter value limit has been thoroughly tested, usually through automated testing programs. The subject of automated testing and code coverage has become quite popular in the Drupal Community, with the `simpletest` unit tester (`http://simpletest.org/`) being the workhorse of choice. Now, unit testing, especially through automated tests (which can be executed when the code is first committed, as well as against future modifications in the code base), is actually part of the implementation cycle itself, and the more you have of it, the more your work will undoubtedly gain in quality. The best modules are built in this way.

*Continued*

So unless you are going to do coding and/or module development, this kind of testing is already done for you. But in any case, unit testing can only go so far. Acceptance testing is actually a different kind of testing, of the "black-box" variety; it is concerned with making sure the requirements are actually present as features in the finished product.

**Acceptance Test 5-1**

- ❑ Test Clean URLs and automatic generation of SEO-friendly paths.
- ❑ Create a blog entry, and verify the generated URL alias.
- ❑ Try it with an apostrophe.
- ❑ Change the configuration for blog aliases, and make sure the whole URL reflects the changes.
- ❑ Change it back to ./blog/{user name}/title, and verify that it is working properly.

Here is a list of the user stories allocated to the initial Prototype Milestone (the complete list can be seen in Figure 4-7, in Chapter 4):

- ❑ A Workshop Leader can approve applications to join the workshop.
- ❑ A Workshop Leader can suspend Members and Publishers.
- ❑ A Workshop Leader can manage affinity groups.
- ❑ A Workshop Leader can broadcast messages to Members.
- ❑ A Workshop Leader can do everything Workshop Members and Publishers can do.

The decision to include initial affinity groups and message broadcasting at this early stage was made because of the huge architectural impact of these user stories. Postponing their implementation until a later stage would run the risk of decisions about which module(s) to use, configuration, and other aspects having a huge impact on other decisions already taken.

The first two and the fifth user stories are supported by off-the-shelf Drupal Administration tools. You'll deal with them in a moment.

What about the implementation of the third and fourth user stories?

**It is not common practice to number user stories. Nor do the user stories for the On-Line Literary Workshop project have anything to do with specific chapters. However, numbering is used here for reference purposes.**

# A Workshop Leader Can Manage Affinity Groups

The implementation of this user story is a great example of how you can follow best practices offered by the Agile approach to development, in a bite-sized chunk. First of all, the card-conversation-confirmation template allows you to have the client write the Acceptance Test before you even start implementation. Then, a lexical analysis of the card allows you to set up a robustness diagram showing the basic business objects, or building blocks, for the solution, while at the same time migrating everyone involved toward a common language. This common language helps to fine-tune the design and will guarantee good semantics in the configuration (menu items, labels, even names used for variables and functions if coding is necessary), and allows you to make sure your card is properly written into the bargain. And finally, the robustness diagram allows you to map your business objects to actual Drupal modules, or make it very clear whether a custom module needs to be developed.

See User Story 5-1.

### User Story 5-1

A Workshop Leader can manage affinity groups.

**Card**

A Workshop Leader can create, list and review, configure and delete groups to which users of the On-Line Literary Workshop belong. When a new user joins the on line community, she is made a member of a certain affinity group. This will give her access to content only visible to group members.

**Conversation**

This can be based on the Drupal contributed module Organic Groups. This module should be used to control access to content on the site.

By virtue of this user story, at a minimum, a test user should be able to access the affinity group homepage. Other user stories will deal with additional associated functionality.

**Confirmation**

**Test 1** — Workshop Leader creates a group called *Haibun* and assigns user **haibun** to it.

**Test 2** — The user haibun logs in and has access to haibun content.

**Test 3** — Workshop Leader modifies the Haibun group configuration.

Figure 5-7 shows the robustness diagram clarifying this functionality. Obviously, this user story is just to get the ball rolling with Organic Groups and its impact on architecture (see below, "Working on the Architectural Baseline") and allows the Workshop Leader to create and initially configure groups to which Workshop Members may belong.

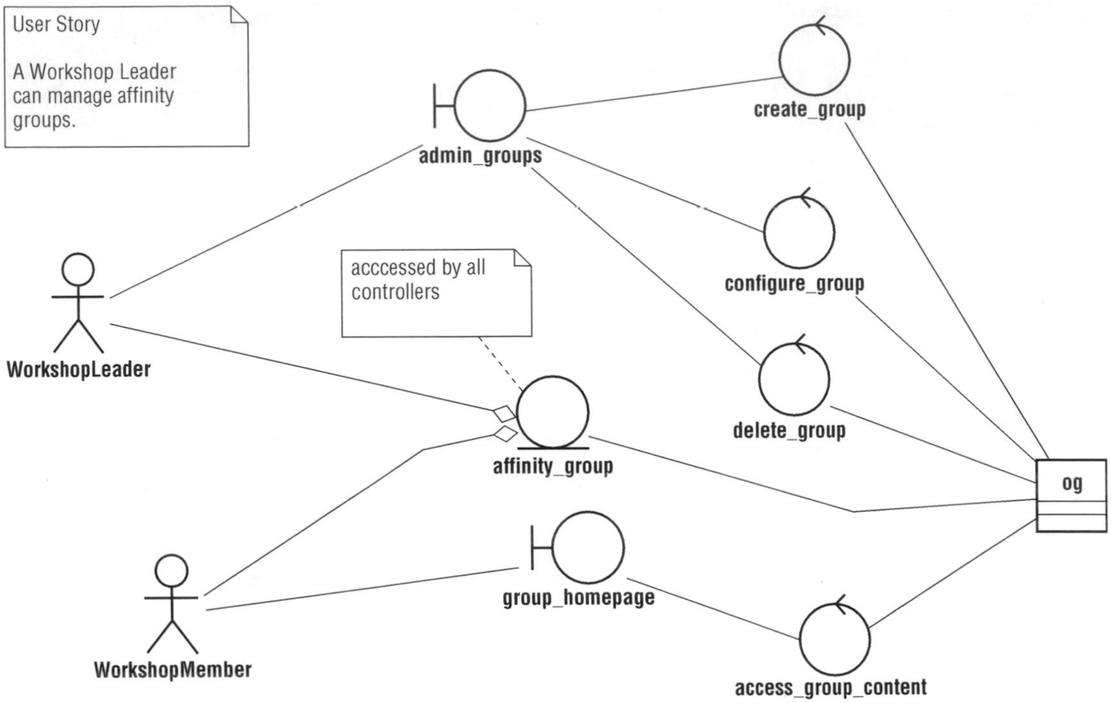


Figure 5-7

Now go ahead and put your newly acquired Drush interface to good use and install the Organic Groups module!

```
victorkane@victorkane:~/Work/Wiley/litworkshop$ drush pm install og--svnsync --
svncommit --svnmessage="Installed og module"↵
Project og successfully installed (version 5.x-7.3).
Project committed to Subversion successfully
victorkane@victorkane:~/Work/Wiley/litworkshop$
```

Now to configure, step through the user story test steps and deploy to the test site:

1. To configure, you first go and enable the module at Administer ➤ Site building ➤ Modules. But wait, the Organic Groups module Enable checkbox is grayed out, and it says "Depends on: Views (missing), Views_rss (missing)."
2. Go back to Drush, and install Views (you'll certainly be needing it anyway):

```
victorkane@victorkane:~/Work/Wiley/litworkshop$ drush pm install views --svnsync --
svncommit --svnmessage="Installed views module"
Project views successfully installed (version 5.x-1.6).
Project committed to Subversion successfully
victorkane@victorkane:~/Work/Wiley/litworkshop$
```

3. Go back to Administer ➤ Site building ➤ Modules, and enable the following checkboxes:

- Organic groups
- Organic groups access control
- Views
- Views RSS
- Views Theme Wizard
- Views UI

4. Click on the "Save configuration" button.

   You will see some comforting info printed at the top of the screen in the info box, like the following:

   - "Organic groups module enabled. Please see the included README file for further installation instructions."
   - "Installing views."
   - "Views module installed tables successfully."
   - "The node access table has been rebuilt."
   - "The configuration options have been saved."

5. Head over to Administer ➢ User management ➢ Access control, and enable all Organic Groups and Views permissions for the dev role.

7. Creating a group actually boils down to creating an item of content type group. So you need to pay a visit to Administer ➢ Content management ➢ Content types and click on the "Add content type" tab in order to create a content type called *group*.

**Previously, the Organic Groups module did this for you by automatically creating a module (code)-based group content type. But now, with CCK giving you the possibility of adding arbitrary fields to a custom content type, you gain a lot of flexibility by rolling your own.**

8. For now, leave it as simple as possible, but be sure to enable the group node option, as well as to disable promotion to front page, enable Create new revision, and disable comments. The workflow section should look something like Figure 5-8.

9. Next, you must allow Workshop Leaders to create items of content type *Group*, which is the same thing as saying, "A Workshop Leader can create a group." You do this by visiting Administer ➢ User management ➢ Access Control and assigning the permissions related to the newly created content type. Clicking "Save content type" brings up the complete list of content types so far, as shown in Figure 5-9.

   Big Red Security update alert! It turns out there has been a new Drupal core release, patching some recently discovered security holes.

10. Leave everything you are doing, grab a fresh copy of the new Drupal security release, and copy it over the existing installation, being careful not to write over your

./sites/default/settings.php or other site-specific details . . . or, if you followed our CVS checkout instructions in the last section in this chapter (aren't you glad you did?), simply open up a terminal to the Drupal document root and do the following:

```
victorkane@victorkane:~/Work/Wiley/litworkshop$ cvs update -dPr DRUPAL-5-12
? .cvsignore
? files
? sites
cvs update: Updating .
P CHANGELOG.txt
P install.php
P robots.txt
...
victorkane@victorkane:~/Work/Wiley/litworkshop$
```

Be sure to run the update script `http://example.com/update.php`, and you are all set. Phew. Red Alert gone. We are once again legal.

**11.** Now, enable at least one other content type as a legitimate group post. *Literary Piece* is perfect, because you want literary pieces to be able to be shared by groups (either open or closed). Go to Administer ➤ Organic Groups ➤ Organic Groups configuration, and click on the Edit link corresponding to the Literary Piece content type. At the bottom, in the Workflow section, select the option: "Standard group post (typically only author may edit). Sends email notifications." Click on the "Save content type" button, and you should see something like Figure 5-10 on the Organic Groups Configuration page.

**12.** For now, you'll leave the rest of the settings as is, and click "Save configuration."

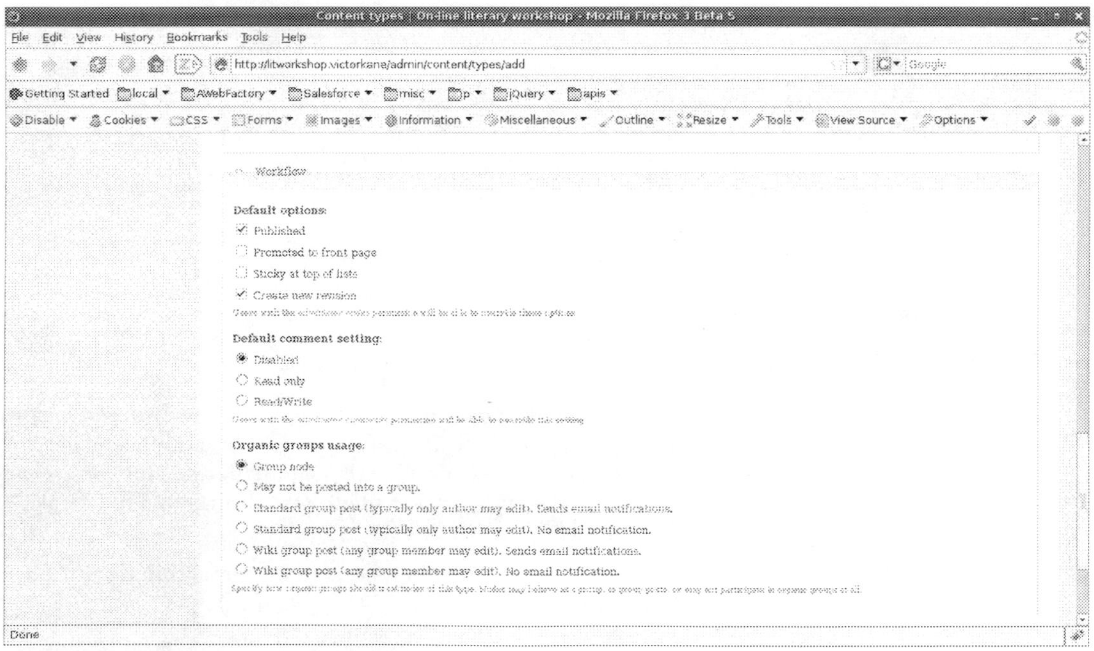


**Figure 5-8**

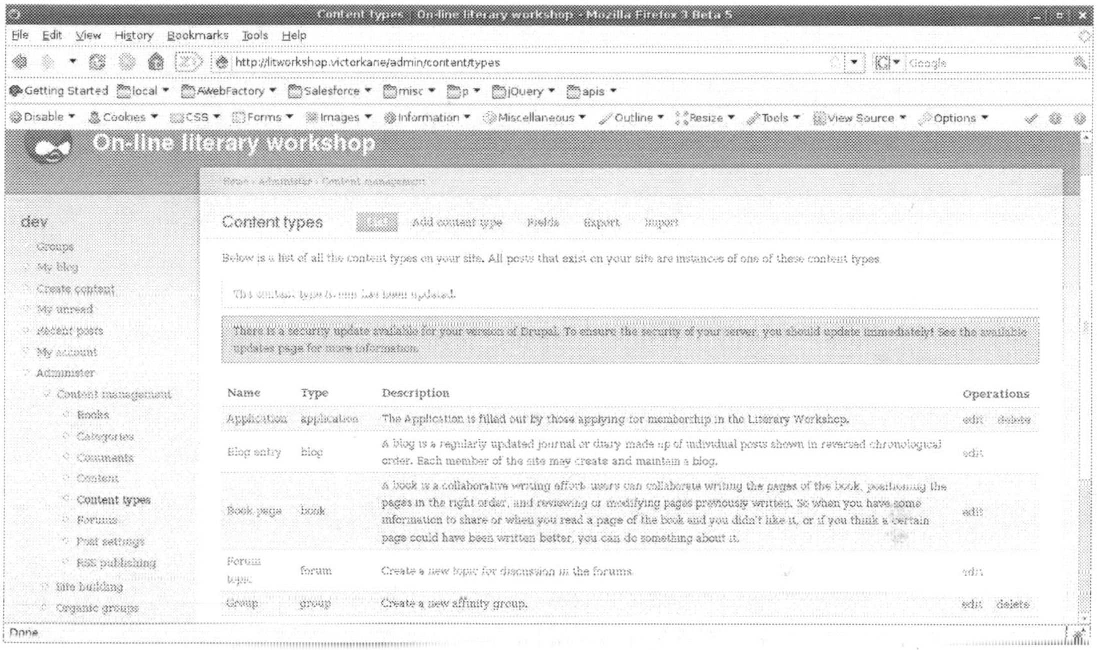

Figure 5-9

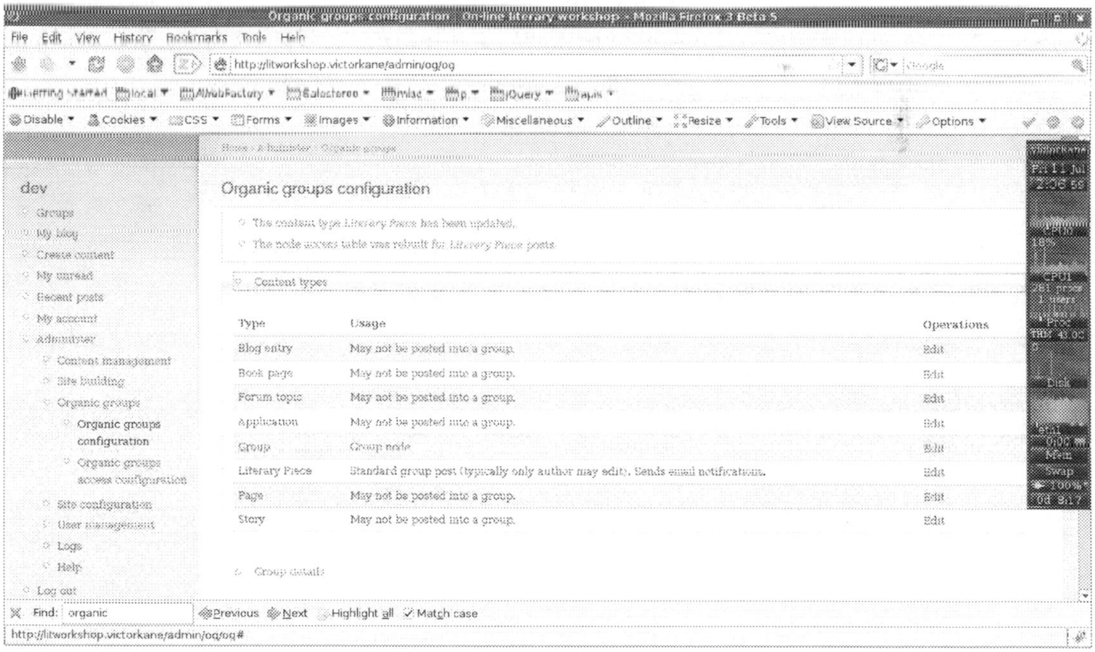

Figure 5-10

Now, when user Pam logs in and wants to create a group, assuming you have called the content type Group (machine-readable name of group) and have supplied an appropriate description, she will see that she can create a new affinity group.

Although Chapter 6 goes into more detail on functionality, let's just make sure this is working:

1. Log in as user pam, click on the "Create content" link from the left-hand-side menu, and click on the Group link to create a new affinity group.
2. Enter **Haibun** as the group name, together with a suitable group description. Put some lorem ipsum into the body, select the closed membership option ("Membership is exclusively managed by an administrator"), and click on the Submit button to create the new affinity group.
3. Now, again from the left-hand-side menu, click on the Groups link for user pam, and you should see the new group listed as in Figure 5-11.

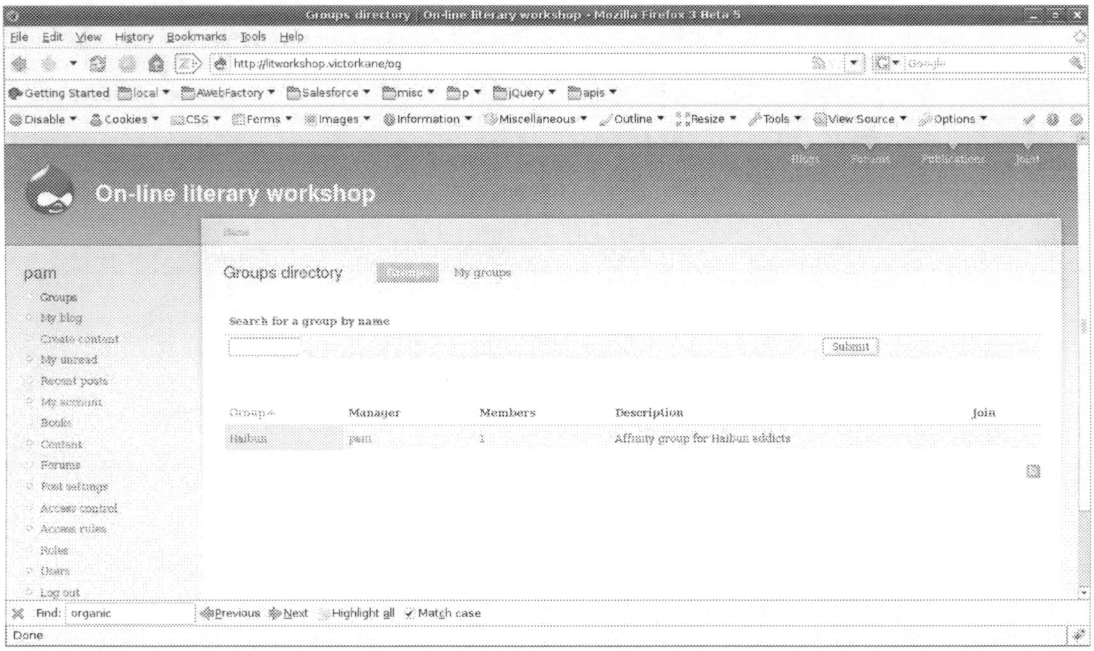


Figure 5-11

4. Click on the link in the Members column showing the number of members (this is not terribly intuitive), which is right now set to **1** (user pam, who created the group and is therefore the group manager). Now click on the "Add members" tab, enter **james** (who was created in Chapter 4) in the List of users to add, and click on the Submit button. The message "1 user added to the group" should appear in the info area on top of the content area. Clicking on the List tab should show both james and pam listed as members.
5. Now log out and log in as james. This user can now click "Groups" and see the Haibun group listed there. Cool — user james can see that he is a member of Haibun. Now, james

clicks "Recent posts" from the left-hand-side menu and clicks his Haibun created earlier and edits it (or creates a new literary piece). Just below the Text area, he sees the Audience checkbox and selects his group Haibun as the group the post will be shown to. He submits his literary piece, then clicks "Groups" again and goes to the Haibun group home page, where james is proud to see his Haibun posted!

6. Now, log in as joyce, and create a new literary piece content type. There is no Audience checkbox for joyce because she is not a member of any affinity group. Log back in as james and create a new literary piece, and you will see that the option is there to post it to the Haibun group. Cool, now log in as user pam, and go to Groups and the Haibun group, and see how productive the members of the literary workshop are!

Well, now is a good time to clean the cache, dump the database, and commit what you have right now to the repository before you go on.

If you are versioning your database dump in ./sites/all/backup/db/litworkshop.sql, you can do the following:

```
victorkane@victorkane:~/Work/Wiley/litworkshop$ drush cache clear
Cache cleared.
victorkane@victorkane:~/Work/Wiley/litworkshop$ drush sql dump > \
sites/all/backup/db/litworkshop.sql
victorkane@victorkane:~/Work/Wiley/litworkshop$ cd sites
victorkane@victorkane:~/Work/Wiley/litworkshop/sites$ svn st
?       CVS
?       default/settings.php
?       default/CVS
?       all/CVS
M       all/backup/db/litworkshop.sql
victorkane@victorkane:~/Work/Wiley/litworkshop/sites$ svn commit -m \
"updated to Drupal 5.8 core release, configured and initially tested organic groups"
Sending        all/backup/db/litworkshop.sql
Transmitting file data .
Committed revision 11.
victorkane@victorkane:~/Work/Wiley/litworkshop/sites$
```

## A Workshop Leader Can Broadcast Messages to Members

In order to implement this user story, the contributed privatemsg may be all that is necessary. The module home page can be found at `http://drupal.org/project/privatemsg`.

Download and install the module. As an exercise, go ahead and enable the module, then follow the instructions so that the user logged in as pam can send some messages to james and joyce, and log in as james and joyce and see if you receive, can reply to, and can use the functionality.

Remember, the complete code base and documentation are available for download at the *Leveraging Drupal* website (`www.wrox.com`).

For each user story allocated to the current Milestone, Pam and I ran all the Acceptance Tests for the Prototype Milestone tasks (based on the list of user stories allocated to this Milestone) and made sure they all passed, after necessary bug-fixing and other modifications had taken place.

See the next chapter to see what the results were and what action was decided on in each case, but agreement was reached that for a Prototype, the Milestone was met.

Commit to the repository, and deploy to the test site.

# What's Left?

In terms of the "Getting initial feedback from the client" goal, your client has participated in the project planning and has written all the user stories. The client was responsible for writing all the Acceptance Tests for the first iteration and participated in executing them. She is now writing the Acceptance Tests for the second Milestone. We're looking good on that score.

In terms of the goals "Finish the user stories with the client," "Plan the project," and "Get the team organized and with the program," you're all set.

There is one area where you still need a tad more work: "Work on the architectural baseline."

# Working on the Architectural Baseline

In the last chapter, you could see that a robustness diagram did a lot of great things for a user story. First off, it tests the semantic consistency of the user story itself, the vocabulary that has to be actually used. Also, it serves as a mini site map showing how a user interacts with the system. And it forms a bridge between *what* the client wants and *how* that is to be implemented; it sheds a first glimpse into what software components are actually capable of supporting that functionality.

**Question: When Do You Do the Robustness Diagrams?**

Answer: As the user story is being written and conversed between development and client staff. Then, as the user story is taken in turn and implemented, you refine it.

**Question: Do You Write All the Robustness Diagrams Together in One Fell Swoop?**

Answer: No, it is a kind of by-product as each user story gets written, conversed, and implemented. It kind of inducts itself into the big picture the architect is searching for, in the course of the process for each iteration.

What needs to be understood here is that the overall picture of the complete shopping list of software components (Drupal modules, mostly, in this case) will actually emerge from the process you are following and should not be pushed or adored in the abstract. With each robustness diagram you do, you will discover one or two contributed Drupal modules you need.

So to see how this stacks up concretely, look back at a couple of user stories and robustness diagrams that got written along the way during this first iteration (or check out the complete set from the *Leveraging*

*Drupal* website), and let's draw the conclusions on the wall: or, rather, on what is called a high-level class diagram showing the most important interfaces (screens?), business objects (entities), and logic (controllers) actually needed to get this show on the road, and how they tie in to Drupal core and contributed modules functionality, as well as other third-party components (feed parsers, rich text editors, etc.).

The robustness diagrams Figure 4-10 (in Chapter 4) and Figure 5-7, taken together with the complete set, give rise to the architecture diagram, with an initial version in Figure 5-12, showing the relationship between the business objects implementing the functionality and Drupal modules forming part of the architecture.

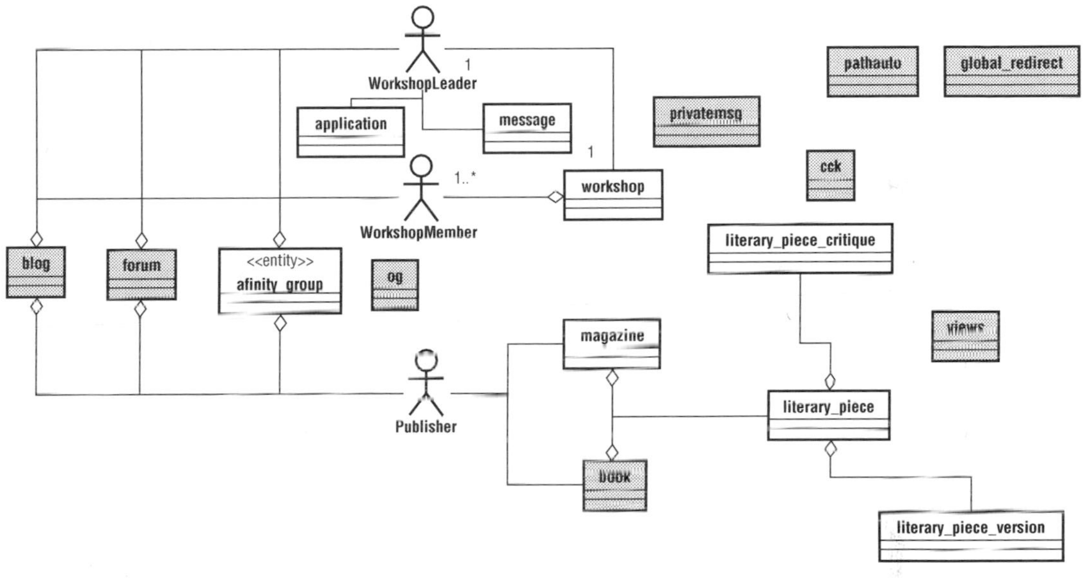


Figure 5-12

# Summary

In this chapter, you have wrapped up the Elaboration phase and made sure that your development environment allows you to easily update both the Drupal core as well as contributed modules, together with as much convenience through the Drupal Shell module as can be brought to bear.

You have confirmed the basic website development workflow on the basis of these tools and have fleshed out the functionality so as to be able to support all the user stories allocated to this Milestone.

You have also detailed a series of Acceptance Tests that have to be run now by Pam, the client, both in order to confirm that you have really got the Milestone deployed, as well as to serve as a springboard for the planning and execution of the next phase, Construction.

# 6

# Pushing the Envelope

So the project is now under way. From your development box, you have access to the code repository, the Trac site, and the application test site, and your client is participating from her workstation or laptop.

Since the envelope is going to be pushed now, with more significant parts of the architecture being implemented, things are going to get substantially more complicated, and communication runs the risk of getting dispersed.

This chapter address all these concerns. In the section, "You've Got Mail," you see private messaging between yourself and the client in full swing. In the section, "Using Your Own dev Affinity Group," you leverage the power of the Organic Groups module to create a special, secure place where development documents can be centralized and shared. You are introduced to the powerful Views module in the section, "Rolling Your Own Document Case and Index," as you find ways of listing and indexing the contents of the dev affinity group content. In the section, "Now, Where Were We?" you review how Trac helps you keep a running sense of where you are on the project, and, indeed, the next few tasks are identified. Finally, the tools used so far are applied to the implementation of some of these tasks in the section, "Browsing and Filtering Views of Literary Pieces."

## You've Got Mail!

After deploying all the work completed in the last chapter to the test site (by committing everything, including a database dump, to the repository, doing an SVN update on the test site, and writing the new database state to the database), try sending a private message to Pam, telling her you need to meet. From the left-hand-side menu, logged in as user dev, go to "My account." Then you will see a new addition: "Private messages" (see Figure 6-1). Follow these steps:

1. Click on "Write private message," and select user **pam** in the "To" field, as in Figure 6-2.
2. Fill in the Subject — **Let's meet** or whatever — and then the Message field, and click on the "Send private message" button.

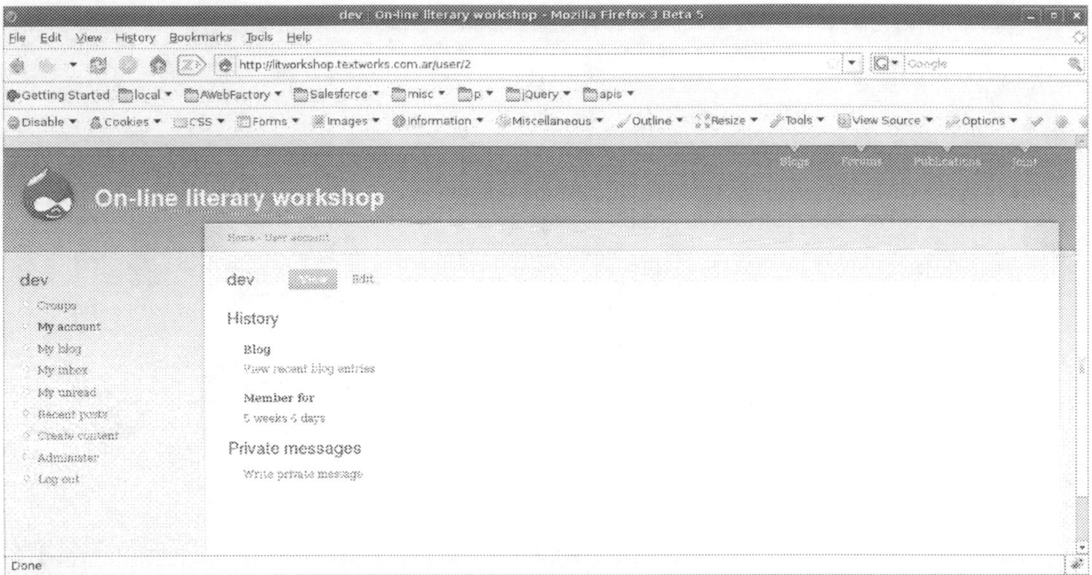


Figure 6-1

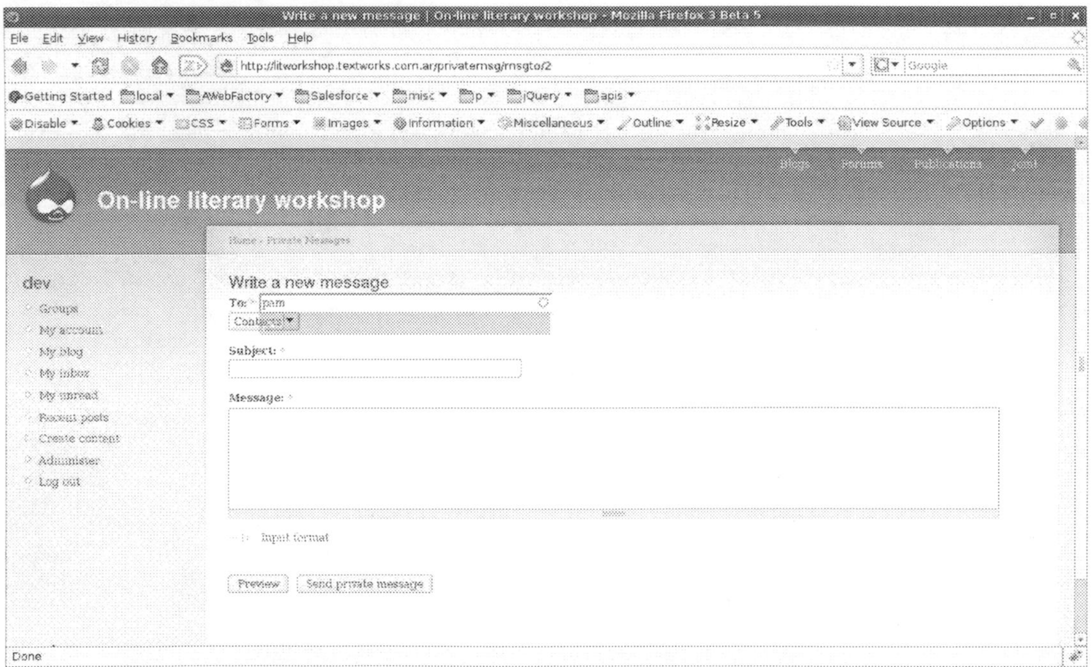


Figure 6-2

3. Now, log out and log in as pam, and you will immediately see two things: on the left-hand-side menu (the Navigation menu with the user name, in this case, pam, as heading), there is a new entry, "My inbox," which right now shows that there is an unread message waiting for the user. And the info box at the top of the content area says, "You have one new *private message*," with the phrase *private message* made clickable. See Figure 6-3.

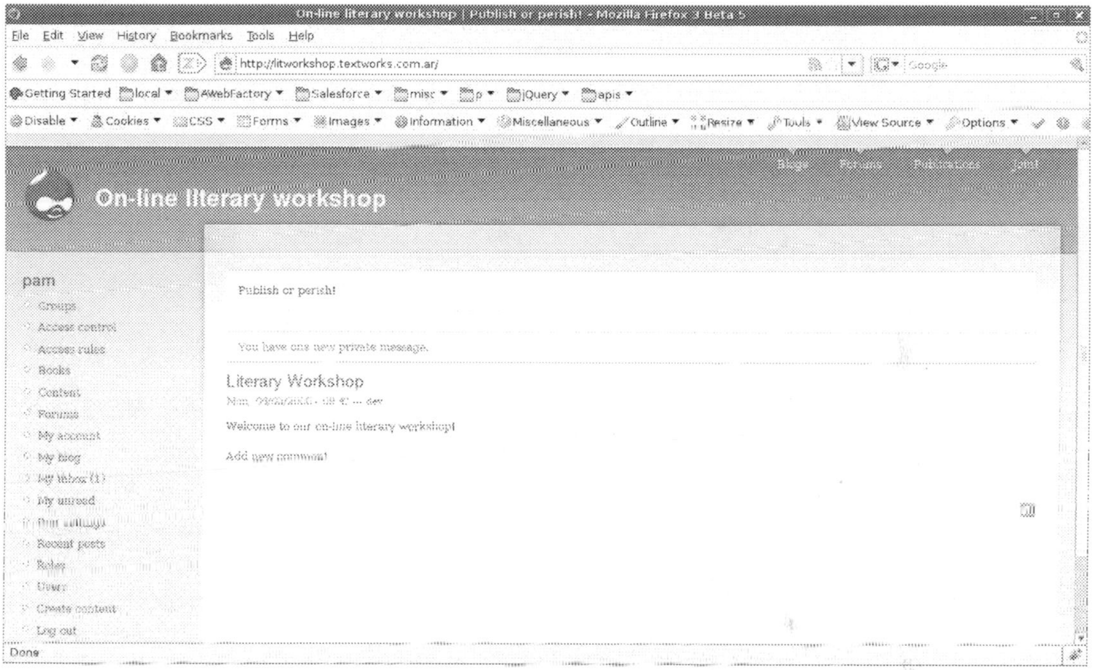


Figure 6-3

User pam clicks on *private message* or the "My inbox" menu item and is taken to her inbox. The "Let's meet" message is highlighted by a red "new" indicator. User pam clicks there to read the message. As shown in Figure 6-4, she has the option to reply to or delete the message, or to go back to list her messages. After she has received a lot of messages, she can even organize them in folders. The operation of the system is quite straightforward.

# Using Your Own dev Affinity Group

You decide to take advantage of the affinity group feature to create an affinity group of your own so that you, other programmers, the graphic designers, Pam, and others of her staff can share documents, Acceptance Tests, and so forth, which only the dev affinity group will be able to access. Cool. Drupal is its own best prototyping tool — it can even self-document itself!

**This means that if you download the Chapter 5 tarball and deploy it and log in as user dev, when you go to Groups and select the dev group, you can see all the user stories and all the Acceptance Tests, links to Trac, and even repository commits and other stuff.**

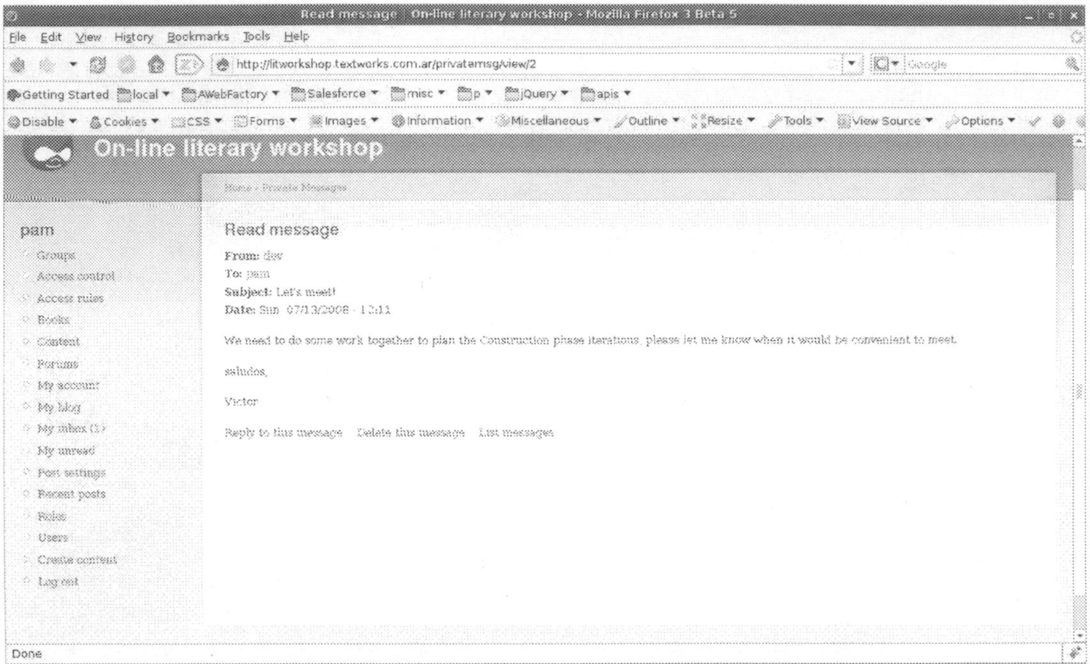


Figure 6-4

Follow these steps to create the dev affinity group.

1. So, logged in as user dev, you hit "Create content" from the Navigation menu, and then click on the "Group–Create an affinity group" link.
2. Fill in the info for Title, Description, and Mission Statement.
3. You want to keep this a closed group (Membership requests section), and, moreover, one that is not even advertised in the group directory, so select the "Private group" checkbox. Clicking on the Submit button creates the group!
4. Now, because the dev group is purposely excluded from the groups directory, when you click "Groups" from the Navigation menu, the group does not appear. However, if you then click on the "My groups" tab, you have access to the group. Then, click "1" in the Members column, and the "Add members" tab. Enter user **pam** in the "List of users" text field, and click "Submit."
5. Now implement two or three content types enabled as group post elements with which to manage the project (right from within itself!). To do this, you need to create the content type and then specify additional fields as needed. These additional fields and their characteristics are described in the tables below. You need to implement the following three content types:

    - User Story
    - Acceptance Test
    - Project Document (for things like the Risk List, Creative Brief, and Styles and Standards Document)

The following table specifies the fields defining the User Story content type, the field labels, the machine-readable name, field type, widget, configuration, and required state for each of the fields composing the content type. The Required Modules column shows which modules must be installed and enabled prior to implementing the content type.

**User Story Content Type (user_story)**

| Field Label | Machine-Readable Name | Field Type | Widget | Configuration | Required/ Multiple | Required Modules |
|---|---|---|---|---|---|---|
| Name | title (default) | | | | | |
| Card | user_story_card | Text | Text Field | 5 rows | Yes/No | CCK |
| Conversation | user_story_conversation | Text | Text Field | 5 rows | No/Yes | CCK |
| Confirmation | user_story_confirmation | Text | Text Field | 5 rows | No/Yes | CCK |

In each of these three content types, you should leave the deprecated Body field label blank, set the "Default options" to Published, and "Create new revision"; set the Organic groups usage to "Wiki group post (any group member may edit). Sends email notifications," and set Private Message "Write to author" links on "Link to node" and "Link to comment" (or, of course, suit yourself!).

The items in the following table are the fields making up the Acceptance Test content type. Notice that the Date and Date API modules must be installed and enabled:

**Acceptance Test Content Type (acceptance_test)**

| Field Label | Machine-Readable Name | Field Type | Widget | Configuration | Required /Multiple | Required Modules |
|---|---|---|---|---|---|---|
| Title | title (default) | | | | | |
| User Story | acc_test_ user_story | Node Reference | Autocomplete Text Field | Content types that can be referenced: User Story | Yes/No | CCK |
| Date Run | acc_test_ date_run | Date | Select List | Granularity: month, day, year | No/No | date, date_api |
| Purpose | acc_test_ purpose | Text | Text Field | 5 rows | No/No | CCK |
| Initial conditions/test prerequisites | acc_test_initial | Text | Text Field | 5 rows | No/No | CCK |
| Observation point | acc_test_ observation_ point | Text | Text Field | 5 rows | No/No | CCK |

*Continued*

### Acceptance Test Content Type (acceptance_test)

| Field Label | Machine-Readable Name | Field Type | Widget | Configuration | Required /Multiple | Required Modules |
|---|---|---|---|---|---|---|
| Test steps | acc_test_steps | Text | Text Field | 5 rows | No/Yes | CCK |
| Post conditions | acc_test_post | Text | Text Field | 5 rows | No/No | CCK |
| Results and recommendations | acc_test_results | Text | Text Field | 5 rows | No/No | CCK |

*You will have to install the Date and Date API (*`http://drupal.org/project/date`*) contributed modules to support fields of type Date for this to work. In any case, a date field is something you will be using often.*

The configuration of the Acceptance Test content type deserves some comments. Figure 6-5 shows the view from Administer ➤ Content management ➤ Content types ➤ Acceptance Test.

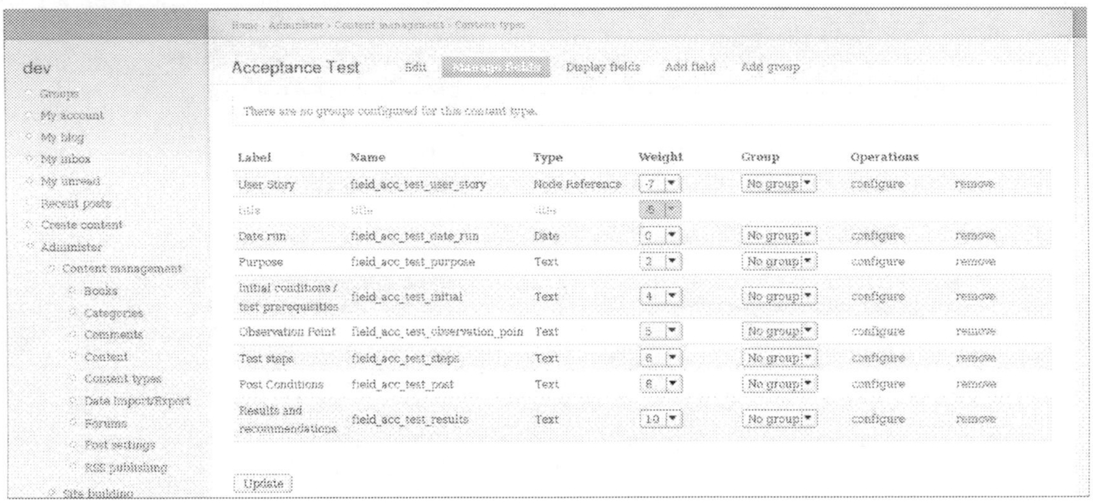


Figure 6-5

Unusually, the User Story is listed first as a linked Node Reference (make sure you check the User Story option in the Content types that can be referenced section), then comes the Title, then the Date the Acceptance Test is run, and then its purpose. Next space is provided to specify the test's initial conditions or prerequisites, such as having logged in as a particular user or being on a certain page. Then the observation point (Where are you standing when you measure this?) can be specified, followed by a series of test steps (click this, do that, do this, go there, etc.). Finally, the post conditions (what the state of the world should be after running the test) are given, followed by a space provided for the person running the test to enter the test results and recommendations.

By the way, as you can see in the following table that specifies the fields defining the Project Document content type, the only explicitly required field is the reference to the user story being tested (without which the creation of the item makes no sense). Don't feel obliged to go into any more detail than absolutely necessary.

#### Project Document Content Type (prj_doc)

| Field Label | Machine-Readable Name | Field Type | Widget | Configuration | Required /Multiple | Required Modules |
|---|---|---|---|---|---|---|
| Title | title (default) | | | | | |
| Discipline | prj_doc_ discipline | Text | Select List | Allowed values list: bm \| Business Modeling req \| Requirements ad \| Analysis and Design imp \| Implementation (after field creation, go back and select this as the default) test \| Test dep \| Deployment ccm \| Configuration and Change Management pm \| Project Management env \| Environment | Yes/No | CCK |
| Abstract | prj_doc_ abstract | Text | Text Field | 5 rows | No/No | CCK |
| Text | prj_doc_text | Text | Text Field | 5 rows | No/Yes | CCK |

Go ahead and create these content types, or else import them from the Leveraging Drupal website. Set permissions for creating and editing these content types for dev and Workshop Leader. (No one else will see them when they click "Create content," and individual content items will be restricted to the dev group.) To start out, add in a couple of the user stories, Acceptance Tests, and a Risk list project document that the project leader can maintain in order to permanently show the "risk" state of the project at all times. Remember to restrict their group access. Figure 6-6 shows how a user story is restricted to the dev group by selecting it in the Audience dropdown list in the Groups section.

Check out this chapter's deployment tarball for exported text versions of all content types, as well as examples of each one.

I hope that you will find them useful for all your future projects using the Drupal CMS Framework.

Figure 6-7 shows the dev group home page (Groups ➤ My Groups ➤ dev) with a few example items added of each kind.

Don't forget to commit and deploy:

```
victorkane@victorkane:~/Work/Wiley$ cd litworkshop/
victorkane@victorkane:~/Work/Wiley/litworkshop$ drush cache clear
Cache cleared.
victorkane@victorkane:~/Work/Wiley/litworkshop$ drush sql \
dump > sites/all/backup/db/litworkshop.sql
```

```
victorkane@victorkane:~/Work/Wiley/litworkshop$ cd sites
victorkane@victorkane:~/Work/Wiley/litworkshop/sites$ svn commit -m \
"added some project docs, acceptance tests and user stories"
Sending        all/backup/db/litworkshop.sql
Transmitting file data .
Committed revision 19.
victorkane@victorkane:~/Work/Wiley/litworkshop/sites$
```

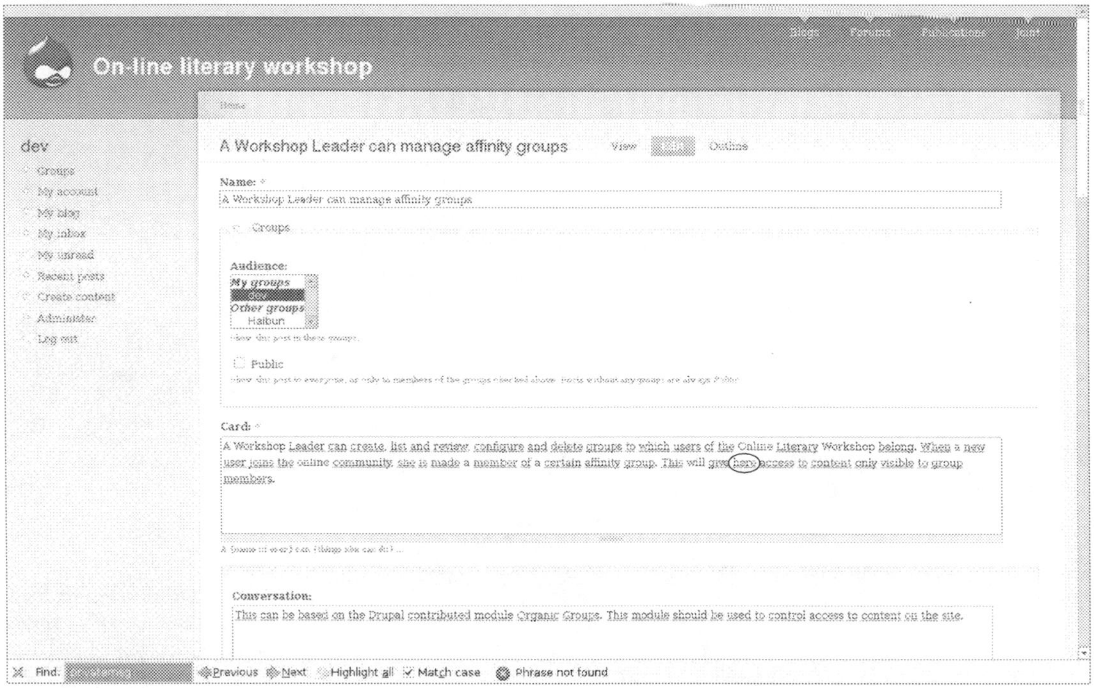


Figure 6-6

# Rolling Your Own Document Case and Index

Well, it is great to be able to access all the project documents in one place and share them wiki style with the client. But Figure 6-7 is a bit overwhelming because you have to scroll a lot and even page through the list to see what you have. The same goes for other group home pages, like the Haibun group home page. Wouldn't it be great if you could see a table with links instead of a long sausage of the actual content itself?

In software development, this is called a *Document Case* (a virtual portfolio of documents) and is fundamental for maintaining a centralized, shared bird's-eye view of all the project documentation. You are going to be able to implement this now, including the possibility of filtering the list according to different criteria.

This is what's great about using Drupal.

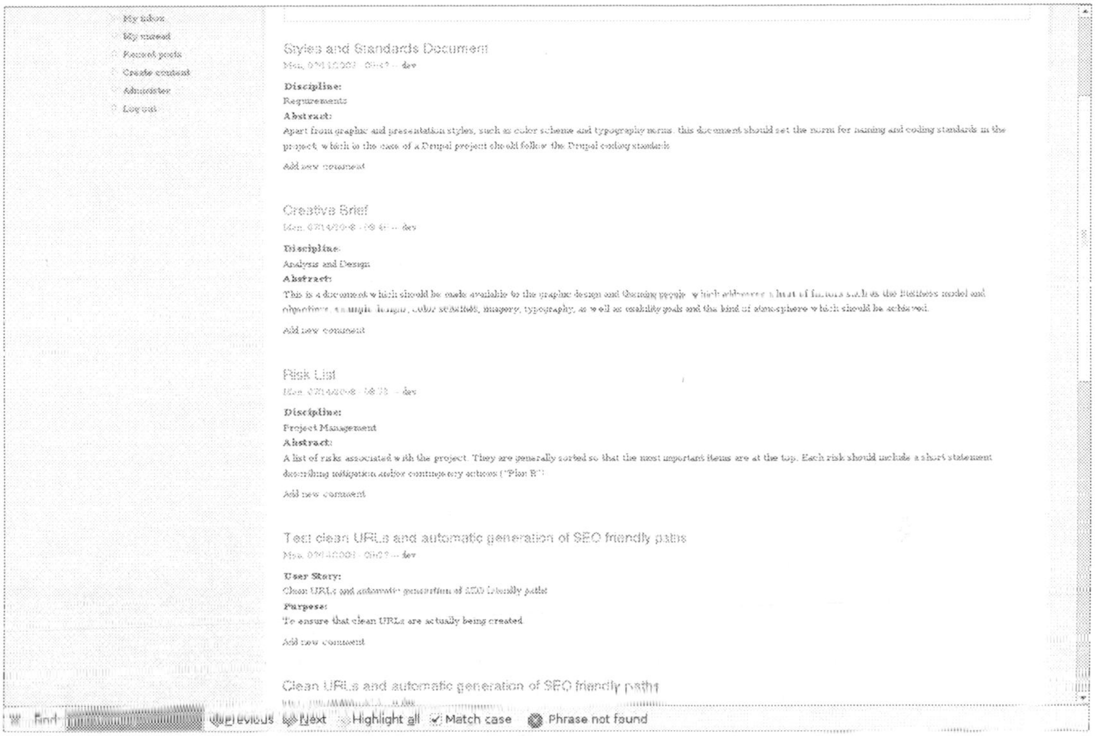


Figure 6-7

## Implementing the Document Case

To solve this first of all in a pretty straightforward manner, you need to start exploring the options offered through the Views module configuration. Up until now, this book has gone into a lot of detail concerning the way you can create custom content types via the CCK module, but you haven't seen anything of its all-important counterpart, the Views module.

> **The All-Important Views Model**
>
> You can find the Views module home page at `http://drupal.org/project/views`. For Drupal 5.x, only Views 1 is available, with many additional features, in usability as well as in basic functionality, added for Views 2, available in Drupal 6.x and beyond. See `http://drupal.org/node/109604` for basic Views 1 Drupal Handbook documentation. For Views 2, the documents come in a wonderful "Advanced Help" format, which will be used by an ever-increasing number of modules and perhaps the Drupal core itself.

As explained in the README.txt file accompanying the Organic Groups module, and as can be seen in Figure 6-8, digging deeper into the Organic Groups configuration page at Administer ➢ Organic Groups ➢ Organic Groups Configuration, it is possible to customize the layout of the group home page by enabling an alternative view whose name is prefixed by *og_ghp_*.

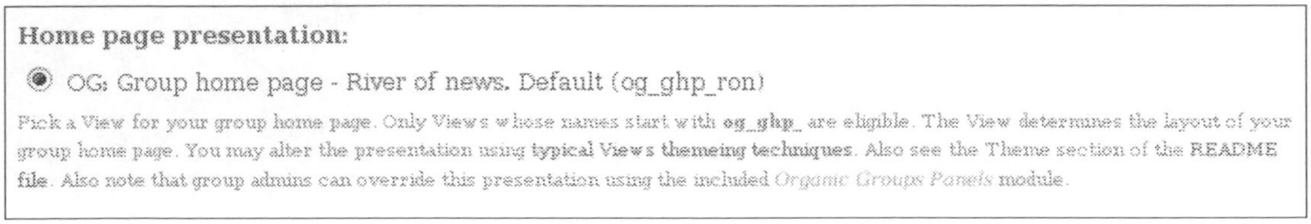

Home page presentation:
OG: Group home page - River of news. Default (og_ghp_ron)
Pick a View for your group home page. Only Views whose names start with og_ghp_ are eligible. The View determines the layout of your group home page. You may alter the presentation using typical Views themeing techniques. Also see the Theme section of the README file. Also note that group admins can override this presentation using the included Organic Groups Panels module.


Figure 6-8

The default view is called *og_ghp_ron* and implements a ''River of News'' layout of content items published by and for the group. You can ''clone'' this view and edit it by following these steps:

1. Go to Administer ➢ Site building ➢ Administer Views. At this point, no custom views have been defined, but by virtue of installing and enabling various modules, there are a host of default views, including several related to Organic Groups (prefixed by *og_*). To reuse og_ghp_ron, you must first add it as a regular view by clicking on the corresponding Add link (see Figure 6-9). You are then taken to the ''Add a View'' form.

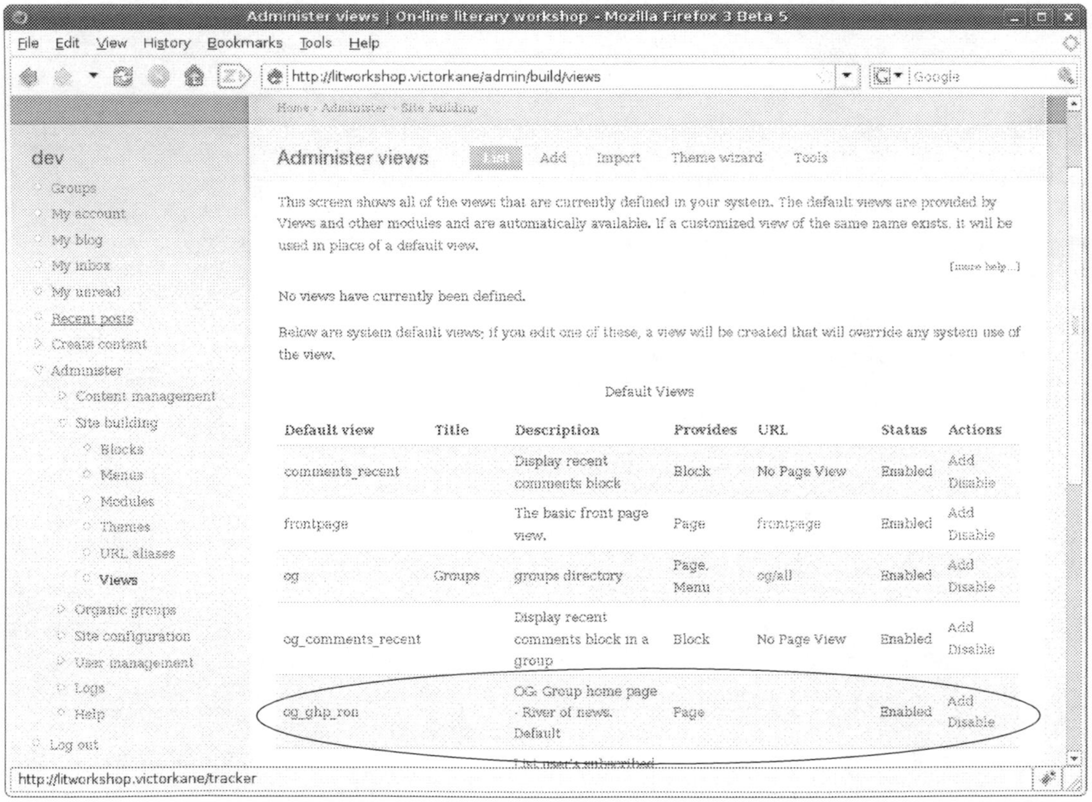


Figure 6-9

2. Simply click on the Submit button at the foot of the page to leave this now editable view unchanged. You are taken back to the Administer ➢ Site building ➢ Administer views page.

3. You are going to create the alternative og_ghp_table view. To start the process, click on the clone link corresponding to og_ghp_ron, as shown in Figure 6-10. You are taken to the "Add a View" form.

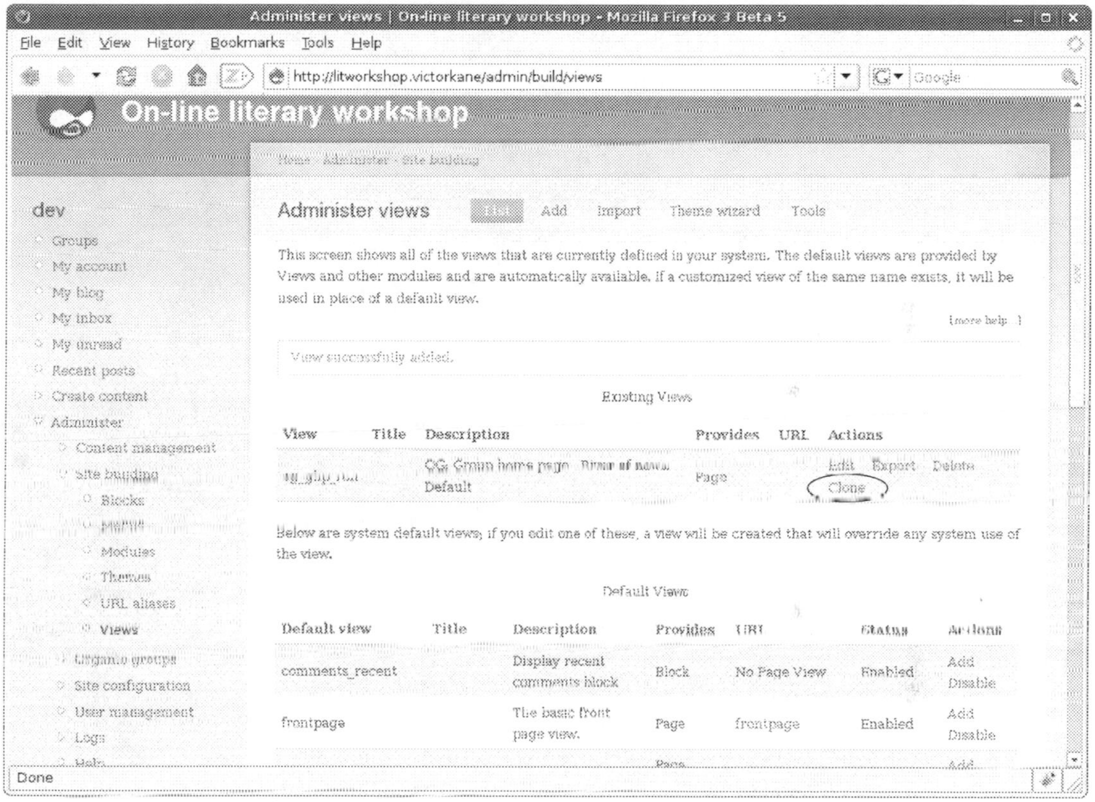


Figure 6-10

4. In the Name field, enter **og_ghp_table**. Leave access as is because this is something handled by Organic Groups access management (dev is a private, closed group unlisted in the group directory). In the Description field, enter **OG: Group home page - Table view. Alternative**. In the Page View section, change the Teaser List to Table View by selecting this entry from the dropdown list. This now obliges you to deliberately specify the fields making up the table columns, which is required in any view not having the Teaser List or Full Nodes View Type.

5. Open up the Fields section. From the Add Field dropdown list, choose Node: Title, and click on the "Add Field" button to the right. Next choose Node: Type, and click on the "Add Field" button. Finally, add Node: Author Name, Node: Updated Time, and Node: Edit link. Fill in suitable entries in the Label fields. Make the first four columns sortable, and set

Default sort as Ascending for Node: Type. Your Fields section should look something like that shown in Figure 6-11.

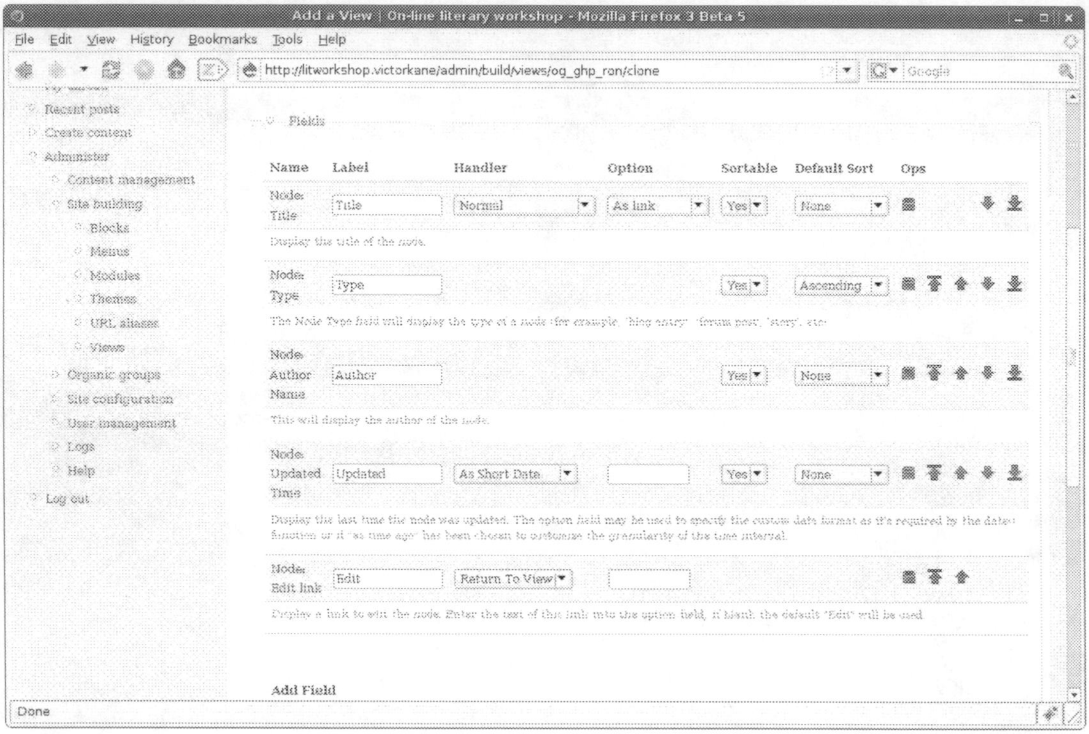


Figure 6-11

6. Scroll down to the bottom of the page without changing anything else for the present, and click on the Save button. *og_ghp_table* is now listed in the list of existing views.

7. Now if you go to the Groups directory, click on "My groups" and the dev group link, things are still as they were before: You will see the River of News layout. However, after you go to Administer ➤ Organic Groups ➤ Organic Groups Configuration and scroll down to the Home page presentation subsection of Group details, *og_ghp_table* is now listed as an alternative (by virtue of the naming convention). Select it, click "Save configuration," and revisit the dev group. It should be very similar to Figure 6-12. Commit and deploy to the test site.

## Views-Sorting Tweak

One of the less intuitive things about using views is that when you designate fields as sortable, as in Figure 6-11, for example, you expect the resulting displayed table (as shown in Figure 6-12) to actually be sorted in real time according to how you click on the table column headings. For example, if you click the Updated heading, you expect the order of the rows to be inverted.

This is not happening, however.

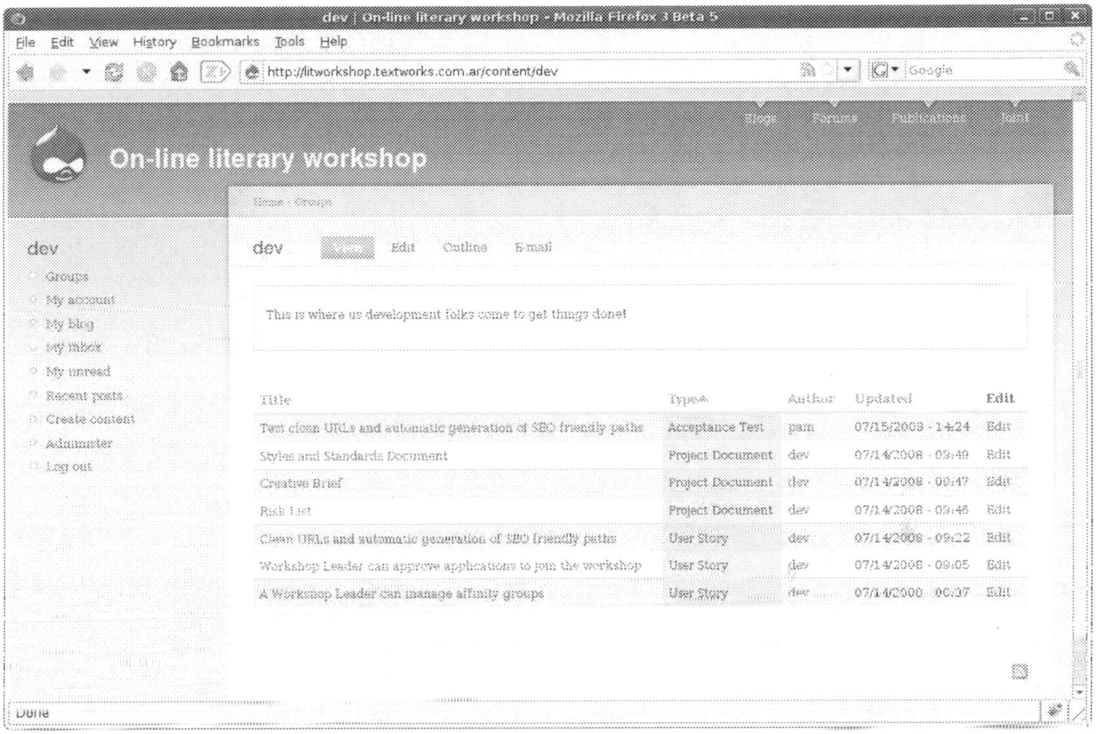


Figure 6-12

Fortunately, the solution is simple, although it involves a decision and is not at all intuitive. The solution is:

1. Go to Administer ➤ Site building ➤ Views Administration, and edit the og_ghp_table view.
2. Open up the last section, Sort Criteria, and remove all sort criteria by clicking the waste-basket icon corresponding to each one (they were placed there in the original design of the og_ghp_ron view).
3. After doing that and clicking on the Save button, you will find that the sortable table headers now work.

If you do add even a single Sort Criteria, however, you will find that they will no longer work. You have to consider the pros and cons on this one.

# Now, Where Were We?

How do you ever know where you are on a project (let's say you have gone to Burning Man at this point, returned, and are blinking at the project on the screen right now)?

Just go to Trac, open up the Roadmap, and take a look at the progress bar. As you can see from Figure 6-13, the Prototype Milestone is done.

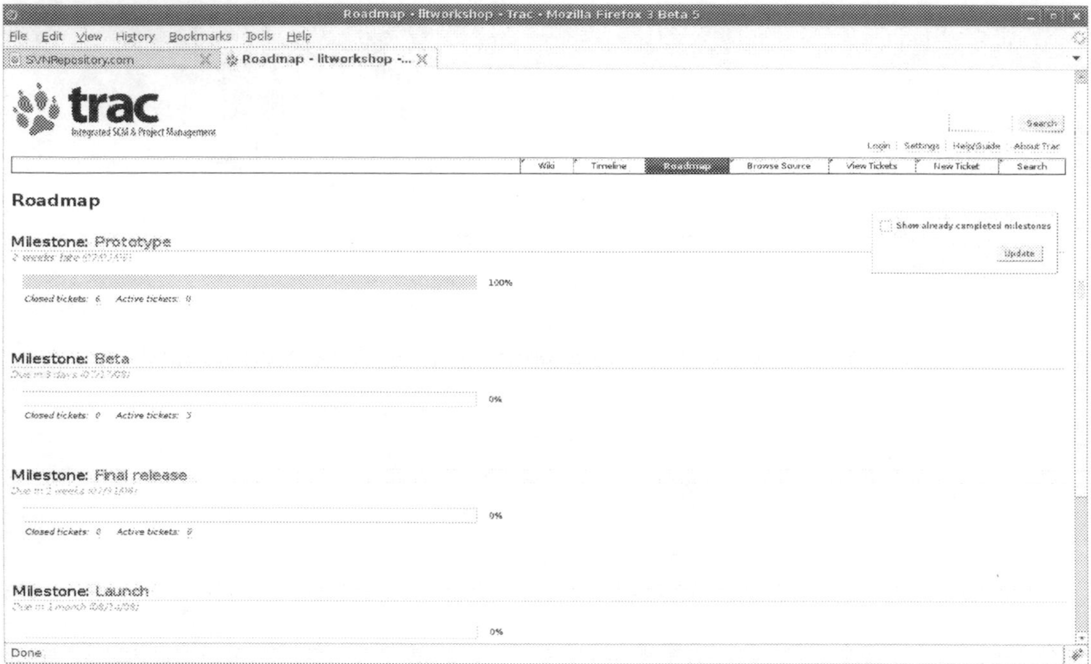


**Figure 6-13**

To see exactly what you are supposed to be doing now, you need to take a look at the user stories assigned to the current iteration, Beta:

- ❑ A Workshop Member can post literary pieces.
- ❑ A Workshop Member can make any post public, private, or visible to an affinity group.
- ❑ A Workshop Member can critique public posts.
- ❑ A Workshop Member can browse public pieces and critiques.
- ❑ A Workshop Member can send and receive messages to and from all Members, Publishers, and the Workshop Leader.

# Creating Role-Specific Navigation Menu Blocks

Much of the functionality involved in the user stories assigned to the Beta iteration already exists. You need to group what functionality you already have in Navigation menu blocks, which are only visible to certain roles. In this case, during a discussion with the client, a decision was made to create several Navigation menus visible only to Administrators, Webmasters, and, for now at least, the Workshop Leader; and to present these menus as handy simplified navigation blocks, containing only those links the Workshop Member actually needs and is likely to use.

The issue should be raised on Trac and added to the Beta milestone task list. To do so:

1. Click "New Ticket" from the top menu bar.
2. Enter **Create simplified navigation block for Workshop Members** in the Short Summary field. Make this task of type enhancement to show that it is actually part of change management, fill in a Full description, and assign it to the current Beta Milestone. The result is shown in Figure 6-14.

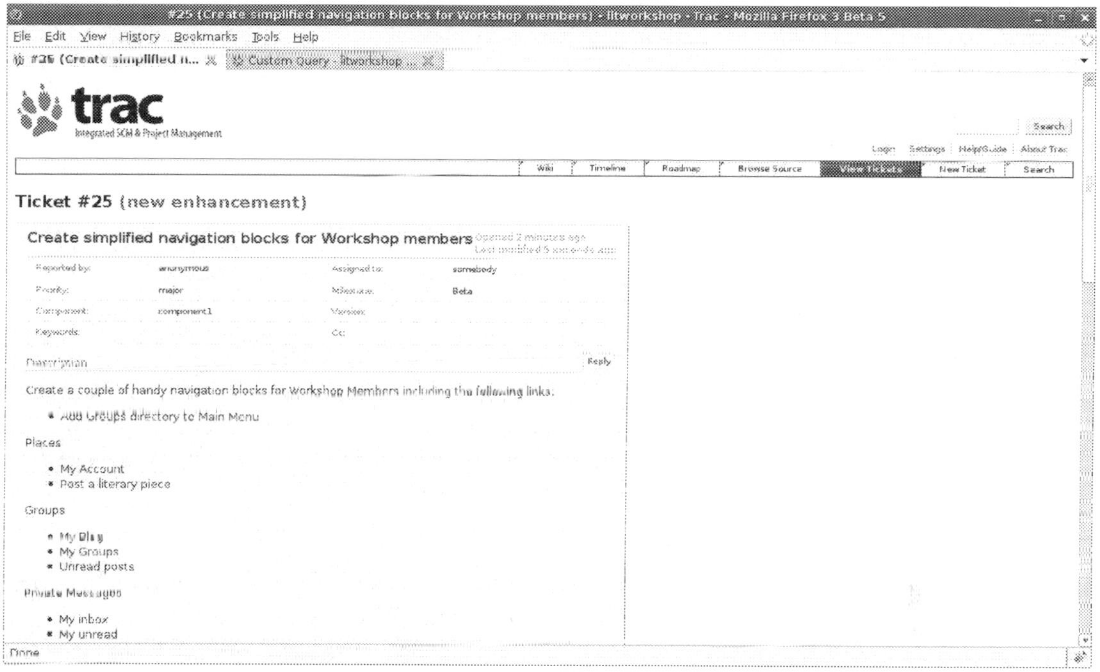


Figure 6-14

3. To implement this in a practical top-down fashion, first go to Administer ➢ Site building ➢ Menu, and add **Groups** to the primary menu.
4. Then go to Administer ➢ Site building ➢ Blocks, and click on the Configure link corresponding to the Navigation block that is currently assigned to the left sidebar. Leave the Custom visibility settings in their default selection (users cannot control whether or not they see this block), and in the "Show block for specific roles" (no checkboxes are currently checked, so that the block is visible to all roles) section, select Admin, Webmaster, and Workshop Leader, then click on the "Save block" button.
5. To create the handy blocks, you could create custom blocks with HTML links, but Drupal offers a much easier and better way: Any menu you create is immediately available as a Block that can be made visible in any region on the page. So, back to Administer ➢ Site building ➢ Menu to create the Places, Groups, and Private Messages menus alongside the Primary Menu, along the lines of the values in the following table. (As Pam reviewed the implementation, we made a couple of changes compared to the issue as it was first raised in Trac.)

**Creating Blocks**

| Menu | Menu Item Title | Description | Path | Weight |
|---|---|---|---|---|
| Primary menu | Blogs | On-Line Literary Workshop blog central! | blog | −10 |
| | Groups | Group directory | og | 0 |
| | Forums | Discussion forums | forum | 2 |
| | Publications | On-line books and magazines | book | 4 |
| | Join! | Join our literary workshop. | node/add/ application | 6 |
| Places | My Account | View your user profile. | user | 0 |
| | Post a literary piece | Create a new literary piece and post as public or private. | node/add/ literary-piece | 2 |
| | Post a forum topic | Post a new topic to one of the forums. | node/add/forum | 4 |
| | Post a blog entry | Create a new blog entry. | node/add/blog | 6 |
| | Private messages | Browse your private messages inbox. | privatemsg/inbox | 8 |
| | Logout | End current session. | logout | 10 |
| Groups | My Groups | List your subscribed groups. | og/my | 0 |
| | Unread posts | New posts to my subscribed groups. | group | 2 |

## Creating the Menus and Navigation Blocks

To create menu Places:

1. Go to Administer ➢ Site building ➢ Menus, and click on the "Add menu" tab. Enter **Places** in the Title field, and hit "Submit."
2. Click on the "Add item" link just below the Menu title *Places*, and add in the My Account entry. Continue in like manner with the other menu items, the Menu Groups and its menu items. You should end up with something similar to Figure 6-15.
3. Now enable the menu blocks automatically generated along with the newly created menus by going to Administer ➢ Site building ➢ Blocks and enabling block Groups in the left sidebar with a weight of 2, and blocking Places in the left sidebar with weight 1. Click "Save blocks."
4. Now click on the configure link for Groups and for Places, and select the "Show block for specific roles" checkboxes for the Admin, Webmaster, Workshop Leader, and Workshop Member roles (the Publisher role will eventually get its own set of navigation blocks in another iteration).

5. Another related touch is to enable the core Tracker module. Go to Administer ➢ Site building ➢ Modules and in the Core–Optional section, enable the Tracker module (Enables tracking of recent posts for users) and click on the "Save configuration" button. Now when user james logs in and goes to My Account, he can see a Track tab along with View and Edit, and there he can see the posts he himself has made, which most people find very convenient.

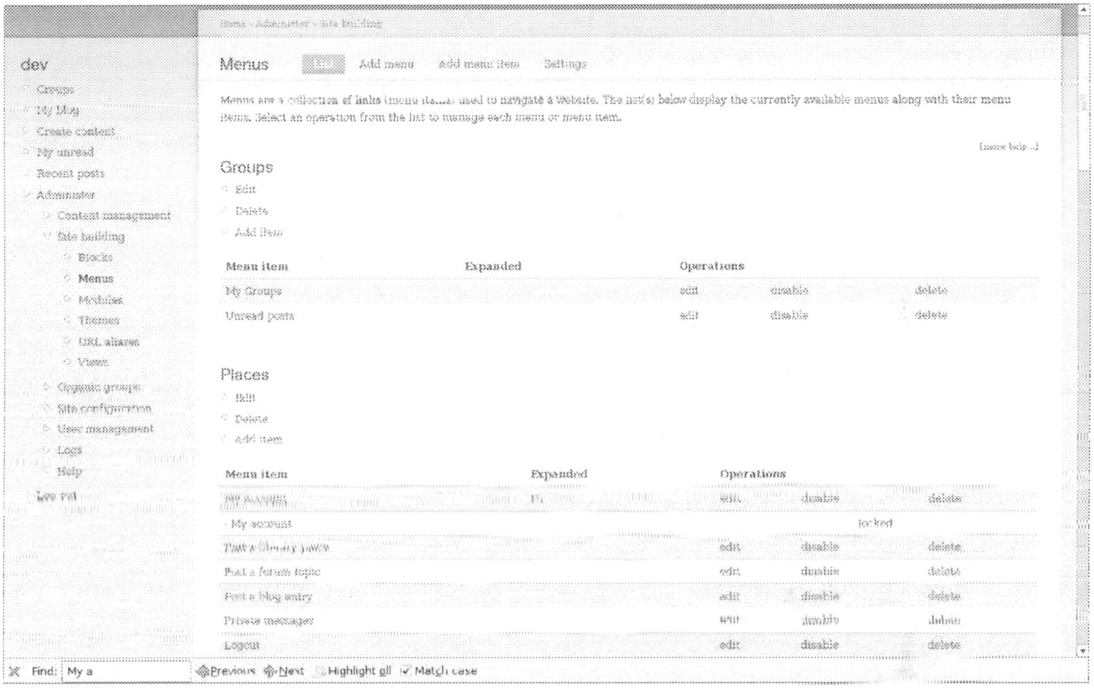


**Figure 6-15**

The gains in usability can be appreciated in Figure 6-16, which shows user James logged in and visualizing his profile page.

Commit and deploy!

# Browsing and Filtering Views of Literary Pieces

Here is where you get to apply what you have learned so far in this chapter to the implementation of Beta Milestone user stories. You have already seen how the Views module allows you to list content items according to various criteria. One common resource often used by Drupal developers for sorting, filtering, and listing content items is the Drupal Taxonomy system, with its Vocabularies, which may be lists of category terms or a set of tags.

In order to implement the user story "A Workshop Member can browse public pieces and critiques," you are now going to see how to create a Vocabulary, add a lists of terms to it, and then apply one or more terms to each literary piece. Then, using the Views module, you will be creating different kinds of lists of literary pieces, including an interactive filter and tag clouds using the Tagadelic module.

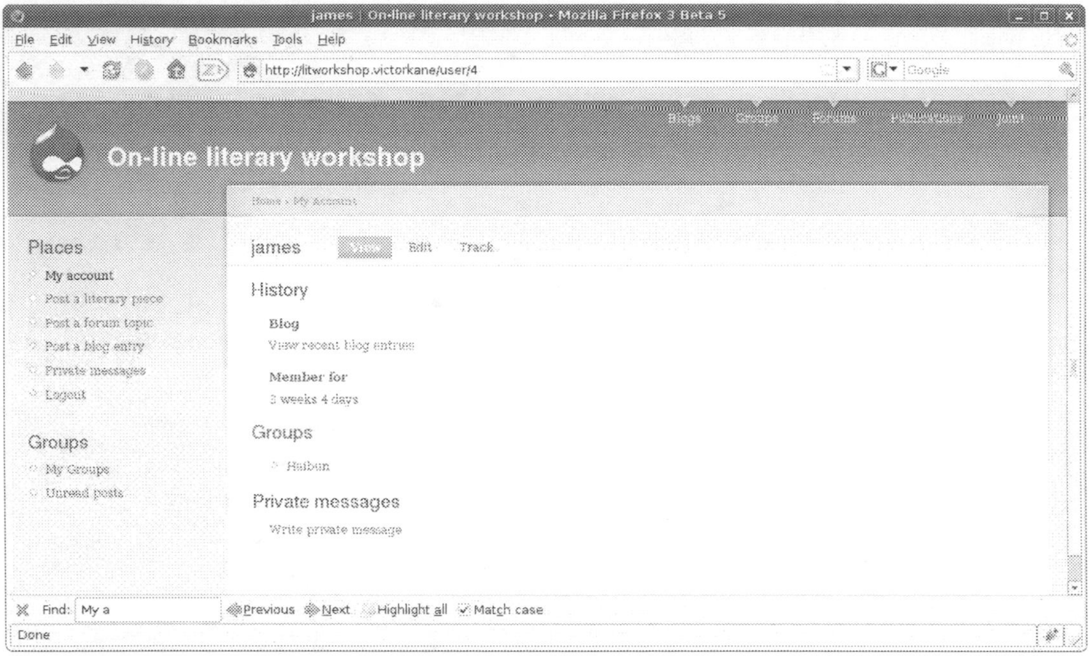


Figure 6-16

## Example: The Beta Milestone

Figure 6-17 shows the one user story not yet implemented for the Beta Milestone: ''A Workshop Member can browse public pieces and critiques.''

So here is what you can do to implement this user story:

1. Create the free-tagging *folksonomy* tagging vocabulary for literary pieces.
2. Create a few literary pieces not designated to any particular private group, created by Workshop Members.
3. Use the Tagadelic module to create a ''tag cloud'' to access literary pieces belonging to a particular category in ''Rivers of News'' format.
4. Create a View to list literary pieces not assigned to any particular private group. Apply filters (i.e., author, tags, date range).
5. Add this View to the Workshop Member Places Navigation menu.
6. Log in as user dev, and go to Administer ➢ Content management ➢ Categories. Here is where you are going to create a Vocabulary to place literary pieces into various categories

and to be able to list and filter them accordingly. Click on the "Add vocabulary" tab, and enter **Tags** in the Vocabulary Name field. Enter **Categories for literary pieces** into the Description field. Select Literary piece as the only Type (content type that will be using these tags). Select the Free-tagging checkbox, and click Submit.

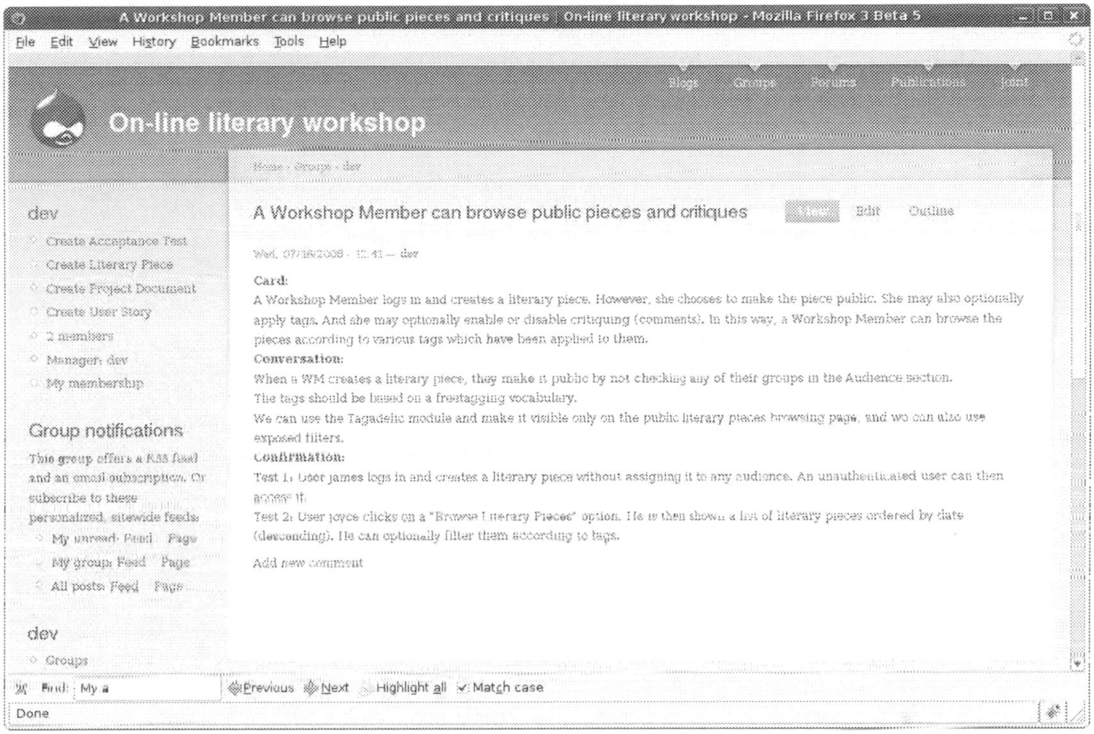


**Figure 6-17**

*The reader should become thoroughly familiar with the extremely powerful Drupal CMS feature, Vocabulary. A good place to start is the Drupal Handbook article, "Taxonomy: A Way to Organize Content"* (`http://drupal.org/handbook/modules/taxonomy`).

7. Now log in as user james, and click on "Post a literary piece" from the Places menu block. Now there is a tag field, just under the Title field. Enter a title, a tag (e.g., Haibun), and a Text. Do not check any audience groups, leaving the post open to the public. Click "Submit."

When you look at the end result (Figure 6-19), you see the tag *Haibun* to the right under the text. This means that there are several literary pieces tagged *Haibun*, and that by clicking on that link, the reader can see all of them together. You can probably immediately detect a problem of a different kind, that being that the desired format for the text (see Edit form in Figure 6-18) is ignored in the end result.

Notice that the formatting is not lost — rather, it "comes back" when you edit the piece. But the view of the text runs all the words together into a single paragraph.

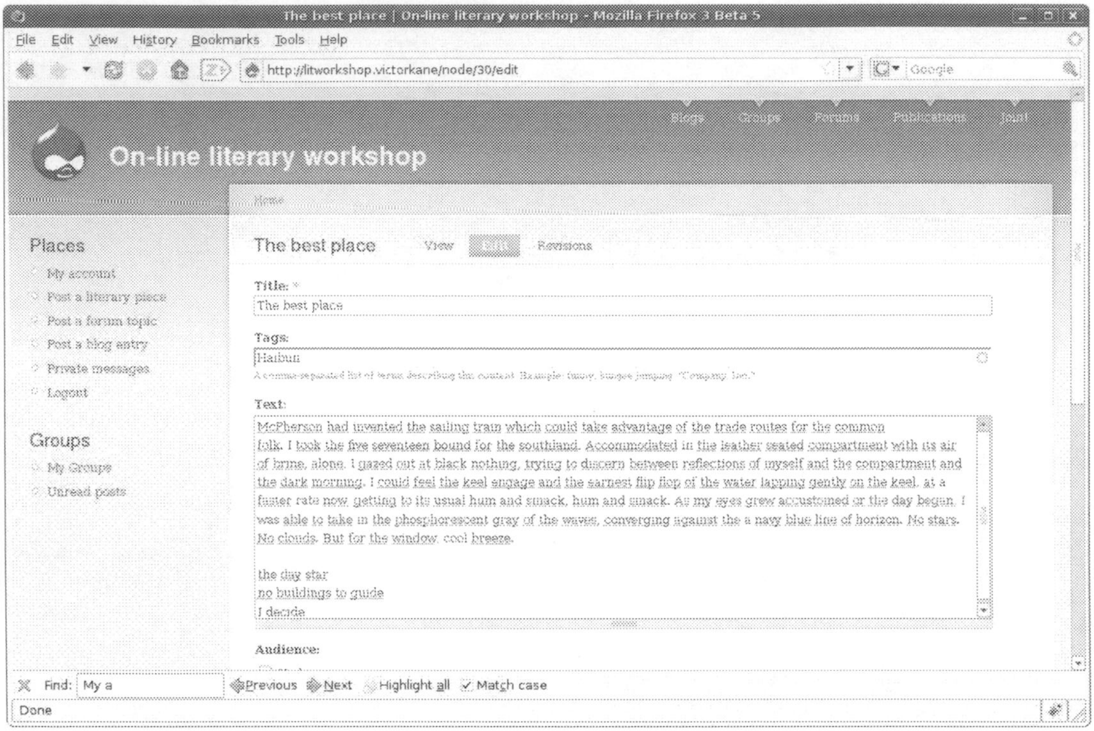


Figure 6-18

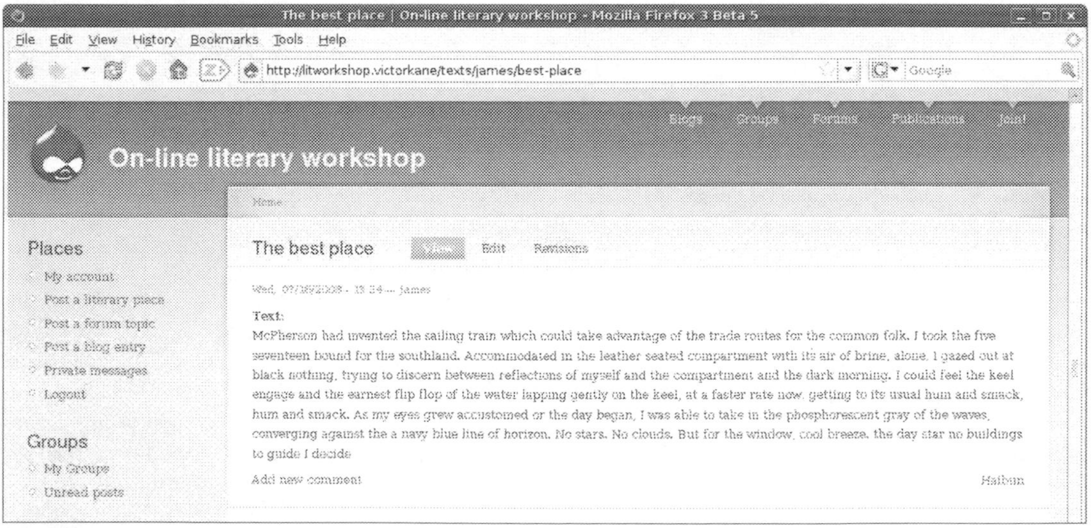


Figure 6-19

## Allowing Filtered HTML Formatting in the Text Area

After investigating for a while to solve this exasperating problem, you will realize that the culprit is the fact that when we created the field for the text, we did not really configure it correctly for a text area. To fix this, follow these steps:

1. Go to Administer ➢ Content management ➢ Content types, and edit the Literary Piece content type.
2. Click on the "Manage fields" tab, and then click on the configure link associated with the field `field_literary_piece_text`. Scrolling down to the Text processing options, you can see that "Plain text" has been selected. That means that when the text is rendered, it is first passed through a filter that strips off new lines and any kind of HTML formatting. This selection is fine for single lines of text and in some other cases, but obviously is not appropriate for literary text.
3. Select "Filtered text" (the user selects the input format). You can do that safely; no data will be affected. Click on the "Save field settings" button.

Now when user james logs in, the problem is automagically resolved. The formatting is now respected. And when he edits the literary piece, more options are visible just below the text field. In fact, they explain what is going on:

```
Web page addresses and e-mail addresses turn into links automatically.
Allowed HTML tags: <a> <em> <strong> <cite> <code> <ul> <ol> <li> <dl> <dt> <dd>
Lines and paragraphs break automatically.
```

Logging back in as user dev, explore this in more detail by going to Administer ➢ Site configuration ➢ Input formats. After carefully reading the information to be found on this page, note the following:

- ❑ Explore how the input formats can be modified by clicking on the configure link for Filtered HTML (the default input format when plain text is not used).
- ❑ Note the filters that make up the input format, and note that the Configure tab allows you to add more HTML tags that can be included.
- ❑ The Rearrange tab allows you to specify the order in which filters are applied as text is processed during the rendering of a content item.

Check out the Drupal Handbook article, "Text Filters and Input Formats" (`http://drupal.org/node/213156`), for more information.

Now go ahead and create two or three literary pieces authored by users james and joyce, and put them into two or three categories by using the tags.

## The Tagadelic Module

Now that tags have been applied to several literary pieces, it would be great to easily access those items by their tags. One way this is commonly accomplished is via a "tag cloud," and in Drupal, you can do this too, using the Tagadelic module.

To do so, first commit (save current state) then use your favorite method for installing the Tagadelic module. I used drush:

```
victorkane@victorkane:~/Work/Wiley/litworkshop$ drush pm install tagadelic
Project tagadelic successfully installed (version 5.x-1.0).
victorkane@victorkane:~/Work/Wiley/litworkshop$
```

Go to Administer ➢ Site building ➢ Blocks, and enable tags in Tags in the left sidebar. Click on the "Save blocks" button. The result can be seen in Figure 6-20.

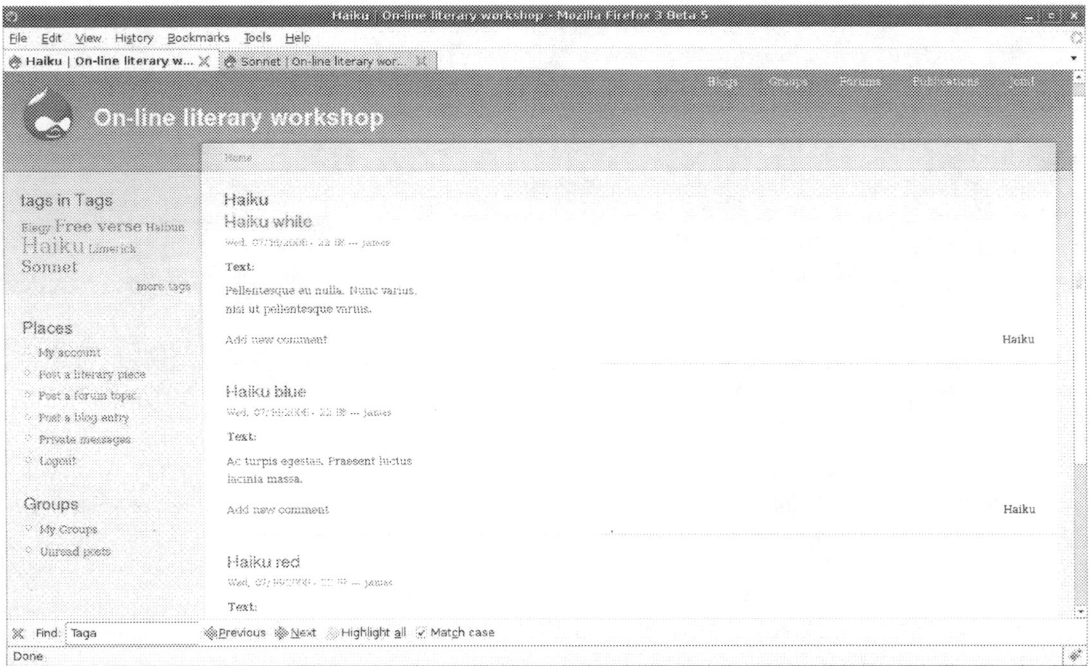

Figure 6-20

Pam says it would be great if it were possible to replace the default title of the *tags in Tags* block with something a little more meaningful to the context. *Genre parade* would do nicely for now. To comply, log in as user dev, and go to Administer ➢ Site building ➢ Blocks. Click on the configure tag corresponding to the *tags in Tags* block. In the Block title field, fill in **Genre parade**, and click on the "Save block" button. Voilá! Commit and deploy.

## Creating the View Itself

The next step is to create a View more convenient for listing that is capable of offering more powerful filtering options. Earlier you modified an existing View to customize the layout of the group home page. You are now going to make a View from scratch. A View is a query generator, and to make it work, you have to provide information about which columns of the database table you wish to include and which search criteria should be invoked to generate the listing. Views also allow you to customize the listings layout and look and feel. And the View not only may be invoked via short snippets of PHP code, but also provides optional block and page renderings. In this case, you are going to use both. Follow these steps:

1. Go to Administer ➤ Site building ➤ Views, and click on the Add tab.
2. Provide a machine-readable name for the view: **genre_browser**. For now, don't select any special access restrictions.
3. Next, add a short description: **Allows the user to browse literary pieces according to genre**.
4. Open the Page section, and select the "Provide Page View" checkbox. Specify a URL for the page: `browse/genre`. For the View Type, select Table View. Type **Browse literary pieces according to genre** in the Title field for the page. Leave the rest of the page items as they are for now at least.
5. Open the Block section. Select the "Provide Block View" checkbox. Here, too, select Table View, and enter **Browse Literary Pieces** as the Title for the block. Put **5** as the maximum number of items to display, and select the More link checkbox.
6. Because you are using the Table View, you need to specify which fields you want displayed as columns in the table. Select Node: Title, and click on the "Add Field" button. Type **Name** in the Label field. Next, add **Taxonomy: Terms for Tags**, and enter **Genre** in the Label field. Then, add the fields **Node: Author name (Label: Author)** and **Node: Updated time (Label: Date)**.
7. Now you just need to specify which content type (node type) you wish displayed; otherwise, all nodes will be displayed. Open the Filters section, and add the Node: Type filter. After clicking on the "Add field" link, select Literary Piece in the Value column. In this way, only nodes of type Literary Piece will be included in the listing.
8. Take a look at what you have up till now. Scroll down to the bottom of the page, and click on the Save button. To view genre_browser in page view first, click the URL `browse/genre`. You should see something similar to Figure 6-21.
9. Two adjustments would be welcome here. Because this is a table view, the number of items per page can be doubled. And the table headings need to be made sortable. Click on the Edit tab, and in the Page section, specify **20** in the "Nodes per Page" field. Then, in the Fields section, select Yes in the Sortable column for Name, Author, and Date.
10. After saving your work, you can now click on the Name, Author, and Date columns to sort the listings table in real time.
11. Now check out the Block View. Go to Administer ➤ Site building ➤ Blocks, and you will see that a new block has appeared, bearing the name *genre_browser*. First, click on the configure link, specify **Browse genre** as the title of the block itself, and click on the "Save block" button. Then enable it for the content region (it's too wide for the left sidebar region, and it is fashionable these days to put navigation blocks at the foot of the page after the page content) with a weight of **1**. Click on the "Save blocks" button.
12. To finish up the current task, you just need to add the View you have tried out onto the Places navigation menu for Workshop Members. To do so, go to Administer ➤ Site building ➤ Menus, and click on the "Add item" link just under the Places heading. Enter **Browse by genre** in the Title field, enter **Browse literary pieces by genre** in the Description field, and enter **browse/genre** (the URL of the page view) in the URL field. Specify a weight of **9**, and click "Submit."

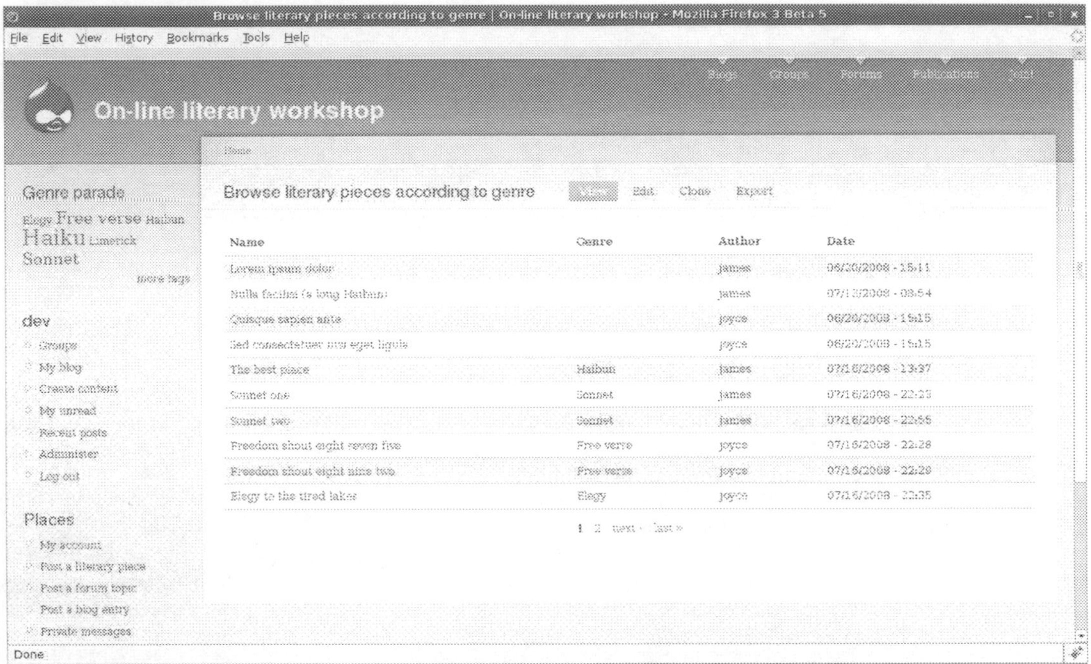

Figure 6-21

13. Now the user can click on the Browse by Genre link in the Places menu, and visualize the listings (20 per page) while the shorter block (first 5 entries) appears on all pages. There is just one thing you need to fix up a little, which is to prevent the block from appearing when the page view does. Go to Administer ➤ Site building ➤ Blocks, click on the configure link corresponding to the genre_browser block, and scroll down to the Page specific visibility settings section. There, select "Show on every page except the listed pages" (the default), and enter **browse/genre** in the Pages text area. While you're at it, add **admin** and **admin/*** on the separate, second, and third lines. Click on the "Save block" button.

    Now, when you select "Browse by genre" from the Places navigation menu, the block ceases to appear, while it does appear on every other page, except administration pages.

14. Commit and deploy.

## *Using Exposed Filters with the View*

The View is fine as far as it goes. The thing is, though, you want to be able to sort what is on the current page in various ways — What if the user would like to filter the content also? Also, this would enable filtering by genre, which does not support real-time sorting.

The solution is to add what the Views module calls *Exposed filters*. To do this, follow these steps:

1. Logged in as user dev, select the page view, and click on the Edit button.
2. Scroll down to the Filters section, and add the following filters under the previously selected Node: Type:

- ❑ Node: Title
- ❑ Taxonomy: Terms for Tags
- ❑ Node: Author Name (for now, select any name to avoid error messages)

3. For each one of these, click on the Expose button.
4. Open the Exposed Filters section, and fill in the Labels: Name, Genre, and Author. And (**important!**) select the checkbox in the Optional column for each of the exposed filters. Click on the Save button. The View will now work with exposed filters. Click on the "Browse by genre" Places navigation menu, and you should see results similar to Figure 6-22, where a search has been made for all the Haikus written by user james whose titles contain the text string *Haiku*.

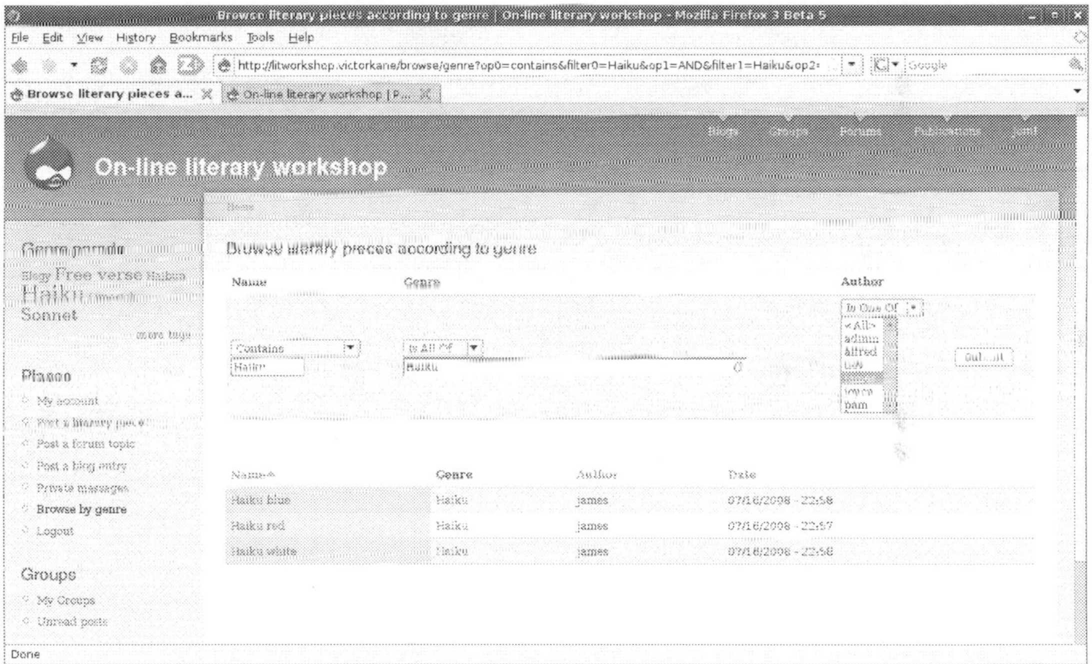


Figure 6-22

# Using Categories and Tag Clouds for Project Management

When you download the chapter tarball, you will see that the author has done the same thing for user stories — creating two vocabularies, one for types of users ("User Stories by Actor"), and another for iterations ("User Stories by Iteration"). Instead of using the free-tagging option, these are single-hierarchy vocabularies to which a fixed, editable series of terms has been added. The "User Stories by Actor" categories, or terms, allow for multiple selections. Explore them by visiting Administer ➢ Content management ➢ Categories, and see how they are used in the various user stories published in the dev group. Two simple Tagadelic module-based tag clouds appear when the dev group home page is visited.

## Summary

In this chapter, you pushed the envelope by adding a large amount of functionality, involving private messaging and affinity groups with their own home page. You also saw the use of the system for project management itself in a variety of ways, something that served admirably as an introduction to the powerful Views module, which complements the Content Construction Kit module you had been using earlier. This module was used to complete the implementation of the user stories corresponding to the Beta Milestone, including a sophisticated listing of literary pieces capable of being sorted and filtered interactively by the site visitor.

In the next chapter, you will explore additional ways of adding functionality, but first and foremost, you will be introduced to the art of becoming an expert Drupal themer in order to give the website application the look and feel desired by the client.

# 7

# Becoming an Expert Drupal Themer

One of the compelling reasons for using Drupal is that it allows you to cleanly override the layout and look and feel of your website, a practice generally referred to as *theming*. This chapter explains how to do this by following "The Drupal Way." By understanding how Drupal renders a page, how the content is passed to the *theming* component of the system, and exactly where and how developers and specialized graphic design people can conveniently affect the final outcome, you can become an expert Drupal themer.

However, our emphasis on theming doesn't mean that we are concerned with graphic design in this chapter. You are not going to come out with a shiny new theme for Drupal here. But you are going to learn how to use existing themes, even bare-bones skeleton themes, and how to use the Drupal theming system to your best advantage.

## On to Theming

So where are we? So far, the following two iterations have been completed:

1. Prototype

    - A Workshop Leader can approve applications to join the workshop.
    - A Workshop Leader can suspend members and publishers.
    - A Workshop Leader can manage affinity groups.
    - A Workshop Leader can broadcast messages to members.
    - A Workshop Leader can do everything Workshop Members and Publishers can do.
    - Clean URLs and automatic generation of SEO friendly paths

2. Beta
    - ❑ A Workshop Member can post literary pieces.
    - ❑ A Workshop Member can make any post public, private, or visible to an affinity group.
    - ❑ A Workshop Member can critique public posts.
    - ❑ A Workshop Member can browse public pieces and critiques.
    - ❑ A Workshop Member can send and receive messages to and from all Members and Publishers and the Workshop Leader.
    - ❑ Create simplified navigation blocks for Workshop Members.

The current iteration is now as follows:

3. Final release
    - ❑ A Workshop Member can start an affinity group with its own forums.
    - ❑ A Workshop Member can post to forums.
    - ❑ A Workshop Member can maintain his or her own literary blog.
    - ❑ A Publisher can browse public content.
    - ❑ A Publisher can broadcast a call for pieces to be submitted for a publication.
    - ❑ A Publisher can select content for inclusion in a publication.
    - ❑ A Publisher can manage an on-line publication.
    - ❑ A Publisher can manage an on-line blog.
4. Initial theming

The last task reflects the fact that in order to launch the site, you need to polish the presentation — have content meet form in an established manner of navigation, searching, layout, color, typography, and look and feel.

It is getting to the point where the architecture and the implementation of the On-Line Literary Workshop have reached a considerable level of complexity.

So here is where the question of theming in Drupal raises its alluring head, and once it is brought in, it will affect the implementation of all other user stories. At this point, you need to deal with it as soon as possible. To get the website done right, your team needs expertise in Drupal theming.

But, what is Drupal theming, precisely?

## Dividing and Conquering Complexity

In July 2006, a team of IBM developers chose to base their ''Using open source software to design, develop, and deploy a collaborative Web site'' project on Drupal, rather than six other Open Source content management solutions. In Part 1 (`www.ibm.com/developerworks/ibm/library/i-osource1`) of what turned out to be a 15-part series (`www.ibm.com/developerworks/ibm/osource/implement.html?S_TACT=105AGX46&S_CMP=LP`), the team explain their reasons for choosing Drupal — then in version 4.7, even though Part 15 of the series covers Drupal 5.x — over its competitors. Although time has passed since then, one of the stringent requirements listed by the team was "separation of presentation and content." With Drupal, they said,

> *The ability to use PHP to move freely between the business logic layer and the presentation layer (using the PHP template engine) was . . . very appealing.*

It is important to understand what is meant here if you wish to leverage "The Drupal Way." Whereas many learned tomes have been written on the subject of multi-tier and layered architecture and the benefits offered by progressive stages of abstraction in the history of software engineering, and justifiably so, perhaps the clearest and simplest exposition for your purposes here is a short article, "Separation: The Web Designer's Dilemma," by Mike Cohen (`www.alistapart.com/articles/separationdilemma`) in May 2004 in *A List Apart*, an important on-line magazine "for people who make websites." The concepts explained in this article are fundamental in understanding why things are the way they are, and rightly so, in the Drupal theming system.

### A Word on Multi-Tier Architecture and Abstraction

Regarding multi-tier, in software applications in general and in website applications and Drupal in particular, there exists a topology of physical layers that share logical responsibility for the work of rendering a page. In the world of software in general, a "three-tier" approach would involve the separation of data persistence, logical processing, and the presentation layer. In website applications, this is embodied in the separation of the database, the web server, and the application logic for which Drupal has responsibility, on the one hand, and then an additional separation within Drupal between the content being marshaled and then being cleanly passed over to a separate procedure specializing in presentation, that is, the layout and look and feel of a requested page. This will be explained more fully in this chapter.

The multi-tier approach itself is based on what is called the *Separation of Concerns*, which divides complicated problems into more manageable and reusable components, which are easier to maintain and scale because they don't interfere with each other. Students of the object-oriented approach will immediately recognize this as an example of the principle of Abstraction. Grady Booch (`www.booch.com/architecture/index.jsp`) sums it up very well in the following words:

> *Software development has been, is, and will likely remain fundamentally hard. To that end, the entire history of software engineering is one of rising levels of abstraction (for abstraction is the primary way we as humans deal with complexity), and we see this reflected in the maturation of our programming languages, platforms, processes, tools, and patterns.*

In distinguishing presentation from structure and content, Cohen writes: "The major reason to separate presentation from the rest of the page is simple: to simplify any change from a slight design adjustment to a full-fledged redesign." The famous CSS Zen Garden (`www.csszengarden.com`) is cited as a starting point, in that the same content is presented in multiple and beautiful ways by changing nothing more than the invoked CSS style sheet. There is a wonderful list of CSS learning resources of all kinds, and in many different languages to boot, at `www.w3.org/Style/CSS/learning`. But you must bear in mind that the ability to use HTML tags "to provide a handle for the designer to apply styles to" is also part of the picture.

"Isolation of content," he adds, "makes adding or updating things easy while maintaining presentational consistency throughout the site." The content includes semantic tags ("like h1-h6, paragraphs, list, em, strong, code, cite, etc.") and "should not require any additional presentational tags or styles in order to fully convey its message."

Structure, then, includes ordered and unordered lists and `<div>` building blocks. But "presentation is pointless without structure. . .[and] it's also pointless to try to separate structure from content." This is because tags like the paragraph tag and heading tags not only set out the structure of a rendered page but also "the browser has a preset way of displaying `<h1>` and `<p>` text, doesn't it?"

This means that presentation necessarily combines layout and style, "which leaves us with . . .presentation and content."

What is fascinating from the point of view of using Drupal as the basis for getting your site done right is what Mike Cohen lays out as "the perfect website separation system":

> *It would store content in a database, allowing the isolation and management of content information. Presentation and structure would be handled together; presentation could be managed with a stylesheet and accompanying structural elements where needed. Structure would best be dealt with through a system of template "packages" built using a server-side scripting language (such as PHP or ASP). Each template "package" could have one or more stylesheets (e.g. CSS Zen Garden), but every template "package" would connect to the same . . .database to retrieve content for display.*

Drupal successfully offers these characteristics: that is what the Drupal theming system is all about, and it is made up of the following:

- ❑ The selected theme engine that interfaces to Drupal core
- ❑ Theme template files written in the corresponding template language
- ❑ Theme style sheets and other theme resources

How does this work? In the following manner: given a semantic element created by Drupal core or a contributed module (say, an image, a block, a link, or a breadcrumb), the module instantiating and controlling the database persistence of that structural element includes a theming function, prefixed, appropriately enough, with the prefix *theme_*. So, for example, you have `theme_image()`, `theme_item_list()`, and `theme_links()` in the component `./includes/theme.inc`, as well as `theme_forum_list()` in the `forum.module`. The wonderful Drupal Documentation folks have provided a list of themeable functions for your use and pleasure; for Drupal 5.x, for example, see `http://api.drupal.org/api/group/themeable/5`. What's that? "Themeable functions"? Well, you see, what you do to modify one of these (e.g., if you don't like the default manner of handling images) is to copy the `theme_image()` function, lock, stock, and barrel (sorry, this isn't OOP, it just acts like it — which is great for our purposes), and you change its name! You stick it in your theme (you'll see an example shortly — your overriding version of the theming function will be placed in a special file called *template.php*) and rename it by replacing the *theme_* prefix with your theme's name. So, here is the default theming function for images for Drupal 5 (see `http://api.drupal.org/api/function/theme_image/5` and tabs for other Drupal releases):

```
<?php

function theme_image($path, $alt = '', $title = '', $attributes = NULL,
                     $getsize = TRUE) {
```

```
    if (!$getsize || (is_file($path) && (list($width, $height, $type,
        $image_attributes) = @getimagesize($path)))) {

      $attributes = drupal_attributes($attributes);

      $url = (url($path) == $path) ? $path : (base_path() . $path);

      return '<img src="' . check_url($url) . '" alt="'
              . check_plain($alt)
  . '" title="' . check_plain($title)
              . '" ' . $image_attributes .
   $attributes . ' />';

    }

  }

  ?>
```

And here, just by way of an example (you will see some working examples for our litworkshop site in a moment), is the "make images square" snippet for an imaginary `newsphoto` theme, from the Drupal Handbook Documentation (from `http://drupal.org/node/21811`):

```
  /**

  * Make images square.

  */

  function newsphoto_image($path, $alt = '', $title = '',
                            $attributes =
  '', $getsize = true) {

    // Always do getimagesize.

    if ($path && (list($width, $height, $type,
        $image_attributes) =
  @getimagesize($path))) {

      //$sizes = _image_get_sizes();
      // To get the below stated IF dynamically filled.

      foreach (_image_get_sizes() as $size) {

        if(in_array($height, $size) ||

           in_array($width, $size) ||

           in_array($height + 1, $size) || // Rounding can cause the
           // displayed to be one pix bigger or smaller then the size in
           // image_get_sizes.

           in_array($width + 1, $size) ||

           in_array($height - 1, $size) ||
           in_array($width - 1, $size)) {
```

```
        // The difference between the real height and the pico height,
        // divided by 2 with a border of 2 pixels.

        $height = round(($size['height'] - $height)/2)+2;

        $width = round(($size['width'] - $width)/2)+4;

        $attributes['style'] .= 'padding:'. $height .'px '. $width .'px;';

        break;

      }

    }

  }

  return '<img src="/' . check_url($path) . '" alt="'
          . check_plain($alt)
. '" title="' . check_plain($title)         . '" ' . $image_attributes .
 drupal_attributes($attributes)
        . '/>';

}

?>
```

As the snippet explains, this function goes in the file template.php in your theme directory, assuming that you are using the default PHPTemplate theme engine in order to override the default mechanism.

So how does that work? To understand that, you need to understand the life cycle of a rendered page and its dynamic structure.

And, of course, to be an expert Drupal themer, you need to comprehend the different kinds of work and levels of expertise corresponding to the different layers and components making up the Drupal theming system spanning the rendering of that page.

So, a typical page is rendered, first, by marshaling its dynamic content from the database, then by structuring it according to a given layout, as specified in your Drupal theme, and finally, it is styled in detail and presented in the browser, again, according to what is specified in your Drupal theme.

## Understanding Dynamic Content

In general terms, what happens when you point your browser at the URL `http://litworkshop.example.com/texts/joyce/elegy-tired-lakes?`

The request is sent by your browser using the HTTP protocol to port 80 of the server in the Internet, whose IP address resolves to `http://litworkshop.example.com`. Assuming that an Apache HTTP server is listening on that port, this server will come to the conclusion that no file exists in the filesystem corresponding to the full URL, and so will search for an index.php or index.html or similar file (according to the Apache configuration) in the document root of the filesystem corresponding to `http://litworkshop.example.com`. There it finds Drupal's index.php file, which it then invokes, handing it the parameter `texts/joyce/elegy-tired-lakes`, effectively telling Drupal to do what it likes with it.

Drupal then goes through its bootstrap, or initiation process, and examines the parameter handed it by the Apache server. It recognizes `texts/joyce/elegy-tired-lakes` as an alias, or synonym, for node/35 (the thirty-fifth content item created in the system) and notes that the operation is not edit, add, or delete, but rather that the request is to view a node.

Given the node ID (35), Drupal loads, or reads, the latest revision of the record from the database and places it into a dynamic node object. It then asks all enabled modules whether they have more data to add before the load process is complete (a module can get in line by implementing the `hook_load` function, which boils down to writing a php function with the name `{name_of_module}_load()`, which adds certain data to the node object.

A similar process then ensues in which those modules that have implemented `hook_nodeapi` and are watching out for the load operation are allowed their moment to add additional data to the node object. The title of the node is then reserved for use as the title of the page being rendered.

Drupal will now apply the appropriate theming function to each structural entity up to and including the node level, by invoking `theme(structual_entity_name, $data_to_output)`. In its inimitable way, very sophisticated support for polymorphism is implemented very simply, thus guaranteeing separation of content from presentation in a highly flexible manner. The convention is to climb up the various theming levels by asking if a theming function is available. When the polymorphic "theme" function is invoked, basically with the type of structural element and the data to be rendered as parameters, Drupal looks on the current theme level to see if there is a theme-level function in existence (`mytheme_image()`). If there is none, it looks to the theme engine, to see if it has a default function. If none is available there, then (and only then) the primitive Drupal theming function itself is called.

> Polymorphism: *"many shapes" for the same thing (for the same name), all bound up in a common interface (see* `http://en.wikipedia.org/wiki/Polymorphism_(computer_science)`*). For Drupal theming, polymorphism is implemented via a series of naming conventions, as explained below.*

So that is why, in order to override how a Drupal image element is rendered, you cut and paste the primitive Drupal `theme_image()` into your theme (e.g., in the template.php file in your newsphoto theme directory), rename it `mytheme_image()`, and have at it! This is all without hacking the default behavior specified in Drupal core, which can be restored or disabled by going to Administer ➢ Site building ➢ Themes and enabling, making default, and configuring any of the themes that come with the standard Drupal release (found in ./themes) or any others you care to download or create yourself (usually placed in ./sites/all/themes).

## Specifying Structure

Drupal comes with the Garland theme enabled by default. How does the Garland theme specify the structure (layout and positioning of structural elements) of the rendered page? Well, actually, you already know a bit about this. Figure 7-1 shows our On-line Literary Workshop in all its structural glory. Notice the shiny new footer message! To include it, go to Administer ➢ Site configuration ➢ Site information, and paste something like the following into the Footer message field:

```
Powered by<a href="http://www.drupal.org" target="_blank"><img src="/images/drupal-
favicon.ico" alt="Drupal rocks!" title="Drupal rocks!" />Drupal</a>
```

You can see that the page consists of several structural elements (each with its own dynamic content) placed in a series of regions (available using the PHPTemplate engine since Drupal 4.7).

You can easily identify these elements and regions if you take a look at the page template file ./themes/garland/page.tpl.php, in the Garland theme directory (see Listing 7-1).

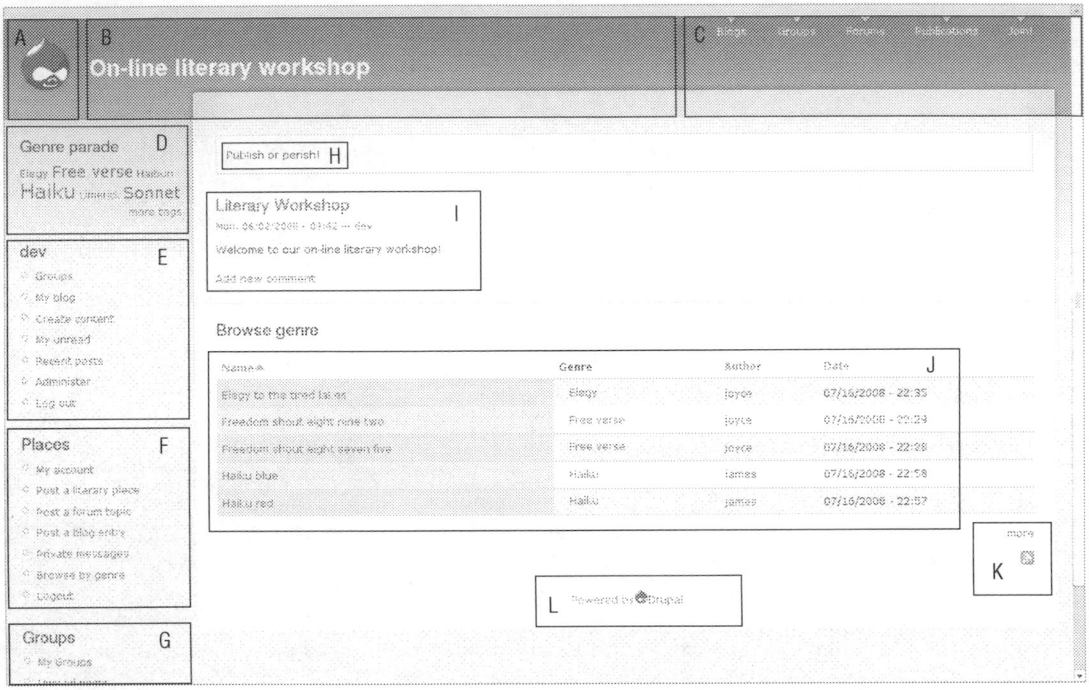


Figure 7-1

**Listing 7-1: The Annotated page.tpl.php (Garland) page template.**

The DOCTYPE (document type declaration) says "XHTML 1.0 Strict, Transitional, Frameset" and has a proper non-relative link to www.w3.org

```
<!DOCTYPE html PUBLIC "-//W3C//DTD XHTML 1.0 Strict//EN"
  "http://www.w3.org/TR/xhtml1/DTD/xhtml1-strict.dtd">
```

xmlns attribute required in XHTML; standard attribute lang sets the language code

```
<html xmlns="http://www.w3.org/1999/xhtml" xml:lang="<?php print $language ?>"
lang="<?php print $language ?>">
```

$head_title for dynamic content of title tag

```
  <head>
    <title><?php print $head_title ?></title>
```

HTML generated by the theme for the head tag, with Drupal core and enabled modules having their chance to add in whatever is necessary

```
    <?php print $head ?>
```

Invocation of all CSS styles and Javascript inclusions, again with each module getting their chance to alter things.

```
    <?php print $styles ?>
    <?php print $scripts ?>
```

The theme adds in its print media stylesheet.

```
    <style type="text/css" media="print">@import "<?php print base_path() .
path_to_theme() ?>/print.css";</style>
    <!--[if lt IE 7]>
```

```
    <style type="text/css" media="all">@import "<?php print base_path() .
path_to_theme()
?>/fix-ie.css";</style>
    <![endif]-->
  </head>
```

Special classes added to body tag as handles for designer styling.

```
  <body<?php print phptemplate_body_class($sidebar_left, $sidebar_right); ?>>
```

The layout nitty gritty.

```
<!-- Layout -->
```

The header is printed out, the first region to be dealt with, including the blocks enabled for that region.

```
  <div id="header region" class="clear-block"><?php print $header; ?></div>

    <div id="wrapper">
    <div id="container" class="clear-block">

      <div id="header">
        <div id="logo-floater">
        <?php
          // Prepare header
          $site_fields = array();
          if ($site_name) {
            $site_fields[] = check_plain($site_name);
          }
          if ($site_slogan) {
            $site_fields[] = check_plain($site_slogan);
          }
          $site_title = implode(' ', $site_fields);
          $site_fields[0] = '<span>'. $site_fields[0] .'</span>';
          $site_html = implode(' ', $site_fields);

          if ($logo || $site_title) {                // element "A"
```

The logo ("A") and site title ("B") are displayed in the header if enabled.

```
            print '<h1><a href="'. check_url($base_path) .'" title="'. $site_title
.'">';
            if ($logo) {
              print '<img src="'. check_url($logo) .'" alt="'. $site_title .'"
d="logo"
/>';                                         // element "B"
            }
            print $site_html .'</a></h1>';
          }
        ?>
        </div>
```

The primary ("C") and secondary menus are displayed if enabled.

```
        <?php if (isset($primary_links)) : ?>
          <?php print theme('links', $primary_links, array('class' => 'links primary-
links')) ?>
        <?php endif; ?>
        <?php if (isset($secondary_links)) : ?>
          <?php print theme('links', $secondary_links, array('class' => 'links
secondary-
```

```
links')) ?>
        <?php endif; ?>

      </div> <!-- /header -->
```

```
The left sidebar is displayed, containing those blocks ("D-E-F-G") enabled for
this region.
```

```
      <?php if ($sidebar_left): ?>
        <div id="sidebar-left" class="sidebar">
          <?php if ($search_box): ?><div class="block block-theme"><?php print
$search_box ?></div><?php endif; ?>
          <?php print $sidebar_left ?>
        </div>
      <?php endif; ?>

      <div id="center">
        <div id="squeeze">
          <div class="right-corner">
            <div class="left-
corner">
```

```
The breadcrumb (not shown on front page).
```

```
          <?php if ($breadcrumb): print $breadcrumb; endif; ?>
```

```
The mission statement ("H").
```

```
          <?php if ($mission): print '<div id="mission">'. $mission .'</div>';
endif; ?>
```

```
The tabs (View | Edit | etc.) (not shown on the front page or for non-
authenticated users) and the Title for the content.
```

```
          <?php if ($tabs): print '<div id="tabs-wrapper" class="clear-block">';
endif;
?>
          <?php if ($title): print '<h2'. ($tabs ? ' class="with-tabs"' : '') .'>'.
$title .'</h2>'; endif; ?>
          <?php if ($tabs): print $tabs .'</div>'; endif; ?>
          <?php if (isset($tabs2)): print $tabs2; endif; ?>
```

```
On some pages a help text is shown.
```

```
          <?php if ($help): print $help; endif; ?>
```

```
Info area for system messages (when content is saved, for example, or if
obligatory fields are missing on forms).
```

```
          <?php if ($messages): print $messages; endif; ?>
```

```
The content itself! ("I")
```

```
          <?php print $content ?>
          <span class="clear"></span>
```

```
RSS Feed icons ("K") for content (main site feed since this is front page).
```

```
          <?php print $feed_icons ?>
```

```
The footer ("L").
```

```
          <div id="footer"><?php print $footer_message ?></div>
      </div></div></div></div> <!-- /.left-corner, /.right-corner, /#squeeze,
/#center -->
```

The right sidebar is displayed, containing those blocks enabled for this region.

```
      <?php if ($sidebar_right): ?>
        <div id="sidebar-right" class="sidebar">
          <?php if (!$sidebar_left && $search_box): ?><div class="block block-
theme"><?php print $search_box ?></div><?php endif; ?>
          <?php print $sidebar_right ?>
        </div>
      <?php endif; ?>

    </div> <!-- /container -->
  </div>
<!-- /layout -->
```

This contains any HTML which a module wants to include just before the closing body tag. Useful sometimes for javascript and for placing certain CSS id's and classes.

```
  <?php print $closure ?>
  </body>
</html>
```

In this way, structural elements are positioned in a given layout and printed out as the content of certain variables. For a complete list of variables available in the page.tpl.php template, see `http://drupal.org/node/11812`.

To see the various regions available, simply go to Administer ➢ Site building ➢ Blocks, which is where you enabled the views-generated `genre_browser` block in the Content region. See Figure 7-2.

Now, how are these regions created, exactly, and what determines their layout? Well, a few things, which are related in the following sections.

## Creating Additional Regions

The default regions are defined in the PHPTemplate theme engine itself (other theme engines, much less commonly used, may or may not support regions, but PHPTemplate is the default and the most often used), specifically in the following snippet taken from around line 20 from the file ./home/victorkane/Work/Wiley/litworkshop/themes/engines/phptemplate/:

```
/**
 * Declare the available regions implemented by this engine.
 *
 * @return
 *  An array of regions. The first array element will be used as the default
region for
 themes.
 */
function phptemplate_regions() {
  return array(
       'left' => t('left sidebar'),
       'right' => t('right sidebar'),
       'content' => t('content'),
       'header' => t('header'),
       'footer' => t('footer')
  );
}
```

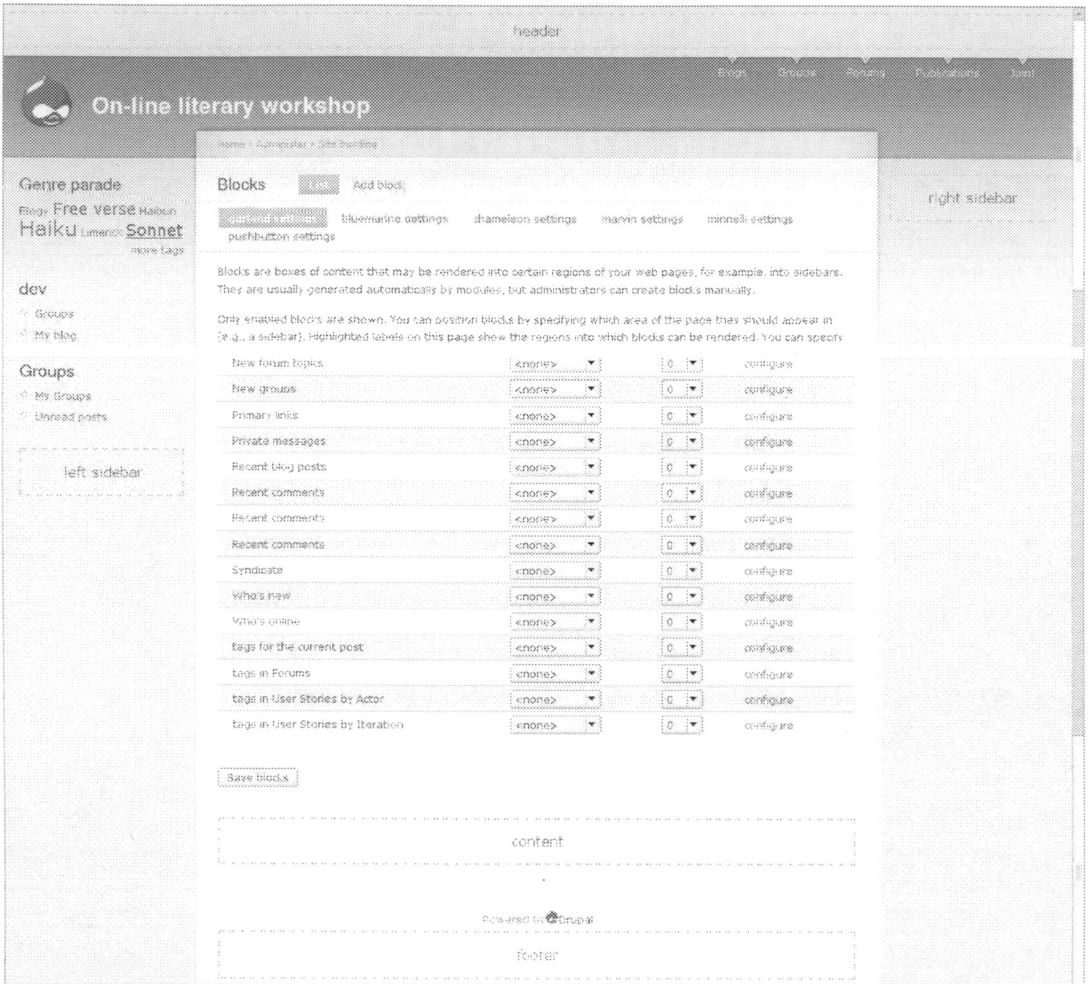


Figure 7-2

Now, if you want to add custom regions, you edit this file, right? Wrong! You override the regions with your own definition, in your own theme. Honoring the same self-styled ''Drupal Way'' polymorphism based on naming conventions, as seen in the case of theming functions, the theme can override the specification of regions by copying it and pasting it into the file template.php, and renaming the function with the name of the theme as prefix.

Let's do that keeping in mind that you don't want to go hacking the Garland theme shipped with the system either. The best practice is to copy the whole theme directory and rename it as your very own.

Copy the Garland theme (`./themes/garland`) to a suitable directory in our own versioned project area, for example, ./sites/all/themes/litgarland. Either copy the Garland theme directory directly, or do the following, as a quick and dirty way of copying and doing away with all the CVS subdirectories (if you checked out Drupal core from the Drupal CVS repository, as recommended, so as to upgrade more easily):

```
victorkane@victorkane:~/litworkshop/themes$ cp -R garland ../sites/all/themes/
victorkane@victorkane:~/litworkshop/sites/all/themes$ mv garland litgarland
victorkane@victorkane:~/litworkshop/sites/all/themes$ find litgarland \( \( -name
CVS -type d \) -o -name .cvsignore \) -exec rm -rf {} \;
```

Let's switch over to our very own newly created Garland-based `litgarland` theme by logging in as user dev, going to Administer ➤ Site building ➤ Themes, and enabling and finally making it default and hitting the "Save configuration" button, as shown in Figure 7-3.

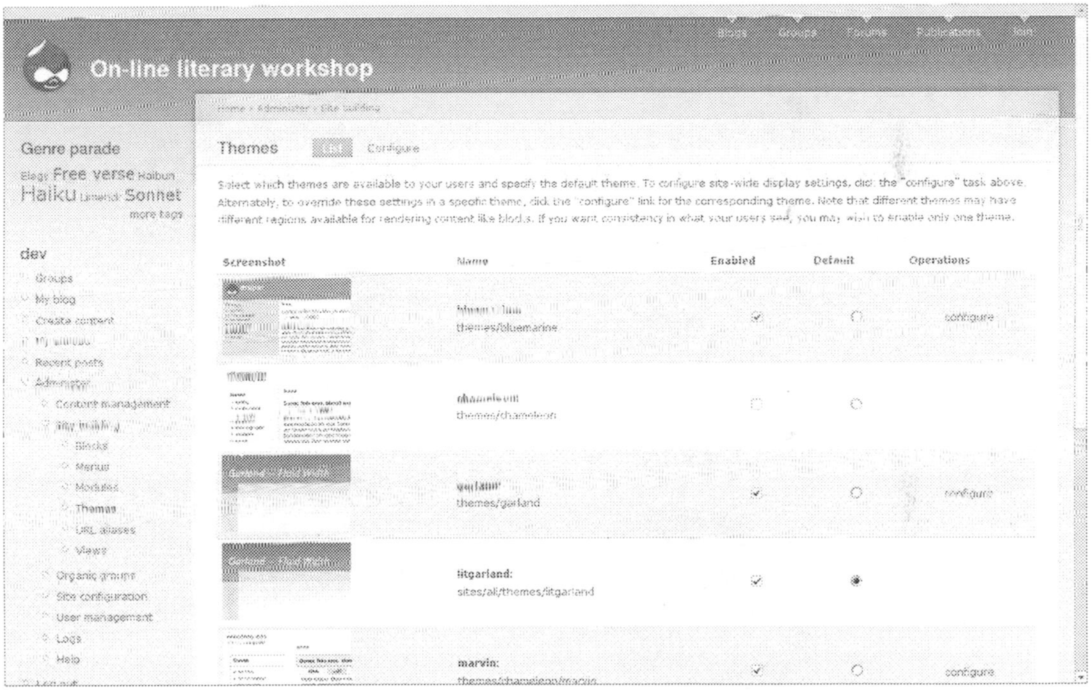


Figure 7-3

Well, nothing much has changed, but you can change that right away by interactively picking a color. Pam was talking about Royal Blue the last time we mentioned the question of color scheme, so do the following:

1. Go to a color scheme site, such as the "[ws] Color Scheme Generator" (`http://wellstyled.com/tools/colorscheme2/index-en.html`), and specify Royal Blue (**#3333FF**) after clicking on "Enter RGB." Nice. That gives you a four-color coordinated scheme: #5050FF, #3838B3, #D3D3FF, and #A7A7FF.
2. After clicking on the "Reduce to 'safe' colors "checkbox, you get #6666FF, #3333CC, #CCC-CFF, and #9999FF.

3. Now, in Drupal, click on the Configure link corresponding to the `litgarland` theme, and you will be taken to the configuration screen for `litgarland`, as seen in Figure 7-4. W00t! An interactive color picker (courtesy of Steve Wittens, coauthor of the theme; see `http://drupal.org/node/91964` for details on the Garland theme and its features)!

4. I put **#3333CC** as both the Base color and the Link color, **#6666FF** for the Header top, and **#CCCCFF** for the Header bottom. Then, I entered my favor Text color **#444444** and clicked on the "Save configuration" button. Now, graphic design is not my strong suit, so you might want to pick one of the 15 garish-to-subtle pre-defined Color sets. The interesting thing is that, when you list all the themes, the new color scheme shows up as the theme preview! Very cool.

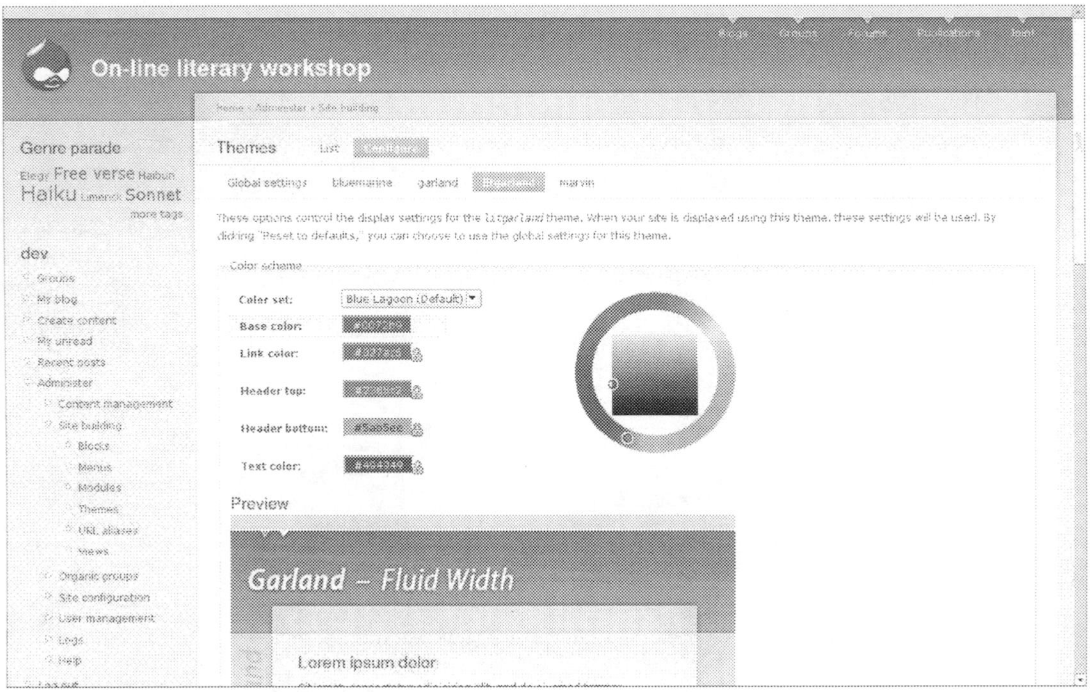


Figure 7-4

## *Adding a Quote Region*

So let's add our own region. Pam has mentioned that she would like a "quote of the day from a famous author" for all pages except the front page, and that it should go where the front-page Mission statement goes.

Well, there is a Quotes module (`http://drupal.org/project/quotes`) that looks active and cool, and that generates blocks. But, hey, roll your own by listing a random quote with a nodequeue. The Nodequeue module is also part of the quiet revolution of modules revolutionizing Drupal (CCK, Views 2, Panels 2, Nodequeue, OG, etc., etc., etc.):

1. Create a content type for the quotes so that Pam can create some of them herself. To make this Agile, instead of making one of the fields of type text, you can create a new free-tagging

multiple-select Vocabulary called *Authors*. So create a content type called *Quote*, using the title field itself for the quote (change the label to *Quote*), and use the default body field for a description and background (change the label to *Background*).

2. Deselect "Promoted to front page" (because even though you want it on the front page, you don't want it as a node but, rather, as part of a block inside our new region), and select "Create New Revision."
3. Disable comments, and make it non-postable to any group. This should be fine for what Pam is looking for. (The content type is included in the downloadable material for this chapter, both as part of the Drupal instance and as an exported content type.)
4. To create the Authors vocabulary so that terms ("authors") can be selected for various quotes, go to Administer ➤ Content management ➤ Categories, and click "Add vocabulary." For the vocabulary name, enter **Authors**. Enter **Authors of quotes, as used in quote of the day** in the description field. Enter **Multiple authors can be selected** in the Help text field. Select Quote as the only Type that authors can be applied to (so while creating or modifying a Quote, the dropdown selection box will appear for authors).
5. Finally, select the "Free tagging," "Multiple select," and "Required" checkboxes, and press the Submit button.

I ran into a problem after creating my first quote, though. The URL was `http://litworkshop.victorkane/content/i-love-deadlines-i-whooshing-sound-they-make-they-fly`. But I would like the word *content* to be replaced by *quote*, so that all my quotes are recognizable right in the URL. To fix this, go to Administer ➤ Site configuration ➤ Pathauto, and open up the Node path settings section. In the "Pattern for all Quote paths" field, enter

```
content/[title-raw]
```

After re-editing, the result should look like Figure 7-5.

So create a few more quotes, just to get the ball rolling. What is cool is that when you reuse an author, you get an automatic dropdown selection list as soon as you type in the first couple of letters in the Author field. That's because in free-tagging vocabularies, the automatic completion widget is used. Figure 7-6 shows this when I added my second Brian Aldiss quote.

Then create a quick View to simply list all your quotes on a page:

1. Go to Administer ➤ Site building ➤ Administer views, click on the Add tab, and enter **quotes** into the Name field.
2. Put **List all quotations** into the Description field. Open up the Page section, select the "Provide Page View" checkbox, and enter **valist-quotes** into the URL field. Select "List View" for View Type.
3. Now open up the Fields section, and add the Node title and Taxonomy Terms for Authors.
4. Next, open the Filters section, and add a Node-type filter. Specify that "Node: Type" *Is One Of* **Quote**. Click "Save."
5. Click on the list-quotes link, and you should see something like Figure 7-7.

Now, because the idea is to create a new region and to stick a random quote in it on every page except the front one, you need to do two things: create the block, then create the region and stick the block there.

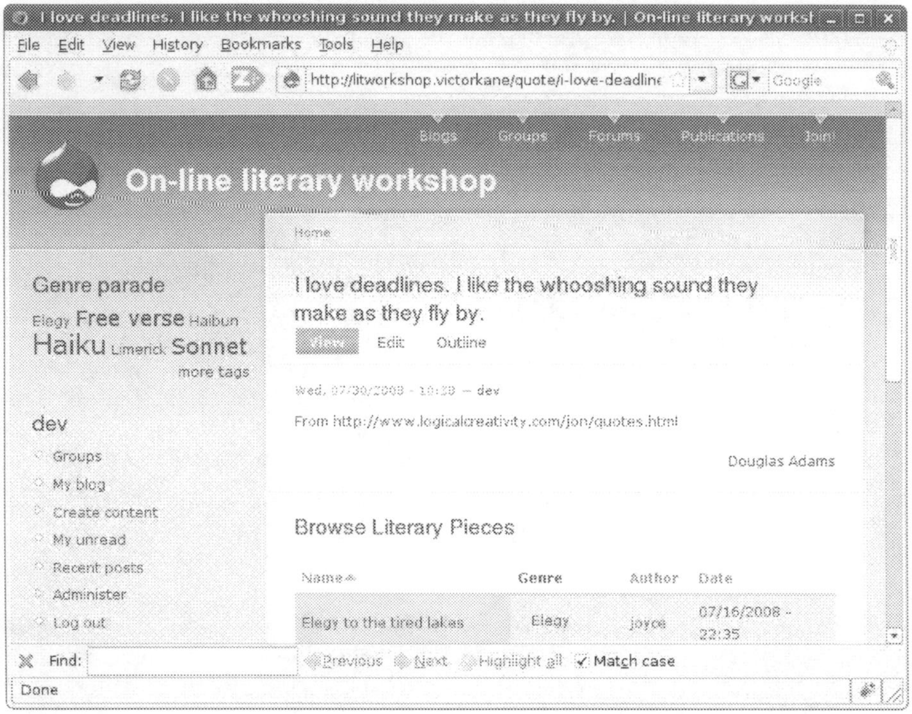


Figure 7-5

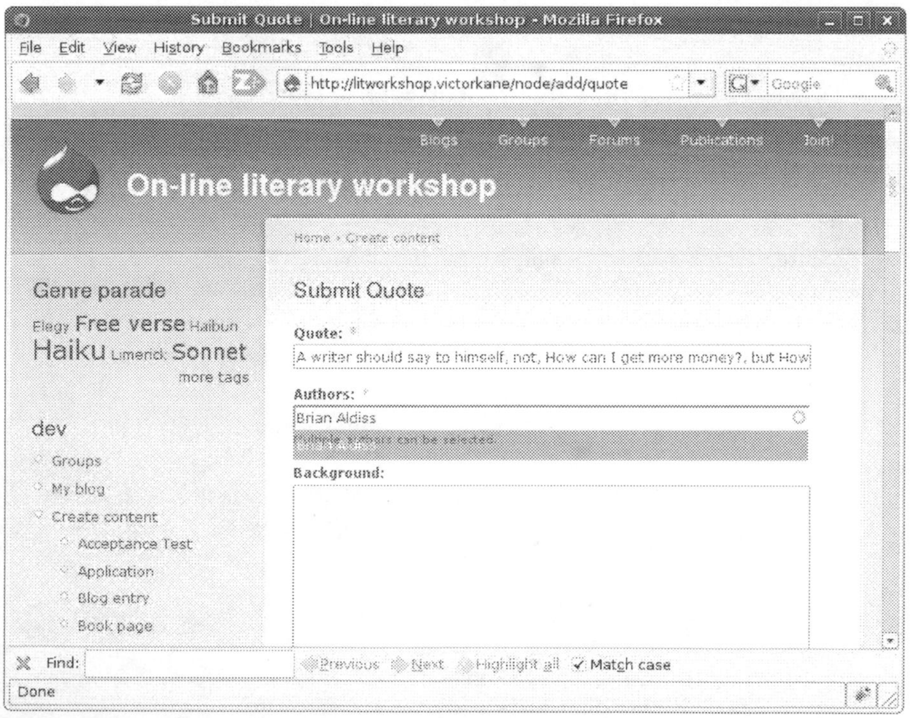


Figure 7-6

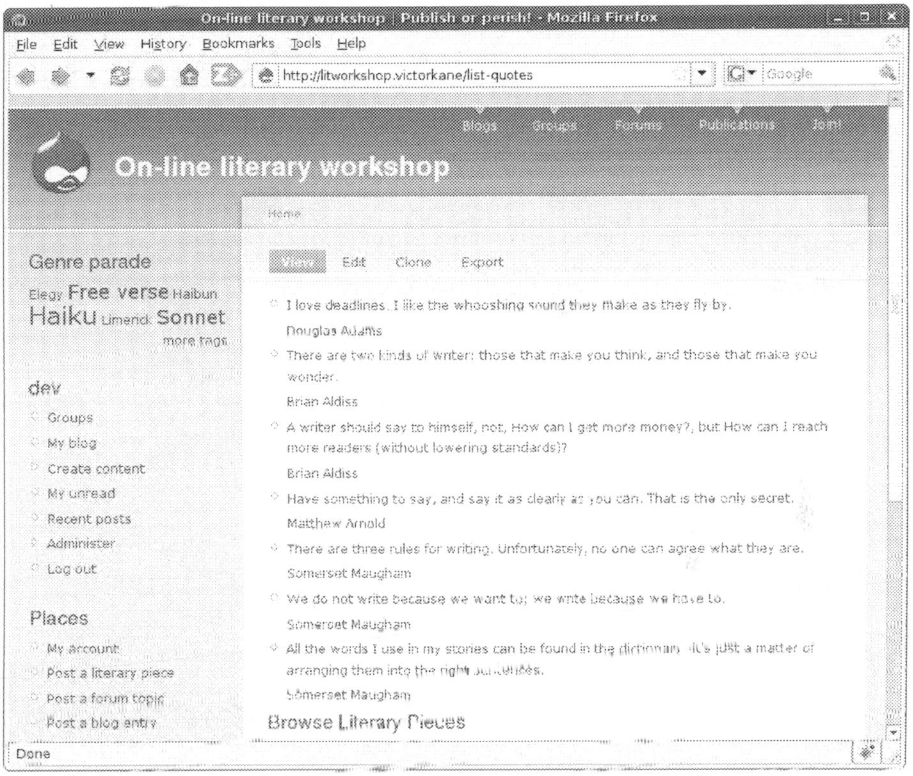


Figure 7-7

## Populating the Quote Region with a Custom Block

First, then, you need the Nodequeue module. You can install it by using the methods presented in earlier chapters, or your own favorite. I used Drush in the following way:

```
victorkane@victorkane:~/litworkshop$ drush pm install nodequeue --svnsync
                                                                  --
svncommit
Project nodequeue successfully installed (version 5.x-2.2).
Project committed to Subversion successfully
victorkane@victorkane:~/litworkshop$
```

Next you follow these steps:

1. Go to Administer ➢ Site building ➢ Modules, and enable the module. Now go to Administer ➢ User management ➢ Access control, assign administer nodequeue permissions to the Admin role, and manipulate all queues and manipulate queues permissions to both the Admin and Workshop Leader roles.
2. Now to create the block containing a single random quote, go to Administer ➢ Content management ➢ Node queue, and hit the "Add node queue" tab.
3. In the Title field, enter **Random Quotation**, then use **0** as the Queue Size (no limit). Inside the "Link for 'add to queue' Text" field, type **Add this quote**. Similarly, for the field called "Link For 'remove from queue' Text," enter **Remove this quote** entry.

4. Enable the appropriate roles so you can add nodes to the queue, and select "Quote" as the type of node to be added to the queue. Click on the Submit button. The queue has now been created. [If the Nodequeue module has just been installed, be sure to visit Administer ➢ User management ➢ Permissions (Access Control in Drupal 5), and grant permission to manipulate queues.]
5. Now, at Administer ➢ Content management ➢ Node queue ➢ View (tab), use the automatic-completion (thank goodness) "Select title to add field" to add all your quote nodes to the queue. Or, as you add quotes, once you create them, you can click on the Node Queue tab that now appears alongside the View, Edit, and other node access tags, and then click the "Add to queue" link for the Random Quotation nodequeue.
6. Go to Administer ➢ Site building ➢ Blocks, and click on the "Add block" tab. Enter **Random Quotation** in the "Block description," and the following PHP code exactly as written into the Block body (it simply instructs the Nodequeue module to fetch a random content item from nodequeue 1, which we have just created):

   ```
   <?php print nodequeue_fetch_random(1); ?>
   ```

7. Open the Input format section just below the text area, and select the PHP code input format (otherwise the PHP will not get executed). Then click on the "Save Block" button. You will now see the Random Quotation block listed with the other disabled blocks.
8. For texting purposes, enable the block in the header region, and click on "Save Blocks."

Now, every time you refresh your browser, you'll get a different quote in the header region. It's not where you want it, and it's not formatted like you want it, but it works! Great start.

## Enabling the Block in a New Region

In a moment, you will see various ways to control the formatting. For now, the objective is to create a new region on the page and enable this block there.

To register the new block, you need to copy the following code from ./litworkshop/themes/engines/phptemplate/phptemplate.engine:

```
/**
 * Declare the available regions implemented by this engine.
 *
 * @return
 *   An array of regions. The first array element will be used as the default
 *   region for
 themes.
 */
function phptemplate_regions() {
  return array(
       'left' => t('left sidebar'),
       'right' => t('right sidebar'),
       'content' => t('content'),
       'header' => t('header'),
       'footer' => t('footer')
  );
}
```

and paste it at the end of the ./litworkshop/sites/all/themes/litgarland/template.php file, then modify it as follows (note change to function name):

```
function litgarland_regions() {
  return array(
       'left' => t('left sidebar'),
       'right' => t('right sidebar'),
       'content' => t('content'),
       'content_top' => t('content top'),
       'header' => t('header'),
       'footer' => t('footer')
  );
}
```

This means that the region "content top" will now be made available to the page template as the variable `$content_top`. So now, when you go to Administer ➤ Site building ➤ Blocks, you are able to directly assign the Random Quotation block to the newly created content top region for the `litgarland` theme!

Do so, and hit "Save blocks." Of course, the immediate result is for the block to disappear completely because nowhere is it specified where the region should be positioned. You saw earlier in the Annotated page.tpl.php file how the HTML generated for the `$header`, `$footer`, `$content`, and other regions are positioned. So you now need to do the same for `$content_top`!

Around line 66 of ./litworkshop/sites/all/themes/litgarland/page.tpl.php, simply specify this with a single PHP statement, just below the printing of the breadcrumb and mission elements, as follows:

```
          <?php if ($breadcrumb): print $breadcrumb; endif; ?>
          <?php if ($mission): print '<div id="mission">'. $mission .\
'</div>'; endif; ?>
          <?php print $content_top ?>
```

The block will now appear just before the title of the current node, so if you log off, and visualize `/texts/james/sonnet-two`, every time you refresh the browser, you will get a random quotation just above the content item. You should be seeing something similar to Figure 7-8.

# Specifying Style

The layout specification is completed in the layout section of the style.css style sheet, which separates out styling important for this aspect of presentation, as opposed to typography, the color scheme, and similar styling specifications.

In practically all themes, these will generally be found in a separate style sheet called *style.css*. A notable exception is the Zen theme, as you will see shortly, which names this style sheet with the name of the theme or subtheme. (This is explained in an explanatory `style.css` stub.) The Zen theme also sports a separate layout.css file, so that people with different skill sets can edit different files and thus lessen the possibility of a web designer breaking the layout.

In terms of styling, before you get to styling the quotation, see if you can fix the footer a little; if you look at it (see Figure 7-9), the image is really too close to the words and needs a little padding out. You can give it a color background, too.

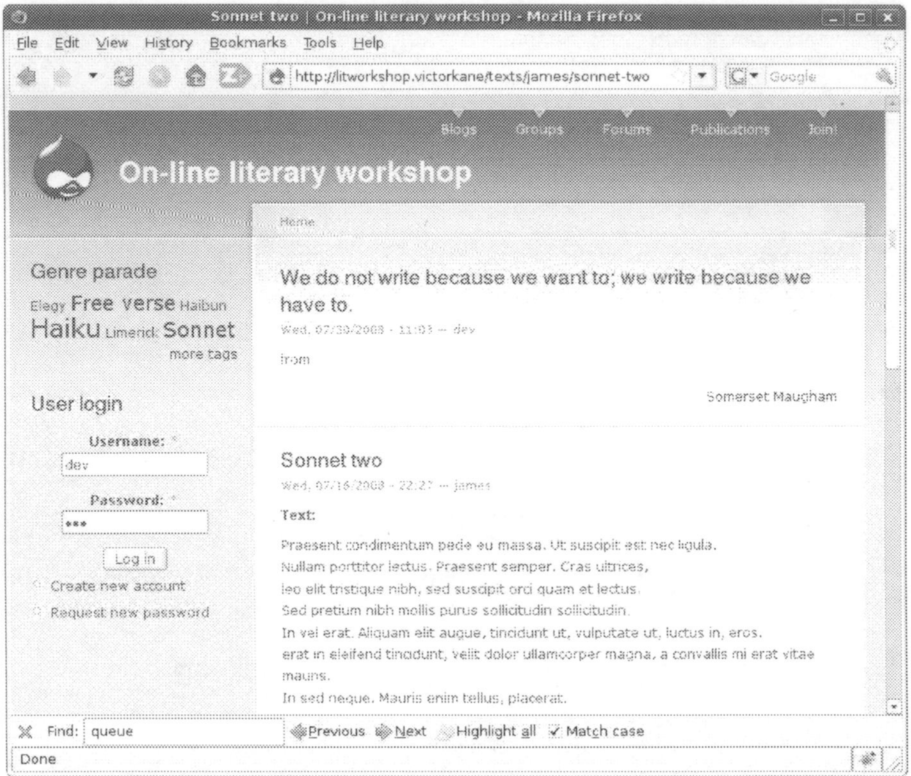

Figure 7-8

A very useful, indeed, invaluable tool for quickly analyzing how to do this is the Firebug add-on for the Firefox browser (install at `https://addons.mozilla.org/en-US/firefox/addon/1843`). Figure 7-9 shows an inspection of the Drupal icon image in the footer, giving a fair number of clues on how you should modify the style sheet to pad out the image.

You can see that the link is enclosed in #footer id, so to pad out the icon a little so that it isn't so close to the words surrounding it, add in the following CSS code at the end of the theme's style.css file:

```
/* footer image formatting */
#footer a img {
  padding: 0 5px;
}
```

Figure 7-10 shows the results of these efforts.

Now, the next step is to theme the Random Quotation block, but beforehand, in order to really leverage Drupal, and to do it right, you need to select and reuse a solid theming platform. In the following section, you do this by standing on the shoulders of giants.

## Synching Your Work with the Repository and the Test Site

At this point, you have installed the Nodequeue module, created a region, and used it. If you haven't synched your work recently, now's the time.

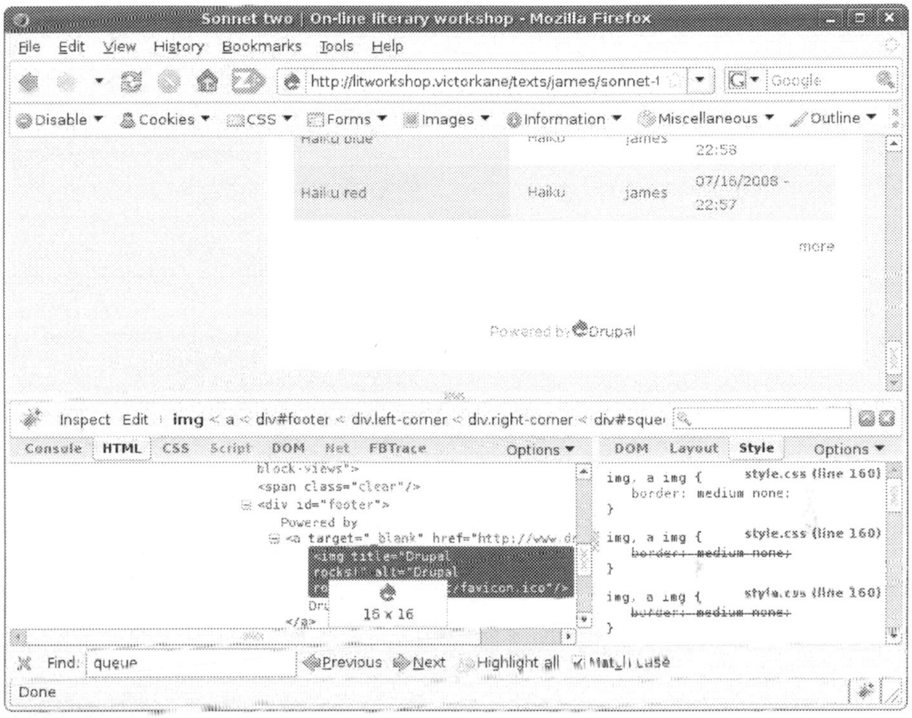


Figure 7-9

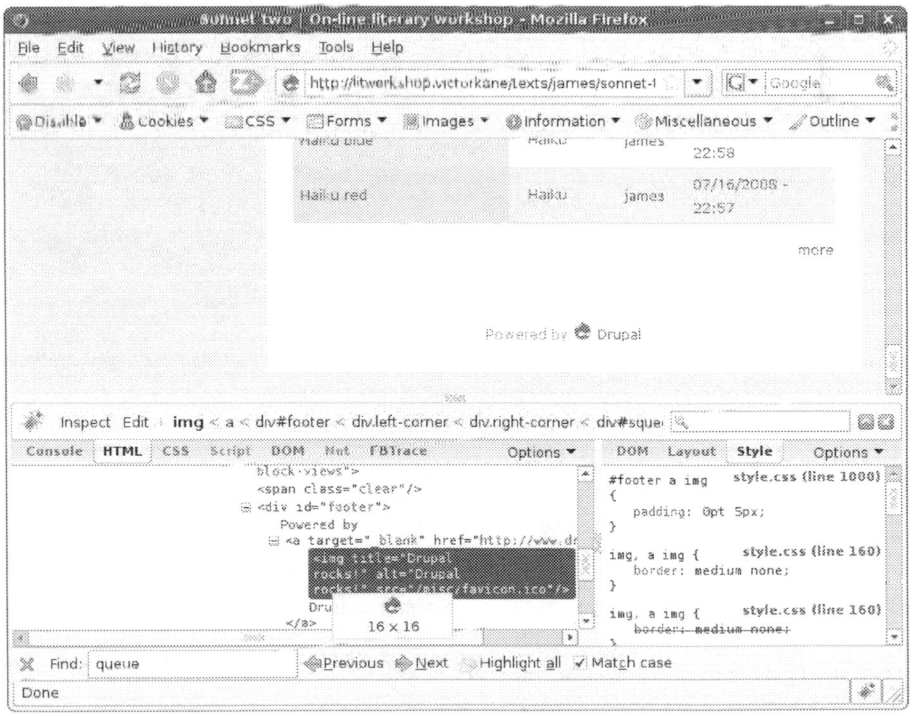


Figure 7-10

Go to ./sites in your workstation, and find out the status of the SVN working copy (notice the shorthand "svn st" used in place of "svn status"):

```
victorkane@victorkane:~/litworkshop/sites$ svn st
?       CVS
?       default/settings.php
?       default/CVS
?       all/CVS
?       all/themes/litgarland
victorkane@victorkane:~/litworkshop/sites$
```

If you had Drush install the Nodequeue module and commit this change to the repository, there is nothing to do there. But you need to synch the database changes, and Drush does not install themes, so you will have to add the new `litgarland` theme to the repository yourself. Do the following:

```
victorkane@victorkane:~/litworkshop/sites$ cd ..
victorkane@victorkane:~/litworkshop$ drush sql dump >\
sites/all/backup/db/litworkshop.sql
victorkane@victorkane:~/litworkshop$ cd sites
victorkane@victorkane:~/litworkshop/sites$ svn add \
all/themes/litgarland/
A          all/themes/litgarland
A   (bin)  all/themes/litgarland/logo.png
A          all/themes/litgarland/style.css
A          all/themes/litgarland/comment.tpl.php
A          all/themes/litgarland/images
A   (bin)  all/themes/litgarland/images/bg-navigation.png
A   (bin)  all/themes/litgarland/images/bg-content-left.png
A   (bin)  all/themes/litgarland/images/bg-navigation-item.png
A   (bin)  all/themes/litgarland/images/bg-content-right.png
A   (bin)  all/themes/litgarland/images/bg-content.png
A   (bin)  all/themes/litgarland/images/bg-navigation-item-hover.png
A   (bin)  all/themes/litgarland/images/bg-bar.png
A   (bin)  all/themes/litgarland/images/body.png
A   (bin)  all/themes/litgarland/images/bg-bar-white.png
A   (bin)  all/themes/litgarland/images/menu-expanded.gif
A   (bin)  all/themes/litgarland/images/bg-tab.png
A   (bin)  all/themes/litgarland/images/menu-leaf.gif
A   (bin)  all/themes/litgarland/images/menu-collapsed.gif
A   (bin)  all/themes/litgarland/images/gradient-inner.png
A          all/themes/litgarland/node.tpl.php
A          all/themes/litgarland/block.tpl.php
A          all/themes/litgarland/template.php
A          all/themes/litgarland/print.css
A          all/themes/litgarland/fix-ie.css
A   (bin)  all/themes/litgarland/screenshot.png
A          all/themes/litgarland/minnelli
A   (bin)  all/themes/litgarland/minnelli/logo.png
A          all/themes/litgarland/minnelli/style.css
A   (bin)  all/themes/litgarland/minnelli/screenshot.png
A          all/themes/litgarland/minnelli/color
A   (bin)  all/themes/litgarland/minnelli/color/base.png
A          all/themes/litgarland/minnelli/color/color.inc
```

```
A  (bin)  all/themes/litgarland/minnelli/color/preview.png
A         all/themes/litgarland/color
A  (bin)  all/themes/litgarland/color/base.png
A         all/themes/litgarland/color/preview.css
A         all/themes/litgarland/color/color.inc
A  (bin)  all/themes/litgarland/color/preview.png
A         all/themes/litgarland/page.tpl.php
victorkane@victorkane:~/litworkshop/sites$ svn commit -m \
"Added litgarland theme,enabled nodequeue and added a content \
top region to house a random quotation block based on the \
nodequeue module"
Sending        all/backup/db/litworkshop.sql
Adding         all/themes/litgarland
Adding         all/themes/litgarland/block.tpl.php
Adding         all/themes/litgarland/color
Adding   (bin) all/themes/litgarland/color/base.png
Adding         all/themes/litgarland/color/color.inc
Adding         all/themes/litgarland/color/preview.css
Adding   (bin) all/themes/litgarland/color/preview.png
Adding         all/themes/litgarland/comment.tpl.php
Adding         all/themes/litgarland/fix-ie.css
Adding         all/themes/litgarland/images
Adding   (bin) all/themes/litgarland/images/bg-bar-white.png
Adding   (bin) all/themes/litgarland/images/bg-bar.png
Adding   (bin) all/themes/litgarland/images/bg-content-left.png
Adding   (bin) all/themes/litgarland/images/bg-content-right.png
Adding   (bin) all/themes/litgarland/images/bg-content.png
Adding   (bin) all/themes/litgarland/images/bg-navigation-item-hover.png
Adding   (bin) all/themes/litgarland/images/bg-navigation-item.png
Adding   (bin) all/themes/litgarland/images/bg-navigation.png
Adding   (bin) all/themes/litgarland/images/bg-tab.png
Adding   (bin) all/themes/litgarland/images/body.png
Adding   (bin) all/themes/litgarland/images/gradient-inner.png
Adding   (bin) all/themes/litgarland/images/menu-collapsed.gif
Adding   (bin) all/themes/litgarland/images/menu-expanded.gif
Adding   (bin) all/themes/litgarland/images/menu-leaf.gif
Adding   (bin) all/themes/litgarland/logo.png
Adding         all/themes/litgarland/minnelli
Adding         all/themes/litgarland/minnelli/color
Adding   (bin) all/themes/litgarland/minnelli/color/base.png
Adding         all/themes/litgarland/minnelli/color/color.inc
Adding   (bin) all/themes/litgarland/minnelli/color/preview.png
Adding   (bin) all/themes/litgarland/minnelli/logo.png
Adding   (bin) all/themes/litgarland/minnelli/screenshot.png
Adding         all/themes/litgarland/minnelli/style.css
Adding         all/themes/litgarland/node.tpl.php
Adding         all/themes/litgarland/page.tpl.php
Adding         all/themes/litgarland/print.css
Adding   (bin) all/themes/litgarland/screenshot.png
Adding         all/themes/litgarland/style.css
Adding         all/themes/litgarland/template.php
Transmitting file data .................................
Committed revision 29.
victorkane@victorkane:~/litworkshop/sites$
```

Now go to the test site, and deploy all your changes by updating the working copy and synching the database, as explained in the last few chapters. Test that your changes are successfully deployed to the test site.

## *Weak and Strong Points in Separation of Concerns with Drupal*

It is worthwhile noting that while Drupal excels in establishing a clean separation between the presentation, data, and application logic layers, it does have one weak spot where separation of concerns is concerned. Drupal fails miserably at separating business objects and application configuration. This leads to a great deal of difficulty in maintaining production and test sites at times when you are close to launch and while debugging is going on, and even scheduled modifications on development and test sites, when people are adding and modifying content on the production site. Several solutions have been proposed (and promised!) for this problem; one of the best seems to be the article "Development Environment for Drupal" (`http://ceardach.com/blog/2008/06/development-environment-drupal`), by Kathleen Ceardach, and her database scripts, packaged into a fully fledged Drupal module (`http://drupal.org/project/dbscripts`).

But in theming, Drupal is at the height of elegance. Compared to other CMS frameworks, you have no non-semantic HTML in the data marshaling layer, no layout hard-coded into the node (page content) building phase or into the application logic. In addition, you have layout added in a separate page rendering process, which delegates regions, blocks, panels, and panes to their own rendering process culminating in an XHTML and CSS invocation to finally render the look and feel of a page in a host of feathered mini-layers.

# Standing on the Shoulders of Giants — Reusing the Zen Theme

You have the theme. From now on, the theme grows with your website application. It has been conceived and designed with change in mind and will change constantly during its entire life cycle.

As you add more functionality in the implementation of each of the user stories, you will be adding more theming, so the presentation layer, now installed in the project, can properly contain the content.

This is going to get complicated in a hurry. And there are so many stumbling blocks along the way — anticipating all of the HTML entities and Drupal structural elements, cross-browser compatibility, and a host of other things. Time for reuse! This book recommends using the Zen theme (`http://drupal.org/project/zen`) as the foundation for all your themes until you don't know any better and can go off and fend for yourself in all things theming.

And, as you will soon see, when it comes time to upgrade to Drupal 6, to Drupal 7, and beyond, you will have a helping hand, standing on the shoulders of the giants standing on the shoulders of giants!

Listen to the seminal podcast (where the creator of the Zen theme, Jeff Robbins of Lullabot, dialogs with the maintainer and re-creator of the Zen theme, John Albin Wilkins), which can be found at `www.lullabot.com/audiocast/podcast-55-john-albin-wilkins-and-zen-theme`. Next, study the Zen theme documentation (currently at `http://drupal.org/node/193318`). Then join me in the next sections, as we port our budding theme to Zen, creating a Zen subtheme, and then use it to theme the Random Quotation block.

> *If you are using Drupal 5.x at this time, go ahead and install the Theme Settings module (*`http://drupal.org/project/themesettings`*), which is supported by the Zen theme and is part of Drupal core in Drupal 6.x and beyond. You will also have to install the dependency Theme Settings API module (*`http://drupal.org/project/themesettingsapi`*).*

## Creating Subthemes

To create the subtheme, which serves as an override of custom Zen functionality, following the instructions in the official documentation, you first download the Zen theme itself, suitable for the Drupal release you are using. Next:

1. Copy the STARTERKIT folder to a zenlitworkshop folder. You now have a new subtheme at ./sites/all/themes/zen/zenlitworkshop, which needs just a little configuration to get you started.
2. You can start with a liquid layout, so copy ./sites/all/themes/zen/layout-liquid.css to ./sites/all/themes/zen/zenlitworkshop/layout.css.
3. In order to override print media styles, copy ./sites/all/themes/zen/print.css to ./sites/all/themes/zen/zenlitworkshop/print.css.
4. Copy ./sites/all/themes/zen/zen.css to ./sites/all/themes/zen/zenlitworkshop /zenlitworkshop.css.
5. As per the documentation, "Edit the template.php and theme-settings.php files in your sub-theme's folder; replace ALL occurrences of 'STARTERKIT' with the name of your subtheme."
6. Go to Administer ➢ Site building ➢ Themes, and enable and make default the `zlitworkshop` theme. Click on the "Save configuration" button.

Well, everything got really plain-looking all of a sudden! And a bit of a mess. Head over to Administer ➢ Site building ➢ Blocks, and fix up the blocks as they were before. The new theme already has a content top region, so make sure Random Quotation is positioned there and that `genre_browser` is assigned to the new content bottom region, then hit "Save blocks." And all the blocks should be organized as before. If not, make any necessary adjustments.

While we are on the Blocks Administration page, you can see that there are a lot of other regions already implemented by the Zen theme which the `zenlitworkshop` subtheme has inherited. You can see them marked in yellow.

Now everything is ready for your designer and the installation of a custom-designed theme. Let's make things a bit more presentable, however, and take a look around and see where things are.

I made the following changes to ./litworkshop/sites/all/themes/zen/zenlitworkshop/zenlitworkshop.css, and things look a little less scary now:

```
body
{
  background-color: #d3d3ff;
}
...
#content-inner
{
  background-color: #fff;
}
/* This makes a big difference! */
#mission, #content-top, #content-area, #content-bottom, .feed-icons{
  padding: 5px;
}
#mission /* The mission statement of the site (displayed on homepage) */
{
  background-color: #e9e9ff;
}
```

You will probably come up with a great many more suggestions! Our new tabula rasa can be seen in Figure 7-11.

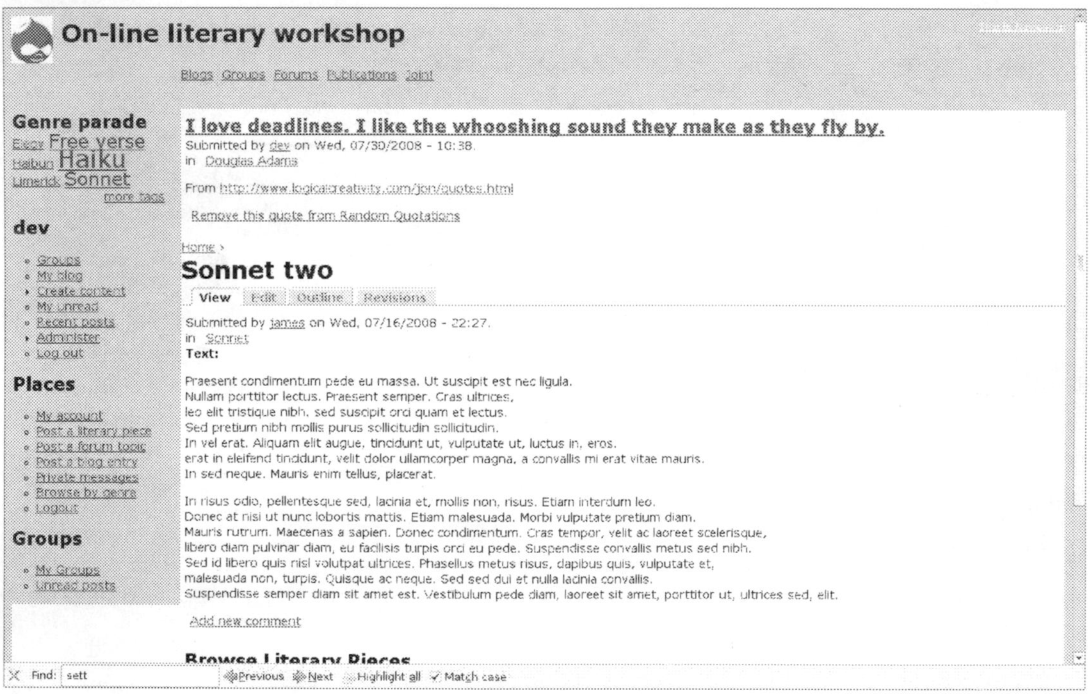

Figure 7-11

Now is a good time to dump the database and commit your changes, after adding the new theme to the SVN repository.

## Applying the Subtheme to the Quotation Block

There are a couple of things left to do with respect to the Quotation block. It should:

- Not appear on the front page, where the mission statement goes.
- Have the same background as mission statement.
- Only show title and clickable author.

### Fixing It So That the Quote Doesn't Appear on the Front Page

In order for the quote not to appear on the front page, you need to do the following:

1. Add a conditional statement in its rendering in the file ./litworkshop/sites/all/themes /zen/zenlitworkshop/page.tpl.php. The first thing you should notice about this file is that it doesn't exist. That's because you only override templates on a need-to basis. And you should override it in the typical Drupal way: cut and paste plus naming conventions. Copy the main Zen theme file to the subtheme directory, and ./zen/zenlitworkshop/page.tpl.php will be executed in lieu of ./zen/page.tpl.php.
2. Edit the subtheme template override in a text editor, and look for the following code block:

```
<?php if ($content_top): ?>
  <div id="content-top">
    <?php print $content_top; ?>
  </div> <!-- /#content-top -->
<?php endif; ?>
```

3. Add in the following conditional so that the block is not shown on the front page:

```
<?php if ($content_top && !$is_front): ?>
  <div id="content-top">
    <?php print $content_top; ?>
  </div> <!-- /#content-top -->
<?php endif; ?>
```

4. Test that by going to the front page and verifying that the Random Quotation block is no longer shown there.

### Creating a Background for the Quote Block

Now, let's give the Quote block the same look and feel as the Mission Statement.

1. In the file ./sites/all/themes/zen/zenlitworkshop/zenlitworkshop.css, give the mission and the content-top divs the same background color:

```
#mission /* The mission statement of the site (displayed on homepage) */
{
  background-color: #e9e9ff;
}
```

```
#content-top /* Wrapper for any blocks placed in the "content top"
region */
{
  background-color: #e9e9ff;
}
```

2. All that's left is to theme the look and feel of the quote content item itself. For this purpose, make a template specified just for nodes of type Quote, by using another polymorphic naming convention inherent in "The Drupal Way."

3. It turns out that all nodes are rendered in the content area according to the general node.tpl.php template. If you wish to override this for any particular content type, you specify a template for this by naming it accordingly: in this case, copy ./sites/all/themes/zen/node.tpl.php to ./sites/all/themes/zen/zenlitworkshop/node-quote.tpl.php, and, thanks to the naming convention, the changes you make to this template will only affect nodes of type Quote.

4. Basically, an eraser is going to be the best writer here: the first cut should look something like this (achieved by simply erasing lines, since you only want the title and the taxonomy):

```
<div class="node <?php print $node_classes ?>" id="node-<?php print \
$node->nid; ?>"><div class="node-inner">

  <?php if ($page == 0): ?>
    <h2 class="title">
      <a href="<?php print $node_url; ?>"><?php print $title; ?></a>
    </h2>
  <?php endif; ?>

  <?php if (count($taxonomy)): ?>
    <div class="taxonomy"><?php print t(' in ') . $terms; ?></div>
  <?php endif; ?>

</div></div> <!-- /node-inner, /node -->
```

5. Cool! It's starting to look much cleaner already! Now let's get rid of "in" and put in a typical quotation dash for the author, stop letting the quote be a link, and reduce its size also. End result:

```
<div class="node <?php print $node_classes ?>" id="node-<?php print\
$node->nid; ?>"><div class="node-inner">

  <?php if ($page == 0): ?>
    <p class="quote">
      <?php print $title; ?>
    </p>
  <?php endif; ?>

  <?php if (count($taxonomy)): ?>
    <div class="taxonomy"><?php print t(' - ') . $terms; ?></div>
  <?php endif; ?>

</div></div> <!-- /node-inner, /node -->
```

6. Now you may need to right-justify the author. Of course, you do this with CSS by adding the following to the end of the file ./litworkshop/sites/all/themes/zen/zenlitworkshop/zenlitworkshop.css:

```
/* Random Quote block */
#content-top .taxonomy {
  margin-left: 400px;
}
```

The results of your labors should look similar to Figure 7-12. A much cleaner quotation block! Add the newly created files to your SVN working copy, and commit your changes.

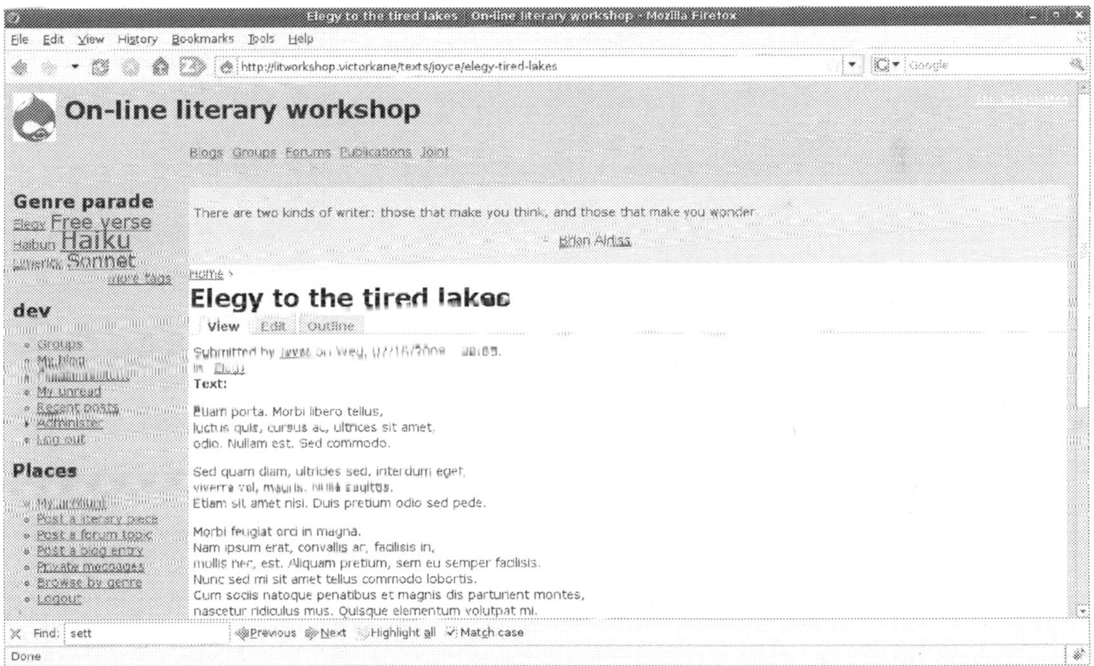


Figure 7-12

# Summary

Well, you are not going to become an expert Drupal themer just from reading this chapter. What has been covered, on the other hand, is everything you need in order to start out practicing to become one. You have seen the philosophy and character of the Drupal theming system itself, based on a clean separation of content and presentation. You have seen how Drupal goes about rendering a page of dynamic content, and you have seen how the presentation can be overridden — in structure, layout, and styling — by managing the various elements making up the Drupal theme. And finally, you have seen how to go about creating a subtheme of the Zen theming component, in order to create a rock-solid theming platform for your projects. The presentation layer is now installed and will be considered in all future chapters of the book as the project matures.

# Part III
# Upgrading Your Drupal Site

# 8

# Upgrading to Drupal 6

Upgrading from one Drupal release to another is what you call a *nontrivial* task. As such, you really need to follow in the footsteps of those who are more experienced and can show you the pitfalls and possible problems you may encounter. For this reason, before even describing the basic steps, a recommended reading list is presented at the beginning, rather than at the end of this chapter.

Then the basic steps are outlined, and then you are taken by the hand and led through the complete detailed procedure you can later put to use yourself, using a real-world example, my blog, `http://awebfactory.com.ar`. It has been running for about three years now on Drupal, since October 2005. It started out on Drupal 4.4 or so. On the blog, there is an article on how I upgraded from Drupal 4.7 to Drupal 5.x ("Updating awebfactory.com.ar from 4.7 to Drupal 5"; `http://awebfactory.com.ar/node/223`).

There is even a before-and-after thumbnail, because I changed over to a custom theme. This time, however, I will be more than satisfied if I can get the same theme working as is under Drupal 6.x

So, here we go.

## Recommended Reading

The more you know, the better! Before upgrading, study the following references:

- Drupal Handbook upgrade pages: `http://drupal.org/upgrade`
- The UPGRADE.txt file found in the document root of the Drupal 6.x file tree is by all accounts the best (if not only) reference material; as well as the documentation that comes with each Drupal module.
- Greg Knaddison (greggles) has published an excellent video on the basic process of upgrading from Drupal 5.x to Drupal 6.x, part of the *Mastering Drupal* series. The video is available free online at `www.masteringdrupal.com/screencast/upgrading-to-drupal-6`.
- Special Forum on `drupal.org` dedicated to upgrade problems and advice
- Converting 5.x themes to 6.x: `http://drupal.org/node/132442`. A little technical, but might come in handy. See `http://drupal.org/update`, `http://drupal.org/update/theme`, and `http://drupal.org/update/modules`.

# Upgrading — The Basic Process

Here are the steps to follow to upgrade from Drupal 5.x to Drupal 6. These are discussed in full detail in the sections that follow.

> **Before you even start, it is important that you both back up and copy your production website to a test site, where you can roll up your sleeves and work happily in full knowledge of the fact that it is impossible for you to do any serious damage. When the upgrade is complete, or at least tested, it can be copied, or the same steps followed again, on the production site.**

1. Shift everything over to a test site. (You may already have one, but this is just to make sure you're acting on the real McCoy, just in case you are not using version control.)
2. Update everything to the latest Drupal 5.x version available, not only for Drupal core, but also for all the modules you are using.
3. Test everything running in the latest and brightest 5.x version.
4. Make a module inventory, and see which modules might not yet have been upgraded to a Drupal 6.x version. The modules you have installed are the most important factor in determining how easy or difficult, or even possible, the upgrade process will be.
5. Switch to the default Drupal theme. Research whether or not your theme is available in a version for Drupal 6 by visiting the theme's project page (e.g., `http://drupal.org/project/amadou`) and seeing if there is a recommended Drupal 6 version, or by locating your theme from the list at `http://drupal.org/project/Themes`.
6. Disable all modules. Now, do not uninstall any of the modules — you don't want to disturb your data. You just want to leave the field clear for the Drupal 6.x core database upgrade to take place first.
7. Update the Drupal core.
8. Update each of the modules and the theme.
9. (Pinch yourself: It's alive!) Re-running All Site Acceptance Tests.
10. Deploying.

Now for true confessions: exactly what happened to `http://awebfactory.com.ar` as I went through each of these steps? Here is the 10-point program:

# Step 1: Shifting Everything over to a Test Site

To start, you want to make a test site. I made a test site on my Ubuntu-fueled laptop by first creating a virtual host pointing to a work directory, added a line to /etc/hosts to create a pseudo-subdomain locally, and then restarting the Apache HTTP server (as described in an earlier chapter).

Next, I needed to transfer the production site to the new local test site. If you have been following this book, then you already know how. In any case, I will quickly review three ways of doing this (outlined in the following sections).

## Installing Using a Complete Backup from Your Hosting

If you have CPanel or the like, there is an icon or a link pointing you to the page where you can create a full backup of your site, with instructions on how to download it. Once you have it on your local disk, you will see that it is a tarred or zipped copy of everything you possess on the site, including all your settings, counters, quotas, logs, databases, certificates, and what have you. The idea is that this file can be uploaded to a new hosting site to make a clone of your previous one.

However, you are interested in just two directories, which you will see after opening up the compressed archive file: your home directory and the dumps of the contents of your database. On my CPanel backup, my home directory was in homedir and the document root was below that (public_html). So I could copy out the Drupal files directly to my test filesystem.

The database dump was in the MySql directory. The file was named username_drpl1.sql, in accordance with the host server username.

The last task before starting up the local test mirror is to insert the SQL file into the database, using the database administration tool included with Cpanel, `PhpMyAdmin`.

If there is no way to get a compressed archive of your host filesystem to download conveniently as a single file (albeit many megabytes), the next best thing might be to simply FTP the files to your test system. You will have to use `PhpMyAdmin` or similar to access a copy of your database, in order to guarantee that the site you are upgrading to Drupal 6.x contains all the latest changes.

Then use `PhpMyAdmin` or similar on your test site to create the test database and insert the downloaded database dump from the production site, and you should be all set to go.

## Quick and Dirty on the Command Line

Here's what I did: I logged into hosted server via ssh and used the command line to first dump the MySql database to a convenient place (usually ./site/all/backup/db) and then tar up and compress the whole file structure. Follow these steps:

1. The information you need is the name of the database together with the database user and password:

```
username@awebfactory.com.ar [~]# cd public_html/sites/all/backup/db
username@awebfactory.com.ar [~/public_html/sites/all/backup/db]# grep \
mysql ../../../default/settings.php
$db_url = 'mysql://username:password@localhost/databasename';
username@awebfactory.com.ar [~/public_html/sites/all/backup/db]#
mysqldump -u\
 username -p databasename > awebfact.sql
```

```
Enter password:
username@awebfactory.com.ar [~/public_html/sites/all/backup/db]# ls
./  ../  awebfact.sql
username@awebfactory.com.ar [~/public_html/sites/all/backup/db]#
```

As an alternative with very large databases, gzip the result directly, like this:

```
username@awebfactory.com.ar [~/public_html/sites/all/backup/db]#
mysqldump -u \
username -p databasename | gzip > awebfact.gz
```

2. Tar the whole Drupal installation, including this database dump:

```
awebfact@awebfactory.com.ar [~/public_html/sites/all/backup/db]#
cd ../../../..
awebfact@awebfactory.com.ar [~/public_html]# tar cvzf ../awebfactory.tgz .
```

3. You now download the tarball (`awebfactory.tgz`) and untar it in your test site document root:

```
victorkane@victorkane:~/Work/AWebFactory/awebfactory.com.ar/public_html$
tar xvzf
../awebfactory.tgz
```

4. Now create the local database, create the user with a password with access to only that database, insert the database dump into the newly created test database, and fire up the local mirror! Here are the final steps (you can find them in the file INSTALL.mysql.txt, in the Drupal document root):

```
victorkane@victorkane:~/Work/AWebFactory/awebfactory.com.ar/public_html
$ mysqladmin\
 -u adminuser -p create databasename
Enter password:
victorkane@victorkane:~/Work/AWebFactory/awebfactory.com.ar/public_html
$ mysql -u\
 adminuser -p
Enter password:
Welcome to the MySQL monitor.  Commands end with ; or \g.
Your MySQL connection id is 508
Server version: 5.0.51a-3ubuntu5.1 (Ubuntu)

Type 'help;' or '\h' for help. Type '\c' to clear the buffer.

mysql> GRANT SELECT, INSERT, UPDATE, DELETE, CREATE, DROP, INDEX,
ALTER, CREATE
    ->   TEMPORARY TABLES, LOCK TABLES
    -> ON databasename.*
    -> TO 'username'@'localhost' IDENTIFIED BY 'password';
Query OK, 0 rows affected (0.03 sec)

mysql> quit
```

```
Bye
victorkane@victorkane:~/Work/AWebFactory/awebfactory.com.ar/public_html\
$ mysql -u username -p databasename < sites/all/backup/db/awebfact.sql
Enter password:
victorkane@victorkane:~/Work/AWebFactory/awebfactory.com.ar/public_html$
```

All set, you have the mirror running now on the test site!

> **Common Caveats**
>
> Cat got your .htaccess file? Layout, CSS weird? Clean URLs no longer working, resulting in "404 Not Found" errors? You used a method to copy the files that omitted Linux "hidden files" (the ones starting with a dot: like .htaccess). Solution: copy in the .htaccess file from a fresh Drupal install.
>
> What's that? .htaccess file is there, but things just not right, maybe your browser is offering to download php pages instead of serving them? The problem might be that the .htaccess file is specifically adjusted to your production site environment. Copy it to the test site using the same method you used to copy the other Drupal files.

# Step 2: Updating to the Latest Drupal 5.x Version Available

Our main objective is to update to Drupal 6.x. Now, the scripts that are run by the release upgrade procedure have been written, debugged, and enhanced on the basis of the latest Drupal 5.x version available at that point. As a result, if you attempt an upgrade from an earlier version of Drupal 5.x, you will not be playing with a full deck, and you are sure to run into problems because the upgrade scripts will not find things as they expect.

## *Updating to 5.x Steps*

Follow these basic steps to get all your modules updated correctly:

1. First, make sure that the site is running as you expect it to on the test site. Then, save a copy of .htaccess, robots.txt and, of course, sites/default/settings.php and any other file you have modified outside of the files and sites/all directories. Finally, get ruthless and erase the Drupal core completely, leaving only the sites and files directories.
2. Now use any one of the methods you have seen in earlier chapters and install the latest Drupal core. Ten bonus points if you do it using CVS (don't forget .cvsignore).

   Another way is to untar a freshly downloaded Drupal 5.x tarball (right from the download link on `http://drupal.org`) into a directory, erase the sites subdirectory, and then copy the whole file tree into the Drupal Document root directory. Finally, merge your custom specifications into the new sites/default/settings.php file, .htaccess file (if you have made any custom modifications), robots.txt, and so on, using as reference the copies you saved in Step 1. You don't want to simply keep the old versions since they may have been improved or may have undergone security fixes.

**Question: How Do I Switch to Using CVS on an Existing Drupal Installation?:** Answer: First plain old erase everything except for the ./sites and ./files directory, unless you are using a custom .htaccess and/or robots.txt file for some reason. Then using a text editor, create a .cvsignore file in the document root, telling CVS to ignore ./sites/default/settings.php and any other special file you don't want overwritten when updating CVS. Note that starting with Drupal 6.x, the core will cease to overwrite your settings.php file, but with Drupal 5.x you need this. Secondly, check out the core. If your Drupal install is in, say, ./public_html, then check out to that specific directory from the directory just above it. For example, to check out Drupal 5.9 to directory public_html, type:

```
cvs -z6 -d:pserver:anonymous:anonymous@cvs.drupal.org:/cvs
/drupal co -d
public_html -r DRUPAL-5-9 drupal
```

3. Then, `update.php` must be run (the first of many times) in case there are database tasks to be performed as part of the update. This has to be done whenever the core or any module is updated. In this case, run it once for the Drupal core update. Later on, it will be run for the modules update. To run it, access it, as admin User #1 (hopefully), via the browser: `http://awebfactory.com.ar/update.php`.

4. `update.php` may complain about your not being User #1 (you know, that first user you created with super privileges but never used again, and whose password you have hopelessly forgotten). Never fear, following the instructions in the PHP doc comment: using a text editor, change the following:

   ```
   $access_check = TRUE;
   ```

   to

   ```
   $access_check = FALSE;
   ```

   `update.php` will even warn you about changing it back after you're done (see Figure 8-1). Ah, the Drupal way! After running the update script, you will be told of any modifications made to the database. Figure 8-1 shows the screen following an update from Drupal 5.x to Drupal 5.9.

*For doing the upgrade from 5.x to 6.x, you actually should be User #1, anyway. So if you don't have the password documented, go ahead and change the password for that user, and document that. If you are stuck without an alternative user with full permissions, get out from behind the eight ball by changing User #1 manually. For example, log in to PhpMyAdmin, and select the appropriate Drupal database. Select the users database. Browse. Disregard record 0. Edit the record with UID equal to 1. Supply a brand-new password by editing the field* `pass` *using the function* `MD5`*. Good old PhpMyAdmin will tell you that this is equivalent to the SQL statement:*

```
"UPDATE `databasename`.`users` SET `pass` = MD5( 'newpassword' ) WHERE \
`users`.`uid` =1 LIMIT 1 ;"
```

*Switch to that User #1 for the remainder of the upgrade process.*

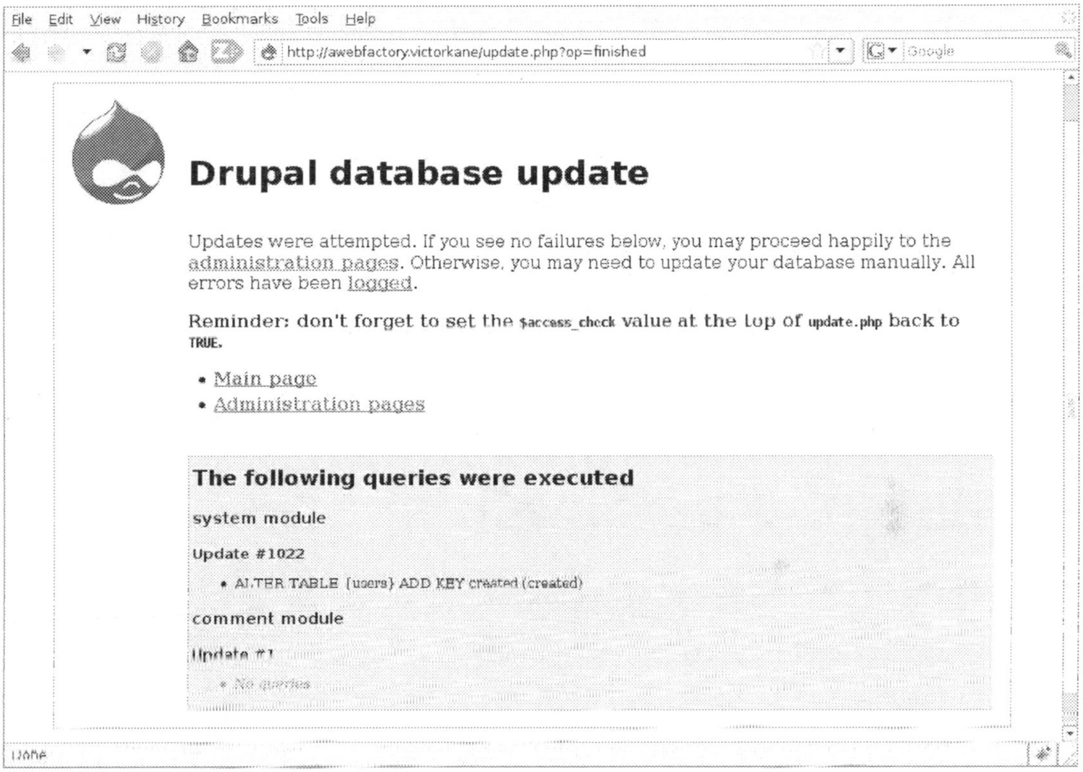


Figure 8-1

5. Once the Drupal core has been updated, each of the modules must be updated. There is an excellent module, called, appropriately enough, the *Update Status module*, that actually shows you the status of your modules and which ones need updating. One of the benefits of upgrading to Drupal 6 is that this module becomes part of the Drupal core. I had installed it in my blog when it first came out.

6. Before you do anything else, go to Administer ➤ Logs ➤ Status report.

You can see immediately see that you have two problems, as shown in Figure 8-2. (In Drupal, these are red. In the figure, they're the gray highlighted areas in the center panel with ⊗ marks next to them.)

One problem is that the "File system" is "Not writable." And yet you know it exists. What gives? As the message indicates, you have to "change the current directory's permissions so that it is writable." One way is to give full permissions in that directory (somewhat insecure), and another, better way is to make the Apache HTTP server user and group the owners of that directory. On many systems, that owner is nobody; on Debian and Ubuntu, it is *www-data*. You can do that with your favorite file manager, or from the command line, after changing directories to the Drupal document root, type:

```
$ sudo chown -R www-data:www-data files
[sudo] password for victorkane:
$
```

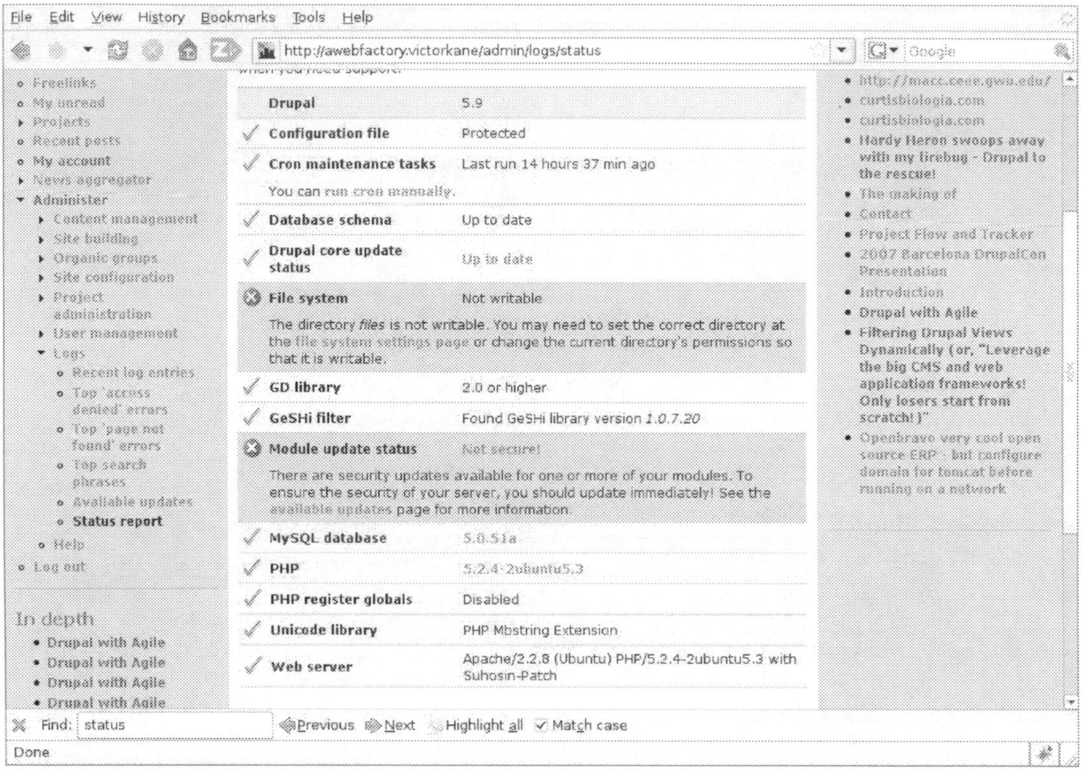


Figure 8-2

After doing so, the red File System warning will change to a nice, green "File systemWritable (public download method)" message.

Now, click the Available Updates link in the Module update status red warning block. You are taken to Administer ➤ Logs ➤ Available updates. Just to be sure, click on the "Check manually" link. Drupal will compare the versions of your installed modules with those in the Drupal CVS code repository.

## The Sad State of My Modules

In Figure 8-3, you are shown the resulting status. As you can see, my modules status is in a sad state, just as I'll warrant yours might be — something that must be remedied before contemplating the upgrade to Drupal 6.

Studying Figure 8-3, you can see there are really a lot of modules to update. The first thing you should try is the "I'm feeling lucky" approach, which, after carefully dumping the database into a SQL file to capture the current state of the system, is to download and install all the modules that need updating, run `update.php` so that the database can be brought in sync with the new versions of the modules, and then test.

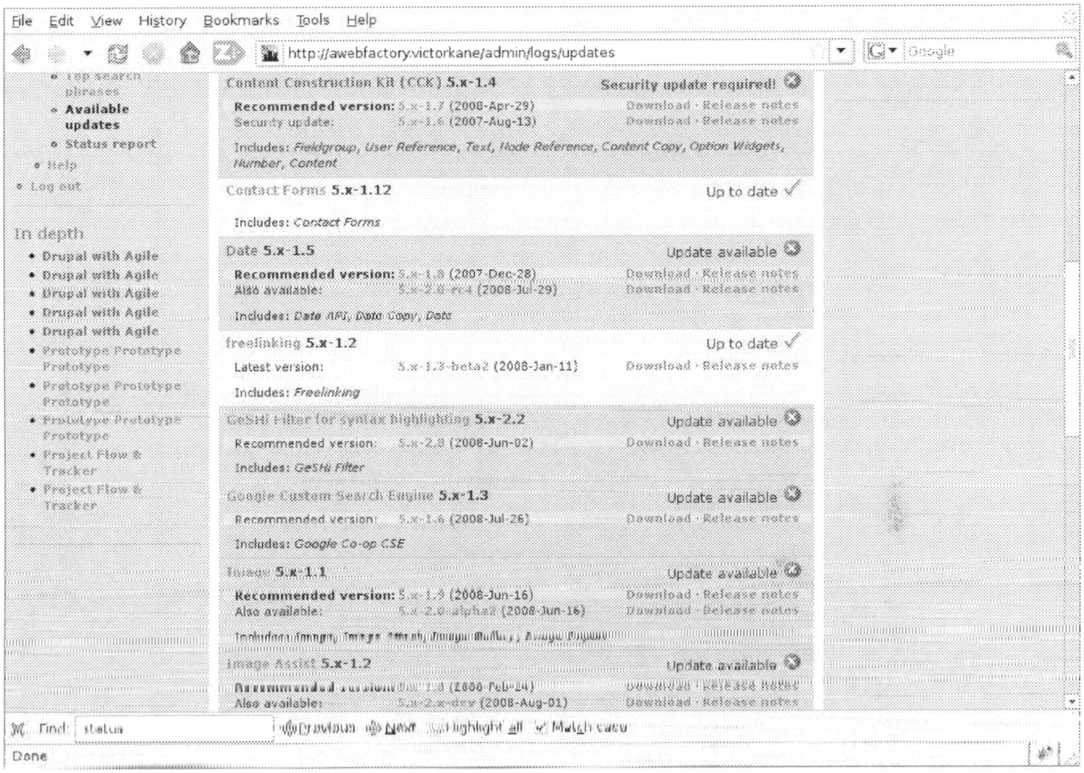


Figure 8-3

In most cases, you should be fine. If you encounter problems with a given module, go back by restoring the database to its previous state and then perhaps installing all except that problem module, then after saving the state, try again with the problem module and carry out the appropriate troubleshooting (including a very important visit to the issue queue of the offending module, where a solution is almost sure to be found). In most cases, however, you won't have any problems. By the way, this is why you should update your modules frequently! Now, with the Update Status module, what used to be a chore is made quite simple.

## Doing What I Did

Given Figure 8-3, I downloaded (using the handy Download link) and installed the latest 5.x-compatible versions of the following modules, using the recommended versions in each case:

- Archive
- CAPTCHA
- CCK
- Date
- GeSHi Filter for syntax highlighting (which I use for code listings)

- Google Custom Search Engine
- Image
- Image Assist
- Project
- Project issue tracking
- S5 presentation player
- Service links
- Tagadelic
- TinyMCE WYSIWYG Editor (for rich text editing: to update, download the latest version of the module and then the latest version of TinyMCE itself — as recommended by module instructions — from the Moxiecode Systems site, `http://tinymce.moxiecode.com/`). This is not covered by the GPL license, and third-party code is not kept in the Drupal CVS repository, which. . .is for Drupal code. I usually install this on one site and then keep a compressed tarball on hand for easy copying to other sites.

You can even use a command-line trick to streamline the downloading process, using wget:

1. Right-click on the Download link for each module on the Update status page marked in red that you are going to update, and copy the link location.
2. On the command line, type **wget**, and then paste in the link and hit [Enter].
3. You can download all the compressed module tarballs very quickly. Place them all in a suitable directory, and erase the modules you are going to update from ./sites/all/modules completely (but conserve any needed fonts and/or third-party files like TinyMCE or JavaScript libraries unless you are going to download a newer version).
4. Copy in all the fresh files (after all, you do have a backup from the production site).

> *What needs to be stressed here is that in a bulk update like this, you should restrict yourself to the latest stable versions of the modules you are actually using. If you want to try out the spanking-new version 2 of a module packed with new shiny features, do it when you know the system has been completely updated and works with all the stable versions first.*

When I invoked the "run the database upgrade script" link, I immediately got an error message:

```
user warning: Table 'awebfact_drpl1.captcha_points' doesn't exist query:
SELECT module,
 type FROM captcha_points WHERE form_id = 'update_script_selection_form' in
/home/victorkane/Work/AWebFactory/awebfactory.com.ar/public_html/includes/ ↩
database.mysql.inc on line 172
```

I bravely clicked on the Update button, expecting the `captcha` update script to take care of that problem. (Were it not to do so, perhaps I needed to upgrade to an older version first, and then to the newer version.)

I then got a host of additional warnings in red to the same effect, and some others too, followed by a listing of all the database changes carried out. I saved the page for future reference and then bravely clicked on the "Main page" link.

Things were OK, because the database update scripts had cleared away the problems. But then I started getting an insistent warning in red on pages that had source code, saying, many times:

```
GeSHi library error: sites/all/modules/geshifilter/geshi is not a directory.
GeSHi library error: sites/all/modules/geshifilter/geshi is not a directory.
```

A review of the README file made me remember that, just like TinyMCE and CAPTCHA (needed extra Open Source font files), additional third-party files required by the module and not kept in the Drupal CVS repository were required and sorely missed. A careful reading of the README.txt file in this module explained the dependency:

```
DEPENDENCY
----------
This module requires the third-party library: GeShi (Generic Syntax
Highlighter, written by Nigel McNie) which can be found at
  http://qbnz.com/highlighter
See installation procedure below for more information.
```

Instead of copying back in what I had before (always an option), I headed to that site to get the latest version, and:

```
Download the GeSHi library (version 1.0.x) from  http://qbnz.com/highlighter
  and place the entire extracted 'geshi' folder (which contains geshi.php)
  in the geshifilter directory (e.g. as /sites/all/modules/geshifilter/geshi)
```

Then I headed to the Administer page and got a WSOD (white screen of death) with the following warning:

```
Fatal error: require_once() [function.require]: Failed opening required
'sites/all/modules/geshifilter/geshi/geshi.php'
(include_path='.:/usr/share/php:/usr/share/pear') in
/home/victorkane/Work/AWebFactory/awebfactory.com.ar/public_html/
sites/all/modules/geshifilter/geshifilter.inc on line 33
```

And yet, the file was there, gosh darnit! Ah, the permissions were weird in the file I had unpacked into the directory, and the Apache HTTP server couldn't see it. I normalized the permissions to the same as the other PHP files. You can do this with your favorite file manager. I did it from the command line, of course, like this, recursively setting all the php files from the ./geshi directory on down:

```
$ sudo chmod -R 644 *.php
```

The red errors went away. But the `geshi` filtering stopped working. Instead of beautifully syntax-colored code, I got:

```
 [geshifilter-code] <?php // on the fly id and description for view $view =
views_create_view('dealers_in_luck', 'Dealers still in luck'); // title, table
view, pager on and 5 nodes-a-page... check out views.module for other params!
views_view_add_page($view, t('Crisis? What crisis...?'), NULL, 'table', true,
5, '', 1, false); // we specify fields, necessary because this is a table view;
first the node title views_view_add_field($view, 'node', 'title', false, 0,
'views_handler_field_nodelink'); // show us the monthly sales volume too
(view, db table, db field, ... and handler views_view_add_field($view,
```

```
'node_data_field_dealer_monthly_sales_volu', 'field_dealer_monthly_sales_
volu_value',
 false, 0, 'content_views_field_handler_group'); // filters now; first, just show
car dealers views_view_add_filter($view, 'node', 'type', '=', 'dealer', ''); //
just published ones at that views_view_add_filter($view, 'node', 'status', '=',
1, ''); // show me all of the ones with more than 500 sales volume per month
views_view_add_filter($view, 'node_data_field_dealer_monthly_sales_volu',
'field_dealer_monthly_sales_volu_value_default', '>=', '500', '');
views_load_cache(); views_sanitize_view($view); print views_build_
view('embed', $view, array(), false); ?> [/geshifilter-code]
```

The filters weren't working!

I headed to the Administer page and was confronted by another red warning:

```
One or more problems were detected with your Drupal installation. Check the status
 report for more information.
```

I went to the status report and was told "Database schema Out of date." Aha! The system needed `update.php` to be run a second time! This could be either very good or very bad. I ran `update.php` again.

This time, no error messages. Upon clicking the link to run the database upgrade script, there were no more red error messages, but upon completion, I got:

```
The following queries were executed
project_issue module
Update #5200

    * Failed: The update was aborted for the following reasons:
          o The Comment upload module is not enabled.

      This and all subsequent updates of Project issue were safely aborted. Correct
the problems listed above, then re-run update.php, click 'Select versions', select
update 5200 for project_issue, and click 'Update'.

      Note: you will most likely need to disable the Project issue module
 temporarily in order to resolve the issues above. If necessary, please refer to
 Project issue's UPGRADE.txt for further details regarding this upgrade problem.
```

I went to Administer ➤ Site building ➤ Modules and saw that, true enough, the Comment upload module was missing. I downloaded this module from `http://drupal.org/project/comment_upload` and installed it. Upon refreshing the page, its checkbox was grayed out, but I clicked on the "Save configuration" button anyway.

*As a Drupal aside, the Geshi syntax was working now, probably because clicking on the "Save configuration" button on Administer ➤ Site building ➤ Modules refreshes the cache of variables in memory, and that seems to have done the trick.*

So, now to execute `update.php` again! And indeed, the project_issue module happily reported on no fewer than eight database modifications it had carried out.

I clicked on the "Administration page" link. Behold! A site with no red error messages! I went to Administer ➤ Logs ➤ Available updates. Green, all green.

Ah, so many modules! So little time!

**How to Find Error Messages When You Get the White Screen of Death (WSOD)**

The WSOD occurs when there is an error preventing any output to the screen. As a result, you don't get the benefit of seeing what is going on, and you are therefore rendered clueless as to how to solve the problem. So whether or not you are a programmer, you do need to know two things: first, how to turn PHP error messaging on; and second, where to find the error messages.

You can ask your Hosting provider to turn error messaging on, but on many hosting sites, you can have your own php.ini file in the document root directory. If it is there, make sure it includes the following line, at least while the site is under development (the php.ini file explains the meaning of many error levels and includes examples of how to include and/or exclude single or multiple entries):

```
error_reporting  =  E_ALL
```

Then look at your Apache HTTP server's error logs, to see what is going on when the WSOD occurs. The exact location of these logs varies with different operating systems and distributions, but you will find it at locations like /var/log/apache2/error.log or /var/logs/httpd/error_log.

Tip: To watch your log entry being made in real time, open up an ssh session, go to the log directory, enter the following command, and watch this window as you enter the WSOD (or refresh the screen):

```
# tail -f error.log
```

The error log will tell you if you have run out of memory, or whether a required PHP file is missing, and so on.

# Step 3: Testing Everything in the Upgraded 5.x Version

At this point, you need to test the site, making a blog entry and uploading images as usual. The first time I used image assist to position an image within a TinyMCE editor text area, I saw a lot of messages saying that the images had been regenerated. But thereafter, everything worked as before. Got my site back again. Project and project issues were working (had used that starting a couple years ago to track web application projects on the site in collaboration with others).

If your site seems to be working well, just pay a couple of visits to make sure everything is problem-free:

1. Go to Administer ➢ Logs ➢ Recent log entries, where there should be no error messages from the recently updated modules. Don't worry if there are. If error message persist, visit the module's issue queue, which is listed on the module's home page (which you can reach directly from Administer ➢ Logs ➢ Available updates, assuming that you have the Update

Status module installed, via the View all pending issues link). You should not attempt the upgrade if there are error messages.

2. Pay a last visit to Administer ➤ Logs ➤ Available updates, just to make sure that everything is absolutely up-to-date just prior to actually going ahead with the upgrade.

At this point, you should immediately back up the database and the complete filesystem so that if difficulties are encountered while upgrading to Drupal 6.x, you will at least have this shiny new upgraded 5.x site to fall back on.

# Step 4: Making a Module Inventory

You have now come to the moment of Drupal module truth. In an ideal world, when you are upgrading from Drupal 5.x to 6.x, you need to replace each installed module with its Drupal 6.x release counterpart. However, it might happen that there is no stable or production-ready version available for a given module. (The Drupal module repository listings for a given category, e.g., `http://drupal.org/project/Modules/category/90`, will show you which modules are stable with the sign "Recommended for version 6.x" accompanied by a green checkmark.) If there is no stable release, or at least a good release candidate, then you may need to forgo that functionality until such a time as a release is issued. But you need to know this ahead of time because the lack of an available stable release of a module might well enter into your decision on whether the time is even ripe for upgrading — which is why this needs to be researched before actually going through with the upgrade.

A release upgrade is a good time to actually upgrade the architecture of the site itself and to decide if you really need to go on with all the installed modules. Perhaps some of them have been ported to the core; perhaps some of them have more attractive alternatives or can be implemented using simpler building blocks of your own. For example, in my case, I decide to eliminate the project and project issue modules in favor of the content types and views modules–based solution that was developed in an earlier chapter for the development documentation for the On-Line Literary Workshop site.

It might be a good time to change the theme, also.

From `http://awebfactory.com.ar`, the following table is a list of all the installed modules and whether or not they will be continued into the Drupal 6.x version of the site, replaced, or discontinued.

**Modules Inventory**

| Module Name | Recommended Drupal 6.x Version? | Notes |
|---|---|---|
| `adsense` | Development version only (at time of writing) | |
| `archive` | Yes | |
| `captcha` | Yes | |
| `cck` | Yes | Upgrades only possible from Drupal 6.3 and later |
| `comment_upload` | | Not using (functionality to be replaced) |

**Modules Inventory**

| Module Name | Recommended Drupal 6.x Version? | Notes |
|---|---|---|
| contact_forms | Yes | |
| date | Yes | |
| freelinking | Yes | |
| geshifilter | Yes | |
| google_cse | Yes | |
| image | Yes | |
| img_assist | Yes | |
| og | Yes | |
| project | | Not using (functionality to be replaced) |
| project_issue | | Not using (functionality to be replaced) |
| s5 | Development version only in both Drupal 5 and 6 | Depends on third-party software |
| service_links | Yes | |
| tagadelic | Yes | |
| tinymce | Yes | Depends on third-party software |

# Step 5: Switching to the Default Drupal Theme

At this point, you are ready to continue with the process by disabling the modules and the custom theme, if any, prior to updating the Drupal core itself. The purpose here is part of the upgrade strategy of dividing the complexity into three main parts:

- Core
- Modules
- Themes

Once the core is working, the modules can be upgraded as much as possible, and on that clean deck, with the system working, the problems originating with converting custom and semi-custom theming solutions from 5.x to 6.x can be dealt with in an isolated manner.

Upgrading themes from one Drupal release to another is always going to require some effort, and this is especially so when upgrading from Drupal 5.x to Drupal 6.x, because on top of the usual run of changes in function names and parameters, there are significant changes that went into effect on the theme engine front starting with Drupal 6.x — this sort of thing should. The Drupal Handbook documentation actually has a great theming overview (see `http://drupal.org/theme-guide`), accurate from a Drupal 6.x and up vantage point, which will undoubtedly help a great deal. See the section, "Step 8b: Upgrading the Theme," later in this chapter for some concrete examples.

# Step 6: Disabling All Contributed Modules

The steps for this are straightforward: Go to Administer ➢ Site building ➢ Modules, and disable all non-core modules. Because of dependencies between modules, you may need to disable an initial group, hit the "Save configuration" button, then disable a second group of modules upon which there no longer exist dependencies. In fact, it is very common for this procedure to be repeated several times.

However, do not uninstall any of the modules. Unless you plan on discontinuing the use of that module, uninstalling it will destroy all content and data associated with that module. The goal here is not to disturb your data, but to simply leave the field clear for the Drupal 6.x core database upgrade to take place first.

*The big exception to not uninstalling modules before performing the upgrade procedure is the Update Status module, which, because it is now part of the Drupal core, specifically requires you not only to disable it before upgrading the Drupal core, but also to uninstall it, thereby removing all traces of it from the database so that it does not clash with the new codebase. To do this, go to Administer ➢ Site building ➢ Modules and disable the module, then click on the "Save configuration" button. Then (and only then), click on the Uninstall tab, select the "Update status" checkbox, and click on the Uninstall button.*

# Step 7: Updating the Drupal Core

There are just two prerequisites here:

Firstly, you really need to be logged in as User #1 (the first user ever created). If you are logged in as an Admin user with full permissions, you can change the password of User #1 if you cannot recall it. (It should be written in a safe place with other site documentation.)

Secondly, if this happens to be a production site, you should definitely go to Administer ➢ Site configuration ➢ Site maintenance, and go off-line by selecting the Off-line radio button and clicking on the "Save configuration" button. That way, users who happen upon the site during this whole process will be warned that the site is undergoing maintenance while it is inaccessible.

Then carry out the following steps:

1. Make sure you have a backup of the Drupal 5.x state of the files and database as it was before disabling the theme and modules, to fall back on in case of emergency and from which to extract site-specific files and info, such as ./sites/default/settings.php, which holds your database access and other important settings, perhaps a custom .htaccess or robots.txt file, and the like. And, of course, the all-important graphic assets, usually found in the files directory.

2. Install the standard Drupal 6.x distribution, either via CVS or by unpacking a downloaded tarball (remembering always never to forget about the .htaccess file).
3. This is very important: make sure you deal with ./sites/default/settings.php properly. It cannot be overemphasized that there are changes to the file in Drupal 6.x, so you want to actually use the new default file default.settings.php as a basis. First of all, make doubly sure that you have saved the old settings.php file somewhere else. Then delete it. Copy the default.settings.php file to settings.php (copy, do not just move or rename). Edit settings.php, inserting your site-specific information, especially the database URL containing your settings (i.e., `$db_url='mysql://username:password@localhost/databasename';`).
4. Delete all the old versions of installed modules (usually in ./sites/all/modules).
5. Install the new Drupal 6.x versions of those modules you will be continuing to use. You will want to copy in the third-party dependencies (TinyMCE, S5, fonts for the graphical version of the Captcha module, etc.) from the backup of the 5.x site, or else download fresh versions from their third-party project pages.
6. Run `http://example.com/update.php`. (The current session still has User #1 logged in with full permissions!)

I ran into an unforeseen problem immediately (probably because I was using the old settings.php file). The session somehow was not honored, and I was told I didn't have permissions to run `update.php`. So I did the following: In Drupal 6.x, you can no longer hack `update.php` itself in the old sense; you need to modify a new access permissions section in ./sites/default/settings.php. So I copied the original settings.php to settings.php.old, and then added the database access details into a new settings.php file copied from the new default.settings.php file now provided by Drupal 6.x. In the new settings.php file I specified:

```
$update_free_access = TRUE;
```

Then I could run `http://example.com/update.php` and had the advantage of going with the new version of `settings.php`, a must.

I was greeted with an overview Drupal database update page, with a lot of good advice on it, which has already been mentioned in these pages. So I hit "Continue." On the next page, I was asked if I wished to select the updates, which you don't want to do unless you have a really good reason to stray from the suggested defaults. I didn't either, so I hit the "Update" button. Eighty-eight updates were to be carried out.

After a while, I was greeted with a long success page, which was the same as Figure 8-4, but greatly enlarged by several sections. First, it printed out many info lines in green:

```
Saving an old value of the welcome message body for users that are pending
administrator approval. However, you should consider modifying this text, since Drupal
can now be configured to automatically notify users and send them their login
information when their accounts are approved. See the User settings page for details.
Drupal can check periodically for important bug fixes and security releases using the
new update status module. This module can be turned on from the modules administration
page. For more information please read the Update status handbook page.
```

```
Drupal now has separate edit and delete permissions. Previously, users who were able
to edit content were automatically allowed to delete it. For added security, delete
permissions for individual core content types have been removed from all roles on your
site (only roles with the "administer nodes" permission can now delete these
types of content). If you would like to reenable any individual delete permissions,
you can do this at the permissions page.
Blog API module does not depend on blog module's permissions anymore, but provides
its own 'administer content with blog api' permission instead. Until this
permission is assigned to at least one user role, only the site administrator will be
able to use Blog API features.
All date fields using the jscalendar widget have been changed to use the text widget
instead, since the jscalendar widget is no longer supported. Enable the Date Popup
module to make a jQuery popup calendar available and edit the field settings
to select it.
```

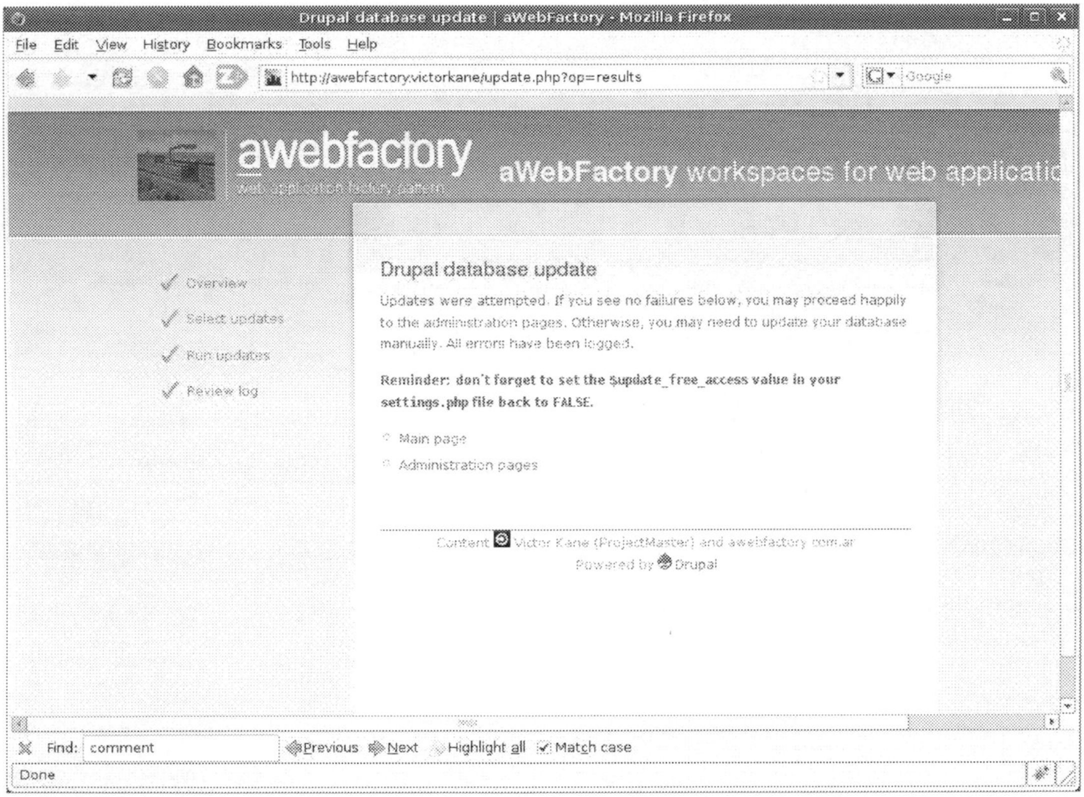


Figure 8-4

Then came a more disturbing but non-catastrophic red warning area with the following two messages:

```
user warning: Unknown column 'f.nid' in 'field list' query: INSERT
INTO image SELECT DISTINCT f.nid, f.fid, f.filename FROM files f INNER JOIN node n ON
f.nid = n.nid WHERE n.type='image' AND f.filename IN
('_original', 'thumbnail', 'preview') in
/home/awebfact/public_html/sites/all/modules/image/image.install on line 252.
```

and

```
user warning: Table 'awebfact_drpl1.file_revisions' doesn't
exist query: DELETE FROM file_revisions WHERE EXISTS (SELECT * FROM image WHERE
image.fid = file_revisions.fid) in /home/awebfact/public_
html/sites/all/modules/image/image.install on line 255.
```

Next came a nice, reassuring central area showing that I had succeeded:

```
Updates were attempted. If you see no failures below, you may proceed happily to the
administration pages. Otherwise, you may need to update your database manually. All
errors have been logged.
Reminder: don't forget to set the $update_free_access value in your
settings.php file back
to FALSE.
```

And there were no errors below, so w00t! Upgrade a success.

Next came the gray area below, showing me what changes had been made to the database, listing all queries.

I hit the "Main page" link, and since my session had been knocked out, I went to `http://awebfactory.com.ar/user` to log in as User #1 again. I then went to the Administration pages (`http://awebfactory.com.ar/admin`).

There I was told that:

```
One or more problems were detected with your Drupal installation. Check the status
 report for more information.
```

After clicking on the status report link, I was told that access to `update.php` was not protected (which I corrected by re-editing ./sites/default/settings.php as described above) and that Update notifications had not been enabled. I clicked on the module administration page link to remedy that, enabled the Update status module (now in the Core section), and clicked on the "Save configuration" button.

# Step 8a: Enabling the Modules

Enabling the modules can be via the old "I'm feeling lucky" mode, or, if you have special cause for concern after actually having read some of the module documentation, it can be done in a series of steps — the "sure fire" modules first, then the question marks, then the difficult cases, one by one.

For each step, the process is, go to Administer ➢ Site building ➢ Modules and enable the module(s), then run `http://example.com/update.php`.

I went ahead and enabled all the modules in the Content construction kit section, the Archive module, and the Date, Date Copy, the Date Popup, and the Date Repeat modules. I enabled the Geshi filter, then Image and Image Assist modules, Organic groups and Organic groups access control, then the Contact Forms, Freelinking, Google CSE, S5 book, Service links, and TinyMCE modules. I enabled the Captcha and Text Captcha modules, and finally, the Tagadelic module.

I was then informed that the content access permissions needed to be rebuilt. But first, I decided to run `update.php`. This turned out to be an uneventful repetition of the last time (the work seemed to have been done thanks to the mere presence of the modules beforehand during the Drupal core update), and I seemed to be all set. I revisited the Administration pages and was told once again about the access permissions, and that there were some problems with the Drupal installation. I clicked the status report to find out what problems there might be first. Oh, it was about the need to rebuild the access permissions. I went ahead and clicked the link that was offered, which took me to Administer ➢ Content management ➢ Post settings, where I confirmed that I was sure I wanted to rebuild the permissions on the site content. (I had used organic groups to manage access permissions to content in Drupal 5.) The process finished well, and the upgrade seemed to be all done.

The site seemed to be working fine. I was soon sent back to the Administration pages and told that the Date Timezone module required me to set the site's timezone name, and the update status module told me that no update data was available (I could check manually or else run `cron`). I checked manually and saw that Module and theme update status was: "up to date." I clicked the "set the timezone name" link, was taken to Administration ➢ Site configuration ➢ Date and time, and simply confirmed the same configuration as in the previous release. Upon returning to the Administration pages, there were no more pesky but useful and informative red warnings.

The only thing remaining now was to update my custom Drupal 5.x theme to Drupal 6.x.

Before attempting to do so, I backed up the database into ./sites/all/backup/db/awebfactory.sql and then did a complete backup of the filesystem. The upgrade to Drupal 6.x was complete except for the theme and the blocks that had been supported before.

One other problem I ran into was that my archive (supported by the archive module) had disappeared! I went to Administer ➢ Site configuration ➢ Archives and re-selected the checkbox beside the blog content type, and this problem was rectified.

# Step 8b: Upgrading the Theme

For most Drupal users, upgrading the theme will be about finding the Drupal 6.x version of the theme they have been using, installing it, and configuring it in a similar fashion to its Drupal 5.x counterpart.

Before you even start messing with the theme, make sure that you have an administration theme you can trust. That way, if your site breaks because of a faulty theme, you can at least disable it temporarily should that be necessary.

In my case, though, I had a custom Drupal 5.x theme I had to upgrade myself.

First of all, I read over the recommended "Converting 5.x Themes to 6.x" article at `http://drupal.org/node/132442`.

Following the instructions I found there, I did the following with my theme:

**Steps Taken to Adapt a Simple Custom Drupal Theme to Drupal 6.x**

| Steps | Description |
|---|---|
| Create an initial .info file | Example (awebfactory.info):<br>`name = awebfactory`<br>`description = AwebFactory blog theme.`<br>`core = 6.x`<br>`engine = phptemplate` |
| There is no Step 2: The custom theme is very simple, consisting only of a few files. | awebfactory.info<br>node.tpl.php<br>style.css<br>page.tpl.php<br>screenshot.png<br>/images |

So I headed over to Administer ➤ Site building ➤ Themes, and apparently by virtue of the .info file, there was my theme! I enabled it and selected it as the default, then hit the "Save configuration" button.

But I got the following fatal error:

```
Fatal error: Call to undefined function adsense_display() in
/home/victorkane/Work/AWebFactory/awebfactory.com.ar/public_html/
sites/all/themes/awebfactory/page.tpl.php on line 27
```

OK, I didn't expect it to be that easy. Ah, a problem with the adsense module, which must have changed somehow. I guess that's what Greg Knaddison meant when he said, "Read up first." Well, lucky I'm using a test site!

*What are you to do in a situation like this? Stay calm! First off, see if the module is even there. You may have forgotten to include it. Second, read the module documentation. Third, check out the module issues and support queues. And if still necessary, fourth, fire off a question in the hugely active Drupal Support Forum. Then, stay there to help out others who come along with the same question!*

Actually, you should do what everyone forgets to do: look at what the error message is saying: "call to undefined function"! First, head over to the documentation of the module . . .oops! Where's the module? I forgot to include the module in the module inventory, and I forgot to even install it. Undefined function, indeed! Since I realize that this may happen more with me than with you, I should perhaps just correct this chapter, but I said I would report realistically on the whole process, and who knows, this could happen to someone else, so . . .:

1. Include the omitted module in the module inventory (site documentation).
2. Go to `http://example.com/admin` so the Admin theme kicks in.
3. Install the module.
4. Disregard all messages until you run `update.php`.
5. Site's up!

Cool. Now the theme is running. That's it! But wait: where are my blocks? Head over to Administer ➢ Site building ➢ Blocks. There are my blocks! They are all assigned to the right sidebar region. Maybe if I hit "Site configuration," they will show up again! Nope. Who took my blocks?

Calming down, and drinking some more of that fine Argentine *yerba mate*, I notice that being on Administer ➢ Site building ➢ Blocks, I should be seeing all the blocks marked in yellow, shouldn't I? Ah, there's only one block showing up like that! *Content*. The content block. I guess I should be grateful for that because otherwise nothing would be showing up at all.

I head over to "Converting 5.x Themes to 6.x" section of the Drupal handbook (`http://drupal.org/node/132442`) and gratefully click on the "Defining block regions" link.

It says that regions are defined in the .info file:

```
regions[left] = Left sidebar
regions[right] = Right sidebar
regions[content] = Content
regions[header] = Header
regions[footer] = Footer
```

But my theme doesn't use any but the standard regions, so that is not my problem. Ah! A little further down, it says:

```
 "The variable names for side bar block regions and footer has been changed.
In 5.x the regions "left", "right" and "footer" used the variables $sidebar_left,
 $sidebar_right and $footer_message inside page.tpl.php. This was ancient cruft that
 was needed in 4.6 and below.
To make it cleaner and more straight forward, the three regions create variables of
$left, $right and $footer just like any other region. $footer_message is still
used but it's for the footer message set from site information administration page."
```

Cool! So, using a text editor, I edit my theme's page.tpl.php file and make this correction.

- Before:

```
<div id="sidebar_right">
<?php if ($sidebar_right) { ?>
  <?php print $sidebar_right ?>
<?php } ?>
</div>
```

- After:

```
<div id="right">
<?php if ($right) { ?>
  <?php print $right ?>
<?php } ?>
</div>
```

Got my blocks back! But...they are not where they are supposed to be! Instead of floating off to the right, they have all fallen down into the content area and you can't see them unless you scroll down. What gives?!

A few minutes working with the magic Firebug add-on for Firefox (don't leave home without it: `https://addons.mozilla.org/en-US/firefox/addon/1843`) showed me what the problem was. Because I had changed the ID attribute to `right` instead of `sidebar_right`, I had to make a corresponding change in the CSS file. Instead of:

```
#sidebar_right{
    width: 210px;
    float: right;
}
```

I needed:

```
#right{
    width: 210px;
    float: right;
}
```

So now I had my blocks, but…they were in the wrong order. Better change the weights…. But wait, where are the weights in the block configuration form so I can order my blocks? (Figure 8-5 shows the Drupal 5 block admin page, and Figure 8-6 shows the same page in Drupal 6.) What gives?

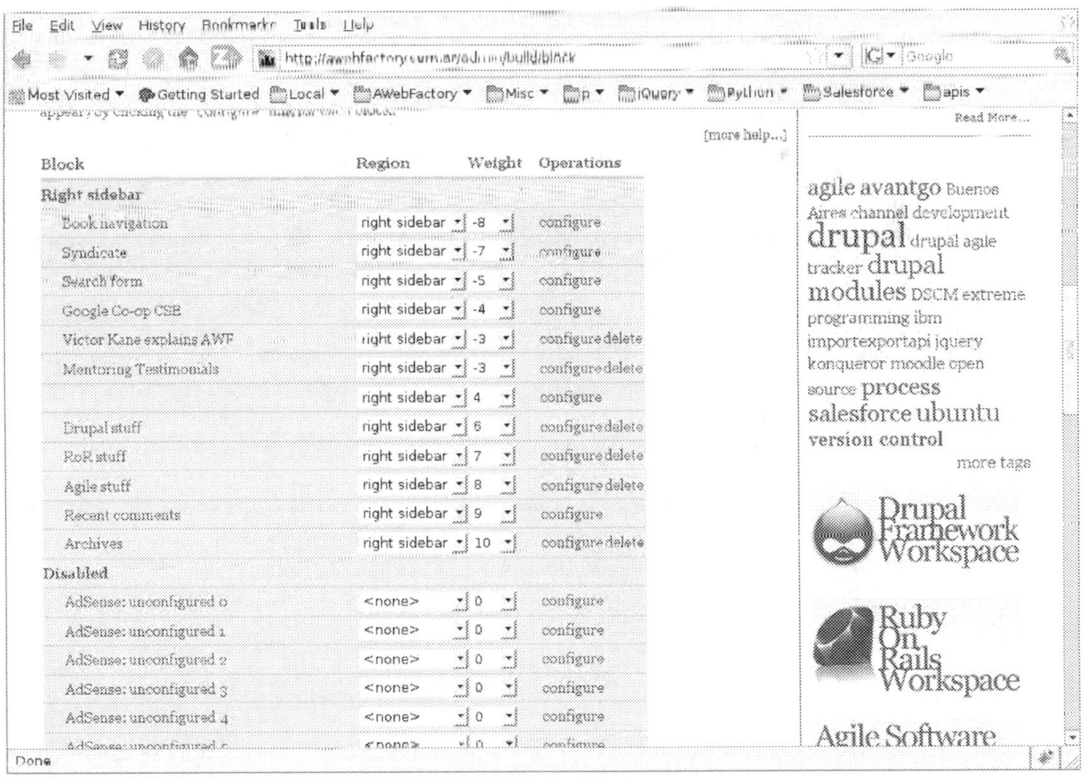

Figure 8-5

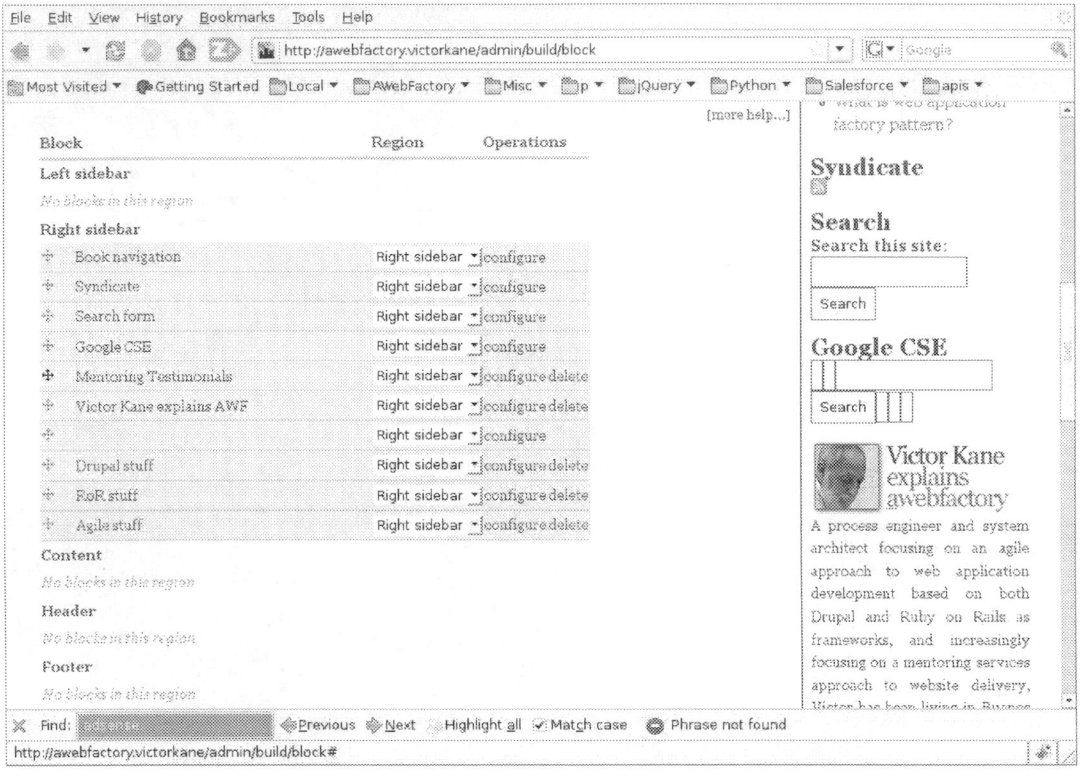


Figure 8-6

Oh my, AJAX admin goodness! You don't need weights; you can just move them up and down by dragging the move icon on the left-hand side of each block entry in the table. One of the great reasons for upgrading to Drupal 6!

Just one more weird thing happened. I never administer the site as User #1, which is considered bad, insecure practice. So I logged in as my usual Admin user and was told to check the status report, so I clicked on "status report." The adsense module was complaining about the Publisher ID not being set, so I clicked on the handy link to the module settings page . . . and got an "Access Denied" page.

Accordingly, I went back to the Administration pages and looked for the first one in the "User management" section, good old "Access control" . . . and it wasn't there! OMG! The usability team strikes again. Well, actually, I have to be open-minded. I suppose *Permissions* is a little more intuitive than *Access control*, especially for you, gentle reader, who has never had to figure out that "Access control" was where you set the permissions. But it is in second place now, under "Access rules." All over the world, thousands of Drupal administrators are going to "Access rules" and realizing that is not what they want, then going back and remembering to go to the second one. Well, that's progress for you.

So I hit "Permissions" and . . . set my permissions for the Admin role.

And to this day, you can see the results of the work done here, at `http://awebfactory.com.ar`, proudly running Drupal 6.x! And then 7.x, and so on and so forth.

## Step 9: Re-running All Site Acceptance Tests

Here is where having acceptance tests really pays off. They can always serve as regression tests to make sure your site is functioning correctly after major overhauling.

Basically, testing the site consists of going through all of the ways users interact with the site (all the use/test cases) to make sure functionality behaves as expected.

In the case of a blog, this is pretty straightforward, but even so, it is handy to have a documented list of use cases to run through. That way, you can delegate the testing to another person and get even better insights on how things really are.

> **As an important part of this testing procedure, do make sure that all your content is still there before deploying to production.**

## Step 10: Deploying

After ensuring that you have your backup for the production site, just erase it and replace it with both code and database from your upgraded test site. If users other than yourself can add content to your production site, you will have to come up with a way to move anything added since you dumped the database to do the upgrade on your test site, even if it's only by manually re-entering a couple of posts and comments. On extremely busy sites where this is not an alternative, the test site should serve as a way of perfecting the procedure and assembling all the necessary files; then the production site should be taken off-line and the upgrade procedure carried out there. Of course, you can simply use your usual deployment method, perhaps by running an update against the site repository.

## Summary

In this chapter, you have seen a complete upgrade from Drupal 5 to Drupal 6 for a simple but nontrivial Drupal site, involving the Drupal core itself and a fair number of modules. The steps for carrying out this upgrade, the best practices to be followed, including the recommendation of using a test site, and the sources of gaining insight into the pitfalls and detailed information that might be necessary are outlined.

The steps have been followed, and the upgrade has been carried out. In the following chapters, you will be exploring the added benefits of Drupal 6, which unfetters us in terms of placing the functionality and presentation theme for our example website application, the On-Line Literary Workshop, on a rich and firm foundation.

# 9

# Upgrading to Drupal 6 Revisited

So you've decided to upgrade your site to Drupal 6! This section is meant to guide you through that process, after having gleaned from both experience and the best advice out there the concrete steps you should follow. The eight steps involved in any upgrade are:

1. Shift everything over to a test site (you may already have one, but this is just to make sure you are acting on the real McCoy, just in case you are not using version control).
2. Update everything to the latest Drupal 5.x version available, not only for Drupal core, but also for all the modules you are using.
3. Test everything running in the latest and brightest 5.x version.
4. Make a module inventory, and see which modules might not yet have been upgraded to a Drupal 6.x version. The modules that you have installed are the most important factor in determining how easy or difficult, or even possible, the upgrade process will be.
5. Switch to the default Drupal theme. Research whether or not your theme is available in a version for Drupal 6.
6. Disable all modules. Now, do not uninstall any of the modules — you don't want to disturb your data. You just want to leave the field clear for the Drupal 6.x core database upgrade to take place first.
7. Update the Drupal core.
8. Update each of the modules and the theme.

Pinch yourself: It's alive!

However, even though each of these steps will always be present, they may vary in significance and the amount of work involved and the problems encountered in each case. The aim here is to cover as much of what you will realistically come up against rather than sharing yet another abstract guide; the material presented here is based on a single, although very representative and decidedly nontrivial, case study.

### Shifting Everything over to a Test Site

In this example, it is assumed that the whole site is maintained under version control, but in a very Drupal-specific manner:

- Drupal core was originally checked out and updated as different releases came out, directly from the Drupal CVS repository.
- The ./sites directory is then physically removed and replaced with a development branch (HEAD) of an SVN repository.

The reasons for this are quite simple: It is so easy to carry out a Drupal core update on the command line that any other method used is asking for trouble. You will see an example presently. On the other hand, just because the Drupal community, for reasons of its own, sees fit to version its development in a CVS repository is no reason why you should. You can use Git, Mercurio, or, as is the case here, SVN, as more modern and more versatile alternatives.

So, shifting over to a test site involves the following steps:

1. Dump the database to a text file capable of being versioned.
2. Commit everything from ./sites on down to the SVN development repository.
3. Create a new database on the test site.
4. Check out the latest Drupal 5.x version from the Drupal CVS repository, into the new application document root, like this: $ cvs -z6 `-d:pserver:anonymous:anonymous@cvs.drupal.org:/cvs/drupal` co -d www -r DRUPAL-5-10 drupal.
5. Edit ./sites/default/settings.php so that Drupal will be able to speak to the newly created test site database.
6. Edit the file .cvsignore in the root directory to contain "./sites/default/settings.php" so that future updates won't overwrite that file.
7. Check out the development version from the SVN repository by executing a command similar to the following: `$ svn co http://mysvnaccount.svnrepository.com/svn/litworkshop/trunk/sites sites sites`.
8. Insert the file ./sites/all/backup/db/litworkshop.sql into the MySql database.

And you're done. Point your browser at the domain or subdomain corresponding to the document root, and you should be good to go.

## Update Everything to the Latest Drupal 5.x Version

In Chapter 7 you did this, but in case you are working with a site that has not been updated, if your site is still at Drupal release 4.7.x, then you need to update to the latest version of Drupal 5.x first. Then, all modules must be updated to their latest version available because it is that version that will have taken into account the best logic necessary for upgrading to Drupal 6.x.

As explained earlier, take the time to test your site with the latest and greatest modules, and make sure nothing is broken or out of the ordinary, because later on, you won't know if any unexpected behavior is due to the upgrade to Drupal 6.x or the upgrade carried out at this stage.

Then you are ready for the next step, taking the module inventory.

# Module Inventory for the On-Line Literary Workshop

At this point, you need to know all about all your contributed modules, that is, those that are not part of Drupal core (those that are not included as part of the regular Drupal release). For each one, you need to know whether there exists a recommended or at least stable version for Drupal 6.x, and you need to research in the issue queues for each one of them for common caveats, pitfalls, and other problems encountered by others who have already carried out the upgrade.

| **module name** | **Recommended Drupal 6.x version?** | **notes (as of August 2008)** |
|---|---|---|
| `cck` | Yes | Completely rewritten and enhanced. Must use Drupal 6.3 or later to avoid problems upgrading. |
| `date` | Yes | Great number of new features |
| `drush` | Yes | |
| `globalredirect` | Yes | |
| `nodequeue` | rc1 | rc1: Release Candidate 1 |
| `og` | Yes | |
| `pathauto` | Yes | |
| `privatemsg` | No | The HEAD version is for Drupal 6. |
| `tagadelic` | Yes | |
| `themesettings`, `themesettingsapi` | Part of core | Disable and uninstall completely, just like `update_status` module. |
| `token` | Yes | |
| `update_status` | Part of core | Disable and uninstall completely. |
| `views` | Yes | Completely rewritten and enhanced |

# Preparatory Steps before the Point of No Return

There are a few preparatory steps to follow before replacing the Drupal core and modules with their Drupal 6.x counterparts:

1. Log in as User #1 (Admin).
2. Switch back to the default Drupal theme (`themes/garland`).
3. It's necessary to disable and completely uninstall the update status module, since it has ended life as a contributed module and has now begun life as part of the Drupal core. But there is no need to disable all non-core modules, because by their presence they will automatically update, given the manner in which Drupal 6 upgrades. You'll have to deselect modules and click on the "Save configuration" button several times because module dependencies will gray out the checkboxes next to those modules being used as a dependency by another module.

   *Do not disable, in actual fact, the other non-core modules. I tested this procedure several times, and the whole procedure went much more smoothly by leaving all the modules enabled except* `update_status` *and* `themesettings`*, as described above. Again, it bears repeating that the latter are special because they are now part of Drupal core, and vestiges of their old versions as contributed modules will cause problems.*

4. Once the Update Status module and the Theme Settings and Theme Settings api modules are disabled, click on the Uninstall tab, and select the checkbox next to the Update Status module. Click Uninstall to delete it from the system completely, because it will be in the Drupal core with Drupal 6 and the existing tables will cause problems if they are not removed entirely from the database. Leave all the other modules in this list alone, and do not uninstall them, because you don't want to destroy any content or configuration settings.

# Physically Replacing the Drupal 5 Contributed Modules

Because all contributed modules in ./sites/all/modules are under SVN version control, you don't have any choice, actually, and must proceed as follows, first removing them from SVN and then adding them in:

```
~/litworkshop/sites$ svn rm all/modules/date
~/litworkshop/sites$ svn rm all/modules/drush
~/litworkshop/sites$ svn rm all/modules/globalredirect
~/litworkshop/sites$ svn rm all/modules/nodequeue
~/litworkshop/sites$ svn rm all/modules/og
~/litworkshop/sites$ svn rm all/modules/pathauto
~/litworkshop/sites$ svn rm all/modules/privatemsg
~/litworkshop/sites$ svn rm all/modules/tagadelic
~/litworkshop/sites$ svn rm all/modules/themesettings
~/litworkshop/sites$ svn rm all/modules/themesettingsapi
```

```
~/litworkshop/sites$ svn rm all/modules/token
~/litworkshop/sites$ svn rm all/modules/update_status
~/litworkshop/sites$ svn rm all/modules/views
~/litworkshop/sites$
~/litworkshop/sites$ svn committ -m "removed all Drupal 5 \ contributed modules
preparatory to Drupal 6 upgrade - do not check out this revision"
```

Next, download and decompress all the Drupal 6 module version replacements you'll need except `themesettings`, `themesettingsapi`, and `update_status` to be omitted, and postpone the `privatemsg` module until the upgraded system is stable to ./sites/all/modules. Once the system is up and running, these directories will be added to version control once again, and committed *en bloc*.

## Update Drupal Core and Run the Update Script

If you have Drupal core under version control, simply change the directory to the Drupal document root and execute the following:

```
~/litworkshop/sites$ cvs update -dPr DRUPAL-6-3
```

replacing DRUPAL-6-3 with the latest version if greater. Otherwise, delete all the Drupal core files and replace them with the latest Drupal 6.x version no earlier than 6.3

*It bears emphasizing that in ./sites/default there is a new file called default.settings.php that changes your basic default settings file. This file should be used as the basis for your new settings.php file, which should simply be a copy of default.settings.php with your database URL inserted in the appropriate place, plus any other site-specific changes you deem necessary.*

Then you want to follow these steps:

1. Still logged in as Admin (User #1), execute `http://litworkshop.example.com/update.php`. The result should be the Overview page of the Drupal database Update Wizard.
2. After clicking "Continue," you have the chance to select updates before clicking on the Update button. After doing so, 81 updates are carried out, and you should be taken to what is essentially a success page, which includes some informational messages in green, possible warnings in pink (which tend to be ignored unless they stop the show), general information, and links to the main and administration pages, as well as the SQL query of all the updates that were executed. It is definitely a good idea to save this page for future reference. Then, click on the "Administration pages" link to continue.
3. Go to Administer ➤ Site building ➤ Modules, and hit the "Save configuration" button to clear the cache. Now that the smoke has cleared, you can go in and see what you have. At this point, the site should be basically navigable and recognizable, with some things broken since some functionality depends on the theme that has been disabled. For example, Figure 9-1 shows how the quote block is still working but is now divested of its theming and placed on the left-hand side, but that the Genre parade block is still there. The views-supported Browse Literary Pieces block, however, has disappeared.

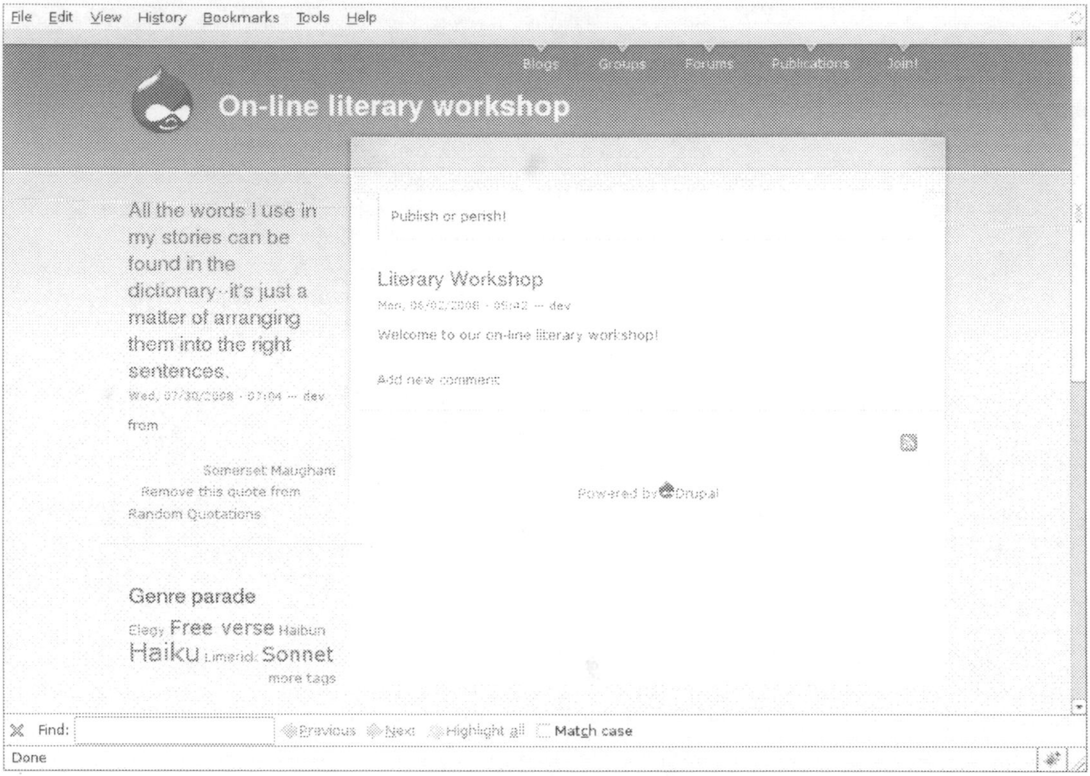


Figure 9-1

4. Now head over to Administer ➤ User management ➤ Permissions (this used to be called *Access control*). Scrolling down, you can see that there are additional permissions added for node content, and a wonderful Ajaxy improvement is that the names of the roles are now always visible as you scroll down the page. (See Figure 9-2.) Apply the new permissions as needed.

# Solving Problems with Organic Groups

At this point, before attacking the theme or the Views situation, you may need to solve some Organic Groups problems.

Log out as Admin and log in as dev. When you do this, you can see that you have two concrete problems:

- ❑ Escaped PHP is showing up in the "My groups" View.
- ❑ The group home pages are no longer showing the group's posts.

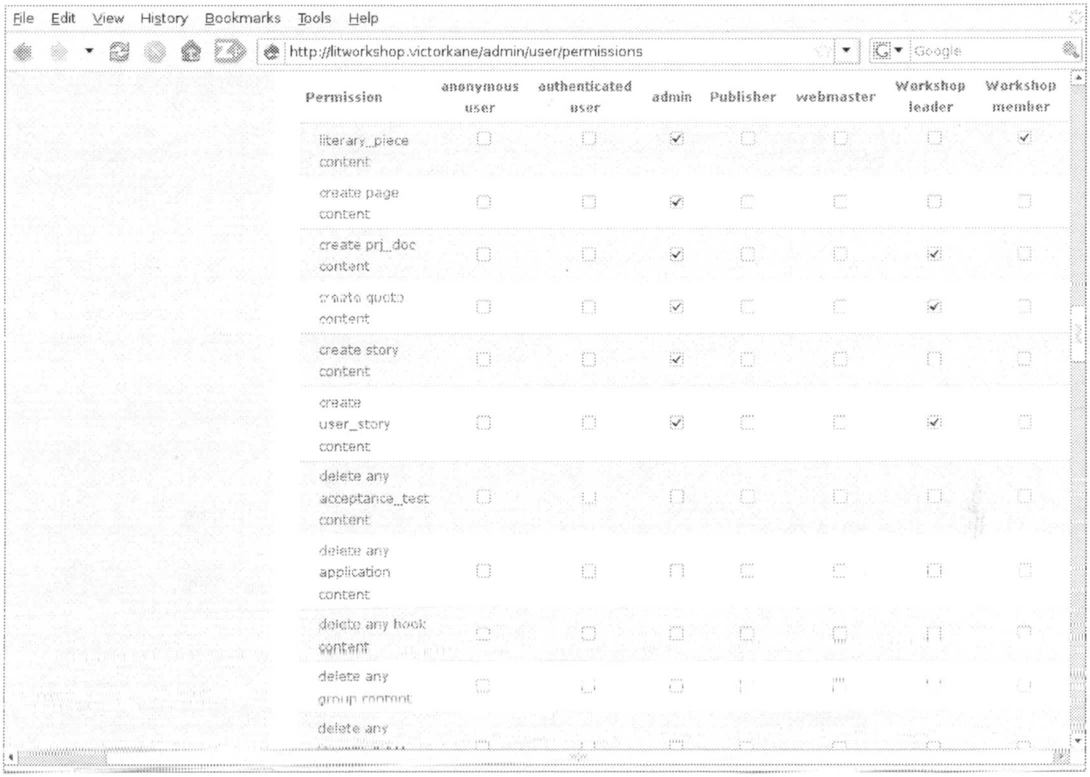


Figure 9-2

# Escaped PHP Showing up in My Groups View

When you click on the Groups main item at the top of the page, you get a correct listing of the groups directory; in this example, this lists the Haibun group, its manager, and the number of members. (The dev group, which houses the project documentation, is configured not to be listed in the groups directory.) So far, so good. But when you click on the "My groups" tab, the screen shows escaped PHP in the header and in the footer, as shown in Figure 9-3.

This is a known, closed issue upon upgrading to Drupal 6, and is "perfectly normal." You simply need to understand clearly what is happening and then fix it. First off, in Drupal 6, the whole ability to use PHP snippets through an optionally applied filter to content items has been wisely abstracted out into its own core module. If one enables this module, then, assuming that you have the correct permissions, you can create a page, specify the PHP filter instead of the Full HTML filter, for example, and specify content as:

```
<?php print '<p>' . $date . 'Welcome</p>'; ?>
```

as an alternative to HTML or plain-text content. Now, what are you doing when you click on the "My groups" tab? You are invoking a View, specifically the `og_my` View, which has a header and a footer and which need to be expressed in terms of PHP, in order to include a link to the list of groups you belong to (your *subscriptions*) in OPML format. There's the rub. For this to happen, a series of conditions has to be met:

1. First off, go to Administer ➤ Site building ➤ Modules, and ensure that the new core PHP filter module is selected. If it is not, select the checkbox and enable the module as usual by clicking on the ''Site configuration'' button.
2. Return to Groups ➤ My groups. If the problem persists, you will need to edit the View. This is remarkably simple. If you mouse over the area just under the ''My groups'' heading visible at the top of the content area in Figure 9-3, three tiny, very handy links appear, allowing you to click them to easily edit, export, or clone the View being presented (see Figure 9-4).

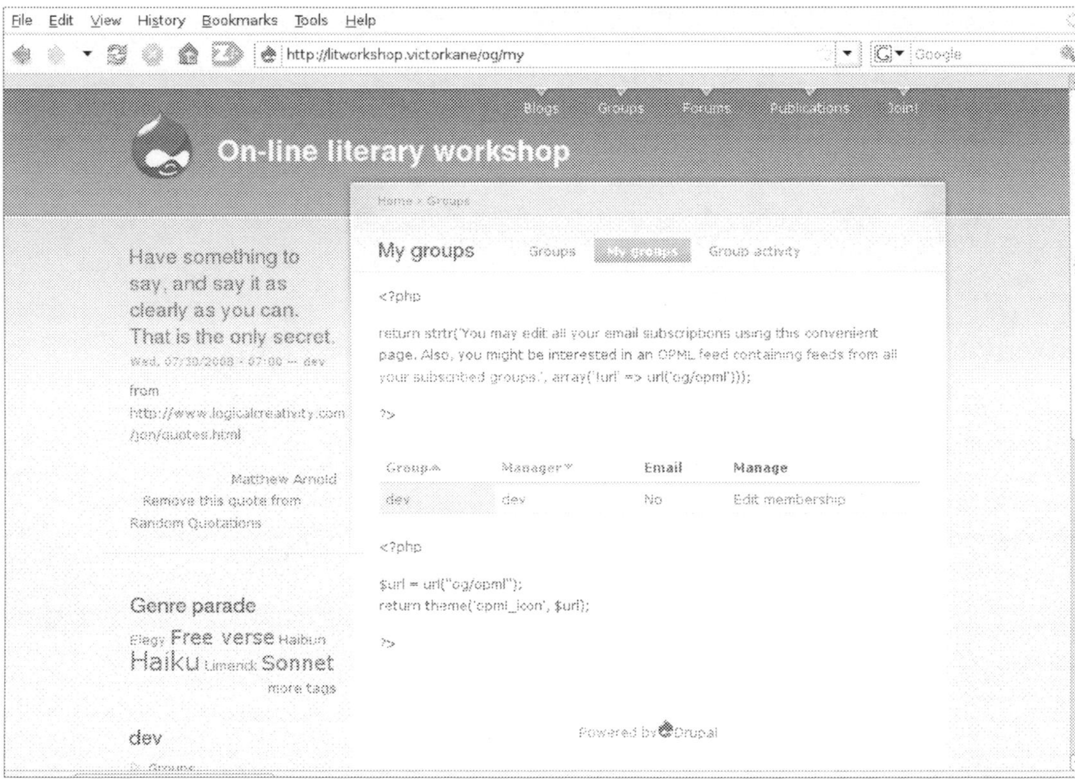


Figure 9-3

Figure 9-4

3. Click on the [Edit] link. Of course, you can accomplish the same thing by going to Administer ➤ Site building ➤ Views and opting to edit the `og_my` View. Once you are at Administer ➤ Site building ➤ Views ➤ Edit view ''`og_my`,'' you make first contact with the all-new Views 2 editing screen, which manages to show everything in a relatively small area, and through the

use of Ajax, makes editing or creating a View very handy and straightforward. At the top of the page is an information item that tells you about the all-new advanced Help module, which you will come to in a moment (it deserves a chapter in itself). What you need now is to look at the ''Basic settings'' section in the second column. This shows settings like the Name (Page), Title (My groups), Items per page, and so on of the page display that concerns us at this point. Notice that both the header and footer have Full HTML links next to them. That is the problem. Change the Header input filter first by clicking on the ''Full HTML'' link.

Full HTML changes to bold, and if you scroll down just a little, you can see that a new work area has opened up, allowing us to edit the header. Figure 9-5 shows how the page looks after opening up the Input filter section and clicking on the PHP code radio button.

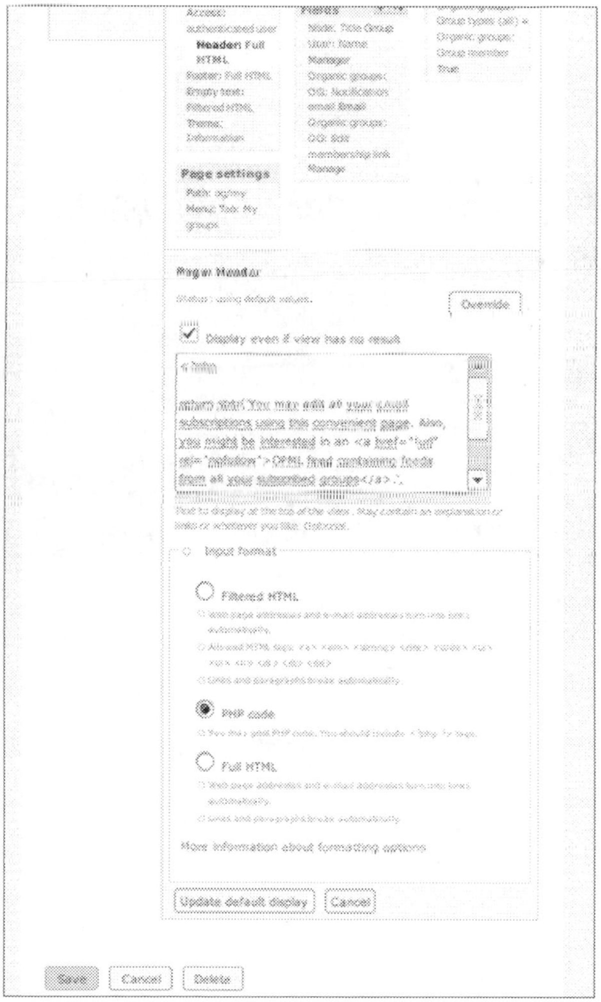


**Figure 9-5**

4. Click on the ''Update default display'' button, and repeat the process for the footer, and then click on the ''Save'' button for your changes to take effect. Figure 9-6 shows that the ''My groups display of escaped PHP'' problem has been solved.

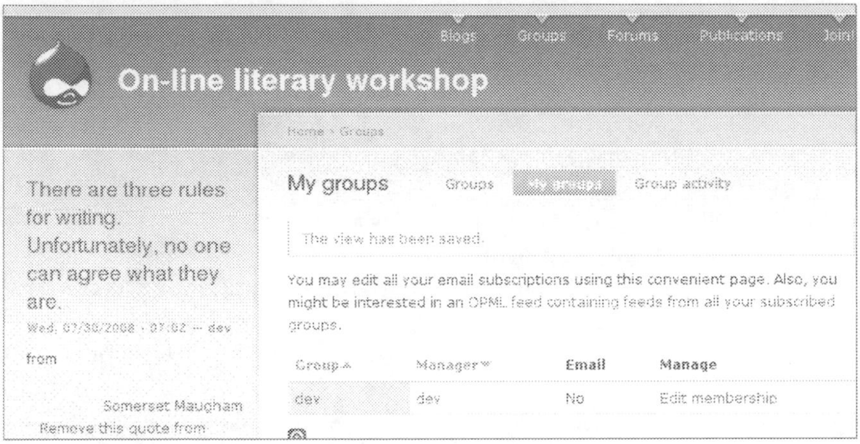


Figure 9-6

## Group Home Pages No Longer Showing the Group's Posts

This was a big problem. Figure 9-7 shows how the dev group home page shows the description of the group and then lists the posts that have been made within the group. Figure 9-8 shows how the listing of the group's posts has been lost.

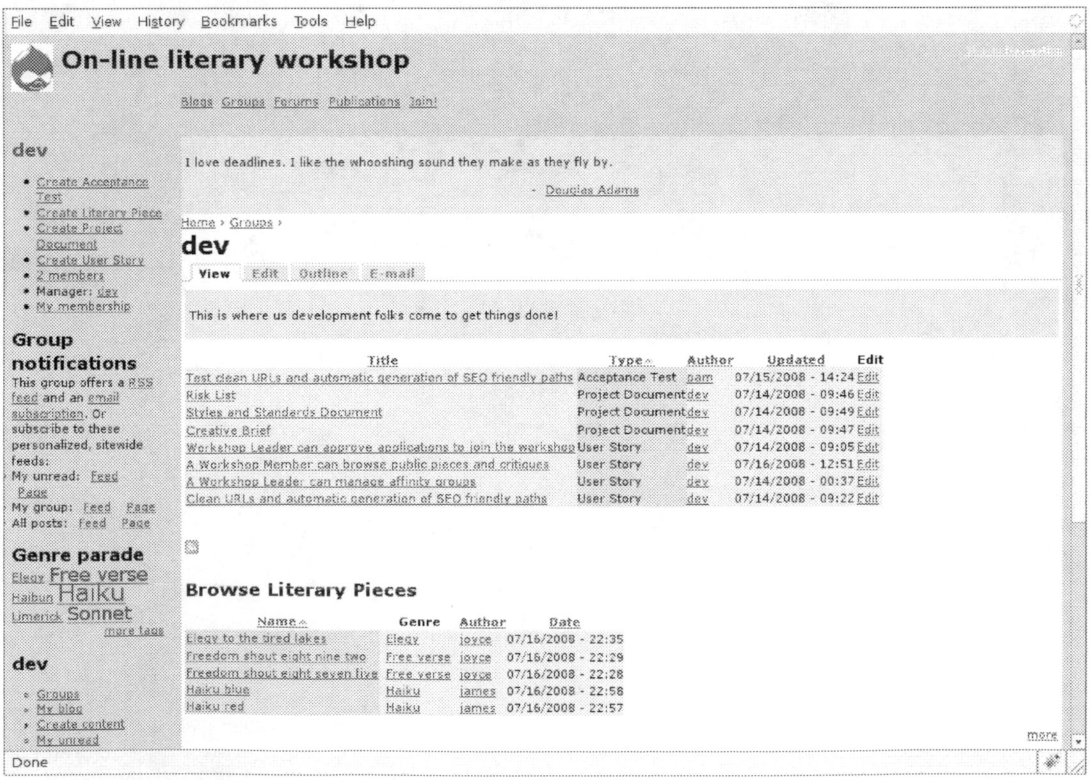


Figure 9-7

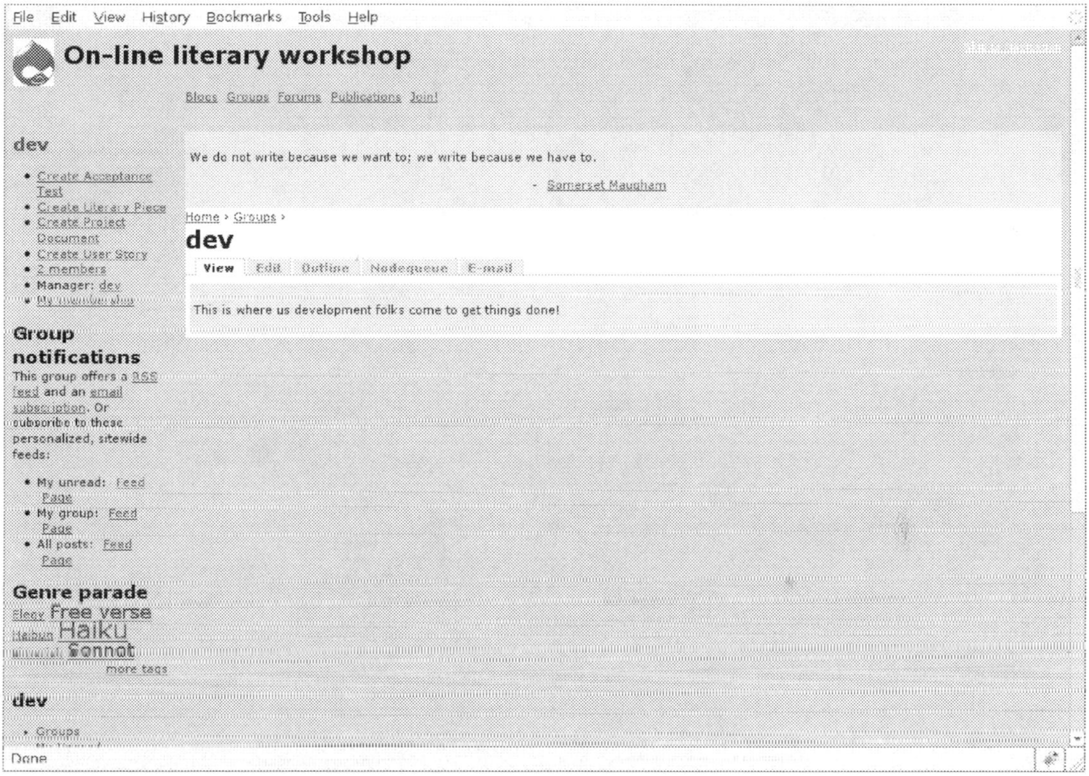


Figure 9-8

As you recall from Chapter 6, this is handled by a specially implemented view, by default called *og_ghp_ron* (group home page River of News), which you then learned how to override with `og_ghp_table` via the user interface by going to Administer ➤ Organic Groups ➤ Organic Groups Configuration and choosing from the list of all views having the *og_ghp_* prefix. Before you go scrambling to do that exact same thing now, bear in mind the following excerpt from the Drupal 6 Organic Groups README.txt:

```
"The user interface for selecting alternate Views for your group homepage is gone.
You may still select an alternate view by setting 'og_home_page_view' variable in
your settings.php. Alternative, just customize your og_ghp_ron View. You can
always revert it if it breaks"
```

So probably what's going on is that the variable `og_home_page_view` is stuck with the value it was given via the user interface in Drupal 5 (`og_ghp_table`), and so does not invoke `og_ghp_ron`, the new default. Why doesn't it just invoke `og_ghp_table`, then? Heading over to Administer ➤ Site building ➤ Views shows that all the views that you created in Drupal 5.x are now missing.

So what about importing `og_ghp_table` from the Drupal 5.x version (still running on the test site) and seeing if that will just work?

1. In the old version, go to Administer ➤ Site building ➤ Views, and click the export link corresponding to `og_ghp_table`.
2. Select and copy the code.

3. In the new version, click on the Import tab, and paste in the code.
4. Leaving the view name blank, click on the `Import` button. The result can be seen in Figure 9-9.

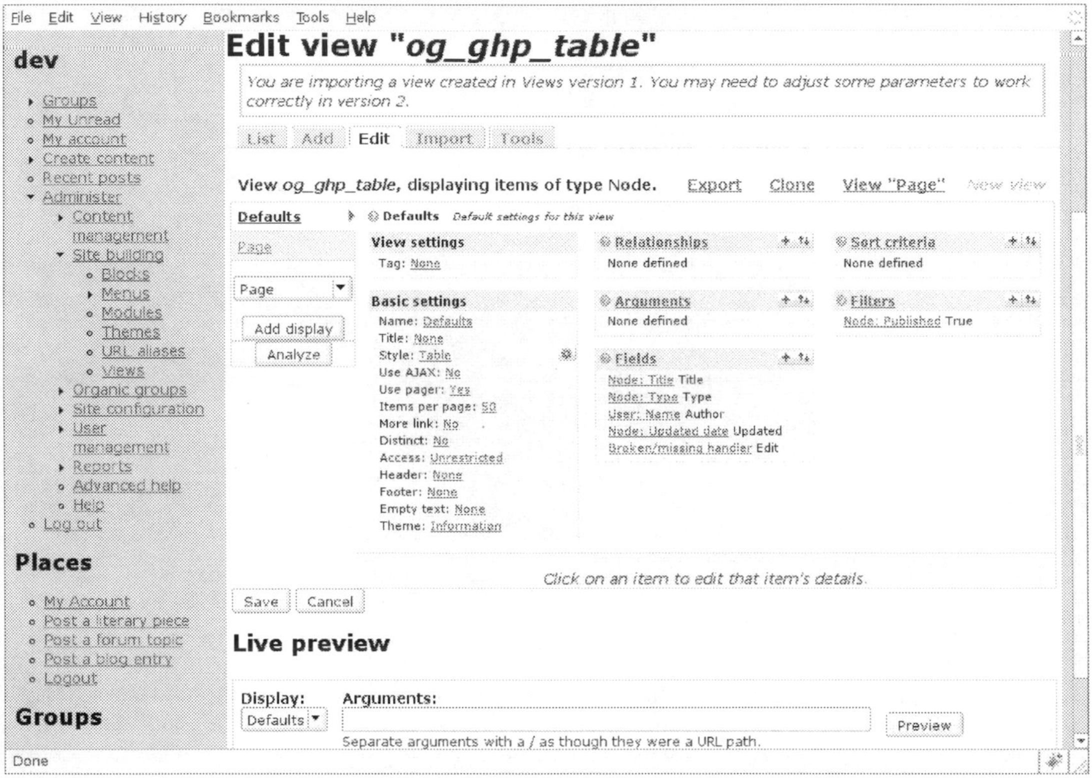

**Figure 9-9**

The warning clearly states:

```
"You are importing a view created in Views version 1. You may need to adjust
some parameters to work correctly in version 2."
```

After studying the default `og_ghp_ron` parameters for the default display, make the following changes:

1. Remove the Page display by selecting it from the tab at the right and hitting the Remove button.
2. Add the ''og'' tag (views have tags now, so it is easy to sort and view them for administrative purposes).
3. Add the Organic groups: Groups argument, so that the view can be invoked for any group simply by the Organic Groups module providing the node ID of the group whose home

page is being displayed. That is how the view `og_ghp_ron` works, and this view needs it also in order to work. When you click the + icon in the Arguments section, a work area opens up below, allowing you to choose a category of arguments (choose "Organic Groups"), and then within that category, the item Groups. See Figure 9-10.

The fields were already imported, so no changes there!

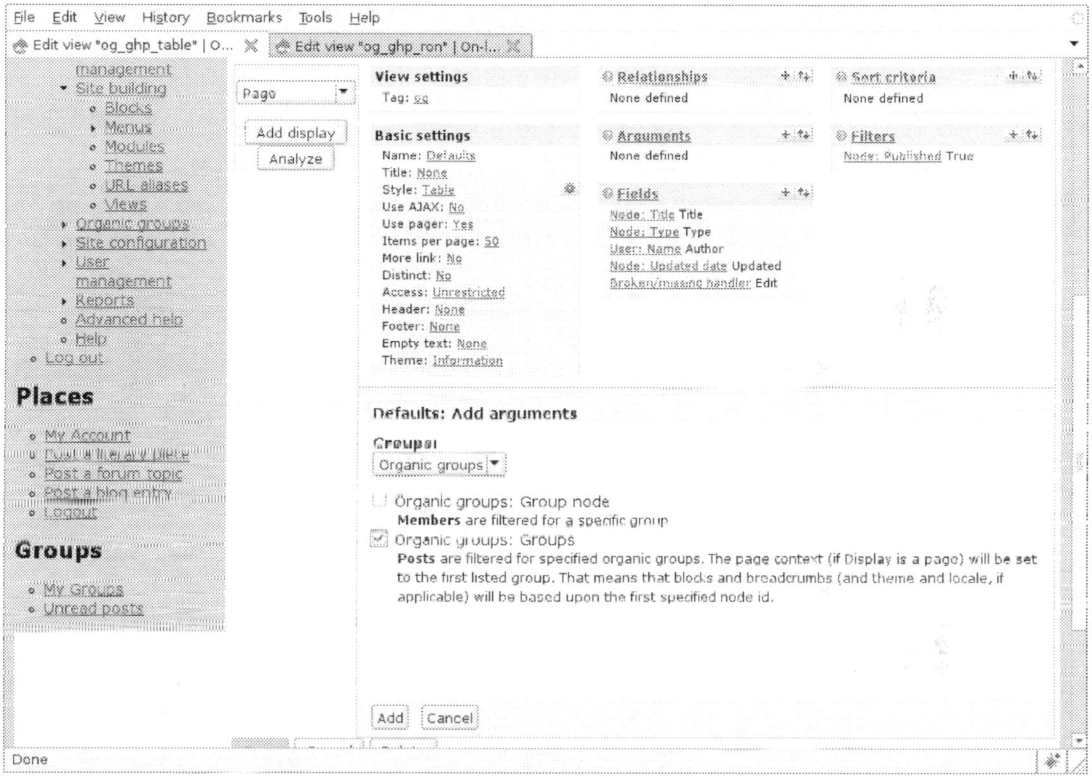

**Figure 9-10**

4. Add the same sort criteria and filter as `og_ghp_ron`.

Now the really cool thing is that you can actually get a live preview to see if the view is working as you configure it. That's how you know you're done!

The last time I edited the dev group node, I noted down that its node ID was 21 (well, not really, but if you go to "My groups" again in another browser window, click "dev," then hit the Edit tab, the URL will be `/node/21/edit`, meaning that the NID of the group node for the dev group is 21). So if you scroll down to the "Live preview" section, provide **21** as the argument (or **20** for the Haibun group), and click on the Preview button, you will see the results right there, plus be shown the SQL query executed (Views is, indeed, a SQL query generator) and other useful information. The Views 2 user interface has improved by leaps and bounds! See this in action in Figure 9-11.

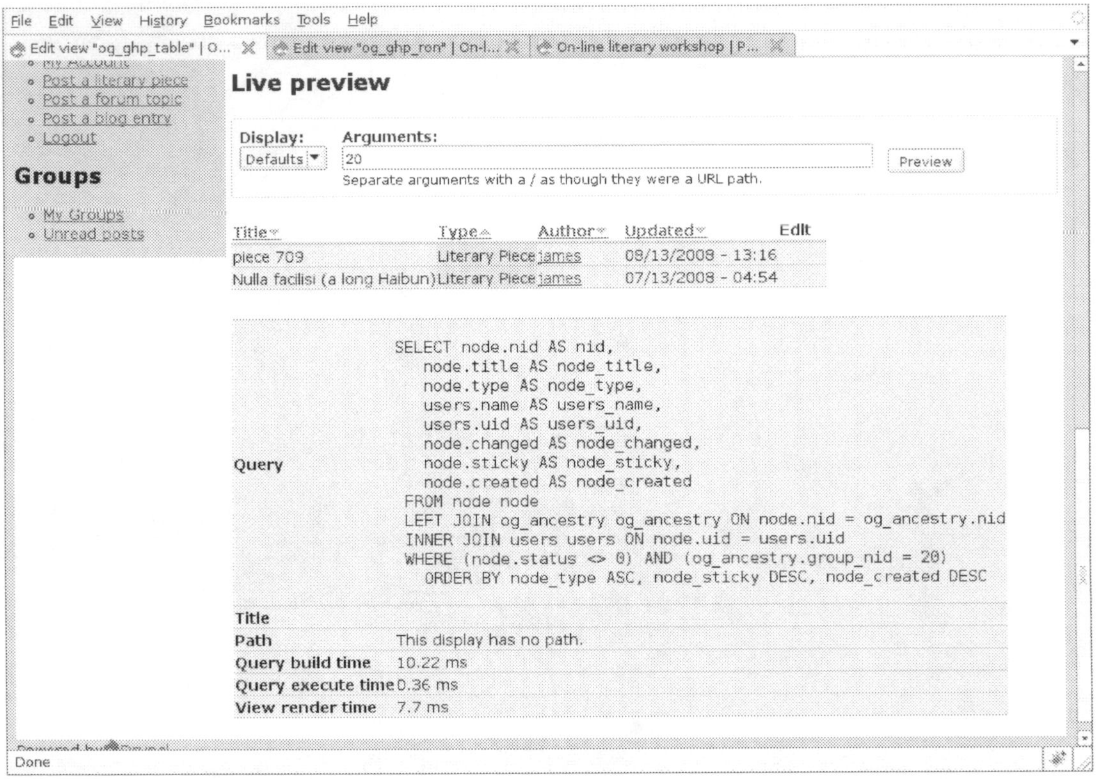


**Figure 9-11**

Save your work, go to the "My groups" page, and then click "dev" — lo and behold, you have your group home page restored!

# Getting the Old Views Back

You have already gotten one of the old views back. There is another view missing from your website application which you had fixed up to appear in every page footer — the Browse Literary Pieces view (see how it is present in Figure 9-7 and absent in Figure 9-8).

Following the same procedure as before, export the view (`genre_browser`) from the test site that is still running Drupal 5.x, and import it onto the new site. This time you need a block display you can then configure as before in Administer ➤ Site building ➤ Blocks.

The view imports well, with its page and block displayed. Everything is almost all set to go, except that in the Fields section, while the node title, author username, and date of last update have imported correctly, one field is described as having a broken or missing handler. If you edit the view on the test site just to see what's going on, you see that this field was actually Taxonomy: Terms for Tags, with label Genre:

1. Click the + icon to add in the closest thing you can find (Taxonomy: Term) and give it the same label, and then remove the broken field.

2. Positioning the field is a breeze! Click on the double-arrows icon, and then in the work area, drag 'n drop! Awesome.
3. Now, fix the filters:

    3a. Go in and fix the Node type filter, which needs to specify **Literary Piece**. Upon fixing that and hitting the Update button, "Live preview" already shows that the view is practically working again!

    3b. Remove the broken handler.

    3c. Click on the + icon in the Filters section, and in the work area select Taxonomy from Groups.

    3d. Select the checkbox next to Taxonomy: Vocabulary ("Filter the results of 'Taxonomy: Term' to a particular vocabulary").

    3e. Click on the Add button, and immediately you get to choose which vocabulary you wish to filter by.

    3f. Leave "Is one of" as the operator, select Tags as the vocabulary, and click on the Update button. The Live Preview is really shaping up!

    3g. Click "Taxonomy: Vocabulary" once again, and hit the Expose button, to make the view the same as it was before.

4. Go ahead and save the view.
5. Go to Administer ➢ Site building ➢ Blocks, assign the genre browser block (which now appears after the creation of the view of the same name) to the Content bottom region, and click on the Configure button.
6. As you did before, in the Page specific visibility settings, make sure that the option "Show on every page except the listed pages" is selected, and then in the text area, list, one per line, the following exceptions:

    ```
    browse/genre
    admin/*
    ```

    This avoids the listing showing up with, erm, the listing, and avoids it showing up on Admin pages.
7. Fill in a Title and save the block.

Figures 9-7 and 9-8 should now be identical.

# Installing the Advanced Help Module

When you were fixing the `og_my` and `og_ghp_table` views, you saw the following information message at the top of the View Edit form:

```
If you install the advanced help module from http://drupal.org/project/↩
advanced_help, Views will provide more and better help. Hide this message.
```

This Advanced Help module can also be used by you for your sites, so it is certainly well worth downloading and installing. It enables placing an arbitrary number of Help links that pop up pure HTML Help pages into a small separate browser window. Really awesome, and yet another part of the solid advance in Drupal usability that comes with each release, by leaps and bounds. Follow these steps:

1. Download the module and install it in the usual way.
2. Go to Administer ➢ User management ➢ Permissions, and grant all three Advanced Help permissions to all authenticated user roles.
3. After saving the permissions, head over to Administer ➢ Views. To the left of each View title bar can now be found a tiny question-mark icon, which turns bright blue when moused over.
4. Clicking on the question-mark icon brings up the help associated with that link in a small browser window. See Figure 9-12.

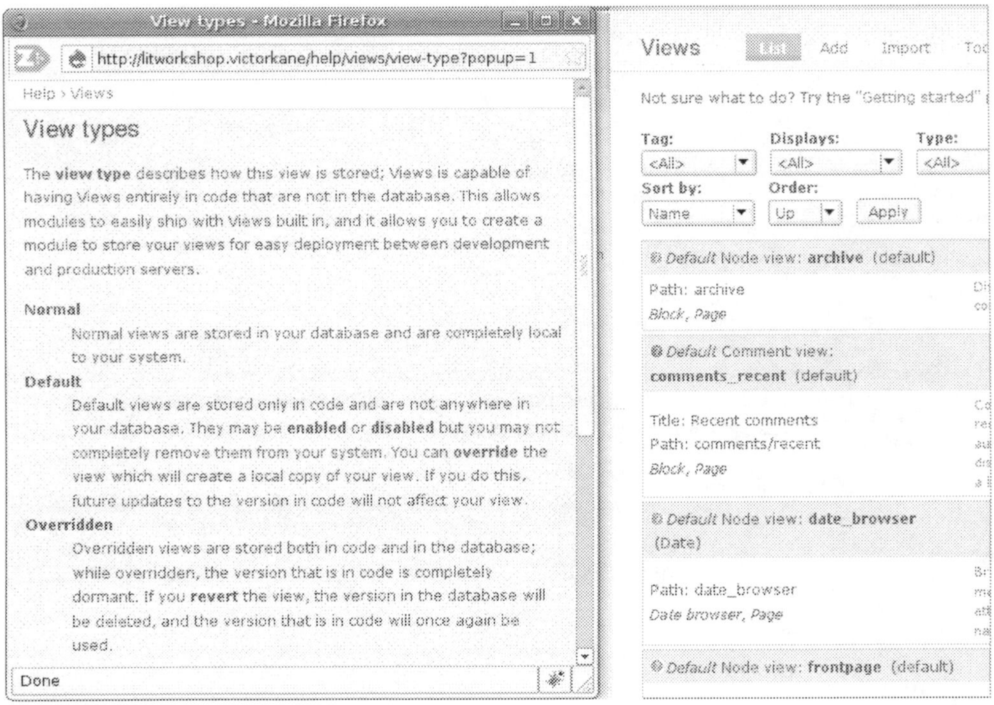

Figure 9-12

There has never been anything like this in Drupal before. Clicking on the Views link in the pop-up breadcrumb takes you to the index, where you can get a full education in Views 2. Also, try it for context-sensitive help while actually editing a view. Clicking the Help icon next to, say, Arguments, will bring up detailed help on the subject. This is also available for the Node Queue module. You can find more on Advanced Help and how to make use of it for your own sites later on in this book.

# Upgrading Your Zen Theme to Drupal 6.x

At the end of Chapter 7, you created a subtheme based on the Zen theme system. In order to upgrade it to Drupal 6.x, you are going to have to be a bit drastic because it is a huge jump, but you will still be able to put your prior work to good use:

1. Copy your subtheme over to some safe location outside your site. Then remove all themes from the ./sites/all/themes directory. If they are under version control, use SVN for this as follows:

```
~/litworkshop/sites$ svn rm all/themes/litgarland/ all/themes/zen/
~/litworkshop/sites$ svn commit -m "Removed Drupal 5 contributed themes
during upgrade to Drupal 6"
```

2. Download the latest version of the Zen theme for Drupal 6 from the project site (`http://drupal.org/project/zen`), and install it under ./sites/all/themes.
3. Create a fresh copy of the subtheme by renaming a copy of ./sites/all/themes/zen /STARTERKIT to ./sites/all/themes/zen/zenlitworkshop.
4. Rename ./sites/all/themes/zen/zenlitworkshop/STARTERKIT.info to ./sites/all/themes/zen/zenlitworkshop/zenlitworkshop.info. This general description and specification file is required for all themes, starting with the Drupal 6 release, as explained in Chapter 8.
5. Edit it with a text editor, and rename all occurrences of STARTERKIT **zenlitworkshop**, change the name field value to **On-line literary workshop theme**, and change the description field value to **Zen based theme for the On-line literary workshop**.
6. Edit ./sites/all/themes/zen/zenlitworkshop/template.php and ./sites/all/themes/zen/zenlitworkshop/theme-settings.php with a text editor also, and rename all occurrences within each one of STARTERKIT **zenlitworkshop**.
7. Because you used a liquid layout previously, copy ./sites/all/themes/zen/zen/layout-liquid.css to ./sites/all/themes/zen/zenlitworkshop/layout.css, being careful not to overwrite any changes you might have made to this file. One way to do this is using the diff in Linux (or the great Windiff in Windows). Notice how the filename is renamed to plain *layout.css*.
8. Copy ./sites/all/themes/zen/zen/print.css to ./sites/all/themes/zen/litworkshop/print.css.
9. Copy ./sites/all/themes/zen/zen/zen.css to ./sites/all/themes/zen/zenlitworkshop/zenlitworkshop.css. Notice how the filename is renamed. This is the main style sheet for your subtheme.
10. Now, what about the other changes that were specific to the Drupal 5.x version of the `zenlitworkshop` theme? Copy the `quote` content type-specific suggestion node-quote.tpl.php file into ./sites/all/themes/zen/zenlitworkshop along with the template node.tpl.php. You can do the same with the page.tpl.php file. Neither the latter nor node.tpl.php has changed significantly.

> *The node-quote.tpl.php will have no effect whatsoever on nodes of type* `quote` *if it is placed in the* `zenlitworkshop` *subtheme directory until it is also accompanied by the template file from which it is derived, node.tpl.php. Both have to be there. See* `http://drupal.org/node/223440` *for the explanation.*

**11.** Now, a lot of changes have been made to zen.css, so the 5.x version of zenlitworkshop.css cannot be simply copied over. You need to copy the changes made to it over to the new zenlitworkshop.css.

**12.** So, how do you know what changes you made to zenlitworkshop.css? By using the UNIX utility `diff` in the following manner: head over to the 5.x version of the `litworkshop` zen subtheme you saved in a different location, and on the command line change directories to the `zenlitworkshop` subtheme. Then do the following (comparing the main style sheet to the original one of that version):

```
~/zenlitworkshop$ diff zenlitworkshop.css ../zen.css
34d33
<     background-color: #d3d3ff;
106,111d104
<     background-color: #fff;
<   }
<
<   /* This makes a big difference! */
<   #mission, #content-top, #content-area, #content-bottom, .feed-icons{
<     padding: 5px;
116d108
<     background-color: #e9e9ff;
121d112
<     background-color: #e9e9ff;
244d234
<     background-color: #d3d3ff;
736,740d725
<
<   /* Random Quote block */
<   #content-top .taxonomy {
<     margin-left: 400px;
<   }
~/zenlitworkshop$
```

Not too bad! Go ahead and effectuate the same changes to the new zenlitworkshop.css file.

> *Starting with release 6.x, a new change in Drupal obliges you to clear the Drupal theme registry whenever you add or remove functions and/or templates. You are not adding or removing any functions in template.php in this case, but you are adding a template (node.tpl.php), required for node-quote.tpl.php. For your changes to go into effect when you enable the new subtheme, clear the theme registry by visiting Administer ➢ Site configuration ➢ Performance and clicking the Clear Cached data button at the bottom of the form.*

You have now prepared your subtheme. After making sure the standard Drupal theme is specified as the default administration theme, clear the Drupal theme registry, enable the `zenlitworkshop` theme, and make it the default theme. Voilá! After all this work, it will be necessary to do some work to make your original theme prettier, but all in good time.

# The All-New Devel Module

Before you commit all your work and call it a day on the upgrade path, it will be well worth the effort to include the all-new Devel module in the mix. Just as Earl Miles (merlinofchaos) has made a tremendous contribution with the Panels (you will see this in a later chapter), Views, Nodequeue, and Advanced Help, as well as the Update Status modules, Moshe Weitzman has also, as the author of Organic Groups and a host of other work in the Drupal Community, including the Devel module.

The Devel module (`http://drupal.org/project/devel`), even though it has not made an appearance yet in this book, has been around for quite some time. It has been popular since its inception, since it makes available a host of helper and utility functions (summary of all database queries for the current page complete with execution times, easy clearing of the cache, reinstallation of modules, access to Drupal variables, a block for running PHP snippets on the fly, etc.). It had already established its "Don't leave home without it" status. And now, starting with Drupal 6, it includes what is billed (justifiably so) as the "Firebug for Drupal theming," the *Theme developer*.

Follow these steps to install and get started with this module:

1. Download and install the module as usual, then enable all the Devel family, the Devel, Devel generate, Devel node access, Macro, Nodequeue generate, and Theme Developer modules.
2. Click on the "Save configuration" button.
3. Head over to Administer ➢ User management ➢ Permissions, and grant all permissions to the Admin role, and none to any other role, in the Devel module and devel_node_access module sections. A common misconception is that Devel should not be installed on production sites because it uses too many resources. Nothing could be further from the truth. It is essential on all sites, including production sites. Simply do not grant any permissions to any role other than the Admin role.
4. After saving permissions, go to the main page. Already, in the lower-left-hand corner, is a transparent gray box with a checkbox and the label "Themer info." Select the checkbox, and immediately in the upper-right-hand corner appears the "Drupal Themer information" window, with the message, "Click on any element to see information about the Drupal theme function or template that created it." Because you know some theming went into the random quote block, click on the Haiku tag in the Genre parade block, just to get off the main page, and on the new page (/category/tags/haiku), select "Themer info" again, and immediately mouse over the random quote area, which will immediately highlight with a red wireframe similar to the Firebug inspect mode. Click on the highlighted area, and then click on the bottom of the "Themer info" screen, on a box that says "Array, 50 elements"). You should see something like Figure 9-13.

The statement bears repeating: There has never been anything like this in Drupal before. Selecting the object on the screen, you are told that it was rendered by the block.tpl.php template invoked via a theming function at the time the page.tpl.php template was invoked to render the page, and that the first invoked the node.tpl.php template in order to render the object itself. The node-quote.tpl.php file was the one actually used via the polymorphic-like naming conventions common to the Drupal theming system, as discussed in Chapter 7. And it was done in 9.01 ms (milliseconds). Additionally, you have before you in the array display (bordered by gray and yellow) all the information about the node itself (the attributes of the `$node` object itself). No more using PHP `print_r` statements in the code and templates to see what's what.

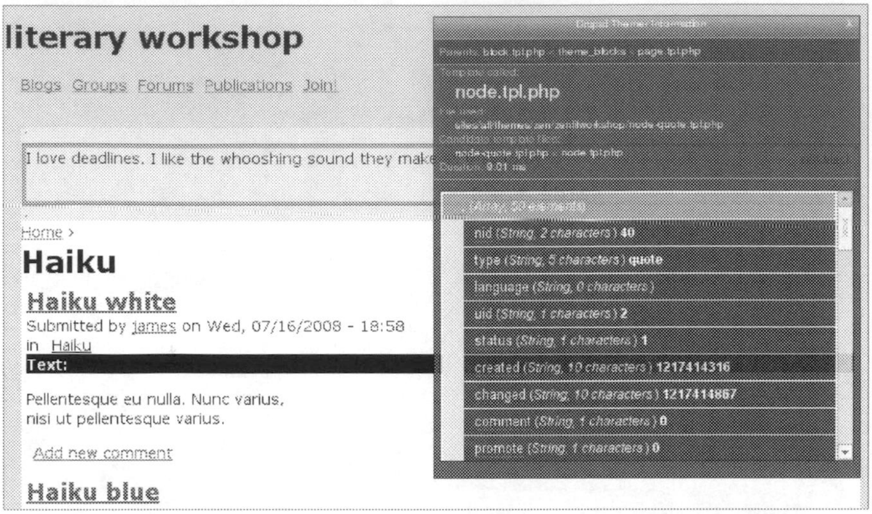


Figure 9-13

To configure the Themer, follow these steps:

1. Go to Administer ➢ Site configuration ➢ Devel Themer. There is an option there to display a theme log at the foot of each page, essentially the same information as in the pop-up browser window, but somewhat more complete and copyable for documentation purposes.
2. To configure the Devel module itself, go to Administer ➢ Site configuration ➢ Devel settings, where you can enable and disable all kinds of options. As someone trying to get the most out of Drupal, you should experiment a lot with these options, and you will learn a great deal at every step.

   For example, enable "Collect query info" and "Display query log," saving the configuration and going to any page, for example /texts/joyce/elegy-tired-lakes. At the bottom of the page, you can now see all the database queries that were necessary to render the page. It is a little overwhelming at first, but yes, Drupal is a database-intensive framework. You can even see the session information. But when it comes time to seeing where the bottlenecks are and making sure you don't have repeated queries and the like, this tool is invaluable.
3. Now enable three of the development blocks, just for the sake of familiarity. Go to Administer ➢ Site building ➢ Blocks, and enable the "Execute PHP" block in the Footer region, the Development and "Switch user" blocks in the left sidebar.

> **Security Alert! At the time of writing this chapter, a security announcement was made by the Drupal Security Team involving multiple vulnerabilities, and maintenance releases were immediately made for Drupal 6.x and 5.x (the past release is always supported in tandem with the current release). When you see that, you drop what you are doing and install the maintenance releases. With Drupal 6.x, just with the Update Status module enabled, the following is shown in the info area**

**at the top of the content area every time you hit an Admin page so you can't miss it (which is a tremendous example of security awareness and responsiveness):**

```
"There is a security update available for your version of
   Drupal. To ensure the security of your server, you
   should update immediately! See the available updates
   page for more information."
```

4. From the Development block, you can disable and enable the Theme Developer (try it); you can empty the cache (so if you add a template to your theme, that's a single-click way of clearing the theme registry and having it enter the scheme of things immediately); you can execute the `PHPinfo` function and see all your system characteristics; you can run cron; and . . . you can access the Variable Editor!

   On this last note, let's try it. After backing up the database, click on the Variable Editor link and scroll down the page until you see the `og_home_page_view` variable. Click on the associated Edit link on the far-right-hand side of the screen. Very carefully, in the textarea, change the `og_ghp_table` value to **og_ghp_ron**. You should see something like Figure 9-14 (notice the handy URL).

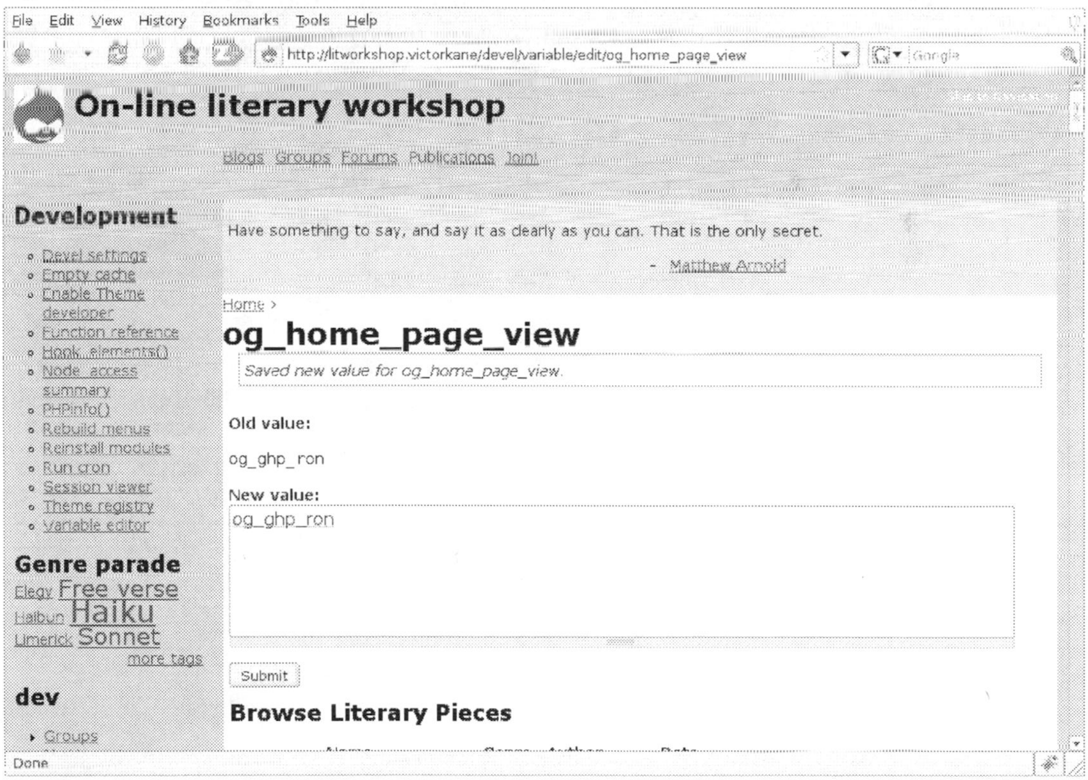


Figure 9-14

5. Now, in another browser window, check out the Haibun group home page. Instead of the table view that took so much work getting into shape, you will now see the default River of News blog-like display for the group's posts.

6. Now, carefully change the value back to `og_ghp_table`. Home ➤ Groups ➤ Haibun now shows your table style display as before! Neat using the Devel module, isn't it? Don't leave home without it! Of course, you have to be careful about what you are doing.

7. So let's execute some PHP code! After backing up the database (again), execute the following harmless block of code by entering it into the Execute PHP block you enabled in the Footer section:

```
global $user;
dprint_r($user);
```

   And hit the Execute button. You will see a prettily printed out display of the `$user` object with all its attributes.

And finally, the Switch user block will allow you to masquerade as james immediately, create some content, and see things as james sees them, without having to log out and log in as james and remember that password too. Of course, because james doesn't have access to the Devel module, you will have to log out and then log in as user dev again, but in any case, this is a very useful feature that you will find yourself using time and again.

# Committing and Deploying to the Test Site

Just as a word of reminder, you must add all the third-party modules in ./sites/all/modules as well as the spanking new Zen subtheme back into the SVN repository. To do so, use either your favorite GUI (RapidSVN or TortoiseSVN) or the command line. Don't forget to include the database dump, and to go ahead and commit also. With this upgrade you have hit a major milestone in the project.

Luckily, deploying the upgrade to the test site is relatively easy:

1. Log into your test site, and place it in maintenance mode (go to Administer ➤ Site Configuration ➤ Site maintenance, select Off-line, and hit the ''Save configuration'' button).

2. Replace the Drupal core files with the 6.x version, and copy the ./sites/default.settings.php file to settings.php, being careful to preserve your site-specific database information.

3. In the ./sites directory, carry out this command to update your themes and modules:

```
$ svn update
```

4. Now, remove all tables from your database (zap it completely — this is a test site, and production content need not be backed up and restored), and restore ./sites/all/backup/litworkshop.sql to the database.

And you're good to go!

# Summary

In this chapter, you have seen, once again, a complete upgrade from Drupal 5 to Drupal 6 for a simple but nontrivial Drupal site, involving the Drupal core itself and a fair number of modules. The steps for carrying out this upgrade, the best practices to be followed, including the recommendation of using a test site, and the sources of gaining insight into the pitfalls and detailed information that might be necessary are outlined and gone over step by step.

This second time around proved to be quite an eye-opener, because the views and og modules each brought with them quite a bit in terms of added functionality and possibilities, not to mention the Devel module: I can truly say, after writing this chapter, that if I had not been familiar with Drupal before, I surely would start using it now.

In the following chapters, you will be exploring even more of the added benefits of Drupal in its latest releases, as the On-Line Literary Workshop approaches its Beta and Final release versions, on its way to launch and life as a Drupal installation profile.

# Part IV

# Getting the Most out of Drupal 6.x

# 10

# Installing and Using Drupal 6 Fresh out of the Box

To show how Drupal 6, with its enhanced functionality, can really kick-start your website application right out of the box, in this chapter you will develop a self-contained website application without installing a single additional module, with the exception of the ever-present CCK (and associated Date) and Views modules, which everyone automatically installs as a matter of course without giving it a second thought, and without which Drupal would not be Drupal.

The project, "Translation Studio," consists of a multi-user, multilingual translation studio capable of being used by both Translators looking for work and Clients who need to get their translations done. Clients upload the work that needs to be done, a Translator Team Leader assigns the work to registered Translators, and the Translators log in and create bilingual or multilingual versions of the same document. When the work is ready to be downloaded, the Client is notified and logs in to access and download his or her translations. Translators are paid a standard rate through an off-site financial arrangement.

You will build this step by step, and, of course, as usual, the self-contained and fully functional code for the chapter is freely downloadable.

> *Please note that just as in the case of the On-Line Literary Workshop, the steps to be followed in building this website application mirror the best-practices workflow presented in Chapter 1 (see the Main Process Workflow diagram and the explanation accompanying it at the start of the chapter). Without exception, all successfully built and launched website applications I have been involved in have followed a workflow similar to this, while all failures I have been associated with resulted from a failure, for some reason, to follow them.*

This time you will be following that workflow in a single chapter. The steps, tailored to the example shown here, are as follows:

1. Install Drupal on a LAMP stack.
2. Design and build the architecture.

3. Create the business objects.
4. Create the site user workflows.

# Step 1: Installing Drupal — Easier Than Ever Before

For the first time, Drupal comes with an interactive Installation Wizard that guides you through every step of the way. When you have finished the installation process, a settings file will be correctly configured and will point toward your newly created database, which will be automatically populated with the necessary tables and data. A good reference section on installing Drupal 6 can be found in the Drupal Handbook Documentation at `http://drupal.org/getting-started/6/install`.

## Downloading Drupal

First of all, go to `http://drupal.org` and in the upper-right-hand corner you will see the Download block. Click on the latest version of Drupal. You will be taken to the Download link. Click "Download Drupal 6.x," and save drupal-6.x.tar.gz (where *x* will be the latest version of the Drupal 6 release) to your local desktop or laptop.

As noted in earlier chapters, however, best practices for Drupal release installation is to grab the Drupal files via CVS, since this makes for super simple updates and eliminates human and FTP errors entirely. See:

- "Doing It with CVS" (Chapter 2)
- "Update Drupal Core and Run the Update Script" (Chapter 9)

## Unzipping and Preparing Files for Upload

In this chapter, let's take the approach simplest for people not familiar with using the command line, in which you transfer all the files to your hosting server using an FTP client. Use your usual file manager to unzip the downloaded file to the desktop or any other convenient folder. There's just one chore to take care of — go to ./sites/default, and copy the default.settings.php file to a new file called *settings.php* in the same folder. While both files need to be present, Drupal will automatically install your settings info in this new file you have created.

## Uploading Files

Next, navigate to that folder with your favorite FTP client. On Windows and Mac, you might use FileZilla (`http://filezilla.sourceforge.net/`), on Ubuntu gFTP, for example. Now follow these steps:

1. Make sure that "hidden" files are visible, since it is essential not to leave out the .htaccess file in the upload.
2. In the destination panel of your FTP client, connect to the document root of the domain or subdomain where you have decided to install Drupal. If this is not a full-blown production install, you will be best served by at least creating a subdomain using your CPanel or hosting panel, which will associate a subdomain like `http://translationstudio.example.com`

with a subdirectory immediately below your main document root. In this way, you have the best of all possible worlds: You don't hog the document root itself on your hosting server, but you can address all images and other files with an "absolute relative" path, such as "/files/images/special-icon.png." In other words, by using a subdomain, Drupal resides in a subdirectory but thinks it is in a document root.

3. Transfer all your files to the destination folder on your hosting server.
4. Before you create the database you will be using for your Drupal installation and running the Installation Wizard, there is just one chore to do, which is to make the uploaded ./sites/default/settings.php file writeable for all users (-rw-rw-rw-, or 666 in Linux). Once the install process is over, the file permissions can be changed back (-r--r--r--, or 444) for security reasons. Your FTP client should allow you to do this in a straightforward manner (in most cases, by right-clicking on the file and finding this feature among the options offered in a dropdown list).

## Creating the Database and User for the Drupal Installation

For security reasons, you want to create a new database user with full permissions over a single, new database to which no other user has permissions. Your hosting panel will offer you one or more ways of doing this. In order to run Drupal's Installation Wizard, you should then have three pieces of information handy:

- The name of the new database
- The name of the user with full privileges over this database
- The user password

I used PhpMyAdmin, as described in Chapter 2: I headed straight for privileges, and clicked on the "Add a new User" link, then filled in the details and noted the three items of info (database name and user, password) on a new sticky Tomboy note (use your own favorite sticky notes app), clicked on the "Create database with same name and grant all privileges" option, and clicked on the Go button.

## Running the Drupal Install Wizard

Now for the fun part. Point your browser at the new installation URL, and you should see something similar to Figure 10-1.

The fascinating "Choose language" option shows that you are in the presence of a truly modern piece of software capable of being localized to an ever-increasing number of languages, and that the localization process can take place right here and now in the installation process.

Even though you will be incorporating both localization (l10n) and internationalization (i18n) in this mini-application, the main localization language will be English. So follow these steps:

1. Click "Install Drupal in English." Behind the scenes, Drupal will attempt to create the directory ./sites/default/files, and in most hosting scenarios, it will be able to do so. Should that not be the case, you will see a warning like that shown in Figure 10-2, and you will have to create the directory manually and make sure Drupal can write to that directory, and then click the "Try again" link at the bottom of the screen.

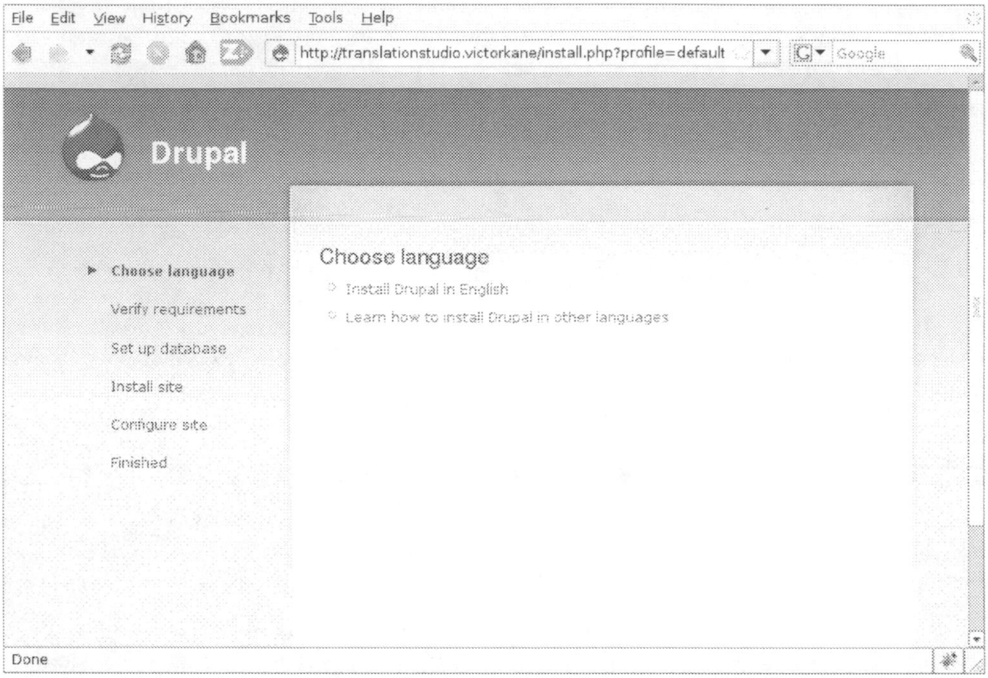


Figure 10-1

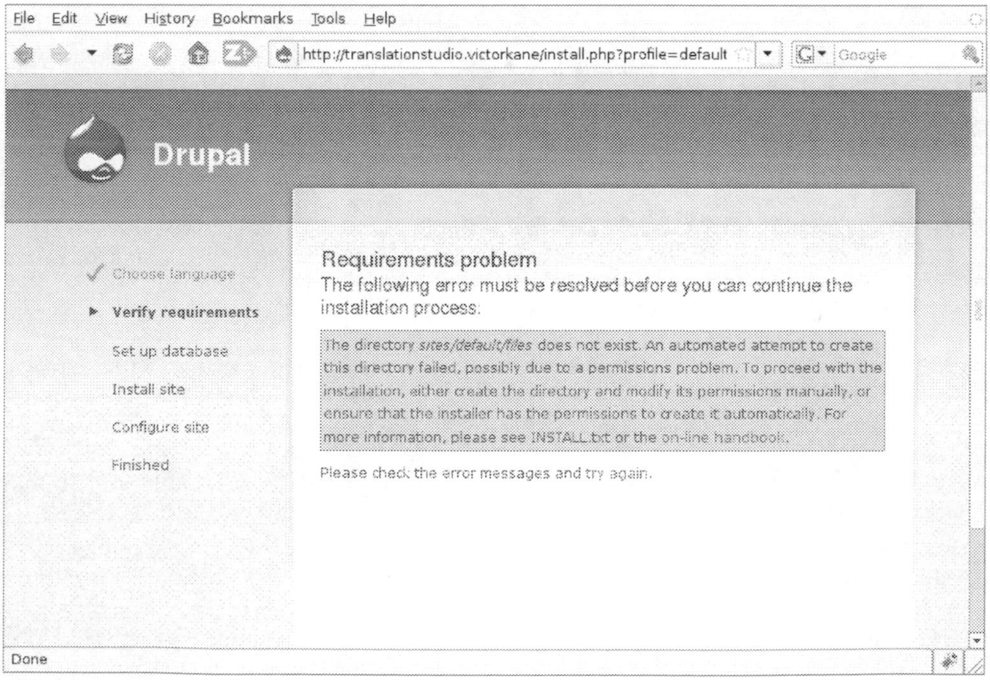


Figure 10-2

2. You are then taken to the Database Configuration page, where you should simply copy in the three items of information you noted down when you created the database. See Figure 10-3.

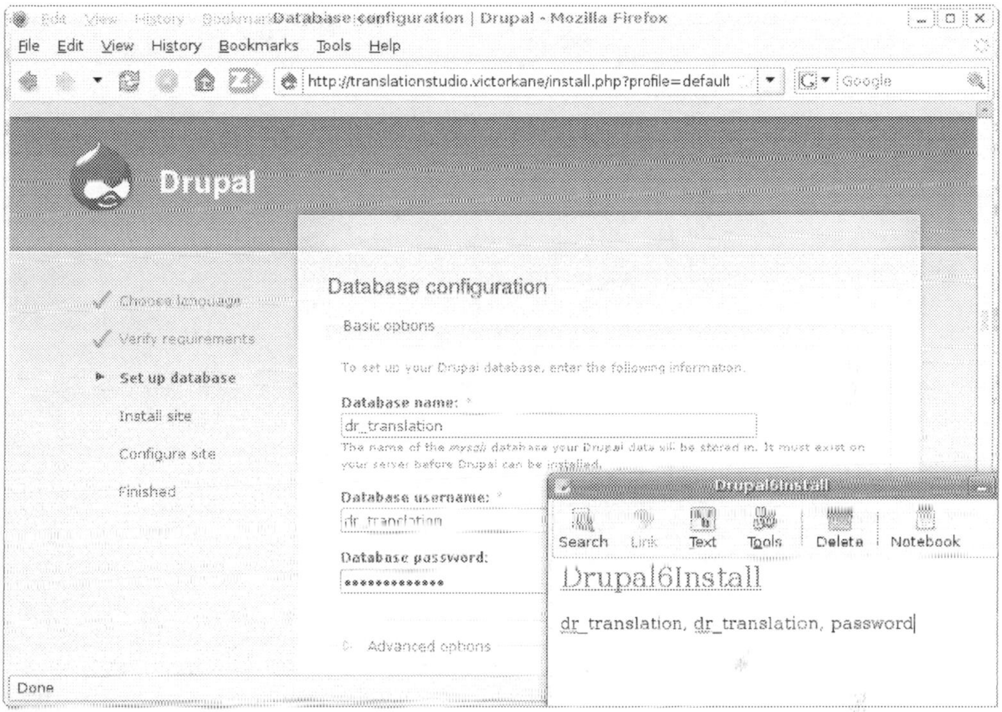

Figure 10-3

3. Click "Save and continue." The next page is very convenient. First of all, the following warning is displayed:

> *All necessary changes to ./sites/default and ./sites/default/settings.php have been made, so you should remove write permissions to them now in order to avoid security risks.*

4. After that, you are asked to fill in site-specific information. This information includes a Site e-mail address, all the particulars for the administration account, and Time Zone information. You also get an automatic enabling of Clean (SEO friendly) URLs together with the comforting message: "Your server has been successfully tested to support this feature," as well as the option of automatically enabling the Update Notifications feature, so that you will be automatically notified when new releases are available for the Drupal core and modules.

   Of particular interest on this page is the very cool password validation Ajax widget, which not only tells you if the repeated password matches, but also informs as to the relative strength (low, medium, high) as well as how to achieve a strong rating. See Figure 10-4.

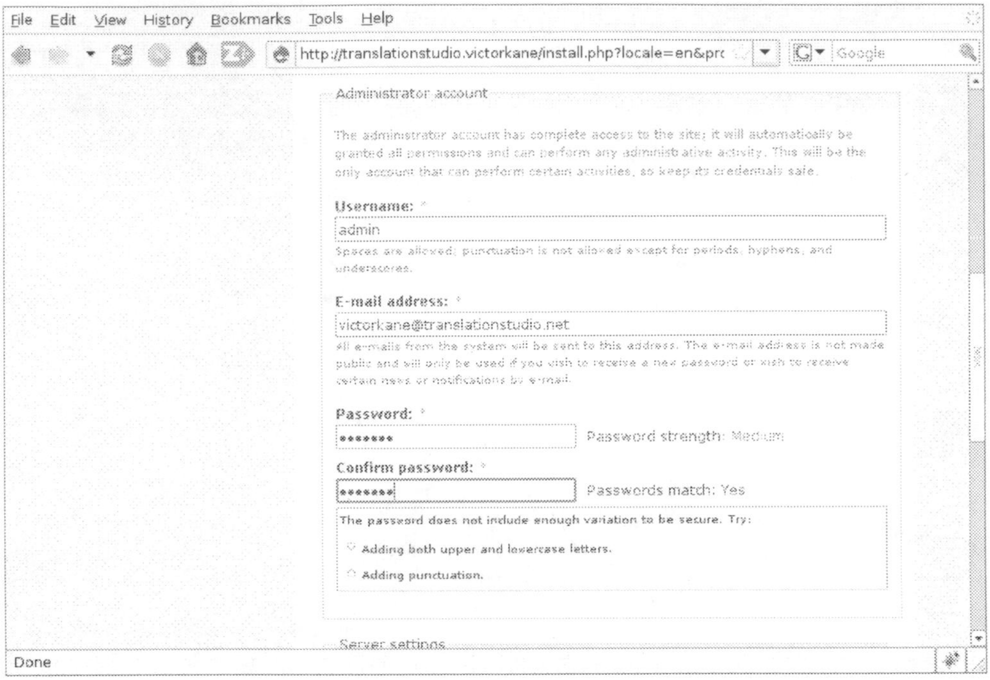

Figure 10-4

5. Click on the "Save and continue" button, and you are taken to the Drupal Installation Complete page, where you can see that you have successfully passed through all stages: You've chosen your localization language, you've verified requirements, you've set up the database, you've installed and configured the site, and you can now visit its front page. If the Installation Wizard had trouble sending out a confirmation e-mail to the new Admin account, you are so warned. After clicking on your new site link, you find yourself on the front page already logged in as the Administration account user.

# Step 2: Designing and Building the Architecture

At this point, you can start with a bilingual site, both from the point of view of l10n and of i18n, and build a functional foundation for the application you have in mind.

Let's take a quick look at the functional scope and then map that to a domain model, including business objects and Drupal modules.

## Application Scope and Domain

In Chapter 1, you saw that before attempting to build any website, it is very important to follow a certain workflow. Mapping out the scope and domain will allow for the production of a very significant amount of cheap (mental) development and will simplify the whole process, since that process concretely comprises a series of implementation steps involving design and implementation. This is in opposition to the expensive kind of development, which you need to avoid like the plague, because it involves doing work and then throwing it away as a substitute for thinking and dialog, as well as building without a plan and changing high-impact architectural components during or even after implementation.

A little scope and domain work clarifies things and simplifies development.

Figure 10-5 shows the scope and functionality of what is required for the mini-application.

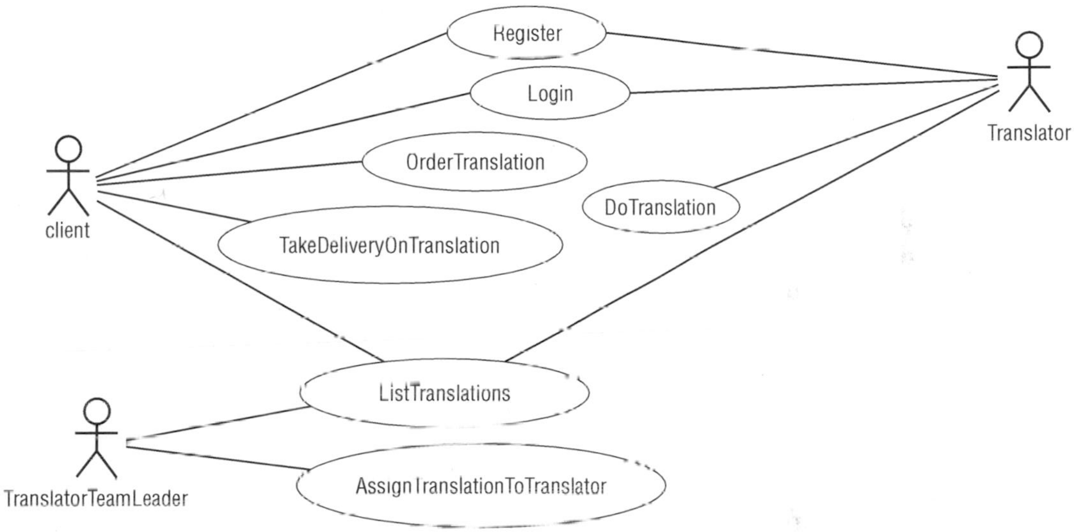


**Figure 10-5**

Figure 10-6 shows the domain of classes and objects required to implement the mini-application, relating these in general to Drupal modules.

## *Creating Roles and Users*

The following best practices make things fall into place naturally as you go along. The roles are made abundantly clear from the scope diagram (see Figure 10-5). And the fact that this can be prototyped right into Drupal makes it all the more natural and exciting, since you are doing analysis and design together with building, all in one go. The following roles are created with sample users:

| Role | User |
|---|---|
| Client | client1<br>client2 |
| Translator | translator1<br>translator2 |
| Translator Team Leader | teamleader |

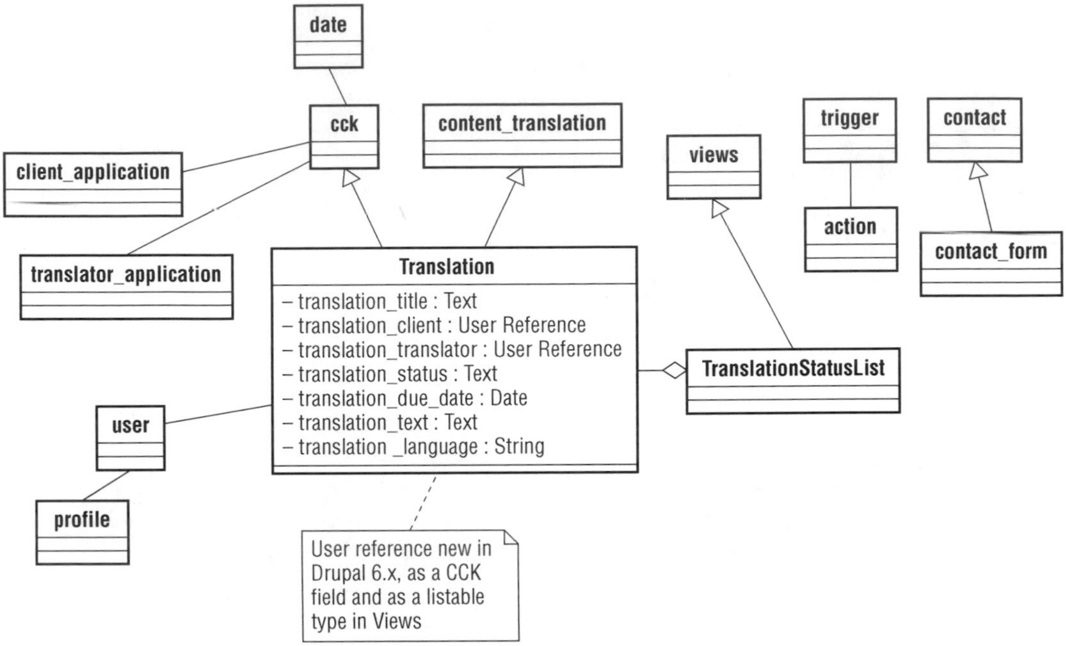


Figure 10-6

To create these roles, do the following:

1. Go to Administer ➢ User management ➢ Roles, and create the roles. The result should be similar to Figure 10-7.
2. Go to Administer ➢ User management ➢ Users, and create the users. The result should be similar to Figure 10-8.

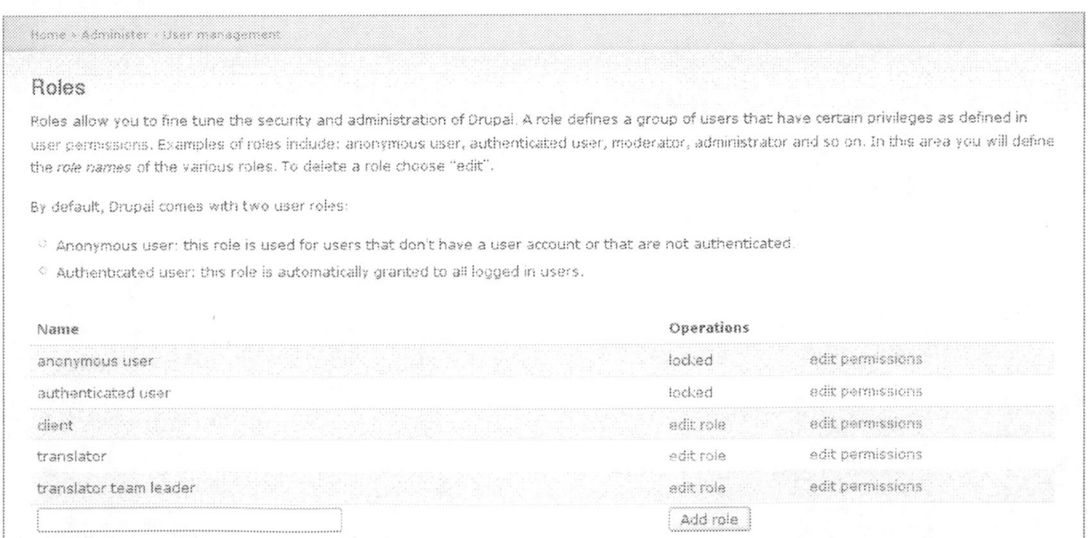

Home › Administer › User management
Roles
Roles allow you to fine tune the security and administration of Drupal. A role defines a group of users that have certain privileges as defined in user permissions. Examples of roles include: anonymous user, authenticated user, moderator, administrator and so on. In this area you will define the role names of the various roles. To delete a role choose "edit".
By default, Drupal comes with two user roles:
Anonymous user: this role is used for users that don't have a user account or that are not authenticated.
Authenticated user: this role is automatically granted to all logged in users.
Name
Operations
anonymous user
locked
edit permissions
authenticated user
locked
edit permissions
client
edit role
edit permissions
translator
edit role
edit permissions
translator team leader
edit role
edit permissions
Add role


Figure 10-7

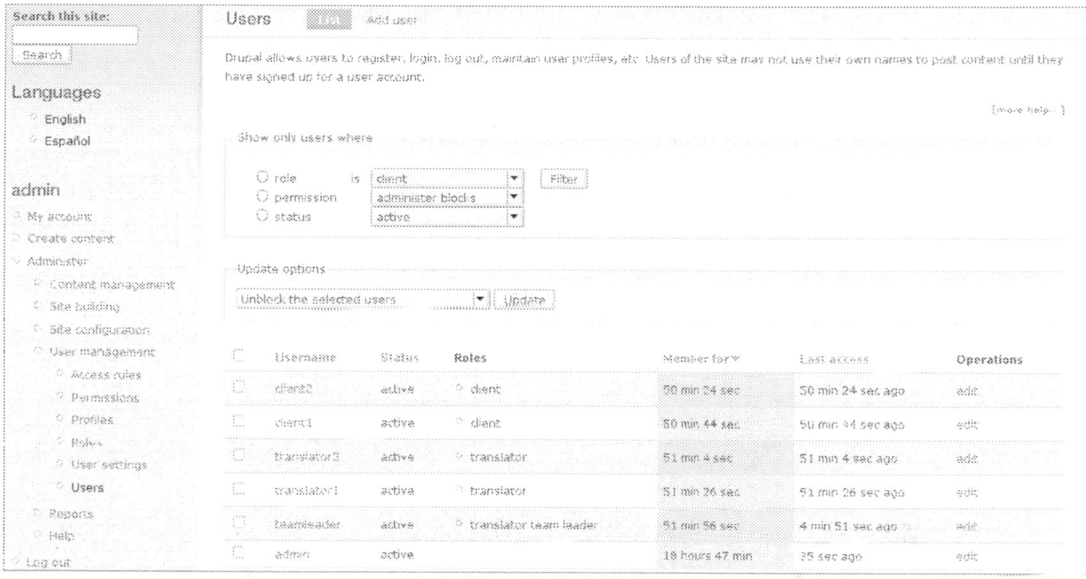

Figure 10-8

## Installing and Enabling Modules

As a result of our analysis and design (scoping the roles and user stories, abstracting out the domain), the following modules should be installed:

- Content Construction Kit
- Date
- Views

To do this, follow these steps:

1. Download all three modules and upload all the files, in their directories, via FTP to ./sites/all/modules.
2. Go to Administer ➤ Site building ➤ Modules, and enable the following modules:
   - Content (all modules)
   - Contact
   - Content Translation
   - Date (all modules except Date PHP4–unless necessary for your environment)
   - Locale
   - OpenID
   - PHP Filter
   - Profile
   - Trigger

- Upload
- Views (all modules)

3. Go to Administer ➤ User management ➤ Permissions, and enable permissions as per the following table:

| Permission | Client | Translator | Translator Team Leader |
|---|---|---|---|
| Access site-wide contact form | x | x | x |
| Access content | x | x | x |
| Create page content | | | x |
| Delete own page content | | | x |
| Edit any page content | | | x |
| Edit own page content | | | x |
| Search content | x | x | x |
| Use advanced search | x | x | x |
| Translate content | x | x | x |
| Upload files | x | x | x |
| View uploaded files | x | x | x |
| Access user profiles | x | x | x |

*Permissions in the node section will be set after the business objects are created (see below).*

## Making the Site Bilingual

Things are kept very simple and straightforward when you always bear in mind the user stories and the domain. To implement the user stories concerning translations and the domain class Translation itself, the website must be made fully bilingual.

Follow these steps:

1. Go to the Drupal translations download page (`http://drupal.org/project/Translations`), and download the Spanish translation for Drupal 6.x, which you will be using as an example, to your local machine. Unpack it into a convenient directory, and then copy all the files right into the Drupal installation directory.

   *Prior to Drupal 6.x, individual language (.PO) files were imported into the selected language one by one. With Drupal 6.x, a language copied with all its subdirectories (modules, profiles, themes) into the Drupal installation directory can be made part of the Drupal installation process, or added at any time, either as the default or as an alternative language.*

2. Go to Administer ➢ Site configuration ➢ Languages, and click on the "Add language" tab. Select Spanish (Español) from the dropdown list, and click "Add language." The language translation files you have copied into the Drupal installation are automatically imported, and the language is enabled. See Figure 10-9.

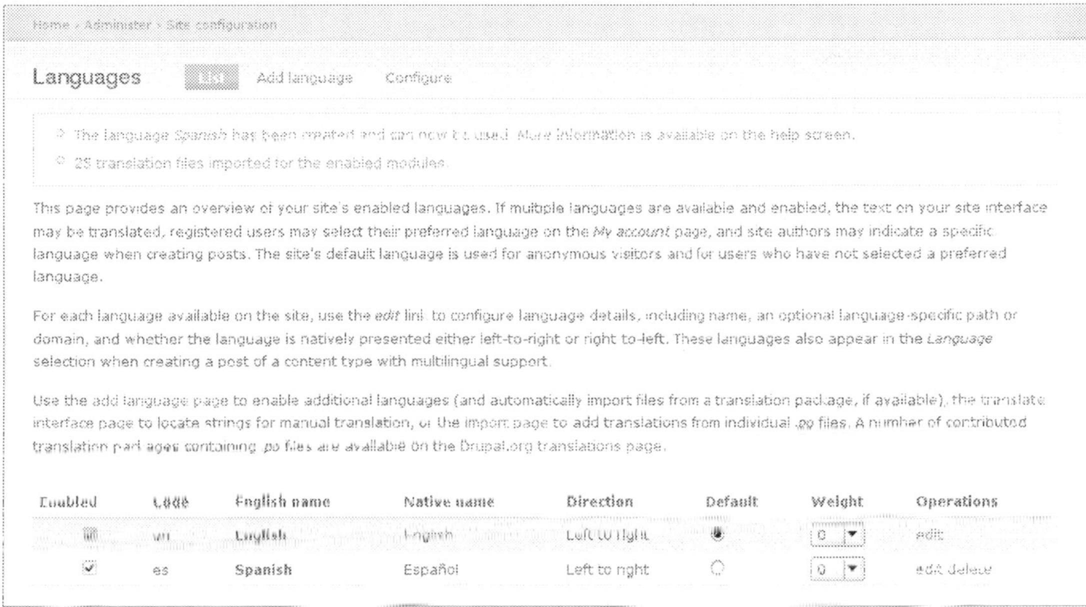


Figure 10-9

3. Now hit the Configure tab, select "Path prefix with language fallback" as the Language Negotiation option, and click "Save settings." With this option not equal to None and with two or more languages enabled, you are now able to enable the Language switcher block and make the site dynamically bilingual.

4. Go to Administer ➢ Site building ➢ Blocks, and enable the Language switcher block into the Left sidebar region. Drag it to the top using the Drag to reorder "move" icon, then hit the "Save blocks" button at the foot of the page.

5. Go to the front page, and the result should be similar to Figure 10-10. Try clicking alternatively on the English and Español links, and you will see the interface as well as the content of the Drupal default welcome page appear in each language in turn.

6. There's just one more thing to do, which is to enable multilingual support with translation for all content types. Go to Administer ➢ Content management ➢ Content types, and edit the Page content type. Scroll down to the Workflow settings section and open it, and select Enabled, with translation option under Multilingual Support. Hit the "Save content type" button. Do the same for the Story content type.

The site is now bilingual.

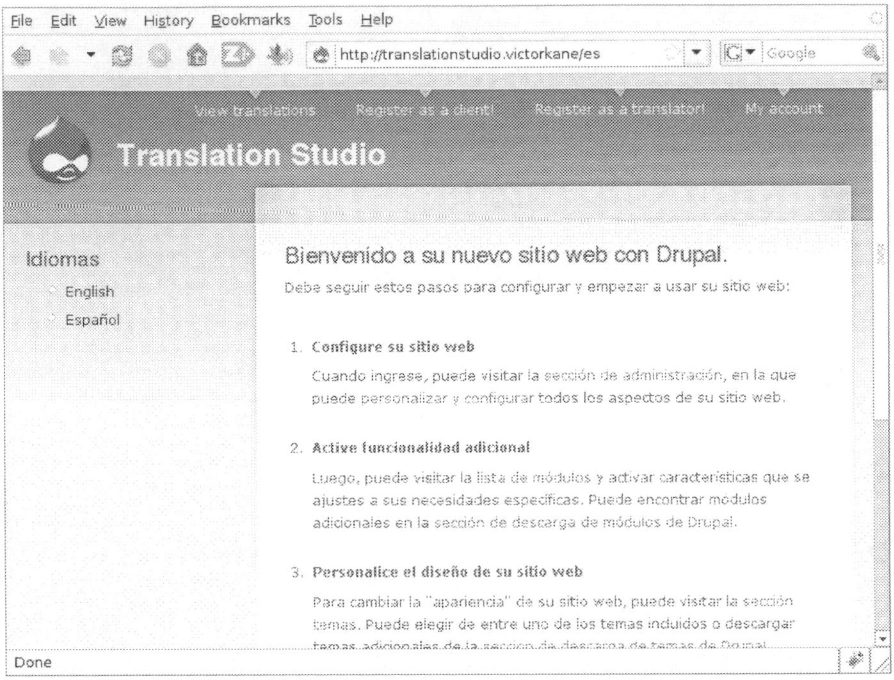


Figure 10-10

To try it out, let's make a bilingual static page as our Welcome page, viewable in both languages:

1. Log in as user teamleader.
2. Click "Create content," and then click on the Page option. In the Title field, enter **Welcome to the Translation Studio!** In the Body field, enter **Now you can get your translations done for the next business day! Just register, and upload a free trial translation. When it's ready, you'll be notified by e-mail, then come in and access your work: it's all ready for you!**
3. In the Language field, select English instead of the default Language neutral. Then click on the Save button. You will see the English version.
4. At this point, hit the Translation tab. As in Figure 10-11, you will see that there exists an English version, but that no Spanish version is at yet available. Click on the "Add translation" link in the right-hand column.

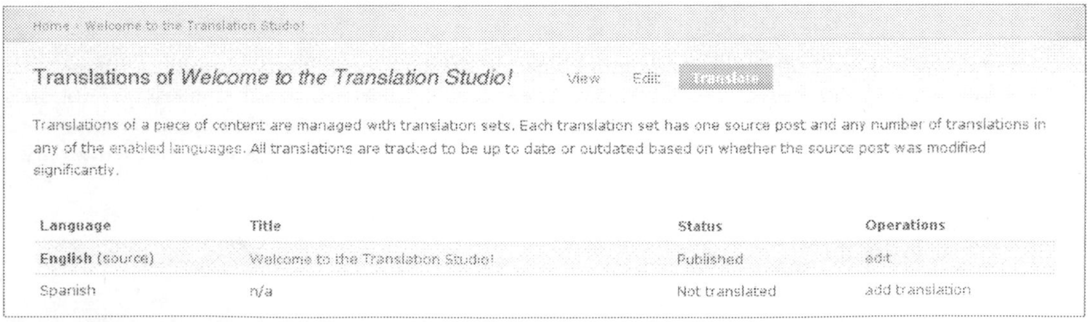


Figure 10-11

5. The Title and Body fields have been filled in with the English versions. Replace them with the following:

| Field | English | Español |
|---|---|---|
| Title | Welcome to the Translation Studio! | Bienvenidos al Estudio de Traducciones! |
| Body | Now you can get your translations done for the next business day! Just register, and upload a free trial translation. When it's ready, you'll be notified by e-mail, then come in and access your work: it's all ready for you! | Ahora puede tener tus traducciones listas para el próximo día laboral! Solo registrarse, y subir una traducción de prueba gratis. Cuando esté lista recibirá una notificación por correo electrónico, entonces puede visitar la página y acceder a su trabajo: está todo listo para Ud. |

*The Language field is fixed as Spanish.*

6. Click Save, and now there are two versions of the same page, one in English and one in Spanish. Try it: click Spanish in the Languages block, and you will see the Spanish version; click English in the Idiomas block, and you will see the English version.

7. Go to Administer ➤ Site configuration ➤ Site information, and at the bottom of the page, enter **node/1** as the Default front page.

The site is bilingual, indeed (see Figures 10-12 and 10-13).

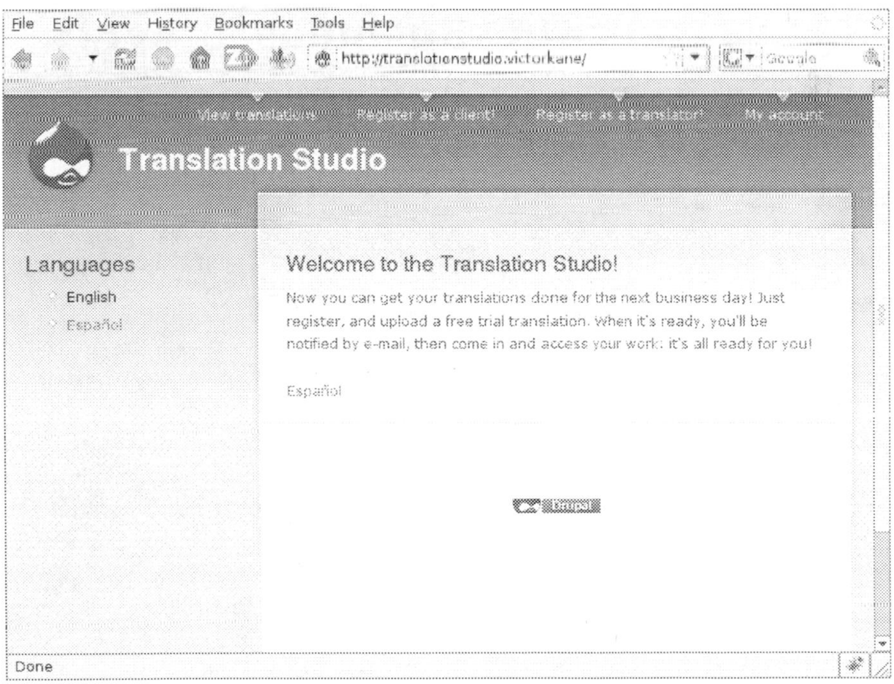


Figure 10-12

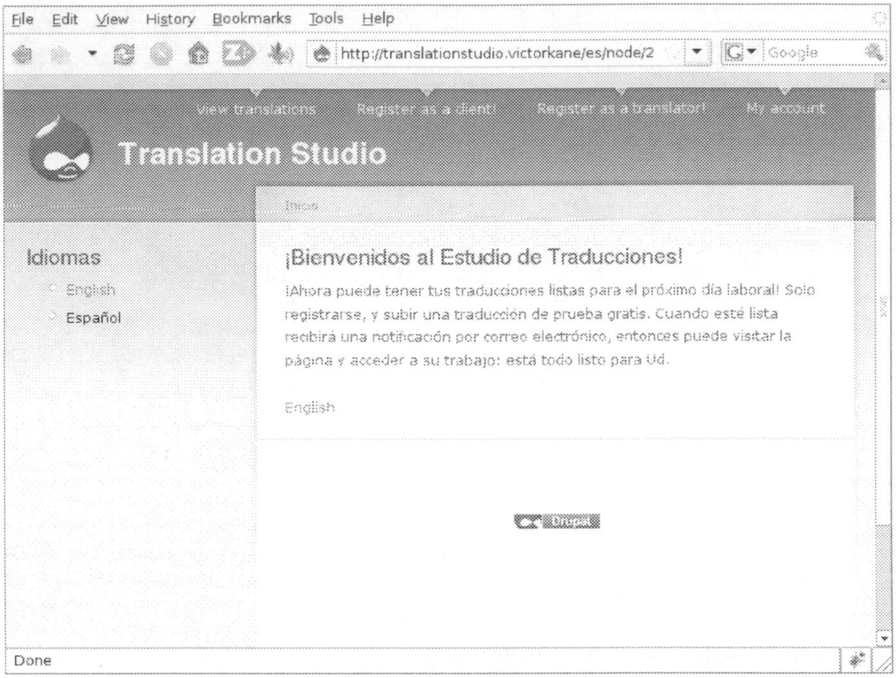


Figure 10-13

# Step 3: Creating the Business Objects

Normally in Drupal, you click the ubiquitous user login block to either log in or register to become a new user. Given the objectives here, however, you can do away with the regular user login/registration block and configure Drupal so that only the Translator Team Leader can register users. Instead of registering directly, Clients will fill out a Client Application form, Translators will fill out a Translator Application form, and the Translator Team Leader will then manually create the users, assign them to the appropriate roles, and send them notifications with login instructions. Of course, with the use of additional modules, this process could be automated, but in this chapter, the aim is to provide an example based mainly on the Drupal core.

You will need a total of three content types, the two kinds of applications with their corresponding fields, and the translation content type itself.

To create the translation content type, do the following:

1. Go to Administer ➢ Content management ➢ Content types, and click on the "Add content type" link.
2. Enter **Translation** in the Name field, and **translation** in the Type field. Enter **Create a multilingual text to be translated** in the Description field. In the Submission form settings section, leave the Body field label blank so as not to use the default Body field. In the Workflow settings, in Default options, check Published and Create new revision. In Multilingual support, select Enabled, with translation. And leave Attachments Enabled. Click "Save Content Type."

3. Click "Manage Fields," and then the "Add a new field" link. The first field to be created is the Client field because each translation will be uploaded by a Client. In Drupal 6, not only is it possible to add a user reference without having to add a contributed module, other than Content Construction Kit itself, but the user interface for adding and maintaining additional fields has been greatly improved and streamlined compared to prior Drupal releases.

4. Enter **translation_client** in the Field name (the internal name will be *field_translation_client*), and enter **Client** in the Label field. Use the dropdown list to select "User reference" for the Field type, and click Continue. Immediately there appears an additional select list for the Widget type, which you should set as Autocomplete Text field. Upon clicking Continue, only then does the rest of the configuration appear. Near the bottom of the page, select Client as the only User role that can be referenced, and click "Save field settings."

   Also improved in the Manage fields tab of the content type is the ability to drag and drop fields to indicate the ordering of fields in the form.

5. Now, let's just add an advanced touch, if you like, to the Client field: a PHP-specified default value. Because the Client is almost always going to be creating translations, it would be good if the Client field had the Client's own username already filled in by default automatically. In order to do this, there being no option other than the specification of specific users, you are obliged to use a few lines of Drupal-specific PHP. Click on the Configure link for the field_translation_client field, and click on the "Default value" link; then enter the following snippet into the PHP code text area:

```
global $user;
if ($user -> roles[3]) {
  $uid = $user -> uid;
  return array(
    0 => array ('uid' => $uid),
  );
}
else {
  return array();
}
```

   If the user is of role Client, then the field is populated with the current user; otherwise, a null default value is returned. Although this is perhaps not necessary, it is included for completeness in order to show the high degree of flexibility of the Drupal content framework.

6. Create the rest of the fields according to the following table:

| Field Label | Machine-Readable Name | Field Type | Widget | Configuration | Required Field |
|---|---|---|---|---|---|
| Title | title (default) | | | | Yes |
| Client | field_translation_client | User reference | Autocomplete Text Field | Client role, default value via PHP code snippet provided in this section. | Yes |
| Translator | field_translation_translator | User reference | Autocomplete Text Field | Translator role, no default | No |

| Field Label | Machine-Readable Name | Field Type | Widget | Configuration | Required Field |
|---|---|---|---|---|---|
| Status | field_translation_status | Text | Select list | New<br>Assigned<br>Completed<br>Needs work<br>Ready<br>(copy and paste these values as is) | Yes |
| Due date | field_translation_due_date | Date | Text Field with jQuery pop-up calendar | | No |
| Text | field_translation_text | Text | Text area (multiple rows) | Plain text | No |

After you've dragged the fields into a logical order, the result should look something like Figure 10-14.

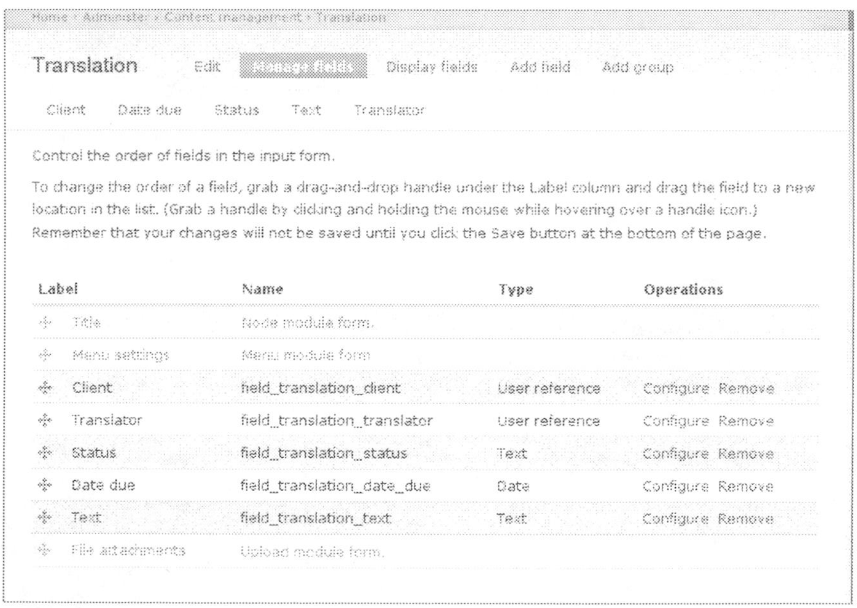


Figure 10-14

7. One more task here is to set both content type-level permissions as well as, starting with CCK version 2, available for Drupal 6 and later, the amazing feature of field-level permissions, both for viewing and editing. Go to Administer ➤ User management ➤ Permissions, and set the following permissions:

| Permission | Client | Translator | Translator Team Leader |
|---|---|---|---|
| content_permissions_module | | x | x |
| Edit field_translation_client | | x | x |
| Edit field_translation_date_due | x | x | x |
| Edit field_translation_status | x | x | x |
| Edit field_translation_text | x | x | x |
| Edit field_translation_translator | | x | x |
| View field_translation_client | | x | x |
| View field_translation_date_due | x | x | x |
| View field_translation_status | x | x | x |
| View field_translation_text | x | x | x |
| View field_translation_translator | | x | x |
| Node module | | | |
| Access content | x | x | x |
| Administer nodes | | | x |
| Create page content | | | x |
| Create translation content | x | x | x |
| Delete any translation content | | | x |
| Delete own page content | | | x |
| Delete own translation content | x | x | x |
| Delete revisions | | | x |
| Edit any page content | | | x |
| Edit any translation content | | x | x |
| Edit own page content | | | x |
| Edit own translation content | x | x | x |
| Revert revisions | | x | x |
| View revisions | | x | x |

8. Now create the Client Application (client_application) content type, entering **Expectations and objectives in making use of the site** as the Body field label. Configure by disabling comments and attachments, enabling Published and Create new revision attributes, and allowing Multilingual support (Enabled) in order to get an idea of language preferences.

Grant full permissions to anonymous users on this content type, basing yourself on the following fields:

| Field Label | Machine-Readable Name | Field Type | Widget | Configuration | Required Field |
|---|---|---|---|---|---|
| Name | title (default) | | | | Yes |
| Expectations and objectives in making use of the site | body | | | | |
| E-mail | field_client_email | Text | Text field | | Yes |

9. Finish up by creating the Translator Application (translator_application) content type, entering **Reasons for applying for an account as Translator as Body field label**. Again, configure by disabling comments and attachments, enabling Published and Create new revision attributes, and allowing Multilingual support (Enabled) in order to get an idea of language preferences by virtue of which language the applicant actually uses. Add the following fields (after doing so, don't forget to grant full editing permissions on the content type and, individually, each of these fields, in Administer ➢ User management ➢ Permissions):

| Field Label | Machine-Readable Name | Field Type | Widget | Configuration | Required Field |
|---|---|---|---|---|---|
| Name | title (default) | | | | Yes |
| Reasons for applying for an account as Translator | body | | | | |
| E-mail | field_client_email | Text | Text field | | Yes |

# Step 4: Creating the Workflows

Now it is time to implement the rest of the user stories corresponding to the roles you have created. The flow of interactions each of the users will be having with the website can best be modeled as workflows, each of which will now be implemented in turn:

- Registration workflow
- The Client's workflow
- The Team Leader's workflow
- The Translator's workflow

## Implementing the Registration Workflow

Translators and Clients will post applications, while Team Leaders will approve them and register Translators and Clients as new users.

1. Go to Administer ➤ User management ➤ User settings, and specify that only site administrators can create new user accounts. Click "Save configuration" at the bottom of the page.
2. Disable the User login/registration block entirely (don't worry, it is always accessible at `http://example.com/user` in case you get stuck without it).
3. Disable the block at Administer ➤ Site building ➤ Blocks by selecting `<none>` for the User login block region and clicking "Save blocks."
4. Click on the configure link corresponding to the Navigation block, and enable it only for the Translator Team Leader role. This will make for a cleaner and less confusing navigation scheme, with most users not being confronted with a lot of options they don't need, while other more straightforward forms of navigation will be provided as each user role's workflow is developed.
5. However, since this effectively removes the navigation block for User #1, it is a great time to follow best practices and create an Admin role to which a new user dev is assigned, which should be used for everyday administration and site configuration tasks. This role should always have all permissions assigned, so permissions have to be revised each time a module is installed and enabled or a new content type created.

   *This tedious task can be eliminated by installing the Admin Role module (`http://drupal.org/project/adminrole`), "a little helper [module] to maintain an administrator role which has full permissions."*

6. In addition, let's enhance the Translator Team Leader role to that of a nontechnical site administrator so she can create and administer user accounts. Simply go to Administer ➤ User management ➤ Permissions, and enable absolutely all permissions to that role except for the more technical permissions (which will be confusing for her). The following table outlines which permissions the Translator Team Leader should have:

| Permission | dev | Translation Team Leader |
|---|---|---|
| Administer blocks | x | |
| Use PHP for block visibility | x | |
| Administer comments | x | x |
| Administer site-wide contact form | x | x |
| Use PHP input for field settings (dangerous — grant with care) | x | |
| Administer filters | x | |
| Administer languages | x | x |
| Translate interface | x | x |
| Administer menu | x | |

| Permission | dev | Translation Team Leader |
|---|---|---|
| Administer content types | x | |
| Administer nodes | x | x |
| Administer search | x | x |
| Access administration pages | x | x |
| Access site reports | x | |
| Administer actions | x | |
| Administer files | x | |
| Administer site configuration | x | |
| Select different theme | x | |
| Administer taxonomy | x | x |
| Administer permissions | x | x |
| Administer users | x | x |
| Administer views | x | |
| Access all views | x | x |

7. Now create several entries in the Primary Menu. To set up navigation option for the Client, go to Administer ➤ Site building ➤ Menus, and then click "Primary links." Set up the menu items as shown in the following table:

| Menu Link Title | Description | Path | Weight |
|---|---|---|---|
| Register as a client! | Register as a client to start uploading translations! | node/add/client-application | 0 |
| Register as a translator! | Register as a translator to start work right away! | node/add/translator-application | 2 |
| My account | Log in/access your account | user | 4 |
| Logout | | logout | 6 |

8. Now, to implement the registration workflow itself, you need to configure an e-mail to be sent to the Team Leader user whenever a Client or Translator Application is created. Then

the Team Leader can read the application and, if she decides to honor it, register the person as a new user on the site, with the appropriate role, and have that user notified in turn.

This can be implemented by taking advantage of Drupal's built-in trigger and action duo, which has already been enabled. Go to Administer ➢ Site configuration ➢ Actions, select "Send e-mail. . ." from the "Make a new advanced action available" dropdown list, and hit Create. You are immediately taken to the "Configure an advanced action" page. Enter **Notify team leader of application by e-mail** in the Description field. Provide an appropriate e-mail address in the Recipient field (this will be a static e-mail, belonging to the Team Leader user). Enter **New Application** in the Subject field, and in the Message field, enter the following:

```
%title has sent a %node_type from %site_name .

Please visit %node_url .

%title wrote:

%body
```

and hit the Save button. Now head over to the Triggers page to establish conditions under which the action should be invoked. Go to Administer ➢ Site building ➢ Triggers. From the Trigger: "After saving a new post drop-down list, Choose an action," select "Send e-mail" and hit Assign.

9. To complete the picture, you need to create a View and place it on the Team Leader menu so that she can easily list the applications and act upon them when she logs in.

   Go to Administer ➢ Site building ➢ Views, and click Add. Enter **applications** in the View name field and **List client and translator applications** in the View description field. Enter **application** in the View tag field (a cool way of grouping together all views having to do with applications), and leave the default Node View type selected. Click Next.

10. Select the fields to be displayed. To add the first, click the + icon next to the Fields block. In the Groups dropdown list, choose Node, select Node: Title, and click Add. The Configure field "Node: Title" dialog appears.

11. Type **Name** in the Label field, and select the "Link this field to its node check box," then click Update. Select + again, select Node group, and then select Node: Type and Node: Post date, and click Add. Click on the up and down arrows to rearrange the order of the fields, and move the Post date field down into third position.

12. Click on the Save button to create the view. The info area announces, "The view has been saved."

13. In the Basic Settings section, click Style, and in the work area below, select Table and hit Update. Configure the table to have each field sortable, with *Post date* as the default sort. Specify a Descending sort order, and hit Update again. Click on the Save button again.

14. Because you want this to be a list of applications, click the + icon in the Filter section. Choose the Node group, select Node: Type, and hit Add. The Operator should be set to "Is one of," and the Node type should have both Client Application and Translator Application checked. Click Update, and then "Save the view."

15. You now need to add a Page display. Select Page and hit "Add display." In the Page settings section, click on the None link in order to edit the attribute labeled *Path*. In the work area that opens up, type **view/applications** in the text field to complete the URL for the page, and hit Update.
16. Click on the Save button.
17. Again, in the Page settings section, click on the "No menu" attribute of Menu. Select Normal menu entry, and in the Title field that then appears, enter **View applications**. Click on the "Update and Save" button.

Now, when the Team Leader logs in, the View applications menu item appears in her navigation block, as can be seen in Figure 10-15.

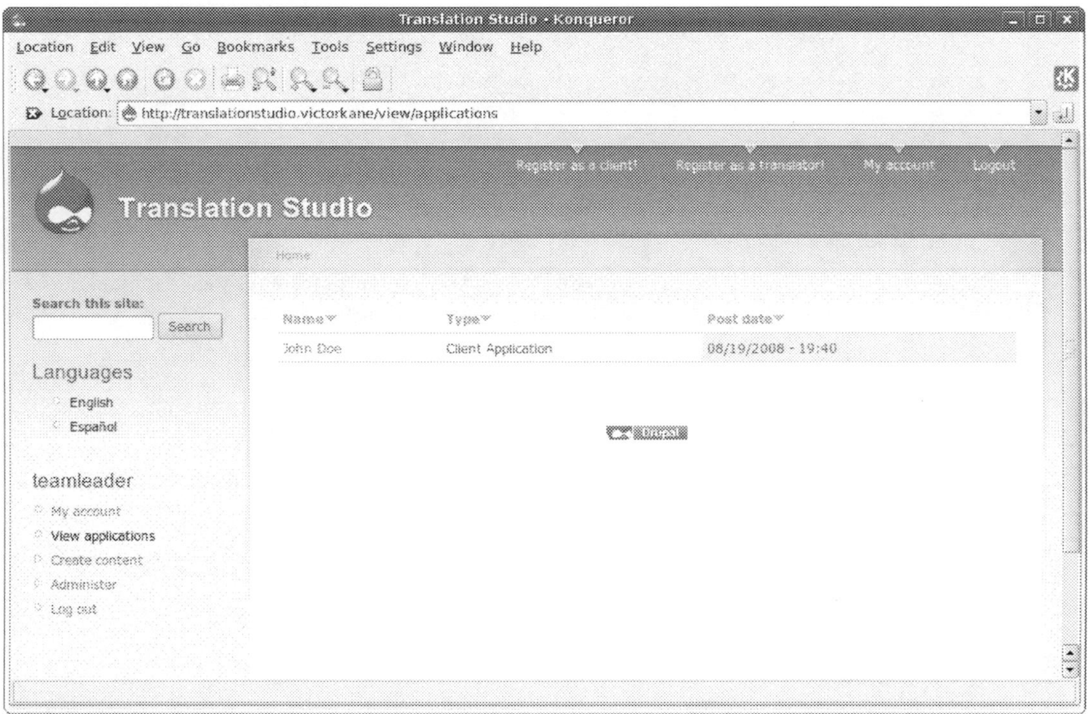


Figure 10-15

She can access John Doe's application by clicking on "John Doe." To actually create a user account for this applicant (again, this is a process that can be automated, but that is beyond the scope of this comprehensive but simple chapter example), the Team Leader may right-click "Administer" from the teamleader menu on the left sidebar to open it in another browser window or to tab the Administration pages menu, a stripped-down version of what dev sees, thanks to your configuration of her permissions. (See Figure 10-16.) From there, she clicks "Users" in the User management group and is taken to Administration ➤ User management ➤ Users. She clicks on the "Add user" tab and places the name provided in the application form in the Username field, the contents of the E-mail field into the E-mail address field, provides a password that the user can later change herself, checks the Client checkbox in the Roles section, checks the "Notify user of new account" checkbox, and selects the same language that the application has chosen (or leave in *English* by default).

Returning to the list of user accounts on the system at Administration ➢ User management ➢ Users, John Doe is now listed as a user of role Client (Figure 10-15).

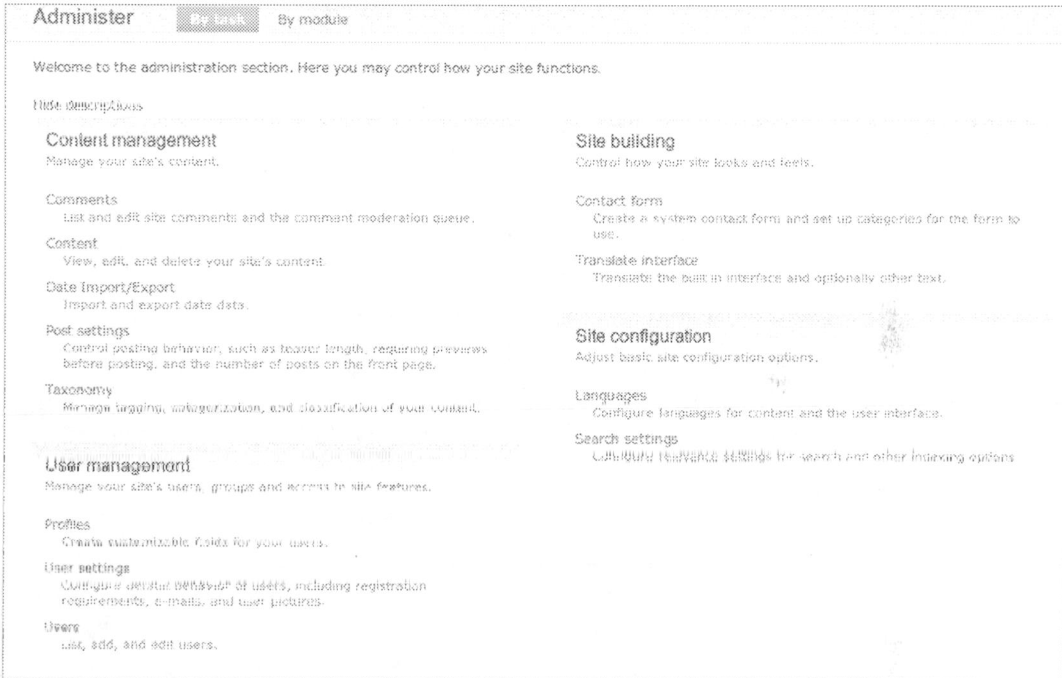


Figure 10-16

## Implementing the Client's Workflow

The Client's workflow involves

- Creating a text for translation.
- Viewing all texts being translated and their status.
- Accessing any translation for downloading.

Let's use the primary menu not only for the Client's and Translator's registration requests, login and logout, but also for the Client's main navigation options once they are logged in.

So to set up the navigation option for the Client, follow these steps:

1. Go to Administer ➢ Site building ➢ Menus, and then click on the Primary links. You have already added menu items to the primary menu.

2. Complete the setup as shown in the following table:

| Menu Link Title | Description | Path | Weight (or just drag into appropriate position) |
|---|---|---|---|
| New translation | Upload a new translation | node/add/translation | -6 |
| Register as a client! | Register as a client to start uploading translations! | node/add/client-application | 0 |
| Register as a translator! | Register as a translator to start work right away! | node/add/translator-application | 2 |
| My account | Log in/access your account | user | 4 |
| Logout | | logout | 6 |

3. Log in as Client John Doe, and create a couple of texts to be translated. Click "New Translation" at the top of the screen. Type in **Translation One** in the Title field. Click anywhere within the "Date due" field to test the delights of the jQuery pop-up calendar, and enter a due date 1 or 2 days later than the current date. Select English as the document language, and enter any appropriate short text. Click on the Save button (remember that the Team Leader will be automatically notified of this event by e-mail). You should see something like Figure 10-17.

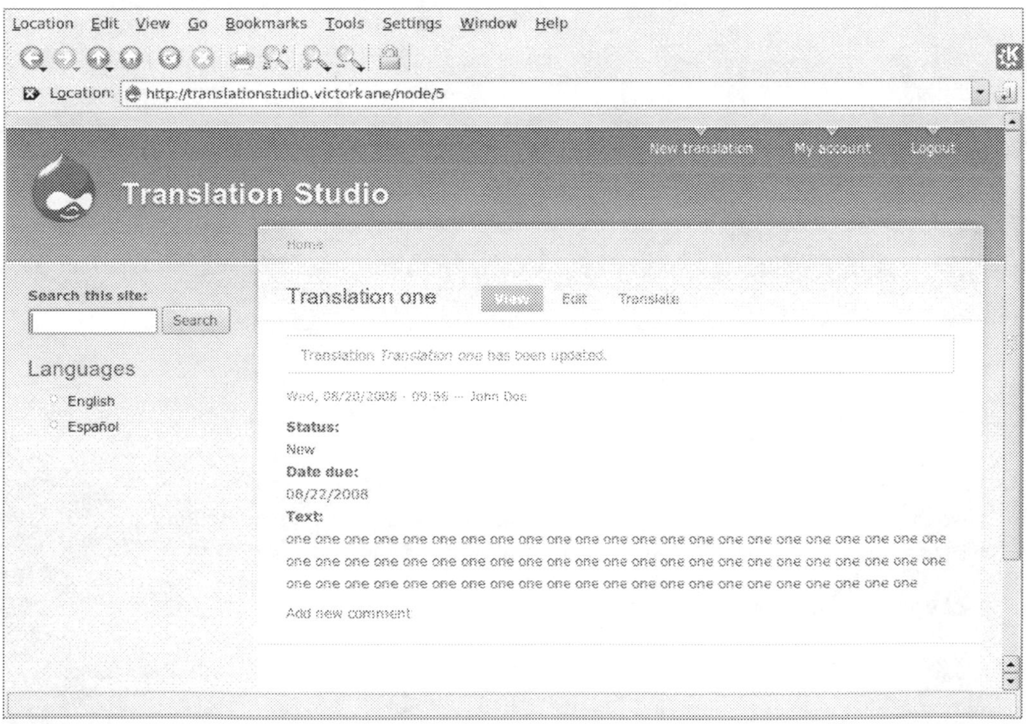


Figure 10-17

Before you create Translation Two in the same way, it is really clear that a short help text is required, so that the Client always chooses either Spanish or English, and that the kind of translation required, either English to Spanish, or vice versa, is made clear. So:

1. Logged in as user dev (I use Firefox for my dev session and Konqueror or IE under wine on Ubuntu for my other user sessions), go to Administer ➢ Content management ➢ Content types, and edit the Translation content type. Open up the Submission form settings, and insert the following text into the Explanation or submission guidelines text area:

   **If submitting an English text for translation into Spanish, please indicate that by setting the Language selector to English. On the other hand, Spanish texts to be translated into English should have the Language selector set to Spanish.**

   **Si está presentando un texto en inglés para su traducción al español, por favor que lo indique mediante el seteo del indicador de Idioma a inglés. Por otro lado, los textos en español que deben ser traducidos al idioma inglés deben tener su selector de idioma puesto en español.**

2. Now, logged in as Client user John Doe, hit "New translation," and the form should look like Figure 10-18.

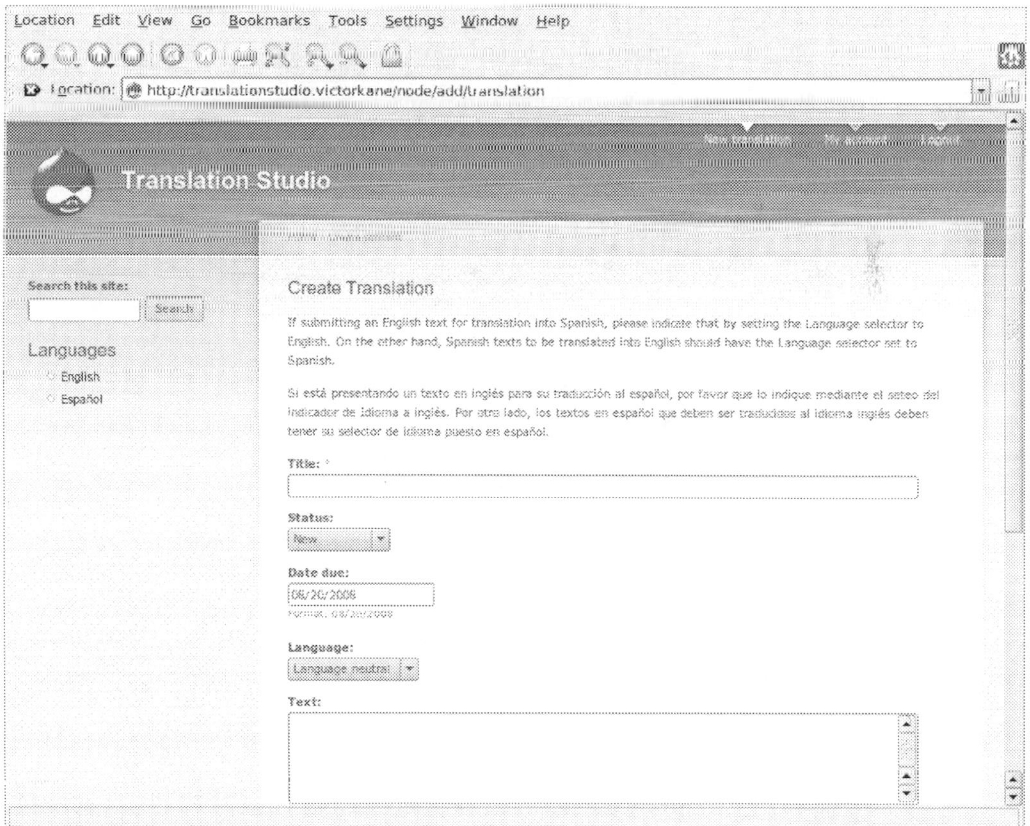


Figure 10-18

Complete Translation two.

3. Now, logged in as dev, you need to implement a table view allowing Clients to visualize a list of their current translations, sorted by status and due date. Go to Administer ➤ Site building ➤ Views, and click on the Add button. Enter the items in the appropriate fields as shown in the following table:

| For This Field | Enter This Item |
|---|---|
| View name | **translations** |
| View Description | **List translations sorted by status and due date** |
| View tag | **translation** |
| View type | **Node** |

4. Click Next. Select the following items as indicated in the following table:

| For This Item | Specify |
|---|---|
| Add fields | Node: Title (Link this field to its node)<br>Content: Text: Status–field_translation_status<br>Content: Date: Date due–field_translation_date_due |
| Add filters | Node: Type = Translation<br>Node: Language = Current user's language<br>User: Current `True` |
| Basic settings | Table style, making all fields Sortable, with Date due as Default sort, with Default sort order as Descending |

5. Click Update, and then click Save.
6. In Basic settings, select Distinct as Yes.
7. In Basic settings, specify Use pager as Full pager.
8. Add a Page display with Path as view/translations.
9. I exported the view so that you may import it as an alternative to going through all the above steps by going to Administer ➤ Site building ➤ Views, hitting the Import tab, pasting in the code, and hitting the Import button (yes, this is PHP code that can be placed in any module to create the view on the fly):

```
$view = new view;
$view->name = 'translations';
$view->description = 'List translations sorted by status and due date';
$view->tag = 'translation';
$view->view_php = '';
$view->base_table = 'node';
$view->is_cacheable = FALSE;
$view->api_version = 2;
$view->disabled = FALSE; /* Edit this to true to make a default view
disabled
 initially */
```

```
$handler = $view->new_display('default', 'Defaults', 'default');
$handler->override_option('fields', array(
  'title' => array(
    'label' => 'Title',
    'link_to_node' => 1,
    'exclude' => 0,
    'id' => 'title',
    'table' => 'node',
    'field' => 'title',
    'relationship' => 'none',
  ),
  'field_translation_status value' => array(
    'label' => '',
    'link_to_node' => 0,
    'label_type' => 'widget',
    'format' => 'default',
    'multiple' => array(
      'group' => TRUE,
      'multiple_number' => '',
      'multiple_from' => '',
      'multiple_reversed' => FALSE,
    ),
    'exclude' => 0,
    'id' => 'field_translation status value',
    'table' => 'node_data_field_translation_status',
    'field' => 'field_translation_status_value',
    'relationship' => 'none',
  ),
  'field translation_date_due_value' => array(
    'label' => '',
    'link_to_node' => 0,
    'label_type' => 'widget',
    'format' => 'default',
    'multiple' => array(
      'group' => TRUE,
      'multiple_number' => '',
      'multiple_from' => '',
      'multiple_reversed' => FALSE,
    ),
    'exclude' => 0,
    'id' => 'field_translation_date_due_value',
    'table' => 'node_data_field_translation_date_due',
    'field' => 'field_translation_date_due_value',
    'relationship' => 'none',
  ),
));
$handler->override_option('filters', array(
  'type' => array(
    'operator' => 'in',
    'value' => array(
      'translation' => 'translation',
    ),
    'group' => '0',
    'exposed' => FALSE,
    'expose' => array(
      'operator' => FALSE,
      'label' => '',
```

```
      ),
      'id' => 'type',
      'table' => 'node',
      'field' => 'type',
      'relationship' => 'none',
    ),
    'language' => array(
      'operator' => 'in',
      'value' => array(
        '***CURRENT_LANGUAGE***' => '***CURRENT_LANGUAGE***',
      ),
      'group' => '0',
      'exposed' => FALSE,
      'expose' => array(
        'operator' => FALSE,
        'label' => '',
      ),
      'id' => 'language',
      'table' => 'node',
      'field' => 'language',
      'override' => array(
        'button' => 'Override',
      ),
      'relationship' => 'none',
    ),
    'uid_current' => array(
      'operator' => '=',
      'value' => 1,
      'group' => '0',
      'exposed' => FALSE,
      'expose' => array(
        'operator' => FALSE,
        'label' => '',
      ),
      'id' => 'uid_current',
      'table' => 'users',
      'field' => 'uid_current',
      'relationship' => 'none',
    ),
  ));
  $handler->override_option('access', array(
    'type' => 'none',
    'role' => array(),
    'perm' => '',
  ));
  $handler->override_option('use_pager', '1');
  $handler->override_option('distinct', 1);
  $handler->override_option('style_plugin', 'table');
  $handler->override_option('style_options', array(
    'grouping' => '',
    'override' => 1,
    'sticky' => 0,
    'order' => 'desc',
    'columns' => array(
      'title' => 'title',
      'field_translation_status_value' => 'field_translation_status_value',
```

```
    'field_translation_date_due_value' =>
'field_translation_date_due_value',
  ),
  'info' => array(
    'title' => array(
      'sortable' => 1,
      'separator' => '',
    ),
    'field_translation_status_value' => array(
      'sortable' => 1,
      'separator' => '',
    ),
    'field_translation_date_due_value' => array(
      'sortable' => 1,
      'separator' => '',
    ),
  ),
  'default' => 'field_translation_date_due_value',
));
$handler = $view->new_display('page', 'Page', 'page_1');
$handler->override_option('path', 'view/translations');
$handler->override_option('menu', array(
  'type' => 'none',
  'title' => '',
  'weight' => 0,
));
$handler->override_option('tab_options', array(
  'type' => 'none',
  'title' => '',
  'weight' => 0,
));
```

10. Now go to Administer ➤ Site building ➤ Menus, and add the view you have just made to the Primary menu, which ends up having six items:

| Menu Link Title | Description | Path | Weight(or just drag into appropriate position) |
|---|---|---|---|
| New translation | Upload a new translation | node/add/translation | -6 |
| View translations | View a list of all your translations ordered by date and status | view/translations | -4 |
| Register as a client! | Register as a client to start uploading translations! | node/add/client-application | 0 |
| Register as a translator! | Register as a translator to start work right away! | node/add/translator-application | 2 |
| My account | Log in/access your account | user | 4 |
| Logout | | logout | 6 |

At this point, the Client user John Doe will be able to click View translations from the primary menu and see a list of the translations, sortable by status and due date, as in Figure 10-19.

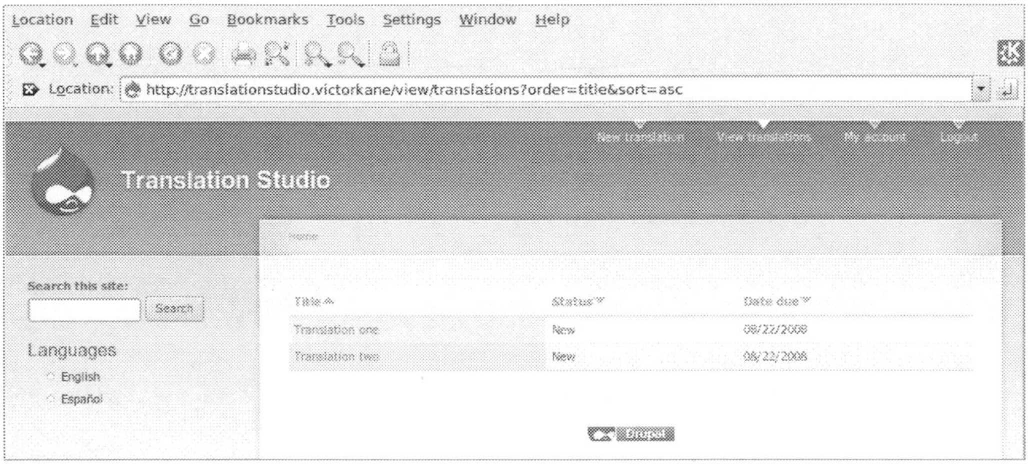


Figure 10-19

Unfortunately, no work has yet been done on them; otherwise, he could click and download his translation!

# Implementing the Translator Team Leader's Workflow

If you look at the scope diagram (Figure 5-8), you can see that the Team Leader is an extremely busy user, since a link is drawn between that user and many of the user stories. In the steps that follow, these user stories can be divided into two main categories, namely, having to manage registrations and having to manage the translations themselves. This divides our implementation of the user stories into these two parts.

## Team Leader Registration Workflow

Let's check this out in a bit more detail than we did above. Here are the steps:

**Team Leader Registration Workflow Steps**

| User/System | Action |
|---|---|
| Jane Doe | Clicks Register as a Client. |
| The System | Presents node/add/client-application. |
| Jane Doe | Completes name and e-mail and clicks on Save button. |

**Team Leader Registration Workflow Steps**

| User/System | Action |
|---|---|
| The System | Client application saved with Jane Doe's data.<br>Mail sent to Team Leader using template specified in Administer ➢ Site configuration ➢ Actions:<br>`%title has sent a %node_type from %site_name .`<br>`Please visit %node_url .`<br>`%title wrote:`<br>`%body` |
| The Team Leader | ❑ Receives following e-mail:<br>"Jane Doe has sent a Client Application from Translation Studio. Please visit `http://translationstudio.textworks.com.ar/node/8.`<br>"Jane Doe wrote: 'Hope to be able to get my work done well. I've tried at least 25 other sites and they haven't worked out, so I'm hoping yours is better.'"<br>❑ Visits /node/8 directly from the mail, or else accesses site and finds her application from the View Applications list. Jane Doe's application is reviewed.<br>❑ In another browser tab or window visits Administer ➢ User management ➢ Users and clicks on "Add user."<br>❑ Specifies the username and e-mail provided in the client application, specifies password, assigns new user to client role, selects the "Notify user of new account" checkbox, and clicks "Create new account." |
| The System | Creates new user Jane Doe. Sends her a welcoming e-mail notifying her of her new account by checking the option "Notify user of new account." |
| Jane Doe | Jane Doe receives the following mail:<br>"Jane Doe,<br>"A site administrator at Translation Studio has created an account for you. You may now log in to `http://translationstudio.textworks.com.ar/user` using the following username and password:<br>username: Jane Doe<br>password: janedoe33<br>"You may also log in by clicking on this link or copying and pasting it in your browser:<br>`http://translationstudio.textworks.com.ar/user/reset/10/1219262189/3add858ff4439d8f086460e1707539ca.`<br>"This is a one-time login, so it can be used only once. After logging in, you will be redirected to `http://translationstudio.textworks.com.ar/user/10/edit` so you can change your password."<br>— Translation Studio team |
| Jane Doe | Logs in. |

Refer to Figure 10-20 to see Jane's first login.

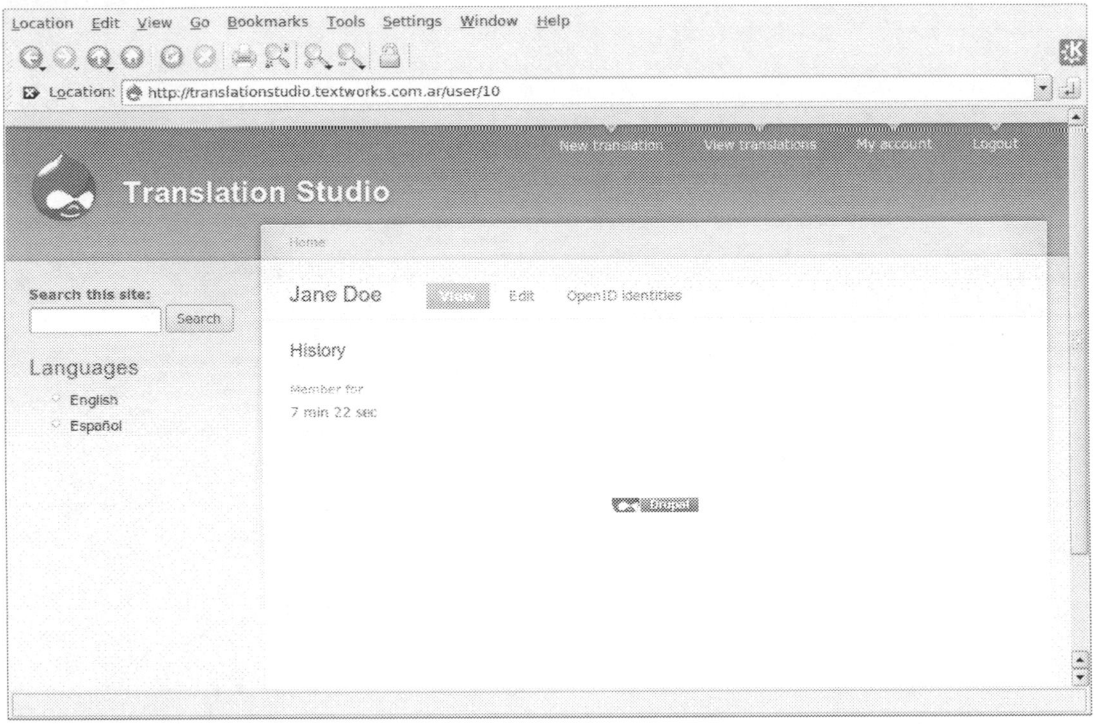


Figure 10-20

Not bad for an off-the-shelf Open Source and free CMS!

## Team Leader's Translation Workflow

But the beat goes on! Let's now see the workflow that is followed as Jane uploads a text for translation, and how the Team Leader will be notified and assign the work to a Translator.

### Team Leader's Translation Workflow Steps

| User/System | Action |
|---|---|
| Jane Doe | Logs in. |
| Jane Doe | Clicks "New translation." |
| The System | Presents node/add/translation. |
| Jane Doe | Completes Title, Language, Date due, Text fields, and clicks on the Save button. |
| The System | Translation saved. Team Leader notified and sent link via e-mail. |

**Team Leader's Translation Workflow Steps**

| User/System | Action |
|---|---|
| The Team Leader | Team Leader receives following e-mail: "Chinese Women's Hockey Team wins Semi-finals and has sent a translation from Translation Studio. Please visit `http://translationstudio.textworks.com.ar/node/9."` *Note: the template needs to be generalized, but it gets the job done for now.* |
| The Team Leader | Accesses the translation directly via the link in the mail. |
| The Team Leader | Edits the translation and, because of permissions, sees more fields. Assigns translation to translator1, sets Status to Assigned. |

The interesting thing is to compare, given how you have configured the permissions, how the user Team Leader sees the translation (Figure 10-21, showing the additional Team Leader menu block in the left sidebar, plus access to more fields), as opposed to how the client sees it (Figure 10-22, showing access to fewer fields and no navigation blocks).

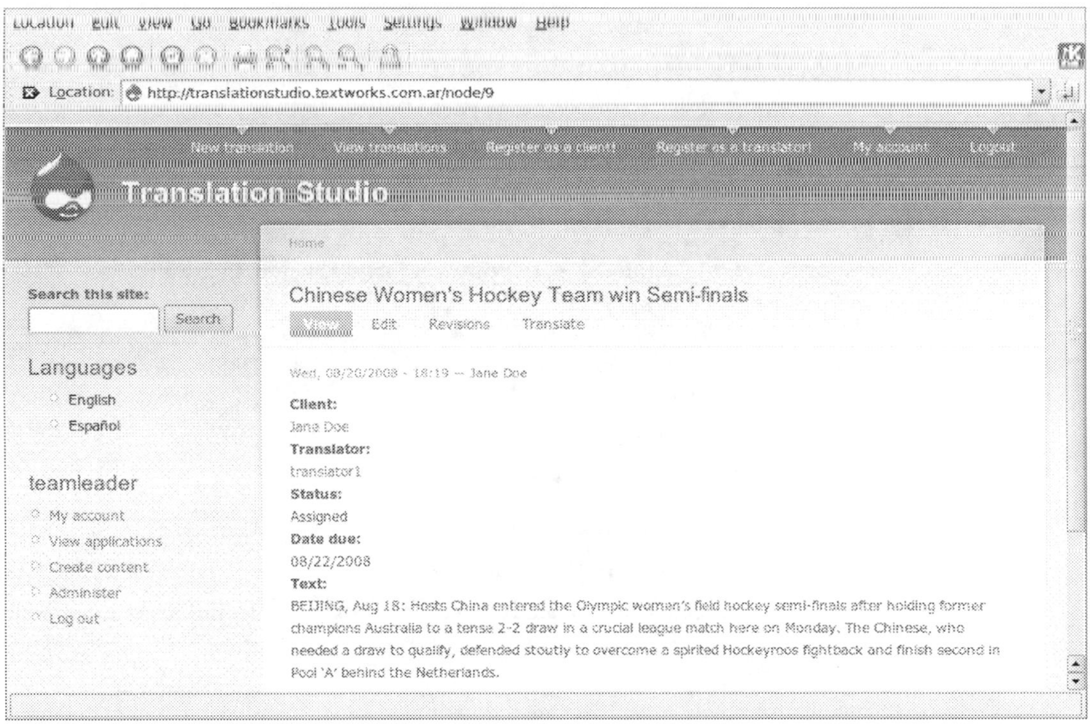


Figure 10-21

Figure 10-22

## Implementing the Translator's Workflow

The Translator is also automagically notified of translations assigned to her, but via an RSS feed! To create the required view, follow these steps:

1. Log in as dev, and go to Administer ➢ Site building ➢ Views. Click the Clone link associated with the Translations view.
2. Enter **translations_by_translator** in the View name field, and click Next.
3. Click Save.
4. Remove the filter: User: Current `True`.
5. Click the + icon in the Arguments section.
6. Select Content: User reference: Translator (field_translation_translator). Configure to Display empty text if argument not present and if argument does not validate. Click Update, and then click Save.
7. Select "existing Page display." Change the Path to **view/my-job-list**. Click Update and then Save.
8. Add a display of type feed! Change Style to **Row**. Specify "Attach to the Page display." Specify the Path of view/my-job-list/feed. Click Save.

The result can be seen in Figure 10-23, complete with an orange RSS icon for the Translator to subscribe to. And here is code for the view all ready to be imported:

```
$view = new view;
$view->name = 'translations_by_translator';
$view->description = 'List translations sorted by status and due date';
$view->tag = 'translation';
$view->view_php = '';
$view->base_table = 'node';
$view->is_cacheable = FALSE;
$view->api_version = 2;
$view->disabled = FALSE; /* Edit this to true to make a default view disabled
 initially */
$handler = $view->new_display('default', 'Defaults', 'default');
$handler->override_option('fields', array(
  'title' => array(
    'label' => 'Title',
    'link_to_node' => 1,
    'exclude' => 0,
    'id' => 'title',
    'table' => 'node',
    'field' => 'title',
    'relationship' => 'none',
  ),
  'field_translation_status_value' => array(
    'label' => '',
    'link_to_node' => 0,
    'label_type' => 'widget',
    'format' => 'default',
    'multiple' => array(
      'group' => TRUE,
      'multiple_number' => '',
      'multiple_from' => '',
      'multiple_reversed' => FALSE,
    ),
    'exclude' => 0,
    'id' => 'field_translation_status_value',
    'table' => 'node_data_field_translation_status',
    'field' => 'field_translation_status_value',
    'relationship' => 'none',
  ),
  'field_translation_date_due_value' => array(
    'label' => '',
    'link to node' => 0,
    'label_type' => 'widget',
    'format' => 'default',
    'multiple' => array(
      'group' => TRUE,
      'multiple_number' => '',
      'multiple_from' => '',
      'multiple_reversed' => FALSE,
    ),
    'exclude' => 0,
    'id' => 'field_translation_date_due_value',
```

```
      'table' => 'node_data_field_translation_date_due',
      'field' => 'field_translation_date_due_value',
      'relationship' => 'none',
    ),
  ));
  $handler->override_option('arguments', array(
    'field_translation_translator_uid' => array(
      'default_action' => 'empty',
      'style_plugin' => 'default_summary',
      'style_options' => array(),
      'wildcard' => 'all',
      'wildcard_substitution' => 'All',
      'title' => '',
      'default_argument_type' => 'fixed',
      'default_argument' => '',
      'validate_type' => 'none',
      'validate_fail' => 'empty',
      'id' => 'field_translation_translator_uid',
      'table' => 'node_data_field_translation_translator',
      'field' => 'field_translation_translator_uid',
      'relationship' => 'none',
      'default_options_div_prefix' => '',
      'default_argument_user' => 0,
      'default_argument_fixed' => '',
      'default_argument_php' => '',
      'validate_argument_node_type' => array(
        'client_application' => 0,
        'page' => 0,
        'story' => 0,
        'translation' => 0,
        'translator_application' => 0,
      ),
      'validate_argument_node_access' => 0,
      'validate_argument_nid_type' => 'nid',
      'validate_argument_vocabulary' => array(),
      'validate_argument_type' => 'tid',
      'validate_argument_php' => '',
    ),
  ));
  $handler->override_option('filters', array(
    'type' => array(
      'operator' => 'in',
      'value' => array(
        'translation' => 'translation',
      ),
      'group' => '0',
      'exposed' => FALSE,
      'expose' => array(
        'operator' => FALSE,
        'label' => '',
      ),
      'id' => 'type',
      'table' => 'node',
      'field' => 'type',
      'relationship' => 'none',
    ),
    'language' => array(
```

```
      'operator' => 'in',
      'value' => array(
        '***CURRENT_LANGUAGE***' => '***CURRENT_LANGUAGE***',
      ),
      'group' => '0',
      'exposed' => FALSE,
      'expose' => array(
        'operator' => FALSE,
        'label' => '',
      ),
      'id' => 'language',
      'table' => 'node',
      'field' => 'language',
      'override' => array(
        'button' => 'Override',
      ),
      'relationship' => 'none',
    ),
  ));
  $handler->override_option('access', array(
    'type' => 'none',
    'role' => array(),
    'perm' => '',
  ));
  $handler->override_option('use_pager', '1');
  $handler->override_option('distinct', 1);
  $handler->override_option('style_plugin', 'table');
  $handler->override_option('style_options', array(
    'grouping' => '',
    'override' => 1,
    'sticky' => 0,
    'order' => 'desc',
    'columns' => array(
      'title' => 'title',
      'field_translation_status_value' => 'field_translation_status_value',
      'field_translation_date_due_value' => 'field_translation_date_due_value',
    ),
    'info' => array(
      'title' => array(
        'sortable' => 1,
        'separator' => '',
      ),
      'field_translation_status_value' => array(
        'sortable' => 1,
        'separator' => '',
      ),
      'field_translation_date_due_value' => array(
        'sortable' => 1,
        'separator' => '',
      ),
    ),
    'default' => 'field_translation_date_due_value',
  ));
  $handler = $view->new_display('page', 'Page', 'page_1');
  $handler->override_option('path', 'view/my-job-list');
  $handler->override_option('menu', array(
    'type' => 'none',
```

```
    'title' => '',
    'weight' => 0,
  ));
  $handler->override_option('tab_options', array(
    'type' => 'none',
    'title' => '',
    'weight' => 0,
  ));
  $handler = $view->new_display('feed', 'Feed', 'feed_1');
  $handler->override_option('row_plugin', 'node_rss');
  $handler->override_option('row_options', array(
    'item_length' => 'default',
  ));
  $handler->override_option('path', 'view/my-job-list/feed');
  $handler->override_option('menu', array(
    'type' => 'none',
    'title' => '',
    'weight' => 0,
  ));
  $handler->override_option('tab_options', array(
    'type' => 'none',
    'title' => '',
    'weight' => 0,
  ));
  $handler->override_option('displays', array(
    'page_1' => 'page_1',
    'default' => 0,
  ));
```

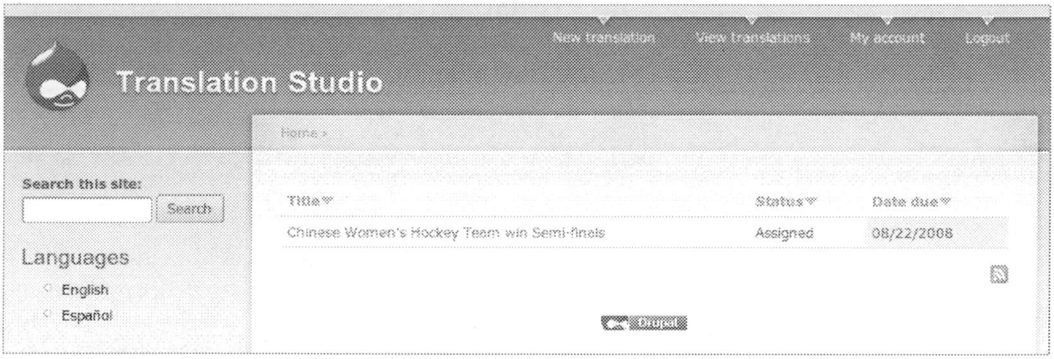


Figure 10-23

But how will the Translator find his customized job list? Obviously, the Team Leader could mail the RSS feed to each of them, or they could be told how to figure it out. But with just one extra touch, you can do something a bit cooler. Let's create a custom block only visible to Translators logging in or on the front page, that provides them with a direct link to their translations job list. Follow these steps:

1. Go to Administer ➢ Site building ➢ Blocks, and click "Add block." Type in **Translators job list** in the Block description field, and leave the Title field blank. Open up the Input format

section, and select PHP code for the input format (not the most secure thing in the world, but hey, just this once!).

2. In the Block body itself, insert the following exactly as it is here (no trailing spaces after the ?> closing tag):

```
<?php
global $user;
print '<h3>' . t('Hello') . ', ' .  $user -> name . ', click \
<a href="/view/my-job-list/' \
. $user -> uid . '">' . t('here') . '</a> ' .  t('to see job list') .
'</h3>';
?>
```

3. Select the checkbox corresponding to Translator in the "Show block for specific roles" section. In the "Show block on specific pages" section, select "Show on only the listed pages," and list the following, each on a separate line:

```
<front>
node/1
node/2
user
user/*
```

The result can be seen in Figure 10-24.

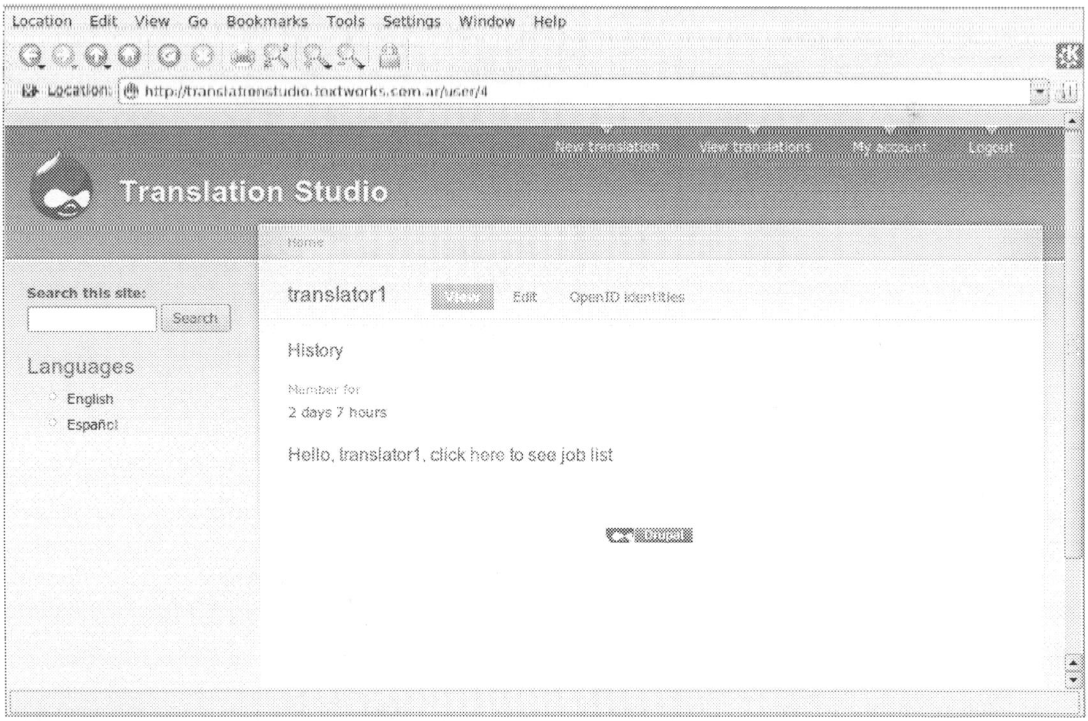


Figure 10-24

The Translator can simply access the list, choose a translation to work on, and change its status to Ready so that the Client knows the work can be downloaded.

# Summary

In this chapter, you made a complete self-contained mini-application on a fresh install of Drupal 6.x.

In doing so, you got the chance to see some fine new functionality built right into this Drupal release, including its convenient Ajaxified admin interface, its support for business objects modeling and for more-flexible-than-ever query generation, as well as a fully localized and bilingual application framework with off-the-shelf support for workflows.

In the next chapter, we'll see where we are with the On-Line Literary Workshop and move forward on that front.

# 11

# Full Swing Agile Approach to Drupal Development

This is actually the best part of the book, and the most representative of real-world work. Distracted by upgrades and other wonderment and a lot of stuff going on, you need to get back on track and bring the project to successful closure.

Now, at what stage is the project? How do you even know? Well, that's the reason for the Agile approach . . . a kind of Google Map of your project: Pan out for the big vision, zoom in to any area of detail you can easily get your head wrapped around, and break off, just a single task to get done and make another step forward. That way, you never get that jackrabbit-in-the-headlights paralysis feeling as complexity overwhelms you and you don't know which way to turn.

This may seem obvious, but it is the single most frequent cause of delays in website application development, as complexity and contemplation and infinite choices rob your time and energy. With Agile, it's like spreading all the cards on the table, taking a moment to put them in order together with the client, then using good old-fashioned worker discipline to reduce implementation to the process. This process is like plucking a card, getting it done, showing it off, feeling good, and then taking another card and another until it's all done.

So this chapter is a road that's going to lay itself, as you take a card, one at a time, and get it done. To work through the chapter, take the code from Chapter 7, and work through all the activities that follow below. As an alternative, you can simply download the tarball for this chapter and see the functionality already working as you read through this chapter.

Now, it has been a few chapters since you were working with the On-Line Literary Workshop. To get back in the driver's seat, the best thing to do is to see which iterations are already done, then run the Acceptance Tests (the confirmation section of each user story, and an associated full-blown Acceptance Test for that user story if there is one) for all of the user stories in those iterations. Then take the first user story not yet implemented . . . and do it.

To see a list of all user stories, log in as user dev, and then click on the groups' primary menu link. This is because the dev group (which the development and client users are members of) is unlisted in the regular group directory. What you see in the dev group is simply the same thing you see at any group page — the listing from what was left as the default group home page view, `og_ghp_table`. You need to hone your project tools a smidgen to make them more useful (which, in this use case — that is, coming home from Burning Man and getting back to work — can readily be seen as woefully inadequate, since you need to hone your project tools so as to be able to quickly see what your progress has been and how far you have come along in the implementation of user stories).

# Honing the Project Tools

I can hear some of you asking, "What is the percentage of time you spend creating tools, as opposed to the amount of time you spend actually getting any work done?" Ah, no, this is the nature of the beast, or business! Always reserve a significant amount of time to fashion tools: This will make you more productive very quickly and is part of the work itself. You should get used to this in the software business.

**Problem: You need to be able to list all user stories and sort them by iteration.**

**Solution**: Make a view to list user stories sortable and filterable by iteration, and make it available on the dev group home page in a new menu block called *project*.

**Problem: If you are in a user story and an Acceptance Test has been written for that user story, you need to have a link that will take you straight to the Acceptance Test.**

**Solution**: Add an Acceptance Test node reference field to the User Story content type, so you can see which ones are related and add additional fields to include additional Acceptance Tests.

## *Adding an Acceptance Test Node*

Let's implement the second one first:

1. Go to Administration ➤ Content management ➤ Content types, and click on the Manage Fields link corresponding to the `user_story` content type.
2. Click on the "Add field" tab, and enter **user_story_acc_test** in the Field name field, **Acceptance Tests** in the Label field, and select "Node reference" from the Field type dropdown list.

3. Click on the Continue button, select "Autocomplete text field" from the dropdown list in the Widget type field, and click on the Continue button again. For the Number of values, select Unlimited. *"'Unlimited' will provide an 'Add more' button so the users can add as many values as they like."* Now, that is cool — and only available with Drupal 6 and later.

   *Previously, three fields were added, then you had to save the node, and another three fields were added; this way you can add as many fields as you like in a single edit. The Acceptance Test must already exist, of course. Indicate Acceptance Test as the only node type that can be referenced, and click on the "Save field settings" button.*

4. From the listing of fields in the "Manage fields" tab, drag the new field down into last place, just after the Confirmation field, and click on the Save button.
5. Now, try it! From the list on the dev organic group home page, click "Clean URLs and automatic generation of SEO friendly paths" user story (if the title field is not clickable, go to Administer ➢ Site building ➢ Views, click on the title field, and specify that it should link to the node). At the bottom, in the Acceptance Test field, type in **clean**, and the widget will offer the already existing Acceptance Test "Test Clean URLs and automatic generation of SEO friendly paths." Click on what is offered. Save your work. Now when you view the user story, you can navigate directly to the Acceptance Tests. And while viewing any of the associated Acceptance Tests, you can navigate right back to the user story. Awesome.

## Make a View to List User Stories

Having solved the second problem, tackle the first ("view user stories by iteration"):

1. First of all, create a Taxonomy vocabulary of terms called *Iteration*. Add the names of the iterations you were using in Trac: **Prototype**, **Beta**, **Final release**, and **Launch**.
2. Go to Administer ➢ Content management ➢ Taxonomy, and click on the "Add vocabulary" tab. Type in **User Stories by Iteration** for Vocabulary name, a suitable description field ("**An iteration in the development process**"), and a suitable Help text ("**Please indicate which iteration the user story has been allocated to in the project planning**.").
3. Indicate "User Story" as the only content type this vocabulary will be used to categorize, and click on the Save button.
4. Back at the listing of taxonomy vocabularies, click on the "Add terms" link for the newly created vocabulary. Add the four terms, one after another (when you click on the Save button, you are brought right back to the "Add term" Form).
5. One last cool thing: When you click "List terms," you can drag Prototype to the top so that it will be listed first, then click on the Save button.
6. Make another vocabulary called *User Story Status*, also applicable to the User Story content type, containing the terms **In progress**, **Test pass**, and **Test fail**. Add another vocabulary, called *User Stories by Actor*, listing all the actors. Of course, the actors may be implicit in the title of the user story, but this way you can easily click the applied vocabulary term and browse all the user stories related to that actor.

7. Edit each of the user stories according to the following table. But before you do, note that if you only want to edit one or two, just to quickly put in the basic details, the form is very big and you'll feel as if you've bypassed the details (e.g., "Conversation," "Confirmation," "Acceptance Tests"). Don't worry! You will be filling this information in later in order to get to the Save button. It would be better to have a collapsible User Story Details group so that it is quick and easy to add a user story that comes to your mind while you are developing.

| Actor | User Story | Iteration | Status |
|---|---|---|---|
| Workshop Leader | Can approve applications to join the workshop.<br>Can suspend Members and Publishers.<br>Can manage affinity groups.<br>Can broadcast messages to Members.<br>Can do everything Workshop Members and Publishers can do. | Prototype | Test pass |
| Webmaster | Clean URLs and automatic generation of SEO-friendly paths. | Prototype | Test pass |
| Workshop Member | Can post literary pieces.<br>Can make any post public, private, or visible to an affinity group.<br>Can critique public posts.<br>Can browse public pieces and critiques.<br>Can send and receive messages to and from all Members and Publishers and the Workshop Leader.<br>Can create simplified navigation blocks for Workshop Members. | Beta | Test pass |
| Workshop Member | Can start an affinity group with its own forums.<br>Can post to forums.<br>Can maintain his or her own literary blog. | Final Release | |
| Publisher | Can browse public content.<br>Can broadcast a call for pieces to be submitted for a publication.<br>Can select content for inclusion in a publication.<br>Can manage an on-line publication.<br>Can manage an on-line blog.<br>Can do initial theming. | Final Release | |
| Webmaster | Can administer the website configuration.<br>Can install new updates and functionality.<br>Can prepare production server.<br>Can optimize production environment and carry out deployment.<br>Can package web application as Drupal installation profile. | Launch | |

8. Go to Administer ➢ Content management ➢ Content types, and click on the "Add group" tab. Type in **User Story Details** in the Label field, and select Collapsed so that the fields in this group will be collapsed by default.

9. Click Add. Now, drag the Conversation, Confirmation, and Acceptance Tests fields so that they belong to the new group. This can be done the old way, by editing each field and manually indicating the group the field belongs to, or by simply dragging them under the group and leaving them slightly indented, as per Figure 11-1.

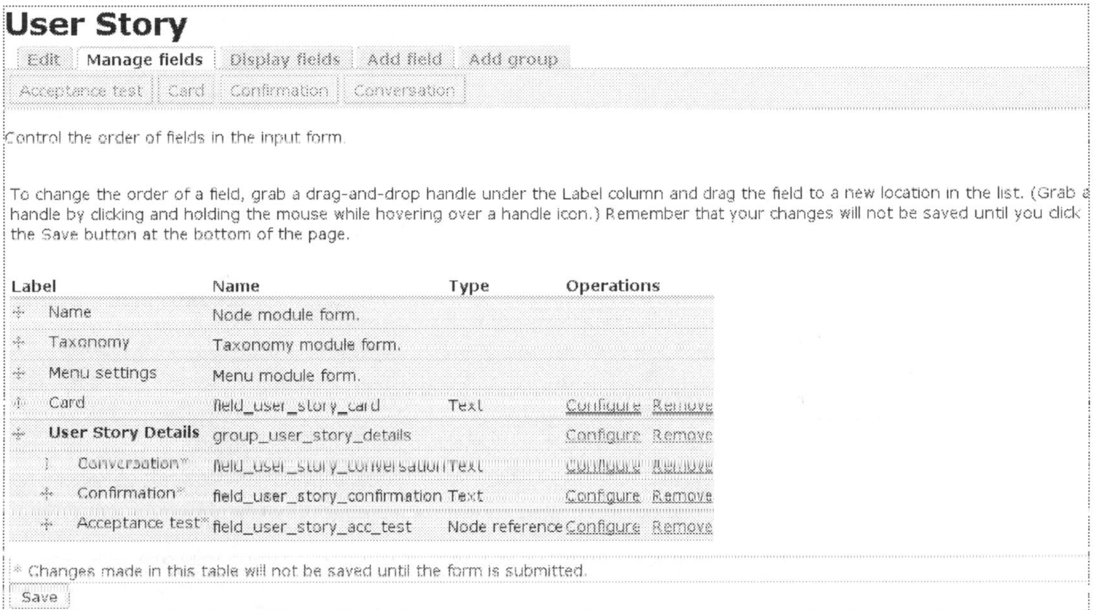


**Figure 11-1**

10. Make sure that all of the user stories in the previous table exist and that they are only accessible to the dev audience by so indicating in the Audience field. This is internal dev business, after all.

## Making the User List Available

So, now you know where you are! Let's leave the Launch iteration to later chapters, and go through the implementation of the Final Release functionality in the rest of this chapter.

But you need to complete the solution to the first tooling problem, namely, "Make a view to list user stories sortable and filterable by iteration, and make it available on the dev group home page in a new menu block called *project*." To do so, follow these steps:

1. Go to Administer ➤ Site building ➤ Views, and click Add. Enter **user_stories** in the View name field, and **List user stories sortable and filterable by iteration** in the View description field. Enter **user stories** in the View tag field (a cool way of grouping together all views having to do with applications), and leave the default Node View type selected. Click Next.

2. Select the fields to be displayed. To add the first, click on the + icon next to the Fields block. In the Groups dropdown list, choose Node, select Node: Title, and click Add. The *Configure field "Node: Title"* dialog appears.

3. Type **Name** in the Label field, and select the "Link this field to its node" checkbox, and then click on the Update button. The Live Preview already shows all nodes in the system! Before you filter the view, finish the fields list. Select + again, select the Taxonomy group, and select Taxonomy: All terms and click Add. Type **All attributes** in the label field, select "Link this field to its term page," and click on the Update button. Select + again, but this time select the Taxonomy group and then select Taxonomy Term. Type in **Iteration** for the label. Select "Link this field to its taxonomy term page," and click on the Update button again. (Note that it is not necessary to specify any vocabulary here since that is handled in the filters section; see below.)

4. Click on the Save button to create the view. The info area announces *"The view has been saved."*

5. In the Basic Settings section, to the right of the Style label, **Unformatted** is selected by default. Click on the Unformatted link, and in the work area below, select Table, and click on the Update button. Configure the table to have each field sortable, with *Title* as the default sort. Specify an Ascending sort order, and click on the Update button again. Click on the Save button again.

6. Click the + icon in the Filter section. Choose the Node group, select Node: Type, and click on the Add button. The Operator should be set to "Is one of," and the Node type should have User Story checked. Click on the Update button and then the "Save the view" button.

7. Click on the + icon in the Filter section again. Choose the Taxonomy group, and select Taxonomy: Term ID. Click on the Add button. The extra settings configuration appears. Select the "User Stories by Iteration" Vocabulary and the Dropdown selection type widget. Click on the Update button.

8. In the filter configuration that appears next, select the operator "Is one of," select all four of the terms so that the list will initially include all User Stories, and click on the "Reduce duplicates" checkbox. Click on the Update and then the Save buttons.

9. Click on the Taxonomy: Term ID filter link again, and now click on the Expose button so that users can filter the view produced. Place **Iteration** in the label field, and click on the Update and "Save the view" buttons.

10. Add another filter. This filter won't be exposed, but rather a filter to avoid user stories being shown once for one vocabulary and once for another: You need a filter to only include queries associated with the "User Stories by Iteration vocabulary." Click on the + icon in the Filters section, and add a Taxonomy: Vocabulary filter set to only include "User Stories by Iteration." Save the view.

11. You now need to add a Page display. Select Page in the dropdown list on the left-hand side, and then click on the "Add display" button. In the Page settings section, click on the None link next to the Path attribute. Type **view/user-stories** in the text field, and click on the Update button. Configure the Use pager attribute to Full pager, and click on "Update default display" since any display will require a pager. Configure the Items per page to 20.

12. Click Save.

For your convenience, the following code can be used to directly import the view, assuming the content types and taxonomies already exist and are configured as per the indications in this chapter:

```
view = new view;
$view->name = 'user_stories';
$view->description = 'List user stories sortable and filterable by \
iteration, actor and status';
$view->tag = 'user stories';
$view->view_php = '';
$view->base_table = 'node';
$view->is_cacheable = FALSE;
$view->api_version = 2;
$view->disabled = FALSE; /* Edit this to true to make a default \
 view disabled initially */
$handler = $view->new_display('default', 'Defaults', 'default');
$handler->override_option('fields', array(
  'title' => array(
    'label' => 'Title',
    'link_to_node' => 1,
    'exclude' => 0,
    'id' => 'title',
    'table' => 'node',
    'field' => 'title',
    'relationship' => 'none',
  ),
  'name' => array(
    'label' => 'Iteration',
    'link_to_taxonomy' => 1,
    'exclude' => 0,
    'id' => 'name',
    'table' => 'term_data',
    'field' => 'name',
    'relationship' => 'none',
  ),
  'tid' => array(
    'label' => 'All attributes',
    'type' => 'separator',
    'separator' => ', ',
    'empty' => '',
    'link_to_taxonomy' => 1,
    'limit' => 0,
    'vids' => array(
      '1' => 0,
      '5' => 0,
      '2' => 0,
      '3' => 0,
      '4' => 0,
      '7' => 0,
    ),
    'exclude' => 0,
    'id' => 'tid',
    'table' => 'term_node',
    'field' => 'tid',
```

```
      'override' => array(
        'button' => 'Override',
      ),
      'relationship' => 'none',
    ),
  ));
  $handler->override_option('filters', array(
    'type' => array(
      'operator' => 'in',
      'value' => array(
        'user_story' => 'user_story',
      ),
      'group' => '0',
      'exposed' => FALSE,
      'expose' => array(
        'operator' => FALSE,
        'label' => '',
      ),
      'id' => 'type',
      'table' => 'node',
      'field' => 'type',
      'relationship' => 'none',
    ),
    'tid' => array(
      'operator' => 'or',
      'value' => array(),
      'group' => '0',
      'exposed' => TRUE,
      'expose' => array(
        'use_operator' => 0,
        'operator' => 'tid_op',
        'identifier' => 'tid',
        'label' => 'Iteration',
        'optional' => 1,
        'single' => 1,
        'remember' => 0,
        'reduce' => 0,
      ),
      'type' => 'select',
      'vid' => '4',
      'id' => 'tid',
      'table' => 'term_node',
      'field' => 'tid',
      'hierarchy' => 0,
      'relationship' => 'none',
      'reduce_duplicates' => 1,
    ),
    'vid' => array(
      'operator' => 'in',
      'value' => array(
        '4' => 4,
      ),
      'group' => '0',
      'exposed' => FALSE,
```

```
    'expose' => array(
      'operator' => FALSE,
      'label' => '',
    ),
    'id' => 'vid',
    'table' => 'term_data',
    'field' => 'vid',
    'override' => array(
      'button' => 'Override',
    ),
    'relationship' => 'none',
  ),
));
$handler->override_option('access', array(
  'type' => 'none',
  'role' => array(),
  'perm' => '',
));
$handler->override_option('items_per_page', 20);
$handler->override_option('use_pager', '1');
$handler->override_option('style_plugin', 'table');
$handler->override_option('style_options', array(
  'grouping' => '',
  'override' => 1,
  'sticky' => 0,
  'order' => 'asc',
  'columns' => array(
    'title' => 'title',
    'name' => 'name',
  ),
  'info' => array(
    'title' => array(
      'sortable' => 1,
      'separator' => '',
    ),
    'name' => array(
      'sortable' => 1,
      'separator' => '',
    ),
  ),
  'default' => 'title',
));
$handler = $view->new_display('page', 'Page', 'page_1');
$handler->override_option('path', 'view/user-stories');
$handler->override_option('menu', array(
  'type' => 'none',
  'title' => '',
  'weight' => 0,
));
$handler->override_option('tab_options', array(
  'type' => 'none',
  'title' => '',
  'weight' => 0,
));
```

## Creating a Block Menu to Easily Access the New View

All that remains is to create the block menu *project* for admin and client (Workshop Leader) roles:

1. Go to Administer ➤ Site building ➤ Menus, and click on the "Add Menu" tab. Type in **project** in the Menu name and **Project** in the Title fields, and **Menu** for accessing project documentation in the Description field. Click Save.
2. Click on the "Add item" tab. Enter **view/user-stories** in the Path field and **User stories** in the Menu link title field. In the Description field, enter **List user stories sorted and filtered by iteration, actor, and status**. And click on the Save button.
3. Now head over to Administer ➤ Site building ➤ Blocks, and enable the newly created Project block (whenever you create a menu in Drupal, a menu block is automatically created and may be enabled in any region supported by the current theme) in the left sidebar region, then drag it down to fourth place, just above Genre parade. Remember to click on the "Save blocks" button at the bottom of the page in order for your changes to go into effect.
4. You now want to configure the block so that it is only visible to the Admin and Workshop Leader roles. You do this by clicking on the configure link corresponding to the Project block and selecting the checkboxes for these roles in the "Show block for specific roles" section. Click on the "Save block" button.

Now you have a shiny new Project menu block in the left sidebar when you are logged in, say, as user dev. Click on the User Stories link, and you should see the results of all our labor; the first problem has now had its solution implemented. Figure 11-2 shows the page after the Final Release filter has been applied.

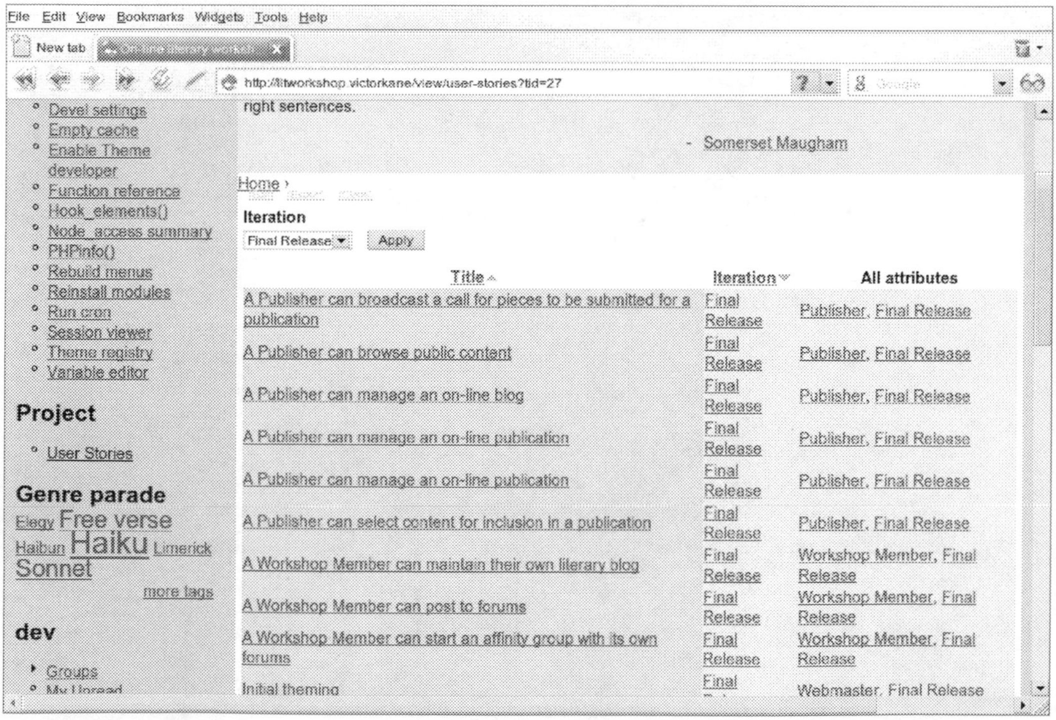


Figure 11-2

# Implementing the User Stories

After working through the last section, you can now take any user story not yet in progress (which is all of them at this point) and implement it!

Such is the joy of keeping it simple when you use the Agile approach to software development: Since you have already divided everything into bite-sized chunks and have distributed these into a planning timeline, when you just take one, you only have to wrap your head around that while you're implementing it. So you can come back from Burning Man, log in as user dev, click on the User Stories link in the Project block menu, orient yourself in terms of which iteration you are in, which user stories have been implemented, take one, put your feet up with your laptop in your lap, and work on it:

## Workshop Member: Starting an Affinity Group with Its Own Forums

This user story is an ideal place to jump right in.

Click on this user story and edit it. Set the User Story status to "Test fail," and click Save right away. Now, if a clutch server is down and you get the call and spend an hour fixing that, when you come back to your work here, you can see which user stories are in progress (Of course, if you prefer, you could just add an **In progress** term to the User Story status taxonomy vocabulary . . . just because I am a natural miser in terms of using resources doesn't mean you have to be.)

### Working with the Conversation and Confirmation Sections

Now, what you want to do here is think aloud in the Conversation section about how you are going to implement this, so a record is kept of how the story was implemented. A typical entry now in the Conversation section could be:

**Conversation**

A Workshop Member can start an affinity group with its own forums.

```
Group enable forums.
```

Enter this by editing the user story:

1. Click and open up the User Story Details section, and enter text in the first available Conversation text area. Remember, if they are all filled up, you can click "Add another item" right then and there thanks to Drupal and jQuery magic.
2. Now, use the Confirmation section to lay out raw material for a future Acceptance Test. Add something like the following (explaining how forums can be enabled as visible only to a given group):

**Confirmation**

User james logs in and decides to create a new group he wants to list in the groups directory for Flash Fiction Enthusiasts. Once the group is created, user joyce logs in,

> joins the group, and starts a group forum topic. User james logs in and leaves a comment on joyce's topic. But user gertrude, not a member of the Flash Fiction Enthusiasts group, cannot access this forum topic, either from the group home page or from the Flash Fiction forum itself.

3. Click the Save button.

   Figure 11-3 shows the user story as you will see it after taking another distracting call.

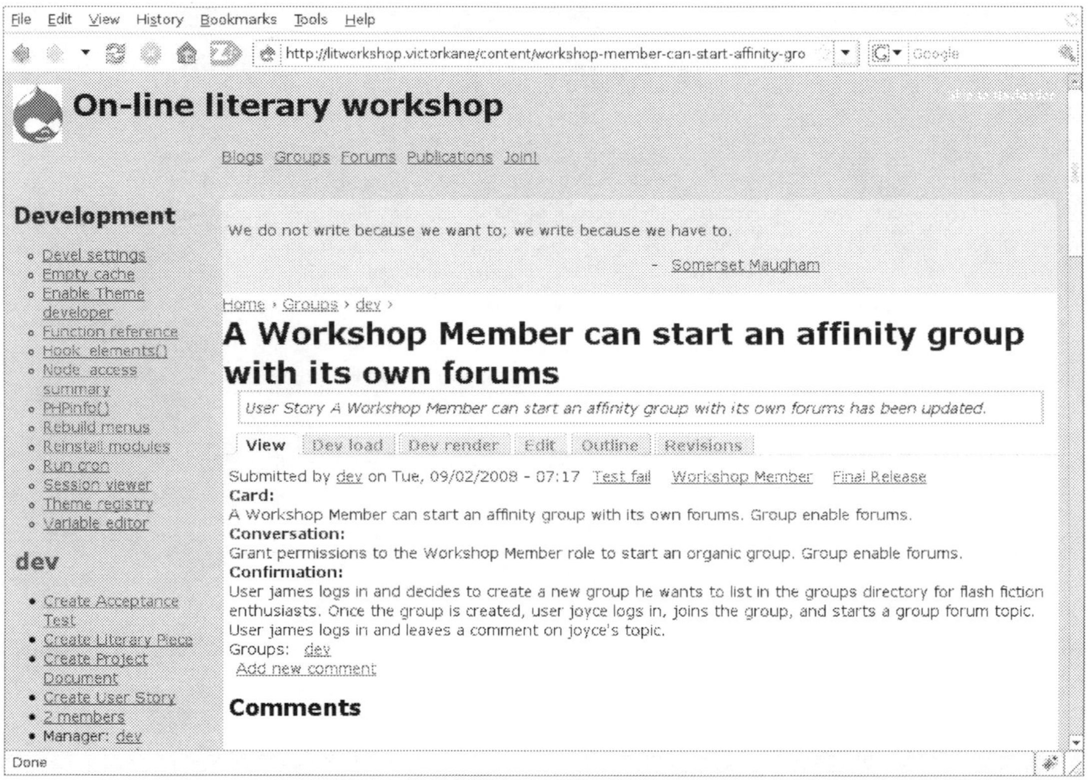


Figure 11-3

4. The first part is simple: Go to Administer ➤ User management ➤ Permissions, and make sure the Workshop Member role has been granted the following permissions in the Forum Module section:

| Module | Permission |
|---|---|
| Node module | Create group content.<br>Edit own group content. |
| Forum module | Create forum topics.<br>Edit own forum topics |

## Making Options Appear in the Place Menu

Now (using another Firefox profile, or else another browser) log in as user james, a Workshop Member. Looking at the Confirmation section for guidance after another phone call unsuccessfully trying to sell me a well-known telecommunications gadget or car insurance, you can see that the first problem you are going to come across is that even though james has permission to create a group, that option does not appear in the Places menu. To make this happen, do the following:

1. Go to Administer ➢ Site building ➢ Menus, and click on the Places menu.
2. Click on the "Add item" tab, and enter **node/add/group** in the Path field, and **Create your own group** in the Menu link title. Click Save. Now you can see all the menu items — go ahead and reorder them according to your own preferences by dragging them up and down.
3. Now, the new option appears in user james' menu. Logged in as user james, click on the "Create your own group" link. Enter **Flash Fiction Enthusiasts** in the Title field and **Join us for flash fiction fun** in the description field, which will appear in the group details block as well as in the group directory. Add a mission statement.
4. In the Membership Requests section, although you could choose Moderated so that membership requests would have to be approved, choose Open so that membership requests are accepted immediately. Select the List in the groups directory checkbox, and click Save.

## Adding a Forum Topic

Upon running the Confirmation Test, you get a "fail": User joyce can join the group, but when he accesses the group home page, the corresponding group block does not include an option to create a forum topic that can optionally only be accessed by Flash Fiction Enthusiasts.

To remedy this problem, do the following:

1. Log in as user dev (or access the browser that is logged in as that user, if you are using the recommended method of having two sessions open in different browsers simultaneously), and go to Administer ➢ Content management ➢ Content types, and edit the Forum topic content type.
2. Open up the Organic groups section, and select the Standard group post (typically only the author may edit). No e-mail notification option. Click on the "Save content type" button.
3. Before running the Confirmation Test, as dev go to Administer ➢ Content management ➢ Forums, and click on the "Add forum" tab. Type in **Flash Fiction** in the Forum name field, choose Literary Forms as the parent, and click Save.
4. Now run the Confirmation Test again.

User joyce logs in (supposing he is not yet a member of the Flash Fiction Enthusiasts group). He clicks on the Groups primary menu option and sees the Flash Fiction Enthusiasts group listed in the groups directory, then clicks the Join link. Upon being asked, "Are you sure you want to join the group?" he clicks on the Join button and is told in the info area just above the content region: "You are now a member of the Flash Fiction Enthusiasts." The user clicks the group home page link (Flash Fiction Enthusiasts) and sees that so far there have been no posts in this group. He sees the Flash Fiction Enthusiasts block menu at the top of the left sidebar and sees that he has the option of creating a forum topic or a literary piece as an internal post of the group, only accessible by members. He clicks on "Create forum topic," types in **What is flash fiction really?** in the Subject field, selects Flash Fiction from the Forums dropdown list, and types in a suitable text in the Body textarea field. He leaves the Audience checkbox for Flash Fiction Enthusiasts selected and hits Save. Then user joyce logs out.

User james logs in, clicks on the My Groups link in the Groups menu block in the left sidebar, then elects to visit the Flash Fiction Enthusiasts group. He sees that joyce has posted "What is flash fiction really?" and clicks the link to access it. He finds himself in the Flash Fiction Forum and reads the forum topic. He leaves a comment.

Well, this time, the Confirmation Test passes!

One question, however: What happens if a Workshop Member who is not a member of the group accesses the group page or this forum topic? The answer is that newly created user gertrude, assigned a role of Workshop Member, logs in, clicks Groups, clicks on the Flash Fiction Enthusiasts group home page link in the group directory, and sees the group mission statement, but is told:

> *"No public posts in this group. Consider joining this group in order to view its posts."*

Awesome. As user dev, go in and edit the user story Confirmation section to include this as part of the test:

> **Confirmation**
>
> User james logs in and decides to create a new group he wants to list in the groups directory for flash fiction enthusiasts. Once the group is created, user joyce logs in, joins the group, and starts a group forum topic. User james logs in and leaves a comment on joyce's topic.

Mark the User Story status as "Test pass" and click Save.

Now click on the User Stories link in the Project menu block in the left sidebar, filter for our current iteration — select Final Release and click on the Apply button — and take another user story to implement.

## A Publisher Can Browse Public Content

This is the next user story on the pile of cards.

From the User Story Details section:

> **Conversation**
>
> Enable the Places menu block for publishers.
>
> Modify the browse/genre view to include the genre taxonomy term as an exposed filter.

## Enabling the Places Menu Block

To enable the places menu block for publishers also (they will only see the links for which they are granted permission), do the following:

1. Go to Administer ➤ Content management ➤ Blocks, and click on the Configure link for the Places block. Select the checkbox corresponding to the Publisher role in the "Show block for specific roles" section, and click on the "Save block" button.
2. To complete the "Browse literary pieces according to genre" view so that it performs as advertised, go to Administer ➤ Content management ➤ Views, and click on the Edit link corresponding to the view genre_browser.
3. Click on the + icon in the header of the Filters section, and in the work area, select Taxonomy from the dropdown list. Select the checkbox next to the Taxonomy: Term ID option. Click on the Add button. The work area now asks you to select the Vocabulary that the taxonomy term should belong to, as well as the selection widget type.
4. Select Tags and Dropdown, and click on the Update button. Now the work area asks you to confirm the Operator ("Is one of"), the terms (do not select any), and offers an Expose button. Click the Expose button, enter **Genre** in the Label field, then click on the Update button, and finally click Save.

The exported code for the new version of *genre_browser*, which you can conveniently import if you prefer, is as follows:

```
$view = new view;
$view->name = 'genre_browser';
$view->description = '';
$view->tag = '';
$view->view_php = '';
$view->base_table = 'node';
$view->is_cacheable = FALSE;
$view->api_version = 2;
$view->disabled = FALSE; /* Edit this to true to make a default \
 view disabled initially */
$handler = $view->new_display('default', 'Defaults', 'default');
$handler->override_option('fields', array(
  'title' => array(
    'label' => 'Name',
    'link_to_node' => 1,
    'exclude' => 0,
    'id' => 'title',
    'table' => 'node',
    'field' => 'title',
    'relationship' => 'none',
  ),
  'name' => array(
    'label' => 'Genre',
    'link_to_taxonomy' => 0,
    'exclude' => 0,
    'id' => 'name',
    'table' => 'term_data',
    'field' => 'name',
```

```
      'relationship' => 'none',
    ),
    'name_1' => array(
      'id' => 'name_1',
      'table' => 'users',
      'field' => 'name',
      'label' => 'Author',
    ),
    'changed' => array(
      'id' => 'changed',
      'table' => 'node',
      'field' => 'changed',
      'label' => 'Date',
    ),
  ));
  $handler->override_option('filters', array(
    'type' => array(
      'operator' => 'in',
      'value' => array(
        'literary_piece' => 'literary_piece',
      ),
      'group' => '0',
      'exposed' => FALSE,
      'expose' => array(
        'operator' => FALSE,
        'label' => '',
      ),
      'id' => 'type',
      'table' => 'node',
      'field' => 'type',
      'relationship' => 'none',
    ),
    'title' => array(
      'operator' => 'contains',
      'value' => '',
      'group' => '0',
      'exposed' => 1,
      'expose' => array(
        'use_operator' => 0,
        'operator' => '',
        'identifier' => 'filter0',
        'label' => 'Name',
        'optional' => 1,
        'remember' => 0,
      ),
      'case' => 1,
      'id' => 'title',
      'table' => 'node',
      'field' => 'title',
      'relationship' => 'none',
    ),
    'vid' => array(
      'operator' => 'in',
      'value' => array(
        '2' => 2,
```

```
      ),
      'group' => '0',
      'exposed' => FALSE,
      'expose' => array(
        'operator' => 'vid_op',
        'label' => 'Genre',
        'use_operator' => 0,
        'identifier' => 'vid',
        'optional' => 1,
        'single' => 1,
        'remember' => 0,
        'reduce' => 0,
      ),
      'id' => 'vid',
      'table' => 'term_data',
      'field' => 'vid',
      'relationship' => 'none',
    ),
    'uid' => array(
      'id' => 'uid',
      'table' => 'users',
      'field' => 'uid',
      'exposed' => 1,
      'expose' => array(
        'identifier' => 'filter2',
        'label' => 'Author',
        'operator' => '',
        'optional' => '1',
        'single' => '0',
      ),
    ),
    'tid_1' => array(
      'operator' => 'or',
      'value' => array(),
      'group' => '0',
      'exposed' => TRUE,
      'expose' => array(
        'use_operator' => 0,
        'operator' => 'tid_1_op',
        'identifier' => 'tid_1',
        'label' => 'Genre',
        'optional' => 1,
        'single' => 1,
        'remember' => 0,
        'reduce' => 0,
      ),
      'type' => 'select',
      'vid' => '2',
      'id' => 'tid_1',
      'table' => 'term_node',
      'field' => 'tid',
      'hierarchy' => 0,
      'relationship' => 'none',
      'reduce_duplicates' => 0,
      'override' => array(
```

```
        'button' => 'Override',
      ),
    ),
  ));
  $handler->override_option('access', array(
    'type' => 'none',
    'role' => array(),
    'perm' => '',
  ));
  $handler->override_option('title', 'Browse literary pieces according to genre');
  $handler->override_option('header_format', '1');
  $handler->override_option('footer_format', '1');
  $handler->override_option('empty_format', '1');
  $handler->override_option('items_per_page', '20');
  $handler->override_option('use_pager', TRUE);
  $handler->override_option('style_plugin', 'table');
  $handler->override_option('style_options', array(
    'columns' => array(),
    'default' => '',
    'info' => array(
      'title' => array(
        'sortable' => TRUE,
      ),
      'name_1' => array(
        'sortable' => TRUE,
      ),
      'changed' => array(
        'sortable' => TRUE,
      ),
    ),
    'override' => FALSE,
    'order' => 'asc',
  ));
  $handler = $view->new_display('page', 'Page', 'page_1');
  $handler->override_option('path', 'browse/genre');
  $handler->override_option('menu', array(
    'type' => 'none',
    'title' => '',
    'weight' => 0,
  ));
  $handler->override_option('tab_options', array(
    'type' => 'none',
    'title' => '',
    'weight' => 0,
  ));
  $handler = $view->new_display('block', 'Block', 'block_1');
  $handler->override_option('title', 'Browse Literary Pieces');
  $handler->override_option('header_format', '1');
  $handler->override_option('footer_format', '1');
  $handler->override_option('empty_format', '1');
  $handler->override_option('items_per_page', '5');
  $handler->override_option('use_pager', TRUE);
  $handler->override_option('style_plugin', 'table');
  $handler->override_option('style_options', array(
    'columns' => array(),
```

```
        'default' => '',
        'info' => array(),
        'override' => FALSE,
        'order' => 'asc',
    ));
    $handler->override_option('block_description', 'Genre browser');
```

Figure 11-4 shows that the publisher alfred logged in and after having clicked the "Browse by genre" link in his Places block menu, applied the Genre filter of Haiku.

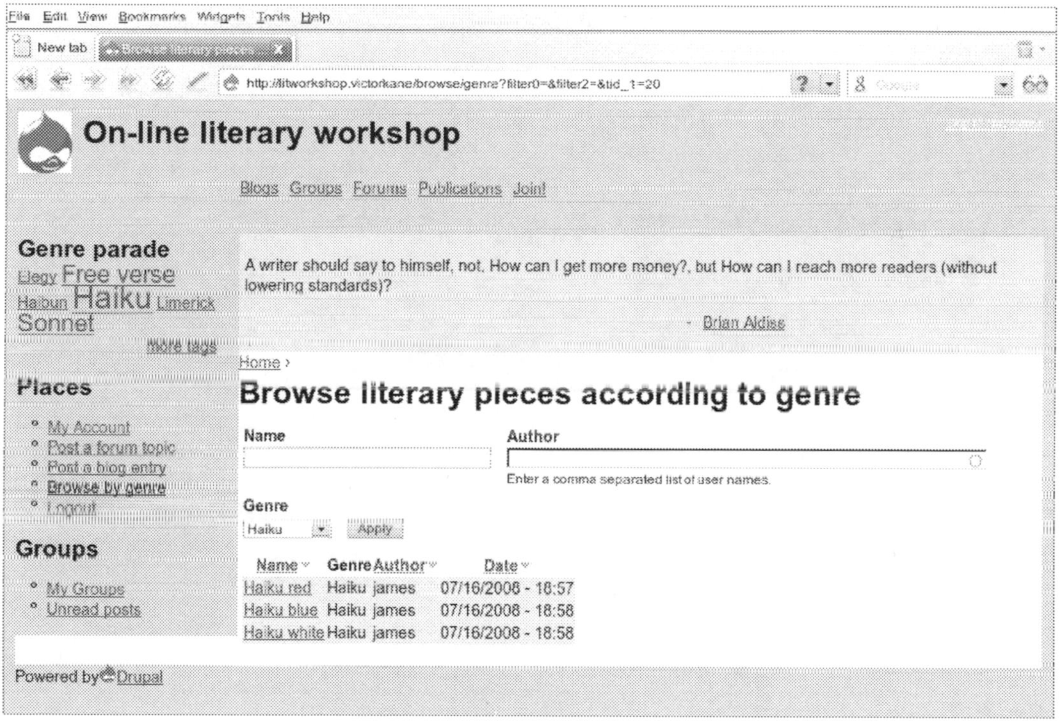


**Figure 11-4**

It is now time to execute the confirmation test.

> **Confirmation**
>
> User alfred logs in and can browse public literary pieces by genre, author, and title from his Places menu block, or else in sequential form via the paged listing at the foot of the page, or finally via the Genre parade tag cloud.

Since this is now fully implemented, you can now set the User Story status to "Test pass."

5. Browse User Stories from the Project menu block again, and take another card from the pile.

## A Publisher Can Select Content for Inclusion in a Publication

From the User Stories section of the user story:

> **Conversation**
>
> Grant the Publisher Role permission to add content to books, to administer book outlines, and to create new books, because the content type book is only being used for publications.

> **Confirmation**
>
> It is assumed that a Publication already exists, and that the User Story "A publisher can browse public content" has already been implemented. User alfred logs in, clicks on the "Browse by genre" link, and applies the Flash Fiction genre filter. He clicks any of the pieces and then after viewing the piece, clicks on the Outline tab. He chooses a book in the Book outline section and then a precise point of inclusion in the hierarchy of that book in the Parent item field. He clicks on "Update book outline," then clicks on the Publications primary menu item. The selected Publication, when chosen, should show the piece as part of the publication at the point of inclusion.

Run the Confirmation Test and set the User Story status to "Test pass."

You are now ready for the next user story.

## A Publisher Can Manage a Publication

The *Conversation* section of this user story is quite straightforward about the basis for the implementation of this user story.

> **Conversation**
>
> During the implementation in the section "Publisher can select content for inclusion in a publication," the Publisher role is granted permission to add content to books, to administer book outlines, and to create new books, because the content type book is only being used for publications.
>
> Place node/add/book on the Places menu under the menu title "Create publication pages." A publication page might be a brand-new publication by virtue of being a Parent node, or else a new book page might be created and attached to an existing Publication (book hierarchy) on the fly.

You should be able to implement all of this via the administration interface. For permissions, you go to Administer ➢ User management ➢ Permissions as usual, while menus (and hence menu blocks) are managed via Administer ➢ Site building ➢ Menus. Figure 11-5 shows the Places menu configured in the corresponding Administration page.

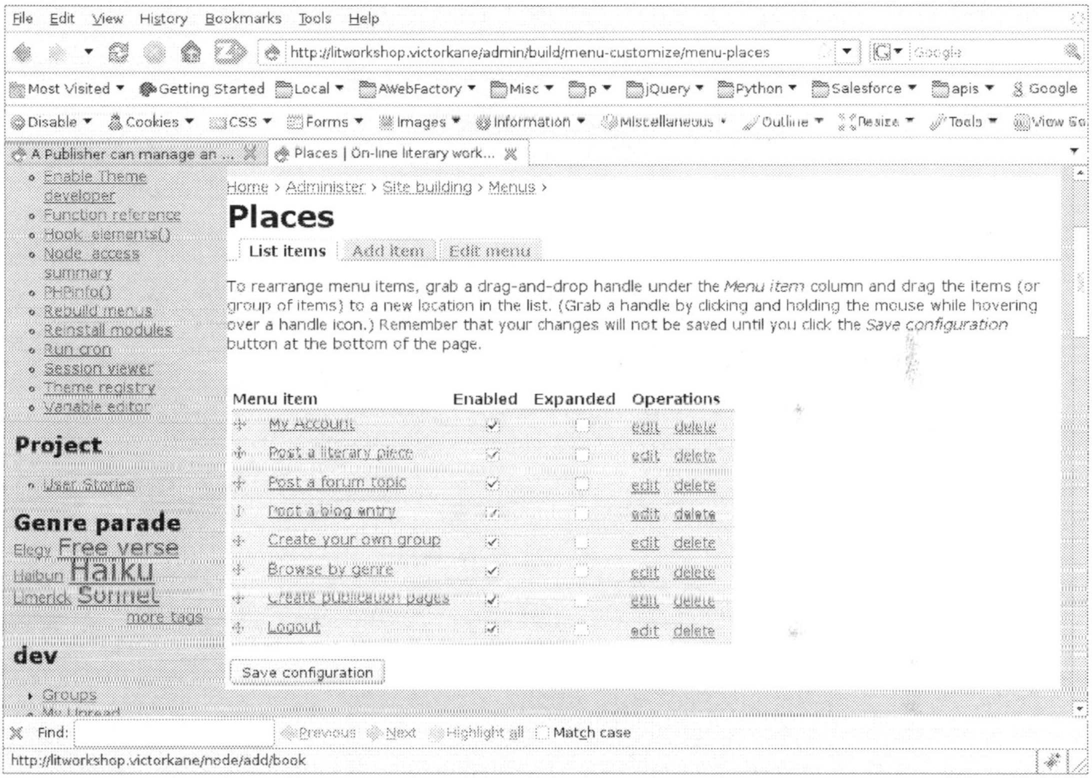

Figure 11-5

As usual, the requirements themselves are better documented in the Confirmation section.

**Confirmation**

It is assumed that the user story in the section "Publisher: Selecting Content for Publication Inclusion" has been implemented. It is assumed that the Flash Fiction genre tag and some example literary pieces of this kind have been posted on the site.

User alfred logs in and decides to create a new publication called *Flash Fiction Roundup*. He creates a book page from his Places block menu, and in the Book outline section selects the `<create a new book>` option. Then, as a child page of this parent book page corresponding to the new publication, he creates an issue of the magazine as a child page. The publication automatically appears in the Publications list.

*Continued*

> User alfred then browses content and makes use of the Outline tab found on all literary pieces content items to assign some pieces to the new issue book page of his new publication.
>
> Only the Publisher role should have access to this functionality, Workshop Members, for example, do not.

To implement this user story, follow these steps:

1. Log in as gertrude, and create three literary pieces with Flash Fiction placed into the Tags field.
2. Log in as alfred. Click the Create publication pages link, and enter **Flash Fiction Roundup** in the Title field. Type **This is a monthly roundup of flash fiction work among workshop members here at the on-line literary workshop** in the Body field. Select `<create a new book>` in the Book outline section. Click Save.
3. Click on the "Add child page" link, and type in **Autumn 2008**. The new publication is immediately listed when he clicks on the Publications primary menu item (by virtue of being the designated top-level page of the book hierarchy).
4. Click on the "Browse by genre" link, and apply a genre filter for Flash Fiction. Figure 11-6 shows the kind of results you should see on your site.

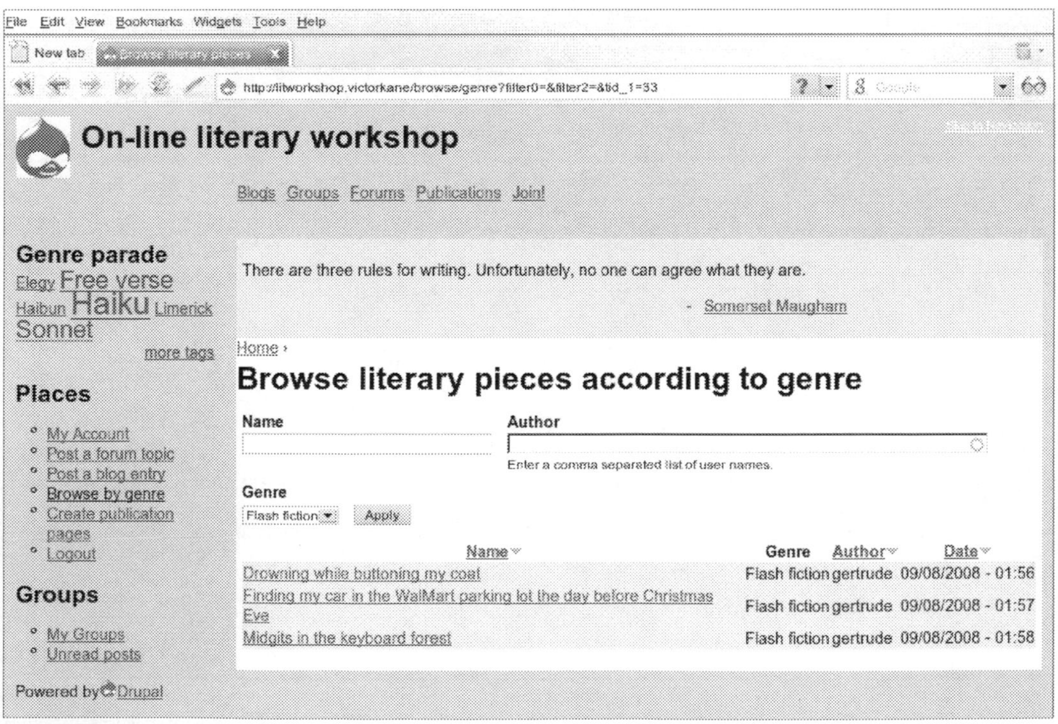


Figure 11-6

5. Click your equivalent of a literary title, like "Drowning while buttoning my coat," and just below the title you will see two tabs: View and Outline, as a result of alfred having been granted the role of Publisher. Click on the Outline tab, and choose Flash Fiction Roundup as the book this literary piece will form a part of. Immediately, jQuery goodness opens up a section asking you to specify the immediate parent item within that book's hierarchy. Choose Autumn2008. Repeat this process with the other two Flash Fiction literary pieces.

   Now, click on the Publications primary menu item. "Flash Fiction Roundup" appears in the list. Click it, and then the "Autumn 2008" issue link. The result should look similar to Figure 11-7.

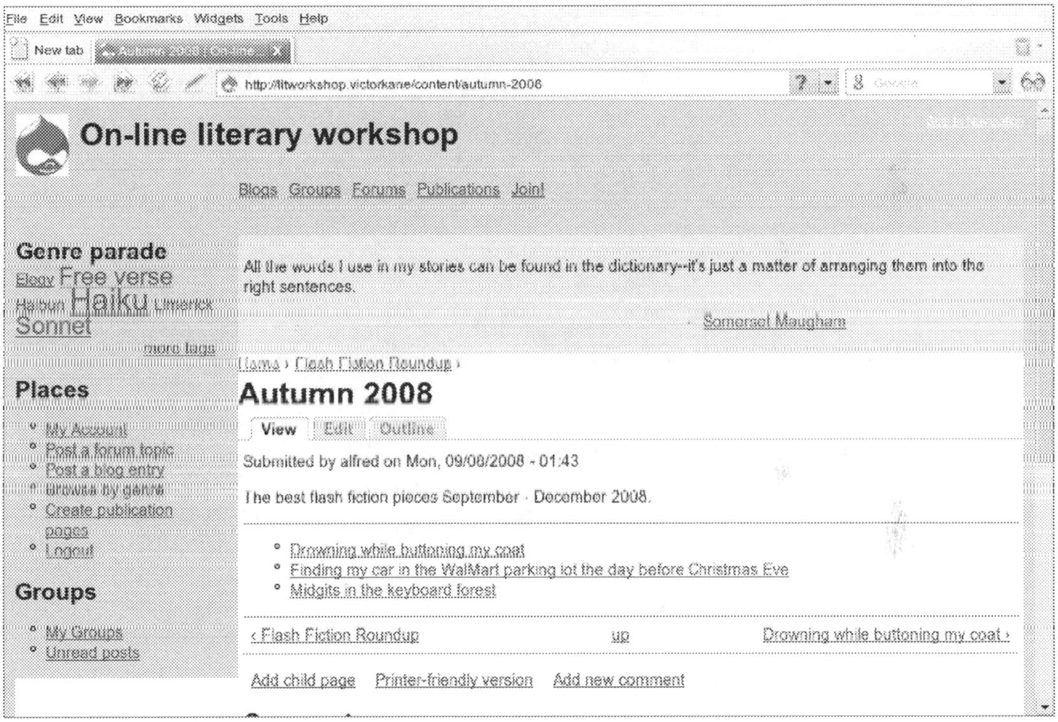


Figure 11-7

6. Complete the Confirmation Test by ensuring that a Workshop Member can see neither "Create publication pages" in their Places menu block, nor the Outline tab when they browse public content.

7. Set the User Story status of this user story to "Test pass," and take another card allocated to the Final Release iteration.

## A Publisher Can Broadcast a Call for Pieces to be Submitted for a Publication

From the section: "User Story Details."

**Conversation**

Enable the private message module, and grant the appropriate permissions.

Again, the requirements are understandable and mainly accessible as well in the testing documentation.

**Confirmation**

User alfred sends a message to several Workshop Members he has had his eye on, asking them to answer with material for the magazine. They are notified of the message when they log in and may access it.

To accomplish this, do the following:

1. Go to Administer ➢ Site building ➢ Modules, and make sure the Private messages module is enabled.
2. Go to Administer ➢ User management ➢ Permissions, and make sure the permissions in the following table are granted in the privatemsg module section:

| Permission | Admin | Publisher | Workshop Leader | Workshop Member |
|---|---|---|---|---|
| Administer privatemsg settings | X | | X | |
| Create new folder | X | X | X | X |
| Read all private messages | X | | | |
| Read privatemsg | X | X | X | X |
| Write privatemsg | X | X | X | X |

3. Visit Administer ➢ Site building ➢ Blocks, and enable the Privatemsg links block to appear just under the Places menu block.

User alfred logs in and clicks "My Account" in the Places menu block. A Send Message link has appeared on his profile page, just below "View recent blog entries." alfred clicks on the "Send Message" link, fills in the list of Workshop Members he wishes to invite to contribute content for his publication in the "To" field, and types in a suitable message in the Message field. Figure 11-8 shows the "Send message" page.

alfred clicks on the Send button and is told:

> *"Private message has been sent to gertrude, james, joyce."*

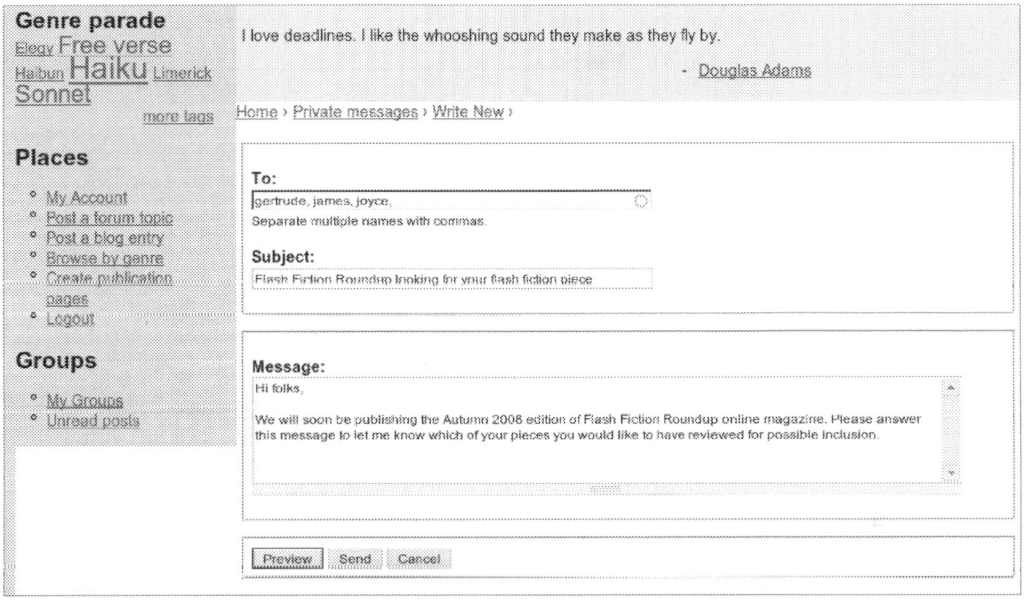


Figure 11-8

Log in as james, and you will find that a new Messages block has appeared just below Places. james clicks on the "Inbox (1 new)" link and sees that he has a message from alfred. He clicks on the Message Subject link, is told that the message is between several Workshop Members, and reads the message.

Well, the Confirmation Test has already been passed, so user dev can set the User Story status to "Test pass."

## Initial Theming

In Chapter 7, the theming chapter, you learned a lot about the guts and nuts and bolts of Drupal theming, but you may have been surprised or even disappointed by the simplistic and rather ugly appearance of the On-Line Literary Workshop at the end of that chapter.

Implementing the "Initial theming" User Story will give you a chance to beautify your application, using what you have already learned as well as presenting a couple of new tweaks.

From the section "User Story Details."

> **Conversation**
>
> Select and download a theme from oswd.org, and carry out an initial implementation of it on the basis of the currently implemented Zen subtheme.

This is just the initial theming, so our requirements aren't excessively stringent.

> **Confirmation**
>
> The overall aesthetic appearance corresponds in terms of layout, color scheme, and typography to the original downloaded XHTML/CSS theme.

After working with Chapter 7, you undoubtedly have acquired the foundation to become an expert Drupal themer. The time has certainly arrived to shed the rustic wireframe. The OSWD (Open Source Web Design, "a site to download *free* web design templates and share yours with others," can be found at `www.oswd.org/`) theme to be implemented in this chapter is "A Bit of Pastel" (`www.oswd.org/design/preview/id/2744`), and it will be used as a basis only, because its CSS includes and confuses many layout and style issues already dealt with admirably by the Zen theme itself. What you really want to extract from the theme is the logo, layout, and block and region theming ideas; the color scheme; and, of course, the typography.

Unpack the theme into a working directory, and simply invoke index.html with a browser, as seen in Figure 11-9.

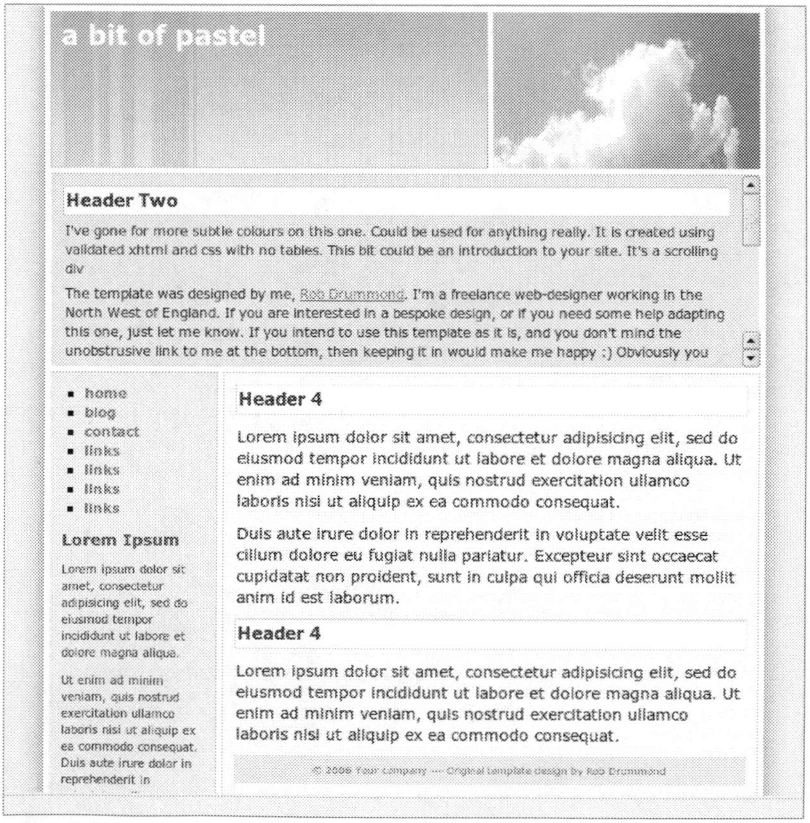


Figure 11-9

Analyzing the theme components, you can see that it is comprised of an index.html file that contains the layout and all content, semantic and otherwise, along with a style sheet (design.css) and three images in a subdirectory. Of the three images, one is the header background, one is a kind of "cloud" logo, and the third is used for the shadow border effect. Of course, whereas the On-Line Literary Workshop uses a liquid layout, this theme has a fixed-width blog-like layout, so you won't be able to take advantage of this third image since it is hard-coded to a fixed-width layout.

## Getting the Header in Place

Your current subtheme is to be found at ./sites/all/themes/zen/zenlitworkshop. Copy the clouds.jpg and left2.jpg files into the main theme directory, where the Drupal logo logo.png is currently located.

The best thing is to have the background image occupy all of the `#header` div. But the image is designed for a fixed-width layout, so one thing you can do is to take a vertical sliver with the gradient and have it repeat horizontally, forgoing the left-hand design.

On Ubuntu the author used Gimp to select a vertical sliver of the left2.jpg file only 10 pixels wide containing just the *image gradient* (), and then did Image/Crop to the selection from the menu. You can save a file like this in PNG format, in the theme directory, and name it *header-back.png*.

In zenlitworkshop.css, the main style sheet for our Zen subtheme, change the #header definition to the following (ca. line 46):

```
#header
{
  height: 150px;
  background: transparent url(header-back.png) repeat-x;
}
```

The result should be similar to that seen in Figure 11-10.

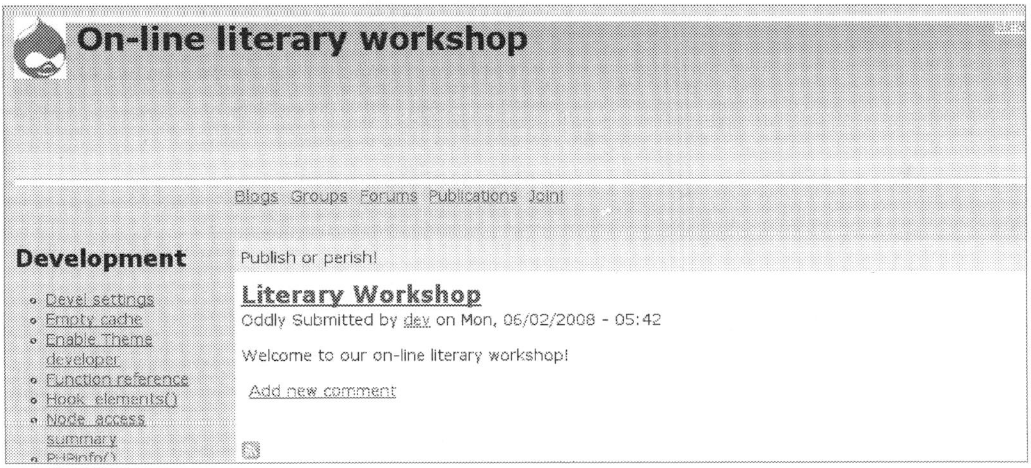


Figure 11-10

Now to position and color the site name and move the logo to the right side and replace our old friend the druplicon (Drupal icon) with clouds.jpg: Inspecting the druplicon with the Firebug Firefox plug-in inspires the following changes, which can be seen in Figure 11-11 (seen later in the chapter).

## *Invert the Printing of `div#site-name` and `div#logo` in page.tpl.php*

By editing page.tpl.php, you can affect the way each and every page gets rendered, in this case, the site name and logo.

- Before:

```
            <?php if ($logo): ?>
              <div id="logo"><a href="<?php print $base_path; ?>" title="<?php
print t('Home'); ?>" rel="home"><img src="<?php print\
$logo; ?>" alt="<?php print t('Home'); ?>" id="logo-image"\
 /></a></div>
            <?php endif; ?>
            <?php if ($site_name): ?>
              <?php
                // Use an H1 only on the homepage
                $tag = $is_front ? 'h1' : 'div';
              ?>
              <<?php print $tag; ?> id='site-name'>
                <a href="<?php print $base_path; ?>" title="<?php print \
t('Home'); ?>" rel="home">
                  <strong><?php print $site_name; ?></strong>
                </a>
              </<?php print $tag; ?>>
            <?php endif; ?>
```

- After:

```
            <?php if ($site_name): ?>
              <?php
                // Use an H1 only on the homepage
                $tag = $is_front ? 'h1' : 'div';
              ?>
              <<?php print $tag; ?> id='site-name'>
                <a href="<?php print $base_path; ?>" title="<?php print \
t('Home'); ?>" rel="home">
                  <strong><?php print $site_name; ?></strong>
                </a>
              </<?php print $tag; ?>>
            <?php endif; ?>
            <?php if ($logo): ?>
              <div id="logo"><a href="<?php print $base_path; ?>" title="<?php
print t('Home'); ?>" rel="home"><img src="<?php print \
$logo; ?>" alt="<?php print t('Home'); ?>" id="logo-image" /></a></div>
            <?php endif; ?>
```

## CSS Layout and Styling Changes

Now that you have successfully placed the elements, a few more styling tweaks are necessary:

1. Change the padding of `div#site-name`, in layout.css, and modify `h1#site-name`.

    - Before:

    ```
    h1#site-name, div#site-name
    {
      margin: 0;
      font-size: 2em;
      line-height: 1.3em;
    }
    ```

    - After:

    ```
    h1#site-name, div#site-name
    {
      margin: 0;
      padding .5em 0 0 .5em;
      font-size: 2em;
      line-height: 1.3em;
    }
    ```

2. Change the color of `#site-name a`, in zenlitworkshop.css, about line 72.

    - Before:

    ```
    #site-name a:link,
    #site-name a:visited
    {
      color: #000;
      text-decoration: none;
    }
    ```

    - After:

    ```
    #site-name a:link,
    #site-name a:visited
    {
      color: #fff;
      text-decoration: none;
    }
    ```

3. Modify `div#logo` in about line 94 of layout.css.

   - Before:

```
#logo
{
  margin: 0 10px 0 0;
  padding: 0;
  float: left;
}
```

   - After:

```
#logo
{
  margin: -45px 0 0 0;
  padding: 0;
  float: right;
}
```

4. Modify the `div#skip-to-nav` link

   - Before:

```
#skip-to-nav
{
  float: right;
  margin: 0 !important;
  font-size: 0.8em;
}

#skip-to-nav a:link, #skip-to-nav a:visited
{
  color: #fff; /* Same as background color of page */
}
```

   - After:

```
#skip-to-nav
{
  float: right;
  margin: -15px 0 0 0 !important;
  font-size: 0.8em;
}

#skip-to-nav a:link, #skip-to-nav a:visited
{
  color: transparent; /* Same as background color of page */
}
```

## Configure Logo to Point to clouds.jpg

In order to accomplish this, go to Administration ➢ Site building ➢ Themes, and configure the logo to not be the default, but to point to clouds.jpg.

## Results So Far

In this section, you are going to carry out more styling tweaks, by editing the main style sheet for your theme, zenlitworkshop.css. Figure 11-11 shows the look and feel achieved up till now.

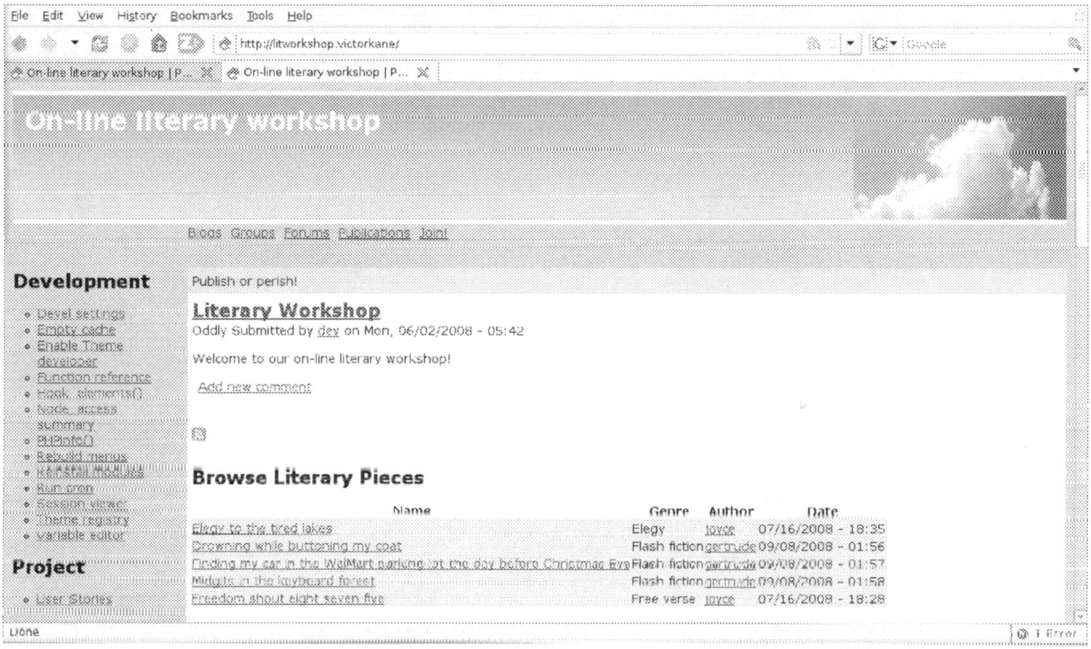

Figure 11-11

Now just a few more touches before you finish with the header: "white snapshot border on left and right of clouds image, plus background outside `div#page` as per original." To do so, follow these steps:

1. First of all, make the body background color light gray in zenlitworkshop.css:

```
body
{
  background-color: #eee;
}
```

2. Create the white border around the header elements, in layout.css:

```
#header
{
  border-left: 5px solid #fff;
}
...
```

```
#logo
{
  margin: -45px 0 0 0;
  padding: 0;
  float: right;
  border-left: 5px solid #fff;
  border-right: 5px solid #fff;
}
```

3. The result can be seen in Figure 11-12.

Figure 11-12

## Theming the Primary Menu

Oops, there are no primary menus in the OSWD theme. Well, let's take the header typography and color scheme as a cue. Make the following modifications in zenlitworkshop.css:

```
#navbar
{
  margin-top: .5em;
}

#primary li {
  background: #fff;
  border: 1px solid #ccc;
}

#primary li a{
  padding-left: 1em;
  text-decoration: none;
  color: #00103e;
}

#primary li a:hover{
  text-decoration: underline;
}
```

The result can be seen in Figure 11-13.

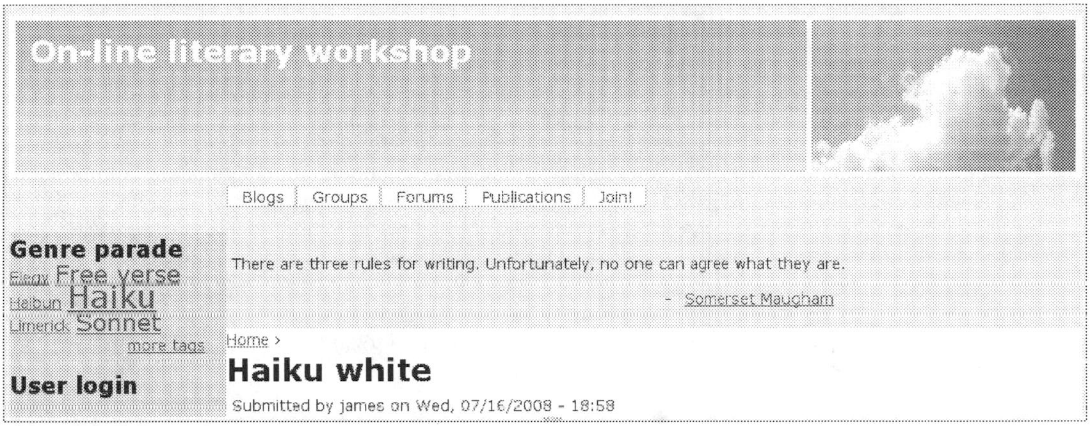


Figure 11-13

## Theming the Quotations Block and the Left Sidebar Regions

You can theme the quotations block and the left sidebar regions by continuing to edit the principal Theme style sheet, zenlitworkshop.css. Sometimes you want to override the default styling of the Zen theme itself, by copying over portions from the Zen style sheets and modifying them, as seen in these steps:

1. Make the background color for the quotations block the same as the Header Two block in the original.

```
  #content-top /* Wrapper for any blocks placed in the "content top"
region */
  {
    background-color: #dbe4ff;
    margin-left: 2px;
     border:1px solid #d1c2ff;
  }
```

2. Theme the sidebar like the original:

```
  #sidebar-left
  {
    width: 190px;
    margin-left: 5px;
    margin-top: 5px;
    background-color: #f0ebff;
    border:1px solid #d1c2ff;
  }
```

```
#sidebar-left-inner
{
  font-size: 80%;
}
```

3. To theme the links, copy to zenlitworkshop.css the links section from the parent Zen theme htmlentities.css file, which are empty, then add a generic anchor tag element and fill in attributes from the original OSWD theme.

```
/** links **/
/* The order of link states are based on Eric Meyer's article:
 * http://meyerweb.com/eric/thoughts/2007/06/11/who-ordered-the-
link-states
 */

/* VK: added this in to prevent having to repeat generic elements */
a {
  text-decoration: none;
  color: #666;
}

a:link
{
}

a:visited
{
}

a:hover,
a:focus
{
  color: #900;
}

a:active
{
}
```

4. Now, in zenlitworkshop.css, theme the block and title headers like the Lorem Ipsum block header in the original sidebar:

```
h1.title, /* The title of the page */
h2.title, /* Block title or the title of a piece of content when it \
is given in a list of content */
h3.title /* Comment title */
{
  margin: 0;
  color: #001d8f;
}
```

The results of these steps can be seen in Figure 11-14.

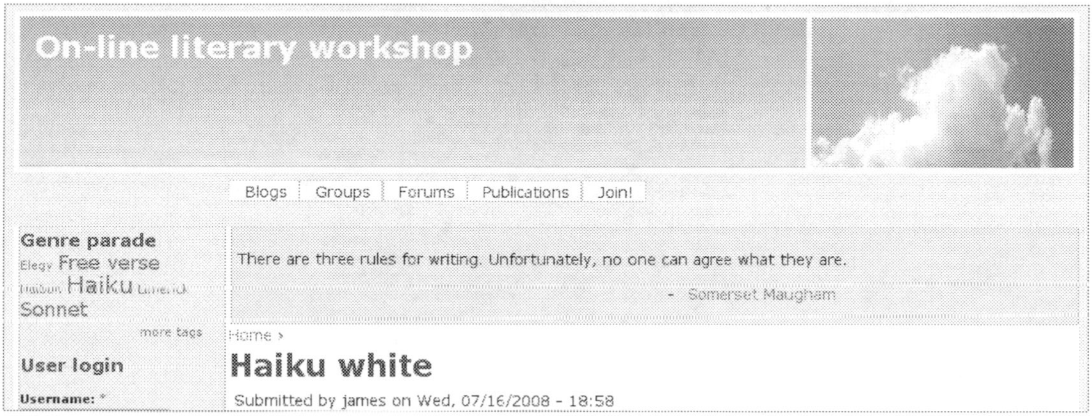


Figure 11-14

## *Theme the Main Content Area*

Now it is time to turn your attention to the look and feel of the main content area, also by editing zenlit-workshop.css.

1. To base the main content area theming on the original, modify zenlitworkshop.css as follows:

```
#content-area /* Wrapper for the actual page content */
{
  background-color: #f5f7ff;
  border: 1px solid #dbc2ff;
  font-size: 90%;
}
```

2. And in the same file, theme `#content-bottom` the same as `#content-top`:

```
  #content-top /* Wrapper for any blocks placed in the "content top"
region */
  {
    background-color: #dbe4ff;
    margin-left: 2px;
        border:1px solid #d1c2ff;
  }

#content-bottom /* Wrapper for any blocks placed in the "content \
bottom" region */
  {
    background-color: #dbe4ff;
    margin-left: 2px;
        border:1px solid #d1c2ff;
  }
```

The result can be seen in Figure 11-15.

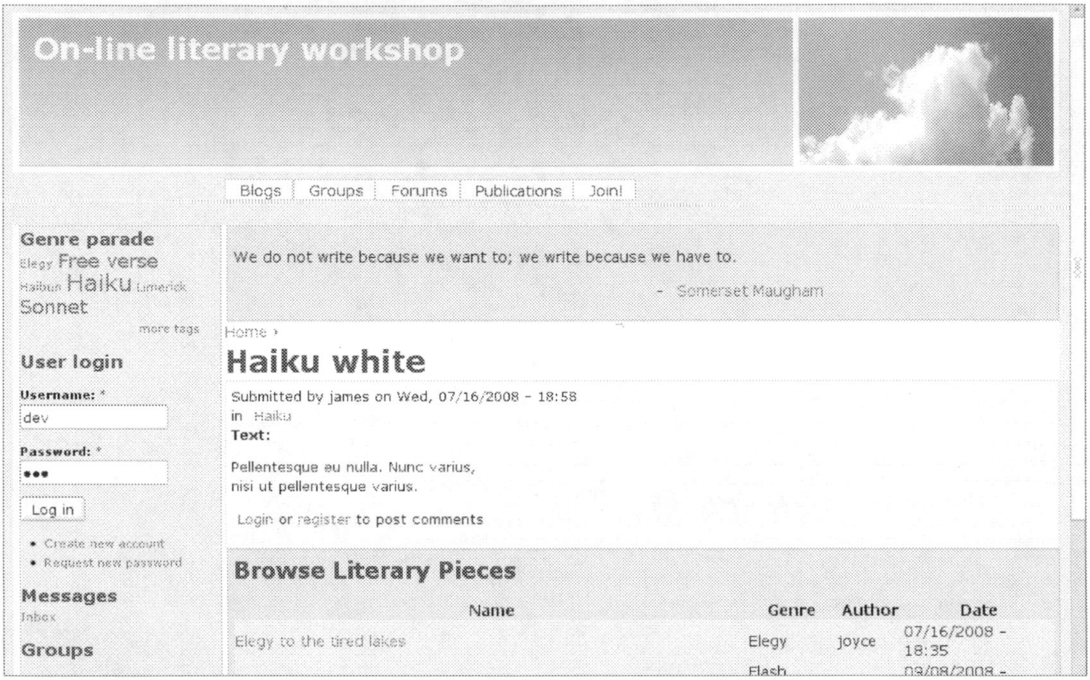


Figure 11-15

Well, perhaps the On-Line Literary Workshop theme will win no prizes for its theme, but it does serve as an example of what can be done relatively easily in terms of migrating toward "non-Drupal" themes.

## Theme the Footer

In order to change the Footer, you can edit the "semantic content," that is, the words, images, and links that are going to appear in that region. You can then style that content by editing zenlitworkshop.css.

1. Go to Administer ➢ Site configuration ➢ Site information, and remove the rather amateurish Footer message:

```
Powered by<a href="http://www.drupal.org" target="_blank"><img src="/misc
/favicon.ico" \
alt="Drupal rocks!" title="Drupal rocks!" />Drupal</a>
```

2. Now, let's enable the Powered by Drupal block in the content-bottom region at Administer ➢ Site building ➢ Blocks.
3. Then, go to Administer ➢ Site building ➢ Menus, and create the Footer links (footer-links) menu. For now, just add **Theme based on BIT OF PASTEL from OSWD**, pointing to `http://oswd.org`.
4. Go back to the blocks administration page and enable the new menu, also in the content-bottom region.

Right now, there is a problem because the footer you have created looks like Figure 11-16.

**Figure 11-16**

You need to remove the block title entirely, theme the listed menu like the primary menu, and float the Powered by Drupal element in-line with it.

At Administer ➤ Site building ➤ Blocks, click on the Configure link corresponding to the Footer links menu block. Enter **<none>** in the Block title field, and click on the "Save block" button. Then, make the following modifications and additions to zenlitworkshop.css:

```
  #content-bottom /* Wrapper for any blocks placed in the "content \
bottom" region */
  {
    background-color: #dbe4ff;
    margin-left: 2px;
        border: 1px solid #d1c3ff;
    font-size: 90%;
  }

  #content-bottom ul li
  {
    display: inline;
    list-style-type: none;
    padding: 0 0.5em;
    margin
  }

  div#block-views-genre_browser-block_1 {
  }

  div#block-menu-menu-footer-links {
    float: left;
  }
  div#block-menu-menu-footer-links ul {
    margin: 1em 0 0 4em;
    padding: 0;
    font-size: 90%;
  }

  div#block-menu-menu-footer-links ul li {
    background: #eee;
    border: 1px solid #ccc;
  }

  div#block-system-0 {
```

```
    margin-top: .8em;
    margin-right: 200px;
    float: right;
  }

  div#block-system-0 .content {
    background: #eee;
    border: 1px solid #ccc;
  }
```

The results can be seen in Figure 11-17.

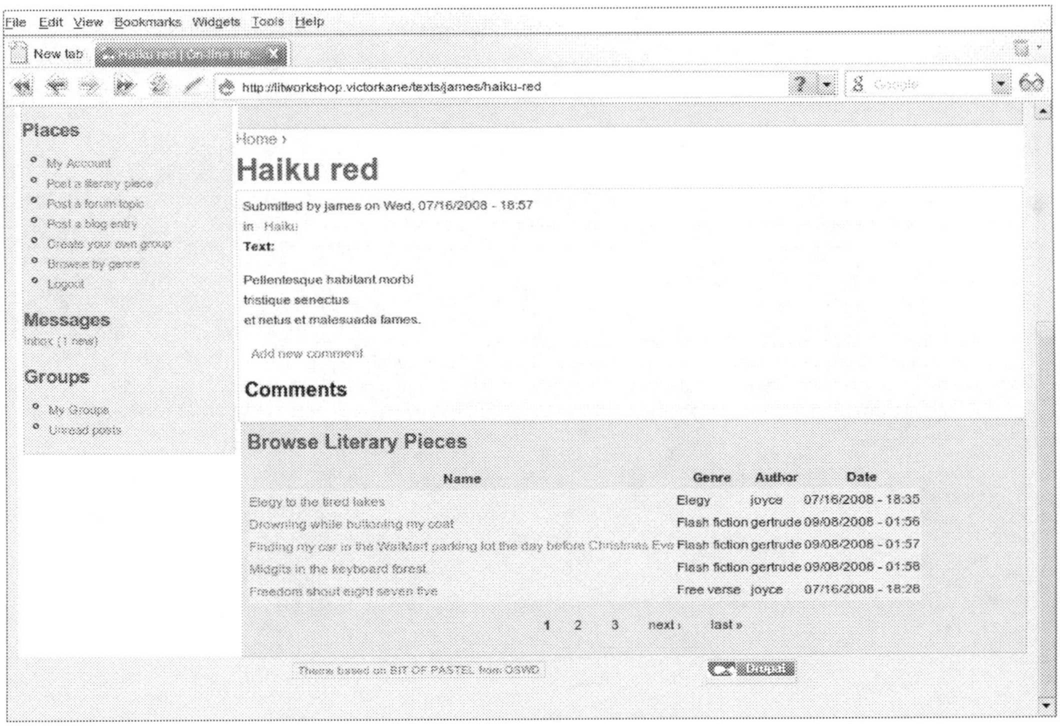

Figure 11-17

And you're done with the initial theming user story. Of course, there are many things that could be optimized, enhanced, and added, but certainly you have an initial theming for the final release and can mark the User Story status as "Test pass."

# On-Line Blog Functionality

In this section, you will enable basic blog functionality, then add in "service links" (Digg, Technorati, etc.) for each post, add an author information block, as well as a block showing the most recent posts, and a blogroll block. In so doing, you will see that while Wordpress (`http://wordpress.org/`) may be a great choice as a blog platform per se, with Drupal you can have the same functionality without giving up any of the tremendous flexibility and power of a full-blown CMS framework. This does require a little effort. The work required is outlined, as usual, in the corresponding user stories.

The Card, Conversation, and Confirmation sections of the user stories concerning blog functionality are identical for the Publisher and Workshop Member roles.

**Card**

A user can manage his or her own blog.

**Conversation**

Enable the core Drupal blog module and grant permissions to the user. Access to the blog posting link should be included in the Places menu block. Pathauto should be configured so as to create an SEO-friendly URL for the user's individual blog. On the right hand side (sidebar), there should be an author info, a blogroll, and a recent posts block for the blog. Enable the service links module.

**Confirmation**

User can log in and immediately post to his or her own blog. Users' posts are immediately published to the site blog River of News, and also to his or her own individual blog (which has the general features associated with blogs — author info, blogroll, recent posts), which has a unique URL that the user can publish. Service links should be present.

You can find these in the following user stories included in the Drupal website you can download for this chapter:

- A Publisher can manage an on-line blog.
- Workshop Members can maintain their own literary blogs.

Running the Confirmation Test for the Publisher User Story, at this point alfred can log in and click the "Post a blog entry" item in the Places menu block. When alfred posts a blog entry, it can be found in the general Blogs primary menu item River of News for all blogs, as well as in alfred's own individual blog. [The URL can be found in the "View recent blog entries" link on the user's profile page, accessible via the My Account link in the Places menu. This URL is SEO-friendly (`http://litworkshop.victorkane/blogs/alfred`).]

Lacking are the three blocks to be found in the right sidebar when individual blogs are accessed.

## Implementing Service Links

The Service Links module allows you to add Digg, del.icio.us, reddit, Technorati, and similar links to nodes. Download and install it from `http://drupal.org/project/service_links`.

Next, do the following:

1. Enable the module at Administer ➢ Site building ➢ Modules.
2. Grant the Access Service Links permission to all roles, and the Administer Service Links permission to roles Admin and Webmaster by visiting Administer ➢ User management ➢ Permissions.
3. Configure the module at Administer ➢ Site configuration ➢ Service links. Select the checkbox next to "Blog entry" in the "Node types" section. Select whichever bookmark links (Digg, Facebook, etc.) and search links (Technorati) you wish. Select Teasers and full-page view in the Service links in the Nodes dropdown list. Select Image and text links in the Service links Style dropdown list. And click on the "Save configuration" button.

Figure 11-18 shows the service links at this stage of development when viewing the Publisher alfred's own blog.

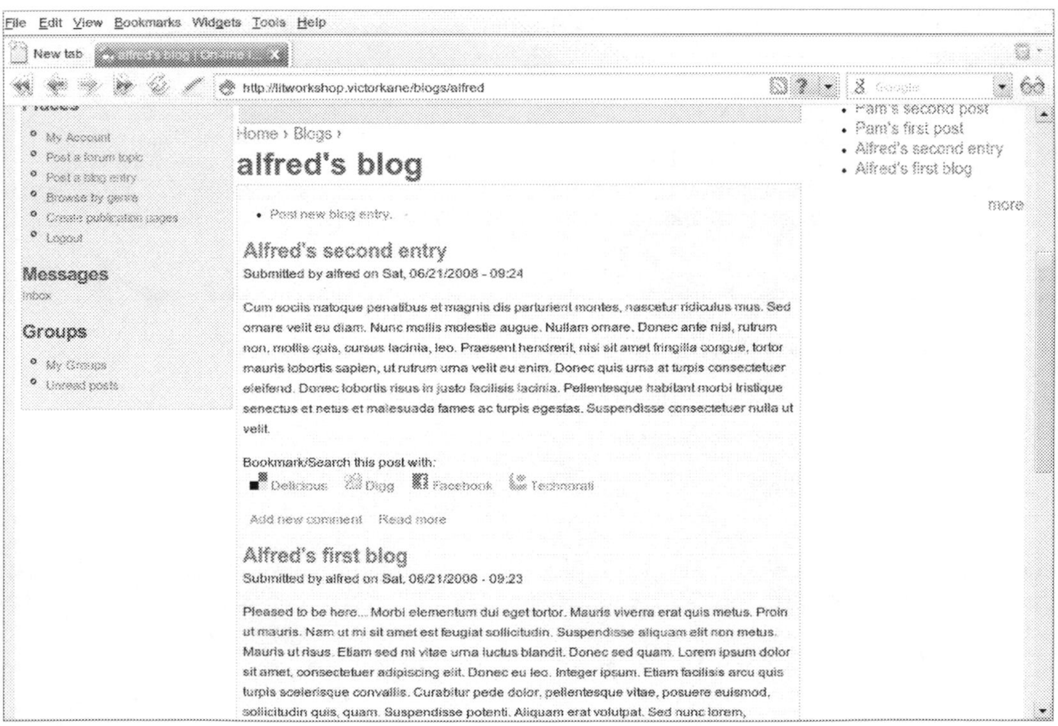


Figure 11-18

## Implementing the Author Info Block for Individual Blogs

Carry out the following steps in order to implement the "Author Info Block," so common on many blogs.

1. Logged in as user dev, go to Administer ➤ Site building ➤ Modules, and enable the core Drupal Profile module.
2. Go to Administer ➤ User management ➤ Profiles, and study up on how to add custom fields and tabbed categories of fields to the user profile. In order to comply with the Confirmation Test of the current user story, in the "Add new field" section click "single-line textfield," and enter **Author** into the Category field. Enter **Name** in the Title field and **profile_author_name** in the Form name field. In the Explanation field, type **Enter your name as it will appear in the Author Info block**. Click on the "Save field" button.
3. In the "Add new field" section, click "multi-line textfield," and enter **Author** into the Category field. Enter **Blurb** in the Title field and **profile_author_blurb** in the Form name field. Enter **Give us a little blurb about yourself, as it will appear in the Author Info block**.

   Figure 11-19 shows Administer ➤ User management ➤ Profiles after these two fields have been configured.

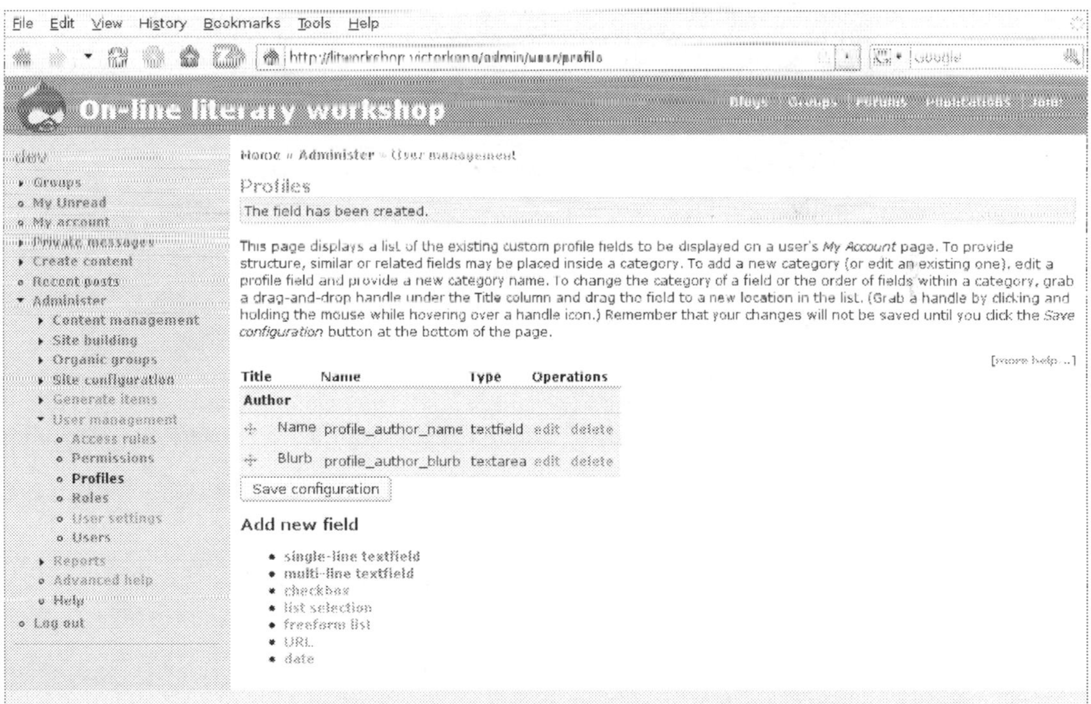


Figure 11-19

4. Log in as alfred and go to My Account. Click on the Edit tab. Because you specified Author as the category for both fields, an Author tab is now automatically configured and appears

next to the Account tab (where you can edit username, password, etc.) when a user edits his or her account. To try this out, click on "author" and enter a name, for example, **Alfred Knowles**, and a short bio, and then click Save. When alfred returns to My Account, there is now an Author section.

5. Now for the "Drupal is awesome" moment. Go to Administer ➤ Site building ➤ Blocks, and enable the . . . Author information block! Assign it to the right sidebar region, and click on the "Save blocks" button. Now click the Configure link for this block, enter **<none>** in the Block title field, and select all three items in the "Profile fields to display" section. In the "Show blocks for specific roles" section, select Publisher, Workshop Leader, and Workshop Member. In the "Page-specific visibility settings" section, select the "Show on only the listed pages" option, and type in:

```
blog/*
blogs/*
blogs/*/*
```

each on a separate line. Click on the "Save block" button. Make sure it is at the top of the right sidebar items.

6. Go to Administer ➤ User management ➤ Permissions, and enable the "access user profiles permission for all users."

Figure 11-20 shows this feature in the case of the URL `/blog/james/james-first-entry`.

## Implementing Recent Posts Block

The Recent Blog Posts block comes with Drupal off the shelf. Simply enable it in the same way as you did the Author Information block.

## Implementing the Blogroll

The Blogroll is best implemented using the Drupal Link module, which allows you to create a content type field of type link, say, in a Blogroll content type, so that a view can easily be made with a block display entitled *Blogroll*, listing the URL portions of each blogroll content item, to create a classic blogroll.

The link module may be downloaded from `http://drupal.org/project/link`.

After testing and making sure everything works, you can now set the User Story status for the blog functionality user stories for the Final Release iteration to "Test pass."

The remaining user story for the current iteration, "A Workshop Member can post to forums," is directly supported by standard Drupal functionality also, as we have seen. Awesome!

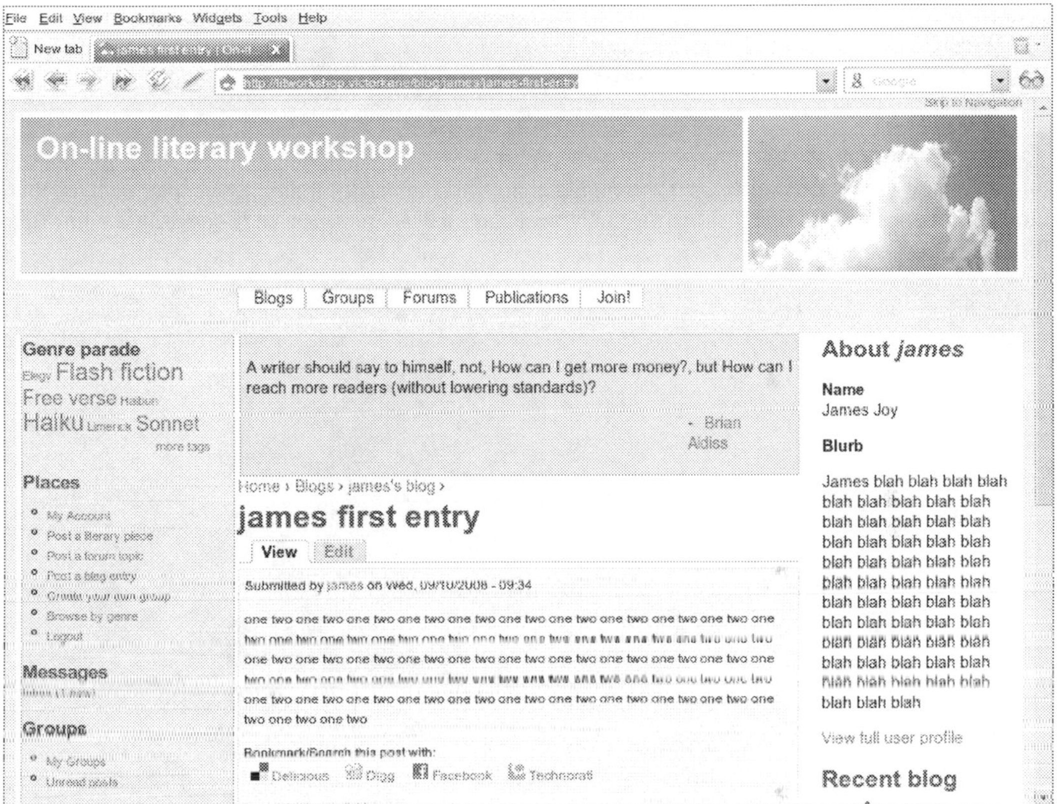


Figure 11-20

# Summary

In this chapter, you first honed your project tools, and then you were able to list all your user stories and sort them by iteration, and were able to link user stories and Acceptance Tests. You were then quickly able to find out where you were on the project on a Monday bleary morning by listing and filtering the user stories according to the current iteration.

You then followed a wild adventure implementing and testing each and every one of them in order to complete the Final Version iteration. Amazingly enough, in this chapter alone, that included the possibility of Workshop Members creating and managing their own affinity groups on the fly, as well as a complete framework for Publishers to easily browse and filter literary pieces in order to assemble and publish individual issues of their own on-line publications. It also included the possibility of broadcasting private messages to Workshop Members and inviting them to contribute material.

You then adapted the wireframe theme you have been using for quite a while now to an Open Source freely available template downloaded from the Open Source Web Development website. As a result, the On-Line Literary Workshop now looks decidedly spiffy, not at all identifiable right off the bat as a ''Drupal'' site.

And as if that were small potatoes, you finished off the chapter setting up a complete self-contained blogging framework so that Workshop Members and Leaders, as well as Publishers, can have their own blogs, publishable with an SEO-friendly URL and complete with typical blog-like Author Information, Blogroll, and Recent Posts blocks.

In the remaining chapters of this book, you will learn how to complete deployment, learn about what future releases of Drupal will have to offer, and review options to base your development on commercial service-supported distributions of Drupal.

# 12

# The jQuery Chapter

After Katherine Bailey's excellent series of articles (see "The Lowdown on jQuery in Drupal": `http://raincitystudios.com/blogs-and-pods/katherine-bailey/the-lowdown-jquery-drupal`), there is certainly less mystery in the Drupal world concerning the use of the JavaScript library, which (in its own words) "is a fast, concise, JavaScript Library that simplifies how you traverse HTML documents, handle events, perform animations, and add Ajax interactions to your web pages" (see "jQuery: The Write Less, Do More, JavaScript Library" home page: `http://jquery.com/`). And articles such as Katherine's certainly illuminate any AHAH problems developers tend to encounter.

But, what is Ajax? And what is AHAH? How do you wrap your head around the whole Rich Internet Application framework question? Also, why did Drupal chose jQuery over other extremely serious contenders? And what can rich internet middleware do for an application like the On-Line Literary Workshop?

## Anatomy of a Rich Internet Application Framework

In this section, you will first be introduced to the basics of what are known as Rich Internet Applications, something that has emerged as a way of giving the same sturdiness and quick response to Internet applications as that enjoyed by desktop applications, thanks to a lot of progress in the use of JavaScript in web browsers. You will be introduced to the Document Object Model (DOM) as a way of accessing all browser objects, and will learn how to access the DOM both with CSS and with JavaScript.

### The Basics

Ajax (see `www.riaspot.com/articles/entry/What-is-Ajax-`) basically exploits an object found in most browsers called XMLHttpRequest (a.k.a. XHR), which allows the browser to carry out an HTTP request to the server without refreshing the page. Using JavaScript, the data returned by the server (which may have nothing to do with XML) may be parsed and then used to modify a DOM element (see `www.w3.org/TR/DOM-Level-2-Core/introduction.html`) in the served page, also without refreshing the page. This makes a web application behave much more like a regular desktop application, and this is referred to as *RIA: Rich Internet Application*.

Now, when the data is taken as it is received from the server and plunked into a DOM element (using innerHTML read/write DOM element access, again, supported by major browsers), that is called AHAH: Asynchronous HTML and HTTP. The main thing is that the response from the server cannot be XML or anything other than pure text or valid XHTML or HTML.

This sounds simple but is not so simple, because it involves multiple processes running on multiple hosts in constant communication. This book has already discussed the serving of static and dynamic pages, and understood them. Figure 12-1 shows this in the context of the serving of a static HTML page from the filesystem in the server.

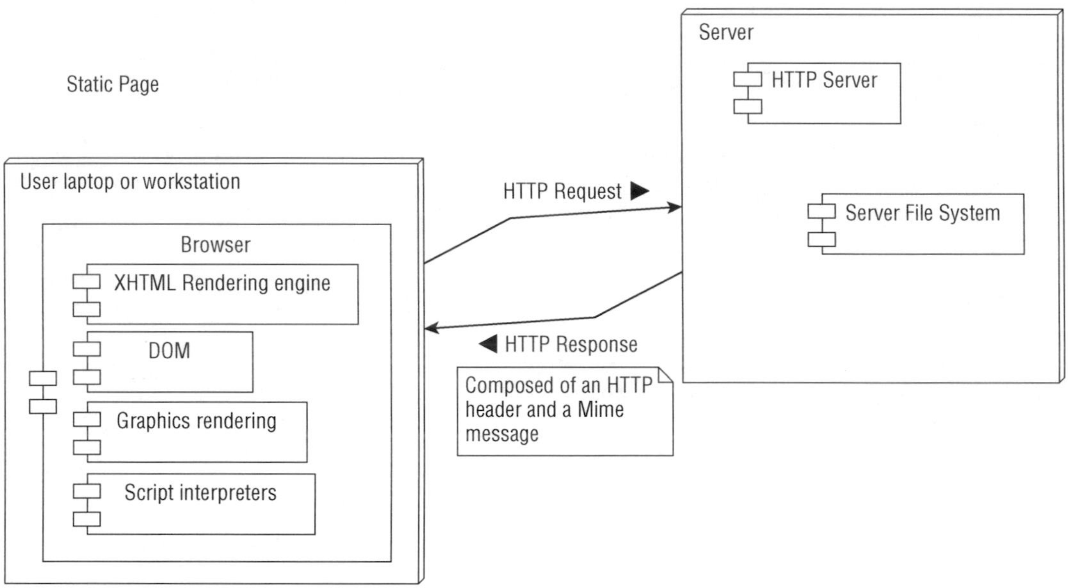


**Figure 12-1**

Looking at it very simply, the browser sends an HTTP request to the server, like `http://litworkshop.lit/cool-haikus/haiku-red.htm;` the HTTP server searches for `haiku-red.htm` in the `cool-haikus` subdirectory just off the document root; and if it is found, its contents are read and sent back to the browser using the HTTP protocol, with a header and a MIME message so the browser knows what to do with it. The page is rendered — a DOM is instantiated in a browser window and displayed.

With Drupal, the architecture is just a tad more complicated, as you saw in Chapter 7 when Drupal theming was dealt with. Instead of having to draw all the content from files having different MIME types in the server filesystem, the HTTP server talks to Drupal, and Drupal talks to a relational database (MySQL, Postgres, Oracle, etc.) or maybe even to a Web Service or a computer storage cloud like Amazon S3, and assembles the XHTML page complete with optionally compressed associated CSS style sheets and JS scripts. Then all of that is handed over to the HTTP server, which hands it off to the browser making the request, which sees it as if it were a static HTML page.

The reason a lot of stuff like Ajax, AHAH, and JavaScript libraries like jQuery seem so difficult for website developers to get started with is because people tend to lose the notion of where it lives, between the HTTP server, the MySQL database, the PHP code, and browser window, with all kinds of code executing inside different components and servers at the same time. So Figure 12-2 shows the architectural basis, in terms of components, of how a typical Drupal page is rendered: The request is received by the Apache HTTP server process, which figures out via the URL that "this is a job for Drupal." Drupal is booted, and also on the basis of the URL asks the MySQL process for a bunch of data, and in a separate process that was described in Chapter 7, the page is marshaled in its various layers as a stream of bytes sent to the browser, which takes the HTML and goes from there in order to make things happen in the browser window.

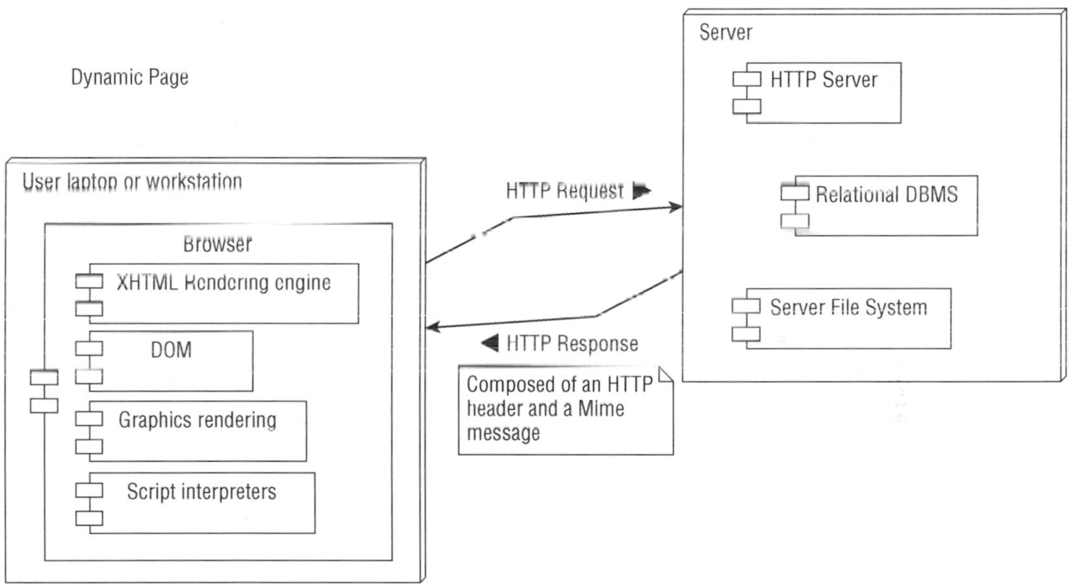


Figure 12-2

So what are the accessible components of a fully rendered page, and how can you get at them?

## Getting at the DOM with CSS

One way you can get at them is via CSS (Cascading Style Sheets). You have already seen how in the last chapter, you were able to theme the footer in many ways. How was it possible to get at the elements of the page to do the styling? The following snippet was used:

```
#content-bottom /* Wrapper for any blocks placed in the "content bottom" region
*/
{
```

```
background-color: #dbe4ff;
margin-left: 2px;
border:1px solid #d1c2ff;
font-size: 90%;
}
```

The browser takes the HTML, generates and instantiates the DOM, then applies this snippet to specify the background color, the border, font size, and left margin for the entire `content bottom` region. That is, it *selects* an object within the Document Object Model, then *applies* certain attributes of this object.

You can see this clearly using the DOM inspector in the Firefox browser, which ''inspects the structure and properties of a window and its contents.'' Go to the home page of the On-Line Literary Workshop and invoke the DOM inspector from the Tools menu (install the Add-on if not present, from `https://addons.mozilla.org/en-US/firefox/addon/1806`). Now, do what CSS (and as you shall soon see, jQuery also) does: find the `content bottom` element. Figure 12-3 shows the DOM inspector with the `#content-bottom` selected.

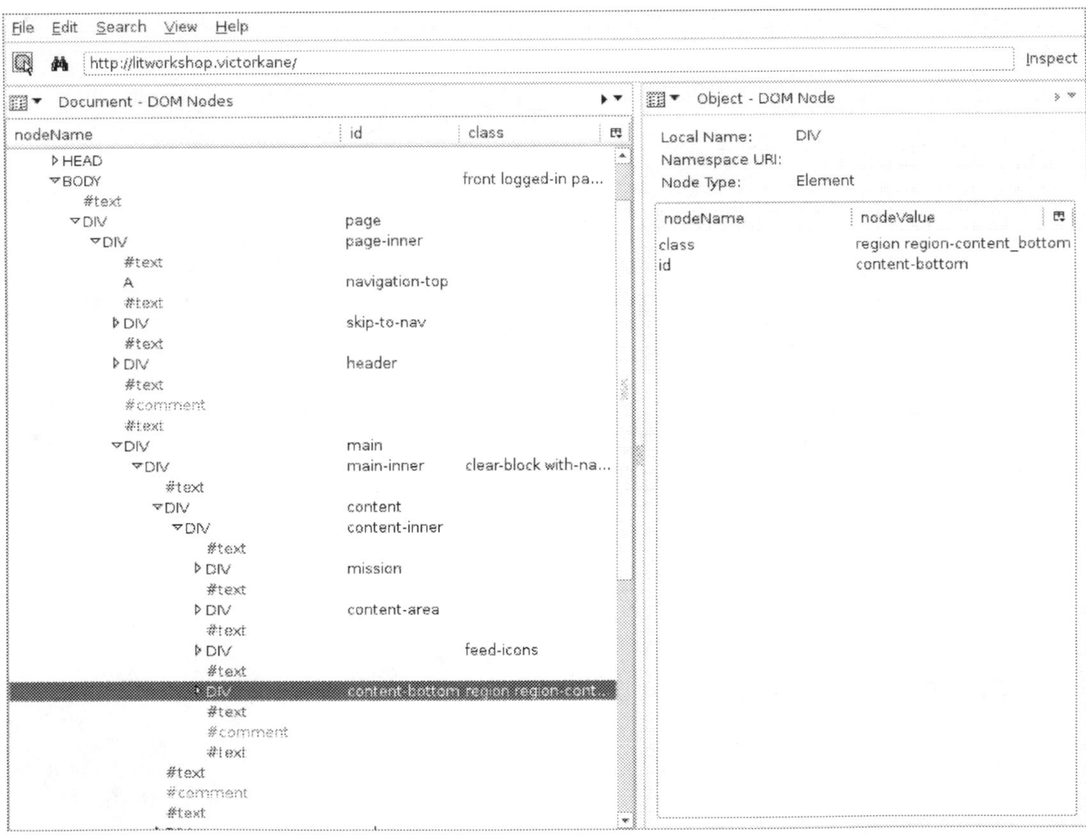


Figure 12-3

It is interesting to see the entire hierarchy. And you can find out much more than you could possibly want to know by selecting different values from the dropdown list at the top right, currently set to Object–DOM Node, including the Style Rules and the Computed Style (the end result of all styles on this object).

So, this is the end result of the style sheets being applied to the object hierarchy making up the document when a page is served. But what happens, for example, if you want to alter any object's attributes (their *value*) on the fly, without re-serving the page, and in response to an event of some kind, such as the user clicking or moving his or her mouse over an object? Answer: you can do it with JavaScript!

## Getting at the DOM with JavaScript

With JavaScript you can:

- Access any DOM element and the value of its properties.
- Modify the appearance of an already rendered page by modifying the value of any element's properties.
- Change the DOM structure itself by adding or eliminating elements, and modifying the content of an already rendered page and not simply its appearance.
- Enable actions to be carried out in response to events that may occur, such as what a user does upon interacting with the page.
- Animate objects with special effects and even movements.
- Use Ajax and AHAH operations to dynamically modify the content of the page via requests to a server, without having to refresh the page.

So where does JavaScript live? Answer: in the browser. It is downloaded as a script by having been included in a `SCRIPT` tag, just as a CSS style sheet when it is included in a `LINK` tag, or an image when it is referenced in an `IMG` tag. Then, at different moments, it is interpreted and executed in the browser's memory space. That is important to bear in mind.

So let's see a simple example of pure JavaScript that modifies the DOM after the page has been rendered.

1. Go to Create content➤Create page, type in **JavaScript example one**, and set the Body input format to Full HTML.
2. Enter the following in the Body field:

```
<div id="section1">
<p>Haikus</p>
</div>
<div>
<ul id="section2">
```

```
<li>option 1</li>
<li>option 2</li>
</ul>
</div>
<div>
<a href="/texts/joyce/elegy-tired-lakes" id="section3" title="click to \
 read" name="click to read">Elegy to the tired lakes</a>
</div>
```

The result can be seen in Figure 12-4.

**Figure 12-4**

3. Now, let's add in some JavaScript to alter the DOM after it has been rendered. Edit the content/javascript-example-one page content item as follows:

```
<script type="text/javascript">
function alterDiv() {
   var section1 = document.getElementById("section1");
   section1.innerHTML = "<h2>Some Haikus</h2>";
   var section2  = document.getElementById("section2");
   section2.innerHTML = "<ol><li>Haiku Red</li><li>Haiku \
 Blue</li><li>Haiku Green</li></ol>";
   var section3 = document.getElementById("section3");
   section3.innerHTML = "<img
src='/sites/all/themes/zen/zenlitworkshop/clouds.jpg' \
 alt='clouds' />";
}
</script>
<body onload="alterDiv();">
<div id="section1">
<p>Haikus</p>
</div>
<div>
<ul id="section2">
<li>option 1</li>
<li>option 2</li>
</ul>
</div>
<div>
<a href="/texts/joyce/elegy-tired-lakes" id="section3" title= \
"click to read" name="click to read">Elegy to the tired lakes</a>
</div>
```

First you add the JavaScript code between the `<script>...</script>` tags. The `alterDiv()` function is defined. Three variables — `section1`, `section2`, and `section3` — are declared, and they are assigned the DOM element having the same `id` attribute. Notice that the DOM element is located via the `document.getElementById()` function. Then the "unofficial" (but present in all major browsers) innerHTML DOM element attribute is assigned some valid XHTML, effectively modifying it on the fly. This is achieved by assigning to the DOM element `body`'s `onload` attribute an invocation of the `alterDiv()` function invocation. This is extremely important, since the `onload` event will only be triggered and the `alterDiv()` function executed after the page is fully loaded; otherwise, the JavaScript would not work.

Going into detail about what the JavaScript actually does to each one of the `<div>` tags, here is the "before" and "after" XHTML, as the JavaScript is executed after the page has been fully loaded:

- Before:

```
<div id="section1">
  <p>Haikus</p>
</div>
<div>
  <ul id="section2">
    <li>option 1</li>
    <li>option 2</li>
  </ul>
</div>
<div>
  <a href="/texts/joyce/elegy-tired-lakes" id="section3" title="click \
 to read" name="click to read">Elegy to the tired lakes</a>
</div>
```

- After:

```
<div id="section1"><h2>Some Haikus</h2></div>
<div>
 <ul id="section2">
  <ol>
    <li>Haiku Red</li>
    <li>Haiku Blue</li>
    <li>Haiku Green</li>
  </ol>
 </ul>
</div>
<div>
  <a name="click to read" title="click to read" id="section3" \
href="/texts/joyce/elegy-tired-lakes"><img alt="clouds" \
 src="/sites/all/themes/zen/zenlitworkshop/clouds.jpg"/></a>
</div>
```

The `<h2>` tag replaces the `<p>` tag in *section 1*, the `<ol>` is inserted into *section 2*, and the logo `<img>` is inserted into the link in *section 3*. The result can be seen in Figure 12-5.

Figure 12-5

However, "The Drupal Way" has its own way of loading CSS and JavaScript elements, to ensure that they are only loaded once and that this is done in the most efficient way possible. One does not go simply sticking `<SCRIPT>` tags into pages willy-nilly. Drupal has a PHP function that may be invoked for both, rich in parameters, which enables you to properly separate content (pages) from programming logic. That way, the individual editing the content does not have to deal with `<SCRIPT>` tags, and the programmer (who will be working with PHP, CSS, and JavaScript files in the theming directory, and not in a content page, as in this simple example) can simply edit a text file, which is much cleaner. As you will see in a moment, you can do the same thing in a much cleaner fashion using jQuery.

# Anatomy of jQuery and Its Plug-Ins

*jQuery* is a JavaScript library that has become very prominent in its own right recently, and adopted not just by Drupal, of course, but by many other frameworks and companies, such as Microsoft and Nokia. You will first be introduced to the library and its relationship with Drupal, and then immediately see a short example programmed right into a Drupal content page, an easy way to get started. The actual process workflow of this example will be shown. Finally, a full-blown theming example implemented by editing PHP template files will be introduced.

## jQuery Itself

The Drupal community chose to include the jQuery JavaScript Library (see `http://jquery.com/`) as part of its core distribution. The rationale here is the same as that of Drupal itself: Just as one should never start from scratch in creating a website application, but instead can gain enormously from using a CMS framework that enables you to use, use, and reuse tried and tested components; likewise, you do not want to start from scratch when it comes to the tricky process of the JavaScript layer of the application. On September 1, 2006, Steven Wittens, writing enthusiastically about the then-upcoming Drupal 5.x release, said in his blog (`http://acko.net/blog/jquery-is-in-drupal-core`):

> *"After a long wait, the awesome jQuery library has finally been committed to Drupal core. jQuery 1.0 will be part of the next major Drupal release, for which the code freeze is about to begin.*

*While we did take advantage of jQuery to add some minor glitter to our JavaScript features, the main advantage is that it makes it easier to develop JavaScript features. Using a simple CSS-based syntax, you can manipulate any element in the page easily. Loading in chunks of HTML through Ajax is a snap too."*

After all, jQuery definitely follows "The Drupal Way." Drupal most probably opted for jQuery because of its small, lightweight size — it being based on a small, disciplined core and plug-ins to extend its functionality — and its use of a hook-like callback approach for easy extensibility.

It is no coincidence that the jQuery home page includes Drupal architecture itself. So in many places on that site, you can see a lot about how Drupal takes great advantage of the library, just in simple things like the Autocomplete widget, collapsible form areas, file upload widgets, and more.

## Our `onload()` Example Implemented with jQuery

Follow these steps:

1. Go to Create content➤Create page, type in **jQuery example one**, and set the Body input format this time to "PHP Code." (If that format type is not available, go to Administer➤Site building➤Modules, and make sure that the PHP filter module is enabled.)
2. Enter **jQuery example one** in the Title field and the following in the Body field:

```
<?php
  drupal_add_js(
    '$(document).ready(function(){
      $("#section1").replaceWith("<h2>Some Haikus</h2>");
      $("#section2").replaceWith("<ol><li>Haiku Red</li><li>Haiku \
Blue</li><li>Haiku Green</li></ol>");
      $("#section3").replaceWith("<img \
src=\'/sites/all/themes/zen/zenlitworkshop/
clouds.jpg\' alt=\'clouds\' />");
    });',
    'inline'
  );
?>

<div id="section1">
  <p>Haikus</p>
</div>
<div>
  <ul id="section2">
    <li>option 1</li>
    <li>option 2</li>
  </ul>
</div>
<div>
  <a href="/texts/joyce/elegy-tired-lakes" id="section3" title= \
"click to read" name="click to read">Elegy to the tired lakes</a>
</div>
```

The result should be identical, as shown in Figure 12-5. However, the JavaScript has been greatly simplified.

- Before:

```
<script type="text/javascript">
function alterDiv(  ) {
   var section1 = document.getElementById("section1");
   section1.innerHTML = "<h2>Some Haikus</h2>";
   var section2  = document.getElementById("section2");
   section2.innerHTML = "<ol><li>Haiku Red</li><li>Haiku \
Blue</li><li>Haiku Green</li></ol>";
   var section3 = document.getElementById("section3");
   section3.innerHTML = "<img
src='/sites/all/themes/zen/zenlitworkshop/clouds.jpg' \
 alt='clouds' />";
}
</script>
<body onload="alterDiv();">
```

Notice also the need for the `onload` statement, no longer required thanks to the `jQuery document.ready()` function, which automatically executes after the page is fully loaded.

- After:

```
<?php
  drupal_add_js(
    '$(document).ready(function(){
      $("#section1").replaceWith("<h2>Some Haikus</h2>");
      $("#section2").replaceWith("<ol><li>Haiku Red</li><li>Haiku \
Blue</li><li>Haiku Green</li></ol>");
      $("#section3").replaceWith("<img \
src=\'/sites/all/themes/zen/zenlitworkshop/
clouds.jpg\' alt=\'clouds\' />");
    });',
    'inline'
  );
?>
```

Speaks for itself, doesn't it?

So, in the context of the workflow of processes interacting between the browser, the HTTP server, Drupal, and the RDBMS database (e.g., MySQL), you can now clearly see at what point the CSS and JavaScript files are included, as shown in the diagram of Figure 12-6.

# A Theming Example

Let's immediately do some fancy stuff to the quotes that appear on each page of the On-Line Literary Workshop in an example brazenly stolen from the jQuery home page example. You don't know it yet, but all you need to do is to figure out the selector, chain in an event function, and pipe some action into that.

Earlier on in the theming chapter, you created a special PHP template for the nodes of the *quote* content type. Edit this file (./sites/all/themes/zen/zenlitworkshop/node-quote.tpl.php) in a text editor.

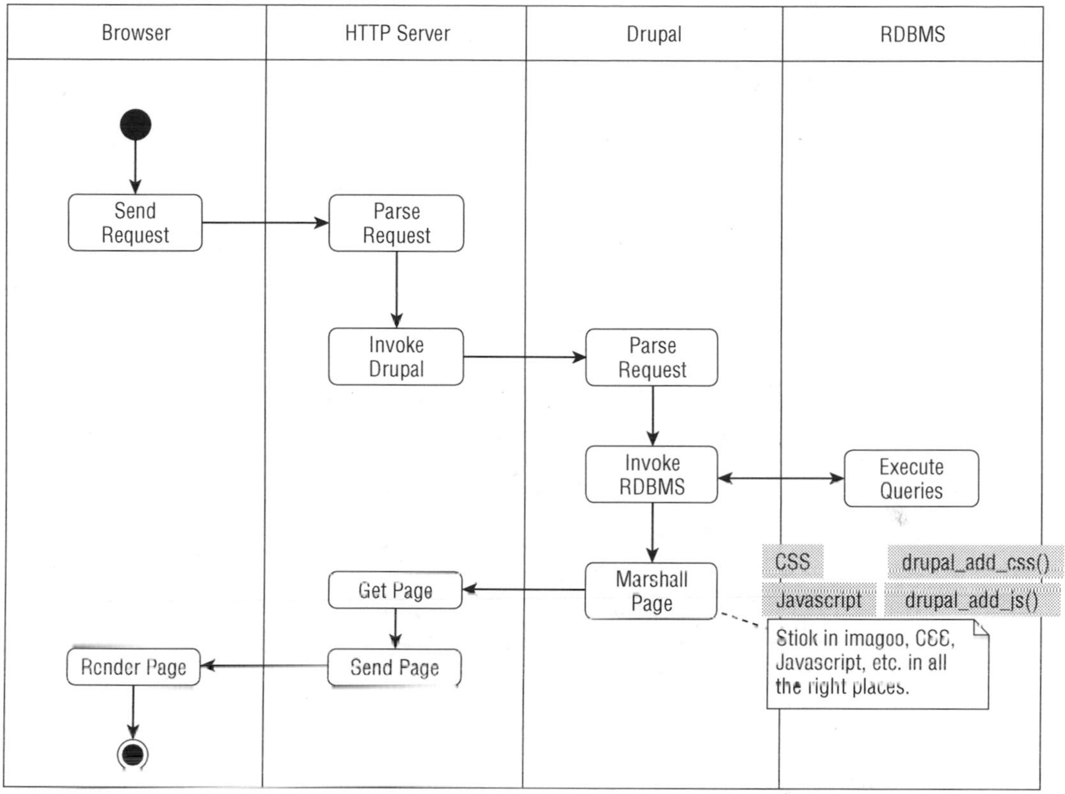


Figure 12-6

- Before:

```
<div class="node <?php print $node_classes ?>" id="node- \
<?php print $node->nid; ?>"><div class="node-inner">

  <?php if ($page == 0): ?>
    <p class="quote">
      <?php print $title; ?>
    </p>
  <?php endif; ?>

  <?php if (count($taxonomy)): ?>
    <div class="taxonomy"><?php print ' - ' . $terms; ?></div>
  <?php endif; ?>

</div></div> <!-- /node-inner, /node -->
```

- After:

```
<div class="node <?php print $node_classes ?>" id="node- \
<?php print $node->nid; ?>"><div class="node-inner">
```

```
<?php  drupal_add_js(path_to_theme() . '/quotebello.js'); ?>


        <?php if ($page == 0): ?>
          <p class="quote">
            <?php print $title; ?>
          </p>
        <?php endif; ?>

        <?php if (count($taxonomy)): ?>
          <div class="taxonomy"><?php print ' - ' . $terms; ?></div>
        <?php endif; ?>

      </div></div> <!-- /node-inner, /node -->
```

The HTML generated by Drupal and sent to the browser whenever the content is of type "quote" includes the following line in the `<head>` tag section:

```
<script type="text/javascript" src="/sites/all/themes/zen/zenlitworkshop/ \
quotebello.js?n"></script>
```

Basically, the result of this script is that whenever a quote content type is displayed, the JavaScript file quotebello.js will be loaded from its location in the Zen subtheme directory, invoked in the title section of the rendered page. Code for quotebello.js:

```
$(document).ready(function(){
  $(".quote").hide();
  //$("p.quote").show("slow");
  //$("p.quote").show(1500);
  $("p.quote").addClass("ohmy").show(1500);
});
```

Basically, this says that when the document is ready, all `<p>` tags of class `quote` should be hidden, and then the class `ohmy` should be added dynamically to objects of that type. Then the effects type function shown should be executed with a speed of 1,500 ms (milliseconds).

**Notice that jQuery derives its power and simplicity and ease of adoption by using the same principles as CSS: First select an element, then specify its attributes. In the case of jQuery, you first select a DOM object, then invoke one or more chained functions whose execution modifies the DOM.**

The neat thing of adding a dynamic class is that the execution real-time effect of fading in and out can be styled in development time just by a graphic designer editing a CSS file, and without having to call in Einstein, the JavaScript programmer. Add the following lines to our old friend zenlitworkshop.css in the Zen subtheme directory to put all the pieces into effect:

```
.ohmy {
  background-color: #abc0ff;
}
```

Now enjoy the animated quotes. By the way, what if it's not working? How do you know the JavaScript code is even loaded? A great way is, as in other cases, by using the Firebug Add-on for Firefox. Figure 12-7 shows the `Script` tag and the quotebello.js script file selected.

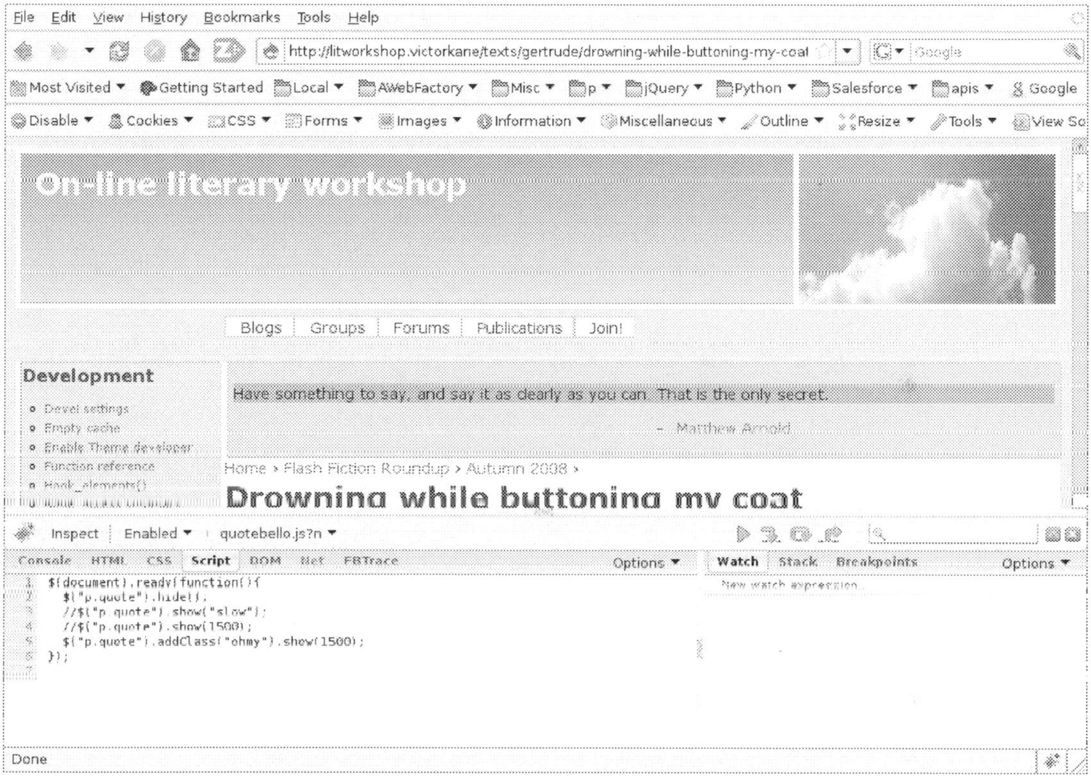

**Figure 12-7**

## Plug-Ins

jQuery elegantly has in common with the "Drupal way" an extremely lightweight footprint, with just the bare essentials in core, in conjunction with an extremely flexible extensibility framework attained thanks to the addition of plug-ins (modules in the case of Drupal).

Let's try one. You can find a complete list of plug-ins by category at `http://plugins.jquery.com/`. One idea, to replace our own homespun effort in the previous example, is the Effects jTypewriter plug-in, which you can find at `http://plugins.jquery.com/project/jTypeWriter`.

1. Download the JS file and install it in the Zen subtheme directory. You need just two changes.
2. First, modify node-quote.tpl.php so that it loads the plug-in also:

```
<div class="node <?php print $node_classes ?>" id="node-<?php print
 $node->nid; ?>"><div class="node-inner">
```

```
<?php  drupal_add_js(path_to_theme() . '/quotebello.js'); ?>
<?php  drupal_add_js(path_to_theme() . '/jTypeWriter.js'); ?>

<?php if ($page == 0): ?>
  <p class="quote">
    <?php print $title; ?>
  </p>
<?php endif; ?>

<?php if (count($taxonomy)): ?>
  <div class="taxonomy"><?php print ' - ' . $terms; ?></div>
<?php endif; ?>

</div></div> <!-- /node-inner, /node -->
```

3. Next, modify quotebello.js so that it reads as follows:

```
$(document).ready(function(){
  $("p.quote").addClass("ohmy").jTypeWriter();
});
```

4. Try out the following parameters to see which you prefer:

```
$(document).ready(function(){
  //$("p.quote").addClass("ohmy").jTypeWriter();
  $("p.quote").addClass("ohmy").jTypeWriter({duration:2.5,type:"word"});
});
```

# Drupal 5.x Uses of jQuery and Other JavaScript Libraries

It is important to review some JavaScript magic that was included in the Drupal CMS Framework before jQuery was introduced, since a lot of it is still prevalent and coexists with jQuery at the present time — the jstools module. Then mention is made of some JavaScript libraries (notably script.aculo.us and Prototype), which are jQuery's "competition" and may still want to be used by Drupal developers in peaceful coexistence with jQuery.

This section also deals with how jQuery is used in the Drupal User Interface itself, and with how development can be synchronized between the two very active Open Source projects. It is very common for many jQuery releases to emerge during the life cycle of a single Drupal release, so ways of keeping the jQuery version up-to-date are discussed.

## *jstools*

Before there was jQuery, there was jstools (`http://drupal.org/project/jstools`), which is an extremely popular collection of modules and libraries developed for Drupal 5.x. Some modules provide direct functionality, while others are dependencies for other modules. They have in common with jQuery two things:

- The objective of "graceful degradation," providing fully usable functionality to pages when JavaScript is not enabled in the browser.
- The attachment of "behaviors" to page elements on the basis of CSS classes.

The most important components of the jstools module set are the following:

- **Activemenu Module** — Upon installation, standard Drupal block menu trees are converted to Ajax trees, that is, when you click a node having children, it opens or closes in place without a page refresh.
- **Jscalendar Module** — A full Drupal integration of Mihai Bazon's DHTML pop-up calendar available for Drupal date fields. It became integrated into the CCK Date field, becoming available as an optional widget.
- **Tabs Module** — This module, also part of the jstools project group of modules, was an early pioneer in that it actually integrated the jQuery tabs plug-in by Klaus Hartl, which can be found at `http://stilbuero.de/tabs`. This was a use of jQuery outside and independent of the main jQuery Drupal integration.

## Prototype and script.aculo.us

But jQuery isn't the only modern JavaScript library, not by a long shot. Ruby on Rails includes the JavaScript duo of prototype and script.aculo.us to provide similar solutions in its framework. Actually, before jQuery was chosen for Drupal, spectacular integration of these libraries was achieved by Ayman Hourieh, who developed a drag-and-drop portal interface very similar to what Earl Miles's Panels modules offer, where you can define the layout and then drag-and-drop functional blocks based on modules to add functionality to your page. See `http://aymanh.com/drag-drop-portal-interface-with-scriptaculous` for the explanation, and `http://aymanh.com/files/portal/` for the spectacular demo.

*I have used this prototype and script.aculo.us with Drupal (to make a Desktop interface application actually, based on the Prototype Windows Class; see* `http://prototype-window.xilinus.com/`*).*

But there is a problem, since both jQuery and Prototype use the `$()` function as an alias for the invocation of the library, and there are no namespaces. On the jQuery site, however, a work-around was published at `http://docs.jquery.com/Using_jQuery_with_Other_Libraries`:

```
var $j = jQuery.noConflict();
     // Use jQuery via $j(...)
     $j(document).ready(function(){
       $j("div").hide();
     });
```

However, `jQuery.noConflict()` did not work with jQuery 1.0.1, the version included with Drupal 5.x. The alternative is to take each of the following files in the Drupal ./misc directory:

- autocomplete.js
- collapse.js
- drupal.js

- progress.js
- tableselect.js
- textarea.js
- upload.js
- update.js

and do the following:

- At the top of the file, add the statement `var $jq = jQuery`.
- Change every instance of `$(...)` to `$jq(...)`.

In version 1.1.x and later, the first line in these files may read:

```
var $j = jQuery.noConflict();
```

However, this does involve patching the ./misc directory, part of the Drupal core; which creates problems when it comes to updating every time a Drupal security release becomes available.

## Drupal 5.x UI

Starting with Drupal 5.x, as described above, the jQuery core became part and parcel of every Drupal release, and all uses of JavaScript were refactored to take advantage of this. As a result, several aspects of the Drupal UI (user interface) took advantage of this.

- **Autocomplete** — When the Autocomplete Widget is used in a CCK field, or when, for example, author information is edited for a node, the Autocomplete Widget is used
- **Collapse** — When a form is divided into fieldset groups, the groups become collapsible, thanks to the use of jQuery, which is handed a selector to locate each fieldset, and a function to support collapsible behavior.
- **Upload** — When you upload a file with the core Drupal Upload module, jQuery is used to provide progress bar behavior.

## The jQuery Update Module

But the jQuery and Drupal development cycles are not, of course, meshed. That is, when Drupal 5 was released, the version of jQuery included with it was version 1.0.1. In all subsequent versions of Drupal 5.x, this remained unchanged. The result was that a point was reached at which Drupal users could not avail themselves of the current version of jQuery, or jQuery plug-ins.

Integration is always a major problem when working with interlocking Open Source community projects. Fortunately, both are as extremely talented as they are active. However, although jQuery was an excellent choice for Drupal, being lightweight and event-centric, the Drupal core was wrapped around what very quickly became an old, and really quite obsolete, version of jQuery.

Enter the jQuery Update module to the rescue. Once installed and enabled in any Drupal 5.x installation, you can copy a more recent version of jQuery to the Drupal ./misc directory that is backward compatible with the core Drupal use of the JavaScript library. This is implemented thanks to John Resig's compat-1.0.js plug-in. Of course, when your Drupal installation is updated with a security release, for example, the newer version of jQuery must again replace the 1.0.1 version included with Drupal.

With time, even the Update module became obsolete, its architecture unable to support later versions of the very dynamic progress characteristic of the jQuery community. So the Update module did become updated itself, twice, the only inconvenience being that each time more files have to be copied to the ./misc directory. However, this is a small price to pay for being able to use the latest version of jQuery, jQuery plug-ins, and jQuery interface (the UI library that allows for drag-and-drop, and a host of other user interface JavaScript goodness).

# Advanced Drupal 5.x Examples

Since jQuery is part of the Drupal core and is used by the Drupal User Interface, and so much fuss is made of it, one is obviously interested in leveraging this spectacular resource that comes for free. But it is not immediately obvious how to go about doing so. To this end, you are presented in this section with three how-tos.

## *Reusing the Collapsible Widget*

Here is a most obvious need and a need not easily answered in Drupal 5.x times: how to extend Drupal widgets themselves based on jQuery. Let's suppose you have a profile themed with a series of sections and that you wish to make each section collapsible. Let's suppose further, for the sake of argument, that these sections will be themed with a template that receives an array of nodes in the variable `$nodes`. The template is invoked via a callback function, along with the parameter `$nodes`. Here is the snippet from the theme's template.php:

```
/**
* Catch the theme_user_profile function, and redirect through the template api
* The user profile will be overridden by this theming function, which sends
*   the variable $nodes to the invoked template.
*/

function phptemplate_user_profile($user, $fields = array()) {
  // Pass to phptemplate, including translating the parameters to
an associative array. The element names are the names that the
variables
  // will be assigned within your template.

  // Get all the nodes associated with the user profile via the node
profile module
  $profile_node = nodefamily_relation_load($user->node id);
  $profile_nid = $profile_node[0] -> nid;
  if ($profile_nid) {
    // Specify section header names for user profile editing page
```

```
    $nodeNames = jobs_get_node_names();
    $profile = _phptemplate_callback('profile-only-section',
 array('node' => $profile_node[0]));
   $profile_sections = '';
    $profile_node_sections =
nodefamily_relation_load_by_type($profile_nid);
      // here is where the template, its name, and its parameters are specified
    /****
     * logic to show all sections, including empty ones
     *
     */
    foreach ($nodeNames as $sectionComputerName => $sectionName) {
      // if the guy has some info for this node
      $sectionNodes = $profile_node_sections[$sectionComputerName];
      $profile_sections .= _phptemplate_callback('profile-section',
array('name' => $sectionName, 'nodes' => $sectionNodes, 'node_type'
 => $sectionComputerName));
    }
    // Has the user filled out enough info to warrant display?
    $cv_state = some_function_to_tell_us_this($user, $profile_node,
$profile_node_sections);
    return _phptemplate_callback('user_profile', array(
      'profile' => $profile,
      'profile_sections' => $profile_sections,
      'cv_state' => $cv_state,
      'user' => $user,
      'fields' => $fields)
      );
  } else {
   // This is for users not using the node profile module, like
webmaster and admin
    $vars = array(
      'user' => $user,
      'fields' => $fields,
      'picture' => theme('user_picture', $user),
      'categories' => '',
    );
    // Extract each field into its own template.

    foreach ($fields as $category => $items) {
      $vars['category'] = $category;
      $vars['items'] = ''; // reset this variable!

      foreach ($items as $item) {
        // we could use array_merge here but I'm putting them all in for
        // clarity of what variables we have available.
        $vars['title'] = $item['title'];
        $vars['class'] = $item['class'];
        $vars['value'] = $item['value'];

        // run the item template
        $vars['items'] .= _phptemplate_callback('user_profile_item', $vars);
      }
      // Now that we have all the items, run it through our category template.
```

```
        $vars['categories'] .= _phptemplate_callback('user_profile_category', $vars);
      }

      // And put it all in the final wrapper.
      return _phptemplate_callback('user_profile', array('vars' => $vars));
    }
  }
```

That is quite a large function residing in the file template.php in the theme directory. The upshot of it all is to invoke the template, which will actually show the user profile sections and pass it the necessary parameters, especially the array of `$nodes` itself.

Here is the template, which actually makes use of the collapsible behavior built into the Drupal core thanks to jQuery:

```
<div class="profile-section-anchor">
  <a name="<?php echo $node_type . '_node_form' ?>"> </a>

</div>
<div class="profile-section">
  <?php drupal_add_js('misc/collapse.js'); ?>

  <fieldset class=" collapsible collapsed">
  <legend><?php echo $name ?></legend>
   <?php if ($nodes) { ?>
    <?php foreach ($nodes as $node) { ?>
      <?php print node_view($node, false, false, false); ?>
      <form class="profile section-edit-button">
        <input type="button" onClick="self.location='<?php print \
$GLOBALS['base_url'] . '/node/' . $node -> nid . '/edit'; ?>'"
value="<?php echo t('Edit')?>"/>
      </form>
    <?php } ?>
   <?php } ?>
   <?php $max = nodefamily_content_type_get_max($node_type); if
(!($max != 0 && count($nodes) >= $max)) { ?>
     <?php
       $nodeNames = jobs_get_node_names();
       $node_type_label = $nodeNames[$node_type];
      ?>
     <form><input type="button" onClick="self.location='<?php print \
$GLOBALS['base_url'] . '/node/add/' . $node_type; ?>'"
 value="Agregar <?php echo $node_type_label ?>"/></form>
   <?php } ?>
  </fieldset>
</div>
```

It is in lines 3–5, which are highlighted in gray, that the fieldset is inserted into the XHTML so that it acts as a wrapper around each section, having a tag name and class attribute selectors, which will work with the way jQuery manages collapsible fieldsets in Drupal core.

The result is shown in Figure 12-8, where one of the sections ("Institutional information") has been clicked open.

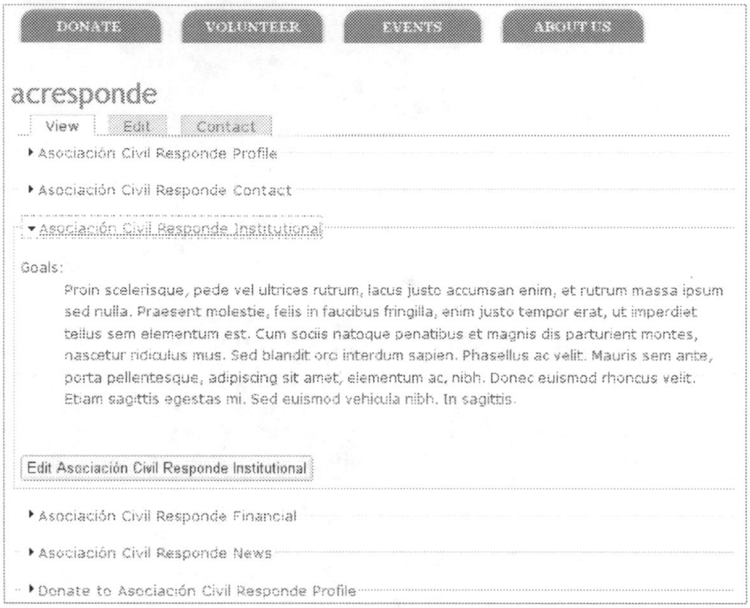


**Figure 12-8**

## Dependent Autocomplete Fields

This is how you can implement an autocomplete nodereference field that depends on a choice made in another such field in Drupal 5.x. Suppose there are three content types:

- Content type one: Company
- Content type two: Contact
- Content type three: Ticket

The Company content type has a nodereference field where Contacts can be filled in (multiple autocomplete field).

Among other fields, the Ticket content type has a select field *type* (phone call, sale, task, bug, hot date, etc.), a single non-multiple nodereference field for Company, and multiple nodereference fields for Contacts involved in the ticket. Since this could involve a company having several thousand contacts distributed among 500 companies, the chance of people with the same name but working in different companies (and actually being different individuals) is high (muchos María Gonzalez y Henry Smith).

Now, any autocomplete function has three fundamental components:

- A handler (a PHP function that will do the actual looking up)
- A MENU_CALLBACK path (URI), which will be invoked by the autocomplete query to access the "handler"
- The special #autocomplete_path selector in a form field

In this example, the three or four Contact nodereference autocomplete fields, by default, already have all this, but the default handler [which lives in the entrails of CCK's nodereference.module, specifically the `nodereference_autocomplete()` function registered by `nodereference_menu()` and referenced in the `nodereference_widget()` function] will unwittingly bring me all Jane Does and María Bustamantes whether they work for the already selected company or not.

To accomplish this, you need three things: a URI (path) for the autocomplete functionality to call a concrete PHP function (the callback function), a way of attaching that trigger to a given field using the autocomplete function, and finally, the implementation of the callback function (the autocomplete handler). These are provided in the following three steps.

## Step 1: MENU_CALLBACK URI Setup

**Question: Where does the code go?**

**Answer**: All the code goes into a module, call it *intranet.module* (create the appropriate intranet.info file first). The only exception is the JavaScript code, which goes into intranet.js in the module directory. I put my modules into ./sites/all/modules/, so the three files would go into ./sites/all/modules/intranet. You can, of course, name the module whatever you want. Just be sure the drupal_add_js function properly invokes the JavaScript file.

```
/**
 * Implementation of hook_menu().
 */
function intranet_menu($may_cache) {
  $items = array();
  $items[] = array(
    'path' => 'intranet/ticket/contact/autocomplete',
    'title' => 'contact autocomplete for ticket',
    'type' => MENU_CALLBACK,
    'callback' => 'intranet_autocomplete',
    'access' => user_access('access content'),
  );
  return $items;
}
```

All we are saying here is that the path intranet/ticket/contact/autocomplete will invoke the function `intranet_autocomplete`, the "handler."

## Step 2: Attach the Overriding URI

In this section, you attach the overriding URI to the Contact autocomplete field with unobtrusive jQuery.

The module continues with the following functions:

```
function intranet_form_alter($form_id, & $form) {
    if ($form['type']['#value'] == 'ticket') {
        $form['#theme'] = 'intra_ticket';
```

```
 }
}
function theme_intra_ticket($form) {
 drupal_add_js(drupal_get_path('module', 'intranet') . '/intranet.js');
}
```

And here is the intranet.js file invoked in the last (short and sweet) function:

```
1  if (Drupal.jsEnabled) {
2    $(document).ready(function() {
3      $("#edit-field-company-0-node-name").blur(function() {
4        companyvalue = $("#edit-field-company-0-node-name").attr("value");
5        re = /\[nid:(.*)\]/;
6        resarray = re.exec(companyvalue);
7        if (resarray) company = resarray[1];
8        $('input.autocomplete[@id^=edit-field-contact-]').each(function () {
9          this.value="http://mentor/intrassa/intranet/ticket/contact/autocomplete/"
+ company;
10         Drupal.autocompleteAutoAttach();
11       });
12     })
13   })
14 }
```

OK, explanations are in order:

- On line 3, an anonymous function is assigned to the `blur` event of the company autocomplete field. The idea is that the user selects a company, and then this anonymous function gets invoked. This anonymous function will first extract the node ID of the selected company via JavaScript's regular expression tools.
- Then, moving right along, on line 8, another anonymous function will iterate over the multiple contact fields (those that start with an `id` attribute of `edit-field-contact-`) and will shove in the new handler URI to which is tacked on the company node ID as parameter to the handler.
- Then, on line 10, `Drupal.autocompleteAutoAttach()` is invoked to fix the autocomplete "community plumbing" (see ./misc/autocomplete.js).

All that is left is the handler itself.

## Step 3: The Handler

This is the Drupal 5.x style with views as an extra data abstraction layer — none of your direct database accessing.

Here it is:

```
/**
*
*/
function intranet_autocomplete($company) {
```

```
  $view = views_get_view('ContactsForASingleCompany');
  $the_contacts = views_build_view('items', $view, array(0 =>
$company), false, false);
  $matches = array();
  foreach ($the_contacts['items'] as $contact) {
    $matches[$contact->node_title . ' [nid:' . $contact->nid . ']']\
 = $contact->node_title;
  }
  print drupal_to_js($matches);
  exit();
}
```

The parameter `$company` is supplied by the calling JavaScript function in intranet.js, and it is used to satisfy the argument of the pre-created View created interactively with the Views module for another purpose and reused here. You iterate over the contacts that the built View brings us, and set up the `$matches` array, which you translate to JSON (Javascript *lingua franca*) before exiting (which is what autocomplete expects).

This is a simple example that should serve as a springboard to any needs along these lines that you may have in your Drupal 5.x systems.

## Making Use of Hierarchical Select (Drupal 5.x)

This is the first of two jQuery-based examples for Drupal 5.x that make use of the aforementioned jQuery Update module (`http://drupal.org/project/jquery_update`). You are going to take a look at the Ajax Goodness of the Hierarchical Select module (`http://drupal.org/project/hierarchical_select`), in order to enhance the user experience when using hierarchical vocabulary select lists. Follow these steps:

1. First install the JQuery Update module just like any other, but after enabling it, the README will instruct you to copy one or more files to the Drupal ./misc directory. If you fail to carry out that copy, you will be warned when you visit the administration pages.

   If you install, say, JQuery Update version 5.x-2.0, once it is enabled at Administer➤Site building➤Modules, you must copy all the JavaScript files found in the ./sites/all/modules/jquery_update/misc directory to the Drupal ./misc directory. These are the files involved:

```
|-- CHANGELOG.txt
|-- LICENSE.txt
|-- README.txt
|-- compat.js
|-- jquery_update.info
|-- jquery_update.install
|-- jquery_update.module
'-- misc
    |-- collapse.js
    |-- farbtastic
    |   '-- farbtastic.js
    |-- jquery.js
    |-- tableselect.js
    '-- upload.js
```

   This may seem like quite a lot, but it means that you can have the latest jQuery version back-ported to Drupal 5 (jQuery 1.2.6 with version 5.x-2.0 of the update module)!

2. Once JQuery Update has been installed and enabled and the appropriate files copied, install the second dependency, JQuery Interface (`http://drupal.org/project/jquery_interface`).
3. Install the Hierarchical Select (version 5.x-3.0-rc3 or later, which requires JQuery Update 5.x-2.0 or later, thus enabling jQuery 1.2.6 or later . . . what a mouthful, but such is the complexity of the difficulties involved . . . ).

   In the example here, the following Hierarchical Select modules were enabled:

   - Hierarchical Select
   - Hierarchical Select Taxonomy
   - Hierarchical Select Taxonomy Views (for exposed filters in Views)
4. Decide which hierarchical taxonomy you are going to use it with. In the example here, there is a taxonomy, called Types, associated with the Story content type, with the following terms, organized as a single hierarchy:

```
Level of Interest
-- Not very interesting
-- Somewhat interesting
-- Very interesting
Popularity
-- Not very popular
-- Quite popular
-- Very popular
Quality
-- High quality
-- Mediocre
-- So-so
```

5. When you create a new story normally, you are presented with a dropdown list showing the hierarchy, and may select a term.

   To enable hierarchical select in Drupal 5.x, however, go to Administer➤Content management➤Categories➤Edit vocabulary, and scroll down to the Hierarchical Select configuration. Select the checkbox "Use the Hierarchical Select form element for this vocabulary," and click on the Submit button.

Now when you create or edit a story, in the Categories section, instead of a full dropdown list showing all possible terms in the hierarchy, you are presented with a dropdown list of only the parent terms, in this case, Level of Interest, Popularity, and Quality. Upon choosing one of these, an additional dropdown box slides out to the right, containing the three alternatives, that is, only those terms that are children of the parent term previously selected. Figure 12-9 shows what this looks like after a child term has been selected.

Figure 12-9

The module is really part of what I would call "the quiet revolution" in Drupal modules, and greatly enhances usability. It comes packaged with integration modules for views (exposed filters), book, menus, and other modules.

Even as it is configured in this example, there are a host of options, involving labels, whether or not the term of the lowest depth only should be chosen or the whole tree, and so on. It is a very useful exercise to play around with the configuration options found when editing the Vocabulary and see how the results differ.

# Validate, Validate, Validate!

A well-designed Form will validate the information a user types into the various fields right in the browser before submitting it to the server, since validation done only on the server is very time consuming. The user would have to press the Submit button, wait for the server to respond, and then have to change information and repeat the process.

You will now see how to accomplish this "The Drupal Way": by using jQuery and a jQuery plug-in, encapsulated in a Drupal module. In this case, both a Drupal 5.x thread and a 6.x thread are provided.

## Drupal 5.x Thread

A very exciting module in the jQuery pantheon is jQuery plug-ins (`http://drupal.org/project/jquery_plugin`), which supports the jQuery Validation plug-in (see `http://plugins.jquery.com/project/validate`), by means of which you can have time-saving Ajax validation in your Drupal forms.

Install and enable the module, which does very little more than provide a single non-redundant and conveniently centralized place to house jQuery plug-ins on a Drupal website installation.

Then, try it out on a test page (create a new content item of type *page*, making sure to specify the PHP input filter):

```
<?php
    jquery_plugin_add('metadata');
    jquery_plugin_add('validate');
    drupal_add_js (
      '$(document).ready(function(){
         $("#commentForm").validate(
```

```
            );}); ',
        'inline');

?>

 <form class="cmxform" id="commentForm" method="get" action="">
 <fieldset>
   <legend>A simple comment form with submit validation and default
 messages</legend>
   <p>
     <label for="cname">Name</label>
     <em>*</em><input id="cname" name="name" size="25" class="hola \
{required:true,minLength:3}" minlength="2" />
   </p>
   <p>
     <label for="cemail">E-Mail</label>
     <em>*</em><input id="cemail" name="email" size="25"  class="required email" />
   </p>
   <p>
     <label for="curl">URL</label>
     <em>  </em><input id="curl" name="url" size="25"  class="url" value="" />
   </p>
   <p>
     <label for="ccomment">Your comment</label>
     <em>*</em><textarea id="ccomment" name="comment" cols="22"></textarea>
   </p>
   <p>
     <input class="submit" type="submit" value="Submit"/>
   </p>
 </fieldset>
 </form>
```

Here is another test page:

```
<?php
    jquery_plugin_add('metadata');
    jquery_plugin_add('validate');
    drupal_add_js (
      '$(document).ready(function(){
         $("#commentForm").validate({
                rules: {
                        cname: {
                                required: true,
                                minLength: 2
                        },
                        cemail: {
                                required: true,
                                email: true
                        },
                }
});
}); ',
```

```
        'inline');

?>

 <form class="cmxform" id="commentForm" method="get" action="">
 <fieldset>
   <legend>A simple comment form with submit validation and default
messages</legend>
   <p>
     <label for="cname">Name</label>
     <em>*</em><input id="cname" name="cname" size="25" class="hola"
minlength="2" />
   </p>
   <p>
     <label for="cemail">E-Mail</label>
     <em>*</em><input id="cemail" name="cemail" size="25"  class="equus" />
   </p>
   <p>
     <label for="curl">URL</label>
     <em>  </em><input id="curl" name="curl" size="25"  class="equus" value="" />
   </p>
   <p>
     <label for="ccomment">Your comment</label>
     <em>*</em><textarea id="ccomment" name="ccomment" cols="22"></textarea>
   </p>
   <p>
     <input class="submit" type="submit" value="Submit"/>
   </p>
 </fieldset>
 </form>
```

## Drupal 6 Thread: An Ajax-Validated Application Form

Let's go into more detail with this jQuery plug-in by using it to add a validation layer to the application form already implemented for the user story, "A Workshop Leader can approve applications to join the workshop." Follow these steps:

1. Install the jQuery plug-ins module for Drupal 6 in the On-Line Literary Workshop website, logging in as user dev.
2. Let's first set up a test page emulating the documentation of this jQuery plug-in at `http://docs.jquery.com/Plugins/Validation#Example`. Create a new content item of type *page*, using input format php:

```
<?php
    jquery_plugin_add('metadata');
    jquery_plugin_add('validate');
    drupal_add_js (
      '$(document).ready(function(){
         $("#commentForm").validate();
       }); ',
      'inline');
```

```
?>
 <form class="cmxform" id="commentForm" method="get" action="">
 <fieldset>
   <legend>A simple comment form with submit validation and default
messages</legend>
   <p>
     <label for="cname">Name</label>
     <em>*</em><input id="cname" name="name" size="25" class="required"
minlength="2" />
   </p>
   <p>
     <label for="cemail">E-Mail</label>
     <em>*</em><input id="cemail" name="email" size="25"
class="required email" />
   </p>
   <p>
     <label for="curl">URL</label>
     <em>  </em><input id="curl" name="url" size="25"  class="url"
value="" />
   </p>
   <p>
     <label for="ccomment">Your comment</label>
     <em>*</em><textarea id="ccomment" name="comment" cols="22"
class="required"></textarea>
   </p>
   <p>
     <input class="submit" type="submit" value="Submit"/>
   </p>
 </fieldset>
 </form>
```

The result can be seen in Figure 12-10.

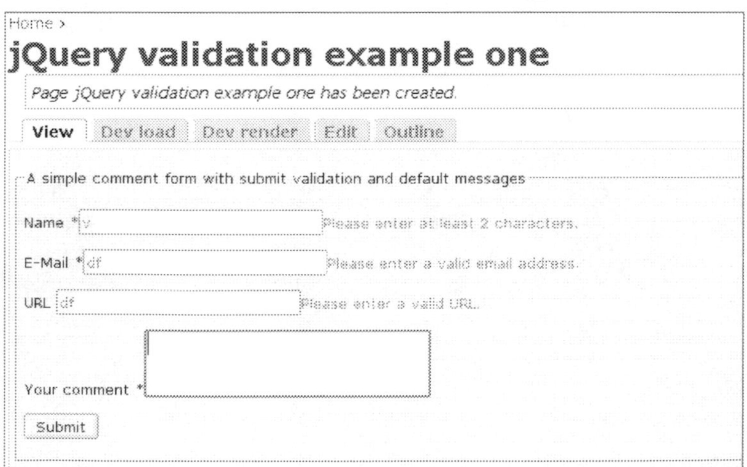


Figure 12-10

## Creating litworkshop.info and litworkshop.module

OK, it works great. Now, how to integrate with the real-world application form using "The Drupal Way"? Well, "The Drupal Way" here might very well indicate that the way to go is to modify the application form on the fly. In order to do so, you need to create a small utility module for your website application (you almost always will have to, anyway) and write just a little bit of PHP. Call this module, appropriately enough, the *Litworkshop module*. Create the directory ./sites/all/modules/litworkshop, and create two text files there:

- litworkshop.info
- litworkshop.module

Notice that the name of the theme used has purposely been called *zenlitworkshop*, so as not to be the same as that of any installed and enabled module. Doing so can cause namespace conflicts (PHP gets very confused with the same name appearing in different places).

The text for litworkshop.info specifies the module name and description. The dependencies must be enabled before it can be enabled itself. Additionally, the package the module will be grouped with on the Administration modules page and the version of Drupal core for which the module is implemented are included:

```
; $Id$
name = Literary workshop utils
description = On-Line Literary Workshop Utility Module.
dependencies[] = jquery_plugin
package = Literary workshop
core = 6.x
```

The text for litworkshop.module starts out with basic module header comment blocks compatible with Drupal coding style (see `http://drupal.org/coding-standards`) and the beginnings of an implementation of `hook_form_alter()`. Implementing this function overrides the default rendering of the form, identified by parameter `$form_id`. Here is the initial version, which simply inserts an `h2` tag at the top of the form, once the new module has been enabled:

```
<?php
// $Id$

/**
 * @file
 * Literary workshop utils
 *
 * On-Line Literary Workshop Utility Module.
 */

/**
 * Implementation of hook_form_alter().
 *
 * Called on all Drupal forms.
 * A switch statement can separate code destined
 * for specific forms.
 *
 */
```

```
function litworkshop_form_alter(&$form, &$form_state, $form_id) {
  switch ($form_id) {
    case 'application_node_form':
      $form['testit'] = array(
        '#value' => '<h2>Validate!</h2>',
        '#weight' => -10
      );
      break;
    default:
      break;
  }
}
```

The form ID is identified using Firebug to reveal the form's HTML and finding the value of a hidden field bearing the name *form_id*, similar to the following:

```
<input type="hidden" name="form_id" id="edit-application-node-form"
value="application_node_form"  />
```

This is shown in Figure 12-11, which also shows how the module (after being enabled) inserts the "Validate!" h2 tag at the top of the form:

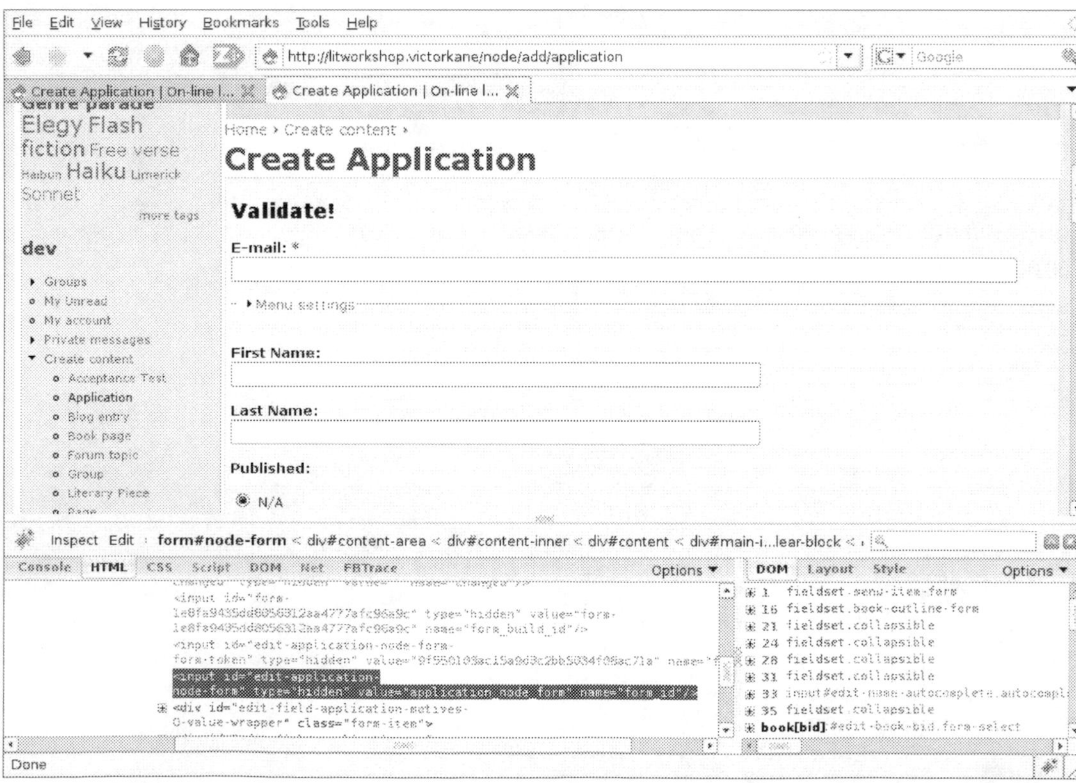


Figure 12-11

You can also find it by doing a text search of the HTML source provided by any browser, of course.

## Getting the Plug-in to Function

Now, to get the plug-in to function, two things are necessary:

1. Load the jQuery Validation plug-in every time this particular form is invoked (e.g., when someone clicks on the Join! primary menu option).
2. Add metadata to the fields you wish to validate.

In order to do the latter, you need to add a "class" attribute to the corresponding field to be validated. To be honest, you need to do a debug `print_r` of the `$form` tree, fortunately passed in as a parameter to the hook you are implementing, so as to know how to specify any particular field. To do this, follow these steps:

1. Add in the following snippet:

```
case 'application_node_form':
  print_r($form);
  break;
```

2. Click "Join!" and if you look at the source, chances are your browser will pretty-print the form. Now, the E-mail field is the most straightforward to deal with since it is simply the title field. Find the following in the (hopefully formatted) `print_r` statement:

```
[title] => Array
    (
        [#type] => textfield
        [#title] => E-mail
        [#required] => 1
        [#default_value] =>
        [#maxlength] => 255
        [#weight] => -5
    )
```

3. Since `$form` is passed in by reference, fortunately, you can simply change it on the fly (which, of course, is the whole idea of what you are trying to accomplish with this example). Here is the completed `litworkshop_form_alter()` hook implementation, specifying validation for the `title` field, which bears the E-mail label (note that the code for loading the jQuery plug-in has been added also):

```
function litworkshop_form_alter(&$form, &$form_state, $form_id) {
  switch ($form_id) {
    case 'application_node_form':
      //Load jQuery Validation plugin
      //$path = drupal_get_path('module', 'litworkshop');
      jquery_plugin_add('metadata');
      jquery_plugin_add('validate');
      //drupal_add_js($path . '/javascript/do_validate.js');
      drupal_add_js (
```

```
            '$(document).ready(function(){
               $("#node-form").validate();
              }); ',
            'inline');
            // Specify how to register each field.
            $form['title']['#attributes'] = array('class' => 'required email');
            break;
          default:
            break;
        }
      }
```

The results of attempting to fill in a value for this field that is not a well-formed e-mail address and then continuing on to the next field can be seen in Figure 12-12.

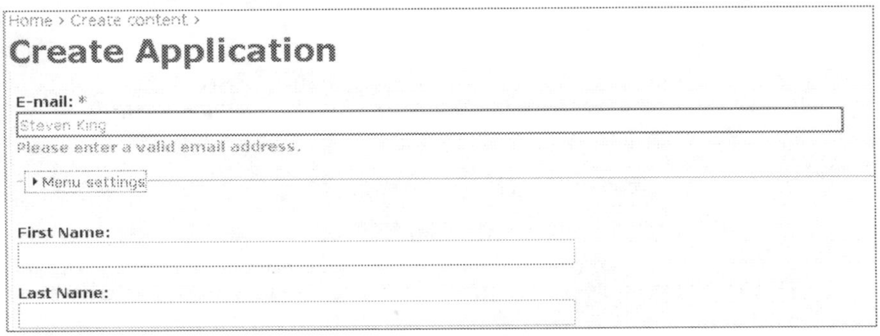


Figure 12-12

# Drupal 6.x jQuery Breakthrough

You get more spectacular widgets in Drupal 6 in the administration fields. Examples of these are what you have seen in use in the fantastic Views 2 user interface, Content Construction Kit fields management, and Menu management administration pages, and widgets that in the Drupal world used to use external "Web 1.0" JavaScript library widgets (like the ubiquitous DHTML calendar used in the jstools module–based jCalendar by Mihai Bazon of HTMLArea fame — see `www.bazon.net/mishoo/`). These are now integrated more seamlessly as jQuery widgets (see Ted Serbinski's page, `http://tedserbinski.com/jcalendar/index.html`, where the current use of Kelvin Luck's jQuery date picker is commented).

And the Drupal use of jQuery plug-ins and the creation of your own widgets and solutions have also become greatly enhanced.

In the hierarchical select examples, you have already seen how easy it is in Drupal 6.x to download any current jQuery plug-in and integrate it into Drupal, and to make full use of jQuery in general.

# An Example jQuery Ajax Alarm Module for Drupal 6.x

In the On-Line Literary Workshop, you want to make sure there is love in the world. That is, in real time, an alarm must inform when there is not a single literary piece without the word *love* in its title.

That could be accomplished via a timer installed whenever literary pieces are viewed. Every time the timer runs down, an Ajax URI may be invoked, which should return `false` if there is no *love*, and `true` if there is. If there is no *love*, an alert should be sent to the browser; otherwise, nothing should be done.

## Creating a Simple View

The first thing to do is to create a simple view that lists the items containing the word *love* in the title. Go to Administer➤Site building➤Views, and create a view with the following characteristics:

| View Configuration | Value |
|---|---|
| Title | Detect literary pieces whose title contains the word *love*. |
| Fields | Node: Title *Name*<br>Taxonomy: Term *Genre*<br>User: Name *Author*<br>Node: Updated date *Date*<br>Node: Sticky *Sticky* |
| Filters | Node: Type = *Literary Piece*<br>Node: Title contains *love* |
| Page display | Include to be able to specify a path. |
| Path | `islove` |

Alternatively, the following code may be imported into a new view or else inserted as file `love_letter_detector.inc` in the Views module directory:

```
$view = new view;
$view->name = 'love_letter_detector';
$view->description = '';
$view->tag = '';
$view->view_php = '';
$view->base_table = 'node';
$view->is_cacheable = FALSE;
$view->api_version = 2;
$view->disabled = FALSE; /* Edit this to true to make a default view
 disabled initially */
$handler = $view->new_display('default', 'Defaults', 'default');
$handler->override_option('fields', array(
  'title' => array(
    'label' => 'Name',
    'link_to_node' => 1,
```

```
      'exclude' => 0,
      'id' => 'title',
      'table' => 'node',
      'field' => 'title',
      'relationship' => 'none',
    ),
    'name' => array(
      'label' => 'Genre',
      'link_to_taxonomy' => 0,
      'exclude' => 0,
      'id' => 'name',
      'table' => 'term_data',
      'field' => 'name',
      'relationship' => 'none',
    ),
    'name_1' => array(
      'id' => 'name_1',
      'table' => 'users',
      'field' => 'name',
      'label' => 'Author',
    ),
    'changed' => array(
      'id' => 'changed',
      'table' => 'node',
      'field' => 'changed',
      'label' => 'Date',
    ),
    'sticky' => array(
      'id' => 'sticky',
      'table' => 'node',
      'field' => 'sticky',
    ),
  ));
  $handler->override_option('filters', array(
    'type' => array(
      'operator' => 'in',
      'value' => array(
        'literary_piece' => 'literary_piece',
      ),
      'group' => '0',
      'exposed' => FALSE,
      'expose' => array(
        'operator' => FALSE,
        'label' => '',
      ),
      'id' => 'type',
      'table' => 'node',
      'field' => 'type',
      'relationship' => 'none',
    ),
    'title' => array(
      'operator' => 'contains',
      'value' => 'love',
      'group' => '0',
      'exposed' => FALSE,
```

```
      'expose' => array(
        'operator' => '',
        'label' => 'Name',
        'use_operator' => 0,
        'identifier' => 'filter0',
        'optional' => 1,
        'remember' => 0,
      ),
      'case' => 1,
      'id' => 'title',
      'table' => 'node',
      'field' => 'title',
      'relationship' => 'none',
    ),
  ));
  $handler->override_option('access', array(
    'type' => 'none',
    'role' => array(),
    'perm' => '',
  ));
  $handler->override_option('title', 'Detect literary pieces whose title \
contains the word love');
  $handler->override_option('header_format', '1');
  $handler->override_option('footer_format', '1');
  $handler->override_option('empty_format', '1');
  $handler->override_option('items_per_page', '20');
  $handler->override_option('use_pager', TRUE);
  $handler->override_option('style_plugin', 'table');
  $handler->override_option('style_options', array(
    'columns' => array(),
    'default' => '',
    'info' => array(
      'title' => array(
        'sortable' => TRUE,
      ),
      'name_1' => array(
        'sortable' => TRUE,
      ),
      'changed' => array(
        'sortable' => TRUE,
      ),
    ),
    'override' => FALSE,
    'order' => 'asc',
  ));
  $handler = $view->new_display('page', 'Page', 'page_1');
  $handler->override_option('path', 'islove');
  $handler->override_option('menu', array(
    'type' => 'none',
    'title' => '',
    'weight' => 0,
  ));
  $handler->override_option('tab_options', array(
    'type' => 'none',
    'title' => '',
```

```
    'weight' => 0,
  ));
  $handler = $view->new_display('block', 'Block', 'block_1');
  $handler->override_option('title', 'Browse Literary Pieces');
  $handler->override_option('items_per_page', '5');
  $handler->override_option('use_pager', TRUE);
  $handler->override_option('style_plugin', 'table');
  $handler->override_option('style_options', array(
    'columns' => array(),
    'default' => '',
    'info' => array(),
    'override' => FALSE,
    'order' => 'asc',
  ));
  $handler->override_option('block_description', 'Genre browser');
```

Running the view by invoking the path `./islove` might yield the results shown in Figure 12-13.

Figure 12-13

## *Implementing the Functionality*

In order to implement this functionality, construct another module, called, for example, todoalarm, for want of a better name. In the directory ./sites/all/modules/todoalarm, create the following two files:

- todoalarm.info:

```
; $Id: $
name = Todo alarm
description = This is a simple jquery + ajax + views based pop-up
 alarm based on the results of a view consulted by a timed process.
core = 6.x
package = "Other"
```

- todoalarm.module:

```
<?php
// $Id: $

/**
* todoalarm module - For Drupal 6
*/

/**
* Implementation of hook_menu().
```

```
*
* This implements the Ajax URL http://example.com/getstatus
* that jQuery function calls with a get in order to see
* if there is love in the world
*/
function todoalarm_menu() {

  $items['getstatus'] = array(

    'title' => 'todos',

    'page callback' => '_todoalarm_ajax_get_status',

    'access callback' => TRUE,

    'type' => MENU_CALLBACK,

  );

  return $items;

}

/*****************************************************
 * Drupal 5 version of hook_menu implementation:
 *
function todoalarm_menu() {
  $items[] = array(
    'path' => 'getstatus',
    'title' => 'todos',
    'callback' => '_todoalarm_ajax_get_status',
    'access' => TRUE,
    'type' => MENU_CALLBACK,
  );
  return $items;
}
 *
 *****************************************************/


/**
* Implementation of hook_nodeapi
*
* This sets the timer under certain operations, such as viewing a node
*/
function todoalarm_nodeapi(& $node, $op, $a3 = NULL, $a4 = NULL) {
  switch ($op) {
    case 'view' :

      if ($node -> type == 'literary_piece') {

        // general universal timer code

        _todoalarm_set_timer();
```

```
      }

      break;
    }
  }

  /* Javascript function inserted in page to set timer
  /* and define Ajax get function */
  /* Invoked by nodeapi hook implementation (see previous) */
  function _todoalarm_set_timer() {
  drupal_add_js(
  'function doit() {
    $.get(base_url + "/getstatus", function(status){
    if (status == "false") {
      var result = confirm("No love!");
      if (result) {
        //setTimeout(doit, 300000);          // five more minutes snooze
        setTimeout(doit, 10000);          // 10 seconds snooze
      }
    }
    });
  }
  $(document).ready(function(){
    setTimeout(doit, 10000);                    // check after one minute
  });',
  'inline'
  );
  global $base_url;
  // nice way to pass parameters from drupal to jQuery!
  drupal_add_js("var base_url = \"" . $base_url . "\";", 'inline');
  }

  /* Callback function installed by hook_menu implementation */
  function _todoalarm_ajax_get_status() {
    /******************************************* Drupal 5 embed view!
    $view = views_get_view('love_letter_detector');
    $todoalarms = views_build_view('items', $view);
    print drupal_to_js(($todoalarms['items'])?false:true);
    ***********************************************************/
    $view_name = 'love_letter_detector';
    $v = views_get_view('love_letter_detector');
    //$v = view::load('love_letter_detector');
    $v -> build();
    $v -> execute();
    print drupal_to_js(($v -> total_rows)?true:false);
    exit;
  }
```

A little explanation for this code:

- The `todoalarm_menu()` function implements `hook_menu()` and implements the Ajax URL `http://example.com/getstatus` that the jQuery function calls with a `GET` request in order to see if there is *love* in the world (i.e., to see if the View returns any nodes including the word *love*).

- Next, the `todoalarm_nodeapi()` function is invoked by Drupal whenever a node is viewed, and its logic invokes the function `_todoalarm_set_timer()` if a node of type literary piece is being viewed.
- The `todoalarm_set_timer()` function adds some in-line jQuery code that defines the function called every time the timer runs down (`doit()`) and then sets the timer itself to 10 seconds.
- The function `doit()`, when called, actually calls the Ajax URI defined by the menu callback function (`/getstatus`), which was configured to point at `_todoalarm_ajax_get_status`.
- The `todoalarm_ajax_get_status` function gets the views object based on its name, and builds and then executes the view. If the result is true, the value `true`, otherwise `false`, is returned. Values are returned (to the JavaScript function invoking the Ajax URI) in JSON format, the *lingua franca* of the JavaScript world.

As always, this module is included in the tarball you may download with each chapter. Try it out, perhaps modifying it here and there.

You can see the results of there being no literary piece with the word *love* in its title in Figure 12-14.

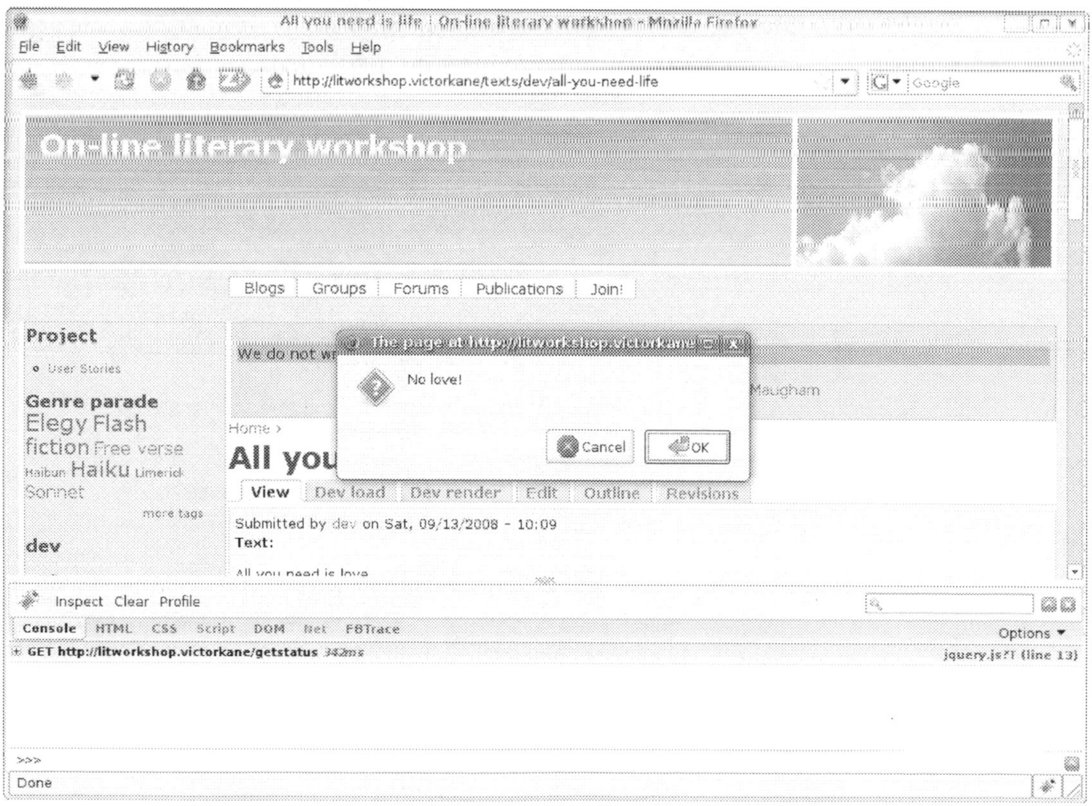


Figure 12-14

The Firebug console `GET` entry may be opened here to reveal the `false` value returned by the Ajax URI.

# Summary

In this chapter, you first delved into the nature of Rich Internet Applications and their capability of making website applications approximate the agility and ease of desktop applications, then learned their history and sorted out the terms (DOM, Ajax, AHAH, etc.) often heard in this context. You were able to learn the architecture of systems leveraging these techniques and understand how many distinct processes communicated with each other among various servers and application instances to achieve the required functionality.

Following this, the chapter discussed why Drupal chose jQuery as its own "Drupal Way" JavaScript library, to be included in every Drupal release. You learned how this brought immense advantages, together with certain difficulties in having to deal with a very old release of jQuery "stuck" in a given Drupal release, and how the JQuery Update module provided an excellent work-around in this sense. You then saw a whole series of concrete examples, capable of being put to good use in future tasks. And jQuery use was contrasted in the Drupal 5 and 6 releases. A complete example of using the jQuery Validation plug-in within the context of Drupal 6 was then demonstrated and explained, together with an additional Ajax example.

All in all, a complex subject was dissected and put to use, and — hopefully — understood clearly, becoming part of the website application arsenal of every reader.

# Part V
# Drupal 7 and the Road Ahead

# 13

# From Drupal 6 to Drupal 7 and Beyond

So, where is it all headed? You often hear that Drupal 7 will be "The One." Drupal 6, as you have seen, represented a huge gain in functionality compared to Drupal 5, which also represented a huge gain in contrast to the previous major release, Drupal 4.7.

In this chapter, you will become acquainted with exactly what changed with the presentation of the Drupal 6 release, and some of the underlying principles guiding Drupal development as it has progressed from one Drupal release to the next, including Drupal 7. A Drupal 7 feature list will be presented, and the architectural style of this release will be analyzed. The battle plans of the various contributed module authors will be reviewed. Finally, you will gain hands-on experience installing Drupal 7 and look toward a minimalist implementation for the On-Line Literary Workshop.

## What's Changed in Drupal 6?

Every Drupal release comes with a CHANGELOG.txt gleaned from the commit logs, including new features and bug fixes, all the way back to Drupal 1.0.0., "Initial release," on January 1, 2001. The log for each of the Drupal 6.x releases (6.1, 6.2, etc.) brought the following major new features:

- A new Schema API, to make it easier to work with databases other than MySQL
- jQuery upgrading to jQuery 1.2.6
- The Update Status module, which continually checks for core and module updates, was added to the core
- Triggers and actions were added to the core to allow custom workflow development
- Support for OpenID
- Any node type can now be posted to a Forum

- Performance gains thanks to conditional loading of include files, a JavaScript aggregator, block-level caching, and a revamped menu system
- New HTML corrector filter
- Installer now themed, and given additional functionality, with a form to include basic site information, the possibility of importing interface translations, as well as the ability to add additional steps programmatically
- Completely revamped theme system to make for easier theming, with an easier configuration made possible via a new .info file, and modules given the possibility of including template files (instead of `theme_` functions inside the module code) capable of being copied right into a user's theme and overridden. Additionally, a new clear-cut pre-process function, as well as theming support for JavaScript functions
- A host of usability enhancements:
    - JavaScript to manually specify teaser portion of body text in nodes
    - Sticky table headers (a boon in setting permissions!)
    - Clean URLs automatically tested via a JavaScript
    - PHP version and Drupal core dependencies strictly enforced for modules via .info file
    - Dynamic check of password strengths
    - Drag-and-drop positioning blocks, menu items, taxonomy vocabularies and terms, forums, profile fields, and input format filters
    - PHP filter now abstracted out into a separate core module (disabled by default for security reasons)
- A host of l10n and i18n language improvements:
    - Support for right to left languages
    - Language detection based on parts of the URL
    - Browser-based language detection
    - The ability to specify a node's language
    - Support for translating posts on the site to different languages
    - Language-dependent path aliases
    - Automatically import translations when adding a new language
    - JavaScript interface translation
    - Automatically import a module's translation upon enabling that module
- Revamped logging system, making it possible to disable database logging (dblog), allowing modules to re-direct logs to other sources besides the database, for example, to a text file, and adding eight error levels according to RFC 3164. A new syslog module for monitoring large Drupal installations was also added
- Improved PostgreSQL support

As you have seen, using Drupal 6 provides a smoother and more solid experience overall, when compared to using previous Drupal releases.

# Killing the Webmaster

Despite these improvements, in September 2007, Dries Buytaert, the originator of Drupal and the Drupal Community, gave a report entitled "State of Drupal Presentation," before the Drupal International Conference held in Barcelona, which I was fortunate enough to attend. The slogan of the report was "Kill the Webmaster," a bloodthirsty but user-friendly motto: The idea is that an NGO (non-governmental organization) or any small or medium-sized business, or a department, section, or business group within a corporation, should be able to create and maintain a website application enabling their community to interact around their goals and activities without having to hire a professional who has to be consulted and depended on to configure and maintain the content of their system. The focus was placed squarely on that percentage of potential users who had tried Drupal, but had then opted for some other alternative because of usability issues. Drupal had lost them forever because they had given up on Drupal — they had come to the conclusion that using Drupal was just too hard. The focus was on how to win over those kinds of users and the way to do it was by building "the killer Drupal 7 release," to be built in compliance with the requirements captured from a survey that ran for 30 days and received more than 1,000 responses. In the survey, people prioritized the following:

- Better media handling
- Moving the content construction kit into Drupal core. CCK, as it is called, has been up till now a contributed module, which, as you have seen in this book, allows the user to create content types with custom fields having built-in data types and an assortment of form widgets to match
- Moving views, or a similar SQL query and report generator, into core. This would complete CCK by offering the off-the-shelf capability of listing content items of various types according to custom-configured and interactive filters and arguments
- Moving a WYSIWYG editor into the Drupal core, so that this functionality is available to users without having to download and install and configure anything ("Kill the Webmaster!")
- Continue to enhance administration usability, and provide tools for the convenient structuring and organization of content
- Continue to improve performance and reduce the resources required to run Drupal
- Automatic upgrading of Drupal core and modules
- Improvements in the node access system, so that non-programmers can configure sophisticated access and security schemes for the data contained in their website application ("Kill the Webmaster!")
- Comprehensive import and export facilities for content and for configuration
- Enhanced Database API (PDO, etc.; see `www.garfieldtech.com/blog/drupal-7-database-plans`)
- Greater connectivity, so that Drupal can integrate Web Services into the mix, and various kinds of APIs. Drupal should be semantic Web-aware and ready (RDF support)
- Continue to enhance usability in general

The overall objective is for Drupal to be as easy to use as the "easier systems" while maintaining the power and flexibility of a web application framework.

This kind of aggressive blueprint for continual progress and evolution, at the risk of losing backward compatibility and obliging Drupal users to constantly update and upgrade (a significant budget in itself), is the Drupal hallmark. Many people new to Drupal constantly question it, saying that they finally learn their way around, only to have everything changed on them brutally every 12 months or so.

But Drupal is only guilty of placing itself squarely in the software industry mainstream — no more, no less. Like continual testing, continual updating and upgrading are part and parcel of all serious software development and deployment because:

- There is a realistic need for continued security updates, something at which the Drupal community excels.
- The Drupal community reflects the full power and creativity of the Open Source business model and places itself squarely on the crest of the wave of the current usability and paradigm revolution.

Drupal refactored continually can open itself to all kinds of developments, not the least among them being the tendency toward open, collaborative, stable, and fully usable website applications capable of interacting with a host of APIs and options for data persistence (i.e., through Web Services rather than through a local database).

# Understanding the Drupal Blueprint from Drupal 7 On

The first news to emerge in Drupal 7 development, however, was not this or that feature, per se, but rather an explosion in the importance placed on testing. "Not because Drupal is buggy," wrote Dries Buytaert while blogging on the Drupal 7 timeline in March 2008 (`http://buytaert.net/drupal-7-timeline`), "but because it makes release management easier, because it leads to better APIs, and because it encourages change and experimentation — something the Drupal community really takes pride in and which is critical to our long term success." In other words, everything was based on a foundation of best practices in software engineering. The more testing coverage (percentage of lines of codes actually tested), the longer development could go on, and the more features that could be included in the Drupal 7 release at code freeze. The aforementioned survey called for a major Drupal release every 12 months, and so the original idea was to have the code freeze in July 2008, based on a tentative release date of March 2009. However, with testing, Dries added that the code freeze could be postponed to November 2008 without requiring more than three months for debugging and stabilization, instead of the usual seven months that would have been required with less test coverage.

All that was needed was the adoption of a good lightweight test framework (perhaps Simpletest — `http://simpletest.org/`) and the mobilization of a high percentage of the Drupal community to participate in whittling down the issue queues and preparing more and more code for committing in time for the code freeze.

Indeed, the Simple Test Framework for Drupal (`http://drupal.org/project/simpletest`) has been in place since October 2004, but as a contributed module. Excitedly, the document home page reads, "SimpleTest 7.x development has been moved to core," which explains why there is no Drupal 7 version.

This is a great step forward in the production of reliable software, proving once again that Open Source software can often be more than a match for proprietary software that can never mobilize hordes of enthusiasts to test things from top to bottom. But also, the extensive documentation (`http://drupal.org/node/291740`) explains how every module author can incorporate unit and functional testing right into the module itself. Later on in this chapter, you will do just that.

This is another reason why Drupal can afford and has every right to progress at neck-breaking speed.

To a great extent, it is a decided advantage that Drupal moves ever forward ... the downside is, as mentioned, that maintaining and upgrading has to become a religious act, in all senses of the word, and not keeping your site as up to date as possible means painting yourself into a corner and creating a certain re-engineering need in the not-so-distant future.

It bears repeating that updating and upgrading is right up there on any Drupal website application budget, but that the plus side is that just by using Drupal, you get a whole security team, for example, working for you.

# Making the Historic Decision to Postpone the Drupal 7 Code Freeze

In May 2008, Buytaert Dries made an important announcement:

> *"Drupal 7 will be ready when it is ready, and more importantly, when the Drupal community is ready for it. At no point, release dates are set in stone, and I'll always continue to listen to input and zeitgeist from the community at large .... I'm willing to adjust release schedules, but I'm not willing to slow down the rate of change and innovation."*

Then, in June 2008, Dries wrote:

> *"While we have made incredible progress with the test infrastructure as well as implemented a dozen of usability improvements, we're still light on feature improvements (such as fields in core). Combined with the late arrival of CCK and Views, and the many Drupal 6 books that are currently being written, it sounds best to postpone the code freeze a little longer. Given the current state of things, the proposed July 15 deadline seems a bit too aggressive to my liking."*

The decision was wisely made not to catapult the active Drupal community and entire user base toward a completely revamped release without first having exhausted all the possibilities of the new Drupal 6 release, to put it through its paces and glean all possible lessons learned in order to allow Drupal to continue to grow as it has always done, in an organic and concrete fashion.

Maturity and intelligence also forge the Drupal hallmark.

# Listing the Drupal 7 Features

Even though you may be using a much earlier release of Drupal and may not even have gotten around to upgrading some of your sites to Drupal 6 yet, since you are using Drupal, it behooves you to know what the future holds, where Drupal is headed, and what benefits are in the offing — which you can appreciate from the Drupal 7 features listed here.

Whether Drupal 7 suffices to "Kill the Webmaster!" remains to be seen. However, the following table gives a partial list of what had been achieved at the time of writing, and even so, it represents and contains major user-friendly enhancements and the removal of many fossilized quirks.

**Drupal 7 Feature List**

| Feature | Description |
|---|---|
| Database | Fully rewritten database layer using PHP 5's PDO abstraction layer, built primarily on an object-oriented paradigm<br>Query builders for INSERT, UPDATE, DELETE, MERGE, and SELECT queries<br>Support for master/slave replication, transactions, multi-insert queries, delayed inserts, and other features |
| Security | Protected cron.php — `cron` will only run if the proper key is provided.<br>Much stronger password hashes compatible with the Portable PHP password hashing framework<br>A pluggable password hashing API supporting alternative hashing and authentication schemes, making it much easier to integrate Drupal authentication into existing and standards-based Enterprise and organizational authentication systems |
| Usability | Drag-and-drop positioning for input format listings<br>Drag-and-drop positioning for poll options<br>Provided descriptions for user permissions<br>Removed comment controls for users<br>Removed display order settings for comment module. Comment display order can now be customized using the Views module.<br>Additional features to the default install profile, and implemented a "slimmed down" install profile designed for developers.<br>Image toolkits are now provided by modules (rather than requiring a manual file copy to the includes directory).<br>Added an Edit tab to taxonomy term pages. |
| News aggregator | Added OPML import functionality for RSS feeds.<br>Optionally, RSS feeds may be configured to not automatically generate feed blocks. |
| Search | Added support for language-aware searches. |
| Testing | A built-in test framework and tests |

In addition, Drupal 7 has made the following changes to module, registry, and Theme system features:

**Drupal 7 Changes**

| Change | Description |
|---|---|
| Refactored "access rules" component of User module | The User module now provides a simple interface for blocking single IP addresses. The previous functionality in the User module for restricting certain e-mail addresses and usernames is now available as a contributed module.<br>Furthermore, IP address range blocking is no longer supported and should be implemented at the operating system level. |
| Removed throttle module | Alternative methods for improving performance are available in other core and contributed modules. |
| Added code registry | Using the registry, modules declare their includable files via their .info file or by virtue of hook_menu, allowing Drupal to lazy-load code as needed, resulting in significant performance and memory improvements. |
| Theme system | Converted the `bluemarine` theme to a tableless layout. |

Whether this suffices to "Kill the Webmaster!" remains to be seen. However, this is just a partial list of what had been achieved at the time of writing, and even so, it represents and contains major user-friendly enhancements and the removal of many fossilized quirks.

# Drupal 7 Architectural Style

Representative of the exciting new Drupal architecture is the new Database API, exclusive support for PHP 5 and later (cutting the shackles that bind and limit to PHP 4), and intense usability concerns.

## *Drupal 7 Database API*

The Drupal 7 Database API describes itself right off the bat as being "built primarily on an object oriented paradigm." It will be instantly familiar to all who have used similar packages in object-oriented languages such as Java or even in scripting languages such as Perl or Ruby. Some examples from the extensive documentation published from very early on in the project make this clear:

```
<?php
$conn = Database::getActiveConnection($target);

$result = $conn->query("SELECT nid, title FROM {node}");

$result = db_query("SELECT nid, title FROM {node} WHERE type = :type", array(
  ':type' => 'page',
));
```

```
$result = db_query("SELECT nid, title FROM {node}");
foreach ($result as $record) {
  // Do something with each $record
}

$record = $result->fetch();              // Use the default fetch mode.
$record = $result->fetchObject();  // Fetch as a stdClass object.
$record = $result->fetchAssoc();   // Fetch as an associative array.

?>
```

Built-in support for master/slave database replication:

```
<?php
$result = db_query("SELECT nid, title FROM {node}", array(), array(
  'target' => 'slave',
));
?>
```

But above and beyond the ease and familiarity for experienced developers, the main thing is that the whole API is built squarely on the industry-standard PDO library available in PHP. In this way, drivers may be written for different RDBMS (as quoted from the Database API documentation):

> *"Each driver consists of several classes derived from parent classes in the core database system. These driver-specific classes may override whatever behavior is needed to properly support that database type. Driver-specific classes are always named for their parent class followed by an underscore followed by the driver name. For example, the MySQL specific version of InsertQuery is named InsertQuery_mysql."*

## Going PHP 5

Another exciting aspect of Drupal architecture is that Drupalistas like Palantir's Larry Garfield promoted, from very early on (2006–2007), the whole struggle against the death embrace of PHP 4 and its crippling limitations as part of an ambitious plan that not only catapulted Drupal into the front line of CMS frameworks, but actually had a huge impact on the entire PHP community as a whole.

This was done first of all as a signal discussion in the Drupal development mailing list and on IRC, and then, via an interproject and interhosting dialog with other major projects and hosting companies to see who would be on board to come out with a pre-announced date after which PHP 4 would no longer be supported, as an influential website, "GO PHP5."

Not only did Drupal free itself of PHP4's shackles, but it also spearheaded an influential movement within the PHP community and was very successful at making PHP go from a scripting language free for all to a serious development contender, as Drupal advanced from "script" to serious CMS website development framework.

## Considering Usability Concerns, Usability Sprints

(Death to the Webmaster!)

Usability in the Drupal administration and configuration user interface has often been cited as one of the essential stumbling blocks preventing a wider and more deserved distribution of the Drupal CMS Framework. The creative "geeks" who have worked so closely together over the years may have overlooked, or postponed, the question of usability in favor of packing in more functionality.

Although the community supported greater functionality and constant refactoring has constantly improved Drupal quality, the hopes of making Drupal more accessible "to the masses" have pushed usability to the fore. You will be informed here of a series of usability studies that were carried out to specify exactly what needs to be changed, of the existence of a group regularly meeting to work on this at `http://groups.drupal.org`. They speak of their hopes for "usability sprints," involving their success at attracting Drupal developers toward work to be done in this area in a massive and concentrated fashion, in order for the objectives to be met.

Also explained are the face-lifting currently under way for `http://drupal.org` itself, and last, but not least, of the spectacular achievements of the Drupal Documentation Team.

## Studying Usability

In June 2007, the Interaction Design and Information Architecture program at the University of Baltimore and a team of eight graduate students in the Research Methods class, taught by professor Kathryn Summers, completed a usability study on Drupal (`http://drupal.org`, "News and Announcements" section). The very fact that this and other studies have taken place show the seriousness of the Drupal community in gearing up for "The One" — Drupal 7 — as a killer application. Instead of the usual geek disdain for usability, here was a community open enough to explore, several times and with experts, the weakest link in the chain: the accusation that Drupal is powerful, Drupal is flexible, but Drupal is too damn hard to use. If Drupal emerges as the leader in its field, it will be because of this honesty and courage.

In a nutshell, the core usability problems with Drupal, the findings in this and in other studies, can be summarized as follows:

- **Better Support for Editing Content in Drupal** — This involves a WYSIWYG content editor that doesn't require a rocket scientist to install, but instead comes directly with a plain Drupal installation.
- **Easier Handling of Input Formats** — This is for nontechnical users to easily balance power with security and configure the kinds of HTML tags and media permitted in the various different content types that are accessible to the various user roles interacting with the system. An example, here, is the many posts to the support forum complaining of users including images in posts, but not being able to see them when visualizing the page.

  *An input format that filtered out the* `<IMG>` *tag was in place. This tag and others needed to be added to the list of allowable, safe tags, but it was difficult to find where in the administration soup this could be done, and then, it was not very intuitive on exactly how to get it done.*

- **Simplification of the Geeky Nomenclature Used to Refer to Content and Content Items: Node, Post, Story** — The general conclusion is that the built-in content type "story" should be changed to "article," and that the descriptions should make it very clear what the differences are between that and, say, "page" (for static and/or information architecture building blocks, or where more metadata is required), or "book" (which allows for section and chapter-like hierarchies).

- **Simplify and Rethink the Administration Areas, Which Most Usability Test Subjects Consider Overwhelming** — Make sure the administration area is seen as separate from the content areas.

  *However, just because WordPress does it this way is no reason for Drupal to do it this way, and there is some controversy on this point. Many users are highly attracted toward "click to edit" and "click to configure" areas; the Zen theme, for example, greatly enhances this experience.*

- **Several Evaluators Wanted a Step-by-Step Instruction on How to Start** — This should include how to get started, a Help API, or even the design of a user experience (UX) capable of being self-explanatory.
- **Change the "Where Did My Content Go" Phenomenon in Drupal** — This phenomenon occurs when you create content but can't find it. And when you do (Administer ➢ Content management ➢ Content), you can filter the content items (nodes) in various ways and apply some bulk operations on a page-by-page basis, but the interface and functionality here have a lot of room for improvement (not to mention being able to find it in the first place). At a minimum, you should be able to carry out bulk operations on all posts of a given content type (i.e., put revision control in place, publish or unpublish, promote to front page, or demote from front page).
- **Determining What a Teaser Is** — Drupal 6 sports a cool, graphic, and interactive manner of separating out the teaser from the body itself, but many first-time users of Drupal have a hard time trying to figure out just what a teaser is in the first place.
- **Blocks Require a Preview Feature to Show How They'll Appear in Regions Once Created** — A user could easily create a blogroll or list of references, or an author information block with an image, using a WYSIWYG content editor. But after creating the block, you could have a hard time seeing what it might look like placed in different regions.
- **The Form for Editing a Post Is Very Confusing** — What does a first-time user (or any user, actually) expect to find when he clicks "Post settings," for example? Is this the ability to add fields? Why wouldn't it? "How do I add new fields?" is a common problem, and something that is way too difficult to find. Gains have been made in Drupal 6 in the actual Wizard you go through to create a field, but there is still a lot of room for improvement before dependencies on Webmasters can be eliminated. Even when users did find the Administer ➢ Content management ➢ Content types ➢ Edit {a content type}, the Add Field tab does not exactly leap out at you, and several evaluators "clicked every other link" but that one in trying to accomplish this feat.
- **The Whole Concept of Business Object Creation Was Not at All Obvious or Intuitive** — In fact, it is indeed one of the strongest points in favor of adopting. Nonetheless, some usability test subjects thought that "content type" was a field that could be added.
- **The Administration Categories Need to Be Reworked** — When faced with the basic administration categories (Content Management, Site Building, Site Information, User Management, etc.), where would you go to create a business object or a forum? Many searched in vain in Site building, perhaps the most commonsense of those available.
- **Where Would You Look, Also, to Set Access Control?** — In Content types? What about "access rules"?
- **There Were Problems about Understanding What Taxonomy Even Is** — This includes its power, how it can be used in conjunction with content types, and how to improve usability with vocabularies of taxonomy terms when you do understand this.

## Usability Group

The Usability Group (`http://groups.drupal.org/usability`) is a serious-minded and highly organized team who recognize the fact that they need to organize separately from the developers. Whereas developers may not have usability front and center when dealing with core functional issues, such as the Database API, or how to optimize the menu system, someone has to in order for gains to be made here. Born themselves at a *usability sprint* at DrupalCon 2008 in Szeged, they have assembled the "top 10" usability areas that must be dealt with for Drupal 7 and have organized *sprints* (or concentrated effort brought to bear on the problem, benefitting from everyone being together at the conference) to deal with them.

For an Open Source community, trying to overcome stumbling blocks over operating system, proprietary software tool compatibility issues, and candidate Web 2.0 replacements, it is an organizational effort striving for user input and striving to get the necessary attention of the leading developers in the community as well because without developer awareness, the necessary code will not get written. This group, an intense confluence of developers, word-mongers, graphic designers, and users, could very well be the envy of large corporations and could hold the key to the success of Drupal 7.

Their top issues as seen through the eyes of users are:

- Where did the help go? There is a great need for context-sensitive help. Furthermore, some felt the help useless when they did find it. And the part of help that did help was confusing in its terminology, which may not even have matched all the corresponding labels. What's a *parent item*?
- Do all the helpful links on the Welcome screen (the one that appears before any content is created) always have to disappear as soon as content is created? Typical reaction when the administrator creates her first node, or post, or story: "Where did the Welcome page go, with its helpful links?"
- Where's the overview on how the whole thing works?
- What's the difference between an *article* (thank goodness it's not called a *story* anymore) and a *page*?
- What are *access rules*? Is that permissions to access content?
- How do we really deal with the need to specify and configure content types, on the one hand, and content creation, management, and edition, on the other? To what extent should they be separate, or conveniently meshed, while being clear, straightforward, and simple to use?
- Teaser, summary, what?
- There is an overwhelming administration interface. We have to go to too many places to accomplish similar tasks, or even a single task. "There are places where the admin interface works fine if you want to delete one or two items, but becomes a nightmare if you need to delete fifty" — Drupal user *starbow*.
- "Where did my content go?"
- How do you enable the built-in WYSIWYG editor? You mean there isn't one? But: "All most people need is a few simple buttons that wrap their content in the appropriate tags and allow them to upload and insert images, audio, and video. This functionality should be part of the default installation of Drupal. If you want an example of a good interface for publishing content, just take a look at the page for creating a post in WordPress, especially the HTML view" (quoted from Drupal user *marketanomaly*).

- Is this an administration page, a content editing page, or is it how the world sees my site?
- How do you make it easier to specify and configure content types?
- How do you eliminating the need for (too much) scrolling up and down?
- What does *Site building* really mean? Is it concerned with development, configuration, or pure content management? Is it the place where users expect to find where to add fields to forms and content types?
- How do you improve usability in the browsing and management of SEO-friendly path aliases?

The Usability Team is cleverly leveraging the built-in issue queues that are part and parcel of `drupal.org` and Drupal 7 development, to channel these concerns toward the developers and graphic design people capable of solving them.

### `drupal.org` Face-Lifting

In parallel with this effort, `drupal.org` itself is undergoing a complete re-design. A special selection process finalized in the awarding of the task to a top design and information architecture firm, and they involved themselves heavily in finding feedback from the community as raw material for their process. They are discovering all the user roles in terms of different community types that interact with `drupal.org`, and the use cases governing that interaction. At the time of writing this book, this process was still in the early stages, but gaining enormous momentum.

A much improved `drupal.org`, the fundamental tool for both using and building Drupal, will no doubt emerge as the fruit of so much effort.

### Documentation Team

The whole problem of documentation is being faced squarely and with a great deal of awareness. Attempting to strike a balance between crowd sourcing and expertise in the development and accessibility of the Drupal handbooks, a whole community-based team, with its own e-mail list, IRC group, and other forms of communication and collaboration, is focusing its efforts on this dire need.

## Projecting Drupal 7 Contributed Module Battle Plans

Building on the solid base of Drupal 6 and the exciting new approaches taken in Drupal 7, the true value and WOW factor of Drupal 7 can only be made fully apparent by projecting what it will be like in terms of what module-level features may be supported by the new code base. In other words, Drupal 7 has become an incredible source of motivation and excitement among module developers.

From aggregators to Xbox aggregation, the whole atmosphere of creativity and refactoring has sparked a veritable movement. And modules are encouraged to be based on incredible engineering, involving flexibility, robustness, and extensibility. Take the aggregation module and its architecture commented by Alex Barth in the Development Seed blog (`www.developmentseed.org/blog/2008/aug/06/improved-aggregator-drupal-7-whats-under-hood`).

There is also a tendency for individual modules to develop synergy and work together. Take the Token module, for example, which exposes the hidden metadata and structure of a content item to the Content

Item Editing Form. Using the Node Title module, for example, one can select from all fields and metadata of a module to automatically generate its title from a formula made up of these tokens. For example, "`[field-make] [field-model] [field-year] Roundup`". And the Pathauto module also uses tokens to enable the administrative configuration of formulas upon which to base the SEO-friendly URL generation of content items on a semantic basis.

This is proof of a growing maturity in the framework. In preparation, many modules underwent a complete rewrite for Drupal 6, something that delayed the production-ready adoption of that release, but which has laid an incredible foundation. Both the Content Construction Kit and Views, for example (which will be in the core, for the most part, with the Drupal 7 release), were completely rewritten from the ground up. From this perspective, the groundwork and implementation of Drupal 7, not only in core, but in the hundreds of contributed modules that extend its functionality enormously and make for the versatility of the framework, have been literally years in the making.

The fact that this is an Open Source community–based project that owes its quality to the fact that development is distributed rather than obeying some "master plan" (that is, Bazaar- rather than Cathedral-based), needs to be stressed in these contexts. Those hoping that more rather than less functionality gets included in Drupal core should participate, even just by testing and providing problem descriptions and perhaps patches, as much as possible. The greater the community participation, the greater the amount of functionality stable enough to be included in the core when Drupal 7 is released.

# Installing Drupal 7

At the time of this writing, there has been no Drupal 7 release of any kind, and the only way of installing it is either by downloading a tarball snapshot or installing via CVS by checking out HEAD. The latter is highly recommended. The initial CVS checkout statement might look a bit cryptic and formidable, but afterward, a simple sweet and short CVS update statement is all you will need to keep abreast of up-to-the-minute development.

In order to create your litworkshop-7 document root, execute the following command from a parent directory:

```
$ cvs -z6 -d:pserver:anonymous:anonymous@cvs.drupal.org:/cvs/drupal checkout -d
litworkshop-7 drupal
```

Since no release is specified, HEAD is assumed.

In other words, these instructions will be the same for Drupal 8, 9, and beyond, before they are released, that is, while they are in active development. Of course, even though developers understand that Drupal cannot migrate its code base from CVS to a more modern version control system overnight, one would hope that beyond Drupal 7, or at least before Drupal 9 becomes a tangible possibility, there will be a migration to SVN or Git or some other more widely adopted present-day alternative.

Henceforward, in order to update your installation after finding out about important development news, simply change the directory to the document root and execute the following command:

```
~litworkshop-7 $ cvs update -dP
```

Couldn't be simpler, could it?

**In case you think that using the command line is only for geeks or is old hat, or passé, new developments highlight the fact that in many cases, it is the easiest, most natural, and certainly the most efficient way to go. In early Fall 2008, Firefox released its Ubiquity add-on, "an extension that allows for the use of dynamic commands in Firefox." This lends a whole new meaning to the expression, "have the world at your fingertips." For example, do you need to translate text you have selected on a page you are browsing? Simply type the add-on hot-key, and then type tr . . . Voilá. Need to calculate something real quick? 2 + 2 = 4! Just like the command line!**

# Developing a Minimalist On-Line Literary Workshop in Drupal 7

Instead of attempting to upgrade the current Drupal 6 version of the On-Line Literary Workshop, let's quickly attempt to develop a minimalist version based on Drupal 7.

Create a database and database user for this installation either on the command line or by using PhpMyAdmin, or similar.

*It bears repeating: To create a new MySQL database and database user all in one, go to Privileges, "Add a New User," and remember to check the "Create database with the same name and grant all privileges" radio button option before hitting the Go button. And you are all set to go.*

1. If you are working on your own workstation or laptop, or virtual or dedicated server, create a virtual host, or if you are working in a shared hosting environment, create a new subdomain, called *litworkshop7*, and point your browser to the document root.

   On a Ubuntu workstation or laptop, one way is to simply add the following to /etc/apache2/sites-enabled/000-default:

```
<VirtualHost *>
  ServerName litworkshop7.hostname
  DocumentRoot /home/victorkane/Work/Wiley/litworkshop-7
  <Directory "/home/victorkane/Work/Wiley/litworkshop-7">
    Options Indexes MultiViews FollowSymLinks
    AllowOverride All
    Order deny,allow
    Deny from all
    allow from all
  </Directory>
</VirtualHost>
```

2. Then perform:

```
$ sudo apache2ctl restart
```

3. Add litworkshop7.hostname to /etc/hosts in order to complete the pseudo-subdomain in your development environment.

Your browser now points to the installation screen, which asks you to select an installation profile, as in Figure 13-1.

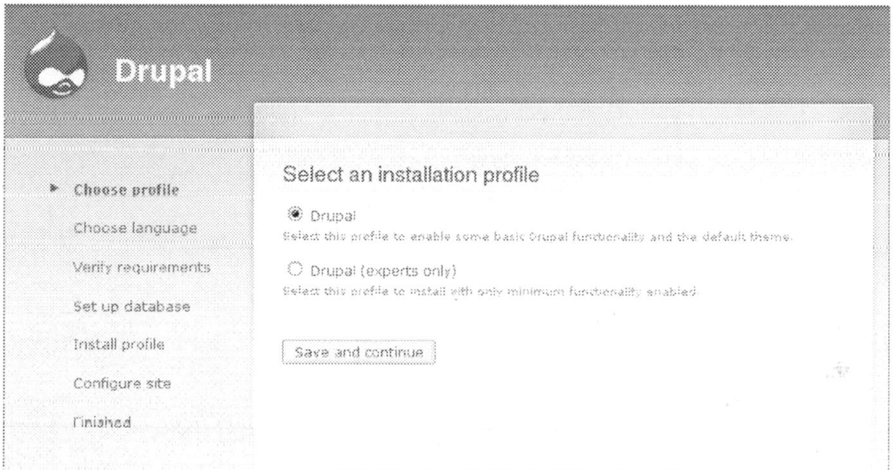


Figure 13-1

4. Leaving the "Drupal (experts only)" option, exciting as it is, for another time, select Drupal, and press the "Save and continue" button. On the next screen, click "Install Drupal in English." More than likely, you will see the error message shown in Figure 13-2.

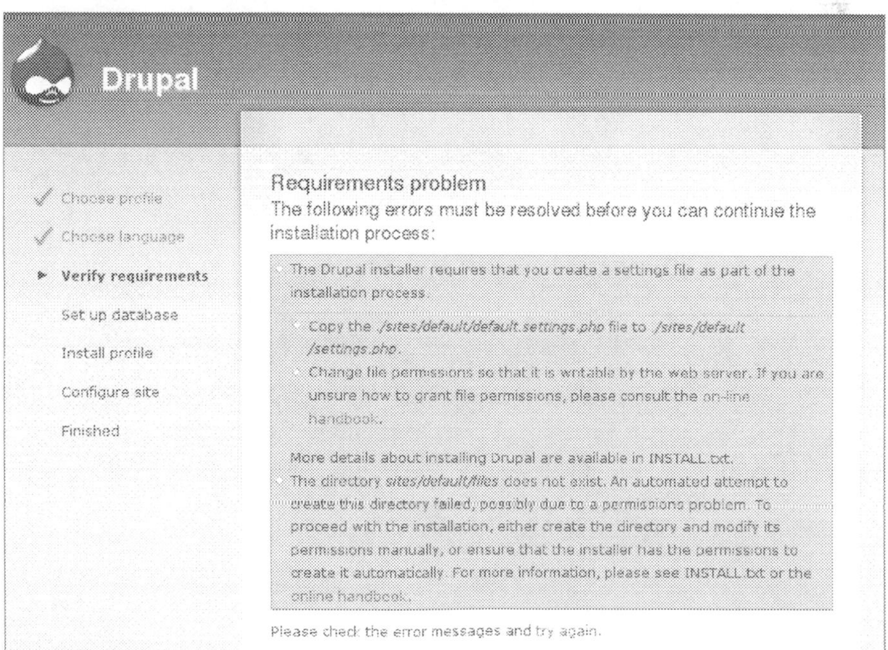


Figure 13-2

5. Well, the Webmaster hasn't been dispatched quite yet. If you have to make the file writable, why not make the directory writable and have the install process take care of the whole thing? OK, gripes aside (reminder to place in issue queue), copy ./sites/default/default.settings.php to ./sites/default/settings.php, and make it writable by the web server. Also, create the ./sites/default/files directory, and make it permanently writable by the web server.

The steps you could take on a Ubuntu workstation would be the following:

1. From the document root:

```
$ mkdir sites/default/files
$ sudo chown www-data:www-data sites/default/files
$ cp sites/default/default.settings.php sites/default/settings.php
$ sudo chmod 666 sites/default/settings.php
```

*"666" means Read + Write privileges for owner, group, and others. "www-data" is the default user for the Apache HTTP server process. However, you can easily configure permissions and other settings using your favorite file manager, as shown in Figure 13-3 (Dolphin/Konqueror in Ubuntu/Kubuntu).*

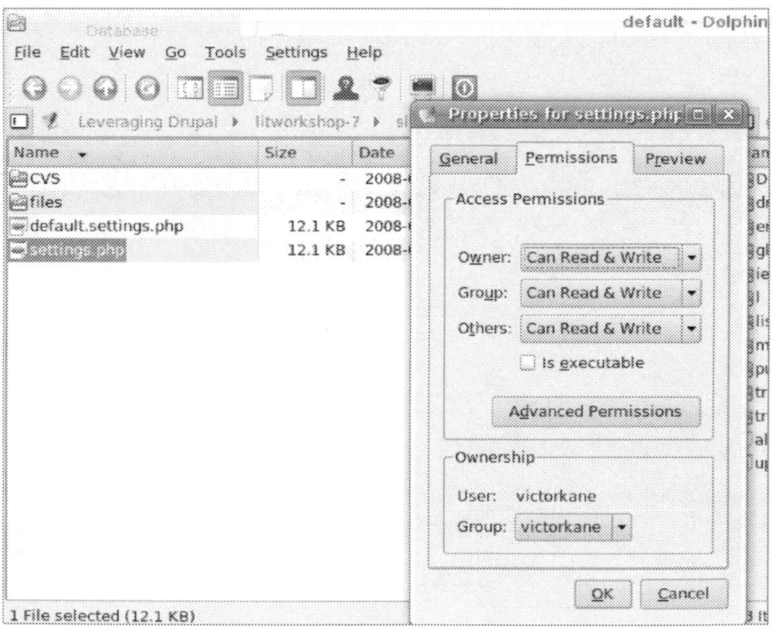

Figure 13-3

2. After completing the installation process, you will "seal up" the settings.php file by removing Write permissions for all users except Owner:

```
$ sudo chmod 644 sites/default/settings.php
```

3. Click "Try again" until you are presented with the Database configuration screen familiar to the Drupal installation process. Click "Advanced options" if you need to specify a remote host, if your database is on a different server, if you need to specify the database port, or if you wish to specify a table prefix so that multiple applications can share the same database. Otherwise, fill in the Database name, username, and password; and click on the "Save and continue" button.
4. You may now configure the site, as in the Drupal 6 installation process, after which, click on the "Save and continue" button. You should see the Drupal installation complete screen, with an error message if Drupal could not send an e-mail notification to the newly created Admin user. Click on the "Your new site" link.

> **If you are installing Drupal off-line, then it is important that you do *not* select "Check for updates automatically"; otherwise, you will be subjected to interminable delays as Drupal tries to connect to `drupal.org` in order to ascertain the update status for the core and modules. You can enable the Update Status module at any time, when you are going to be working on-line.**

5. Go to Administer ➢ Site configuration ➢ Site information, and establish the Site name (On-Line Literary Workshop 7) and slogan (Publish or Perish!).

Drupal 7 has now been successfully installed!

# Creating Literary Pieces

The main goal here is to create the Literary Piece content type and simply have it displayed automatically on the front page for now.

1. Go to the main Administration page. The first thing you notice is that the Content Types link (where you manage the content types that come with Drupal, now Article and Page, as well as the ones you create yourself), which used to be on the left-hand side in the Content Management category, has now been included on the right-hand side in the "Site building" category (see Figure 13-4). This is in answer to the usability concerns mentioned in that section earlier on in the chapter.
2. Go ahead and click the "Content types" link. You can see the off-the-shelf content types listed there, Article and Page (as opposed to Story and Page in Drupal 6 and earlier). Click on the "Add content type" tab.

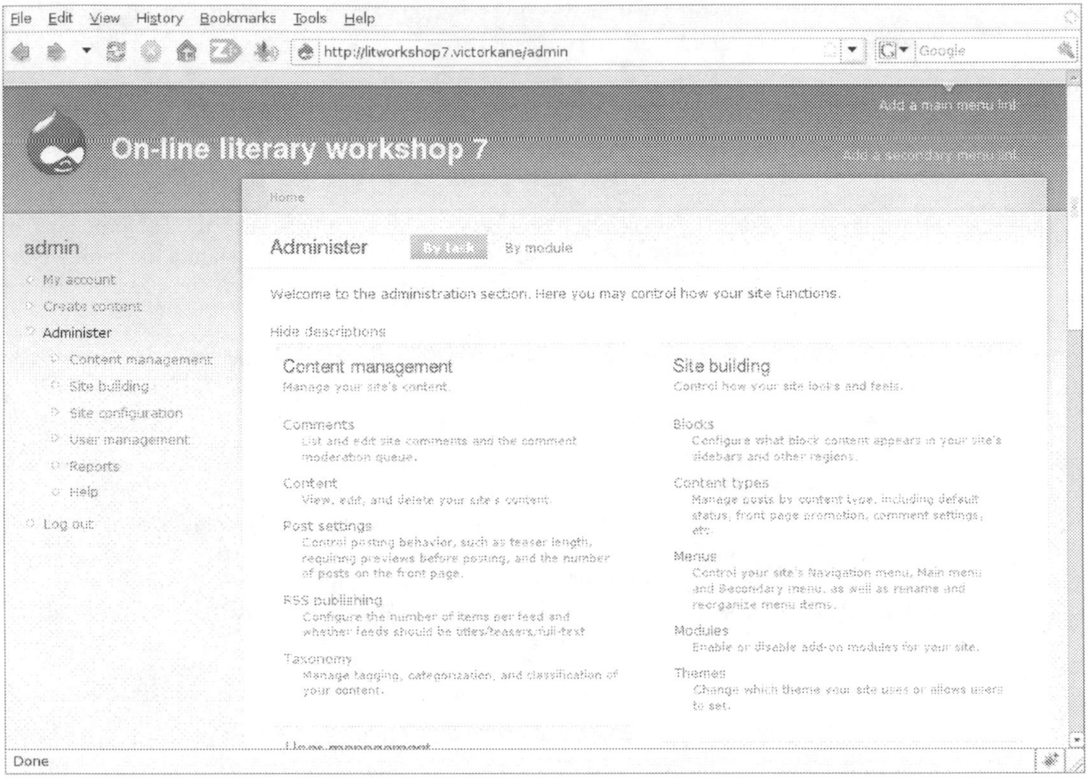


Figure 13-4

3. Type **Literary Piece** in the Name field, and **literary_piece** in the Machine name field. Type **A literary piece a member submits for critique or for possible submission to publications** into the Description field.

4. Open up the "Submission form settings" section. Leave **Title** in the Title field label field, and instead of removing **Body** from the Body field label field as you have done up till now, go ahead and change its label to *Text* by typing **Text** in the body field label field. This is because, unfortunately, at the time of this writing, it is not yet possible to add fields to a custom content type. This functionality is expected shortly in the core in Drupal 7. For now, leave the Workflow and Comments sections at their default values, and click on the "Save content type" button.

5. Go to Create Content, and click on the Literary Piece link. Create a few literary pieces. Then click on the site name in order to return to the front page, and you should see something like Figure 13-5. Not very exciting, to be sure, but we are already running Drupal 7!

Once content types can have fields added to them in Drupal core, it is expected that Views will quickly follow (without the User Interface, which will still be available as a contributed module). Then, it will be possible to create business objects and listings, all without installing any contributed modules at all.

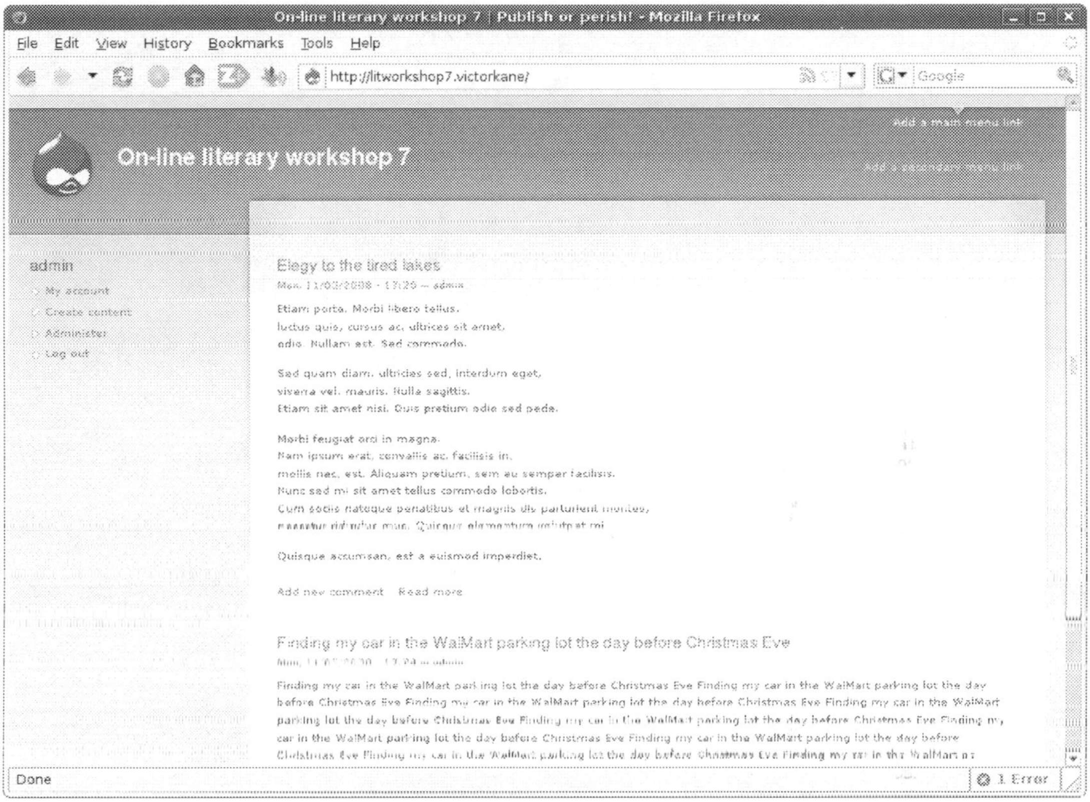


Figure 13-5

# Summary

In this chapter, you have met "The One" — the rock-solid, dependable, powerful and extensible, hugely usable off-the-shelf, killer CMS Framework application, as a community at work, as a blueprint, as a prototype, and as the basis for a minimalistic but fully functional application. You have been introduced to the concerns and sources of inspiration as nothing less than the elimination of dependencies on the tech-savvy "Webmaster" who is necessary for changing even a comma on a site's content, and the concerns that first-time users find Drupal not only powerful, but easy to use: easy enough, that is, to stay with Drupal and to choose it definitively over the competition. And for good reason. You have also seen how this effort is anything but cosmetic, or even confined to the presentation or usability layers (e.g., the inclusion of off-the-shelf WYSIWYG editor) having far-reaching consequences in terms of a complete architectural refactoring effort spanning, indeed, several years, and exemplified by the object-oriented paradigm used in the new Database API, on the one hand, and the Views module, on the other. The inclusion and definitive incorporation of at least basic Views and Content Construction Kit (fields can be added to forms and content types) components, together with the new Database API, for example, show a slow, evolutionary, but definitive trend toward overcoming complexity explosion breakdown via the gradual and case-proven adoption of the object-oriented paradigm itself.

# 14

# Deploying your Application as a Drupal Installation Profile

The goal of this chapter is to comply with the tasks and user stories outlined in the Deployment phase of our project plan. The best way to deploy a website application based on Drupal is by creating an installation profile, and by leveraging the Advanced Help module for context-sensitive help and training.

In the case of the On-Line Literary Workshop, the project you have been building by working your way through this book, I have actually created a downloadable installation profile on the Drupal site, as a way of giving back to the community, so that others may use and help improve the project, and, as always, as a way of obtaining feedback from the community on actual use and thereby enhance quality.

In this chapter, you will learn how to create an installation profile (a.k.a. *distribution profile*) for the On-Line Literary Workshop, how to use it as a deployment tool, and how to use the Advanced Help module as a way of providing on-line context-sensitive help for your users.

## Leveraging the Advanced Help Module

You saw earlier that the Views 2 module, deployed in Drupal starting with release 6.x, optionally uses the Advanced Help module to provide context-sensitive help in the form of stand-alone HTML files accessible via a question-mark icon in all sections of its interactive pages.

Earl Miles, the creator of Views, Panels, and Nodequeue, did not artificially bind his new Help system to the Views module, but instead thoughtfully abstracted it out into a module in its own right, and explains in the documentation that any module can use it.

"Although no general help is available," there is a breadcrumb on every pop-up Help window, whose root is Help. Clicking that link will display a list of modules implementing their own Help system, including the Help module itself. Among the modules supporting help is Advanced Help, which provides valuable assistance. The section "Implementing the On-Line Literary Workshop Help System" explains how any module may easily provide its own context-sensitive help.

## Analyzing the Components of the Views 2 Help System

If you go to Administer ➤ Site building ➤ Views and the Advanced Help module is enabled, you will see a series of question-mark icons next to each entry in the listing of available views on the system, all of which point to the Views-type pop-up Help entry. When you edit a view, for example, love_letter_detector, you will see that each section has a question-mark icon. For example, clicking the icon found in the Relationships section brings up Help ➤ Views ➤ What is Views? ➤ Relationships.

Following what is succinctly explained in the Advanced Help module help (Help ➤ Advanced help ➤ Using advanced help), any module wishing to implement Advanced Help must create a subdirectory, into which an .ini configuration file is placed, along with help-specific HTML, CSS, and image files.

Accordingly, a visit to ./sites/all/modules/views detects the presence of a subdirectory "help," in which can be found a views.help.ini file, together with a host of HTML files, plus a subdirectory of images files.

You can gain insight by studying the Help ➤ Views help index window (see Figure 14-1) in comparison with the following initial fragment of the views.help.ini file:

```
[about]
title = "What is Views?"
weight = -40

[getting-started]
title = "Getting started"
weight = -45

[view-type]
title = "View types"

[display]
title = "Displays"
weight = -30

[display-default]
title = "Default display"
parent = display
weight = -20

[display-page]
title = "Page display"
parent = display
weight = -15
```

```
[display-block]
title = "Block display"
parent = display
weight = -10

[display-attachment]
title = "Attachment display"
parent = display

[display-feed]
title = "Feed display"
parent = display
```

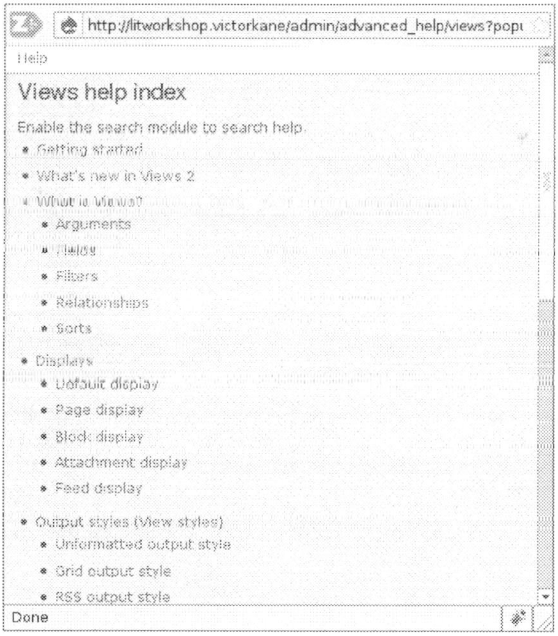


Figure 14-1

## Planning the On-Line Literary Workshop Help System

You have already created a `litworkshop` module as a utility module to place various elements, including jQuery support functions. That will be the place to house the Help system, in a subdirectory help.

As an example, you can provide a clickable on-line Help icon for the title field of the Application form, which has already been embellished with a jQuery validation component.

There will be one entry concerning the Application Form in general, and children help files for various topics.

# Implementing the On-Line Literary Workshop Help System

Creating a custom Help system forms an important part of the deployment process, since on-line, context-sensitive help will greatly enhance the user experience. Thanks to the Advanced Help module, created by Earl Miles for the Views 2 module Help system and then abstracted out into its own module as a stroke of genius, it is quite straightforward to implement. You first create an .ini file in a directory called *help* inside your module structure (i.e., ./sites/all/modules/your module/help). This .ini file will have one entry for each Help page, which have to be written in basic HTML with any HTML editor. The last step is to insert the links to these pages together with a "?" icon into the proper contexts throughout your website.

## Creating the .ini File

Create the directory ./sites/all/modules/litworkshop/help, and place the following .ini file in this directory:

```
[about-litworkshop]
title = About the On-line Literary Workshop
file = about-litworkshop
weight = -10

[applying]
title = Why it is necessary to apply to Join the On-Line Literary Workshop
file = applying
parent = about-litworkshop
weight = 1

[application-form]
title = How to fill out your application form
file = starting-group
parent = about-litworkshop
weight = 2

[getting-started]
title = Getting started
file = getting-started
weight = 1

[joining-group]
title = Joining a literary affinity group
file = joining-group
weight = 2

[starting-group]
title = Starting your own literary affinity group
file = starting-group
weight = 3
```

## Creating One HTML File for Each Entry

Each Help page is written in pure HTML and corresponds to a single entry in the .ini file, as mentioned above.

A file listing of the help subdirectory for the On-Line Literary Workshop module is:

```
litworkshop/sites/all/modules/litworkshop/help$ ls
about-litworkshop.html  getting-started.html  starting-group.html
application-form.html   joining-group.html
applying.html           litworkshop.help.ini
```

Each file consists of pure HTML text (no need for <HTML>, <HEAD>, or <BODY> tags):

```
litworkshop/sites/all/modules/litworkshop/help$ cat about-litworkshop.html
<p>
The On-Line Literary Workshop is a creative social network oriented
 community center where all those who are interested in getting lots
 of practice at writing and critiquing, for fun and profit, as well
as publishing their best literary pieces, are welcome.
</p>
<p>
Publishers hoping to find new talent as well as a place to publish an
on-line literary magazine, are also welcome members of the community.
</p>
```

## Theming in the On-Line Help Icon

Now, add a theming function for the form, and theme in a clickable on-line Help icon pointing to the module's on-line Help. As you remember from the jQuery chapter, the validation system was implemented via `hook_form_alter` by intercepting the rendering and modifying the application form itself. Now, you can add a single statement to add in the little clickable Help icon that invokes the new context-sensitive help item. According to "Using Advanced Help," the following PHP statement will embed a help link:

```
$output .= theme('advanced_help_topic', $module, $topic);
```

Our complete `hook_form_alter` function now looks like this:

```
function litworkshop_form_alter(&$form, &$form_state, $form_id) {
  switch ($form_id) {
    case 'application_node_form':
      //Load jQuery Validation plugin
      $path = drupal_get_path('module', 'litworkshop');
      jquery_plugin_add('metadata');
      jquery_plugin_add('validate');
      //drupal_add_js($path . '/javascript/do_validate.js');
      drupal_add_js (
      '$(document).ready(function(){
         $("#node-form").validate();
       }); ',
      'inline');
      // Specify how to register each field.
      $form['title']['#attributes'] = array('class' => 'required email');
      // Prefix help markup to Title field
      $form['title']['#prefix'] = '<h5>' .
```

```
          theme('advanced_help_topic', 'litworkshop', 'about-litworkshop') .
         ' Find out more about the On-line literary workshop</h5>';
          break;
        default:
          break;
      }
    }
```

The #prefix Form API property is used to simply . . . prefix the markup output by the advanced help topic theming function for the litworkshop module, invoking the about-litworkshop topic.

Figure 14-2 shows how, as a result, the embedded Help icon appears in the Application Form when you click on the Join! menu item.

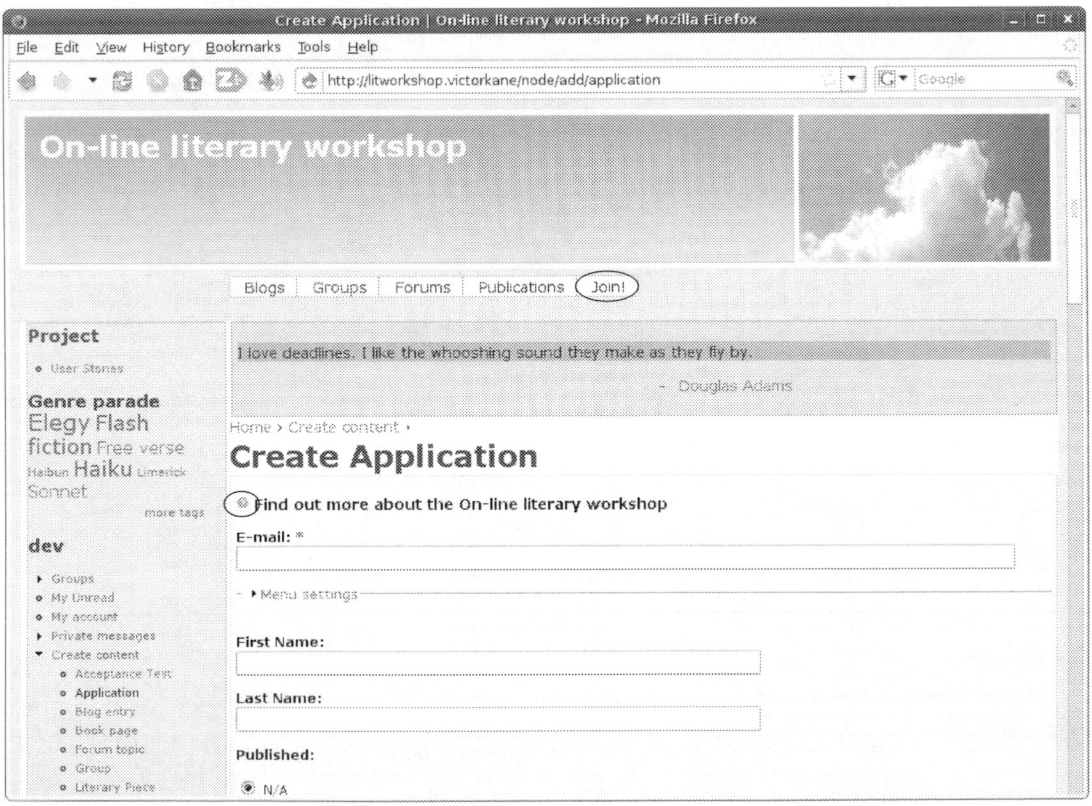


Figure 14-2

Figure 14-3 shows the result of clicking on the embedded Help icon.

Figure 14-4 shows the results of clicking on the On-Line Literary Workshop breadcrumb element.

Your on-line context-sensitive Help system is ready for deployment! Just edit the separate HTML help files, and you are all set to go!

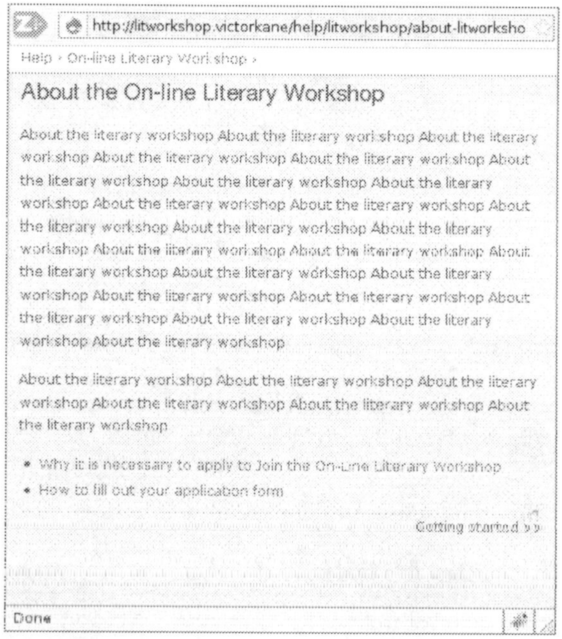

Figure 14-3

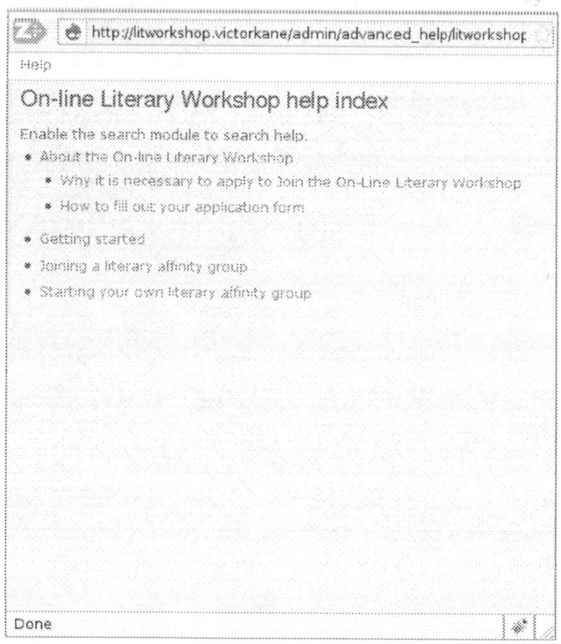

Figure 14-4

# Installing Profiles! Kill the Webmaster!

There's that violent phrase again. Once touted as the ultimate webmaster-slayer in Drupal land, installation profiles would enable a user to download a tarball, install it as she would a fresh Drupal release, but be provided instead with a series of built-in configurations and third-party modules all set up to provide a specific kind of feature set (an on-line newspaper, a pastebin-like application for sharing code snippets, an on-line community, a blog, etc.). This would be huge: A user with no knowledge whatsoever of Drupal could be provided with an off-the-shelf solution for her needs.

However, for some reason, the offerings have been sparse, indeed. Very few installation profiles have been published. Just the plain difficulty level, along with certain gotchas and caveats may go toward explaining why folks are just finding it simpler to do a MySQL dump and simply tarball the Drupal installation and make that available instead. But an installation profile allows you to use the latest, and hence most secure, version of Drupal instead of the one that happened to be used in development, and it is still something that you can definitely leverage to your advantage. Calls are constantly being made for developers to make use of this mode of website application distribution, which would do much to broaden the Drupal user base.

## What Are Installation Profiles?

*Installation profiles* are simply scripts located in the aptly named *profiles* directory, with the suffix .profile, which are designed to programmatically configure Drupal, install and enable modules, and so on, as if someone were following these steps interactively in a browser window.

When you install Drupal (that is, point your browser at the root directory of a freshly unpacked Drupal tarball), you are given a choice of all the installation profiles found in the profile directory. If translation subdirectories are found (e.g., a Spanish translation: .translations/es.po), they are installed also.

The best way to understand what they are is to analyze an existing one. The next section analyzes drupalbin, an installation profile that can be downloaded from `drupal.org`.

## Analyzing Drupalbin: An Example Installation Profile

The drupalbin installation profile is found at `http://drupal.org/project/drupalbin`. It consists of the following:

```
'-- drupalbin
    |-- LICENSE.txt
    |-- README.txt
    '-- drupalbin.profile
```

The profile is simply a PHP file with a series of functions that Drupal executes as it goes through the steps of the installation process. Like most installation profiles, it is patterned on the default Drupal installation profile file. Here is the drupalbin.profile file:

```
<?php
// $Id: drupalbin.profile,v 1.1.4.2 2008/04/02 17:35:36 robloach Exp $

/**
 * @file
```

```
 * Install Profile for DrupalBin - http://drupalbin.com
 */

/**
 * Return an array of the modules to be enabled when this profile is installed.
 *
 * @return
 *  An array of modules to be enabled.
 */
function drupalbin_profile_modules() {
  return array(
    // Core - required
    'block', 'filter', 'node', 'system', 'user',

    // Core - optional
    'color', 'help', 'menu', 'path', 'search', 'taxonomy',

    // GeSHi Filter
    'geshifilter', 'geshinode',

    // Other
    'token', 'pathauto', 'auto_nodetitle', 'clone', 'print'
  );
}

/**
 * Return a description of the profile for the initial installation screen.
 *
 * @return
 *   An array with keys 'name' and 'description' describing this profile.
 */
function drupalbin_profile_details() {
  return array(
    'name' => 'DrupalBin',
    'description' => 'Tool to collaborate and debug code snippets.'
  );
}

/**
 * Return a list of tasks that this profile supports.
 *
 * @return
 *   A keyed array of tasks the profile will perform during
 *   the final stage. The keys of the array will be used internally,
 *   while the values will be displayed to the user in the installer
 *   task list.
 */
function drupalbin_profile_task_list() {
}

/**
 * Perform any final installation tasks for this profile.
 *
 * @param $task
 *   The current $task of the install system. When hook_profile_tasks()
```

```
 *   is first called, this is 'profile'.
 * @param $url
 *   Complete URL to be used for a link or form action on a custom page,
 *   if providing any, to allow the user to proceed with the installation.
 *
 * @return
 *   An optional HTML string to display to the user. Only used if you
 *   modify the $task, otherwise discarded.
 */
function drupalbin_profile_tasks(&$task, $url) {
  // Site information
  variable_set('site_mission', 'Post a code snippet.');
  variable_set('site_frontpage', 'node/add/geshinode');

  // Permissions
  db_query("UPDATE {permission} SET perm = '%s' WHERE rid = %d",
    'create source code node, access content, clone node, search content', 1);
  db_query("UPDATE {permission} SET perm = '%s' WHERE rid = %d",
    'create source code node, edit own source code node, access \
 content, clone node, search content', 2);

  // Taxonomy
  $tags = array(
    'name' => 'Tags',
    'help' => 'Any tags you would like to associate with your code,  \
delimitered by commas (example: Views, CCK, Module, etc).',
    'relations' => '0',
    'hierarchy' => '1',
    'multiple' => '0',
    'required' => '0',
    'tags' => '1',
    'module' => 'taxonomy',
    'weight' => '0',
    'nodes' => array('geshinode' => 'geshinode')
  );
  taxonomy_save_vocabulary($tags);

  // PathAuto
  variable_set('pathauto_node_geshinode_pattern', '[nid]');

  // Automatic Node Titles
  variable_set('ant_geshinode', '2');
  variable_set('ant_pattern_geshinode', 'Code');

  // String Overrides
  variable_set('locale_custom_strings_en',
    array(
      'Printer-friendly version' => 'Download',
    )
  );
}
```

All the functions are prefixed with the installation profile name (the same as the subdirectory under ./profiles):

- `drupalbin_profile_modules()` — The first function, `drupalbin_profile_modules()`, returns an array of modules, present in the ./sites/all/modules directory of the installation tarball, which should be enabled automatically.
- `drupalbin_profile_details()` — The second function, `drupalbin_profile_details()`, returns, as the comment says, the name and description of the installation profile so that it can appear in the list of available profiles, if Drupal finds more than one.
- `drupalbin_profile_task_list()` — The third function, `drupalbin_profile_task_list()`, returns a list of tasks to appear on the left-hand side of the screen, and marked as done by Drupal as the installation process advances. While this is not used here, you will be using it in your own Literary Workshop installation profile.
- `drupalbin_profile_tasks()` — The last function, `drupalbin_profile_tasks()`, first sets some variables, such as the *Site mission*, then sets up some permissions by inserting them directly into the permission database table. Next, a taxonomy vocabulary called *Tags* is created, a pathauto pattern is set, and the automatic nodetitle module is configured. Finally, the default English locale string Printer-friendly version is customized to read as "Download" (this is logical for a code paste bin–type of application).

# Writing the On-Line Literary Workshop Installation Profile

It's time to write your own installation profile for the On-Line Literary Workshop, which will aid not only in deployment, but also in sharing this development with others who can download it from `drupal.org`. The benefits, apart from scoring karma points, are that the more people who use this website application, the more suggestions and bug fixes will come flowing in, improving its quality continually.

To accomplish this, follow the steps outlined in the following subsections, which deal with a clean Drupal installation as the starting point, how to add in the modules and themes that form part of the installation profile, how to include your views as versionable text files easily installed when the user follows the installation procedure, how to prepare the various directories and the scripts that belong there, and finally, how to create the Drupal installation tarball itself.

## Starting with a Clean Drupal Installation Tarball

The first thing to do is to unpack a Drupal 6.x release installation tarball into a working directory. When you have finished your installation profile, it can be tarred up again for easy download. If you want to publish the installation profile on `http://drupal.org` itself, you only need publish the contents to be placed under the ./profile directory. But the goal here is to create a convenient tarball that may be downloaded, with modules and everything. (As always, you may download this as the code corresponding to this chapter, even though the profile is published on `http://drupal.org`.)

Following the Drupal naming convention, the parent of the document root, that is, the root node of the installation profile tarball, is named in the following manner:

```
.
'-- drupal-litworkshop-6.4-1.0
    |-- CHANGELOG.txt
    |-- COPYRIGHT.txt
    |-- INSTALL.mysql.txt
    |-- INSTALL.pgsql.txt
    |-- INSTALL.txt
    |-- LICENSE.txt
    |-- MAINTAINERS.txt
    |-- UPGRADE.txt
    |-- cron.php
    |-- includes
    |-- index.php
    |-- install.php
    |-- misc
    |-- modules
    |-- profiles
    |-- robots.txt
    |-- scripts
    |-- sites
    |-- themes
    |-- update.php
    '-- xmlrpc.php
```

## Copying in the Modules and the Theme

Copy into drupal-litworkshop-6.4-1.0/sites/all/modules all the modules, including the custom litworkshop module. Copy into drupal-litworkshop-6.4-1.0/sites/all/themes the Zen theme and `zenlitworkshop` subtheme.

### What about the .svn Subdir cruft?

Since ./sites/modules and ./sites/themes constitute a working copy of the SVN repository, you need a simple way to copy them to the distribution profile without all the .svn subdirs (where subversion stores all its metadata). `svn export` command to the rescue! For this purpose, the following form is best:

```
$ svn export WORKING-COPY-PATH DESTINATION-PATH
```

This will export the working copy path at revision WORKING to DESTINATION-PATH, a directory that should not exist. For example:

```
$ cd sites
$ svn export modules /tmp/modules
$ svn export themes /tmp/themes
```

Then the directories may be simply copied into the installation profile filesystem under sites.

## Abstracting out the Views into the litworkshop Module

Real women and men don't leave their views in the database.

It's going to be a lot simpler for our installation profile, and for views reuse in general, to abstract out the views we have developed for the On-Line Literary Workshop website application into text files associated with the litworkshop module, via an implementation of `hook_views_default_views()`.

By implementing this hook in a file named according to the file-naming convention found in the Views API and returning an array of views expressed as code, views can be stored in text files rather than configuration settings stored in the database.

To carry this out in the On-Line Literary Workshop, you need to carry out the following steps:

1. Export all the views germane to our application, and transform the output from the export process into code stored in a text file. (In Administer ➤ Site building ➤ Views, each enabled view listed has an Export link.)
2. Write a function implementing `hook_views_default_views()` so that the views cache mechanism will pick up the views, in the same way as those specified by Organic Groups, for example.

The standard way to do this is documented in the file docs.php found in the Views module docs subdirectory. The following function needs to be placed in a file named *MODULENAME.views_default.inc* and will auto-load provided it is found in the module directory or in a subdirectory called *includes*:

```
 function hook_views_default_views() {
  // Begin copy and paste of output from the Export tab of a view.
  $view = new view;
  $view->name = 'frontpage';
...
  // End copy and paste of Export tab output.

  // Add view to list of views to provide.
  $views[$view->name] = $view;

  // ...Repeat all of the above for each view the module should provide.

  // At the end, return array of default views.
  return $views;
}
```

However,

```
<?php
// $Id$

// "Borrowed" from og_views module by Moshe Weitzman
// Declare all the .view files in the views subdir that end in .view
function litworkshop_views_default_views() {
  $files = file_scan_directory(drupal_get_path('module',
 'litworkshop'). '/views', '.view');
  foreach ($files as $absolute => $file) {
```

```
      require $absolute;
      $views[$view->name] = $view;
    }
    return $views;
  }
```

This will be run once by the views cache mechanism and will automatically include and enable all the views present as text files with extension .view in the ./sites/all/modules/litworkshop/views subdirectory.

All that is left to do is to place the views *include* file in the module directory structure, as shown below.

## Exporting the Website Application Views

The views developed thus far are the following:

- genre_browser
- love_letter_detector
- og_ghp_table
- user_stories

Export and place the resulting code of each view into a separate .view text file in the views subdirectory as shown above. Then, delete each view. (Don't worry if you are trying this out on the test site — that's why you use Subversion for version control.) Don't forget, these are php files and require the appropriate prefixed heading, as usual:

```
<?php
// $Id$
$view = new view;
...
```

## The Views Include File

Add the file litworkshop.views_default.inc as shown above.

The litworkshop module now comprises the following files:

```
litworkshop/
|-- help
|   |-- about-litworkshop.html
|   |-- application-form.html
|   |-- applying.html
|   |-- getting-started.html
|   |-- joining-group.html
|   |-- litworkshop.help.ini
|   '-- starting-group.html
|-- litworkshop.info
|-- litworkshop.module
|-- litworkshop.views_default.inc
'-- views
    |-- genre_browser.view
```

```
    |-- love_letter_detector.view
    |-- og_ghp_table.view
    '-- user_stories.view
2 directories, 14 files
```

*You may need to go to Administer ➤ Site building ➤ Views ➤ Tools and hit the "Clear views cache" button in order for these views to reappear in the Administer ➤ Site building ➤ Views list.*

## Preparing the ./profile Directory

Regarding the ./profile directory itself, since you do not want people having to choose which profile to install, but rather wish to automate the whole installation, the first thing to do might be to delete the contents of the ./profiles/default directory so that the only installation profile Drupal will find is your own.

More practically, rename the default subdirectory to *literaryworkshop*, and the name of the .profile file to *literaryworkshop.profile*. Do likewise with the prefix of each function. Your profile directory should look like this:

```
profiles
'-- literaryworkshop
    '-- literaryworkshop.profile
```

Your starting literaryworkshop.profile should look like this:

```
<?php
// $Id$

/**
 * Return an array of the modules to be enabled when this profile is installed.
 *
 * @return
 *   An array of modules to enable.
 */
function literaryworkshop_profile_modules() {
  return array('color', 'comment', 'help', 'menu', 'taxonomy', 'dblog');
}

/**
 * Return a description of the profile for the initial installation screen.
 *
 * @return
 *   An array with keys 'name' and 'description' describing this profile,
 *   and optional 'language' to override the language selection for
 *   language-specific profiles.
 */
function literaryworkshop_profile_details() {
  return array(
    'name' => 'Drupal',
    'description' => 'Select this profile to enable some basic \
Drupal functionality and the default theme.'
  );
}
```

```
/**
 * Return a list of tasks that this profile supports.
 *
 * @return
 *   A keyed array of tasks the profile will perform during
 *   the final stage. The keys of the array will be used internally,
 *   while the values will be displayed to the user in the installer
 *   task list.
 */
function literaryworkshop_profile_task_list() {
}

/**
 * Perform any final installation tasks for this profile.
 *
 * The installer goes through the profile-select -> locale-select
 * -> requirements -> database -> profile-install-batch
 * -> locale-initial-batch -> configure -> locale-remaining-batch
 * -> finished -> done tasks, in this order, if you don't implement
 * this function in your profile.
 *
 * If this function is implemented, you can have any number of
 * custom tasks to perform after 'configure', implementing a state
 * machine here to walk the user through those tasks. First time,
 * this function gets called with $task set to 'profile', and you
 * can advance to further tasks by setting $task to your tasks'
 * identifiers, used as array keys in the hook_profile_task_list()
 * above. You must avoid the reserved tasks listed in
 * install_reserved_tasks(). If you implement your custom tasks,
 * this function will get called in every HTTP request (for form
 * processing, printing your information screens and so on) until
 * you advance to the 'profile-finished' task, with which you
 * hand control back to the installer. Each custom page you
 * return needs to provide a way to continue, such as a form
 * submission or a link. You should also set custom page titles.
 *
 * You should define the list of custom tasks you implement by
 * returning an array of them in hook_profile_task_list(), as these
 * show up in the list of tasks on the installer user interface.
 *
 * Remember that the user will be able to reload the pages multiple
 * times, so you might want to use variable_set() and variable_get()
 * to remember your data and control further processing, if $task
 * is insufficient. Should a profile want to display a form here,
 * it can; the form should set '#redirect' to FALSE, and rely on
 * an action in the submit handler, such as variable_set(), to
 * detect submission and proceed to further tasks. See the configuration
 * form handling code in install_tasks() for an example.
 *
 * Important: Any temporary variables should be removed using
 * variable_del() before advancing to the 'profile-finished' phase.
 *
 * @param $task
 *   The current $task of the install system. When hook_profile_tasks()
 *   is first called, this is 'profile'.
```

```
 * @param $url
 *   Complete URL to be used for a link or form action on a custom page,
 *   if providing any, to allow the user to proceed with the installation.
 *
 * @return
 *   An optional HTML string to display to the user. Only used if you
 *   modify the $task, otherwise discarded.
 */
function literaryworkshop_profile_tasks(&$task, $url) {

  // Insert default user-defined node types into the database. For a complete
  // list of available node type attributes, refer to the node type API
  // documentation at: http://api.drupal.org/api/HEAD/function/hook_node_info.
  $types = array(
    array(
      'type' => 'page',
      'name' => st('Page'),
      'module' => 'node',
      'description' => st("A <em>page</em>, similar in form to a
 <em>story</em>, is a simple method for creating and displaying
information that rarely changes, such as an \"About us\" section
 of a website. By default, a <em>page</em> entry does not allow
visitor comments and is not featured on the site's initial home
 page."),

      'custom' => TRUE,
      'modified' => TRUE,
      'locked' => FALSE,
      'help' => '',
      'min_word_count' => '',
    ),
    array(
      'type' => 'story',
      'name' => st('Story'),
      'module' => 'node',
      'description' => st("A <em>story</em>, similar in form to a \
<em>page</em>, is ideal for creating and displaying content that
informs or engages website visitors. Press releases, site
announcements, and informal blog-like entries may all be
created with a <em>story</em> entry. By default, a <em>story</em>
 entry is automatically featured on the site's initial home
page, and provides the ability to post comments."),

      'custom' => TRUE,
      'modified' => TRUE,
      'locked' => FALSE,
      'help' => '',
      'min_word_count' => '',
    ),
  );

  foreach ($types as $type) {
    $type = (object) _node_type_set_defaults($type);
    node_type_save($type);
  }
```

```
  // Default page to not be promoted and have comments disabled.
  variable_set('node_options_page', array('status'));
  variable_set('comment_page', COMMENT_NODE_DISABLED);

  // Don't display date and author information for page nodes by default.
  $theme_settings = variable_get('theme_settings', array());
  $theme_settings['toggle_node_info_page'] = FALSE;
  variable_set('theme_settings', $theme_settings);

  // Update the menu router information.
  menu_rebuild();
}

/**
 * Implementation of hook_form_alter().
 *
 * Allows the profile to alter the site-configuration form. This is
 * called through custom invocation, so $form_state is not populated.
 */
function literaryworkshop_form_alter(&$form, $form_state, $form_id) {
  if ($form_id == 'install_configure') {
    // Set default for site name field.
    $form['site_information']['site_name']['#default_value'] =
$_SERVER['SERVER_NAME'];
  }
}
```

At this point, you have to ask yourself the question: What constitutes the On-Line Literary Workshop website application? The following need to be specified:

- Modules
- Content items
- Taxonomy vocabularies and their terms
- Nodequeues
- Variables
- The theme

Views have been abstracted out and dealt with separately, so they do not have to be dealt with by the profile script.

The `details` function is as follows:

```
function literaryworkshop_profile_details() {
  return array(
    'name' => 'Drupal (On-line Literary Workshop)',
    'description' => 'Select this profile to enable the On-line  \
Literary Workshop and the literary workshop theme.'
  );
}
```

The `modules` function is as follows (Drupal searches in all the usual places, plus in a modules directory under the installation profile directory itself; you are using ./sites/all/modules):

```
function literaryworkshop_profile_modules() {
    // Core - required
    'block', 'filter', 'node', 'system', 'user',

    // Core - optional
    'blog', 'book', 'color', 'dblog', 'forum',
    'help', 'menu', 'path', 'php', 'profile',
    'search', 'taxonomy', 'tracker',

    // Content construction kit
    'content', 'content_copy', 'content_permissions', 'fieldgroup',
    'nodereference', 'number', 'optionwidgets', 'text', 'userreference',

    // Date/Time
    'date', 'date_api', 'date_copy', 'date_timezone',

    // Literary workshop
    'litworkshop',

    // Mail
    'privatemsg',

    // Nodequeue
    'nodequeue',

    // Organic groups
    'og', 'og_access', 'og_views',

    // Other
    'advanced_help', 'global_redirect', 'token', 'pathauto',
    'todoalarm', 'service_links',

    // Taxonomy
    'tagadelic',

    // User interface
    'jquery_plugin',

    // Views
    'views', 'views_ui',
}
```

Neither the Devel nor the Drush module will form part of the installation profile.

All that is lacking now is for a series of non-interactive configuration steps to be executed. Since they are non-interactive, a simple series of tasks can be scripted in the `literaryworkshop_profile_tasks()` function, without it being necessary to implement the state machine of separate tasks/URL pairs outlined in the comment documenting that function.

Rather, a series of statements can be included that create content types, taxonomy vocabularies, and their terms and set up the value of Drupal variables and the default theme.

The complete literaryworkshop.profile is now as follows:

```
<?php
// $Id$

/**
 * Return an array of the modules to be enabled when this profile is installed.
 *
 * @return
 *   An array of modules to enable.
 */
function literaryworkshop_profile_modules() {
    // Core - required
    'block', 'filter', 'node', 'system', 'user',

    // Core - optional
    'blog', 'book', 'color', 'dblog', 'forum',
    'help', 'menu', 'path', 'php', 'profile',
    'search', 'taxonomy', 'tracker',

    // Content construction kit
    'content', 'content_copy', 'content_permissions', 'fieldgroup',
    'nodereference', 'number', 'optionwidgets', 'text', 'userreference',

    // Date/Time
    'date', 'date_api', 'date_copy', 'date_timezone',

    // Literary workshop
    'litworkshop',

    // Mail
    'privatemsg',

    // Nodequeue
    'nodequeue',

    // Organic groups
    'og', 'og_access', 'og_views',

    // Other
    'advanced_help', 'global_redirect', 'token', 'pathauto',
    'todoalarm', 'service_links',

    // Taxonomy
    'tagadelic',

    // User interface
    'jquery_plugin',

    // Views
    'views', 'views_ui',
}

/**
```

```
 * Return a description of the profile for the initial installation screen.
 *
 * @return
 *   An array with keys 'name' and 'description' describing this profile,
 *   and optional 'language' to override the language selection for
 *   language-specific profiles.
 */
function literaryworkshop_profile_details() {
  return array(
    'name' => 'Drupal (On-line Literary Workshop)',
    'description' => 'Select this profile to enable the On-line \
Literary Workshop and the literary workshop theme.'
  );
}

/**
 * Return a list of tasks that this profile supports.
 *
 * @return
 *   A keyed array of tasks the profile will perform during
 *   the final stage. The keys of the array will be used internally,
 *   while the values will be displayed to the user in the installer
 *   task list.
 */
function literaryworkshop_profile_task_list() {
}

/**
 * Perform any final installation tasks for this profile.
 *
 * The installer goes through the profile-select -> locale-select
 * -> requirements -> database -> profile-install-batch
 * -> locale-initial-batch -> configure -> locale-remaining-batch
 * -> finished -> done tasks, in this order, if you don't implement
 * this function in your profile.
 *
 * If this function is implemented, you can have any number of
 * custom tasks to perform after 'configure', implementing a state
 * machine here to walk the user through those tasks. First time,
 * this function gets called with $task set to 'profile', and you
 * can advance to further tasks by setting $task to your tasks'
 * identifiers, used as array keys in the hook_profile_task_list()
 * above. You must avoid the reserved tasks listed in
 * install_reserved_tasks(). If you implement your custom tasks,
 * this function will get called in every HTTP request (for form
 * processing, printing your information screens and so on) until
 * you advance to the 'profile-finished' task, with which you
 * hand control back to the installer. Each custom page you
 * return needs to provide a way to continue, such as a form
 * submission or a link. You should also set custom page titles.
 *
 * You should define the list of custom tasks you implement by
 * returning an array of them in hook_profile_task_list(), as these
 * show up in the list of tasks on the installer user interface.
 *
```

```
 * Remember that the user will be able to reload the pages multiple
 * times, so you might want to use variable_set() and variable_get()
 * to remember your data and control further processing, if $task
 * is insufficient. Should a profile want to display a form here,
 * it can; the form should set '#redirect' to FALSE, and rely on
 * an action in the submit handler, such as variable_set(), to
 * detect submission and proceed to further tasks. See the configuration
 * form handling code in install_tasks() for an example.
 *
 * Important: Any temporary variables should be removed using
 * variable_del() before advancing to the 'profile-finished' phase.
 *
 * @param $task
 *   The current $task of the install system. When hook_profile_tasks()
 *   is first called, this is 'profile'.
 * @param $url
 *   Complete URL to be used for a link or form action on a custom page,
 *   if providing any, to allow the user to proceed with the installation.
 *
 * @return
 *   An optional HTML string to display to the user. Only used if you
 *   modify the $task, otherwise discarded.
 */
function literaryworkshop_profile_tasks(&$task, $url) {

  // Insert default user-defined node types into the database. For a complete
  // list of available node type attributes, refer to the node type API
  // documentation at: http://api.drupal.org/api/HEAD/function/hook_node_info.
  $types = array(
    array(
      'type' => 'page',
      'name' => st('Page'),
      'module' => 'node',
      'description' => st("A <em>page</em>, similar in form to a \
<em>story</em>, is a simple method for creating and displaying \
information that rarely changes, such as an \"About us\" section \
 of a website. By default, a <em>page</em> entry does not allow \
 visitor comments and is not featured on the site's initial home \ page."),
      'custom' => TRUE,
      'modified' => TRUE,
      'locked' => FALSE,
      'help' => '',
      'min_word_count' => '',
    ),
    array(
      'type' => 'story',
      'name' => st('Story'),
      'module' => 'node',
      'description' => st("A <em>story</em>, similar in form to a \
<em>page</em>, is ideal for creating and displaying content that \
 informs or engages website visitors. Press releases, site \
announcements, and informal blog-like entries may all be created \
with a <em>story</em> entry. By default, a <em>story</em> entry is \
automatically featured on the site's initial home page, and provides \
the ability to post comments."),
```

```
      'custom' => TRUE,
      'modified' => TRUE,
      'locked' => FALSE,
      'help' => '',
      'min_word_count' => '',
    ),
    array(
      'type' => 'application',
      'name' => st('Application'),
      'module' => 'node',
      'description' => st("The <em>Application</em> is filled out \
by those applying for membership in the Literary Workshop."),
      'custom' => TRUE,
      'modified' => TRUE,
      'locked' => FALSE,
      'help' => '',
      'min_word_count' => '',
      'has_title' => TRUE,
      'title_label' => 'E-mail',
      'has_body' => FALSE,
    ),
    array(
      'type' => 'group',
      'name' => st('Group'),
      'module' => 'node',
      'description' => st("Create a new affinity <em>Group</em>."),
      'custom' => TRUE,
      'modified' => TRUE,
      'locked' => FALSE,
      'help' => '',
      'min_word_count' => '',
      'has_title' => TRUE,
      'title_label' => 'Title',
      'has_body' => TRUE,
      'body_label' => 'Body',
      /* REQUIRE OG AND PUT IN OG SPECIFIC SETTINGS */
    ),
    array(
      'type' => 'literary_piece',
      'name' => st('Literary Piece'),
      'module' => 'node',
      'description' => st("A <em>Literary Piece</em> a member \
submits for critique or for possible submission to publications."),
      'custom' => TRUE,
      'modified' => TRUE,
      'locked' => FALSE,
      'help' => '',
      'min_word_count' => '',
      'has_title' => TRUE,
      'title_label' => 'Title',
      'has_body' => FALSE,
    ),
    array(
      'type' => 'quote',
      'name' => st('Quote'),
```

```
      'module' => 'node',
      'description' => st("Create a <em>Quote</em> for random \
display at the top of each page."),
      'custom' => TRUE,
      'modified' => TRUE,
      'locked' => FALSE,
      'help' => '',
      'min_word_count' => '',
      'has_title' => TRUE,
      'title_label' => 'Quote',
      'has_body' => TRUE,
      'body_label' => 'Background',
    ),
  );

  foreach ($types as $type) {
    $type = (object) _node_type_set_defaults($type);
    node_type_save($type);
  }

  // Default page to not be promoted and have comments disabled.
  variable_set('node_options_page', array('status'));
  variable_set('comment_page', COMMENT_NODE_DISABLED);

  // Don't display date and author information for page nodes by default.
  $theme_settings = variable_get('theme_settings', array());
  $theme_settings['toggle_node_info_page'] = FALSE;
  variable_set('theme_settings', $theme_settings);

  // Create the Author and Tags vocabularies applied to Quote \
and Literary Pieces respectively, and add terms to each.
  $vocabulary = array(
    'name' => st('Authors'),
    'description' => st('Authors of quotes, as used in quote of the day.'),
    'help' => st('Multiple authors can be selected.'),
    'nodes' => array('news' => st('Quote')),
    'hierarchy' => 0,
    'relations' => 0,
    'tags' => 1,
    'multiple' => 1,
    'required' => 1,
  );
  taxonomy_save_vocabulary($vocabulary);
  // Define some terms to categorize news items.
  $terms = array(
    st('Brian Aldiss'),
    st('Douglas Adams'),
    st('Matthew Arnold'),
    st('Somerset Maugham'),
    );
  // The taxonomy_form_term form is not in taxonomy.module needs
  // taxonomy.admin.inc to be loaded.
  $form_id = 'taxonomy_form_term';
  require_once 'modules/taxonomy/taxonomy.admin.inc';
  foreach ($terms as $name) {
```

```
      $form_state['values']['name'] = $name;
      $form_state['clicked_button']['#value'] = st('Save');
      drupal_execute($form_id, $form_state, (object)$vocabulary);
    }
    $vocabulary = array(
      'name' => st('Tags'),
      'description' => st('Categories for liteary pieces.'),
      'nodes' => array('news' => st('Literary Piece')),
      'hierarchy' => 0,
      'relations' => 0,
      'tags' => 1,
      'multiple' => 0,
      'required' => 0,
    );
    taxonomy_save_vocabulary($vocabulary);
    // Define some terms to categorize news items.
    $terms = array(
      st('Elegy'),
      st('Flash fiction'),
      st('Free verse'),
      st('Haibun'),
      st('Haiku'),
      st('Limerick'),
      st('Sonnet'),
      );
    // The taxonomy_form_term form is not in taxonomy.module needs
    // taxonomy.admin.inc to be loaded.
    $form_id = 'taxonomy_form_term';
    require_once 'modules/taxonomy/taxonomy.admin.inc';
    foreach ($terms as $name) {
      $form_state['values']['name'] = $name;
      $form_state['clicked_button']['#value'] = st('Save');
      drupal_execute($form_id, $form_state, (object)$vocabulary);
    }

    // Variable settings
    variable_set('admin_theme', 'bluemarine');
    variable_set('theme_default', 'zenlitworkshop');
    variable_set('og_home_page_view', 'og_ghp_table');

    $themes = system_theme_data();
    if (isset($themes['zenlitworkshop'])) {
        system_initialize_theme_blocks($theme);
        db_query("UPDATE {system} SET status = 1 WHERE type = 'theme'
  and name = '%s'", 'zenlitworkshop');
        // Update the menu router information.
        menu_rebuild();
        drupal_rebuild_theme_registry();
    }
  }

  /**
   * Implementation of hook_form_alter().
   *
   * Allows the profile to alter the site-configuration form. This is
```

```
  * called through custom invocation, so $form_state is not populated.
  */
function literaryworkshop_form_alter(&$form, $form_state, $form_id) {
  if ($form_id == 'install_configure') {
    // Set default for site name field.
    $form['site_information']['site_name']['#default_value'] =
$_SERVER['SERVER_NAME'];
  }
}
```

## Caveats

As of this writing, no one has ever shown how to create content types implemented on the basis of the Content Construction Kit during the install process. Nor are nodequeues dealt with. In any case, it is a simple matter to import these cleanly after the fact, and this can be dealt with in the On-Line Help under a topic such as "Interactive tasks required to complement the install process."

## Creating the Drupal Installation Tarball Itself

Change to the parent directory of drupal-litworkshop-6.4-1.0, and execute the following command to create the tarball:

```
$ tar cvzf drupal-litworkshop-6.4-1.0.tgz drupal-litworkshop-6.4-1.0/
```

# Summary

The emphasis in this chapter has been on deployment and the deployment phase of the On-Line Literary Workshop. For this purpose, you have seen how to implement a complete on-line Help system based on Earl Miles's Advanced Help module (first seen with the birth of the Views 2 module). And you have learned what installation profiles are and how the complete website application can be prepared and packaged in this way, once the design and implementation work has been tested and finalized.

# 15

# Acquia Drupal as an Enterprise-Ready Alternative

The Acquia company exists in the best for-profit tradition of the Open Source business model, which is that of providing services paid for by clients built on an Open Source software system — one, that is, published under an Open Source license and available free of charge.

Dries Buytaert, the creator and founder of the Open Source Drupal Community and the founder of the Acquia company, often compares Acquia to Red Hat, as Drupal is to Linux. The rationale here is that Red Hat is a distribution of the freely available Linux operating system, but is not itself freely available since its distribution adds a commercial service in and of itself. And clients have shown that they are willing to pay for that service.

However, I would suggest that the metaphor model might be closer to the following: Acquia is to Drupal as Canonical (the commercial sponsor of Ubuntu) is to Debian, because Acquia Drupal is still provided free of charge under the GPL license, as is the regular vanilla Drupal tarball distribution you can download from the Drupal site itself, which you have been working with in this book. What Acquia provides are the following services:

- Packaging via software integration for the Drupal core and third-party modules
- Integration of the Drupal core with selected third-party modules, based on best practices and tested procedures
- Integration with Mollom, an anti-spam service
- Monitoring via the Acquia Network
- Support

First, Drupal is methodically integrated with a hand-picked collection of powerful modules that can be trusted as the bedrock for Enterprise-ready website applications. One of these modules connects your installed Acquia Drupal website to Mollom, an anti-spam service akin to Akismet. Your website is also monitored on the Acquia Network to check that your website is up and running (Heartbeat service) and to see if any files have been changed (i.e., by an intruder). And finally, you have access to first-class support, something that can let you rest easy as problems arise in the course of the website application life cycle.

As a software engineer, this means having that feeling of safe component reuse from the very start.

# Trying out Acquia Drupal

You should definitely try out Acquia and prove for yourself how the fact that it already comes with many pre-selected modules, an excellent theme, and additional functionality can save you a lot of time and give you a firm base upon which to start your development. This is not to mention the fact that your site will be constantly monitored to see whether it is up and running, and to report on any filesystem changes.

From the Acquia home page (`http://acquia.com/`), when you click on the "Subscribe to Acquia Network" link, you are taken to a product matrix that compares the various Acquia Network Subscriptions (`https://acquia.com/product-matrix`). Single server, 2-3 server cluster, and 4+ server bundles are available for the Community (Free), Standard, Professional, Enterprise, and Elite Product Subscriptions.

There are four main tasks required for generating your Drupal Acquia website application, as follows:

1. Create a subscription.
2. Set up Acquia Drupal.
3. Register with the Acquia Network.
4. Get support.

## *Step 1: Creating a Subscription*

To try out the Single Server site Community Product Subscription (list $200, currently Free), do the following:

1. Click on the Free button. Figures 15-1 and 15-2 show the Acquia Drupal Subscription Form and Checkout screen, respectively.
2. After clicking "Submit Order," you are taken to your "User account" screen (see Figure 15-3), where you can log into your account with your username and password, as per the details sent to your registered e-mail address in the mail entitled, "Acquia account details for username."

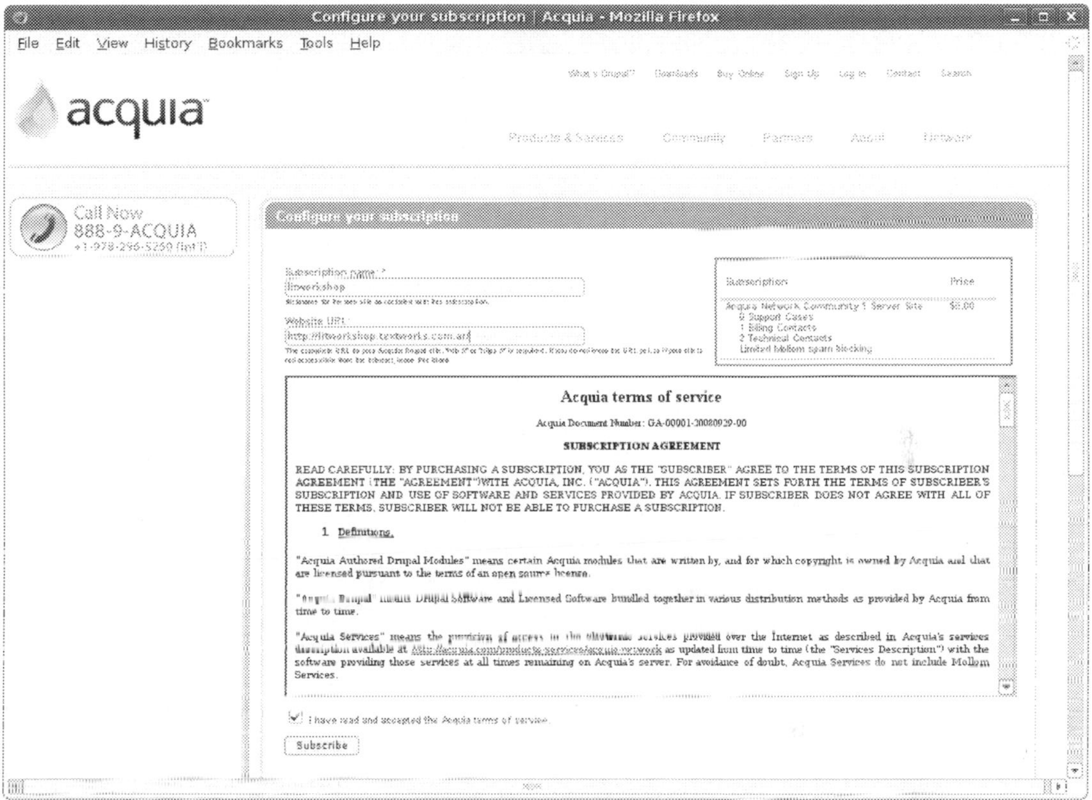


Figure 15-1

3. Click on the Messages tab (Figure 15-4), and access the "Getting started with your new subscription" message, which can be seen in Figure 15-5.

## Step 2: Setting up Acquia Drupal

Click on the Download link (see Figure 15-5) to get to the Download page (see Figure 15-6) and download the full version. Whereas there were update versions and even a way to connect an existing Drupal 6 site to the Acquia Network, I downloaded the full version to set up.

The "Getting started..." message had a handy link to the documentation "on how to install Acquia Drupal and use it with the Acquia Network." I suggest that you go there and download the PDF doc provided because it's chock-full of cool information and it directs you to good old INSTALL.txt. You also should do the following:

1. Unpack the file, and rename the Drupal document root appropriately.

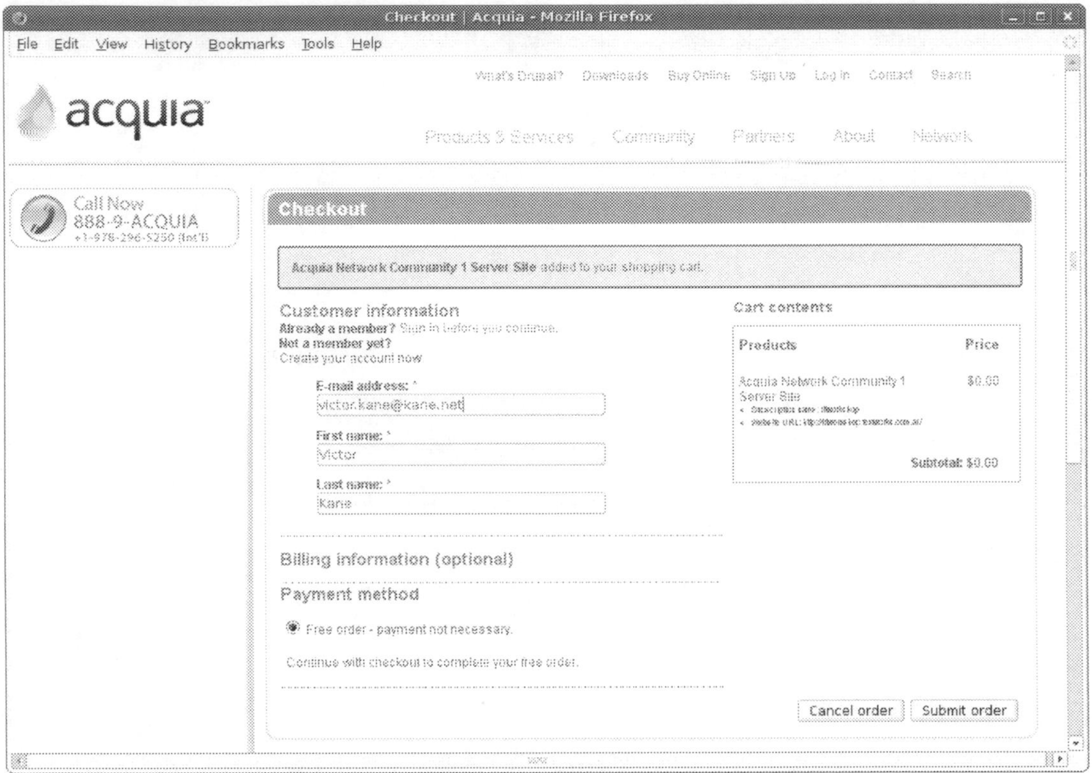


Figure 15-2

2. Copy sites/default/default.settings.php to sites/default/settings.php, and make sure that the Apache server had Write privileges on the latter.

3. Create a MySQL database and user (with full privileges over that database and only that database) for the Acquia Drupal installation.

4. Point your browser at the pre-configured site URL, and supply the database name, username, and password (see Figure 15-7).

The configure site screen is almost exactly the same as the Drupal 6 equivalent, that is, a form to set up the basic site info, administration account, server settings (such as default time zone, and clean URLs information), and check for updates automatically selected. The only difference is that it asks for your "Acquia subscription identifier" and "Acquia subscription key," which can easily be visualized at any time from your `Acquia.com` Network site, when you hit the Subscription tab. See Figure 15-8.

You fill in the necessary info to create the Admin user and click on the "Save and continue" button. Gratifyingly, the process is over and the installation is complete, as seen in Figure 15-9.

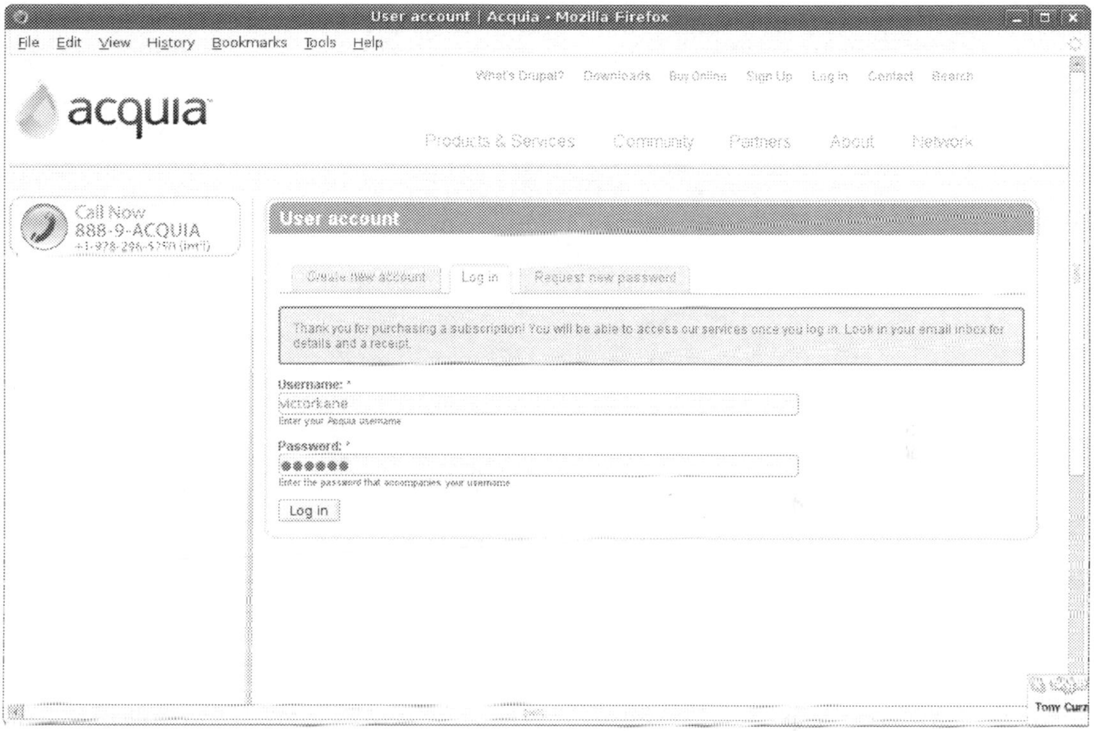


Figure 15-3

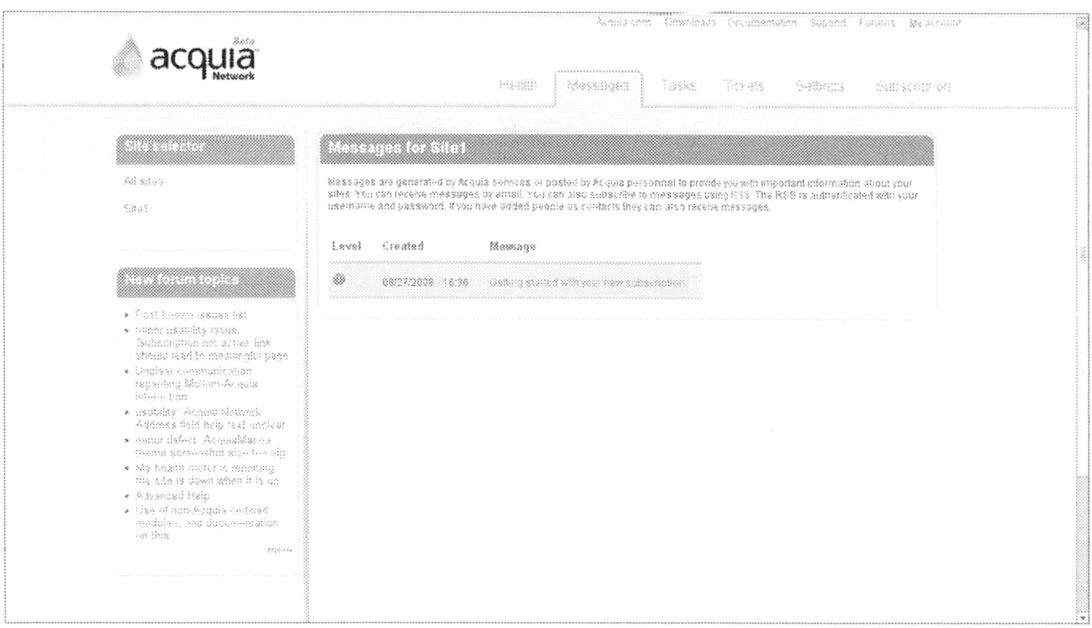


Figure 15-4

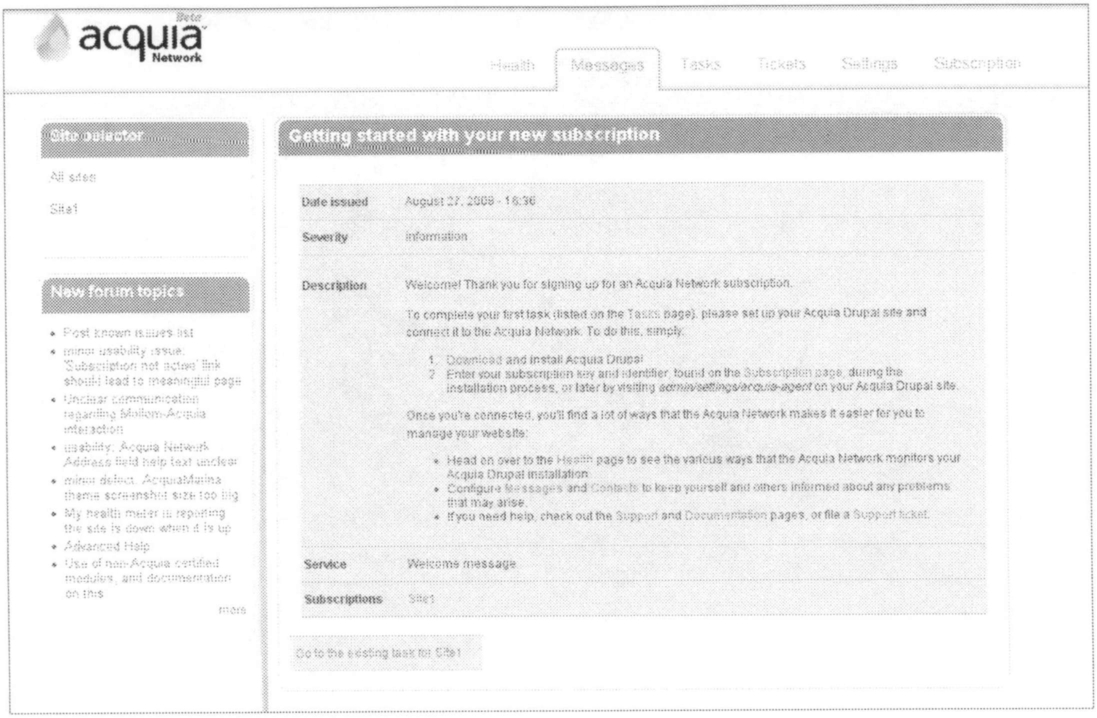


Figure 15-5

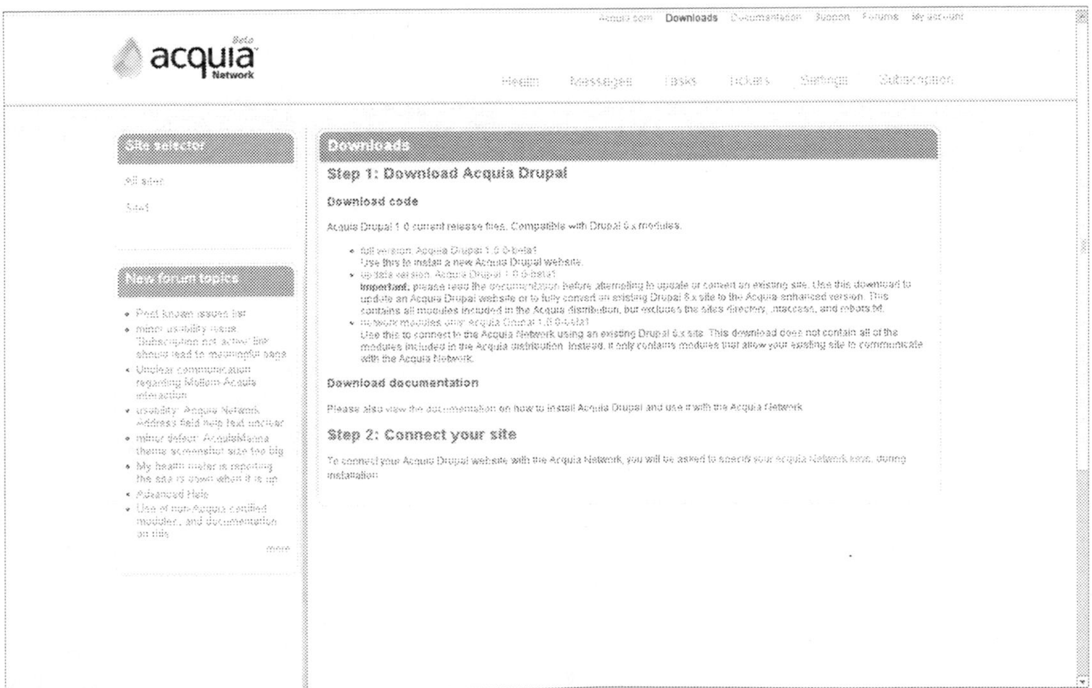


Figure 15-6

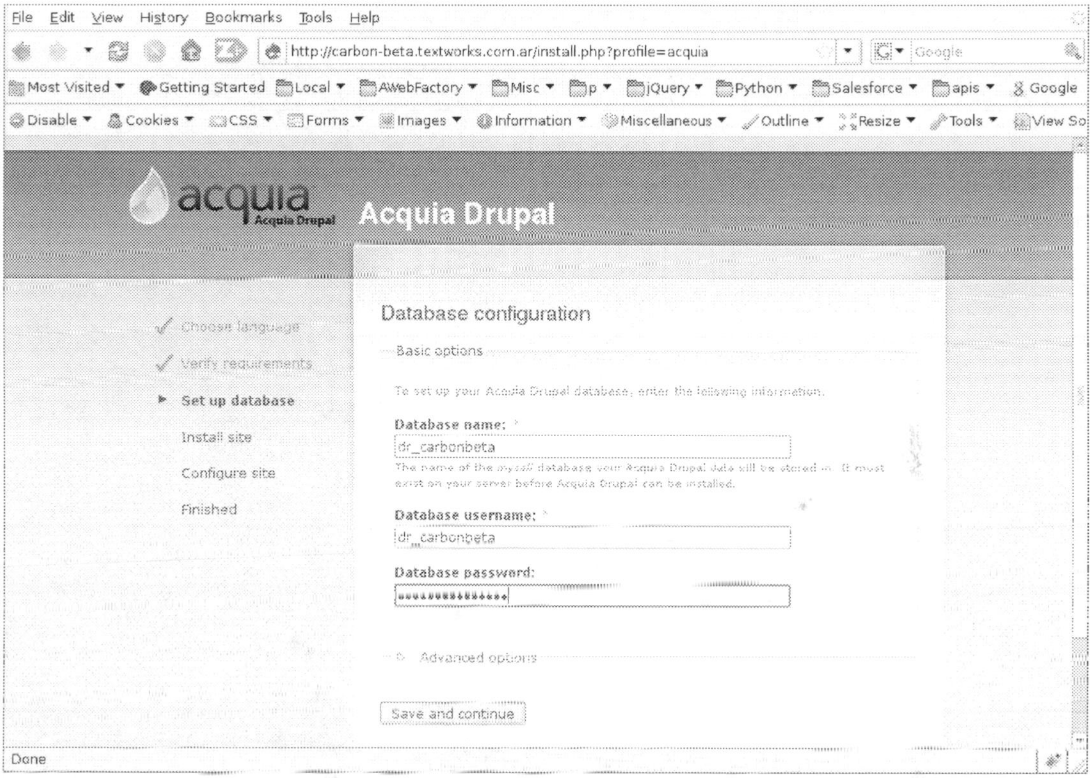


Figure 15-7

## Step 3: Registering Your Website with the Acquia Network

Now, go back to the Acquia account dashboard to guide you through registration. Follow these steps:

1. Click on the Task tab, where you will see a link that says "Task: Connect your Acquia Drupal site to the Network." Click on this link. Basically, as seen in Figure 15-10, you are invited to mark this task as done, because the actual task itself was done when you supplied your Acquia subscription identifier and Acquia subscription key to complete the installation process.
2. Check this task as done, and click on the "Update task" button.

Now, this is one of the first concrete benefits of being part of the Acquia system. Your site is monitored by Acquia 24/7, and you are notified by e-mail should your site go down, and notified again when it goes back up again. This is the Heartbeat service. But, how do you know if your site is properly connected to the monitoring system?

What about my site? Well, it turns out that because litworkshop was a running Drupal site, just by subscribing, its cron (operating system scheduler service) is run every 5 minutes by the Acquia Network and you receive an e-mail giving you a cron summary of successful cron invocations on your site! Click on the Health tab to see a nice Heartbeat uptime report, as in Figure 15-11.

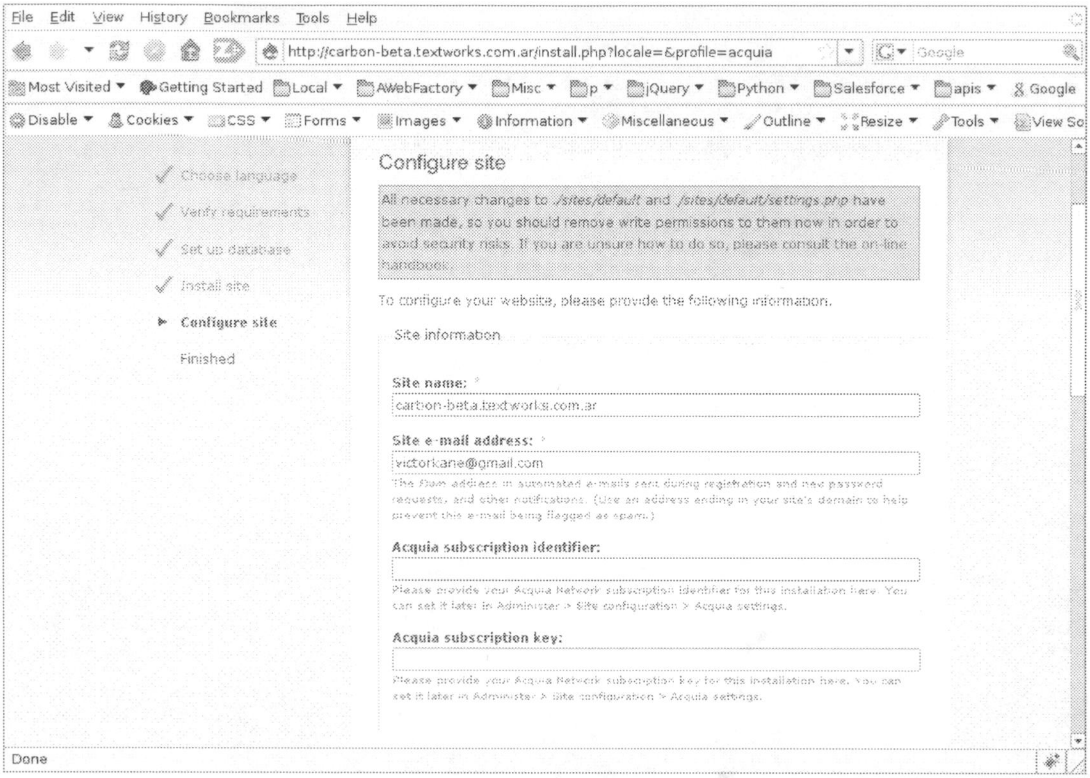


Figure 15-8

Figure 15-9

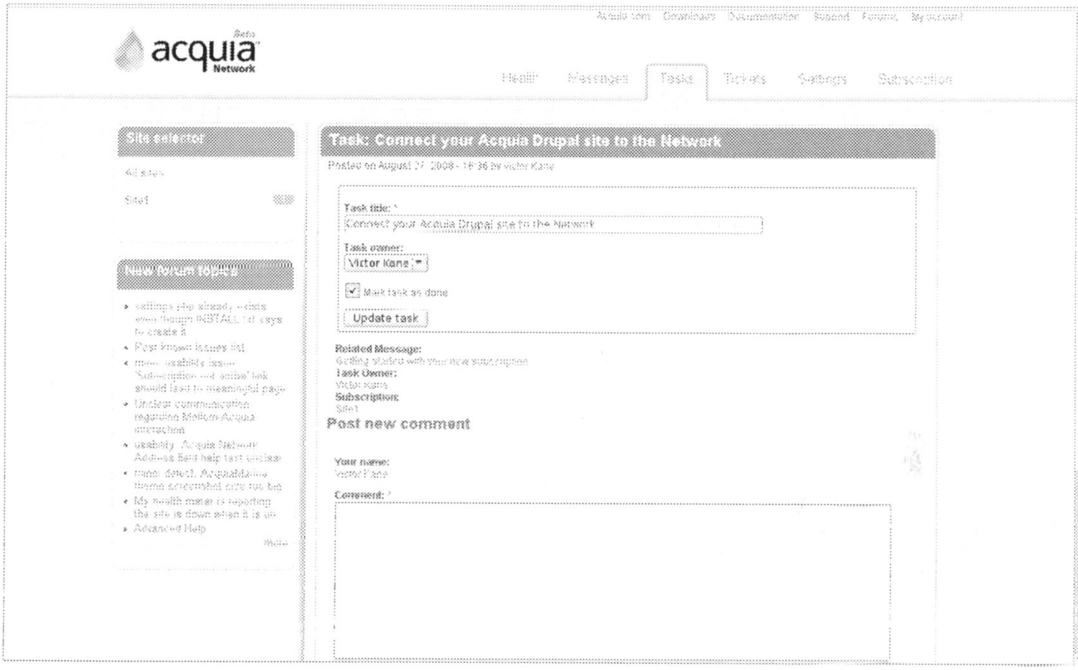


Figure 15-10

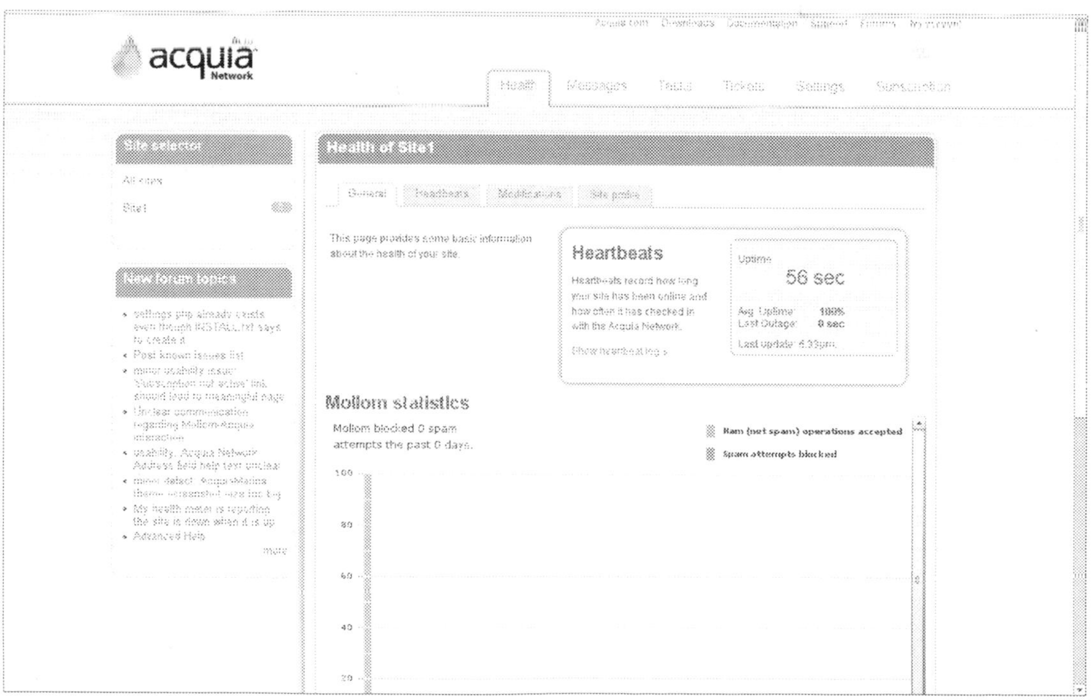


Figure 15-11

To set up cron permanently on your site, the steps that follow show what I did as way of example. But, you will want to have cron running on your site for the monitoring system to be tailored to your needs.

1. Logging in via ssh (secure shell command line) and as root, I typed the following:

```
$ crontab -e
```

2. In the editor that pops up, I added the following, replacing example.com with my own URL:

```
02,32 * * * * /usr/bin/wget -O - -q http://example.com/cron.php
```

   This effectively instructs cron to be run every 30 minutes.

3. Back at my Acquia Network site login, I clicked on the Settings tab. Under my site name, I clicked on the Cron tab and instructed Acquia to let me run cron, and that I would be running it every 30 minutes, as per Figure 15-12. As the Help text states: "This setting determines how long the Acquia Network should wait without receiving a heartbeat before it alerts you that your site may be down."

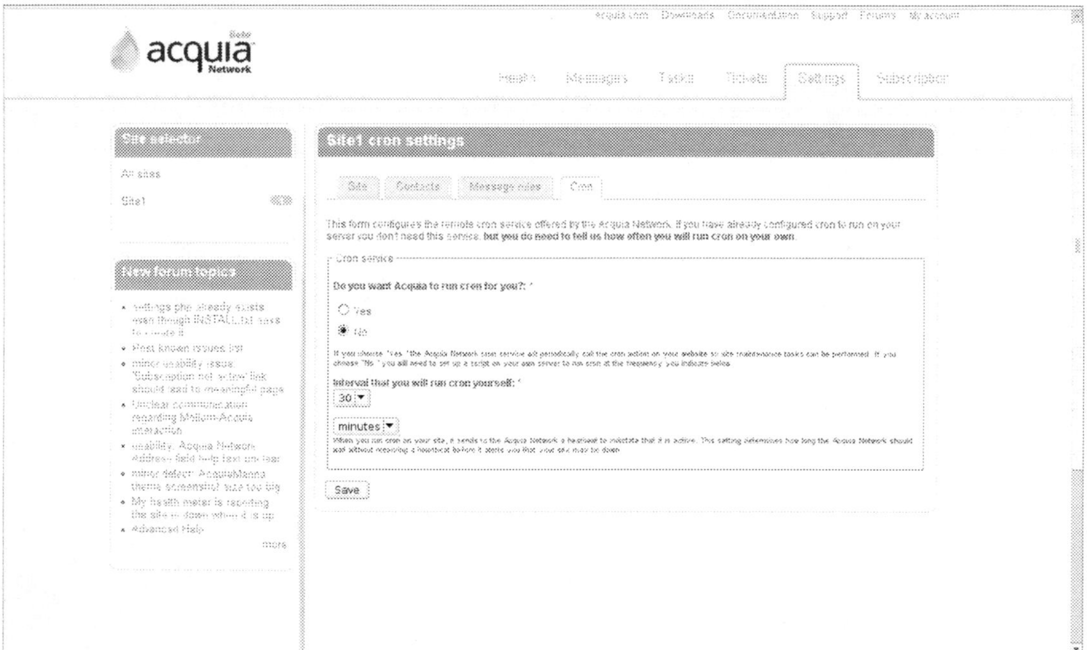


Figure 15-12

After the next period has passed, you should see the heartbeats reflected in the Health tab section (see Figure 15-11).

If, however, your cron job doesn't send in a heartbeat in time, your site will be marked as down, and you will also receive an e-mail to that effect.

## Step 4: Getting Support

Support is one of the things that really distinguishes Acquia Drupal. Use it or lose it! If you get that "What do I do next?" or "How do I do that?" feeling, go right ahead and click on the Tickets tab and click on the "Create a new ticket" button. State the urgency, specify the related subscription and the type of support you require (technical, sales, other), fill in a suitable title and description (as per Figure 15-13), and click Submit.

Figure 15-13

# Exploring the New Acquia Drupal Website Installation

Assuming that you were following along and that you have your Acquia Drupal website up and running, take a look around.

The most noticeable thing is that the administration menu module (`http://drupal.org/project/admin_menu`) is included and enabled by default, providing an extremely convenient dark-colored, thin dropdown Admin menu, with quick access to the most common tasks. This saves a great deal of time and effort. Figure 15-14 shows the easy invocation of Administer ➤ Site building ➤ Modules. The menu also includes Acquia subscription information and informs you how many anonymous and authenticated users are currently visiting the site. The menu is pure CSS-based, with just a few jQuery JavaScript functions for additional tweaking and IE6 support.

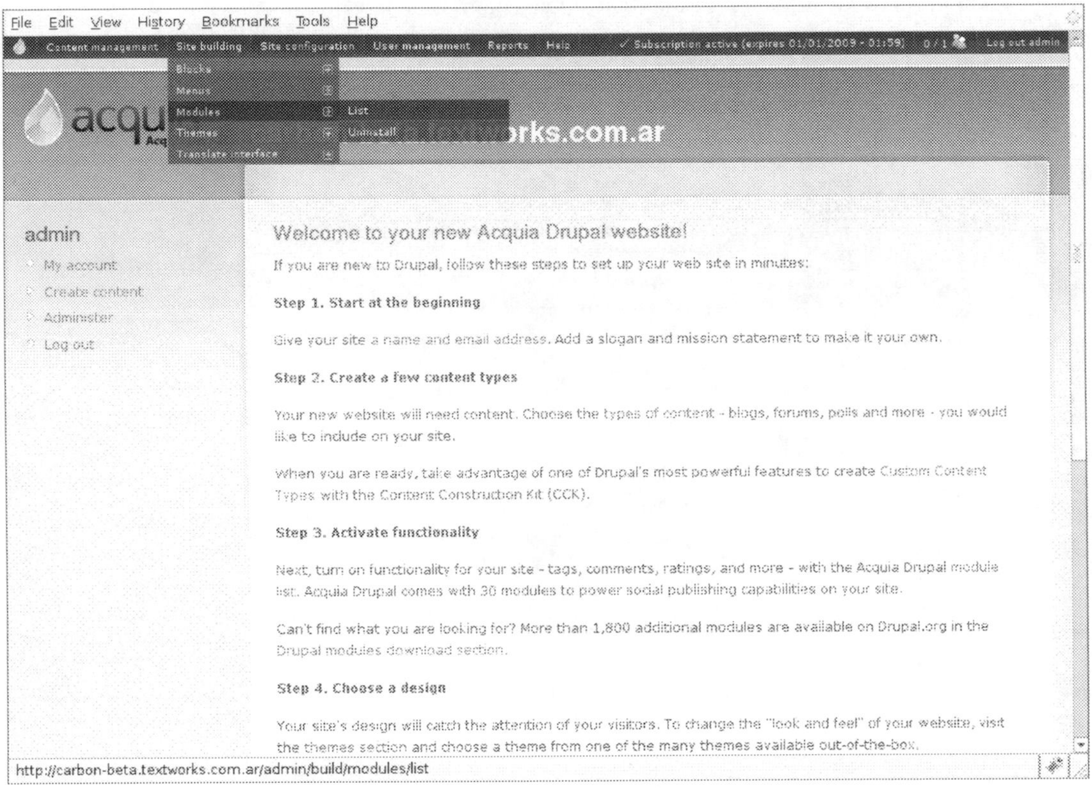


Figure 15-14

At Administer ➤ Site building ➤ Modules, the following modules goodies have been specially integrated into Drupal Acquia:

- Acquia agent and Acquia site information (in the Acquia Network section)
- Administration menu, as mentioned earlier
- Content Construction Kit
- Image module
- The Markdown input filter (for blogging, easy non-HTML styled input)
- Tagadelic (tag cloud)
- Fivestar voting and Voting API

- Google Analytics
- Mollom (Akismet-like spam protection included as part of the Acquia subscription)
- Pathauto
- Token and Token actions
- Views
- Print, including support for e-mailing and PDF export of web pages

The last item, the Print module, does not come with any of the two third-party PDF libraries required for PDF export (dompdf and TCPDF), which one would expect to see here; the reason is that Acquia Drupal is still distributed under the GPL license, just as Drupal itself is.

The Global Redirect module (`http://drupal.org/project/globalredirect`) is recognized for its usefulness. Even though it didn't make the first cut of modules initially included in Drupal Acquia, it will most probably be included in an upcoming version along with Pathauto (which did make the first cut). This is because it, or something similar, is required to avoid duplicate URLs pointing to the same web page.

# Installing Updates

On September 30, 2008, Dries announced on the Drupal site that Acquia Drupal was out of beta (`http://drupal.org/node/315151`). This article explains how the Acquia Network (`http://acquia.com/products-services/acquia-network`), "is a hosted service that helps you with site management (update notifications, spam blocking, cron service, modification detection, etc.) and provides real-time visibility into the health and usage of all your Drupal sites that are connected" to it. In addition, the Acquia Network gives you access to the Acquia Technical Support Team (`http://acquia.com/products-services/drupal-technical-support`). Last but not least, "we are also releasing Acquia Drupal (`http://acquia.com/products-services/acquia-drupal`) today."

Because I was already subscribed, I received a notification e-mail concerning the Drupal release and latest version update, together with instructions. To provide a clear feeling for the quality of Acquia support, I am including the e-mail text in full:

> *A new version of Acquia Drupal has just been released that contains important security and bug fixes for your installation of Acquia Drupal. We recommend that you upgrade to the new version as soon as possible.*
>
> - *Get instructions for upgrading your site.* (`http://acquia.com/network/manuals`)
> - *Download the new version.* (`http://acquia.com/downloads`)
>
> *The release notes for Acquia Drupal 1.0.1-ISR:*
>
> *The Acquia Drupal interim release consists of Acquia's package of Drupal core with a curated set of contributed modules, plus the ability to connect to the Acquia Network. This version includes the following updates:*
>
> - *Change Log*
>
>   *US816: Modified — Updated Drupal core to 6.5. See the full release notes* (`http://drupal.org/node/318701`) *for Drupal 6.5 on* `Drupal.org`.

*US816: Modified — Updated imagecache to 6.x-2.0-beta1*

*US816: Modified — Updated filefield to 6.x-3.x-dev (as of October 8, 2008) since 6.x-3.0-alpha5 is missing a fix in the install code*

*US816: Modified — Updated CCK to 6.x-2.0-RC10 including missing files for advanced help*

*US816: Modified — Updated Views to 6.x-2.0-RC5*

*DS2: Fixed — Updated the Acquia Marina theme to version 6.x-1.1 from (multiple bug fixes)*

The first step was to get the update instructions at `https://acquia.com/network/manuals`, the first step of which was to download the PDF manual at `https://acquia.com/files/downloads/acquia_getting_started_1-0_ISR_01.pdf`. The Migrating and Upgrading section provided a comprehensive and detailed list of instructions.

Following the instructions are best practices for upgrading, based on the "Advanced Migration with the Command Line" section:

1. Make sure the PHP memory limit is greater than or equal to 32 MB; find the following line in your website's php.ini file (in Ubuntu, that is /etc/php5/apache2/php.ini):

```
memory_limit = 32M      ; Maximum amount of memory a script may
consume (16MB)
```

2. Log in on the command line to your site, and place your site in maintenance mode (Administer ➤ Site configuration ➤ Site maintenance).
3. Prepare a gzip'd backup of your database contents:

```
mysqldump -u username -p password databasename | gzip > filename.sql .gz
```

4. Prepare a tarred backup of your site including the database backup:

```
cd drupal-document-root
tar cvzf backup-filename.tgz .
```

5. If this is a production site, test restoring your site using the recently created backup file(s).
6. Check that all non-Acquia integrated contributed modules are *not* present in ./modules/acquia and *are* present in ./sites/all/modules.
7. Download the current Acquia Drupal release (choose the Update version, which omits the sites directory along with the .htaccess and robots.txt files) using wget or curl.

```
wget http://acquia.com/files/downloads/acquia-drupal-1.0.1-ISR.2844-
update.tar.gz
```

8. Replace old Acquia Drupal distribution files with new ones. Because the use of an update via a version control system is not one of the options recommended by Acquia, something like the following is your best option:

Unpack the new release to a new document root, named after the release. For example, if your present document root is /var/www, change the directory to /var and do the following:

```
mysite:/var$ cp www/.htaccess acquia-drupal-1.0.1-ISR-update/
mysite:/var$ cp www/robots.txt acquia-drupal-1.0.1-ISR-update/
mysite:/var$ cp -R carbon-beta/sites acquia-drupal-1.0.1-ISR-update/
mysite:/var$ mv www www-old
mysite:/var$  mv acquia-drupal-1.0.1-ISR-update/ www
```

Shouldn't have even skipped a heartbeat (pardon the pun).

9. Still logged in as Admin (User #1), run `update.php`, click on the Continue button and then the Update button. Figure 15-15 shows a typical result of this operation.

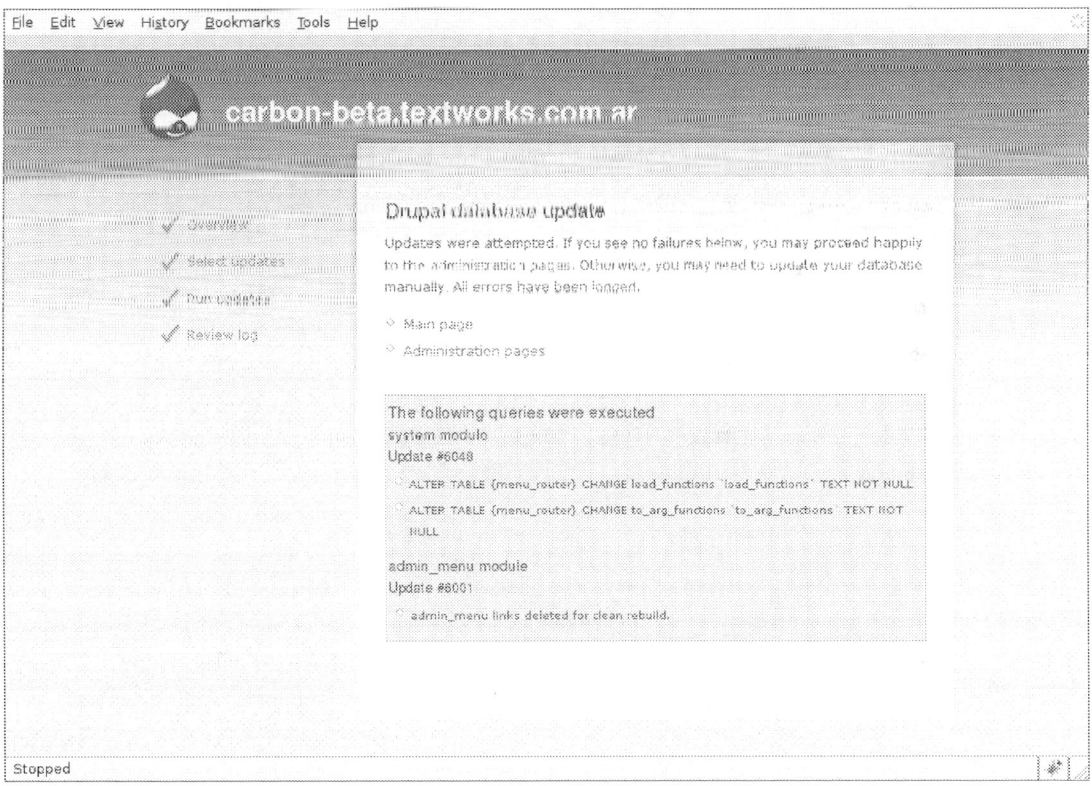


**Figure 15-15**

10. There is no Step 10: You're done!

# Introducing the Acquia Marina Theme

So, any new goodies?

The most obvious is the new theme bundled with Acquia Drupal as of their Release version, developed in partnership with Top Notch Themes and released under the GPL license (see `http://drupal.org/project/acquia_marina` to see the theme and `www.topnotchthemes.com/` for the Top Notch Themes site). By going to Administer ➤ Site building ➤ Themes, you can see the new theme listed, *Acquia Marina*.

Enable it and set it as default.

The theme project page (`http://drupal.org/project/acquia_marina`) specifies an incredible number of special features, including 15 collapsible block regions, optional dropdown primary menu, a set of icons for core and Views blocks, and cross-browser compatibility, all of which goes to explain why it has fast become a favorite on `http://drupal.org`.

Another feature mentioned is that of "advanced theme settings," which actually allow you to have interactive control over the widest number of settings ever before made available via the theme settings facility (part of the core starting with the Drupal 6 release). You can see a partial screenshot at `http://drupal.org/node/315553`, but it is well worth listing the complete list:

- Usual display toggles for Logo, Site name, Mission Statement, and the like
- Usual Logo and Shortcut icon settings
- General settings
  - Fine-tune display of Mission statement
  - Toggle Breadcrumb display
  - Special optional handling for unregistered usernames
  - Incredible fine-tuning over search results display formatting
- Node (content item) settings
  - Toggle author username, post date (including custom handling for each content type!)
  - Toggle new line for each taxonomy term!
  - Full customization of "Read more" and "Add new comment" links, including special handling for full content or teaser content item views
- SEO Optimization
  - Page title customization
  - Meta tags customization

Figure 15-16 shows the theme, with its very attractive color scheme, typography, and an example of its icon set, displaying a newly created page content item.

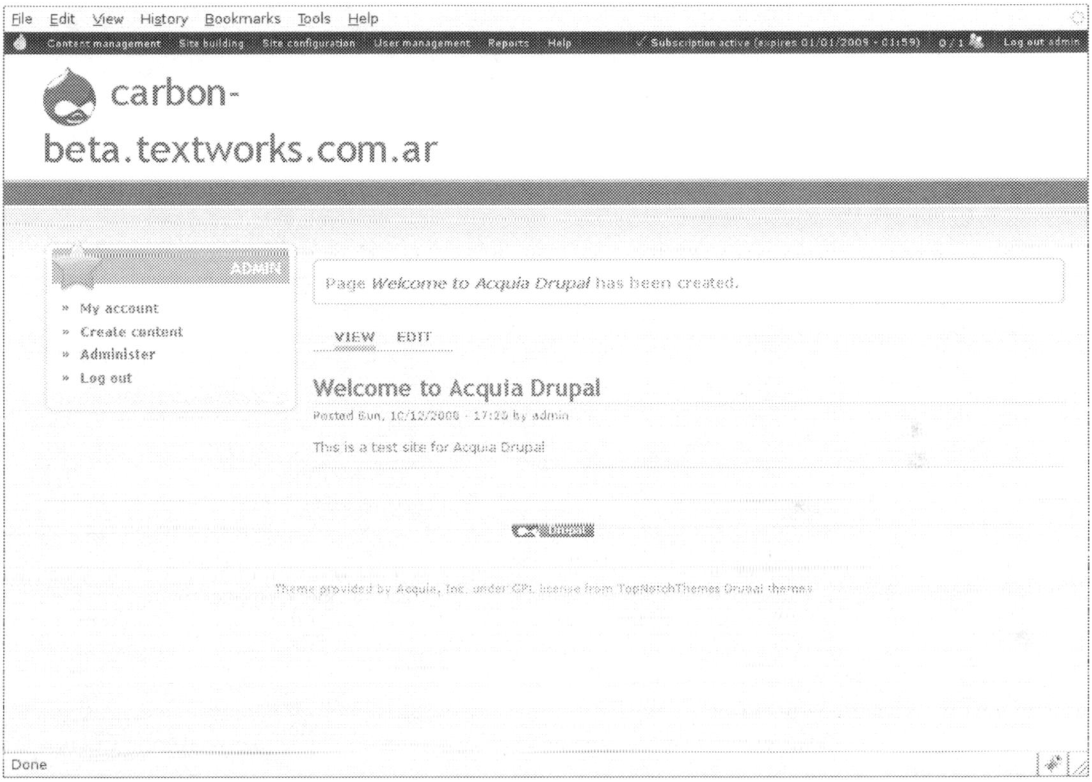


Figure 15-16

# Checking out Mollom

One way to stop spam is by prohibiting user contribution to your website altogether. However, given the character of modern website applications and their dependence on user and crowd sourcing of their content, this is increasingly ceasing to be an option.

That leaves the option of administering comments and content-form submissions manually, but that can be a tedious and error-prone process, indeed.

The Mollom service (see `http://mollom.com`) purports not only to stop spam, or negative content, but also to spot high-quality content, in a positive sense. Its efficiency is, as of this writing, posted on their homepage as 99.84 percent.

The Mollom service (which has in common with Drupal and Acquia Drupal that of being founded also by Dries Buytaert) is integrated into Drupal and Acquia Drupal via the Mollom module (`http://drupal.org/project/mollom`). It is a paid service (although there is a limited free version), but an integral part of and hence bundled with the Acquia Network.

From the "Getting Started with Acquia" manual:

> *"Mollom works by analyzing content submitted to your site then automatically classifying it as 'spam' (bad) or 'ham' (good). Mollom blocks content that it is certain is spam, and lets content be published that it is certain is legitimate. The small percentage of content in between (when Mollom is not certain whether a piece of content is legitimate or not) passes through an extra layer of protection before being published to your website: The user submitting the content is presented with a simple visual or audio CAPTCHA challenge — a 'Completely Automated Public Turing test to tell Computers and Humans Apart' — that humans can easily solve, but generally stops automated 'spambot' contributions dead in their tracks."*

The first step to trying it out is:

1. Enable the Mollom module. Go to Administer ➢ Site building ➢ Modules, and enable the Mollom module in the Other section.
2. Visit Administer ➢ Site configuration ➢ Mollom to enter your Mollom access keys. These keys can be found on your Acquia Network dashboard (click on your Subscription link in the Administration menu) under the Subscription tab, in the "Mollom Spam protection keys" section. Enter your Public and Private keys, and click on the "Save configuration" button. You should see a message similar to the following:

   > *"We contacted the Mollom servers to verify your keys: the Mollom services are operating correctly. We are now blocking spam."*

   followed by a Site usage statistics graph, and a series of configuration options.
3. Select the "Protect comment" form and "Protect story form" settings in the "Spam protection settings" section, and maintain the "Block all submissions on the protected forms until the server problems are resolved" option choice in the "Server settings" section.
4. Go to Administer ➢ User Management ➢ Permissions, and allow anonymous users to:
   - ❑ Access comments
   - ❑ Post comments
   - ❑ Post comments without approval
   - ❑ Create story content
   - ❑ Edit own story content
5. Now, accessing the site as an unauthenticated user (e.g., using a different browser, like Opera), the anonymous user finds a Navigation menu offering a "Create content" option. Clicking there, she is given the option of creating a Story. Click on the Story link, and attempt to make the most sincere post you are capable of. For example, *Title*: "Sincerity is questioned in a recent poll," with any appropriate text in the Body text area. The result is shown in Figure 15-17.
6. Continuing in the same unauthenticated session, create a spamish story (e.g., something copied out of your Gmail Spam directory). The results are shown in Figure 15-18.

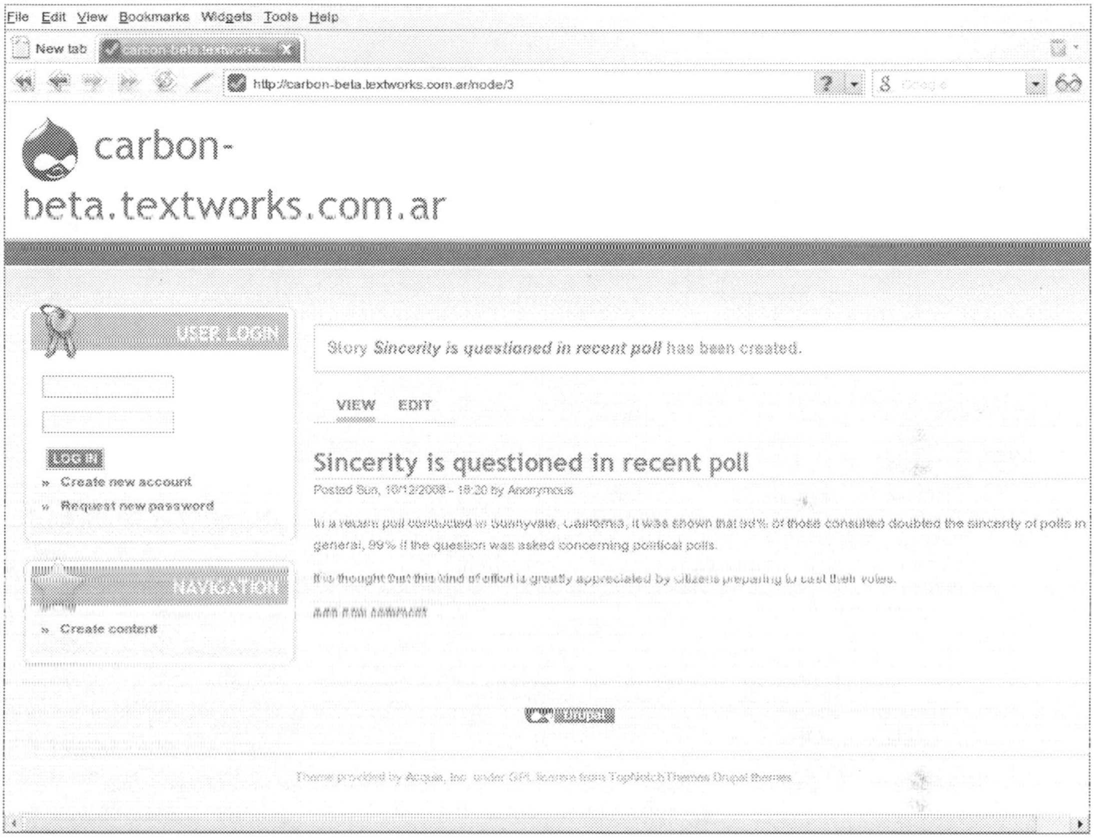


Figure 15-17

7. Fill in the Captcha (play the audio if the image captcha is not clear!) and click Save. If the captcha is filled in correctly, you see the Edit screen once again with no warning; click on the Save button again, and the Story is posted.

8. In your Admin session, go back to the Mollom Admin page (Administer ➤ Site configuration ➤ Mollom).

# Using the Acquia Partner Program

Just as the Acquia Network monitors your website, the Acquia Partner program is a natural resource for those seeking pre-screened service providers from all over the world, whether it be an individual working as mentor or a large company. For all those businesses excited about the alternatives offered by Open Source projects in general and the Drupal CMS framework in particular, the Partner Program could well prove the "missing link" that will enable them to find the service providers they need in the most efficient manner and to obtain the results they expect.

At the same time, the program seems like a great opportunity for those looking for a solid base upon which to build a career in providing Drupal services. You can find out more about it at `http://acquia.com/blog/introducing-acquia-partner-program`.

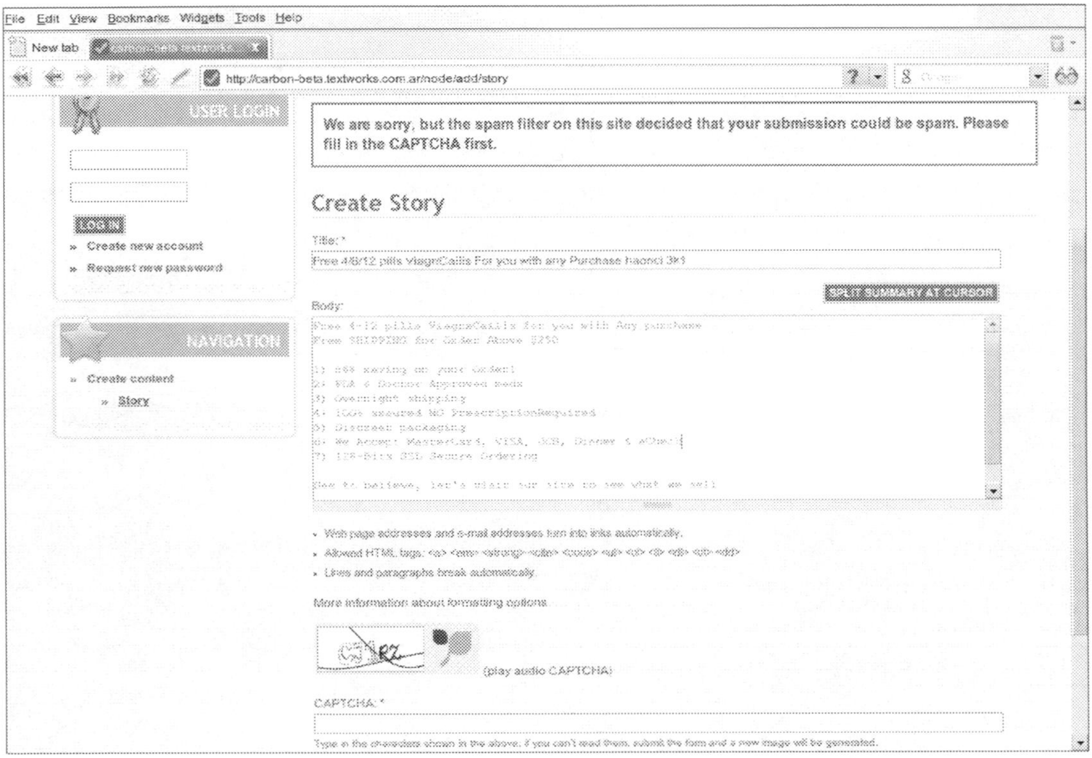


Figure 15-18

# Summary

In this chapter, you heaved a great sigh of relief, as you shifted part of the responsibility for installing and configuring your website application, as well as for keeping it up-to-date, onto the shoulders of Acquia, in the best tradition of software engineering reusability.

You checked out the benefits in terms of maintenance, off-the-shelf productivity, monitoring, and other services, and were able to gain enough experience to tell you whether this path is your best alternative for Leveraging Drupal and getting your site done right.

# Index

## A

# B

# D

# J

## L



## M



## N

# O



# P

# U

# X



# Z